Lecture Notes in
Business Information Processing

558

Series Editors

Wil van der Aalst ⓘ, *RWTH Aachen University, Aachen, Germany*
Sudha Ram ⓘ, *University of Arizona, Tucson, USA*
Michael Rosemann ⓘ, *Queensland University of Technology, Brisbane, Australia*
Clemens Szyperski, *Microsoft Research, Redmond, USA*
Giancarlo Guizzardi ⓘ, *University of Twente, Enschede, The Netherlands*

LNBIP reports state-of-the-art results in areas related to business information systems and industrial application software development – timely, at a high level, and in both printed and electronic form.

The type of material published includes

- Proceedings (published in time for the respective event)
- Postproceedings (consisting of thoroughly revised and/or extended final papers)
- Other edited monographs (such as, for example, project reports or invited volumes)
- Tutorials (coherently integrated collections of lectures given at advanced courses, seminars, schools, etc.)
- Award-winning or exceptional theses

LNBIP is abstracted/indexed in DBLP, EI and Scopus. LNBIP volumes are also submitted for the inclusion in ISI Proceedings.

Renata Guizzardi · Luise Pufahl · Arnon Sturm ·
Han van der Aa
Editors

Enterprise, Business-Process and Information Systems Modeling

26th International Conference, BPMDS 2025
and 30th International Conference, EMMSAD 2025
Vienna, Austria, June 16–17, 2025
Proceedings

 Springer

Editors
Renata Guizzardi ⓘ
University of Twente
Enschede, The Netherlands

Luise Pufahl ⓘ
Technical University of Munich
Munich, Germany

Arnon Sturm ⓘ
Ben-Gurion University of the Negev
Be'er-Sheva, Israel

Han van der Aa ⓘ
University of Vienna
Vienna, Austria

ISSN 1865-1348   ISSN 1865-1356 (electronic)
Lecture Notes in Business Information Processing
ISBN 978-3-031-95396-5   ISBN 978-3-031-95397-2 (eBook)
https://doi.org/10.1007/978-3-031-95397-2

© The Editor(s) (if applicable) and The Author(s), under exclusive license
to Springer Nature Switzerland AG 2025

This work is subject to copyright. All rights are solely and exclusively licensed by the Publisher, whether the whole or part of the material is concerned, specifically the rights of translation, reprinting, reuse of illustrations, recitation, broadcasting, reproduction on microfilms or in any other physical way, and transmission or information storage and retrieval, electronic adaptation, computer software, or by similar or dissimilar methodology now known or hereafter developed.
The use of general descriptive names, registered names, trademarks, service marks, etc. in this publication does not imply, even in the absence of a specific statement, that such names are exempt from the relevant protective laws and regulations and therefore free for general use.
The publisher, the authors and the editors are safe to assume that the advice and information in this book are believed to be true and accurate at the date of publication. Neither the publisher nor the authors or the editors give a warranty, expressed or implied, with respect to the material contained herein or for any errors or omissions that may have been made. The publisher remains neutral with regard to jurisdictional claims in published maps and institutional affiliations.

This Springer imprint is published by the registered company Springer Nature Switzerland AG
The registered company address is: Gewerbestrasse 11, 6330 Cham, Switzerland

If disposing of this product, please recycle the paper.

Preface

This book contains the proceedings of two long-running events held alongside the CAiSE conference relating to the areas of enterprise, business-process, and information systems modeling: the 26th International Working Conference on Business Process Modeling, Development, and Support (BPMDS 2025) and the 30th International Working Conference on Exploring Modeling Methods for Systems Analysis and Development (EMMSAD 2025). More information on the individual events and their selection processes can be found on the following pages.

BPMDS 2025

The Business Process Modeling, Development and Support (BPMDS) working conference has been held for more than two decades, dealing with and promoting research on BPMDS, and has been a platform for a multitude of influential research papers. In keeping with its tradition, the working conference covers a broad range of theoretical and application-based research. BPMDS started in 1998 as a recurring workshop. During this period, business process analysis and design were recognized as central issues in the area of information systems (IS) engineering. The continued interest in these topics on behalf of the IS community is reflected by the success of the latest BPMDS events and the recent emergence of new conferences and workshops devoted to the theme. In 2011, BPMDS became a two-day working conference attached to CAiSE. The goals, format, and history of BPMDS can be found at www.bpmds.org.

BPMDS 2025 received 39 submissions, of which 37 submissions went into peer review. Each of these submissions was reviewed by three members of the Program Committee or sub-reviewers invited by PC members. Finally, 12 high-quality full papers were selected for publication and presentation at the conference. These accepted papers cover a wide spectrum of topics, which we organized under four headers: (1) Business Process Improvement, (2) Human-AI Interplay in Exploring Process Representations, (3) Event Data Extraction, and (4) Probabilistic Approaches to Uncertainty and Prediction in Process Mining.

We want to thank everyone who submitted papers to BPMDS 2025 for sharing their work with us. Furthermore, we want to thank the members of the Program Committee, who made a remarkable effort in reviewing submissions, the organizers of CAiSE 2025 for their help with the organization of the event, IFIP WG8.1 for its continued support and Springer for their assistance during the production of the proceedings.

April 2025

Han van der Aa
Luise Pufahl

EMMSAD 2025

This year is a festive date for EMMSAD, which completes 30 years of existence. The objective of the EMMSAD conference series is to provide a forum for researchers and practitioners interested in modeling methods for systems analysis and development (SA&D) to meet and exchange research ideas and results. The conference aims to provide a home for a wide variety of modeling paradigms, including software modeling, business process modeling, enterprise modeling, capability modeling, service modeling, ontology modeling, and domain-specific modeling. These important modeling paradigms and specific methods continue to be enriched with extensions, refinements, and new languages. Even with some attempts at standardization, new modeling paradigms and methods are constantly being introduced, especially to deal with emerging trends and challenges. Ongoing changes significantly impact the way systems are analyzed and designed. Moreover, they challenge the empirical and analytical evaluation of the modeling methods, contributing to the understanding of their strengths and weaknesses. This may guide researchers toward the development of the next generation of modeling methods and help practitioners select the modeling methods most appropriate to their needs.

EMMSAD 2025 accepted papers in the following five tracks that emphasize the variety of EMMSAD topics: (1) Foundations of modeling & method engineering – chaired by Anne Gutschmidt and Istvan David; (2) Enterprise, business, process, and capability modeling – chaired by Jānis Grabis and Simon Hacks; (3) Information systems and requirements modeling – chaired by Roman Lukyanenko and Marcela Ruiz; (4) Domain-specific and knowledge modeling – chaired by Robert Clarisó and Tiago Prince Sales; and (5) Evaluation of models & modeling approaches – chaired by Qin Ma and Monique Snoeck. More details on the current and previous editions of EMMSAD can be found at http://www.emmsad.org/.

In total, EMMSAD 2025 attracted 37 submissions. The division of submissions between the tracks was as follows: five related to foundations of modeling and method engineering, seven related to enterprise, business, process, and capability modeling, nine related to information systems and requirements modeling, eight related to domain-specific and knowledge modeling, and eight related to evaluation of modeling approaches. Each paper was reviewed by three members of the program committee and received a meta-review by the track chairs. Finally, 16 high-quality papers, comprising 13 full papers and three short papers, were selected.

We wish to thank all the authors who shared their work with us, as well as the members of the EMMSAD 2025 Program Committee and Track Chairs for their valuable, detailed, and timely reviews. Finally, we thank the organizers of CAiSE 2025 for their help in organizing the event, IFIP WG 8.1 for its support, and Springer for their continued support.

April 2025

Renata Guizzardi
Arnon Sturm

BPMDS 2025 Organization

Program Chairs

Han van der Aa — University of Vienna, Austria
Luise Pufahl — Technical University of Munich, Germany

Steering Committee

Selmin Nurcan — Paris 1 Panthéon-Sorbonne University, France
Rainer Schmidt — Munich University of Applied Sciences, Germany
Pnina Soffer — University of Haifa, Israel

Program Committee

Judith Barrios Albornoz — University of the Andes, Colombia
Iris Beerepoot — Utrecht University, the Netherlands
Rob Bemthuis — University of Twente, the Netherlands
Kristof Böhmer — University of Vienna, Austria
Faiza Bukhsh — University of Twente, the Netherlands
Carl Corea — University of Koblenz, Germany
Marco Comuzzi — UNIST, South Korea
Vinicius Stein Dani — Utrecht University, the Netherlands
Johannes De Smedt — KU Leuven, Belgium
Djordje Djurica — WU Vienna, Austria
Andreas Fritsch — Karlsruhe Institute of Technology, Germany
Stefan Jablonski — University of Bayreuth, Germany
Amin Jalali — Stockholm University, Sweden
Mieke Jans — Hasselt University, Belgium
Anna Kalenkova — University of Adelaide, Australia
Timotheus Kampik — Umeå University, Sweden
Agnes Koschmider — University of Bayreuth, Germany
Alexander Kraus — University of Mannheim, Germany
Sander J.J. Leemans — RWTH Aachen, Germany
Henrik Leopold — Kühne Logistics University, Germany
Orlenys López-Pintado — University of Tartu, Estonia
Xixi Lu — Utrecht University, the Netherlands

Niels Martin	Hasselt University, Belgium
Jan Mendling	Humboldt-Universität zu Berlin, Germany
Giovanni Meroni	Technical University of Denmark, Denmark
Selmin Nurcan	Université Paris 1 Panthéon-Sorbonne, France
Adrian Rebmann	SAP Signavio, Germany
Jana-Rebecca Rehse	University of Mannheim, Germany
Kate Revoredo	Humboldt-Universität zu Berlin, Germany
Michael Rosemann	Queensland University of Technology, Australia
Ronny Seiger	University of St. Gallen, Switzerland
Estefanía Serral	KU Leuven, Belgium
Stefan Schönig	University of Regensburg, Germany
Pnina Soffer	University of Haifa, Israel
Francesco Tiezzi	Università di Firenze, Italy
Amy Van Looy	Ghent University, Belgium
Irene Vanderfeesten	KU Leuven, Belgium
Inge van de Weerd	Utrecht University, the Netherlands
Jochen De Weerdt	KU Leuven, Belgium
Karolin Winter	TU Eindhoven, the Netherlands

Additional Reviewers

Luka Abb	University of Mannheim, Germany
Milda Aleknonyte-Resch	Kiel University, Germany
Tijmen Kuijpers	Eindhoven University of Technology, the Netherlands
Luca Mozzoni	University of Camerino, Italy
Jessica Piccioni	University of Camerino, Italy
Sara Pettinari	Gran Sasso Science Institute, Italy
Yorck Zisgen	University of Bayreuth, Germany

EMMSAD 2025 Organization

Program Chairs

Renata Guizzardi	University of Twente, the Netherlands
Arnon Sturm	Ben-Gurion University of the Negev, Israel

Track Chairs

Anne Gutschmidt	University of Rostock, Germany
Istvan David	McMaster University, Canada
Jānis Grabis	Riga Technical University, Latvia
Marcela Ruiz	Zurich University of Applied Sciences, Switzerland
Monique Snoeck	KU Leuven, Belgium
Qin Ma	University of Luxembourg, Luxembourg
Robert Clarisó	Universitat Oberta de Catalunya, Spain
Roman Lukyanenko	University of Virginia, USA
Simon Hacks	Stockholm University, Sweden
Tiago Prince Sales	University of Twente, the Netherlands

Program Committee

Alberto García	Universitat Politècnica de València, Spain
Alexander Bock	University of Duisburg-Essen, Germany
Alixandre Santana	OTH Regensburg, Germany
Dominik Bork	TU Wien, Austria
Andreas L. Opdahl	University of Bergen, Norway
Antonio De Nicola	ENEA, Italy
Arava Tsoury	Ruppin Academic Center, Israel
Ben Roelens	Open Universiteit, the Netherlands
Bentley Oakes	Polytechnique Montréal, Canada
Binny Samuel	University of Cincinnati, USA
Cesar Gonzalez-Perez	Incipit CSIC, Spain
Charlotte Verbruggen	KU Leuven, Belgium
Claudenir M. Fonseca	University of Twente, the Netherlands
Damiano Torre	University of Washington Tacoma, USA
Drazen Brdjanin	University of Banja Luka, Bosnia and Herzegovina
Elena Kornyshova	CNAM, France

Estefanía Serral	KU Leuven, Belgium
Felix Härer	University of Fribourg, Switzerland
Fernanda Baião	PUC-Rio, Brazil
Frederik Gailly	Ghent University, Belgium
Geert Poels	Ghent University, Belgium
George Grossmann	University of South Australia, Australia
Georgios Koutsopoulos	Stockholm University, Sweden
Giuseppe Berio	Université de Bretagne Sud and IRISA, France
Hans Weigand	Tilburg University, the Netherlands
Hans-Georg Fill	University of Fribourg, Switzerland
Iván Alfonso	Luxembourg Institute of Science and Technology, Luxembourg
Jaap Gordijn	Vrije Universiteit Amsterdam, the Netherlands
Janis Stirna	Stockholm University, Sweden
Jennifer Horkoff	Chalmers University of Technology, Sweden
Jenny Ruiz de La Peña	University of Holguin, Cuba
Jesús Sánchez Cuadrado	Universidad de Murcia, Spain
João Paulo Almeida	Federal University of Espírito Santo, Brazil
Jolita Ralyté	University of Geneva, Switzerland
Jose Ignacio Panach	Universitat de València, Spain
Juan De Lara	Universidad Autónoma de Madrid, Spain
Jürgen Jung	Frankfurt University of Applied Sciences, Germany
Knut Hinkelmann	FHNW University of Applied Sciences and Arts Northwestern Switzerland, Switzerland
Kristina Rosenthal	Hochschule Niederrhein University of Applied Sciences, Germany
Kurt Sandkuhl	University of Rostock, Germany
Maria Luiza Campos	Federal University of Rio de Janeiro, Brazil
Marne de Vries	University of Pretoria, South Africa
Martin Henkel	Stockholm University, Sweden
Michael Wahler	Zurich University of Applied Sciences ZHAW, Switzerland
Mira Balaban	Ben-Gurion University of the Negev, Israel
Mohamad Gharib	University of Tartu, Estonia
Oscar Pastor	Universidad Politécnica de Valencia, Spain
Pascal Ravesteyn	Utrecht University of Applied Sciences, the Netherlands
Paul Grefen	Eindhoven University of Technology, the Netherlands
Pedro Paulo F. Barcelos	University of Twente, the Netherlands

Peter Fettke	German Research Center for Artificial Intelligence (DFKI) and Saarland University, Germany
Raimundas Matulevicius	University of Tartu, Estonia
Rebecca Deneckere	Centre de Recherche en Informatique, France
Said Assar	Institut Mines-Télécom Business School, France
Stefan Strecker	University of Hagen, Germany
Sybren De Kinderen	Eindhoven University of Technology, the Netherlands
Tong Li	Beijing University of Technology, China
Tony Clark	Aston University, UK
Valdemar V. Graciano N.	Universidade Federal de Goiás, Brazil
Victoria Döller	University of Vienna, Austria
Yves Wautelet	Katholieke Universiteit Leuven, Belgium

Additional Reviewers

Bastian Kres	Fern Universität in Hagen, Germany
Nedo Aleander Bartels	Fraunhofer Inst. for Experimental Software Engineering, Germany
Marzia De Bartolomeo	AlmavivA, Italy
Lukas Daubner	University of Tartu, Estonia
Iris Mulder	Utrecht University of Applied Sciences, the Netherlands
Alberto Gaspar	Universitat de València, Spain
Sergio Manoel S. da Cruz	Universidade Federal Rural do Rio de Janeiro, Brazil

Contents

Business Process Improvement (BPMDS 2025)

AI-Enhanced Business Process Automation: A Case Study in the Insurance Domain Using Object-Centric Process Mining 3
   Shahrzad Khayatbashi, Viktor Sjölind, Anders Granåker, and Amin Jalali

Identifying Process Improvement Opportunities Through Process Execution Benchmarking 19
   Luka Abb, Majid Rafiei, Timotheus Kampik, and Jana-Rebecca Rehse

Interdependency-Aware Business Process Prioritization for Process Improvements 36
   Lauma Lubane and Marite Kirikova

Human-AI Interplay in Exploring Process Representations (BPMDS 2025)

Human-AI Collaboration for Business Process Modeling with Petri Nets 55
   Timo Schlösser, Martin Forell, Selina Schüler, and Andreas Fritsch

Repairing Process Descriptions by Discovering Deviations from Process Models 71
   Nan Sai, Karolin Winter, and Remco Dijkman

Process Model Complexity Metrics, Cognitive Load and Visual Behavior: A Multi-granular Eye-Tracking Analysis 87
   Thierry Sorg, Amine Abbad-Andaloussi, Ekkart Kindler, and Barbara Weber

Event Data Extraction (BPMDS 2025)

Which Tables are Mine(able)? 107
   Shameer K. Pradhan, Mieke Jans, and Niels Martin

OCPM^2: Extending the Process Mining Methodology for Object-Centric Event Data Extraction 123
   Najmeh Miri, Shahrzad Khayatbashi, Jelena Zdravkovic, and Amin Jalali

Making the Case for Process Analytics: A Use Case in Court Proceedings 141
Milda Aleknonytė-Resch, Anna-Katharina Dhungel, Fabian Elsaeßer, and Arvid Lepsien

Probabilistic Approaches to Uncertainty and Prediction in Process Mining (BPMDS 2025)

Predicting Unseen Process Behavior Based on Log Injection 159
Qian Chen, Karolin Winter, and Stefanie Rinderle-Ma

Toward IoT-Based Process Analytics: Extending Event Knowledge Graphs with Ambiguity 176
Marco Franceschetti, Dominik Manuel Buchegger, Ronny Seiger, and Barbara Weber

Probabilistic Learning of Temporal Uncertainties in Business Processes 193
Michel Kunkler and Stefanie Rinderle-Ma

AI-Driven Modeling and Analysis (EMMSAD 2025)

Assessing the Suitability of Large Language Models in Generating UML Class Diagrams as Conceptual Models 211
Marco Calamo, Massimo Mecella, and Monique Snoeck

Exploring the Influence of Data Characteristics on Machine Learning Outcomes 227
Camilla Sancricca, Pasquale Castiglione, and Cinzia Cappiello

Can an LLM Use Work System Axioms When Describing Work Systems for Requirements Analysis? 245
Steven Alter

Security (EMMSAD 2025)

Forensic Readiness and Privacy: Towards Resolving Software Goal Conflict ... 257
Lukas Daubner, Jakub Harašta, and Raimundas Matulevičius

An Ontological Model of the Phishing Attack Process 274
Ítalo Oliveira, Gerd Wagner, Glenda Amaral, Tiago Prince Sales, Jan-Willem Bullée, Marianne Junger, Dipti K. Sarmah, Maya Daneva, and Giancarlo Guizzardi

HarborLang: Enhancing Maritime Operational Safety Through Cyber
Threat Simulation and Assessment 290
   *Diana Malakhova, Simon Hacks, Anna Alexeeva,
and Thomas Ricardo Pathe*

Evaluation of Modeling Practices (EMMSAD 2025)

Learning Analytics Dashboard with Peer Comparison for Student
Feedback in Conceptual Modeling Education 301
   *Elena Tiukhova, Charlotte Verbruggen, Tinne De Laet, Bart Baesens,
and Monique Snoeck*

Are Code and Design Models Similarly Effective in Understanding
Software Structure and Behavior? 318
   Iris Reinhartz-Berger and Monique Snoeck

Towards a Maturity Assessment Framework for MBSE Adoption: Results
from a Meta-synthesis 335
   Tobias Henoeckl, Charlotte Verbruggen, and Dominik Bork

Modeling of and within Organizations (EMMSAD 2025)

Enhancing C2-Systems: Validation of Goal and Concept Models
with Stakeholders 353
   Jan Lundberg, Kent Andersson, and Janis Stirna

Supporting Collaborative Design by Diagram Briefs in the Early Stage
of Innovation Projects 368
   Tobias Kautz and Robert Winter

A Metamodel for Applying Green BPM Approaches with the EU Taxonomy ... 386
   Ilona Bogatinovska, Finn Klessascheck, Kerstin Andree, and Luise Pufahl

Experience Report: Applying a Capability Heat Map in a Government
Organization 403
   Evelien Groenendal and Ben Roelens

Domain Modeling (EMMSAD 2025)

State of the Art and Research Directions for Visual Conceptual Modeling
in Robotics 415
   Daniel Borcard and Hans-Georg Fill

A Domain-Specific Modeling Method for Designing Conversational
Agents for Coaching: A Case from Health Coaching 431
  Charuta Pande, Hans-Georg Fill, and Knut Hinkelmann

Designing Decision Support Systems for Rural Mobility Enhancement 448
  *Sabine Janzen, Hannah Stein, Lotfy Abdel Khaliq, Florian Hergert,
  and Wolfgang Maass*

Author Index 465

tities, and classify textual information based on prior training on vast datasets. Specifically, LLMs can be fine-tuned or prompted to extract relevant parts and classify them accurately within diverse claim descriptions, reducing reliance on human input and supporting digital transformation in business process management.

Organizations often transition from traditional (as-is) processes to AI-driven (to-be) workflows gradually, resulting in a phase where both process variants operate in parallel. This coexistence allows organizations to evaluate the impact of AI automation on their ongoing processes, but it also presents challenges, as both process variants can influence the process outcomes. To support this, a data-driven approach should analyze both parallel process variants, each representing distinct aspects of the process, thereby enabling a more comprehensive understanding of how automation alters process behavior [9]. Object-Centric Process Mining (OCPM) [22] has emerged as a promising method for analyzing process transformations that enables the simultaneous analysis of multiple perspectives, making it particularly valuable for AI-driven process reengineering. Investigating side effects of process automation is important as indicated in literature [4, 25], where OCPM enable such investigation based on recorded process data. While previous research has demonstrated OCPM's use in analyzing a single business process variant [2, 15, 21], its ability to capture both as-is and to-be process variants simultaneously has yet to be investigated.

To address this gap, this study presents a real-world case from the insurance sector, where the rising volume of claims necessitated AI-driven automation for claim part identification. The study follows the Business Process Reengineering (BPR) framework [18] to examine the transition from a manual as-is process to an AI-enhanced to-be workflow, supported by an LLM [5] for automation. Instead of fully automating claim part management, the LLM model generates leads for investigators, ensuring a balance between AI-driven efficiency and expert oversight and having humans in the loop. The AI implementation adheres to the CRoss-Industry Standard Process for Data Mining (CRISP-DM) methodology [7], providing a structured approach to data understanding, modeling, and deployment.

To evaluate the impact of AI-driven automation, this study applies OCPM to assess process scalability. The evaluation follows $OCPM^2$ [17], an extension of the PM^2 process mining methodology [24], enabling a systematic examination of process evolution. By applying OCPM, this study provides empirical insights into how AI-driven process reengineering enhances scalability while also assessing OCPM's strengths and limitations in analyzing real-world process transformations.

The remainder of this paper is structured as follows: Sect. 2 details the methodology, outlining the application of BPR, CRISP-DM, and OCPM for process evaluation. Section 3 presents the results, examining the impact of AI-driven automation on scalability and process dynamics while evaluating OCPM's advantages and limitations. Finally, Sect. 4 concludes the paper.

Business Process Improvement (BPMDS 2025)

2 Methodology

Figure 1 illustrates the Business Process Reengineering (BPR) framework [18] consisting of 6 phases that are followed in this study. In the *understanding phase*, the

AI-Enhanced Business Process Automatio[n]: Case Study in the Insurance Domain Usi[ng] Object-Centric Process Mining

Shahrzad Khayatbashi[1], Viktor Sjölind[2], Anders Granåker[2], and Am[in Jalali[3]]

[1] Linköping University, Linköping, Sweden
shahrzad.khayatbashi@liu.se
[2] If P&C Insurance, Stockholm, Sweden
viktor.sjolind@if.fi, {anders.granaker,amin.jalali}@
aj@dsv.su.se
[3] Stockholm University, Stockholm, Sweden

Abstract. Recent advancements in Artificial Intelligence (AI), particu[larly] Large Language Models (LLMs), have enhanced organizations' ability to re[engi]neer business processes by automating knowledge-intensive tasks. This aut[oma]tion drives digital transformation, often through gradual transitions that imp[rove] process efficiency and effectiveness. To fully assess the impact of such auto[ma]tion, a data-driven analysis approach is needed - one that examines how t[radi]tional and AI-enhanced process variants coexist during this transition. Ob[ject-] Centric Process Mining (OCPM) has emerged as a valuable method that ena[bles] such analysis, yet real-world case studies are still needed to demonstrate its ap[pli]cability. This paper presents a case study from the insurance sector, where [an] LLM was deployed in production to automate the identification of claim pa[rts,] a task previously performed manually and identified as a bottleneck for s[cal]ability. To evaluate this transformation, we apply OCPM to assess the imp[act] of AI-driven automation on process scalability. Our findings indicate that wh[ile] LLMs significantly enhance operational capacity, they also introduce new p[ro]cess dynamics that require further refinement. This study also demonstrates [the] practical application of OCPM in a real-world setting, highlighting its advanta[ges] and limitations.

Keywords: AI-Driven Automation · Business Process Reengineering · Digita[l] Transformation · Business Process Management

1 Introduction

Artificial Intelligence (AI), particularly in the form of Large Language Models [5], is transforming business processes by automating knowledge-intensive ta[sks,] enhancing operational efficiency. For example, identifying claim parts in the ins[urance] domain is a knowledge-intensive task that traditionally requires human expert[ise due] to the wide variety of claim parts. As claim volumes increase, manual identif[ication] becomes a bottleneck, limiting process scalability. LLMs present a significant op[portu]nity to automate this task by leveraging their ability to understand context, rec[ognize]

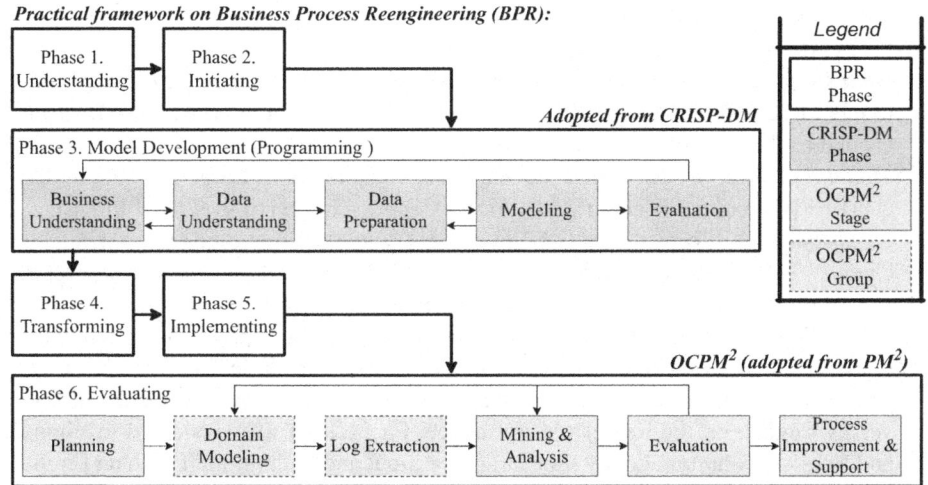

Fig. 1. The followed research methodology based on BPR [18], CRISP-DM [7] and OCPM² [17], an extended version of PM² [24].

objectives of reengineering were defined, emphasizing the role of AI-driven automation in enhancing the scalability of the claim part identification process. This phase involved identifying scalability limitations and key challenges by analyzing the as-is process. Stakeholder interviews and process documentation were conducted to understand manual claim assessments, their associated bottlenecks, and the feasibility of AI-driven automation.

Following this, the *initiation phase* defined the project vision, scope, and requirements. The primary goal was to develop an AI-driven approach for automating the identification of claim parts requiring further investigation. Additionally, data collection strategies were outlined to ensure necessary historical claim data availability for AI model training.

Next, the *model development phase* (referred to as Programming in BPR) was carried out by the technical team, following the CRISP-DM methodology [7] to ensure a structured approach in developing a customized AI model, where its tasks are explained below:

- *Business Understanding*, where the objectives and constraints of AI integration within the claims handling process were defined. Security approval was obtained to ensure compliance with security and privacy regulations. Discussions with domain experts helped establish requirements for claim part identification, ensuring alignment with operational goals. The primary business objective was to automate knowledge-intensive tasks while maintaining acceptable performance and enhancing scalability.
- *Data Understanding*, where data sources, data quality issues, and relevant features were identified. The analysis focused primarily on claim descriptions and notes,

representing the unstructured data sources. Additionally, exploratory data analysis (EDA) [6] was conducted to gain deeper insights.
- *Data Preparation*, a labeled dataset was created by asking claim part investigators to label free-text claim descriptions and notes. This unstructured data served as the ground truth for evaluating the quality of the developed AI solution.
- *Modeling*, where we leveraged the analytical capabilities of Large Language Models (LLMs) to identify claim parts. Various approaches were evaluated to ensure a consistent output format from GPT models [1], with the Structured Output feature in OpenAI APIs found to be the most effective [20]. The prompt engineering process was a collaboration between business domain experts and data scientists.
- *Evaluation*, where the LLM model was assessed using two approaches. First, quantitative evaluation was performed against the ground truth dataset. Second, a language evaluation was conducted to analyze the impact of using the Finnish language versus English on the model's performance. Each claim was processed in Finnish and English by automatically translating the input and combining it with an English version of the instructions. Business validation was further conducted through pilot tests, where human experts reviewed the AI-generated outputs before full deployment.

The *transformation phase* involved conducting pilot studies to evaluate AI integration, estimating the scale of organizational changes, and assessing resource requirements.

The *implementation phase* focused on restructuring workflows and integrating AI into the IT infrastructure. The solution was implemented using serverless components, queuing mechanisms, table storage, and models hosted in an Azure OpenAI Service, ensuring that GPT models operated within a regional data center in Sweden to comply with company policies on data privacy and security. Additional privacy measures were applied, such as masking Personally Identifiable Information (PII) before transmitting data to the AI inference server.

Finally, the *evaluation phase* aimed to assess the impact of AI on process scalability using process mining techniques, following OCPM^2 [17], an extended version of the PM^2 [24] methodology. The process began with the planning stage, where we formulated the key research questions. Next, in the domain modeling, we designed the domain by identifying object types, activities, and their relationships. Following this, we extracted an Object-Centric Event Log (OCEL 2.0) [3] and applied object-centric and traditional process discovery techniques to analyze the AI-driven transformation. OCEL was selected as the data format due to its support for advanced analytical operations such as drill-down, unfolding [13, 14], and ad-hoc filtering (e.g., dicing), which were essential for exploring different process perspectives and ensuring flexible, performance-efficient querying during analysis [11]. The findings were then empirically validated by domain experts to ensure reliability, and we ultimately derived insights to enhance the claims part management process.

3 Case Study

3.1 Process Context

The case study was conducted at *If P&C Insurance*, a property and casualty insurance company serving approximately 4 million customers across the Nordic and Baltic regions [8]. The company offers a comprehensive range of insurance solutions and services tailored to diverse customer segments, including individuals and large corporations. It processes more than 1.4 million claims annually, with half of them handled within 24 h of being reported. This study focuses on a sub-process within the claims handling procedure, specifically aimed at identifying certain types of *claim parts* that require special treatment. Due to confidentiality restrictions, the business terms for these claim parts cannot be disclosed.

This business process operates in the Nordic and Baltic regions across three business areas, each comprising multiple lines of business. In total, there are 77 lines of business where different variations of this process are in place. The process heavily relies on claim handlers to identify claim parts. However, the variations across lines of business make it challenging to train claim handlers, as identifying these components requires specialized business knowledge. In this study, we applied AI to identify claim parts in one specific line of business.

The goal to develop an AI-driven solution was set by the business before the start of the project, based on prior internal analysis and strategic digital transformation objectives. However, the BPR and CRISP-DM phases were essential for tailoring the solution, validating feasibility, aligning stakeholder expectations, preparing the data, and evaluating the impact of the AI system in practice. The project began on 2024-01-30, with the first version of the model developed on 2024-04-16. The model was integrated and deployed in production on 2024-09-25. This study evaluates the impact of this process reengineering on the scalability of the business process, based on data collected over 5 months during which both AI and claim handlers worked in parallel to identify claim parts. Claim handlers continued to work as before, even after the introduction of AI, allowing us to assess its impact on the scalability of the business process.

This section presents the results from phases 3 and 6 of the Business Process Reengineering (BPR) project. It includes both the evaluation outcomes and the main lessons learned during the study. A total of twelve people from the company took part in the project, enabling the implementation of phases 1 to 5 and supporting the first author to evaluate the outcome using OCPM. The team included two data scientists, one software engineer, two subject matter experts, one business owner, one DevOps specialist, one cloud engineer, one data privacy officer, one legal expert, one identity and access management (IAM) expert, one enterprise architect, and one application security specialist. The first author led the work in Phase 6, focusing on the process mining analysis, with support from the second and last authors in providing the required data. The second and third authors were responsible for conducting Phase 3.

3.2 Phase 3: Model Development

The development of the claim part identification model followed the CRISP-DM methodology, ensuring a structured and iterative approach. Close collaboration between

Table 1. Evaluation results of different model versions for Claim Part identification.

Model Version	Language	Accuracy	Precision	Recall	F1_score
v1	eng	0.76	0.83	0.67	0.74
v1	fin	0.77	0.86	0.67	0.75
v2	eng	0.77	0.92	0.61	0.73
v2	fin	0.76	0.85	0.64	0.73
v3	eng	0.7	0.8	0.56	0.66
v3	fin	0.77	0.81	**0.72**	0.76
v4	eng	0.71	0.79	0.61	0.69
v4	fin	0.74	0.76	**0.72**	0.74
v5	eng	0.8	0.81	**0.81**	0.81
v5	fin	0.77	0.83	0.69	0.76

technical team and domain experts played a crucial role in refining requirements and improving model accuracy. Given the importance of precise claim part identification in automated processing, the goal was to develop a model capable of achieving at least human-level performance. The company's baseline analysis revealed that human claim handlers correctly identify 70% of the actual claim parts, meaning that 30% of the true items are missed. This recall value sets a performance benchmark against which the LLM models were evaluated. A balanced dataset was manually labeled by claim part investigators to ensure that model predictions could be assessed reliably.

To evaluate the LLM models, we used Recall as the primary evaluation metric. It was prioritized over F1-score because, in claim processing, false negatives (missed claim parts) have a significantly higher impact than false positives. While the F1-score balances precision and recall, it does not align with real-world priorities, where failing to detect claim parts has a tangible negative financial impact. In contrast, false positives can often be handled through additional validation steps with minimal disruption. Since the consequences of false negatives outweigh those of false positives, maximizing recall is more critical than achieving a perfect balance. By focusing on Recall, the model ensures a higher likelihood of identifying all relevant claim parts, even if some additional filtering is required downstream, which will be handled by investigators.

In the initial Proof-of-Concept, we tested a variety of different models, including the small language model (SLM) Phi-3 from Microsoft and the large language model (LLM) Mistral Large. Our tests showed that these models did not perform adequately when processing input data and prompts in the Finnish language. Since the prompts expose business-specific terminology that is subject to confidentiality restrictions, we are unable to disclose them in this paper. For the production system, we eventually settled on GPT-4o-0806, employing a Chain-of-Thought (CoT) prompt structure with few-shot samples to guide the model in identifying claim parts, and different strategies to produce an output format that could easily be integrated into the system. GPT-4o also seemed to give similar levels of performance in both Finnish and English. Throughout the project, therefore, we kept running two separate analysis processes for each claim

Business Process Improvement (BPMDS 2025)

AI-Enhanced Business Process Automation: A Case Study in the Insurance Domain Using Object-Centric Process Mining

Shahrzad Khayatbashi[1(✉)], Viktor Sjölind[2], Anders Granåker[2], and Amin Jalali[2,3]

[1] Linköping University, Linköping, Sweden
shahrzad.khayatbashi@liu.se
[2] If P&C Insurance, Stockholm, Sweden
viktor.sjolind@if.fi, {anders.granaker,amin.jalali}@if.se,
aj@dsv.su.se
[3] Stockholm University, Stockholm, Sweden

Abstract. Recent advancements in Artificial Intelligence (AI), particularly Large Language Models (LLMs), have enhanced organizations' ability to reengineer business processes by automating knowledge-intensive tasks. This automation drives digital transformation, often through gradual transitions that improve process efficiency and effectiveness. To fully assess the impact of such automation, a data-driven analysis approach is needed - one that examines how traditional and AI-enhanced process variants coexist during this transition. Object-Centric Process Mining (OCPM) has emerged as a valuable method that enables such analysis, yet real-world case studies are still needed to demonstrate its applicability. This paper presents a case study from the insurance sector, where an LLM was deployed in production to automate the identification of claim parts, a task previously performed manually and identified as a bottleneck for scalability. To evaluate this transformation, we apply OCPM to assess the impact of AI-driven automation on process scalability. Our findings indicate that while LLMs significantly enhance operational capacity, they also introduce new process dynamics that require further refinement. This study also demonstrates the practical application of OCPM in a real-world setting, highlighting its advantages and limitations.

Keywords: AI-Driven Automation · Business Process Reengineering · Digital Transformation · Business Process Management

1 Introduction

Artificial Intelligence (AI), particularly in the form of Large Language Models (LLMs) [5], is transforming business processes by automating knowledge-intensive tasks and enhancing operational efficiency. For example, identifying claim parts in the insurance domain is a knowledge-intensive task that traditionally requires human expertise due to the wide variety of claim parts. As claim volumes increase, manual identification becomes a bottleneck, limiting process scalability. LLMs present a significant opportunity to automate this task by leveraging their ability to understand context, recognize entities, and classify textual information based on prior training on vast datasets. Specifically, LLMs can be fine-tuned or prompted to extract relevant parts and classify them accurately within diverse claim descriptions, reducing reliance on human input and supporting digital transformation in business process management.

Organizations often transition from traditional (as-is) processes to AI-driven (to-be) workflows gradually, resulting in a phase where both process variants operate in parallel. This coexistence allows organizations to evaluate the impact of AI automation on their ongoing processes, but it also presents challenges, as both process variants can influence the process outcomes. To support this, a data-driven approach should analyze both parallel process variants, each representing distinct aspects of the process, thereby enabling a more comprehensive understanding of how automation alters process behavior [9]. Object-Centric Process Mining (OCPM) [22] has emerged as a promising method for analyzing process transformations that enables the simultaneous analysis of multiple perspectives, making it particularly valuable for AI-driven process reengineering. Investigating side effects of process automation is important as indicated in literature [4,25], where OCPM enable such investigation based on recorded process data. While previous research has demonstrated OCPM's use in analyzing a single business process variant [2,15,21], its ability to capture both as-is and to-be process variants simultaneously has yet to be investigated.

To address this gap, this study presents a real-world case from the insurance sector, where the rising volume of claims necessitated AI-driven automation for claim part identification. The study follows the Business Process Reengineering (BPR) framework [18] to examine the transition from a manual as-is process to an AI-enhanced to-be workflow, supported by an LLM [5] for automation. Instead of fully automating claim part management, the LLM model generates leads for investigators, ensuring a balance between AI-driven efficiency and expert oversight and having humans in the loop. The AI implementation adheres to the CRoss-Industry Standard Process for Data Mining (CRISP-DM) methodology [7], providing a structured approach to data understanding, modeling, and deployment.

To evaluate the impact of AI-driven automation, this study applies OCPM to assess process scalability. The evaluation follows OCPM^2 [17], an extension of the PM^2 process mining methodology [24], enabling a systematic examination of process evolution. By applying OCPM, this study provides empirical insights into how AI-driven process reengineering enhances scalability while also assessing OCPM's strengths and limitations in analyzing real-world process transformations.

The remainder of this paper is structured as follows: Sect. 2 details the methodology, outlining the application of BPR, CRISP-DM, and OCPM for process evaluation. Section 3 presents the results, examining the impact of AI-driven automation on scalability and process dynamics while evaluating OCPM's advantages and limitations. Finally, Sect. 4 concludes the paper.

2 Methodology

Figure 1 illustrates the Business Process Reengineering (BPR) framework [18] consisting of 6 phases that are followed in this study. In the *understanding phase*, the task: one in which we translated both the input data and prompts from Finnish to English and another where we ran the analysis using input data and prompts in Finnish. The input data, mainly claim descriptions and notes, were masked to eliminate Personally Identifiable Information (PII) before processing by the LLM. In the English version, we also used GPT-4o-0806 to translate input data before processing. All LLMs in use were deployed in an Azure OpenAI service with data residency in Sweden.

As the model evolved through multiple iterations, systematic improvements were made to enhance performance. Table 1 shows the evaluation result for different model versions. As can be seen, version 1 and version 2 fell short of human performance, with recall scores lagging behind the 70% baseline. The initial model used an XML format to produce a stable output format. This approach would occasionally produce slight variations in the output when we expected binary results for a task. In the second version of the model, we switched to the JSON mode API feature [19], which guaranteed that the output was valid JSON, and although there were improvements, we still had not fully solved the issue of unwanted variations in the output.

By version 5, instruction sets were significantly enriched with detailed metadata considerations, such as insurance event timing, which played a crucial role in improving claim part likelihood estimation. We also solved the issue of unwanted variations in the output using the OpenAI Structured Outputs feature that forced the output to adhere to a strict schema [20]. A major refinement in version 5 was the introduction of specialized claim part prompts, which allowed the model to assess the existence of specific components separately, leading to improved prediction scores. The changes enabled the model (version 5) to achieve an 81% recall for the English version, surpassing human performance and demonstrating its ability to automate claim processing with a high degree of accuracy. This milestone was particularly critical for the business, as it allowed for large-scale automation while maintaining consistency in claim assessments.

3.3 Phase 6: Evaluation

We followed OCPM[2] [17], an extended version of the PM[2] [24] methodology, to evaluate the impact of our AI-driven business process reengineering.

Planning: In this stage, we aimed to answer the following four questions:

- *Q1) How have claim handlers effectively identified claim parts?*
- *Q2) How has AI effectively identified claim parts?*
- *Q3) Among the claim parts under investigation, how many claim parts did AI fail to identify but were accurately identified by claim handlers?*
- *Q4) Among the claim parts under investigation, how many claim parts did claim handlers fail to identify but were accurately identified by AI?*

Additionally, we identified various systems from which we needed to extract data.

Domain Modeling: Through multiple iterations, we identified relevant object types based on the questions and designed a business conceptual model in UML notation, illustrating the object types and their relationships within this business process context (see Fig. 2). The identified object types are *Customer, Claim, Claim Note, Claim Part, AI Model*, and *Employee*, where an employee can be either a *Claim Handler* or a *Claim Part Investigator*. All these object types are defined as classes, with *Claim Handler* and *Claim Part Investigator* inheriting from the *Employee* class.

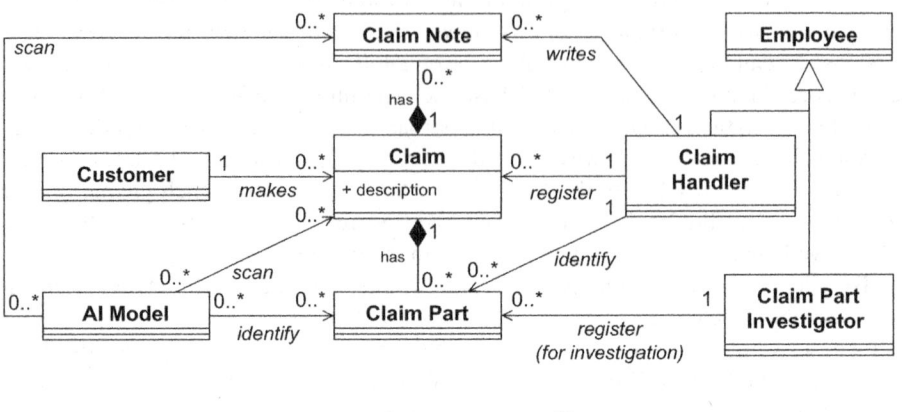

Fig. 2. The conceptual model illustrating the identified object types and their relationships within the claims part identification process.

A customer can make multiple claims, but each claim can be made by only one customer. Each claim can be registered by a claim handler, while a claim handler can register multiple claims. Each claim can have multiple claim notes, and each note is written by a claim handler. A claim handler can also identify claim parts, where each claim part belongs to a specific claim. A claim can have multiple claim parts. An AI model can scan claim descriptions and claim notes to identify claim parts. Additionally, a claim part investigator can register a claim part for further investigation.

In addition, we documented the relation between activities and object types using an "Extraction Matrix", where activities were listed as rows and object types as columns. We do not present this matrix in this paper, as we will show the existence of relations later when we elaborate on verifying the extraction.

In this paper, we used the following acronyms to refer to activities and some object types for the sake of the readability of figures, i.e.: ***CP**: Claim Part*, ***rc**: register claim*, ***cn**: create note*, ***rCP**: report Claim Part*, ***cCPi**: create Claim Part investigation*. These two acronyms refer to activities that enhance the process using AI, i.e., ***sc**: scan claim*, ***pCP**: predict Claim Part*. In the traditional process, after registering the claim and creating notes, a claim handler could identify and report claim parts. Then, a claim part investigator could create a claim part investigation for them, which initiates another process. The integration of AI introduced two additional activities: the AI model scans the claim (reading claim descriptions and claim notes), and it identifies the claim part (referred to as the "predict claim part"). Then, the claim part investigator can register a claim part investigation for them as well.

Implementation and Log Extraction: Extracting logs posed several challenges despite the presence of multiple data warehouses within the company. Fortunately, the company maintained a temporal data warehouse that stored not only claim-related data but also tracked changes to each entity. However, information about individual claim parts had to be extracted from an operational system using a specific KPI. We extracted temporal data that captured all relevant information but filtered the results to retain only one note per claim—the most recent note available prior to the scan claim activity (sc). This filtering step facilitated the transformation of data into the OCEL 2.0 format, as this standard cannot distinguish whether related claim notes have expired. This limitation could be addressed by defining a validity period for object-to-object relations within OCEL 2.0. Notably, this limitation does not exist in all OCED formats, e.g., temporal Event Knowledge Graphs (tEKG) [12] capture snapshots of objects and their relationships at a particular point in time.

We performed a drill-down operation at the employee role level to distinguish between claim handlers and claim part investigators aiming to discover more detailed patterns [16] when analyzing the process. We also verified the log by checking whether all relations identified in the Extraction Matrix were captured. Figure 3 shows the number of relations captured in extracted OCEL 2.0 between each activity and different object types, depicted in the corresponding cells. This heatmap was used to verify the correctness of the extracted OCEL 2.0.

Process Mining Analysis and Evaluation: We analyzed the results by discovering the Object-Centric Directly-Follows Graph (OC-DFG) [22] and Object-Centric Petri Nets (OCPNs) [23] from the extracted OCEL. We found OC-DFG particularly useful for analysis, as we needed to examine all possible paths that could be directly followed to perform different analyses, which we elaborated on later. However, *using any object-centric process model to communicate with stakeholders proved ineffective*. Stakeholders found these models too complex to interpret, even when we reduced the number of object types by selecting a more specific profile (i.e., a set of object types). Despite our efforts to simplify the visualizations, stakeholders still found them difficult to interpret during the final presentation. As a result, while we used OC-DFG to analyze different scenarios, we flattened the filtered OCELs by focusing on the Claim object type (which was related to all activities) and presented the results using a Directly-Follows Graph (DFG). Flattening has been considered as an effective technique to complement OCPM [10]. In this study, stakeholders found these graphs informative, as they improved communication when discussing and investigating different scenarios. Although object-centric models enabled deeper analysis and log filtering for specific insights, DFGs proved more effective for conveying results to end users.

Figure 4 shows the DFG discovered by flattening the log on the claim object type without any filtering. In total, 3743 claims have been registered (rc) in this line of business over 5 months. Among these claims, claim handlers identified claim parts for only 68 claims, i.e., rCP, while AI scanned all claims and identified 1034 claim parts. Please

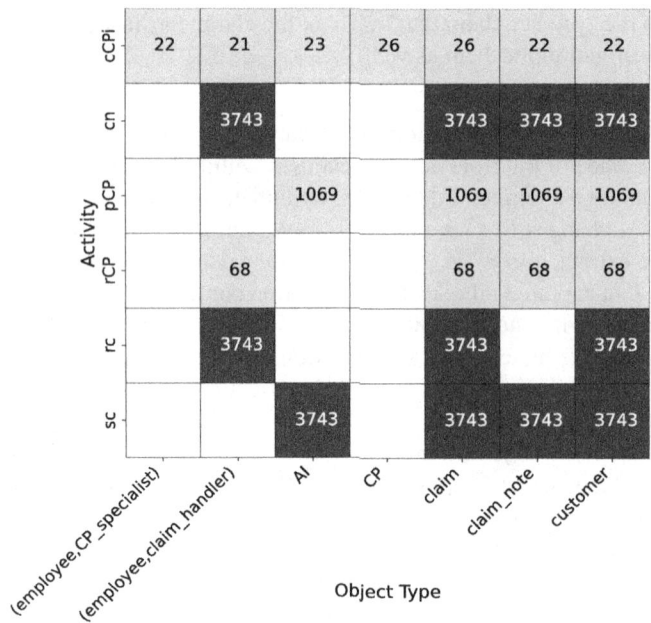

Fig. 3. The verification matrix showing the number of relations between activities and object types in the extracted OCEL with these acronyms used for activity names: *rc: register claim*, *cn: create note*, *rCP: report Claim Part*, *cCPi: create Claim Part investigation*, *sc: scan claim*, *pCP: predict Claim Part*. *CP* is also used as an acronym for *Claim Part* object type.

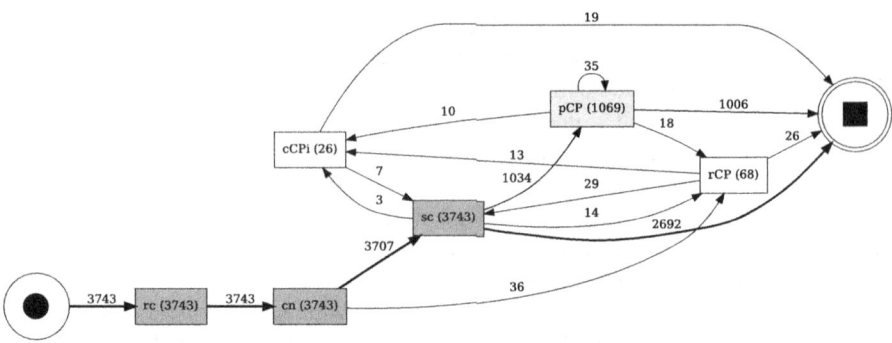

Fig. 4. The discovered Directly-Follows Graph (DFG) of claim part identification process, showing how AI scaled Claim Part identification.

note that the loop in *pCP* occurred because a few prediction results were registered multiple times due to the use of message queues in the architecture, where messages timed out. Therefore, the incoming flow shows the correct number of unique predictions.

As can be seen, claim part investigators have created only a few cases for investigation due to the limited number of investigators currently handling these claim parts.

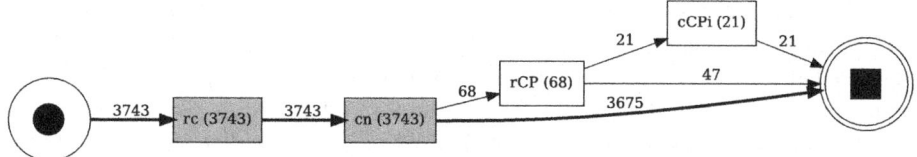

Fig. 5. The discovered DFG depicting human performance in identifying Claim Parts and investigating identified cases.

The number of investigators was sufficient for the traditional process, as they did not investigate all identified claim parts but selected the most important ones based on certain claim features. However, AI significantly scaled the identification process, leading stakeholders to recognize *the need to employ more investigators to handle the increased workload*. This demonstrates that while AI can enhance scalability, it can also shift bottlenecks within the process.

These findings highlight the importance of assessing process reengineering efforts when implementing AI-driven improvements, as other parts of the process may be affected and require additional adjustments. *This highlights the value of analyzing the end-to-end process when improving a part of the process using any AI-driven approach, as improving one specific point in the process may not add value to the organization.*

The identified changes were considered highly valuable by stakeholders and the company, who plan to extend AI usage to other lines of business. Additional questions arose during the evaluation phase, and *OCEL 2.0 proved beneficial by eliminating the need for repeated data extraction and integration for each analysis*, as it retains information about all object types. *OCEL 2.0 also enabled us to query and filter different relations using qualifiers defined for object-to-object and event-to-object relations*, without which we needed to extract and integrate the data to an event log from scratch, increasing data processing time significantly for every analysis. The business was interested in investigating the process and answering questions (Q1-Q4) about how humans and AI contributed to claim part identification. We present the analysis for these questions below.

Q1) How have claim handlers effectively identified claim parts?

To answer this question, we filtered out "scan claim" (sc) and "predict Claim Part" (pCP) events from the log, which were only performed by AI. Additionally, we retained only "create Claim Part investigation" ($cCPi$) events where its claim number could be found among reported Claim Parts (rCP). Figure 5 presents the DFG obtained after filtering the OCEL accordingly and flattening the log based on the claim object type. As can be seen, claim handlers identified 68 claim parts from 3743 claims, indicating that 1.82% of claims contain claim parts. The business experts we interviewed confirmed this percentage, which is too low relative to the expected number of claim parts. This was a key motivation for initiating this project—to scale claim part identification. From these identified claim parts, claim part investigators created 21 cases for further investigation. It is worth mentioning that investigators do not create an investigation case for every identified claim part; instead, they select cases based on specific business criteria.

Q2) How has AI effectively identified claim parts?

To answer this question, we filtered out the "report Claim Part" (*rCP*) events from the log, which were performed solely by claim handlers. Additionally, we retained only "create Claim Part investigation" (*cCPi*) events where its claim number could be found among predicted Claim Parts (*pCP*). The reason for such filtering was that some claim part investigations may have been created based on claim handler reports before the AI would scan the claims. As a result, the AI would predict the claim part only after the investigation had already been created. Therefore, the *cCPi* event would not be attributed to the AI, even though the AI would identify such cases. Figure 6 presents the DFG obtained after filtering the OCEL accordingly and flattening the log based on the claim object type.

As can be seen, AI identified 1034 claim parts (see the frequency of incoming flow to *pCP*) from 3743 claims, indicating that 27.62% of claims contain claim parts. This percentage is expected by the business experts we interviewed, showing the success of claim part identification. Among these identified claim parts, the investigators created 23 cases for further investigation. Please note that the outgoing and incoming flows to *sc* show the order of events that happened in different cases and do not indicate loops.

It is evident from this figure that investigators created some claim parts before AI scanned the claims. Such a shift in their work does not affect the AI outcome, as AI did not know about the created items. Please note that as some *cCPi* were not related to AI (as they were created before AI scanned the claim), they would have been missed if one filtered the traditional log by including only *cCPi* events that are related to AI through an attribute. Thus, *it was experienced that without having OCEL, we could either end up with incorrect analysis or need to perform a complex data processing and re-extracting the log to answer this question.*

If we compare the AI-identified claim parts ratio with the human-identified claim parts ratio, we can conclude that the process has scaled 1420%, a finding confirmed by the business when investigating the cases. However, we do not observe a significant difference when examining the created claim part investigation (*cCPi*). Upon discussing this issue with business stakeholders, we realized that *a lack of investigators is limiting the scalability of the claim part management process*. Since *cCPi* initiates this process, its impact is constrained by this bottleneck. This is an interesting finding, as it highlights how the successful adoption of AI in scaling the identification process creates a bottleneck in another process (i.e., the claim part management process). The company is now working to scale this aspect of the process to fully leverage the benefits of AI-identified claim parts by enabling the processing of a greater volume.

Q3) Among the claim parts under investigation, how many claim parts did AI fail to identify but were accurately identified by claim handlers?

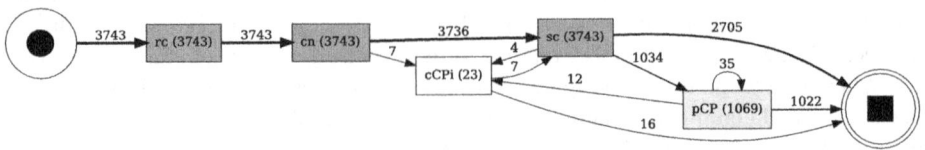

Fig. 6. The discovered DFG depicting AI performance in identifying Claim Parts.

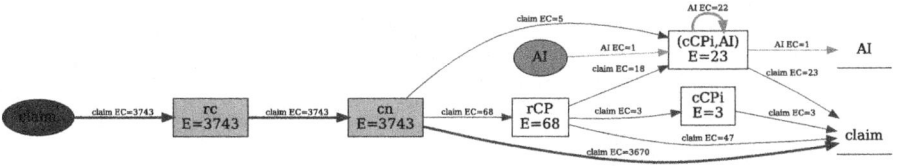

Fig. 7. The discovered OC-DFG separating cases identified by humans alone (*cCPi E=3*) and those identified by AI or AI and humans (*(cCPi,AI) E=23*).

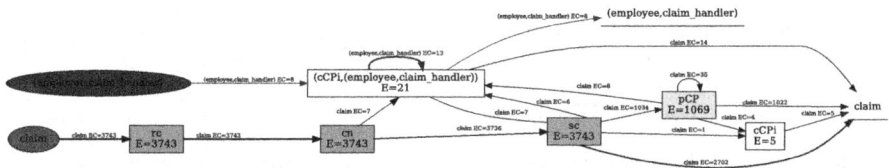

Fig. 8. The discovered OC-DFG separating cases identified by AI alone (*cCPi E=5*) and those identified by humans or AI and human (*(cCPi,(employee,claim_handler)) E=21*).

The claim parts that are under investigation are considered truly identified claim parts by the business as an investigator has approved them by creating an investigation request for them (*cCPi*). Thus, the business was interested in investigating how the process looks like for 26 claim parts for which the investigation request is made (*cCPi* in Fig. 4). To answer this question, we discovered an OC-DFG by applying some specific filtering, as explained below (see Fig. 7).

The overall OC-DFG could answer the question as well, but stakeholders considered it very complex and impractical as it required a lot of effort to be interpreted. Thus, we excluded non-human activities from the log. Also, we only kept *Claim* and *AI* object types and unfolded [13, 14] the log based on *cCPi* and *AI*. The unfold operation enabled us to separate all investigation activities where AI was involved, helping users to visually separate the ones that were only performed by claim handlers. As can be seen from the OC-DFG, there were only 3 investigation cases where the claim handler reported the claim part, and AI missed them. The frequency of *(cCPi,AI)* (23) represents the number of times that both AI or human and AI could identify claim parts.

Q4) Among the claim parts under investigation, how many claim parts did claim handlers fail to identify but were accurately identified by AI?

To answer this question, we only kept *Claim* and *(employee, claim_handler)* object types and unfolded the log based on *cCPi* and *(employee, claim_handler)*. We excluded *rc* as it only performed by the claim handler, then discovered the OC-DFG (see Fig. 8). As can be seen, AI identified 5 cases that claim handlers missed among open to be investigated cases. Figure 9 shows how many investigations were created based on identified cases by claim handlers and AI. As can be seen, AI and claim handlers identified 18 cases among cases under investigation, where claim handlers missed identifying 5 cases, and AI missed identifying 3 cases. The result are all evaluated by discussing identified cases with stakeholders and verifying the correctness based on source systems.

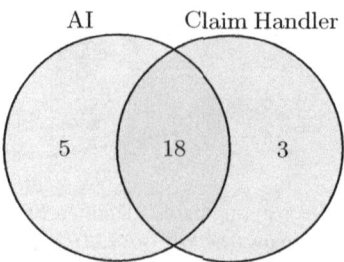

Fig. 9. Number of investigation created based on AI & Human identification.

3.4 Lessons Learned and Discussion

The integration of AI into business processes offers significant opportunities for efficiency gains but also introduces new challenges. We summarize our key findings below.

AI's Impact on Business Process Dynamics. AI-driven process reengineering does not guarantee efficiency improvements across the entire workflow. While AI can remove bottlenecks in one area, it may create new constraints elsewhere, necessitating process-wide adjustments:

- AI successfully eliminated bottlenecks in claim identification but created a backlog in claim investigation, requiring reallocation of resources and workforce adjustments.
- Scaling a single process step does not automatically lead to overall efficiency gains and adding business value. Organizations must ensure that downstream processes can handle the increased workload, either through automation, workforce expansion, or process redesign.
- AI-generated workload growth may exceed human capacity, highlighting the need for a holistic evaluation of AI adoption beyond individual task optimization.

Challenges in Process Mining Visualization and Usability. While process mining provides deep insights, effectively communicating these findings to business stakeholders remains a challenge. Several key visualization issues were identified:

- **Customization is crucial to usability.** Full object-centric models are too complex for non-technical users. Providing both simplified flat models and more detailed object-centric views improves adoption and decision-making.
- **Dynamic exploration capabilities are needed.** Drill-down and unfolding operations enable targeted analysis, reducing the need for repeated log reconstruction and enhancing efficiency.
- **Current open-source tools lack flexibility.** Existing open-source process mining tools do not offer the customization required for seamless stakeholder engagement. Improved visualization frameworks are necessary to bridge the gap between technical insights and business decision-making.

4 Conclusion

This study demonstrates the application of AI-driven automation in scaling business processes within the insurance sector, specifically in the claims part identification process. By leveraging Large Language Models (LLMs) and Object-Centric Process Mining (OCPM), we systematically evaluated how AI enhances process scalability and efficiency. Our findings indicate that AI significantly increased the number of identified claim parts, reducing the manual workload of claim handlers. However, this success also introduced new bottlenecks, particularly in the claims investigation phase, highlighting the need for holistic process redesigns when integrating AI solutions.

The evaluation using OCPM provided valuable insights into the AI-driven transformation, allowing for detailed process analysis and performance tracking. However, our study also uncovered challenges in effectively communicating object-centric process models to stakeholders. While OCPM enabled in-depth analyses, traditional process representations were more understandable and acceptable for business users. These findings emphasize the need for improved visualization techniques to bridge the gap between complex process mining insights and practical business decision-making.

References

1. Achiam, J., et al.: GPT-4 technical report. arXiv preprint arXiv:2303.08774 (2023)
2. Berti, A., Jessen, U., Park, G., Rafiei, M., van der Aalst, W.M.P.: Analyzing interconnected processes: using object-centric process mining to analyze procurement processes. Int. J. Data Sci. Anal. 1–23 (2023)
3. Berti, A., et al.: Ocel (object-centric event log) 2.0 specification. arXiv preprint arXiv:2403.01975 (2024)
4. Bider, I., Jalali, A.: Limiting variety by standardizing and controlling knowledge intensive processes. In: 2016 IEEE 20th International Enterprise Distributed Object Computing Workshop (EDOCW), pp. 1–9. IEEE (2016)
5. Brown, T., et al.: Language models are few-shot learners. In: Advances in Neural Information Processing Systems, vol. 33, pp. 1877–1901 (2020)
6. Camizuli, E., Carranza, E.J.: Exploratory data analysis (EDA). In: The Encyclopedia of Archaeological Sciences, pp. 1–7 (2018)
7. Chapman, P., et al.: Crisp-dm 1.0: step-by-step data mining guide. SPSS Inc **9**(13), 1–73 (2000)
8. If P&C Insurance. About us (2025). https://www.if-insurance.com/about-if/about-us. Accessed: 13 Mar 2025
9. Jalali, A.: Aspect mining in business process management. In: Johansson, B., Andersson, B., Holmberg, N. (eds.) BIR 2014. LNBIP, vol. 194, pp. 246–260. Springer, Cham (2014). https://doi.org/10.1007/978-3-319-11370-8_18
10. Jalali, A.: Object type clustering using Markov directly-follow multigraph in object-centric process mining. IEEE Access **10**, 126569–126579 (2022)
11. Khayatbashi, S., Hartig, O., Jalali, A.: Transforming event knowledge graph to object-centric event logs: a comparative study for multi-dimensional process analysis. In: International Conference on Conceptual Modeling, pp. 220–238. Springer (2023)
12. Khayatbashi, S., Hartig, O., Jalali, A.: Transforming object-centric event logs to temporal event knowledge graphs. In: International Conference on Business Process Management, pp. 300–313. Springer (2024)

13. Khayatbashi, S., Miri, N., Jalali, A.: Advancing Object-Centric Process Mining with Multi-dimensional Data Operations. Springer (2025)
14. Khayatbashi, S., Miri, N., Jalali, A.: OLAP operations for object-centric process mining. In: Accpeted in CAiSE Forum 2025. Springer (2025)
15. Kretzschmann, D., Park,G., Berti, A., van der Aalst, W.M.P.: Overstock problems in a purchase-to-pay process: an object-centric process mining case study. In: International Conference on Advanced Information Systems Engineering, pp. 347–359. Springer (2024)
16. Miri, N., Jalali, A.: Uncovering patterns in object-centric process mining: an approach using drill-down and roll-up techniques. In: Haghighi, P.D., Greguš, M., Kotsis, G., Khalil, I. (eds.) Information Integration and Web Intelligence, pp. 49–54. Springer, Cham (2025)
17. Miri, N., Khayatbashi, S., Zdravkovic, J., Jalali, A.: OCPM^2: extending the process mining methodology for object-centric event data extraction (2025). Accepted in BPMDS 2025
18. Motwani, J., Kumar, A., Jiang, J., Youssef, M.: Business process reengineering: a theoretical framework and an integrated model. Int. J. Oper. Prod. Manag. **18**(9/10), 964–977 (1998)
19. OpenAI. Json mode - openai API. https://platform.openai.com/docs/guides/structured-outputs (2025). Accessed 16 Mar 2025
20. OpenAI. Structured outputs - openai API. https://platform.openai.com/docs/guides/structured-outputs (2025). Accessed 27 Feb 2025
21. Park, G., Aydin, S., Uğur, C., van der Aalst, W.M.P.: Analyzing an after-sales service process using object-centric process mining: a case study. In: International Conference on Process Mining, pp. 406–418. Springer (2023)
22. Aalst, W.: Object-centric process mining: dealing with divergence and convergence in event data. In: Ölveczky, P.C., Salaün, G. (eds.) SEFM 2019. LNCS, vol. 11724, pp. 3–25. Springer, Cham (2019). https://doi.org/10.1007/978-3-030-30446-1_1
23. van der Aalst, W., Berti, A.: Discovering object-centric petri nets. Fund. Inform. **175**(1–4), 1–40 (2020)
24. van Eck, M.L., Lu, X., Leemans, S.J.J., van der Aalst, W.M.P.: PM^2: a process mining project methodology. In: Zdravkovic, J., Kirikova, M.,Johannesson, P. (eds.) Advanced Information Systems Engineering, pp. 297–313. Springer (2015)
25. Vu, H., Haase, J., Leopold, H., Mendling, J.: Towards a theory on process automation effects. In: International Conference on Business Process Management, pp. 285–301. Springer (2023)

Identifying Process Improvement Opportunities Through Process Execution Benchmarking

Luka Abb[1]([✉]), Majid Rafiei[2], Timotheus Kampik[2], and Jana-Rebecca Rehse[1]

[1] University of Mannheim, Mannheim, Germany
{luka.abb,rehse}@uni-mannheim.de
[2] SAP Signavio, Berlin, Germany
{majid.rafiei,timotheus.kampik}@sap.com

Abstract. Benchmarking functionalities in current commercial process mining tools allow organizations to contextualize their process performance through high-level performance indicators, such as completion rate or throughput time. However, they do not suggest any measures to close potential performance gaps. To address this limitation, we propose a prescriptive technique for process execution benchmarking that recommends targeted process changes to improve process performance. The technique compares an event log from an "own" process to one from a selected benchmark process to identify potential activity replacements, based on behavioral similarity. It then evaluates each proposed change in terms of its feasibility and its estimated performance impact. The result is a list of potential process modifications that can serve as evidence-based decision support for process improvement initiatives.

Keywords: Benchmarking · Process Mining · Process Improvement

1 Introduction

Benchmarking is a well-established method for organizations to assess their performance relative to peers, set performance goals, and identify areas for operational improvement [9]. In particular, benchmarking often focuses on business processes [3]. For example, a finance organization might benchmark its purchase-to-pay (P2P) workflow completion rates by comparing them to those of other organizations that use the same standard software, thus facilitating comparability. This comparison allows the organization to contextualize its own completion rate, determining whether its performance is "good" (significantly above the median) or "bad" (below average, based on the overall distribution).

To support such analyses, commercial process mining tools offer benchmarking capabilities based on process-level performance indicators, such as completion rate, automation rate, or average throughput time [10,27]. These indicators tell organizations how well their processes run relative to those of their competitors. However, they do not offer insights on what process improvements would be necessary to match the performance of industry peers.

To address this limitation, it is necessary to move from a high-level comparison of performance indicators to a detailed comparison of the actual business process *execution* [3]. This approach, which we call *process execution benchmarking*, involves the in-depth comparison of two or more event logs that record executions of processes sharing relevant properties, e.g., the process type. Process execution benchmarking can be conducted externally, by comparing process executions with those of similar organizations, or internally, by analyzing event logs from different units within the same company. This latter approach holds significant potential for process improvement: In large, geographically dispersed organizations, operational knowledge often remains isolated within specific divisions or teams [26,31]. This can lead to inefficiencies, as one organizational branch might excel in a particular process but lack the means or incentives to communicate and share their expertise with others [11]. Execution benchmarking addresses this in a data-driven way. For instance, the finance organization could use it to compare the P2P processes in its different country-level branches. By studying the process variants frequently executed in the best-performing branch, it can determine best practices and implement them in other branches as well.

Previous work on comparative analysis of event logs primarily focused on descriptive insights, aiming to uncover and visualize differences in control-flow and performance [32]. In this paper, we instead take a *prescriptive* approach: We introduce a technique that takes an "own" and a "benchmark" event log and identifies actionable [23,30] process changes expected to improve process performance. It outputs a set of behaviorally plausible process modifications, each associated with measures for feasibility and estimated performance impact. The potential modifications can then be sorted, filtered, and compiled into a list of recommended process changes that is provided to a process manager.

Specifically, we concentrate on process changes in the form of activity replacements. This is motivated by the fact that activity selection is critical for process optimization [28]: In many information systems, e.g., ERP systems, the same process can be executed by multiple configurations or pathways. Hence, different organizations or branches often implement different approaches for key process steps, but may not be aware of the impact that their activity-level choices have on their overall process performance. Our technique is meant to make these performance implications visible and provide concrete improvement suggestions based on practices that are already successfully employed by the benchmark.

2 Problem Illustration

To illustrate our technique, we use a standardized purchasing process in two versions, shown in Fig. 1: The "own" version to be improved and the "benchmark" version, from which we draw potential improvements. The process models are for illustration only; our technique does not rely on models. Both process versions include essentially the same four steps: Create a purchase order (PO), assign it to a purchase requisition (PR), release the PO, and post an invoice receipt. However, the first and third step are implemented in different ways. Table 1 shows minimal event logs with the execution variants these models permit.

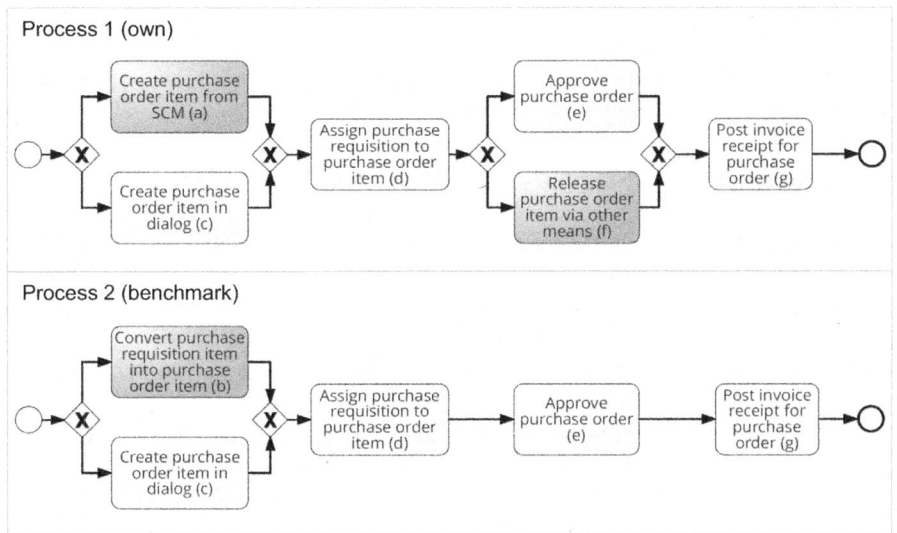

Fig. 1. Running example own and benchmark versions of a (simplified) purchasing process in an SAP ERP system. Disparities are highlighted in blue. (Color figure online)

Table 1. Running example event logs with all execution variants that the respective process models permit.

(a) Event log L_1.

L_1
$\langle a, d, e, g \rangle$, $\langle a, d, f, g \rangle$
$\langle c, d, e, g \rangle$, $\langle c, d, f, g \rangle$

(b) Event log L_2.

L_2
$\langle b, d, e, g \rangle$, $\langle c, d, e, g \rangle$

This example showcases the two modifications that our approach should identify:

(1) **True replacement:** In the own process, a PO can be created from the Supply Chain Management (SCM) system. The benchmark process instead allows PO items to be created by converting items from a PR. Activity b is hence a possible replacement for activity a that could lead to faster process execution, since the PO items do not have to be generated from scratch.

(2) **Choice streamlining:** In the own process, a PO can be released by approval or through other means (e.g., directly, without involving central procurement), consolidated in activity f. The benchmark process always requires approval, which could, e.g., lead to better compliance. On a process level, this simplifies the PO release, but on a log level, it can be interpreted as a replacement, since every execution variant in the own log that would execute activity f at this point will instead contain activity e in the benchmark log.

In the following, we will use this example to illustrate how our technique finds potential improvements to the process.

3 Foundations

Event Logs. Process mining relies on event logs, i.e., collections of data records that capture the execution of processes in organizations. An event log consists of multiple unique cases, where each case represents one complete execution of a process. A case is composed of a sequence of unique events, called a trace. An event is a record of an activity that occurred during the execution of the process.

Formally, an *event log* L is a set of traces, denoted by $L = \{t_1, t_2, \ldots, t_n\}$. Each $t_i, 1 \leq i \leq n$ is a trace, and $n = |L|$ is the number of traces in the event log. A *trace* t is a sequence (totally ordered set) of events corresponding to a single process execution (a case). A trace is denoted as $t = \langle e_1, e_2, \ldots, e_m \rangle$, where each e_i is an event, m is the number of events in the trace, and for e_j, e_k, $1 \leq j < k \leq m$, we say that "e_j occurs before e_k (in t)". An *event* $e = (c, a)$ is a tuple of attributes, with at least two components, where c is a unique identifier for the case to which the event belongs and a is the name of the executed activity. The set of all activities in the event log is denoted as A. A *variant* $v \in [\langle a_1, a_2, \ldots, a_m \rangle \mid \langle (c_1, a_1), (c_1, a_2), \ldots, (c_1, a_m) \rangle \in L]$ is a unique sequence of activity attributes of events that appear in a trace. V denotes a set of variants and $T(v)$ denotes the set of all traces that exhibit a variant $v \in V$.

Ordering Patterns and Behavioral Relations. Within a trace t, the relative ordering of two activities $a, b \in A$ can be described by the ordering pattern $a >_t b$ if a is executed at some point before b (i.e., b eventually follows a) and $a \not>_t b$ otherwise. Based on these patterns, any pair of activities $a, b \in A$ in the event log can be characterized by one of three behavioral relations [1,35]:

Strict Order ($a \to b$). Activity a occurs before b in all traces where both occur:

$$\forall t \in L : a >_t b \text{ and } b \not>_t a$$

A reverse strict order relationship is written as $a \leftarrow b$.

Exclusiveness ($a \# b$). Activities a and b never occur together in any trace:

$$\forall t \in L : a \not>_t b \text{ and } b \not>_t a$$

Interleaving Order ($a \parallel b$). Activities a and b can occur in any order within a trace, i.e., in at least one trace a occurs before b and vice versa:

$$\exists t \in L \mid a >_t b \quad \text{and} \quad \exists t \in L \mid b >_t a$$

Per these definitions, an activity has an interleaving relation to itself if it can repeat within a trace (i.e., is part of a loop) and an exclusive one if it cannot.

4 Technique

Our technique aims to provide a process manager with a list of process changes that could improve process performance. It requires as input two event logs, L_1 and L_2, which capture executions of the own and the benchmark process, respectively. Its output is a list of behaviorally plausible process modifications, each associated with a feasibility and a performance assessment. To identify these modifications, we establish behavioral footprints per activity in both logs (Sect. 4.1) and use these to identify initial activity "matches", i.e. behaviorally plausible replacement options (Sect. 4.2). Replacement options that can be implemented together are grouped into sets, representing potential process changes (Sect. 4.3). Finally, we assess each process change with regard to feasibility (likelihood to result in a valid process) (Sect. 4.4) and expected performance impact (Sect. 4.5). These five steps are summarized in Fig. 2.

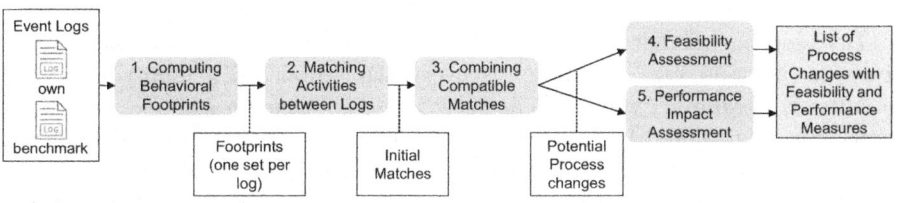

Fig. 2. High-level overview of the proposed technique and intermediary results

We designed this technique based on the following assumptions:

(1) *Same process type:* Both event logs capture the same process type, for example, a purchase-to-pay process. Otherwise, it would hardly be possible to improve one process using data-driven insights from the other.
(2) *Standardized activity names:* Activity names are standardized, i.e., two activities in L_1 and L_2 with the same name refer to the same process step and two activities with different names refer to different process steps. This assumption is realistic in environments where organizations adopt enterprise information systems from a standard software and implement the standardized reference process models that this software contains. This holds, for example, in the SAP environment, where many different organizations implement standardized processes according to the SAP reference model [12].
(3) *Common performance measure:* Both event logs include at least one common case-level performance measure, for example, a successful completion indicator, the throughput time, or a customer satisfaction score.

In the following, we describe the steps of our technique in more detail.

4.1 Computing Behavioral Footprints

The first two steps in our technique aim to establish a set of potential activity replacements that make sense from a behavioral perspective. Intuitively, we only want to replace an activity with one that implements an analogous step in the process, i.e., accomplishes essentially the same advancement towards the process goal. In the running example, it is easy to see that replacing a (creating a PO) with e (releasing a PO) is not a valid change because the latter is always executed after the former in the own process. Replacing a with b, however, might be a valid change, since these two activities are always executed at the start of their respective process version, and they are both exclusive to activity c.

Behavioral relations, as defined in Sect. 3, offer a formal framework for describing how activities relate to each other. In our technique, we use them to algorithmically determine if two activities exhibit the same behavior, which would indicate that they likely implement the same process step. We first construct a relation matrix $R : A \times A \mapsto \{\rightarrow, \leftarrow, \#, \|\}$ for each event log. The behavioral relations that an activity has to all other activities in the same log (i.e., the rows of this matrix) are collectively referred to as its *behavioral footprint*. In the next step, we then use these footprints as a basis to identify plausible replacements.

Deriving the behavioral relations between activities simply from the *existence* of traces (as done, e.g., in simple discovery algorithms [1]) is highly susceptible to noise. For example, when two activities only co-occur in a single trace out of thousands, they would be in a sequential relation according to the definition in Sect. 3, although that trace was likely incorrectly recorded and they are instead exclusive. Similar to, e.g., the inductive miner infrequent [19], we therefore want to consider the frequency of traces when establishing behavioral relations. To this end, we compute scores for the exclusive and interleaving relation types based on their support in the log, i.e., the number of traces that exhibit the respective patterns. We write T_a for the set of traces in which a occurs, $T_{a \wedge b}$ for the subset of T_a in which both a and b occur, $T_{a \wedge \neg b}$ for the subset of T_a in which b does not occur, and $T_{a|a>b}$ for the subset of T_a in which a occurs before b.

The *exclusiveness score* for a and b counts the number of traces that contain only one activity and normalizes it by the overall frequency of the activities:

$$s_\#(a,b) = min(\frac{|T_{a \wedge \neg b}|}{|T_a|}, \frac{|T_{b \wedge \neg a}|}{|T_b|})$$

The *interleaving order score* for a and b computes the difference between the number of traces in which a is executed before b and the number of traces in which b is executed before a:

$$s_\|(a,b) = 1 - \frac{abs(|T_{a|a>b}| - |T_{b|b>a}|)}{|T_{a \wedge b}|}$$

After computing these scores, we first determine if a and b should be considered exclusive; this is the case if $s_\#(a,b) > exc$, where $exc \in [0,1]$ is a threshold parameter to be set by the user. If the activities are not exclusive, we determine if they should be considered interleaving in a similar manner: If $s_{\parallel}(a, b)$ is greater than the threshold parameter $int \in [0, 1]$, a and b are interleaving. Both threshold parameters should be set close to 1, so that exclusive and interleaving relations are only inferred if the great majority of traces exhibit the respective patterns. If there is not sufficient support for either an exclusivity or interleaving order relation, a and b are considered sequential in the direction that is more frequently observed, i.e., $a \rightarrow b$ if $|T_{a|a>b}| > |T_{a|b>a}|$ and $a \leftarrow b$ otherwise.

The output of this step is one matrix with pairwise activity relations for L_1 and L_2 each (see Fig. 3). Each row vector in these matrices is one behavioral footprint of an activity. To differentiate between activity executions in the two logs, we use the notation a_1 and a_2 for the occurrence of activity a in L_1 resp. L_2. Likewise, we denote the sets of activities in L_1 and L_2 as A_1 and A_2.

4.2 Matching Activities Between Logs

Using the behavioral footprints from the previous step, we can identify activity replacements that are behaviorally plausible. Specifically, we consider an activity in L_2 to be a potential replacement for an activity in L_1 iff their behavioral footprints are identical. However, because we cannot assume $A_1 = A_2$—our assumption is merely that $A_1, A_2 \subseteq A$, given A as our global set of activities— and the relation between two activities $a \in A_1$ and $x \notin A_1$ is undefined, it is not possible to establish equivalence based on the full footprint. Instead, we must disregard relations to activities that do not exist in both logs. Two footprints are then considered identical iff their relations to all activities shared between the two logs (i.e., to all activities in the intersection $A_1 \cap A_2$) are identical.

Figure 3 illustrates this for the running example: a, b, and f are not in $A_1 \cap A_2$, so relations to them are not considered in the matching (indicated by greyed columns). (a_1, b_2) is one potential match because their partial footprints (relations to c, d, e, and g, indicated in blue) are identical. In total, there are four behaviorally plausible replacements: (a_1, b_2), (a_1, c_2), (c_1, b_2), and (f_1, e_2).

The output of this step is a set of activity matches. A match (a_1, b_2) implies that activity $a_1 \in A_1$ can be replaced with activity $b_2 \in A_2$. We remove any trivial matches (i.e., an activity matched with that same activity in the benchmark log, like (a_1, a_2)) from this set to get a set of potential replacement options.

4.3 Combining Compatible Matches

In the previous step, we have identified behaviorally feasible pairwise activity replacements, i.e., one activity being replaced by another one in isolation. In this step, we want to combine these isolated replacements into sets of process changes that can be implemented jointly. The rationale for this is that there may be dependencies between replacements, so that a certain replacement can only be implemented or will only lead to better performance, if it is combined with another one. In the running example, it might be the case that replacing a with b would improve performance in those traces that then execute e, but

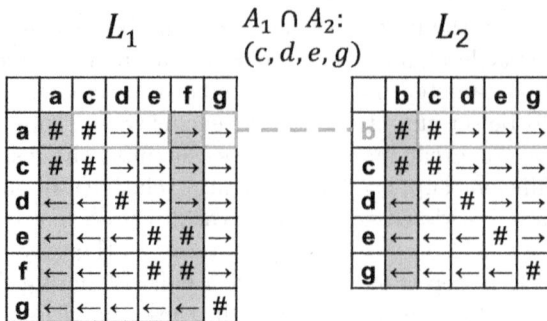

Fig. 3. Matching activities between footprint matrices to find behaviorally plausible replacements in the running example.

not in those that later continue with f. In this scenario, also implementing the replacement (f_1, e_2) will result in an overall higher performance gain than only implementing (a_1, b_2). We hence want to find sets of replacements that can later be jointly assessed for feasibility (Step 4) and performance impact (Step 5).

However, not all activity replacements can be freely combined with one another. Conflicts arise if the same activity in L_1 can be replaced by different activities from L_2. In the running example, both (a_1, b_2) and (a_1, c_2) are potential replacements, but only one of them can be implemented, so we should not show both to a process manager. Therefore, we want to identify sets of changes that are not in conflict with each other and thus can be implemented together. To do this, we construct a so-called compatibility graph (see Fig. 4), which contains one node for each possible replacement and an edge between two nodes iff they are not in conflict with one another, i.e., the two replacements do not refer to the same activity. The fully connected subgraphs of this compatibility graph (including single nodes) correspond to the sets of compatible replacements that are the output of this step. We call each set a potential *process change*.

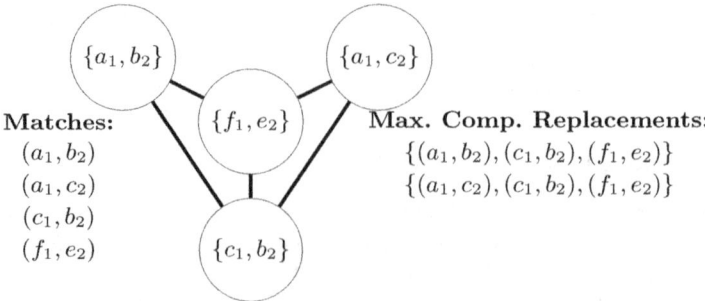

Fig. 4. Matches, compatibility graph, and maximal compatible replacements from the running example. Fully connected subgraphs are also considered changes.

4.4 Assessing the Feasibility of Process Changes

At this stage, we have identified a set of behaviorally plausible process changes. Each process change δ consists of compatible replacement options between activities in L_1 and L_2. However, there is no guarantee that replacing activities with behaviorally similar ones will result in a feasible process. To ensure that the changes we propose can actually be implemented, we need to verify the feasibility of each process change. In the absence of process models, we base this verification on empirical evidence from the benchmark log L_2.

If we want to assess the feasibility of replacement option (a_1, b_2), then for each variant $v_1 \in L_1$ in which a is executed, we could check if L_2 contains a corresponding variant v_2 which is identical to v_1, except that b is executed instead of a. If this is the case for all variants, we have strong evidence that replacing a with b is a valid change to make in the process. However, such exact matches are problematic because they do not account for differences in the benchmark process that are not part of the identified process changes, such as additional activities. They also do not consider the logs' potential incompleteness with regard to the permutations of concurrent or repeated activity executions. Therefore, instead of requiring exact matches of variants, we rely on trace alignments [6] to find those variants in the benchmark log that most closely match the ones from the own log and compute a *feasibility score* for each process change.

For a single replacement (a_1, b_2), let $V_{1,a} \subseteq L_1$ be the set of variants in L_1 where activity a is executed and $V_{2,b}$ the set of variants in L_2 where activity b is executed. We construct new variants in L_1, denoted $V'_{1,a}$, by implementing the replacement (a_1, b_2) for each $v_1 \in V_{1,a}$. This yields a modified variant v'_1, where a is replaced by b, but the other activities remain the same. To assess the feasibility of this replacement, we examine each modified variant v'_1 and find its closest match among the variants in the benchmark log, i.e., the variant in $V_{2,b}$ that has the minimal edit distance (Levenshtein distance [22]) to v'_1. We denote the closest match of v'_1 as $\mu(v'_1)$. We then iterate over all $v_1 \in V_{1,a}$ and compute the average frequency-weighted edit similarity between their modified versions $v'_1 \in V'_{1,a}$ and their closest matches $\mu(v'_1) \in V_{2,b}$:

$$\text{Feasibility}(a_1, b_2) = \frac{\sum_{v_1 \in V_{1,a}} |T_1(v_1)| \cdot \text{EditSimilarity}(v'_1, \mu(v'_1))}{\sum_{v_1 \in V_{1,a}} |T_1(v_1)|}$$

Using edit similarity instead of edit distance normalizes the feasibility score to $[0, 1]$. It is calculated by dividing the edit distance of two variants by the maximum length of these two variants, and then subtracting the result from 1.

For a given process change δ, which may consist of multiple replacement options, we assess the feasibility of a simultaneous implementation of all replacements in δ to the variants in L_1. For each variant $v_1 \in L_1$ in which any of the activities involved in δ are executed, we construct a modified variant v'_1 by applying all replacement options within δ. For example, for the change $\delta_1 = \{(a_1, b_2), (f_1, e_2)\}$ in our running example, there are three affected variants in L_1: $v_1 = \langle a, d, e, g \rangle$, $v_2 = \langle a, d, f, g \rangle$, and $v_3 = \langle c, d, f, g \rangle$. The modified variants after applying δ (replacing a with b and f with e) would be $v'_1 = v'_2 = \langle b, d, e, g\rangle$ and $v'_3 = \langle c, d, e, g\rangle$. We then find the closest match for each variant and compute the feasibility score across all affected variants analogously to the single replacement case. In this example, each modified variant has an exact match, since $\langle b, d, e, g\rangle$ and $\langle c, d, e, g\rangle$ are recorded in L_2. The feasibility score for δ would therefore be 1. For the process change $\delta_2 = \{(a_1, b_2)\}$, meanwhile, the affected variants would be $v_1 = \langle a, d, e, g\rangle$ and $v_2 = \langle a, d, f, g\rangle$. In this case, the modified $v'_2 = \langle b, d, f, g\rangle$ does not have an exact match in L_2 and its closest alignment ($\langle b, d, e, g\rangle$) has an edit similarity of 0.75. Assuming equal frequency of v_1 (which has an exact match) and v_2 (which has a closest match with similarity 0.75), the overall feasibility score for this process change would be 0.875.

4.5 Assessing the Performance Impact of Process Changes

The feasibility score from the previous section provides a means to assess whether it is *possible* to implement a process change. To provide useful recommendations for process improvement, we also need to assess whether a process change will be *beneficial*, i.e., have a (substantial) positive impact on process performance. We also base this assessment on empirical evidence from the benchmark event log: We approximate the expected performance impact of a process change as the difference in performance between the variants in L_1 that are affected by this change and their closest match variants in L_2.

For simplicity, we assume that both logs contain the same single performance measure $\pi(t)$ that assigns a value to each trace t, with higher values corresponding to better performance. The expected performance impact of a process change can then be approximated as the average difference in π between the traces in L_1 where the to-be-replaced activities are executed and their corresponding (closest match) traces in L_2 where the replacing activities are executed.

For a replacement (a_1, b_2), we again construct modified variants from $V_{1,a}$ and find their closest match in $V_{2,b}$ in the benchmark log (see Sect. 4.4). For each v_1 in $V_{1,a}$, we calculate the average performance difference between all traces in L_1 of this variant ($T_1(v_1)$) and the traces in L_2 of its closest match $\mu(v'_1)$:

$$\bar{\pi}(v_1) = \frac{\sum_{t \in T_1(v_1)} \pi(t)}{|T_1(v_1)|}.$$

The expected performance impact across all variants affected by replacement (a_1, b_2) is then calculated as the mean difference between the performance of traces that contain a in L_1 and that of their closest match aligned traces in L_2:

$$\Delta\pi(a_1, b_2) = \frac{\sum_{v_1 \in V_{1,a}} |T_1(v_1)| \cdot (\bar{\pi}(\mu(v'_1)) - \bar{\pi}(v_1))}{\sum_{v_1 \in V_{1,a}} |T_1(v_1)|},$$

For process changes that contain multiple replacements, we follow the same procedure as for the feasibility score: The expected performance impact of a process change δ is calculated with $V_{1,\delta}$ as the set of variants in L_1 in which at least one of the activities to be replaced in δ is executed and $V_{2,\delta}$ the set of variants in L_2 in which at least one of the replacement activities is executed.

4.6 End Result

Our technique outputs a list of process changes consisting of one or multiple activity replacement options, each associated with (1) a measure for feasibility, estimating the possibility to implement the change without further modifying the process and (2) a measure for the expected impact on process performance, indicating the potential benefits of the change. An exemplary output is shown in Table 3. This list can be presented to a process manager, who can use the measures to filter, prioritize, and select the most promising changes for further investigation or implementation. Thereby, we offer evidence-based, prescriptive decision support in process improvement initiatives.

4.7 Discussion

In designing our technique, we made certain decisions that resulted in limitations and could be addressed by potential extensions.

Focus on Event Logs. We recommend process changes based exclusively on the information available in event logs, which capture only a fraction of the information about a process. For instance, a country branch may execute a certain activity due to regulatory requirements and cannot simply replace it, even if that would lead to a faster execution. Our technique might therefore yield false positive recommendations, which a manager must identify and discard.

Concrete Implementation. We opted to prioritize simple and intuitive functions and measures for each step, which, of course, can be adapted. It would, e.g., be possible to extend the approach to consider multiple performance measures with individual weights or to use a utility function that considers feasibility and performance impact to derive a single quality score for each process change. It would also be possible to consider additional preprocessing steps, such as semantic matching in scenarios where activity names are not standardized.

Similarity Between Logs. If the process executions in the two logs are too dissimilar, our technique will not return any meaningful process changes. Consider two distinct processes that share only a start activity. In Step 2, all activities in A_1 would be matched with all activities in A_2, since they all share the same relation to the common start activity. However, the only feasible process change in this scenario would be one that essentially replaces the entire own process with the benchmark one, which is not a useful recommendation. The similarity between the logs can be established beforehand (e.g., [20]), but there is no definite rule for how similar two logs must be to get good results.

Focus on Replacements. Our technique is designed to identify activity replacements as practically relevant process modifications. Other possible modifications, such as adding an activity only found in the benchmark log or removing one that the benchmark does not execute, are not considered in this paper. However, the general ideas of our technique could be applied to these modifications as well.

Behavioral Matching. In Step 1, we use behavioral relations to match activities. It would be possible to additionally consider semantics in this step, i.e., match activities based on the meaning of their labels.

Single Replacements. In Step 2, we only consider 1:1 activity matches. Extending this to n:m matches could accommodate situations where replacements are only feasible when exchanging, e.g., entire choice constructs. This extension would significantly increase the complexity of our technique, as it necessitates identifying such constructs, even when they are nested. Process discovery algorithms address similar challenges and may be a useful starting point for this.

5 Evaluation

Evaluating if our technique finds intended activity replacements requires pairs of event logs with performance measures and labeled differences. Since these are not available in real-life logs, we conduct an evaluation on synthetic data in Sect. 5.1. To also show that our technique can be applied in real-life settings, we conduct a case study on a realistic event log in Sect. 5.2. All code, data, and parameters used in the experiment and the case study are available on GitLab.[1]

5.1 Experiment

We used the Process and Log Generator (PLG) tool [8] to generate 1,000 randomly configured process models. We then created a corresponding benchmark process model for each of them by replacing 1–3 activities in the original model with new ones, keeping track of the replacements to establish a ground truth. In addition, we performed 0–2 activity insertions and deletions per model. These are not found by our technique, but increase the variance between the own and benchmark process and thus make the data more realistic. We then simulated event logs from all models, with 1,000 traces each and control-flow noise, and applied our technique to the 1,000 own and benchmark event log pairs.

We evaluated two aspects of our technique: (1) Whether the initial matches in Step 2 align with the ground truth (using precision and recall) and (2) whether the identified changes are more feasible than those returned by a random baseline. We constructed this baseline by randomly selecting the same number of matches from $A_1 \times A_2$ as the number of matches returned by the technique and then applying Steps 3 and 4 in the same way to both sets of matches. The results are shown in Table 2 (averaged over all log pairs). Precision and recall are relatively high, but do not approach 1. The main reasons for this are incompleteness of either event log, particularly when it comes to larger blocks of concurrent or repeating activities, and noise, which can sometimes lead to incorrect activity relations being derived in Step 1. Overall, however, our technique identifies a great majority of intended matches and produces few false positives.

The average feasibility score is also considerably higher than for the random baseline. This indicates that when the process changes our technique identifies are implemented, the resulting traces are likely to have equivalents with low edit

---

[1] https://gitlab.uni-mannheim.de/jpmac/process-execution-benchmarking/.

Table 2. Mean precision, recall, and feasibility scores achieved in the evaluation.

Aim	Metric	Technique	Baseline
(1)	Precision	0.831	–
	Recall	0.901	–
(2)	Feasibility Score	0.802	0.580

distance in the benchmark logs and therefore be valid process executions. Note that because of the way we have set up this evaluation, feasibility scores close to 1 are unlikely to occur, because the activity insertions and deletions inherently introduce disparities between otherwise corresponding variants.

Evaluating the performance assessment would require simulating the logs such that the traces resulting from specific replacements in the benchmark log demonstrate better performance than their matches in the original log and then showing that our technique assigns good performance measures to them. By design, our approach involves identifying these exact traces in the benchmark log through alignments and calculating a performance difference to the original ones (see Sect. 4.5). This evaluation would therefore not be informative w.r.t. its efficacy. Consequently, we omit an explicit evaluation in this experiment.

5.2 Case Study

To showcase how our technique can be applied in real-life settings and what the recommended changes could look like, we also conduct a small case study on a realistic event log. This event log consists of demo data that was released as part of the SAP Signavio Plug and Gain initiative; it simulates typical executions of a purchasing process in the SAP ERP system. We split this event log into two parts that each correspond to a country-level suborganization. The log of the India organization has a median case duration of about 11 days and acts as the "own" event log in this scenario. The log of the Germany organization, which acts as our benchmark, has a median case duration of about 9 days.

We filter out the 5% least common variants from this event log and then apply our technique. In doing so, we identify five potential process changes that all pertain to the creation of the initial purchase order (Table 3). We can see that, in this dataset, all process changes have a high feasibility, i.e., when the changes would be implemented in the own process, all frequently observed variants have exact matches in the benchmark dataset. However, there are stark differences in their expected performance impact (measured in average hours lost or gained per case): Only the first two changes would lead to a reduction of about 1 and 4 h in average throughput time across all cases, whereas the remaining three are associated with an increase of over 8 h. A straightforward conclusion from these results would be that creating a PO in the SCM leads to considerably slower process executions, and that creating it directly using the "Create PO" dialog window is a faster option.

Table 3. Exemplary list of process changes for the running example

Activities	Replacements	Feasibility	Performance
Create PO item from SCM	Convert PR item into PO item	0.95	−0.97 h/case
Create PO item from SCM	Create PO item in dialog	0.95	−4.42 h/case
Create PO item in dialog	Convert PR item into PO item	0.96	+11.61 h/case
Create PO item from SCM Create PO item in dialog	Convert PR item into PO item	0.96	+8.96 h/case
Create PO item from SCM Create PO item in dialog	Create PO item in dialog Convert PR item into PO item	0.96	+8.24 h/case

6 Related Work

Process Performance Improvement. Improving process performance is the end goal of most process mining initiatives [30], and several studies focus on the performance aspects of event data. Some explore the integration of performance measures with standard process mining analyses, such as process discovery [14], conformance checking [2], and process simulation [5]. Others aim to analyze the performance of running process instances, e.g., by predicting the remaining time of a case [33] or prescribing interventions to avoid negative process outcomes [17].

Another related literature stream investigates how to make process mining results actionable, i.e., move from understanding a process to being able to improve it [30]. This includes technical papers introducing new process mining approaches [16,23,24] as well as case studies and qualitative research about how practitioners utilize process mining results [13,15,30].

Process Variant Analysis. There is substantial process mining literature on analyzing and comparing different versions or variants of the same process (e.g., [4,7,25,29]; see [32] for a comprehensive review). The focus in these publications is on (1) identifying and (2) visualizing differences between two or more process variants, but not on associating these differences with performance implications or making recommendations for process improvement [32]. Most similar to our work is [3], in which event logs from different organizations are initially grouped based on their overall performance, as measured by key performance indicators, and then compared. However, this approach remains descriptive and does not suggest concrete process modifications.

Process Model Matching. While identifying activity correspondences among separate event logs for process execution benchmarking is a novel topic, there has been substantial research on finding these correspondences in process models. This task, called process model matching [21,34], generally has a different objective than process execution benchmarking: Its main purpose is to align or integrate handcrafted process models, whereas execution benchmarking aims to derive process improvement opportunities. Notably, process model matching can also be used for the purpose of process improvement when employed with a reference model [18], but this is not its typical application.

7 Conclusion

In this paper, we have introduced a novel technique for automated process improvement through process execution benchmarking. It relies on behavioral relations to identify potential activity replacements using a benchmark event log and associates them with measures for feasibility and expected performance impact. Our technique can supplement high-level indicator-based process benchmarking by leveraging event logs to recommend to a process manager concrete, actionable process modifications that are expected to improve performance.

In future work, one could explore technical extensions to the approach presented. It would also be worthwhile to conduct a user study with process managers to verify if the outputs are useful for process improvement in practice.

References

1. van der Aalst, W., Weijters, T., Maruster, L.: Workflow mining: discovering process models from event logs. IEEE Trans. Knowl. Data Eng. **16**(9), 1128–1142 (2004)
2. van der Aalst, W., Adriansyah, A., van Dongen, B.: Replaying history on process models for conformance checking and performance analysis. Wiley Int. Rev. Data Min. Knowl. Disc. **2**(2), 182–192 (2012)
3. Aksu, U., Reijers, H.A.: How business process benchmarks enable organizations to improve performance. In: IEEE International Enterprise Distributed Object Computing Conference, pp. 197–208 (2020)
4. Ballambettu, N.P., Suresh, M.A., Bose, R.P.J.C.: Analyzing process variants to understand differences in key performance indices. In: Advanced Information Systems Engineering, pp. 298–313. Springer, Cham (2017)
5. Bisogno, S., Calabrese, A., Gastaldi, M., Levialdi Ghiron, N.: Combining modelling and simulation approaches: how to measure performance of business processes. Bus. Process. Manag. J. **22**(1), 56–74 (2016)
6. Bose, R., van der Aalst, W.: Trace alignment in process mining: opportunities for process diagnostics. In: Hull, R., Mendling, J., Tai, S. (eds.) Business Process Management, pp. 227–242. Springer, Cham (2010)
7. Buijs, J., Reijers, H.A.: Comparing business process variants using models and event logs. In: Enterprise. Business-Process and Information Systems Modeling, pp. 154–168. Springer, Cham (2014)
8. Burattin, A.: PLG2: Multiperspective process randomization with online and offline simulations. In: BPM Demos. CEUR (2016)
9. Carpinetti, L., de Melo, A.: What to benchmark? A systematic approach and cases. Benchmarking **9**, 244–255 (2002)
10. Celonis: How does process mining work? (2024). https://www.celonis.com/process-mining/how-does-process-mining-work/. Accessed 05 Dec 2024
11. Cramton, C.D.: The mutual knowledge problem and its consequences for dispersed collaboration. Organ. Sci. **12**(3), 346–371 (2001)

12. Curran, T., Keller, G., Ladd, A.: SAP R/3 Business Blueprint: Understanding the Business Process Reference Model. Enterprise Resource Planning Series, Prentice Hall PTR, Upper Saddle River (1997)
13. Dees, M., de Leoni, M., van der Aalst, W.M.P., Reijers, H.A.: What if process predictions are not followed by good recommendations? In: BPM Industry Forum, pp. 61–72. CEUR (2019)
14. van Dongen, B.F., Adriansyah, A.: Process mining: fuzzy clustering and performance visualization. In: BPM Workshops, pp. 158–169. Springer, Cham (2010)
15. Grisold, T., Mendling, J., Otto, M., vom Brocke, J.: Adoption, use and management of process mining in practice. Bus. Process. Manag. J. **27**(2), 369–387 (2021)
16. Gröger, C., Schwarz, H., Mitschang, B.: Prescriptive analytics for recommendation-based business process optimization. In: Business Information Systems, pp. 25–37. Springer, Cham (2014)
17. Kubrak, K., Milani, F., Nolte, A., Dumas, M.: Prescriptive process monitoring: quo vadis? PeerJ Comput. Sci. **8**, e1097 (2022)
18. Küster, J.M., Koehler, J., Ryndina, K.: Improving business process models with reference models in business-driven development. In: BPM Workshops, pp. 35–44. Springer, Cham (2006)
19. Leemans, S.J.J., Fahland, D., van der Aalst, W.M.P.: Discovering block-structured process models from event logs containing infrequent behaviour. In: BPM Workshops, pp. 66–78. Springer, Cham (2014)
20. Leemans, S.J., van der Aalst, W.M., Brockhoff, T., Polyvyanyy, A.: Stochastic process mining: earth movers' stochastic conformance. Inf. Syst. **102**, 101724 (2021)
21. Leopold, H., Niepert, M., Weidlich, M., Mendling, J., Dijkman, R., Stuckenschmidt, H.: Probabilistic optimization of semantic process model matching. In: Business Process Management, pp. 319–334. Springer, Cham (2012)
22. Levenshtein, V.I.: Binary codes capable of correcting deletions, insertions, and reversals. Cybernet. Control Theory **10**(8), 707–710 (1966)
23. Park, G., van der Aalst, W.: Action-oriented process mining: bridging the gap between insights and actions. Progress Artif. Intell. **11**(3), 275–290 (2022)
24. Park, G., Van Der Aalst, W.M.: Realizing a digital twin of an organization using action-oriented process mining. In: International Conference on Process Mining, pp. 104–111 (2021)
25. Partington, A., Wynn, M., Suriadi, S., Ouyang, C., Karnon, J.: Process mining for clinical processes: a comparative analysis of four Australian hospitals. ACM Trans. Manag. Inf. Syst. **5**(4), 1–18 (2015)
26. Riege, A.: Three-dozen knowledge-sharing barriers managers must consider. J. Knowl. Manag. **9**(3), 18–35 (2005)
27. SAP Signavio: Process performance indicators in SAP Signavio Process Insights (2024). https://community.sap.com/t5/technology-blogs-by-sap/process-performance-indicators-in-sap-signavio-process-insights-discovery/ba-p/13744670. Accessed 05 Dec 2024
28. Scheer, A.W., Hoffmann, M.: The process of business process management. In: Handbook on Business Process Management 2: Strategic Alignment. Governance, People and Culture, pp. 351–380. Springer, Cham (2015)
29. Schuster, D., Zerbato, F., van Zelst, S.J., van der Aalst, W.M.: Defining and visualizing process execution variants from partially ordered event data. Inf. Sci. **657**, 119958 (2024)
30. Stein Dani, V., Leopold, H., van der Werf, J.M.E.M., Beerepoot, I., Reijers, H.A.: From process mining insights to process improvement: all talk and no action? In: Cooperative Information Systems, pp. 275–292. Springer, Cham (2024)

31. Szulanski, G.: Sticky Knowledge: Barriers to Knowing in the Firm. Sage (2002)
32. Taymouri, F., Rosa, M.L., Dumas, M., Maggi, F.M.: Business process variant analysis: survey and classification. Knowl.-Based Syst. **211**, 106557 (2021)
33. Verenich, I., Dumas, M., Rosa, M.L., Maggi, F.M., Teinemaa, I.: Survey and cross-benchmark comparison of remaining time prediction methods in business process monitoring. ACM Trans. Intell. Syst. Technol. **10**(4) (2019)
34. Weidlich, M., Dijkman, R., Mendling, J.: The Icop framework: Identification of correspondences between process models. In: Advanced Information Systems Engineering, pp. 483–498. Springer, Cham (2010)
35. Weidlich, M., Mendling, J., Weske, M.: A foundational approach for managing process variability. In: Advanced Information Systems Engineering, pp. 267–282. Springer, Cham (2011)

Interdependency-Aware Business Process Prioritization for Process Improvements

Lauma Lubane and Marite Kirikova

Institute of Applied Computer Systems, Riga Technical University, 6A Kipsalas Street, Riga LV-1048, Latvia
lauma.lubane@edu.rtu.lv, marite.kirikova@rtu.lv

Abstract. An organization should routinely change and improve its business processes to be a competitive market player. However, as organizations have limited resources, simultaneously improving all business processes is impossible. Therefore, they should prioritize processes for improvement. Current Business Process Management literature provides various process prioritization approaches; however, process interdependency is often neglected as an impacting factor of successful improvement initiatives, even though it is recognized that improving one business process can impact the performance of other processes. To address the problem of neglecting process interdependency, the interdependency-aware business process prioritization approach is proposed, which includes a method for process interdependency identification and evaluation based on business process architecture and models to obtain interdependency rankings that are used together with the expert-evaluated rankings reflecting such process aspects as process health, importance, and feasibility. The proposed interdependency-aware business process prioritization approach is implemented in one company, and the preliminary results show the practical applicability of the proposed approach.

Keywords: Business Process Management · Business Process Prioritization · Process Interdependency

1 Introduction

Research findings indicate that process-oriented organizations perform better non-financially, which indirectly facilitates better financial performance [1]. Businesses make conscious decisions and investments to organize business processes through Business Process Management (BPM) [2]. Business Process Improvement (BPI), as one of the core BPM concepts, plays an important role in maintaining or enhancing an organization's competitiveness and ability to comply with a rapidly changing external environment. To be or become a market leader, the organization must routinely change and improve its business processes, following its core values and strategic goals [3]. BPM and BPI are resource-intensive activities, and as organizations have limited financial and time resources, they cannot afford to improve all business processes or manage countless BPI initiatives simultaneously. Moreover, even if enough resources are available, managing multiple BPI initiatives simultaneously might become risky and complex as business processes are not isolated and might be mutually influenced [2].

Business process prioritization or selection is a systematic evaluation and conscious decision of what business processes to include in a BPI initiative. Business process prioritization is a part of the process identification phase in the BPM lifecycle [2]. Thus, the organizations prioritize business processes to achieve the following results:

- ensure the success of the BPI initiative since the selection of the appropriate business processes impacts the effectiveness of a BPI initiative [4];
- account for limited resource availability and effectively allocate resources since BPM and BPI are resource-intensive activities [2];
- minimize risks and complexity of multiple BPI initiatives since managing several BPI initiatives simultaneously might become risky and complex because business processes might impact or be impacted by other business processes [2].

As indicated in the American Productivity & Quality Center's (APQC) 2024 survey report [5], developing criteria for BPI project prioritization and managing process interdependency are among the top challenges for practitioners. Similarly, Kerpedzhiev et al. [6] indicate interdependency-aware process prioritization as one of the BPM capability framework's core capabilities in strategic alignment. Despite this reasoning, assessing process interdependency is an underrated part of prioritization [7]. This paper proposes an approach to business process prioritization that respects process interdependency.

The paper is organized as follows: Sect. 2 sets the background of the study; Sect. 3 presents a new method for identifying and evaluating business process interdependencies; Sect. 4 proposes an interdependency-aware business process prioritization approach that is related to and incorporates the results of the method presented in Sect. 3; Sect. 5 describes how the proposed approach was implemented in a company; and Sect. 6 concludes the paper and discusses further research.

2 Background and Related Work

This section briefly reviews existing literature on business process prioritization criteria and discusses related works on process interdependency as a prioritization criterion. It also provides a background on a multi-criteria decision-making technique, which is appropriate for the joint use of calculated and expert-provided values and is adopted in the proposed interdependency-aware business process prioritization approach.

2.1 Process Prioritization Criteria

One of the most widely used groupings is Hammer and Champy's three groups of criteria [8]:

- *Process dysfunctionality (health)* – how ineffective, broken, unhealthy business processes are not performing as expected. In academic literature, the notion of "process health" is used as a synonym for process dysfunctionality. It is considered that the unhealthier a business process is, the higher it should be prioritized for improvement. The health criteria are expressed as process cost, e.g., cost of quality [9]; process time, e.g., variation in process time [10] or the average percentage of process results that match the target time limit [11]; and process quality, e.g., reward rate [12].

- *Process importance* – business process interaction with the organization's internal components (interdependency) and external environment (relevance) that shows how significant processes are to the organization. More important processes are typically improved first. However, organizations should align the BPI efforts with strategic goals to assess the process' importance [13]. Some constructs for measuring process importance are the importance to customers [14], supplier involvement [13], and the number of process executions [15].
- *Process feasibility* – the process potential to be improved successfully. The more feasible a process is, the more likely an improvement effort will succeed. The feasibility dimension includes flexibility criteria as the process performance measure, which captures the process's ability to react to intentional (build-time flexibility) and unexpected changes (run-time flexibility) [2]. Such concepts as complexity [16], formality [17], and automation feasibility [14] are used to estimate process feasibility.

2.2 Process Interdependency as a Prioritization Criterion

Interdependency is perceived as a business process interaction with the internal organization's components and processes [18]. Business process architecture can be used to visualize the dependencies and impact of processes in an organization or a specific department within an organization [2]. According to Dijkman et al., business processes may impact one another in the following 4 ways [19]:

1. *Decomposition* – a process is decomposed into sub-processes, and the level of detail increases.
2. *Specialization* – a process is a specific (or special) variation of another process.
3. *Use* – a process uses the output of another process, i.e., to be executed, process B needs the output of process A.
4. *Trigger* – process B is triggered by another process A; process B does not need the output of process A.

Only a few existing business process prioritization approaches consider process interdependencies as one of the prioritization criteria. Bitomsky et al. use transition rate [12], Kratsch et al. apply use frequency [20], and Fischer et al. utilize shared activity contexts [13] to account for process interdependencies; however, these concepts do not include all relation types. Lehnert et al. incorporate all four relation types but exclude prioritization criteria related to business concepts and qualities that cannot be extracted from data [18]. Most of the proposed prioritization approaches that take into account process interdependencies are data-driven – they use logs for process mining and involve complex calculations and extensive preparation therefore their practical applicability is limited [12, 13, 18, 20].

To capture various aspects of dependency, in the reviewed literature business process interdependency is assessed from the following three perspectives:

1. *Control flow dependency* – defines the logical order of processes [18].
2. *Resource dependencies* – shows which processes share the same resources. Resources can be either humans or IT applications [21].
3. *Data dependencies* – shows business processes that share the same data objects [21].

These three perspectives demonstrate a holistic view of a process as they collectively capture the structural, operational, and informational dimensions of a process.

2.3 Ordinal Priority Approach as a Multi-criteria Decision-Making Technique

Multi-criteria decision making (MCDM) is a discipline that helps decision makers to evaluate, compare and make a choice from a set of alternatives; in other words – make a decision. From this point of view, process prioritization can be considered a decision-making problem where the decision-maker evaluates a number of alternatives (business processes) against defined criteria and chooses the most satisfying alternative [22].

Ordinal Priority Approach (OPA) is a MCDM technique developed by Atae et al. that uses ordinal data as an input [23]. As ordinal, not cardinal, data is analyzed, OPA can simultaneously weigh all three components – alternatives, attributes, and experts. The business process prioritization approach proposed in this paper utilizes OPA for ease of use because research suggests that making relative evaluations is easier than providing precise and absolute judgments [24]. Furthermore, OPA enables experts to assign identical rankings to multiple alternatives or to abstain from ranking altogether [24]. The availability of the Online OPA Solver further enhances its practicality and accessibility for practitioners. To the authors' best knowledge, OPA has not yet been used in process prioritization studies; however, it has been successfully applied in other prioritization problems in such research fields as project management [25], education [26], personal data protection [27], and road safety [28] thus showing potential for application also in BPM.

3 Method for Process Interdependency Identification and Evaluation

To guide the development of an interdependency-aware business process prioritization approach, the following design objectives (DOs) were defined:

DO1: Business process interdependency. Business process prioritization must view process as a part of a process network and consider process dependencies as one of the prioritization criteria.

DO2: Business-driven process prioritization. Respecting problems that arise in applying data-driven business process prioritization, the objective is to adhere to the business-driven approach that does not require extensive use of log data. According to the overview of prioritization criteria discussed in the related works, business-driven process prioritization must rely upon a comprehensive set of process *health, importance*, and *feasibility* measures, which are to be evaluated by experts.

Process interdependency (DO1), as shown by the analysis of the related work, is rarely considered by the experts. Therefore, a method for identifying and evaluating process interdependency was developed and is presented in Sect. 3. When evaluating process interdependency, it is important to identify those processes that have the most significant impact on the overall business process landscape and whose improvement would benefit other processes the most [18]. Therefore, in the process interdependency context, we rank processes from the most impactful to the least impactful processes in a process network with the intention that related processes will also be improved by improving the most impactful process. To account for process dependencies, we propose a method for determining dependency rankings from three perspectives – *control flow, resource*, and *data dependencies* – using graph theory and process modeling elements across four relation types – *composition, specialization, trigger,* and *use* (see Sect. 2.2). The steps of the method for evaluating business process interdependencies are divided into two consecutive phases (Phase I and Phase II).

3.1 Phase I of the Method: Preparation

The first phase is a preparation for a detailed analysis of business process interdependencies. It requires the participation of an analyst knowledgeable in enterprise architecture and business process modeling and the involvement of domain experts.

Step 1.1: Identification of business processes for inclusion in prioritization. In this step, the business processes that are considered for improvement and need to be prioritized are identified. The processes are identified by experts who are familiar with the processes, their impact and relevance in the organization, and their main characteristics. Depending on the scope of the improvement initiative, the processes included in prioritization can be from one or more organizational units or the whole organization. However, the number of processes included in prioritization, preferably, should not exceed 9 as individuals usually cannot compare more than 7 objects (plus or minus two) simultaneously [24].

Step 1.2: Construction of business process architecture diagram. Business process architecture is a high-level abstraction model showing the most important business processes within an organization and their relations [2]. In the context of business process prioritization, a business process architecture diagram must include all business processes that have been selected for prioritization and their relations. Once business processes are identified, business process architecture is constructed. This can be done, for instance, in the enterprise architecture modeling language ArchiMate [29], as per Dijkman et al., showing each type of relation with different container and arrow elements [19]. The architecture is constructed by the analyst who knows the architecture modeling language together with the experts. Figure 1 illustrates an example of business process architecture. BP4 triggers a composed BP1 that consists of BP2 and BP3. The composed process is used by BP5, which has 2 specializations (variants) – BP6 and BP7. Finally, BP8 uses BP5. This example will be used in further explanation of the process interdependency identification and evaluation method.

Step 1.3: Transitioning of business process architecture diagram to process network. In this step, the business process architecture constructed in the previous step is transitioned to a process network [18, 30]. The experts continue to participate in this step to ensure the meaningfulness of the transition. The processes in the network will also be considered for overall process prioritization (Sect. 4). Business process architecture transition to process network is performed based on 4 ways business processes can impact each other listed in Sect. 2.2. First, the *composed* process is either included as one vertex or all its subprocesses are included as separate vertices. Next, *specialization* – the main process is included as a single vertex, or process variants are included as separate vertices. Process variants and subprocesses must hold the same relations as the main process [18]. Finally, *use* and *trigger* relations are incorporated in the process network as edges from used to using and from triggering to triggered processes, respectively. Different arrow types are used to show *use* and *trigger* relations. The constructed business process network is then used to understand *control flow dependencies* in Phase II of the method.

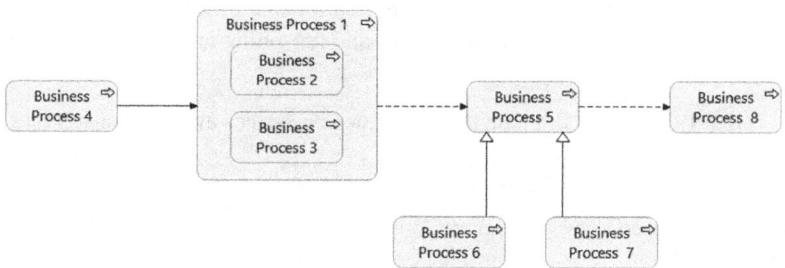

Fig. 1. Example of business process architecture.

Figure 2 demonstrates the process network of the business process architecture shown in Fig. 1. The business process network is constructed in ArchiMate 3.0 notation. Composed BP1 is modeled as a single vertex, excluding its components. BP4 retains its *trigger* relation to BP1. Variants of BP5 (BP6 and BP7) are included as separate vertices, preserving *use* relations from BP1 to BP8. Thus, *use* and *trigger* relations are adjusted accordingly to maintain the same relations as in business process architecture.

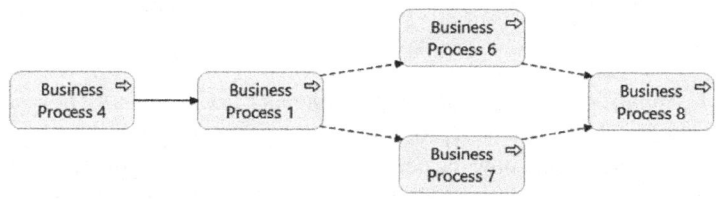

Fig. 2. Example of business process network.

Step 1.4: Construction of business process model diagrams, including resources and data objects. As a final step of Phase I, the business processes that are included in the business process network are modeled using the Business Process Model and Notation (BPMN) that allows organizations to represent their business processes on a detailed level [31]. These models are used in the next phase for evaluating *resource* and *data dependencies*, therefore they must include information about what data or information an activity uses/produces (data object) as well as who performs each activity (resource). Data objects include such objects as documents, files, materials, and data stores while a resource object can be a process participant, IT application, and equipment [2].

3.2 Phase II of the Method: Business Process Interdependency Evaluation

In the second phase, business process interdependencies are identified and evaluated based on the business process network and the detailed process models constructed in step 1.4 in Phase I. A rank is assigned to each business process, identifying processes from the most impactful to the least impactful within the process network based on three perspectives: *control flow, resource,* and *data dependencies* using corresponding matrices. Summary of interdependency identification and evaluation steps, their inputs, outputs and the applied theoretical principles and reasoning are depicted in Table 1.

Table 1. Overview of Phase II Process interdependency evaluation matrices.

Task/step	Applied reasoning	Output
2.1: Control flow dependency evaluation and ranking	Trigger relations – adjacency principle Use relations – reachability principle	Control Flow Dependency matrix
2.2: Resource dependency evaluation and ranking	Only Responsible roles Dependency non-directedness	Resource Dependency matrix
2.3: Data dependency evaluation and ranking	Dependency directedness Trigger relations – adjacency principle Use relations – reachability principle	Data Dependency matrix
2.4: Business process interdependency ranking	Borda count	Business process interdependency rankings

Step 2.1: Control flow dependency evaluation and ranking. Control flow dependency shows the logical order of business processes and how connected the business processes are. This helps to understand how the performance of one business process impacts other business processes and the whole process network [18]. To show whether and how each pair of business processes is related, a Boolean Control Flow Dependency matrix is built using the business process network constructed in Phase I (see Fig. 2) and by applying the following logic:

- As *trigger* relation only activates the target business process and does not impact its performance, a Boolean value "1" is assigned to those business process intersections (from triggering to triggered) [18]. In graph theory, this is denoted as vertex adjacency, which includes only 1-step directed connections of vertices [32].
- *Use* relation is cumulative as the used process performance impacts using processes also indirectly, e.g., process C is impacted by process A through process B [18]. The concept of vertex reachability is applied, determining whether it is possible to move directly or indirectly from process A to process C [32]. If process A is linked to process C, either directly or via other business processes, with a *use* relationship, a "1" is assigned to the intersection of those business processes (from used to using).

If two business processes are not connected with the *use* or *trigger* relations, then a "0" is assigned to those business process intersections in the Control Flow Dependency matrix. Then, the outgoing relations of each business process are counted, showing the total *control flow dependencies* of each business process. Only outgoing relations are included as they denote relations from used to using and from triggering to triggered business process and indicate that the used and triggering business processes should be prioritized over using and triggered business processes based on the premise that improving used or triggering processes will also improve using and triggered business processes. Finally, business processes are ranked from the most impactful (highest rank) to the least impactful (lowest rank) based on the *control flow dependency* counts.

Table 2 depicts the Control Flow Dependency matrix for the business process network in Fig. 2. As BP4 triggers BP1, "1" is assigned to BP4–BP1 intersection. BP1 is used by BPs 6 and 7, therefore "1" is assigned to BP1–BP6 and BP1–BP7 intersections. Similarly, "1" is assigned to BP6–BP8 and BP7–BP8 intersections. As BP1 connects to BP8 via BPs 6 and 7, "1" is also assigned to BP1–BP8 intersection.

Table 2. Example of Control Flow Dependency Matrix.

	BP 1	BP 4	BP 6	BP 7	BP 8	$\sum$	Rank
BP 1	0	0	1	1	1	3	1
BP 4	1	0	0	0	0	1	2
BP 6	0	0	0	0	1	1	2
BP 7	0	0	0	0	1	1	2
BP 8	0	0	0	0	0	0	3

Step 2.2: Resource dependency evaluation and ranking. Resource dependency identifies whether processes share the same resources. It is important to identify and take into account *resource dependencies* as changes in one process might require more or less of a certain resource in another process. *Resource dependencies* are non-directional, meaning that if a role is responsible for completing activities in two processes, it is irrelevant whether process A triggers or uses process B or vice versa [21]. A Resource Dependency matrix is built using detailed business process models constructed in the last step of Phase I. The Resource Dependency matrix shows the count of shared resources between each process pair. To represent the resource non-directionality, shared resource count is assigned to both process intersections, i.e., from process A to process B and from process B to process A. If two business processes do not share resources, then a "0" is assigned to those process intersections in the matrix. Finally, *resource dependencies* are summed up and business processes are ranked from the most dependent (highest rank) to the least dependent (lowest rank).

Step 2.3: Data dependency evaluation and ranking. Data dependencies analyze whether the data objects produced by one process are consumed by other processes. Business process network and the detailed business process models are used to obtain this ranking. Changes in one process might alter the use, quality, or content of data objects, which, if used in other processes, can also impact them. To represent *data dependencies*, a Data Dependency matrix is constructed. The matrix shows a count of shared data objects between each business process pair. The Data Dependency matrix is constructed by counting the number of shared data objects in detailed business process models constructed in the first phase. However, data object dependencies are directed as only the succeeding process can use data objects created in the preceding process, i.e., if the output of process A is a document that triggers or is used in process B, then in the Data Dependency matrix, this resource should be included only in the intersection of process A to B but not B to A [33]. Additionally, if process A impacts process C through the *use* relation via process B, shared data object count is also assigned to process A and process C intersection following vertex adjacency and reachability notions as in *control flow dependency* analysis. To incorporate this logic, the Control Flow Dependency matrix is used in the following way – shared data object count is assigned to business processes identified as having *control flow dependency* in Step 2.1. If two business processes do not share data objects and a *control flow dependency* has not been identified, then a "0" is assigned to those process intersections in the matrix. Next, *data dependencies* are summed up, and processes are ranked from the most impactful (highest rank) to the least impactful (lowest rank). For the example shown in Fig. 2, shared data object counts could be arbitrarily set for illustrative purposes as follows: BP1 generates six data objects used by BP6, and since BP1 precedes BP6, "6" is assigned to BP1–BP6 but not BP6–BP1 intersections. As BP1 impacts BP8 via BPs 6 and 7, a shared document count is assigned to the BP1–BP8 intersection.

Step 2.4: Final ranking of business processes by their interdependency. To calculate the final ranking of business processes by their interdependency, *control flow, resource,* and *data dependency* ranking points are aggregated using the symmetric Borda count where points are assigned to each rank position (highest rank is assigned the highest points, lowest rank is assigned the lowest points) as per Eq. (1) and then summed up. In the case of equal rankings, integers are assigned to those rankings [34].

$$w = m - i, \qquad (1)$$

where w – alternative ranking points;
m – the number of alternatives;
i – ith preferred alternative.

The final ranking is determined by counting the points across the three interdependency perspectives (*control flow, resource,* and *data dependency* perspectives), and final rankings are assigned – the highest rank (i.e., having the most impact on other business processes) is assigned to the business process having the most points, and the lowest rank (i.e., having the least impact on other business processes) is assigned to business process having the least points [34]. Processes with high interdependency are prioritized for improvement as such process performance may improve other process performance [18]. Table 3 illustrates possible final rankings for the processes of Fig. 2.

For each step of Phase II, an algorithm is developed that uses as an input the process architecture and models constructed in Phase I and produces, as an output, the matrices described above. So, Phase II of the interdependency identification and evaluation method can be applied semi-automatically. The final business process' interdependency

Table 3. Final business process interdependency ranking using Borda count.

	Control flow dependency points	Resource dependency points	Data dependency points	$\sum$	Final rank
BP 1	4	4	4	12	1
BP 4	3	2	3	8	2
BP 6	3	2	2	7	3
BP 7	3	0	2	5	4
BP 8	2	3	2	7	3

rankings are used in the interdependency-aware business process prioritization approach that is described in detail in the next section.

4 The Approach for Interdependency-Aware Business Process Prioritization

To fulfill DO2 implies having expert opinions included in the prioritization approach. This section proposes an interdependency-aware business process prioritization approach that incorporates expert assessments across three criteria groupings – *health, importance,* and *feasibility* – with quantified interdependencies from the interdependency evaluation method (Sect. 3). The OPA [22] technique briefly described in Sect. 2.3 was chosen to incorporate both the expert assessments and the identified process' interdependency evaluations due to its flexibility, simplicity, ease of application, and availability of online OPA Solver tool, making the prioritization approach practical in real-world scenarios.

The proposed approach for interdependency-aware business process prioritization is related to the method for business process interdependency identification and evaluation presented in the previous section in the following three ways:

1. The experts chosen in Phase I of the method for business process interdependency identification and evaluation can be involved in the overall process prioritization.
2. The processes for prioritization are the same as those included in the process network identified in Phase I of the method for business process interdependency identification and evaluation.
3. The final process interdependency evaluation obtained in Phase II of the method is used in line with expert evaluations of other criteria in process prioritization.

To comply with DO2 and to apply OPA, the criteria and their evaluation scales must be defined. The prioritization criteria used in this paper are inherited from the related works and align with Hammer and Champy's three criteria groups discussed in Sect. 2.1. However, the approach does not restrict the use of other criteria, while the presence of the interdependency criterion is mandatory. Table 4 shows the criteria, their description, scales, and how the evaluation is obtained. Cost, Time, and Quality refer to process

Table 4. Used business process prioritization criteria.

Criteria and their description	Criteria scales	Evaluation
Cost: the necessity to reduce process cost	Highest rank – most necessity Lowest rank – least necessity	Expert
Time: the necessity to reduce process execution time	Highest rank – most necessity Lowest rank – least necessity	Expert
Quality: the necessity to improve process quality	Highest rank – most necessity Lowest rank – least necessity	Expert
Relevance: process alignment with the organization's goals	Highest rank – most relevant Lowest rank – least relevant	Expert
Interdependency: process interdependency in business process architecture	Highest rank – having the most impact on other processes Lowest rank – having the least impact on other processes	Business proc. network and model analysis
Build-time flexibility: process possibility to be changed from legislative, technological, and organizational perspectives	Highest rank – highest possibility Lowest rank – lowest possibility	Expert
Run-time flexibility: processes ability to tolerate unexpected changes during execution	Highest rank – lowest tolerance Lowest rank – highest tolerance	Expert

health; Relevance and Interdependency denote process *importance*, while Build-time flexibility and Run-time flexibility describe process *feasibility*.

The defined criteria and identified processes are evaluated by process experts and, by applying OPA, final process weights are determined. However, in the proposed approach, the process' interdependency (exclusively) is evaluated by a specific method (as described in Sect. 3) not by experts.

The proposed approach prescribes the following activities for selecting the processes with the highest weight for improvement.

Ranking of criteria. As not all identified criteria are equally important, each expert evaluates and ranks criteria by their perceived criterion importance in prioritizing business processes for improvement. Criteria weighing directly impacts alternative weights and final rankings as alternatives ranked higher in more important criteria (with higher weights) will also be ranked higher [23].

Ranking of alternatives against the criteria. In this step, each business process included in the business process network is evaluated against each criterion by each expert. Only those processes included in the business process network are evaluated by experts. Additionally, as explained previously, experts do not provide an interdependency ranking. Instead, it is obtained by the method described in Sect. 3; thus, the interdependency rankings are the same for all experts. The interdependency rankings are included in the overall ranking after all the expert evaluations have been provided.

Determining the final business process priorities using OPA. As a final step, expert criteria and alternative rankings are inserted in the online OPA Solver 1.4 tool that produces the final expert, criteria, and alternative, i.e., business process weights [35]. The final weights are then further used by experts to help them prioritize business processes for improvement – processes with higher weights have higher priority for improvement, and processes with lower weights have lower priority for improvement.

5 The Evaluation of the Proposed Approach

To observe the feasibility of the proposed interdependency-aware business process prioritization approach, it was applied in a large international company operating in the aviation industry. To limit the number of processes selected for analysis, the scope of the case study was reduced to one department – Human Resources (HR). This department has been selected to demonstrate the applicability of the approach in a context that is not highly industry-specific, making it relevant to a broader range of organizations. The data produced during the implementation of this approach is not provided fully to comply with the company's internal policies.

Firstly, two HR employees were nominated as experts by the head of the division. Both employees have been with the company for several years and have extensive experience in various areas of HR, ranging from payroll to HR service. During an online meeting with both experts, processes to be included in the prioritization were identified and explained in detail. Following these descriptions, an analyst constructed the business process architecture and transformed it into the process network as depicted in Fig. 3. Finally, the 8 business processes included in the network were modeled in BPMN. These activities correspond to Phase I of the business process interdependency identification and evaluation method proposed in Sect. 3.

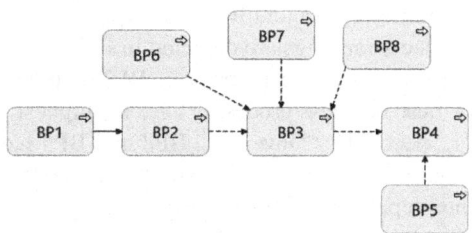

Fig. 3. Case study business process network.

Secondly, four algorithms were applied using process models and the network as an input to obtain process interdependency ranking (as discussed in Sect. 3.2). The resulting Control Flow, Resource, and Data dependency matrices were amalgamated using Borda count, producing interdependency rankings depicted in Table 5. BP6 was ranked highest as it has the largest impact on other processes across all the three interdependency perspectives: hence, its improvement could have the largest positive impact on the whole process network. In contrast, BP4 was ranked as the lowest process partly because it is not used by, and it does not trigger other processes.

Thirdly, the experts assigned rankings for all criteria listed in Table 4 and 8 business processes regarding each criterion. This was organized as an individual activity using predefined ranking templates. These evaluations were supplemented by process interdependency rankings from the previous step. Finally, the data was entered in the Online OPA Solver, which, after solving the MCDM problem, produced criteria and process weights.

Table 5. Case study business process interdependency rankings.

	Control flow dependencies	Resource dependencies	Data dependencies	$\sum$	Final rank
BP 6	7	7	7	21	1
BP 5	6	3	5	14	5
BP 7	7	6	7	20	2
BP 1	6	1	5	12	6
BP 8	7	5	7	19	3
BP 2	7	7	6	20	2
BP 4	5	2	4	11	7
BP 3	6	4	6	16	4

As per expert evaluation, criteria descriptions were clear. The experts considered Quality and Interdependency to be the most important factors by which to prioritize business processes. Thus, the experts confirmed the necessity to consider business process interdependencies when prioritizing processes for improvement. Time and Run-time flexibility were the least important factors from the experts' point of view.

The final business process rankings are depicted in Fig. 4. It shows that BP7 should be prioritized for improvement with the 1st priority, BP3 with the 2nd priority, and BP4 with the 3rd priority as these business processes have the highest weights, i.e., 0.16591, 0.16538 and 0.15822 respectively. Conversely, BP8 and BP5 have the lowest priority for improvement, having the lowest weights – 0.06209 and 0.05943 respectively.

To evaluate how interdependency impacts prioritization results, another simulation was done where interdependency was excluded as one of the prioritization criteria. By excluding interdependency, BP7 was in 4th place, while BP4 had the highest priority for improvement. However, if BP4 had been selected for prioritization, its improvement would have the smallest positive impact on the whole process network as the process is the least impactful (it has the lowest interdependency rank) as opposed to the interdependency rank of BP7. Therefore, the results suggest that interdependency is an important criterion that impacts final business process rankings.

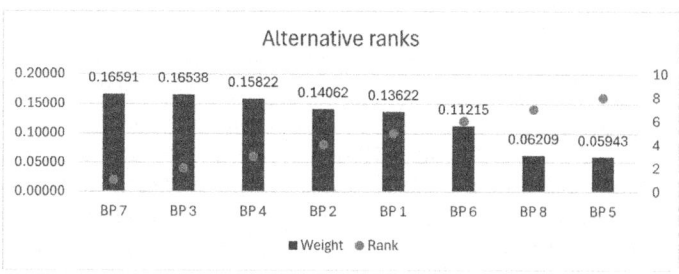

Fig. 4. Case study final business process rankings.

Applying the proposed interdependency-aware business process prioritization approach in a company produced meaningful results; it has proven that interdependency is an important process prioritization criterion that impacts final process rankings and should be considered during prioritization. The application of the approach also showed that combining a semi-automated process evaluation with expert evaluations is possible.

6 Conclusions

Existing business process prioritization approaches practically do not consider business process interdependencies as one of the prioritization criteria. However, interdependency is an important factor as business processes impact and are impacted by other processes. The paper proposes a business-driven approach for prioritizing business processes for improvement while considering their interconnectedness. The proposed prioritization approach includes the use of the semi-automated process interdependency identification and evaluation method, where process interdependencies are identified and evaluated (using business process architecture and business process models) from three perspectives – *control flow, resource,* and *data dependencies* – across four relation types – *composition, specialization, trigger,* and *use*. The results of interdependency evaluation (obtained by the method) are used in the proposed process prioritization approach along with other prioritization criteria. The processes identified in the interdependency evaluation method as elements of the business process network are also evaluated by business process experts in the prioritization approach, where final process weights are determined by applying OPA. The proposed prioritization approach can help practitioners to prioritize business processes for improvement by using business-driven standardized modelling notations (ArchiMate and BPMN) as well as corresponding modeling tools available online.

The proposed approach was implemented in a company from the aviation industry. The obtained results confirmed the applicability of the proposed approach in the company and approved the importance of considering process interdependencies as one of the prioritization criteria.

Nevertheless, the proposed approach has some notable limitations. Firstly, it was implemented in a single case; therefore, to further assess its applicability in practice, it should be evaluated in companies with various sizes, maturity levels, and experience with BPM. Secondly, a small number of experts with contrasting opinions can lead to unreliable results; therefore, more than two experts should be included in evaluations to increase the robustness of results. Thirdly, the presented method for process interdependency identification and evaluation requires organizations to model in detail all business processes included in prioritization. This may imply that the method could work better in organizations with well-established BPM practices and documentation, and the proposed approach may require different levels of effort from organizations to respect the process interdependency. Considering these limitations, future studies should focus on replicating the proposed approach in various case studies and exploring more automated or less time-consuming business process modeling techniques.

References

1. Škrinjar, R., Bosilj-Vukšić, V., Indihar-Štemberger, M.: The impact of business process orientation on financial and non-financial performance. Bus. Process. Manag. J. **14**, 738–754 (2008). https://doi.org/10.1108/14637150810903084
2. Dumas, M., La Rosa, M., Mendling, J., Reijers, H.A.: Process identification. Essential process modeling. In: Fundamentals of Business Process Management, pp. 35–115. Springer Berlin, Heidelberg (2018)
3. Bhaskar, H.L.: Business process reengineering: a process based management tool. Serbian J. Manage. **13**, 63–87 (2018). https://doi.org/10.5937/sjm13-13188
4. Ohlsson, J., Han, S., Johannesson, P., Carpenhall, F., Rusu, L.: Prioritizing business processes improvement initiatives: the Seco tools case. In: Advanced Information Systems Engineering: 26th International Conference, CAiSE 2014, pp. 256–270. Springer (2014)
5. APQC: 2024 Process & Performance Management Priorities & Challenges (2024)
6. Kerpedzhiev, G.D., König, U.M., Röglinger, M., Rosemann, M.: An exploration into future business process management capabilities in view of digitalization: results from a Delphi study. Bus. Inf. Syst. Eng. **63**, 83–96 (2021). https://doi.org/10.1007/s12599-020-00637-0
7. Amoozad Mahdiraji, H., Hafeez, K., Razavi Hajiagha, S.H.: Business process transformation in financial market: a hybrid BPM-ELECTRE TRI for redesigning a securities company in the Iranian stock market. Knowl. Process. Manag. **27**, 211–224 (2020). https://doi.org/10.1002/kpm.1632
8. Hammer, M., Champy, J.: The hunt for reengineering opportunities. In: Reengineering the Corporation: A Manifesto for Business Revolution, pp. 151–170. Harper Collins (1993)
9. Glogovac, M., Filipovic, J., Zivkovic, N., Jeremic, V.: A model for prioritization of improvement opportunities based on quality costs in the process interdependency context. Eng. Econ. **30**, 278–293 (2019). https://doi.org/10.5755/j01.ee.30.3.14657
10. Aqlan, F., Al-Fandi, L.: Prioritizing process improvement initiatives in manufacturing environments. Int. J. Prod. Econ. **196**, 261–268 (2018). https://doi.org/10.1016/j.ijpe.2017.12.004
11. Viontita, S.C., Er, M., Nurkasanah, I., Sonhaji, A.I.: Determining business process improvement priorities at Surabaya City Office for population administration & civil registration. In: 2022 International Conference on Advanced Computer Science and Information Systems (ICACSIS), pp. 211–218. Depok (2022)
12. Bitomsky, L., Huhn, J., Kratsch, W., Röglinger, M.: Process meets project prioritization – a decision model for developing process improvement roadmaps. In: Proceedings of the 27th European Conference on Information Systems (ECIS). Association for Information Systems (2019)

13. Fischer, M., Hofmann, A., Imgrund, F., Janiesch, C., Winkelmann, A.: On the composition of the long tail of business processes: implications from a process mining study. Inf. Syst. **97**, (2021). https://doi.org/10.1016/j.is.2020.101689
14. dos Santos, R.P., Salgado, T.M., Pereira, V.R.: Business process prioritization criteria: a case study in the financial market. RAUSP Manage. J. **57**, 35–48 (2022). https://doi.org/10.1108/RAUSP-07-2020-0155
15. Fleig, C., Augenstein, D., Maedche, A.: KeyPro – a decision support system for discovering important business processes in information systems. In: Mendling, J., Mouratidis, H. (eds.) Information Systems in the Big Data Era. CAiSE 2018. Lecture Notes in Business Information Processing. International Conference on Advanced Information Systems Engineering. Springer, Cham (2018)
16. de Lorena, A.L., Costa, A.P.: A process prioritization model for implementing risk management: the case of a Brazilian Public University. In: IEEE International Conference on Systems, Man and Cybernetics (SMC), pp. 1507–1512. Bari (2019)
17. Ohlsson, J., Han, S., Bouwman, H.: The prioritization and categorization method (PCM) process evaluation at Ericsson: a case study. Bus. Process. Manag. J. **23**, 377–398 (2017). https://doi.org/10.1108/BPMJ-07-2016-0136
18. Lehnert, M., Röglinger, M., Seyfried, J.: Prioritization of interconnected processes. Bus. Inf. Syst. Eng. **60**, 95–114 (2018). https://doi.org/10.1007/s12599-017-0490-4
19. Dijkman, R., Vanderfeesten, I., Reijers, H.A.: Business process architectures: overview, comparison and framework. Enterp. Inf. Syst. **10**, 129–158 (2016). https://doi.org/10.1080/17575.2014.928951
20. Kratsch, W., Manderscheid, J., Reißner, D., Röglinger, M.: Data-driven process prioritization in process networks. Decis. Support Syst. **100**, 27–40 (2017). https://doi.org/10.1016/j.dss.2017.02.011
21. Cherif, C.: Towards a probabilistic approach for better change management in BPM systems. In: Proceedings – IEEE International Enterprise Distributed Object Computing Workshop, EDOCW, pp. 184–189. Institute of Electrical and Electronics Engineers Inc. (2019)
22. Ishizaka, A., Nemery, P.: General introduction. In: Multi-Criteria Decision Analysis: Methods and Software, pp. 1–9. John Wiley & Sons, Incorporated, West Sussex (2013)
23. Ataei, Y., Mahmoudi, A., Feylizadeh, M.R., Li, D.F.: Ordinal priority approach (OPA) in multiple attribute decision-making. Appl. Soft. Comput. **86**, 105893 (2020). https://doi.org/10.1016/j.asoc.2019.105893
24. Javed, S.A., Du, J.: What is the ordinal priority approach? Manage. Sci. Bus. Decis. **3**, 12–26 (2023). https://doi.org/10.52812/msbd.72
25. Faisal, M.N., Al Subaie, A.A., Sabir, L.B., Sharif, K.J.: PMBOK, IPMA and fuzzy-AHP based novel framework for leadership competencies development in megaprojects. Benchmarking **30**, 2993–3020 (2023). https://doi.org/10.1108/BIJ-10-2021-0583
26. Hashemkhani Zolfani, S., Nemati, A., Reyes-Norambuena, P.J., Monardes-Concha, C.A.: A novel MCDM approach based on OPA-WINGS for policy making in undergraduate elective courses. Mathematics **10**, 4211 (2022). https://doi.org/10.3390/math10224211
27. Mishra, V., Gupta, K., Saxena, D., Singh, A.K.: A global medical data security and privacy preserving standards identification framework for electronic healthcare consumers. IEEE **70**, 4379–4387 (2024). https://doi.org/10.1109/TCE.2024.3373912
28. Bouraima, M.B., Kiptum, C.K., Ndiema, K.M., Qiu, Y., Tanackov, I.: Prioritization road safety strategies towards zero road traffic injury using ordinal priority approach. Oper. Res. Eng. Sci. Theory Appl. **5**, 206–221 (2022). https://doi.org/10.31181/oresta190822150b
29. Phillip Beauvoir, Jean-Baptiste Sarrodie: Archi. https://www.archimatetool.com/
30. Voloshin, V.I.: Basic definitions and concepts. In: Introduction to Graph Theory, pp. 1–34. Nova Science Publishers, New York (2009)

31. Object Management Group, Inc.: BPMN.org. https://www.bpmn.org/
32. Yang, F., Duan, P., Shah, S., Chen, T.: Capturing connectivity and causality from process knowledge. In: Capturing Connectivity and Causality in Complex Industrial Processes, pp. 23–38. Springer Cham, Cham (2014)
33. Denolf, J.M., Trienekens, J.H., Wognum, P.M., Van Der Vorst, J.G.A.J., Omta, S.W.F.: Towards a framework of critical success factors for implementing supply chain information systems (2015)
34. Zwicker, W.S.: Introduction to the theory of voting. In: Brandt, F., Conitzer, V., Endriss, U., Lang, J., Procaccia, A.D. (eds.) Handbook of Computational Social Choice, pp. 23–56. Cambridge University Press, New York (2016)
35. Mahmoudi, A., Sadeghi, M., Deng, X., Pan, P.: OPA solver: a web-based software for ordinal priority approach in multiple criteria decision analysis using JavaScript. SoftwareX **24**, 101546 (2023). https://doi.org/10.1016/j.softx.2023.101546

Human-AI Interplay in Exploring Process Representations (BPMDS 2025)

Human-AI Collaboration for Business Process Modeling with Petri Nets

Timo Schlösser, Martin Forell(✉), Selina Schüler, and Andreas Fritsch

Karlsruhe Institute of Technology (KIT), Institute of Applied Informatics and Formal Description Methods (AIFB), Kaiserstr. 89, 76133 Karlsruhe, Germany
timo.schloesser@partner.kit.edu,
{martin.forell,selina.schueler,andreas.fritsch}@kit.edu

Abstract. Business Process Modeling enables organizations to document and improve workflows, but creating process models remains a time-intensive task requiring expertise in formal modeling languages and domain knowledge. Recent advances in Large Language Models (LLMs) have facilitated the automated generation of process models from textual descriptions, yet these LLMs often struggle with ambiguity, inconsistencies, and validation challenges. This work introduces a human-in-the-loop (HITL) approach where an LLM generates clarifying questions to resolve ambiguities, enabling human-AI collaboration through iterative refinements and structured guidance for more accurate process models. Evaluation results demonstrate that the HITL approach resolves ambiguities and improves the syntactic and semantic quality of generated process models. By bridging the gap between automation and human expertise, this approach contributes to the development of reliable and effective methodologies for Business Process Modeling.

Keywords: Business Process Modeling · Petri Nets · Large Language Models · Text-to-Model

1 Introduction

In the rapidly evolving landscape of digital transformation, Business Process Management (BPM) has become indispensable for organizations aiming to understand, document, analyze, and improve their business processes. For these purposes, business processes may be modeled or described in various formats – ranging from textual representations to visual diagrams and executable models [36]. However, creating and maintaining process models is inherently challenging, as it requires significant domain knowledge, proficiency with formal modeling languages, and continuous adjustments in response to organizational changes [1,26].

Various Natural Language Processing (NLP)-based approaches have been proposed for handling these issues. Rule-based methods, such as those described in [9], rely on predefined transformation rules to convert textual descriptions into process models. These approaches require strictly formatted text as input. However, in practice, domain experts frequently describe processes informally, limiting the applicability of rule-based automation.

Recent advances in Large Language Models (LLMs), particularly commercial LLMs such as [3,28,29], as well as open-source LLMs like [22,31], offer new possibilities for process modeling automation. LLMs can interpret complex textual descriptions and handle diverse input formats more flexibly than rule-based methods [14]. However, despite their potential, current LLM-based approaches face limitations in handling ambiguity and incomplete process descriptions, which can lead to errors in generated models. In the context of this paper, we understand ambiguity as textual descriptions that allow for multiple valid interpretations of a process' control flow. These issues are particularly relevant in processes with multiple interacting process components, where dependencies and execution sequences are often implicit rather than explicitly stated.

To address these challenges, we propose a Human-in-the-Loop (HITL) approach that integrates human-Artificial Intelligence (AI) collaboration. Rather than replacing human expertise, it assists process designers in resolving ambiguities within textual process descriptions. It does so by incorporating targeted clarifications, iterative refinements, and structured modeling techniques. This collaborative approach supports the clarity and maintainability of business process models, ensuring their alignment with real-world processes.

To validate our approach, we developed a prototypical implementation and evaluated it on process descriptions with varying structural complexities. The evaluation focuses on processes with multiple interacting control flow patterns, as these present the greatest challenges for LLM-based modeling. Control flow patterns are fundamental constructs describing common routing behaviors, such as sequences, parallel splits and joins, and exclusive choices, used to represent and analyze workflows independently of specific process languages [36]. Our results demonstrate that HITL significantly improves syntactic correctness and semantic accuracy in such cases.

The remainder of this paper is structured as follows: Sect. 2 introduces Business Process Modeling and LLMs. Section 3 reviews automated process modeling approaches. Section 4 details our HITL-based method. Section 5 presents a prototypical implementation, and Sect. 6 discusses evaluation results. Section 7 analyzes implications, followed by conclusions and future directions in Sect. 8.

2 Background

This section presents background on Business Process Modeling (especially quality dimensions of process models), LLMs and HITL systems.

2.1 Business Process Modeling Using Petri Nets

BPM approaches aim to improve the performance of organizations' processes [36]. Business process models form the basis for identifying improvement potential. Various process modeling languages exist, and they differ in accessibility and formal precision [13]. Petri nets have long been recognized as a robust modeling language within BPM due to their formal foundation, supporting structural and behavioral analysis of processes while providing a clear graphical representation [36]. The formal structure of a Petri net consists of places (P), transitions (T), and directed arcs ($F \subseteq (P \times T) \cup (T \times P)$) that connect them. Places represent states or conditions, while transitions represent activities that can change the system's state. The state of a Petri net is defined by its marking, which is represented by tokens distributed across places. The dynamic behavior of a system is modeled through the firing of transitions, which move tokens between places according to the network structure [30].

The quality of process models can be distinguished in syntactic, semantic, and pragmatic quality [19]. In this paper, we focus on syntactic and semantic quality. *Syntactic quality* focuses on the adherence to formal rules and constraints of the modeling language. This includes proper use of modeling elements, correct connectivity between components, and compliance with language-specific restrictions. Syntactic correctness is fundamental, as it ensures that models can be properly interpreted and analyzed using formal methods. *Semantic quality* addresses the accurate representation of process logic and business rules. This dimension evaluates whether the model correctly captures the intended behavior, relationships, and constraints of the business process. Semantic quality is crucial for ensuring that process models serve their intended purpose in supporting business operations and analysis.

2.2 Large Language Models

LLMs represent a major advancement in AI, particularly within the domain of NLP. Most current LLMs are built upon the Transformer architecture [34], which employs self-attention mechanisms to capture intricate relationships within language data and has since become the foundation for most state-of-the-art LLMs [10,12,33]. By leveraging vast datasets of text, LLMs can learn the complex patterns and structures inherent in human language, achieving the capability to understand and generate natural language [25]. The scale of these LLMs, encompassing their extensive parameter counts and substantial training data, enables them to address increasingly sophisticated linguistic tasks [25].

To guide the LLM during output generation, various prompt engineering strategies have been developed to enhance the quality and relevance of the outputs. Among these strategies are (1) *Role Prompting*, which assigns a specific role to the LLM to tailor its responses to align with the expectations of that role [35]; (2) *Knowledge Injection*, which incorporates additional domain-specific information not present during pre-training to mitigate common errors and ensure more accurate outputs [21]; (3) *Few-Shot Prompting*, where examples of input-output pairs are provided to the LLM, enabling it to learn desired response patterns and formats [6]; and (4) *Negative Prompting*, which directs the LLM to avoid specific elements or features during generation, thereby improving output relevance by excluding undesirable content [23].

To further improve the quality and reliability of LLM outputs, this work employs two complementary approaches. First, the *HITL Approach* integrates human expertise into the generation process by providing interactive feedback, refinement, and context-specific adaptation [24]. This approach is particularly suited for tasks requiring high precision and nuanced decision-making. The design of HITL systems involves structuring interaction points to determine when human intervention is necessary, identifying the most effective forms of input, and integrating human feedback into the automated control flow [24]. Second, *Self-Reflection* enables LLMs to autonomously evaluate and refine their outputs through iterative feedback loops [20]. By comparing generated outputs against predefined criteria, LLMs can identify potential improvements, generate corrective feedback, and iteratively refine their outputs. This process does not require additional supervised training or external reinforcement, making it an efficient method for enhancing output quality [20].

3 Related Work

Recent advancements in LLMs have introduced methodologies for automated process modeling, offering an alternative to traditional rule-based process modeling approaches. Research has shown the potential of LLMs to extract and represent complex process semantics from textual descriptions.

GPT-3.5 [27] was employed by [32] for summarization and causal relationship extraction to derive preliminary process models. BERT [7] was utilized alongside GPT-based models by [18] to classify tokens and derive structured elements, resulting in improved accuracy across diverse test scenarios.

A tool leveraging LLMs to generate and refine process models from textual descriptions was introduced by [15], incorporating prompt engineering, error handling, and interactive feedback mechanisms. Extending this perspective, a framework for integrating LLMs into process modeling was introduced by [14], emphasizing methodological approaches such as iterative refinement, role prompting, and validation techniques to ensure sound and accurate process representations. Another approach, presented in [4], integrates LLMs with knowledge graphs to dynamically generate and refine process representations, focusing on decision-making in data-centric processes.

While existing approaches have achieved notable progress in leveraging LLMs for process modeling, challenges persist in analyzing textual process descriptions. These descriptions often exhibit complexity, ambiguity, and inconsistencies, which can hinder the generation of accurate and complete process models. Given the human-centric nature of process models, incorporating domain expertise is critical to resolving ambiguities and maintaining the semantic and syntactic integrity of the generated outputs. However, most current methods integrate human feedback only in post-generation stages, thereby limiting the potential to address issues at their source. The integration of the HITL approach during the early stages of the modeling process offers a promising approach to improve the quality of input descriptions, reduce interpretive ambiguities, and generate process models that more closely align with the intended structure and functionality. This work builds on previous research that demonstrated the potential of LLMs in process modeling [8].

4 Approach

This section presents our approach for generating process models from textual descriptions. To address language ambiguities, we introduce a HITL approach that enhances textual input for LLMs. The process follows three phases: (1) *Pre-Processing*, which resolves ambiguities and structures input descriptions; (2) *Model Generation*, where LLMs convert structured descriptions into a Petri net representation; and (3) *Model Improvement*, which refines the generated Petri nets for greater accuracy and consistency. This structured method bridges the gap between informal text and formal, executable process models.

4.1 Step 1: Pre-processing Using HITL

In the pre-processing phase, an unstructured textual process description provided by a stakeholder is transformed into a structured format suitable for process model generation using LLMs. This phase aims to improve the quality of the textual input by reducing ambiguities through targeted clarifying questions and by structuring it. This structured representation bridges the gap between unstructured natural language and a format optimized for subsequent LLM-based model generation. Figure 1 visualizes an overview of the pre-processing phase using the HITL approach.

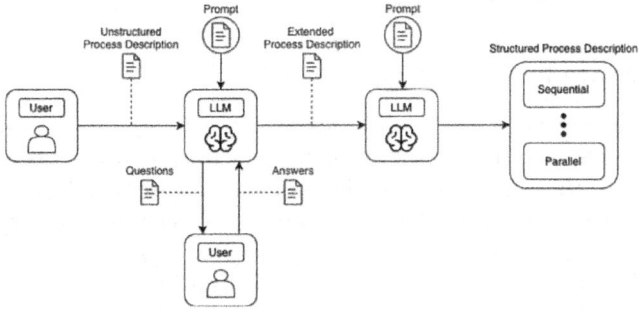

Fig. 1. Transformation of unstructured textual process descriptions into structured process descriptions through targeted clarifications and control flow pattern identification.

The phase begins with an initial analysis of the provided text. Here, the LLM, guided by a prompt to extract activities and their sequential relationships, identifies individual activities and their ordering. This initial analysis establishes a preliminary understanding of the process flow, serving as a foundation for subsequent refinement. Next, the LLM generates targeted clarifying questions. Leveraging a prompt designed to elicit information about specific control flow patterns (sequence, AND-split/join, XOR-split/join, and loops) [2,36]. This question generation process targets each of the four control flow patterns:

1. *Sequence:* Questions like "Does 'process payment' always follow 'check order completeness'?" aim to confirm the strict sequential order of activities.
2. *AND split/join:* Questions like "Can 'quality check' and 'packaging' occur concurrently?" investigate the potential for parallel execution of activities.
3. *XOR split/join:* Questions like "What happens if 'credit check' is declined?" explore decision points and branching logic within the process.
4. *Loops and Cycles:* Questions like "Under what conditions is 'send reminder' repeated?" probe for iterative behaviour and loop conditions.

The user's responses are appended to the original process description as supplementary information, preserving the original text while providing additional context for the LLM. This approach ensures that the LLM has access to both the textual process description and the clarifying details provided by the user, facilitating a more accurate and nuanced understanding of the process. This extended process description then informs the final structuring step.

Finally, the LLM restructures the extended process description into a format organized according to the identified control flow patterns. Guided by prompts to segment and structure the information based on these patterns, the LLM creates a representation with distinct sections for each control flow type that appears in the process description. This segmentation ensures that sequential flows, parallel activities (AND-splits/joins), decision points (XOR-splits/joins), and cycles (Loops and Cycles) are delineated and represented in separate sections within the structured description.

4.2 Step 2: Model Generation

The Model Generation phase, following Pre-Processing, transforms the structured process description into a formal process model (using Petri nets in this implementation, though other modeling languages are possible).

As depicted in Fig. 2, the structured process description is divided into sections corresponding to a control flow pattern. Each section is then processed independently by the LLM. Specifically, the LLM receives targeted prompts focusing on the control flow pattern of the section, generating a partial Petri net model for that specific control flow pattern. For instance, a section representing a parallel activity would be accompanied by a prompt instructing the LLM to generate the corresponding Petri net construct. Using targeted prompts for each control flow pattern, this segmented approach aims to improve the accuracy of modeling individual patterns. By focusing the LLM on smaller sections, the complexity of the modeling task is reduced, allowing the LLM to concentrate on specific challenges in isolation. This focused approach is expected to lead to more precise and robust partial process models.

Once the LLM has generated partial Petri net models for each segment, further prompts guide the integration of these fragments into a complete, cohesive Petri net representing the entire process description. This aggregation step ensures the correct connection and logical flow between the segments, resulting in a unified and accurate process model.

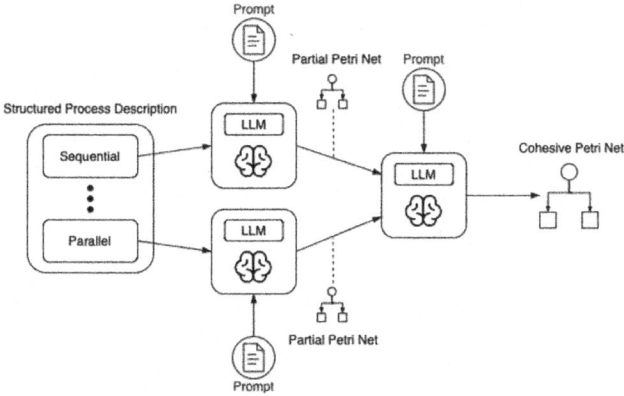

Fig. 2. Two step transformation of the structured process description into partial Petri nets and finally into a complete, cohesive Petri net

4.3 Step 3: Model Improvement Using Self-reflection

To address potential inconsistencies and maintain logical flow across segments, a self-reflection mechanism with iterative feedback loops is used. This process refines the initial Petri net by detecting and correcting common modeling errors, such as incorrect edges or misplaced transitions, thus promoting greater accuracy and consistency in the Petri net.

During *Self-Reflection*, the LLM receives the initially generated Petri net along with a prompt instructing it to review the model for common errors and provide improvement suggestions. The objective is to detect areas that could introduce inconsistencies or inaccuracies. Based on this evaluation, the LLM generates concrete recommendations, such as adjusting connections or clarifying decision logic to enhance accuracy.

In the *Refinement* phase, the LLM applies these suggested improvements to the Petri net. With guidance from a structured prompt, the LLM integrates the proposed modifications, ensuring the updated model adheres to logical correctness and structural integrity.

Finally, the refined Petri net is converted into a JSON file using an LLM with an output parser, enabling seamless integration into various modeling tools.

5 Prototypical Implementation and Process Example

A prototype[1] was implemented using Python, leveraging libraries such as LangChain [16] and Langgraph [17], incorporating prompt engineering strategies to guide the LLM through all processing phases. These strategies include role prompting (positioning the LLM as a Petri net expert), knowledge injection about Petri net constructs, few-shot prompting with examples, and negative prompting to refine question generation.

Table 1. Process description illustrating a scenario with incomplete specification at a decision point. The description details what happens when updates are needed, but lacks information on the alternative path if no updates are required, highlighting an ambiguity

Process Description
The process begins with cleaning and organizing the kitchen workspace. Next, the chef checks for updates to the menu or recipes. If updates are needed, the recipes are either revised or adjusted with new ingredients, moving them into a stage where they are ready to be tested. The updated recipes are then tested by cooking them. Once the testing is done, the recipes are finalized and approved. Finally, the kitchen is prepared for service, and the updated menu is ready for customers.

Users interact through a command-line interface to input process descriptions and respond to clarifying questions generated during the pre-processing phase. Afterward, the entire process is automated, ultimately providing the user with the resulting Petri net as a JSON file. For demonstration purposes, the Horus Business Modeler [11] was used to import the JSON file and visualize the process model.

To demonstrate our approach, we present a simple example process involving a scenario where updates may or may not be required. Specifically, the original process description (Table 1) only defines the actions to be taken when an update is required, without detailing what happens if no update is needed. This lack of detail introduces ambiguity, which can lead to inaccuracies in the generated process model.

By applying the HITL approach, the model generated a set of clarifying questions aimed at resolving the ambiguity surrounding the decision point, as depicted in Table 2. The questions focused on parallelism and decisions in the process, such as: "Is there a decision point after checking for updates to the menu or recipes? If so, what are the possible paths if no updates are needed?" The user responded that if no updates are needed, the process should skip directly to preparing the kitchen for service. Additionally, the user confirmed that revising the recipes and adjusting the ingredients occur independently, allowing them to proceed in parallel without any dependencies.

---
[1] The code is available at https://github.com/KIT-BIS/human-ai-modeling.

Table 2. Clarifying questions and corresponding answers aimed at resolving ambiguities in the process description. The questions address issues of parallelism and decision points, focusing on dependencies between activities and actions if no updates are required.

Questions (LLM)	Answers (Human)
Parallelism and Concurrency	
During the state where updates are required, revising the recipes and adjusting the ingredients occur in parallel. Are there any dependencies between these two activities that need to be considered?	No, there are no dependencies between these two activities. They can occur independently, allowing them to proceed in parallel without coordination.
Decisions and Choices	
Is there a decision point after checking for updates to the menu or recipes? If so, what are the possible paths if no updates are needed?	Yes, there is a decision point after checking for updates. If no updates are needed, the process skips directly to preparing the kitchen for service.

Based on these clarifications, the structured process description generated with the HITL approach included both branches of the decision point, as shown in Table 3. The structured description explicitly states that if no updates are needed, the process skips directly to preparing the kitchen for service. It also details the parallel activities of revising recipes and adjusting ingredients as independent actions. In contrast, the structured description generated without the HITL approach lacks this completeness, as it only specifies the actions to be taken if updates are needed, without addressing the alternative scenario.

Figure 3 presents the Petri nets generated from the process description. The Petri net generated using the HITL-enhanced process description captures both possible branches of the decision point, leading to a more comprehensive model. Specifically, it includes the connection where, if no updates are needed, the process proceeds directly to preparing the kitchen for service. On the other hand, the Petri net generated without the HITL approach omits this branch, resulting in a less accurate representation of the process.

This example demonstrates the advantages of the HITL approach in generating a more complete process description, resulting in a more accurate Petri net. Addressing ambiguities through targeted questions ensured the full representation of the process logic.

Table 3. Comparison of structured process descriptions with and without HITL intervention. The HITL version includes a complete specification of decision points and parallel activities, providing additional clarity on the actions to be taken if no updates are needed, which is missing in the version without HITL.

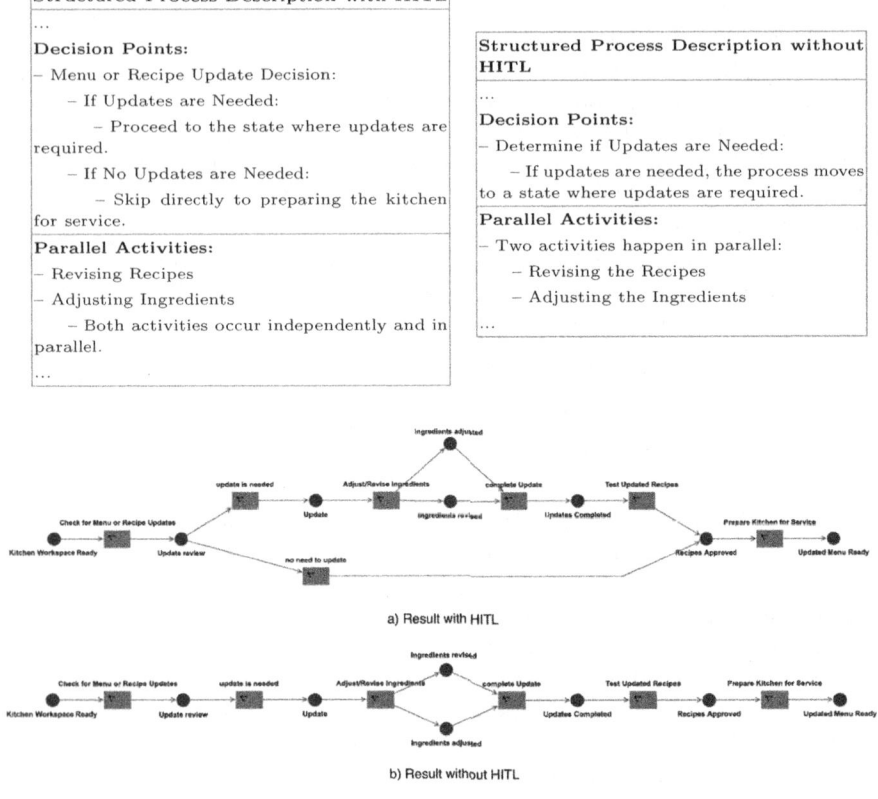

Structured Process Description with HITL
...
Decision Points:
– Menu or Recipe Update Decision:
– If Updates are Needed:
– Proceed to the state where updates are required.
– If No Updates are Needed:
– Skip directly to preparing the kitchen for service.
Parallel Activities:
– Revising Recipes
– Adjusting Ingredients
– Both activities occur independently and in parallel.
...

Structured Process Description without HITL
...
Decision Points:
– Determine if Updates are Needed:
– If updates are needed, the process moves to a state where updates are required.
Parallel Activities:
– Two activities happen in parallel:
– Revising the Recipes
– Adjusting the Ingredients
...

Fig. 3. Comparison of Petri nets generated with and without HITL. The Petri net generated with HITL includes additional branches that clarify decision points, leading to a more complete representation of the process compared to the version generated without HITL.

6 Evaluation

To evaluate our proposed approach for Business Process Modeling, we conducted an experimental evaluation. This section details our evaluation strategy, introduces the used dataset, and presents our model quality metrics and results.

6.1 Evaluation Strategy

Evaluating the effectiveness of our proposed HITL approach involves examining two primary objectives: (1) determining how human-AI collaboration addresses ambiguities and structural complexities in textual process descriptions, and (2) identifying any limitations across different control flow patterns. Existing datasets, such as the Pet Data Set [5], were unsuitable due to their lack of formal reference models and insufficient systematic coverage of specific control flow patterns. Therefore, we developed a custom dataset[2] containing 15 process descriptions, each paired with a manually constructed reference Petri net. These descriptions systematically represent sequential, parallel, XOR decision, cycle, and combination patterns, reflecting real-world complexity. Each scenario was categorized into one of three complexity levels: easy (minimal complexity, single control flow pattern), medium (increased complexity through multiple patterns or additional elements), and hard (multiple interacting control flows, nested structures, or substantial modeling complexity).

To systematically assess the value of human-AI collaboration, we compared two variations of our method: (1) without HITL, in which Petri nets were directly generated from the original textual descriptions, and (2) with HITL, where iterative human feedback was used to clarify and refine the input descriptions before generating Petri nets. Both approaches utilized GPT-4o as the underlying LLM. A modeling expert evaluated the generated Petri nets by assessing their syntactic correctness and semantic accuracy against manually created reference models. The evaluation explicitly examined how integrating human feedback through the HITL methodology influenced modeling accuracy, particularly in ambiguous and structurally complex scenarios reflective of real-world business process challenges.

6.2 Evaluation Metrics

To assess the effectiveness of our LLM-based approach, we employed two evaluation metrics-syntactic correctness and semantic accuracy-to systematically measure the quality of generated Petri nets. An expert evaluator compared each generated model against manually created reference Petri nets. Since multiple valid models may exist for a given process description, our evaluation focused on the alignment of the generated Petri nets with the intended meaning and structure of the original textual descriptions, rather than strict adherence to a single reference model.

Syntactic correctness evaluates whether the generated Petri nets satisfy formal criteria essential for validity, such as the absence of deadlocks, boundedness, the reachability of all states, and the existence of clearly defined start and end places. Petri nets meeting these criteria received a score of 1 (correct), whereas models with syntactical issues received a score of 0 (incorrect).

Semantic accuracy assesses whether the generated Petri nets accurately represent the intended logical dependencies and control flow patterns described in the textual input. For example, if a process description specifies multiple control flow elements such as XOR splits or parallel execution paths, each element

---

[2] The dataset is available at https://huggingface.co/datasets/bis-aifb-kit/process_descriptions_for_modeling.

is individually assessed. A fully correct representation receives a full semantic score (e.g., 2/2 for correctly modeling both XOR splits and joins), while partially correct representations receive proportional scoring. This metric ensures the generated Petri nets faithfully capture the intended business logic and workflow interactions described in the input.

6.3 Results with GPT-4o

This section presents the results of the developed approach for generating Petri nets using GPT-4o, evaluated on a dataset of 15 process descriptions with and without the HITL component. The results are summarized in Table 4, which provides an aggregated overview for each control flow pattern: sequential, parallel, cycle, decision, and combination. The tables display the total syntax and semantic scores for all three descriptions per pattern. The left table shows results without HITL, while the right table presents those with HITL.

Table 4. Aggregated evaluation results comparing the syntax and semantic quality of Petri nets generated with and without HITL. The table highlights differences in the accuracy of modeling different control flow patterns, demonstrating that the HITL approach led to improvements in more complex scenarios (e.g., Combination), while in simpler patterns (e.g., Sequential, Parallel), the approach without HITL often performed better.

Without HITL	Syntax	Semantic	With HITL	Syntax	Semantic
Sequential	3/3	3/3	Sequential	3/3	2/3
Parallel	3/3	12/12	Parallel	2/3	9/12
Cycle	2/3	5/6	Cycle	3/3	5/6
Decision	3/3	9/10	Decision	2/3	9/10
Combination	1/3	6/12	Combination	2/3	8/12

The results indicate that incorporating the HITL approach significantly improved the modeling accuracy for structurally complex process descriptions involving multiple interacting control flow elements. Specifically, with human feedback, semantic correctness increased from 6/12 to 8/12, and syntactic correctness improved from 1/3 to 2/3. This demonstrates that human-AI collaboration effectively resolves ambiguities, enabling the model to better represent process dependencies and logic.

In contrast, the approach without HITL consistently achieved high syntactic and semantic accuracy for simpler scenarios involving Sequential, Parallel, Cycle, and Decision patterns, indicating no systematic weaknesses. However, the integration of HITL had varied impacts on these simpler patterns: semantic accuracy slightly decreased in Sequential (from 3/3 to 2/3) and Parallel scenarios (from 12/12 to 9/12), and syntactic correctness decreased marginally in Parallel scenarios (from 3/3 to 2/3). This variation suggests that while human collaboration is particularly beneficial in resolving complexity and ambiguity, it may introduce minor inaccuracies in simpler scenarios where descriptions are already clear. These findings highlight that the effectiveness of the HITL method strongly depends on the complexity and structural ambiguity of the process descriptions, which will be analyzed further in the discussion section.

7 Discussion

The evaluation results indicate that integrating the HITL approach significantly enhances syntactic correctness and semantic accuracy for process descriptions characterized by multiple interacting control flow elements. The observed improvements suggest that iterative human feedback helps effectively resolve ambiguities and refine complex textual descriptions. Because real-world business processes typically involve combinations of several control flow patterns rather than isolated or clearly defined structures, these results underline the practical value and applicability of human-AI collaboration through the proposed HITL methodology.

At the same time, the evaluation confirms that the fully automated baseline approach (without HITL) consistently achieves reliable modeling performance across simpler control flow patterns, including Sequential, Parallel, Cycle, and Decision structures. This consistency suggests that the automated approach alone is robust for clearly defined scenarios, indicating no systematic weaknesses in handling such patterns. However, incorporating human feedback through HITL demonstrated varied effects for simpler scenarios: in Sequential and Parallel cases, semantic accuracy slightly decreased with human intervention, indicating that additional descriptions might introduce minor deviations rather than enhance clarity.

This finding does not suggest an inherent limitation of HITL, but rather highlights that the methods effectiveness depends on the structural complexity and ambiguity within the original process descriptions. Where textual descriptions are already clear and unambiguous, introducing human input may provide limited or negligible benefit and could even be counterproductive. Consequently, the advantage of the HITL approach emerges clearly when applied to scenarios marked by structural complexity, implicit dependencies, and ambiguity.

Several factors influence the effectiveness of the HITL approach in process modeling:

- *Quality of Generated Questions:* HITL effectiveness depends on how well the LLMs generate clarifying questions. If questions fail to address ambiguities, HITL benefits remain limited and may even introduce additional complexity.
- *Quality of User Responses:* Clear and relevant user feedback is crucial. High-quality responses refine the LLMs's understanding, while vague or inaccurate answers can reduce performance.

- *Integration of Responses:* Effective integration of user feedback into the process description ensures meaningful refinements, preventing redundant iterations or unnecessary changes.
- *Quality of the LLMs:* The overall effectiveness of HITL is influenced by the capabilities of the LLMs. More advanced models handle complex interactions better, while less capable models may struggle, particularly when additional layers of complexity are introduced.

It is also important to emphasize that the proposed approach does not rely on blind acceptance of LLMs outputs. Instead, the generated process model serve as a starting point for human modelers, who remain in control of reviewing, adjusting, and finalizing the process model. This collaborative setup ensures that errors such as hallucinations, overly generic outputs, or prompt failure are mitigated by human oversight. Rather than replacing human expertise, the goal of our HITL methodology is to support it-establishing a Human-AI Collaboration framework where LLMs provide structure and efficiency, and humans provide domain awareness and contextual correctness.

While the results highlight the potential of HITL, some limitations must be considered. The evaluation was conducted on a relatively small dataset of 15 process descriptions, with only three descriptions per control flow pattern. To improve generalizability, a larger and more diverse dataset is needed. Additionally, HITL interactions were provided by a single expert, which could introduce bias. A broader evaluation with multiple experts could provide deeper insights into how different perspectives influence effectiveness.

Another important factor is the reliance on GPT-4o as the underlying LLMs. While GPT-4o is a high-performing commercial model, even advanced LLMs have limitations in handling ambiguities and complex dependencies. Future work should explore how different LLMs, including open-source models, process refinements to assess generalizability.

These limitations highlight areas for further research and improvement, including dataset expansion, multi-expert evaluation, and testing different LLMs to refine the strengths and weaknesses of HITL.

8 Conclusion

This paper introduced a HITL approach for Business Process Modeling with Petri nets, addressing ambiguity challenges in textual descriptions. By incorporating targeted clarifications and iterative refinements, the approach enhances syntactic correctness and semantic accuracy in complex modeling scenarios. Evaluation results confirm HITL's effectiveness, particularly for complex control flow patterns, ensuring robust automation without introducing systematic weaknesses.

Future work could explore adaptive HITL systems that selectively apply human feedback based on perceived structural ambiguity. Expanding the evaluation with real-world datasets and integrating diverse LLMs may further enhance generalizability. Furthermore, introducing multiple domain experts in our collaborative HITL-approach could further improve robustness and mitigate biases. Overall, the embedding of human expertise and automated (LLMs-based) modeling approaches is a promising avenue for building reliable and efficient process modeling systems.

References

1. van der Aalst, W.M.P.: Process Mining: Discovery, Conformance and Enhancement of Business Processes. Springer, Berlin, Heidelberg (2011). https://doi.org/10.1007/978-3-642-19345-3
2. van der Aalst, W., ter Hofstede, A., Kiepuszewski, B., Barros, A.: Workflow patterns. Distrib. Parallel Databases **14**(1), 5–51 (2003). https://doi.org/10.1023/A:1022883727209
3. Antrophic: Claude 3.7 sonnet and claude code (2025). https://www.anthropic.com/news/claude-3-7-sonnet. Accessed 19 Apr 2025
4. Beheshti, A., et al.: ProcessGPT: Transforming Business Process Management with Generative Artificial Intelligence (2023). https://doi.org/10.48550/arXiv.2306.01771
5. Bellan, P., van der Aa, H., Dragoni, M., Ghidini, C., Ponzetto, S.P.: PET: an annotated dataset for process extraction from natural language text tasks. In: Business Process Management Workshops, Münster, Germany (2023). https://doi.org/10.1007/978-3-031-25383-6_23
6. Brown, T.B., et al.: Language Models are Few-Shot Learners (2020). https://doi.org/10.48550/arXiv.2005.14165
7. Devlin, J., Chang, M.W., Lee, K., Toutanova, K.: BERT: pre-training of deep bidirectional transformers for language understanding (2019). https://doi.org/10.48550/arXiv.1810.04805
8. Forell, M., Schüler, S.: Modeling meets large language models. In: Modellierung 2024 Satellite Events. Potsdam, Germany (2024)
9. Friedrich, F., Mendling, J., Puhlmann, F.: Process model generation from natural language text. In: CAiSE. London, UK (2011). https://doi.org/10.1007/978-3-642-21640-4_36
10. Grattafiori, A., et al.: The Llama 3 Herd of Models (2024). https://doi.org/10.48550/arXiv.2407.21783
11. Horus software GmbH: Business Modeler (2024). https://www.horus.biz/de/produkte/business-modeler/. Accessed 19 Apr 2025
12. Jiang, A.Q., et al.: Mistral 7B (2023). https://doi.org/10.48550/arXiv.2310.06825
13. Koschmider, A., Oberweis, A., Stucky, W.: A petri net-based view on the business process life-cycle. Enterp. Model. Inf. Syst. Archit. (EMISAJ) **13**, 47–55 (2018). https://doi.org/10.18417/emisa.si.hcm.4
14. Kourani, H., Berti, A., Schuster, D., van der Aalst, W.M.P.: Process modeling with large language models (2024). https://doi.org/10.48550/arXiv.2403.07541
15. Kourani, H., Berti, A., Schuster, D., van der Aalst, W.M.P.: ProMoAI: process modeling with generative AI. In: International Joint Conference on Artificial Intelligence (2024). https://doi.org/10.24963/ijcai.2024/1014
16. LangChain: Introduction — LangChain (2024). https://python.langchain.com/docs/introduction/. Accessed 19 Apr 2025

17. LangChain: LangGraph Quick Start (2024). https://langchain-ai.github.io/langgraph/tutorials/introduction/. Accessed 19 Apr 2025
18. Licardo, J.T., Tanković, N., Etinger, D.: A method for extracting BPMN models from textual descriptions using natural language processing. Procedia Comput. Sci. **239**, 483–490 (2024). https://doi.org/10.1016/j.procs.2024.06.196
19. Lindland, O., Sindre, G., Solvberg, A.: Understanding quality in conceptual modeling. IEEE Softw. **11**(2), 42–49 (1994). https://doi.org/10.1109/52.268955
20. Madaan, A., et al.: Self-refine: iterative refinement with self-feedback (2023). https://doi.org/10.48550/arXiv.2303.17651
21. Martino, A., Iannelli, M., Truong, C.: Knowledge injection to counter large language model (LLM) hallucination. In: The Semantic Web: ESWC 2023 Satellite Events. Hersonissos, Crete, Greece (2023). https://doi.org/10.1007/978-3-031-43458-7_34
22. MetaAI: Llama 3.2: Revolutionizing edge AI and vision with open, customizable models (2024). https://ai.meta.com/blog/llama-3-2-connect-2024-vision-edge-mobile-devices/. Accessed 19 Apr 2025
23. Miyake, D., Iohara, A., Saito, Y., Tanaka, T.: Negative-prompt inversion: fast image inversion for editing with text-guided diffusion models (2023). https://doi.org/10.48550/arXiv.2305.16807
24. Mosqueira-Rey, E., Hernández-Pereira, E., Alonso-Ríos, D., Bobes-Bascáran, J., Fernández-Leal, A.: Human-in-the-loop machine learning: a state of the art. Artif. Intell. Rev. **56**(4), 3005–3054 (2023). https://doi.org/10.1007/s10462-022-10246-w
25. Naveed, H., et al.: A Comprehensive Overview of Large Language Models (2024). https://doi.org/10.48550/arXiv.2307.06435
26. Oberweis, A.: Modellierung und Ausführung von Workflows mit Petri-Netzen. Vieweg+Teubner Verlag, Wiesbaden (1996). https://doi.org/10.1007/978-3-322-81039-7
27. OpenAI: GPT-3.5 Turbo fine-tuning and API updates (2023). https://openai.com/index/gpt-3-5-turbo-fine-tuning-and-api-updates/. Accessed 19 Apr 2025
28. OpenAI: Hello GPT-4o — OpenAI (2024). https://openai.com/index/hello-gpt-4o/. Accessed 19 Apr 2025
29. OpenAI: Introducing GPT-4.5 (2025). https://openai.com/index/introducing-gpt-4-5/. Accessed 19 Apr 2025
30. Reisig, W.: Understanding Petri Nets: Modeling Techniques, Analysis Methods, Case Studies. Springer, Heidelberg (2013). https://doi.org/10.1007/978-3-642-33278-4
31. Sanseviero, O., Schmid, P.: Introducing gemma 3: the developer guide (2025). https://developers.googleblog.com/en/introducing-gemma3/. Accessed 19 Apr 2025
32. Simon, C., Haag, S., Zakfeld, L.: Experimente zur GPT-3.5-unterstÃtzten Entwicklung von Prozessmodellen. Anwendungen und Konzepte der Wirtschaftsinformatik p. 8 (2023). https://doi.org/10.26034/lu.akwi.2023.4570
33. Team Gemini, et al.: Gemini: a family of highly capable multimodal models (2024). https://doi.org/10.48550/arXiv.2312.11805
34. Vaswani, A., et al.: Attention is all you need (2023). https://doi.org/10.48550/arXiv.1706.03762
35. Wang, R., et al.: Role prompting guided domain adaptation with general capability preserve for large language models (2024). http://arxiv.org/abs/2403.02756
36. Weske, M.: Business Process Management: Concepts, Languages, Architectures. Springer, Heidelberg (2024). https://doi.org/10.1007/978-3-662-69518-0

Repairing Process Descriptions by Discovering Deviations from Process Models

Nan Sai[✉], Karolin Winter[ID], and Remco Dijkman[ID]

Department of Industrial Engineering and Innovation Sciences, Eindhoven University of Technology, Eindhoven, The Netherlands
{n.sai,k.m.winter,r.m.dijkman}@tue.nl

Abstract. Business processes can be captured in various forms, ranging from unstructured textual descriptions to formalized process models. This increases the risk of having deviating representations of what should describe the same process. To address this issue, this paper presents an approach for identifying deviations between process descriptions and process models and subsequently repairing these deviations in the process descriptions. Thus, it complements existing research that by now mainly focused on repairing process models. The proposed approach employs process structure trees, mapping elements from the textual description to tree nodes, and subsequently discovering deviations. Afterwards, new process fragments for the deviating parts of the description are generated by means of sentence templates and a Large Language Model. To repair the identified deviations, those fragments are then used to replace the deviating ones resulting in a description more closely aligned with the process model. The approach is empirically evaluated using an existing dataset wherein deviations are introduced. The findings show that our method can discover and repair deviations reliably and efficiently.

Keywords: Deviation Discovery · Business Process Repair · Natural Language Processing · Process Trees

1 Introduction

Business process management aims at monitoring and improving how work is performed within companies [7], where the work is represented in the form of a business process. Business processes can be represented in the form of natural language process descriptions, process models or event logs [6]. These diverse representations can lead to a fragmentation of process information [1] and deviations among them [6], posing serious problems for companies [1]. For example, deviations indicating circumvention of important regulations could result in compliance violations leading to severe fines. In this paper, we consider two types of representations, process descriptions and process models.

To cope with fragmented process information, one key challenge is to discover and correct deviations among different process representations. Prior research addressed discovering inconsistencies between natural language descriptions and process models [2,17,20] or process model repair, e.g., [8,9,19]. However, process description repair remains limited, mostly identifying missing activities [21]. Alternatively, other methods generate entire process descriptions from models [4,13,14,18]. However, repairing only deviating parts of process descriptions may be more desirable to ensure that the (rest of the) textual description remains correct and recognizable to users. Therefore, this paper introduces an approach to: i) detect deviations between process models and descriptions, and ii) repair descriptions without altering the entire text. It addresses missing activities in descriptions and models and control-flow routing deviations.

To achieve this, we propose a three-phase approach. First, a Large Language Model (LLM) converts the process description into an intermediate representation. Second, process structure trees are compared to this representation to detect deviations. Using process trees allows minimal alterations by identifying the smallest sub-tree containing the deviation. Third, the parts of the description referring to this sub-tree are replaced, for which we rely on a combination of sentence templates as presented in [18] and an LLM for refining and correcting the sentences. The effectiveness of the proposed method is demonstrated based on experimental results evaluated at each phase.

The remainder of the paper is organized as follows. First, a running example and preliminaries are presented in Sect. 2. The example is then used in Sect. 3 to illustrate our deviation discovery and process description repair approach which is evaluated and discussed in Sect. 4. After outlining related work in Sect. 5 the paper concludes with a summary and outlook on future work in Sect. 6.

2 Running Example and Preliminaries

To illustrate the problem of repairing process descriptions, consider the running example presented in Fig. 1 depicting a simplified process of customized manufacturing of 3D prints. Our aim is to discover deviations between a process description and a process model and then repair the deviating parts in the description. Thereby, we focus on two types of deviations. First, *missing activities*, e.g., in the running example, activity `send model` is present in the process model but not in the process description. Second, we consider control-flow mismatches regarding both, the *execution order of tasks* as well as *gateways*. Consider, e.g., in the process model, `check if color is in stock` which is performed as the first activity. However, this is in contradiction to the process description where first `inspect sketches` and `refine them` should happen before, i.e., we observe a mismatch in terms of execution order. In addition, a parallel gateway is present in the process model but a decision between the two branches is defined by the process description resulting in a mismatch linked to gateways.

After discovery of deviations, we provide a mechanism to repair the process descriptions. Thereby, we opt for the least intrusive repair actions by identifying the minimal scope of a deviation. To do so, we make use of process trees. So far, process trees have been used for example to repair process models by identifying

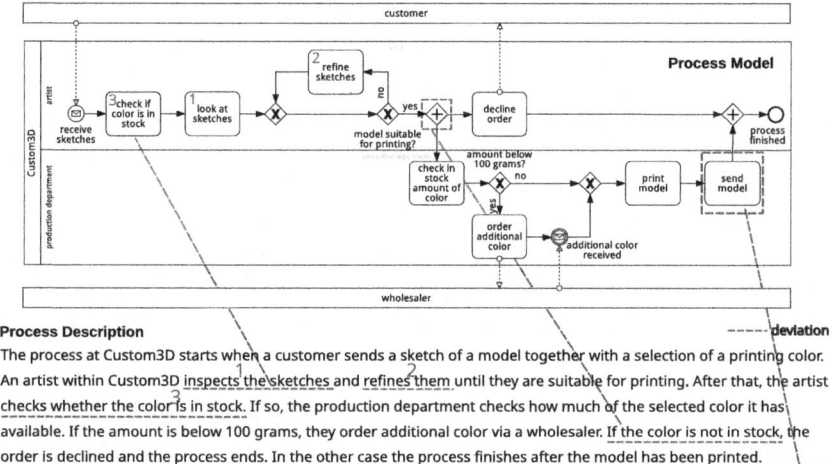

Fig. 1. Running Example to Illustrate the Problem Statement

deviating sub-processes through comparison with event logs [11]. Process trees are particularly suitable for comparing extracted relationships and detecting deviations, as their hierarchical sub-tree structure allows for precise and local repair of processes. The process tree divides the entire process into different hierarchical sub-trees, and can contain different control flow structures such as sequences ($\rightarrow$), exclusive choices ($\times$), parallel executions ($+$) or loops ($\circlearrowleft$). In this paper, we consider the following assumptions to simplify process trees [3] in order to facilitate comparison between process trees and descriptions. We do not allow nested nodes with the same operator, operators with a single child, or redundant τ-leaves, for instance, $\rightarrow (a, \tau, b)$ simplifies to $\rightarrow (a, b)$.

3 Deviation Discovery and Process Description Repair

Figure 2 depicts the proposed approach taking a process description and a process tree, as input and producing a repaired process description. In-between there are three intermediate phases, *Data Transformation and Preparation* (Sect. 3.1), *Deviation Discovery* (Sect. 3.2) and *Process Description Repair* (Sect. 3.3).

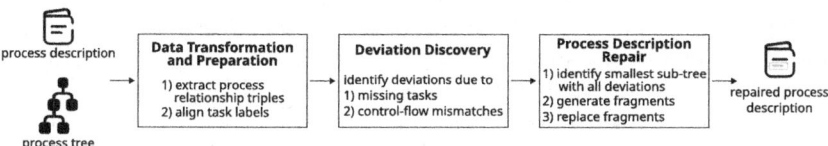

Fig. 2. Overview of Deviation Discovery and Repair Approach

3.1 Data Transformation and Preparation

As depicted in Fig. 2, during the first phase of the approach the process description is transformed into a set of task label aligned process relationship triples. Informally speaking, relationship triples capture relations between process elements like tasks or operators and indicate their location in the text, effectively transforming textual descriptions into structured data to enable more effective deviation detection later on. Their definition and extraction procedure is outlined in the following. In order to account for synonyms between the description and the process tree we furthermore align task labels in this step of the approach.

Process Relationship Triple Extraction from Process Descriptions. In this step the process description D is transformed into a structured representation consisting of, what we call, a set of process relationship triples. To formally define this, the set of tasks present in the description is denoted as A_D, the set of control-flow operator labels as $C_D = \{\times_n, +_n, \circlearrowleft_n |\ n \in \mathbb{N}\}$. Those comprise, similar to process trees, parallel and exclusive gateways as well as loops and carry an index, e.g., $loop_1$ to distinguish different control nodes of the same type.

Definition 1 (Process Relationship Triples). *Given the set of process description tasks A_D and the set of control-flow operator labels C_D, we define a process description D as its set of process relationship triples as follows*

$$D = \{(a, b, p) | (a, b) \subseteq (A_D \cup C_D) \times (A_D \cup C_D), p \subseteq \mathbb{N}\}$$

A process relationship triple (a, b, p) indicates that in sentence number p, there is a flow from task or operator a to task or operator b. Hence, sequences, indicated by $\rightarrow$ in a process tree, are implicitly captured. We add positional information in order to determine the location of the deviation in the description during later repair. Considering the running example in Fig. 1, one possible process relationship triple is ($loop_1$, "checks whether the color is in stock", [3]). To realize this transformation of descriptions into a set of process relationship triples, we use GPT-4o[1] to execute three prompts through the provided API.[2] *Prompt 1* provides the definition of relationship triples including a detailed description of various types of process elements including operators $\times, +, \circlearrowleft$, and tasks and how to recognize their unique characteristics. *Prompt 2* provides an example of a specific process description and what the extracted relationship triples look like. *Prompt 3* directs to extract all relationship triples from the provided process description and organize them by sentence.

Aligning Task Labels. Now, we address the challenge of identifying synonyms between task labels in the process description and the process tree. For example, "inspect the sketches" from the description corresponds to "look at sketches" in the model. Such correspondences are identified through aligning each task label within the extracted set of process relationship triples with its counter part in the process tree in case there exists one (see Algorithm 1).

---

[1] https://platform.openai.com/docs/models#gpt-4o.
[2] https://github.com/NanSais/Repairing-Process-Descriptions-by-Discovering-Deviations-from-Process-Models.git.

Algorithm 1. Task Label Mapping

1: **Input:** $P = \{(e, r) \in A_D \times A_T \mid \text{sim}(e, r) \geq \gamma\}$.
2: **Initialization:** $G \leftarrow \emptyset$, $U_D \leftarrow \emptyset$, $U_T \leftarrow \emptyset$.
3: **for** $\ell = 1, 2, \ldots, k, \text{ where } k = |P|$ **do**
4:     Let $\sigma(P)[\ell] = (e_\ell, r_\ell)$.
5:     **if** $e_\ell \notin U_D$ **and** $r_\ell \notin U_T$ **then**
6:         $G \leftarrow G \cup \{(e_\ell, r_\ell)\}$
7:         $U_D \leftarrow U_D \cup \{e_\ell\}$
8:         $U_T \leftarrow U_T \cup \{r_\ell\}$
9:     **else if** $e_\ell \in \mathcal{R}_{\text{loop}}$ **and** $e_\ell \notin U_D$ **then**
10:        $G \leftarrow G \cup \{(e_\ell, r_\ell)\}$
11:       $U_D \leftarrow U_D \cup \{e_\ell\}$
12:     **else**
13:        skip
14:     **end if**
15: **end for**
16: **Final Mapping:** $M : A_D \to A_T$, $M(r) = e \iff (e, r) \in G$.

Algorithm 1 takes as input a set P containing all pairs (e, r) with $e \in A_D, r \in A_T$ whose similarity score $\text{sim}(e, r)$ is at least γ.

To calculate the similarity score, task labels are first encoded using the sentence-transformers/all-mpnet-base-v2[3] model, producing vector representations, then cosine similarity between these vectors is calculated yielding a similarity score between 0 and 1. To illustrate this, consider the three process model tasks $r_1 = $ "look at sketches", $r_2 = $ "refine sketches", and $r_3 = $ "decline order" and the task in the description $e_1 = $ "inspect the sketches" as present in the running example. The corresponding similarity scores between all possible pairs are then given as $\text{sim}(e_1, r_1) = 0.93$, $\text{sim}(e_1, r_2) = 0.67$, $\text{sim}(e_1, r_3) = 0.05$. Through setting a similarity threshold $\gamma \in [0, 1]$[4] we receive the set P, e.g., in the above example with $\gamma = 0.6$, we get $P = \{(e_1, r_1), (e_1, r_2)\}$.

One challenge Algorithm 1 addresses is to prevent mapping elements twice. For example, element $e_1 = $ "inspect the sketches" could be potentially mapped to two elements $r_1 = $ "look at sketches" and $r_2 = $ "refine sketches". This could lead to ambiguities because we might allow unreasonable relationship triples, e.g., ("refine sketches", "refine them", p). Consequently, we need to ensure to receive a one-to-one mapping in Algorithm 1 as explained in the following.

Algorithm 1, l. 2: First, we initialize empty sets G (mapped pairs), U_D (mapped description tasks), and U_T (mapped process tree tasks).

Algorithm 1, ll. 4–7: Now, we iterate over sorted pairs $\sigma(P)[\ell] = (e_\ell, r_\ell)$. If neither e_ℓ nor r_ℓ is mapped, we add (e_ℓ, r_ℓ) to G and mark them as mapped in U_D and U_T. To get sorted pairs, we use their similarity score. To illustrate, assume an additional task e_2 with $\text{sim}(e_2, r_1) = 0.94$. Then $P = \{(e_2, r_1), (e_1, r_1), (e_1, r_2)\}$; pair (e_2, r_1) is mapped first, (e_1, r_1) is skipped, and (e_1, r_2) is mapped next. Thus, we achieve optimal mapping by considering both elements equally while sorting pairs by similarity scores.

---

[3] https://huggingface.co/sentence-transformers/all-mpnet-base-v2.
[4] In this case we set $\gamma = 0.6$ to strike a balance between the quantity and quality of matches, ensuring that there are enough matching pairs with reasonable similarity, however, other values of γ are possible depending on the use case.

Algorithm 1, ll. 8–10: Here we consider the special case of tasks occurring in loops. Such tasks can be present multiple times under different labels or contexts in the set of process relationship triples. For this, we define a loop subset $\mathcal{R}_{\text{loop}}$ containing all tasks from A_D occurring in a process relationship triple of the form $(\text{loop}_i, \text{task}_j, p_k)$. If $r_\ell \in \mathcal{R}_{\text{loop}}$ and not yet mapped, add (e_ℓ, r_ℓ) to G, map e_ℓ in U_D, but leave r_ℓ unmapped in U_T, allowing reuse. For instance, task $e_2 =$ "refine them" matches r_2 but, due to the loop relation (loop_1, e_2, p), r_2 remains available for further matching.

Algorithm 1 ll. 11–15: In all other cases, we skip the pair. The result is a set containing the final mapping, e.g., $G = \{(\text{"inspect the sketches"}, \text{"look at sketches"}), ...\}$

Based on set G, we can define the task label aligned process description.

Definition 2 (Task Label Aligned Process Description). *Let the task label mapping function be given as*

$$\phi : A_D \to A_D \cup A_T, e \mapsto \begin{cases} r, & \text{if } (e,r) \in G \\ e, & \text{otherwise} \end{cases}$$

We define the set of aligned process description tasks as $A'_D = \{\phi(e) \in A_D \cup A_T\}$ Accordingly, the process description with aligned task labels is defined as

$$D' = \{(a,b,p) | (a,b) \subseteq (A'_D \cup C_D) \times (A'_D \cup C_D), p \subseteq \mathbb{N}\}$$

For the example given above, D' will then, e.g., contain ("inspect the sketch", "refine sketch", p_1) instead of ("look at sketch", "refine them", p_1).

3.2 Deviation Discovery

Now we identify deviations caused by i) missing tasks in both, the description and process tree, ii) control-flow mismatches. As input we consider again the process tree as well as the aligned process relationship triples set D' from the previous step. We receive a set of missing tasks A_m and a set of deviating relationship triples D_{dev}.

Missing Tasks. In this step we determine the delta between tasks present in the process description and in the process tree, i.e., all tasks that are either missing from the process tree or the process description. The set of tasks with these characteristics is given as $A_m = A'_D \triangle A_T$. To illustrate this, consider, for example, the task "send model" in Fig. 1. This task is present in the model but not in the description, so it is flagged as missing and added to A_m. Similarly, tasks present in the process description but not in the tree are added to A_m.

Control-flow Mismatches. After identifying deviations caused by missing tasks, we now turn to deviations caused by control-flow mismatches. In order to clearly distinguish between those two causes, i.e., to avoid discovering deviations that are actually caused by a task being missing and not a real control-flow deviation, we exclude the set of relationship triples containing missing tasks from the following steps, i.e., we consider as input $D'_{cf} = \{(a,b,p) \in D' | a, b \notin A_m\}$.

Algorithm 2 depicts how a relationship triple (a, b, p) is verified based on a given process tree T and is divided into three steps, I–III. These three steps are proposed because, depending on the structure of the process relationship triple, different sub-trees with different root nodes $\rightarrow, \times, +$ and $\circlearrowleft$ have to be considered. Verifying a triple (a, b, p) involves then checking all possible sub-trees for two conditions, i) element a must be in the set of output nodes for a sub-tree or the root node itself, ii) element b must be the first node of a (directly following) sub-tree of which a is an output or root node. Thereby, we refer to output nodes as the set of tail nodes of a branch of the process sub-tree which would be connected to its following branch, rather than only the bottom nodes of the branch. Definition 3 summarizes how the output nodes and the first node are determined. Its details are explained along each Step I–III in Algorithm 2.

Definition 3 (Get Output Nodes and First Node). *Let n be a node in the process tree T, where n.parent denotes its parent node, n.children represents its child nodes, and n.value refers to its label. None means no first node. The traversal functions $output\_nodes(n)$ and $first\_node(n)$ are defined as follows:*

$$output\_nodes(n) = \begin{cases} \{n.parent\}, & \text{if } (n.children = \emptyset \text{ and } n.value \neq \tau) \\ & \vee (n.value = '\circlearrowleft' \text{ and } n.children \neq \emptyset) \\ output\_nodes(last(n.children)), & \text{if } n.value = '\rightarrow' \text{ and } n.children \neq \emptyset \\ \bigcup_{c_i \in n.children} output\_nodes(c_i), & \text{otherwise} \end{cases}$$

$$first\_node(n) = \begin{cases} n & \text{if } n.children = \emptyset \\ first\_node(n.children[1]) & \text{if } n.value = '\rightarrow' \text{ or } n.value = '\circlearrowleft' \\ n & \text{if } n.value \neq '\rightarrow' \text{ and } n.value \neq '\circlearrowleft' \\ None & \text{otherwise} \end{cases}$$

Algorithm 2, Step I. Here, we verify whether a given process relationship triple conforms to a sub-tree with $\rightarrow$ as the root node. This is the case if there exists a sub-tree with a sequence node ($\rightarrow$) as root, having "a" as an output node and "b" as the first node of the subsequent branch. Consider a simple tree (Fig. 3a) with separate branches for A and B connected through a sequence node; here, the triple (A, B, p) conforms. For a more complex scenario (Fig. 3b), two sub-trees exist–one rooted at $\rightarrow$ and another at XOR. Initially, (A, B, p) conforms to the full tree due to A and silent node τ outputs followed by B. Since silent nodes (τ) are unobservable, i.e., we replace them with their parent nodes, allowing verification of (XOR, B, p). Thus, $output\_nodes(n)$ in Definition 3 returns either its parent or itself for leaf nodes, depending on whether n is a silent transition τ, and recursively traverses the last child if n is $\rightarrow$. Similarly, $first\_node(n)$ returns n for leaf nodes and recursively traverses the first child if n is $\rightarrow$.

Algorithm 2, Step II. Next we consider sub-trees with operators $\times$ and $+$. A process relationship triple (a, b, p), conforms if i) node a is either $+$ or $\times$, and ii) a branch of that node where b is the first node exists. For example, the exclusive operator in Fig. 3b has a direct sequence with the "A" task and the "B" task in the process relationship triples: ("XOR_1", "A", p_1), ("XOR_1", "B", p_1). Similarly, if a parallel or exclusive operator node is directly connected to a $\rightarrow$ node in the process tree structure, the first node of that branches sub-tree (where

Algorithm 2. Relationship Triple Verification $\mathcal{V}_{rel}$

```
 1: Input: (a, b, p) ∈ D'_cf, a process tree T
 2: Step I:
 3: if ∃n ∈ T s.t. n.value =→ then
 4:     if ∃i s.t. node(a) ∈ traverse(n.children[i]) then
 5:         if traverse_first_node(n.children[i + 1]).value = b then
 6:             Return True
 7:         end if
 8:     end if
 9: end if
10: Step II:
11: if ∃a' ∈ T s.t. a'.value ∈ {+, ×} then
12:     if ∃j s.t. traverse_first_node(a'.children[j]).value = b then
13:         Return True
14:     end if
15: end if
16: Step III:
17: if ∃x ∈ T s.t. x.value =↺ then
18:     if a =↺ then
19:         if traverse_first_node(x.children[1]).value = b then
20:             Return True
21:         end if
22:     else if b =↺ then
23:         if node(a) ∈ traverse(x.children[1]) then
24:             Return True
25:         end if
26:     end if
27: end if
28: Return False
```

$\rightarrow$ is the root node) will be connected to the parallel or exclusive operator in the process relationship triples. Thus, $output\_nodes(n)$ in Definition 3 recursively traverses all children if n is a × or + node, while $first\_node(n)$ returns n directly for such nodes.

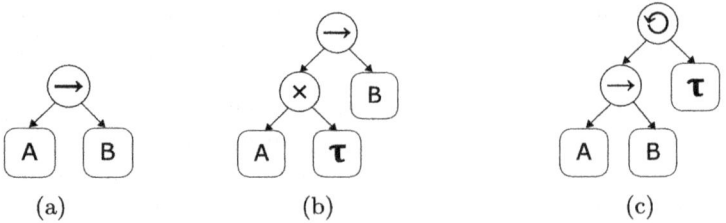

Fig. 3. Examples of Process Trees

Algorithm 2, Step III. The third step addresses sub-trees with operators ↺ as root nodes. A relationship triple (a, b, p) conforms if either: i) node a is ↺, and b is the first node of its first branch; or ii) node b is ↺, and a is the output node of its first branch. For instance, in Fig. 3c, the sub-tree rooted at ↺ has "A" as the first node and ↺ as its output node, conforming the triples ("$loop_1$", "A", p_1) and ("B", "$loop_1$", p_1). Thus, $output\_nodes(n)$ in Definition 3 returns n if n is a ↺. Similarly, $first\_node(n)$ recursively traverses the first child if n is a ↺.

Algorithm 2 focused on verification of process relationship triples individually. However, relationship triples referring to the same operator must also correspond to the same operator node in the tree. Therefore, we also check if the relationship triples with the same operator relate to a single operator node. If not, they are marked as deviating and added to the set D_δ.

In summary, the set of deviation relationships D_{dev} can be represented as

$$D_{dev} = \{(a,b,p) \in D' \mid a \in A_m \lor b \in A_m \lor (a,b,p) \in D_\delta \lor \mathcal{V}_{rel}((a,b,p)) = \text{False}\}$$

3.3 Process Description Repair

After obtaining the sets of missing tasks A_m and deviating relationship triples D_{dev}, the last phase of the approach comprises the actual process description repair as indicated in Fig. 2. To realize it, we first identify the smallest sub-tree containing all deviations. Second, we generate process description fragments for the deviating parts and third, we insert or replace those fragments at the correct position in the process description.

Smallest Sub-tree Identification. Algorithm 3 determines the smallest sub-tree containing all discovered deviations by identifying the lowest common ancestor (LCA) of the nodes corresponding to tasks included in either A_m or D_{dev}.

Algorithm 3. Find Lowest Common Ancestor

1: **Input:** Input: N — Set of nodes defining the target subtree
2: paths ← empty list
3: **for** each node in N **do**
4:    path ← FINDPATH(root, node)
5:    **if** path is not None **then**
6:       append path to paths
7:    **else**
8:       **return** None {Node not found in the tree}
9:    **end if**
10: **end for**
11: lca ← None
12: **for** i from 0 to (minimum length of paths) -1 **do**
13:    current_node ← paths[0][i]
14:    **if** all paths have current_node at index i **then**
15:       lca ← current_node
16:    **else**
17:       **break**
18:    **end if**
19: **end for**
20: **return** LCA // the lowest common ancestor node

The algorithm employs depth-first search from the root, using a helper function FindPath to record paths from the root to each target node. Collected paths are compared node by node to identify their longest common prefix. The last matching node is the LCA, root of the smallest sub-tree. A special case arises with the → node, connecting multiple sequential sub-trees. Selecting this node as the root might include unrelated sub-trees. To handle this, branches without deviations are pruned by retaining only branches between the first and last relevant nodes. This ensures the sub-tree contains only deviation-related branches.

Finally, positional information from deviation triples maps this sub-tree back to the process description, concentrating repairs precisely and effectively.

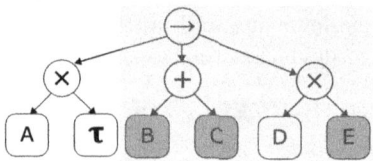

Fig. 4. Example of Smallest Subtree Identification Containing Deviations

An example of an identified smallest deviation sub-tree is illustrated in Fig. 4, where nodes B, C, and E constitute the deviation. Applying Algorithm 3 identifies the top → node as their common root node. However, the leftmost branch under this node does not include deviations and is thus pruned. Consequently, the smallest deviation sub-tree is highlighted by the yellow box. Despite this optimization, the sub-tree still includes non-deviating parts, i.e., the branch containing D.

Generating Process Description Fragments. After identifying the smallest sub-tree containing all deviations, the next step is to generate the corresponding process description fragments. First, we generate description fragments based on process description templates presented in [18]. Those fragments consist of short sentences that describe sub-processes, ensuring all known elements are accurately represented. Since the templates are incomplete sentences, we only need to fill in the tasks to complete them. The operator node of the process tree determines which template to use. Because process trees have a nested structure, templates should be filled recursively from the bottom up, preserving the hierarchy and flow. However, such template-based fragments can lack fluency and contain inconsistencies. We therefore use an LLM to refine the fragments. This two-step approach ensures completeness and improves readability. For example, the process sub-tree "+(Prepare invoice, Pack goods)" is generated into a raw description fragment "2 procedures are executed in an arbitrary order: Prepare invoice, Pack goods" based on the template. The LLM then refines it into "Prepare invoice and pack goods at the same time". If decision rules exist, they are also incorporated into the generated fragments.

Replacing Fragments. Finally, these refined descriptionsfragments are made to replace the deviated parts of the original descriptions in their entirety without affecting the other non-deviating parts. This is because when identifying the smallest sub-tree that contains all deviations, it may inevitably contain some non-deviating parts. Therefore, it is also necessary to identify the relationship triples that contain these tasks based on the full range of tasks contained in the smallest sub-tree, and re-identify the sentences that need to be replaced. The localization of the sentences that need to be replaced will be achieved by the p (sentence number) in the process relationship triples. The identified sentences are then replaced with improved description fragments, thus effectively restoring the accuracy and consistency of the process representation.

4 Evaluation

The dataset and gold standard generation are described in Sect. 4.1 and the evaluation method and results in Sect. 4.2. The dataset including the gold standard and the prototypical implementation of our approach are publicly available[5].

4.1 Dataset and Gold Standard Generation

As baseline for our dataset we take the dataset from [12] because it contains pairs of model and process descriptions which are available in .BPMN format.[6] We selected three description model pairs named after their identifiers V_k09, R_j04, V_G01 in the original dataset. Thereby, we chose the models with the highest score 5 because those reflect the descriptions most accurately. We manually created gold standards for expected outcomes at relationship triples extractions, deviation discovery and description repair. While doing so, we identified two issues: i) vague descriptions hindering precise deviation discovery and repair, and ii) incomplete coverage of all deviation types. To address this, we generate "ideal" descriptions with less vagueness and adjust models for alignment. Additionally, we introduce two new datasets per ideal description, covering different deviation types. For V_k09, deviations include a missing exclusive gateway and two missing tasks in the description. For R_j04, they involve a missing parallel gateway and two missing tasks in the process model. V_G01, contains no missing tasks or gateways, but control-flow deviations are introduced by swapping an exclusive and parallel gateway, and swapping two task positions.

4.2 Evaluation Method and Results

This section presents results for each of the three phases and key steps (cf. Fig. 2). Each experiment is repeated five times, and results are averaged to ensure reliability by reducing random fluctuations and outliers. For *Process Description Transformation and Preparation* and *Deviation Discovery*, we evaluate precision, recall, and F1 score. For *Process Description Repair*, both original and repaired descriptions are compared to the gold standard for consistency. For this, we use GPT4o structured prompting to assess consistency based on core process alignment (50%) and sequence accuracy (50%), using a 0-to-1 scale where 1 represents an exact match. Core Process Alignment refers to whether the overall steps and workflow in the description match those in the gold standard. Sequence accuracy refers to whether the specific tasks are carried out in the same order as in the

---
[5] https://github.com/NanSais/Repairing-Process-Descriptions-by-Discovering-Deviations-from-Process-Models.git.
[6] We used PM4Py [5] to convert the BPMN models to process trees.

gold standard. This method prioritizes process accuracy over textual similarity, resulting in more objective evaluation of repair improvements. Since the second and third phases depend on the first phase's quality, additional experiments use gold standard relationship triples as inputs to avoid follow-up errors.

Process Description Transformation. Evaluation of extracted relationships involves both, identification and label alignment. We conduct an evaluation with positional information p and one without. This enables assessment of the ability to extract different parts of process relationship triples. Outputs are compared to the gold standard, with results presented in Table 1. Adding sentence numbers lowers precision, recall, and F1 scores, suggesting that positional information complicates extraction. The R_j04 dataset performs significantly worse than others. Analysis reveals that while task extraction is nearly perfect, errors arise from redundant parallel gateway identification. The process description connects tasks sequentially using "and" (e.g., "The payment is made through an app, and the successful repair is confirmed."), yet these were misinterpreted as parallel despite lacking explicit indicators like "at the same time." This misinterpretation largely explains the lower scores for R_j04.

Table 1. Evaluation Results for Relationship Triples

Data	deviation type	relationship triples extraction (without sentence number)			relationship triples extraction		
		Precision	Recall	F1	Precision	Recall	F1
V_k09	missing gateway (in text)	0.916	0.894	0.904	0.760	0.741	0.750
	missing2tasks (in text)	0.926	0.860	0.892	0.661	0.624	0.642
R_j04	missing gateway (in model)	0.782	0.725	0.752	0.688	0.637	0.662
	missing2tasks (in model)	0.541	0.550	0.545	0.467	0.475	0.470
V_g01	gateway order	0.794	0.733	0.761	0.697	0.640	0.666
	tasks order	0.834	0.800	0.817	0.750	0.720	0.735

Deviation Discovery. The quality of deviation discovery is evaluated by comparing the identified deviant sentences to those in the gold standard with results depicted in Table 2. Deviation discovery performs best with gold standard relational triples, achieving high precision, recall, and F1 scores, especially in V_g01 and V_k09. Notably, recall consistently reaches 1, ensuring all true deviant sentences are discovered. Precision remains high but not perfect due to considering adjacent sentences to address scattered process information. Performance declines when using previous step outputs instead of gold standard triples, particularly in R_j04, where precision and F1 scores drop significantly due to accumulated inaccuracies. Despite recall remaining high (1 or near 1) across datasets, lower precision indicates some non-deviant sentences are mislabeled, leading to unnecessary repairs. In summary, while recall ensures comprehensive deviation discovery, reduced precision increases repair workload.

Process Description Repair Based on Deviations. The repair results based on identified deviations are shown in Table 3. Across all datasets and deviation types, the repair process enhances alignment with the gold standard descriptions. When using gold standard relationship triples, the repaired descriptions

Table 2. Evaluation Results for Deviation Discovery

Data	deviation type	deviation location (gold relationship triples)			deviation location		
		Precision	Recall	F1	Precision	Recall	F1
V_k09	missing gateway (in text)	1	1	1	0.360	1	0.503
	missing2tasks (in text)	0.600	1	0.750	0.700	0.800	0.697
R_j04	missing gateway (in model)	0.500	1	0.667	0.267	1	0.408
	missing2tasks (in model)	0.800	1	0.889	0.571	0.950	0.707
V_g01	gateway order	1	1	1	0.754	1	0.857
	tasks order	1	1	1	0.581	1	0.698

consistently achieve higher scores compared to the original descriptions, indicating good alignment. Even when using potentially flawed output from the previous steps, the repair still yields better results. Although the initial step of the R_j04 dataset shows lower performance, the repair phase improves scores. This is because the initial step mainly affects the localization of deviant sentences, while the repair step focuses on identifying and reconstructing the corresponding sub-trees. The earlier results show that deviant sentences are almost perfectly identified, though some non-deviant sentences are misclassified. As a result, the repair step always includes the deviant parts, with variations only in the extent of non-deviant content also repaired. In summary, the input quality in the first two steps has minimal impact on the repair's effectiveness in refining the process description, influencing only the extent of necessary corrections.

Table 3. Evaluation Results for Description Repair

Data	deviation type	(gold relationship trips)		non-repair	repair
		non-repair	repair		
V_k09	missing gateway (in text)	0.95	0.98	0.87	0.914
	missing2tasks (in text)	0.92	0.95	0.888	0.94
R_j04	missing gateway (in model)	0.95	0.97	0.906	0.944
	missing2tasks (in model)	0.9	0.95	0.866	0.94
V_G01	gateway order	0.75	0.85	0.8	0.88
	tasks order	0.86	0.9	0.84	0.86

5 Related Work

This work presents two core contributions, i) deviation discovery between process models expressed as process trees and process descriptions and ii) repair of process descriptions based on the process tree and the discovered deviations.

For i), existing work focused on inconsistency detection between textual sources and process models, e.g., [2], alignment between process descriptions and process models, e.g., [17] and assessing compliance between regulatory documents and process models [20]. In contrast, we aim at precisely locating deviations through considering process models in the form of process tress allowing to identify a minimal process sub-tree for which repair actions are initiated. The aforementioned papers have also not focused on repair.

Related work for the second core contribution of this paper, i.e., process description repair focused, i.a., on generating an entire process description from an existing process model, e.g., [4,13,14,18]. In contrast, we focus on just repairing the deviating parts of a description which has the advantage that non deviating parts of process descriptions are kept in their original state, i.e., we only interfere at the most minimal level. One work that is closely related to ours is [21]. However, we take a broader approach by not only repairing deviations linked to missing activities but also for example to wrong order of activities. Complementary approaches focused on process model repair, e.g., [8,9,19]. Such approaches could be integrated into our framework to complement it further by allowing repair in both directions, model and description.

We use LLMs to transform process descriptions. Related work in this direction concentrates mainly on process model generation, e.g., Declare or BPMN models [10] or using Chatbots for generating process models from text, e.g., [12]. Further related work focused on extracting resource information from process descriptions using LLMs, e.g., [15,16].

6 Conclusion

Processes can be captured in diverse representations, ranging from formal process trees to natural language descriptions or event logs. Manual alignment among these different representations is challenging, yet essential due to the volume of processes in companies. To deal with this, we proposed an approach to i) detect deviations between process trees and natural language process descriptions, and ii) repair these descriptions by correcting only deviating parts, preserving as much original text as possible. Experiments show accurate deviation localization with high recall and effective repairs. They also confirm the effectiveness of the repair process, as significant improvements in alignment with the gold standard are achieved after corrections, even with initially imperfect inputs.

Although effective, the proposed approach has some limitations. The lack of ability to model long-range dependencies in the process tree itself may leave some deviations unrecognized, while the reliance on GPT-4o poses a challenge to reproducibility. Additionally, the risks associated with large language models, such as output variability, illusions, and cue sensitivity, remain unaddressed. Future research should focus on mitigating these risks. Moreover, we plan to extend the approach to deviations linked to other perspectives than control-flow and including event logs as additional source of information.

References

1. van der Aa, H., Leopold, H., Mannhardt, F., Reijers, H.A.: On the fragmentation of process information: challenges, solutions, and outlook. In: Enterprise, Business-Process and Information Systems Modeling. LNBIP, vol. 214, pp. 3–18. Springer (2015). https://doi.org/10.1007/978-3-319-19237-6_1
2. van der Aa, H., Leopold, H., Reijers, H.A.: Comparing textual descriptions to process models - the automatic detection of inconsistencies. Inf. Syst. **64**, 447–460 (2017). https://doi.org/10.1016/J.IS.2016.07.010
3. van der Aalst, W.: Process Mining - Data Science in Action, 2d edn. Springer (2016). https://doi.org/10.1007/978-3-662-49851-4
4. Aysolmaz, B., Leopold, H., Reijers, H.A., Demirörs, O.: A semi-automated approach for generating natural language requirements documents based on business process models. Inf. Softw. Technol. **93**, 14–29 (2018). https://doi.org/10.1016/J.INFSOF.2017.08.009
5. Berti, A., van Zelst, S., Schuster, D.: Pm4py: A process mining library for python. Software Impacts **17**, 100556 (2023). https://doi.org/10.1016/j.simpa.2023.100556, https://www.sciencedirect.com/science/article/pii/S2665963823000933
6. Carmona, J.: The alignment of formal, structured and unstructured process descriptions. In: van der Aalst, W., Best, E. (eds.) PETRI NETS 2017. LNCS, vol. 10258, pp. 3–11. Springer, Cham (2017). https://doi.org/10.1007/978-3-319-57861-3_1
7. Dumas, M., Rosa, M.L., Mendling, J., Reijers, H.A.: Fundamentals of Business Process Management, 2nd edn. Springer (2018). https://doi.org/10.1007/978-3-662-56509-4
8. Fahland, D., van der Aalst, W.: Model repair - aligning process models to reality. Inf. Syst. **47**, 220–243 (2015). https://doi.org/10.1016/J.IS.2013.12.007
9. Genga, L., Rossi, F., Diamantini, C., Storti, E., Potena, D.: Model repair supported by frequent anomalous local instance graphs. Inf. Syst. **122**, 102349 (2024). https://doi.org/10.1016/j.is.2024.102349
10. Grohs, M., Abb, L., Elsayed, N., Rehse, J.: Large language models can accomplish business process management tasks. In: Business Process Management Workshops. LNBIP, vol. 492, pp. 453–465. Springer (2023). https://doi.org/10.1007/978-3-031-50974-2_34
11. Guan, W., Cao, J., Gu, Y., Qian, S.: Aimed: an automatic and incremental approach for business process model repair under concept drift. Inf. Syst. **119**(C) (2023). https://doi.org/10.1016/j.is.2023.102285
12. Klievtsova, N., Benzin, J., Kampik, T., Mangler, J., Rinderle-Ma, S.: Conversational process modelling: state of the art, applications, and implications in practice. In: Business Process Management Forum. LNBIP, vol. 490, pp. 319–336. Springer (2023). https://doi.org/10.1007/978-3-031-41623-1_19
13. Kluza, K., Znamirowski, M., Wiśniewski, P., Jemioło, P., Ligęza, A.: Generating descriptions in polish language for BPMN business process models. In: Rutkowski, L., Scherer, R., Korytkowski, M., Pedrycz, W., Tadeusiewicz, R., Zurada, J.M. (eds.) ICAISC 2020. LNCS (LNAI), vol. 12416, pp. 357–368. Springer, Cham (2020). https://doi.org/10.1007/978-3-030-61534-5_32
14. Leopold, H., Mendling, J., Polyvyanyy, A.: Generating natural language texts from business process models. In: Ralyté, J., Franch, X., Brinkkemper, S., Wrycza, S. (eds.) CAiSE 2012. LNCS, vol. 7328, pp. 64–79. Springer, Heidelberg (2012). https://doi.org/10.1007/978-3-642-31095-9_5

15. Mustroph, H., Barrientos, M., Winter, K., Rinderle-Ma, S.: Verifying resource compliance requirements from natural language text over event logs. In: Business Process Management. LNCS, vol. 14159, pp. 249–265. Springer (2023). https://doi.org/10.1007/978-3-031-41620-0_15
16. Mustroph, H., Winter, K., Rinderle-Ma, S.: Social network mining from natural language text and event logs for compliance deviation detection. In: Cooperative Information Systems. LNCS, vol. 14353, pp. 347–365. Springer (2023). https://doi.org/10.1007/978-3-031-46846-9_19
17. Sànchez-Ferreres, J., van der Aa, H., Carmona, J., Padró, L.: Aligning textual and model-based process descriptions. Data Knowl. Eng. **118**, 25–40 (2018). https://doi.org/10.1016/J.DATAK.2018.09.001
18. Silva, T.S., Avila, D.T., Flesch, J.A., Peres, S.M., Mendling, J., Thom, L.H.: A service-oriented architecture for generating sound process descriptions. In: 23rd IEEE International Enterprise Distributed Object Computing Conference, EDOC, pp. 1–10. IEEE (2019). https://doi.org/10.1109/EDOC.2019.00011
19. Vinci, F., de Leoni, M.: Repairing process models through simulation and explainable AI. In: Business Process Management - 22nd International Conference, BPM. LNCS, vol. 14940, pp. 129–145. Springer (2024). https://doi.org/10.1007/978-3-031-70396-6_8
20. Winter, K., van der Aa, H., Rinderle-Ma, S., Weidlich, M.: Assessing the compliance of business process models with regulatory documents. In: Conceptual Modeling. LNCS, vol. 12400, pp. 189–203. Springer (2020). https://doi.org/10.1007/978-3-030-62522-1_14
21. Zeng, Q., Tang, X., Ni, W., Duan, H., Li, C., Xie, N.: Missing procedural texts repairing based on process model and activity description templates. IEEE Access **8**, 12999–13010 (2020). https://doi.org/10.1109/ACCESS.2020.2965160

Process Model Complexity Metrics, Cognitive Load and Visual Behavior: A Multi-granular Eye-Tracking Analysis

Thierry Sorg[1]($^{\boxtimes}$), Amine Abbad-Andaloussi[1], Ekkart Kindler[2], and Barbara Weber[1]

[1] Institute of Computer Science, University of St. Gallen, St Gallen, Switzerland
{thierry.sorg,amine.abbad-andaloussi,barbara.weber}@unisg.ch
[2] DTU Compute, Technical University of Denmark, Kongens Lyngby, Denmark
ekki@dtu.dk

Abstract. Complexity metrics are widely used to estimate the difficulty of understanding process models. However, the relationship between these metrics and the concept of cognitive load, which captures the difficulty experienced by users, is not fully understood in the process modeling literature. In neighboring fields like Software Engineering, researchers could only to a limited degree establish a relationship between complexity metrics and users' cognitive load. To investigate the extent to which such a relationship exists in the process modeling field, we conduct an eye-tracking experiment that assesses how a suite of metrics, capturing both the essential complexity inherent to the process specifications and the accidental complexity emerging from the model layout, aligns with users' cognitive load during model comprehension tasks. Our findings show that the used metrics suite aligns well with users' cognitive load. Moreover, our analysis of users' behavior suggests that different levels of model complexity yield distinct visual behaviors. The implications of our work extend to both practice and research, validating a comprehensive suite of complexity metrics and delivering a multi-granular approach that can be reproduced in other experiments to enable the analysis of users' cognitive load and behavior on simple but also complex models.

Keywords: Process models · Complexity metrics · Cognitive load · Visual behavior · Difficulty · Eye tracking

1 Introduction

Process models can be used at different stages in the life cycle of an information system, from development to operation, supporting engineering tasks but also fostering the communication between various stakeholders [13]. Graphical representations of process models are supported by visual notations. These notations present an integral part of the language of software engineering used

© The Author(s), under exclusive license to Springer Nature Switzerland AG 2025
R. Guizzardi et al. (Eds.): BPMDS 2025/EMMSAD 2025, LNBIP 558, pp. 87–103, 2025.
https://doi.org/10.1007/978-3-031-95397-2_6

for decades [25]. Historical examples such as the early Goldstine and von Neumann program flowchart [17] alongside contemporary examples such as the Unified Modeling Language (UML[1]) and Business Process Model and Notation (BPMN[2]) unequivocally demonstrate that visual notations are designed purposely for humans. Therefore, graphical artifacts stemming from visual notations (e.g., process models) need to be understandable.

In the literature, complexity metrics have been proposed to estimate the difficulty of understanding process models [10,23,24], but the relationship between these metrics and the concept of cognitive load, which captures the difficulty experienced by users, remains largely unexplored in the field of process modeling. Ultimately, complexity metrics need to align with users' cognitive load in order to reflect the difficulty of comprehending process models. However, studies in neighboring fields like software engineering had inconclusive results on the link between complexity metrics and cognitive load [11,18,27]. As a result, the robustness of existing complexity metrics is still open to debate.

This work aims to address this issue by investigating the relationship between complexity metrics and cognitive load. Moreover, to explain the cognitive processes underlying the comprehension of process models, our work takes a step further by exploring the way users' visual behavior unfolds over time when conducting tasks on simple and complex process models.

Our research questions are formulated as follows: **RQ1: Does process model complexity as captured by existing complexity metrics align with measures of users' cognitive load?** and **RQ2: How do users' visual behaviors evolve over time during comprehension tasks on process models of varying complexity?** To explore these questions, we employ a comprehensive set of metrics designed to quantify two distinct types of complexity: *essential complexity*, which arises from the inherent logic and requirements of the process specifications embedded in the model, and *accidental complexity*, which stems from the way the model is represented, structured, or laid out, rather than its core functionality. Subsequently, through a controlled eye-tracking experiment, we investigate at a coarse-grained level how tasks on simple models and tasks on models with essential and accidental complexities affect users' cognitive load. We capture the construct of cognitive load using subjective, performance, physiological and behavior measures, thereby covering the different dimensions of this construct [9]. Our findings show that when the suite of complexity metrics differentiates two models, a distinction is also observed in estimates of users' cognitive load. Then, at a fine-grained level, using physiological and behavioral measures, we focus on exploring users' visual behavior and investigating its dynamics over time, across tasks on simple models, as well as tasks on models with essential and accidental complexities. Our findings, herein, suggest that performing tasks with varying complexity levels underlies different behavioral patterns associated with information search and inference, which can be clearly distinguished with eye-tracking.

---

[1] See. uml.org.
[2] See. bpmn.org.

This work has implications for both practice and research. For the former, we validate a comprehensive suite of metrics that can be reused in practical settings to estimate process model complexity and associated difficulty. Considering RQ1, one of the contributions of this work lies in the methodology. Indeed, we have developed data collection and analysis methods (cf. Sect. 3) that are suitable not only for small static models (e.g. images of models), but also for large models (i.e., models that can be navigated and zoomed). This makes our methods applicable to settings with models of realistic size, increasing ecological validity. As for the latter, our multi-granular research method is suitable for validating emerging complexity metrics at a coarse-grained level through a wide array of cognitive load measures. Moreover, for RQ2, at a fine-grained level, our work shows how process models and continuous measurements from eye-tracking can work together to identify cognitive activities such as information search and inference. This contribution paves the way for further research and development of adaptive software systems capable of recognizing cognitive activities in order to provide context-specific support to users. The remainder of this paper is structured as follows. Section 2 presents the notions and concepts relevant to this work. Section 3 explains our research method. Sections 4 and 5 present our findings and discuss them, respectively. Finally, Sect. 6 concludes the paper.

2 Background and Related Work

This section introduces theoretical concepts related to this work. Section 2.1 introduces process models and complexity metrics. Section 2.2 presents the cognitive load theory and the measures to capture cognitive load. Finally, Sect. 2.3 introduces relevant visual behavior analysis techniques.

2.1 Process Model Complexity

The literature includes a variety of metrics to measure process model complexity, rooted in fields like software engineering, graph theory, and information theory [22]. Based on existing studies [1,4], complexity metrics can be categorized into those measuring essential complexity and those measuring accidental complexity. Essential complexity metrics focus on features inherent to the complexity of the process specifications encoded in the model. For example, [22] proposed a suite of metrics capturing dimensions reflecting the essential complexity of process models, which covers their *size, density, partitionability, connector interplay, cyclicity*, and *concurrency*. Accidental complexity metrics, in turn, capture features related to the model layout and representation. The metrics of [7] (i.e., *edges style, crossing edges, edge angles*, and *symmetry in blocks*) as well as the *consistency flow* metric presented in [8] capture different features reflecting the accidental complexity of process models. In our experiment, we use the aforementioned metrics to capture both essential and accidental complexities and to investigate their impact on users' cognitive load. For further information about these metrics, we refer the reader to our online appendix[3].

---
[3] Online appendix: https://doi.org/10.5281/zenodo.15067310.

The majority of the studies investigating complexity metrics in the process modeling literature have used comprehension measures [24,29,30] (i.e., comprehension time and accuracy), error rates [22], and subjective assessments of users' perceived difficulty [29]. To the best of our knowledge, the only study that relied on the cognitive load theory and used the associated measures focused on complexity metrics for declarative (constraint-based) process models [2]. Our work differs from [2] by focusing on imperative (flow-based) process models, which have different characteristics and have wider adoption in practice. Moreover, our work aims to reinforce and extend the findings of [22,24,29,30] by taking a cognitive perspective, supported by a wide array of subjective, performance, physiological and behavioral measures, to investigate users' cognitive load and behavior at different granularity levels.

2.2 Cognitive Load Theory and Measurements

Cognitive Load Theory (CLT) views human working memory as having limited capacity [9,33]. When this limit is reached, people experience cognitive overload, which impedes their performance and increases errors [9]. CLT identifies three types of cognitive load: intrinsic, extraneous, and germane [32]. Intrinsic load comes from the inherent complexity of the material being studied. In process modeling, this refers to the essential complexity of process models (cf. Sect. 1) [2,4]. Extraneous load arises from how poorly the material is presented. In process modeling, this stems from the accidental complexity of process models (cf. Sect. 1) [2,4]. Germane load involves building mental schemes to process new information efficiently using knowledge from long-term memory [32]. This study examines how essential and accidental complexities in process models influence intrinsic and extraneous loads, respectively, leaving germane load aside. To limit germane load's impact, our within-subject experiment controls factors affecting intrinsic and extraneous loads while keeping germane load-related factors constant (see Sect. 3.2).

Cognitive load can be captured using a set of measures [9], which we describe in the following paragraphs:

Subjective Measures. These measures aim to subjectively assess the difficulty of a task (e.g., model comprehension). A notable example is the 5-point perceived difficulty Likert scale (ranging from *very easy*, i.e., low cognitive load to *very difficult*, i.e., high cognitive load), which is typically used in the literature [2,31].

Performance Measures. These measures capture the user's performance when solving a task [9]. In the context of comprehension tasks, comprehension accuracy (i.e., the correctness of the answer provided by the user) and comprehension time (i.e., the time taken to provide an answer) are typically used [2,14,31] such that low comprehension accuracy and high comprehension time are indicators of increased cognitive load [2,9,31].

Physiological Measures. Eye-tracking technology enables continuous collection of eye-gaze and pupillary measurements as users perform tasks, offering finer temporal granularity and potentially more precise insights into cognitive load [19,20,34]. Eye-trackers capture gaze data, which is aggregated into fixations [19] using fixation detection algorithms. A fixation represents the duration the eyes remain still on a specific stimulus point. The eye-mind hypothesis suggests that fixations correspond to concurrent mental processing [20]. In [16], the authors found that fixations lasting 250–500 ms reflect mental processing, while those exceeding 500 ms indicate deep mental processing. Additionally, pupillary features can be used to compute the low/high index of pupil activity (LHIPA) [12], an indicator of cognitive load based on the ratio of low to high frequencies in pupil size oscillations, where low LHIPA values signify high cognitive [12].

Behavioral Measures. The continuous stream of data provided by eye-trackers allows also capturing users' visual behavior, from which cognitive load-related measurements can be derived [9,19,34]. The concept of an Area of Interest (AOI) is central to behavioral analyses. In a nutshell, an AOI denotes a spatial area of the stimulus that has information relevant to a particular analysis [19]. In our study, each process model element denotes a distinct AOI. In [6], the authors used the *AOI run count* (i.e., the number of entries and exits to an AOI) to capture users' visual associations between AOIs. This measure reflects the user's mental effort to cognitively integrate information distributed over several parts of the model and thus can be used as a cognitive load indicator. A variant of this measure has been used in Empirical Software Engineering too and has been demonstrated to align well with users' cognitive load [18].

Physiological and behavioral measurements provide continuous data, unlike performance measures (e.g., comprehension accuracy, time) and subjective measures (e.g., post-task surveys), which are collected after task completion. This implies that a fine-grained cognitive load analysis should rely on physiological or behavioral data. However, performance and subjective measures are still vital as they offer a reference for comparison. Section 3.1 will outline the measures used to study the impact of essential and accidental complexity on users' cognitive load across the analysis.

2.3 Visual Behavior Analysis

Eye-tracking reveals users' cognitive load and behavior changes over time [19]. The AOIs over time plot [19] shows the sequence of AOIs a user visits while performing a task. For process comprehension, this plot displays the sequence of process model elements a user has visited to solve a task. Visits and revisits to AOIs also offer insights into user behavior [19]. A *visit to an AOI* refers to the time separating the entry and exit to an AOI [19], while *revisits to an AOI* denote the number of times an AOI was revisited through a specific time interval (e.g., throughout a task) [19]. Based on these two measures, it is possible to compute a *revisit ratio* $\rho_{revisit} = \frac{\#(revisits)}{\#(totalvisits)}$. The associated value can range from 0 for a pure stimulus discovery with no revisit, to 1 for a very large number of revisits. The AOIs over time plot and the revisit ratio will be used in this study to explore users' behavior (cf. Sect. 3.1).

3 Research Method

This section presents the method followed to design our study (cf. Sect. 3.1). Moreover, it introduces our experimental procedure (cf. Sect. 3.2) and the approaches used to set up the data collection and analyze the collected data (cf. Sect. 3.3).

3.1 Study Design

Research Model. *Deductive Research Model.* This hypothesis-testing model is designed to investigate the relationship between essential/accidental complexity measures, and users' cognitive load. Figure 1 depicts our research model.

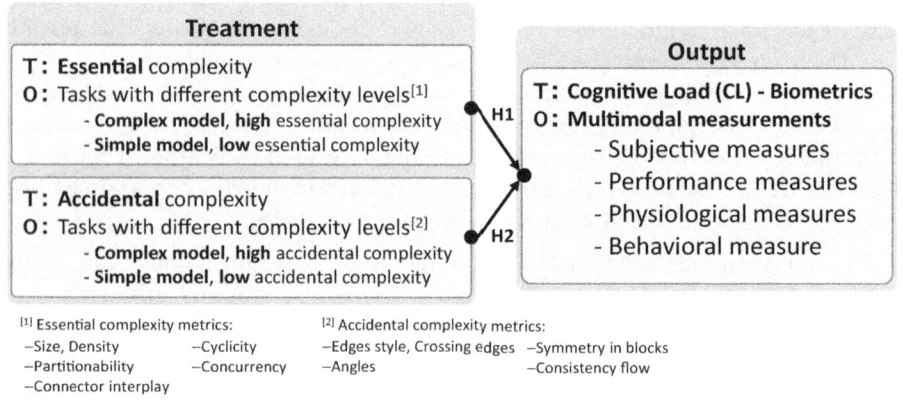

Fig. 1. Research model for hypothesis testing. **T**: theoretical construct. **O**: Operationalization of constructs. This figure is available in the online appendix (https://doi.org/10.5281/zenodo.15067310).

In the *Treatment* part, essential and accidental complexities are our theoretical constructs. We operationalize each construct in simple and complex models following the set of complexity metrics introduced in Sect. 2.1. As *Output*, cognitive load denotes our theoretical construct. It is operationalized with the cognitive load measures introduced in Sect. 2.2. We formulate the following hypotheses:

- **H1** Models with high essential complexity yield higher cognitive load than models with low essential complexity.

– **H2** Models with high accidental complexity yield higher cognitive load than models with low essential complexity.

To validate these hypotheses, the relationship between process model complexity (as captured by the complexity metrics in Fig. 1) and users' cognitive load is investigated at a coarse-grained task level where users will be provided with comprehension tasks on models with either low or high complexity. Afterward, the collected cognitive load measures will be compared across the two conditions. The outcome of this investigation will help us address **RQ1**, i.e., *Does process model complexity as captured by existing complexity metrics align with measures of users' cognitive load?*

Inductive Research Model. The second research model is an exploratory model that follows the Goal, Question, Metric (GQM) template [5] as presented in Table 1. The goal of this exploratory model is to delve deeper into the comprehension of simple and complex process models by examining, at a fine-grained level, users' behavior when solving comprehension tasks. Therein, we pose the following research question: **RQ2**, *How do users' visual behaviors evolve over time during comprehension tasks on process models of varying complexity?* To address this question, we will analyze plots of AOI's visits over time and fixation duration over time. We will also compute measures related to comprehension time, the number of deep mental processing fixations and the revisit ratio.

Table 1. Inductive research model - Description of the inductive research goal with the derived research questions and associated measures. This model is inspired by the Goal, Question, Metric (GQM) template [5]

Goal	Purpose	Explore, at fine-grained level
	Issue	the way users solve comprehension tasks
	Object	with simple and complex process models.
Question	**RQ2**	*How do users' visual behaviors evolve over time during comprehension tasks on process models of varying complexity?*
Measures		Comprehension time, number of deep mental processing fixations and revisit ratio

Material. To investigate the hypotheses and achieve our research goals, we designed several process models. These include a simple model with low essential and accidental complexities, and two complex models where we intentionally increased essential and accidental complexity, respectively. The simple model and the high essential complexity model differ in size, density, partitionability, connector interplay, cyclicity, and concurrency (cf. Fig. 1). Similarly, the simple model and the high accidental complexity model differ in layout, including edge style, crossings, angles, block symmetry, and flow consistency (cf. Fig. 1). The process models use the core BPMN 2.0 elements (start/end events, edges, activities, and gateways) and incorporate five key workflow patterns for sequence, concurrency, choice (exclusive and inclusive), and repetition. These elements are common in real-world process models [26]. Also, such a set is sufficient to create models with low and high essential and accidental complexities. A model with high essential complexity is designed by modifying it repeatedly until each measure of essential complexity individually indicates that the model is more complex than all simple models. A similar process is applied to models with high accidental complexity. In addition, to avoid the impact of domain knowledge on the models' comprehension, we have anonymized the models' activities using random letters. The process models used in the experiment are available in our online appendix (see footnote 3).

Our experiment comprises a series of tasks, each one consisting of a question (i.e., *Given this model, is the following assertion valid?*) asking the participant to validate (by choosing *yes*, *no* or *I don't know*) an assertion related to one model (e.g., *In this process, if activity BA is executed, activity AZ never occurs, and conversely.*). Assertions are designed to involve two activities always graphically separated with the same distance in the model to avoid confounding factors, emerging from the varying number of activities relevant for each task and the changing distance between the task-relevant activities, which may both contribute to users' cognitive load. Moreover, all the assertions are formulated in a positive form as mixing them with negative assertions can have confounding effects on users' cognitive load. Finally, to avoid a potential learning effect due to repeated presentation of a model, we limited the number of distinct assertions to two. In total, we designed 6 tasks, 2 for each model. The tasks used in the experiment are available in our online appendix (see footnote 3).

Participants. Twenty-seven people with Computer Science or Information Systems background participated in the experiment, which took place at the University of St. Gallen. Fourteen participants (11 men, 3 women) declared prior knowledge of BPMN. The rest of the participants (8 men, 5 women) declared no prior knowledge. The participants' average age was around 30 ($\mu = 31.19, \sigma = 7.31$).

3.2 Experimental Procedure

We conducted a within-subject experiment in a controlled lab environment. Each session began with a familiarization phase, including an introduction to the BPMN subset used in the experiment (cf. Sect. 3.1) and a detailed explanation of each possible assertion (as defined in Material, Sect. 3.1) to ensure participants understood the tasks. This was followed by a quiz with four tasks similar to the experiment, where participants could receive help (e.g., reminders of gateway definitions). After the quiz, we discussed each answer to confirm understanding and asked participants to self-assess task difficulty using a 5-point Likert scale. Finally, participants completed a demographic survey.

Although this eye-tracking experiment is conducted in a controlled environment, some human factors can impact data quality [19]. To address this, participants are given final instructions before calibration, including reminders to maintain their head and body position during recording. After calibration, the session begins with a *test* task to familiarize participants with the procedure, though they are not told it is a dummy task (excluded from analysis). This approach helps avoid bias from unfamiliarity with the setup. To mitigate learning effects, tasks are presented in different orders for each participant. For each task, participants answer a validation question (i.e., validating an assertion, as explained in Sect. 3.1) and a self-assessment question on model understanding difficulty using the 5-point Likert scale.

The detailed explanations as well as the mitigation of the learning effect are among factors that contribute to limit the participant's germane load. They reduce the volume of new information to process to the extent required for the completion of a given task, thereby reducing the need to build mental schemes to process this information.

3.3 Data Collection and Analysis Procedure

Data Collection Using EyeMind. Data collection occurred in two phases: an initial (unrecorded) phase using surveys and questionnaires (cf. Sect. 3.2) and a second (recorded) phase using process models and tasks as stimuli (cf. Sect. 3.1). For the recorded phase, we used a Tobii X3-120 eye-tracker on a 24″ monitor (1920 × 1080 resolution). Following guidelines [19], we controlled lab lighting to minimize recording issues. We also used the open-source tool EyeMind [3] to manage the experiment protocol and map gaze data to process model elements automatically.

Using static stimuli (e.g., non-interactive images of small process models) is common for data collection, as it ensures a consistent mapping between gaze coordinates and on-screen elements, simplifying eye-tracking analysis [19]. However, dynamic stimuli enable the use of large models (like ours) and navigation through them. For this reason, we chose dynamic stimuli for data collection, as they better reflect the scale and complexity of real-world models and enhance the ecological validity of the insights. This functionality is well-supported by EyeMind [3].

Data Analysis. The analysis of the collected data is divided into two parts associated with each research model (cf. Sect. 3.1). The following paragraphs summarize the data analysis for each part, while the Python notebooks in our online appendix (see footnote 3) provide more detail on the used analysis procedures.

Deductive Analysis. This coarse-grained analysis addresses RQ1. First, we filtered out data compromised by technical issues in eye-tracking capture. We collected 149 recordings from 150 tasks performed by 25 out 27 participants, as 2 participants had recording problems due to large calibration offsets, and 1 participant is missing 1 task. In the second step, we calculated cognitive load measures (cf. Fig. 1) and derived descriptive and inferential statistics. We used the non-parametric Wilcoxon Signed-Rank test (single-tailed) to establish if the mean differences between the pairs of indicators of cognitive load, associated with low and high complexity process models, are statistically significant. This test does not require normally distributed data.

Inductive Analysis. This fine-grained analysis addresses RQ2. We started by analyzing participants' visual behavior using three types of plots for all trials (i.e., task instances). The first type shows sequences of AOIs visited over time (AOIs over time plots [19]), the second replicates the first with an overlay highlighting observed trends, and the third displays the evolution of fixation duration over time. Examples are shown in Fig. 2. We then grouped the trial plots based on the initial task categories from the experiment design: tasks on the simple model (low essential and accidental complexities), tasks on the high essential complexity model, and tasks on the high accidental complexity model. This enabled us to compare visual behaviors across categories, revealing distinct patterns.

Table 2. Descriptive and inferential statistics. Abbreviations: CL: Cognitive load, Desc.: Descriptive, Inf.: Inferential, #: Number of observations (i.e., pairs of indicators of cognitive load), Comp.: Comprehension, N.: number, P.: Processing, D.: Deep, LHIPA: Low/High Index of Pupil Activity, M_{Simple}, $M_{Complex}$: calculated means for models with low and high complexity, respectively. A p-value $< .05$ means that the results of pairwise comparisons are significant.

Measure of CL	H1: Essential complexity				H2: Accidental complexity			
	Desc. (Mean)			Inf.	Desc. (Mean)			Inf.
	#	M_{Simple}	$M_{Complex}$	p	#	M_{Simple}	$M_{Complex}$	p
Perceived difficulty	50	0.620	2.360	<.001	50	0.620	2.280	<.001
Comp. accuracy	50	0.980	0.660	<.001	50	0.980	0.880	0.025
Comp. time	49	44.938	145.137	<.001	49	44.938	104.020	<.001
AOI run count	49	88.163	232.120	<.001	49	88.143	204.540	<.001
N. Mental P. fix.	49	27.857	85.520	<.001	49	27.857	71.200	<.001
N. D. Mental P. fix.	48	4.250	12.320	<.001	47	4.250	11.876	<.001
LHIPA	48	1.320	0.636	<.001	48	1.320	0.786	<.001

4 Findings

4.1 Deductive Analysis

This analysis addresses *RQ1* (cf. Sect. 3.1) with the left side of Table 2 investigating *H1* (on essential complexity) and the right side investigating *H2* (on accidental complexity). Overall, the descriptive statistics suggest that compared to a simple model with low essential and accidental complexities, models with high complexity are perceived as more difficult, have lower comprehension accuracy and require more comprehension time. In addition, when reading those complex models, the participants exhibited a higher AOI run count, more fixations reflecting mental processing (i.e., duration in the range [250, 500 ms]) and deep mental processing (i.e., duration >500 ms) as well as lower LHIPA values. According to the background presented in Sect. 2.2, the trends of all these measures suggest that models with high essential or accidental complexity cause higher cognitive load than simple models. This proposition is confirmed by the inferential statistics of the individual measures in the left and right sides of Table 2, all returning significant values, which in turn, respectively, confirm *H1* on essential complexity and *H2* on accidental complexity.

4.2 Inductive Analysis

This analysis addresses *RQ2* (cf. Sect. 3.1). Herein, we have made a number of observations throughout our inductive analysis of the collected data. These observations reoccurred across several participants. For sake of brevity, we present these observations in this section through the visual behavior of a single representative participant (P22). This participant performed simple, complex tasks with essential complexity and complex tasks with accidental complexity (as illustrated in Fig. 2). We refer to the appendix (see footnote 3) for a more general overview on the behavior of all participants.

In Fig. 2, Graph a2 is created from a1 by adding an overlay showing the envelope, which estimates the curve covering all points. The envelope appears as a dash-dotted black line. Figure 2 b2 anc c2 are constructed in a similar manner. The envelope graphically describes how a participant discovers AOIs (i.e., the elements of the process model) during the task. In a first phase, it shows a relatively fast pace with a steep slope (approximated by a dashed light gray line) of the curve. Then, in a second phase, it takes a slower pace (approximated by a dashed dark gray line). As the task progresses, the curve approaches a plateau, suggesting a state of equilibrium where no further AOIs are discovered and more back-and-forth movements occur between AOIs already visited, as shown in the first row of Fig. 2 (in particular b1). This pattern holds for the majority of our participants (cf. Appendix (see footnote 3)).

In Fig. 2 a1, b1 anc c1, among all the visits to AOIs, we marked in black the two AOIs (activities) required to answer the task (assertion validation) question. We define a *discovery phase* as the time period that extends from the beginning of the task until the participant has located both activities (i.e. when both vertical lines appear in Graphs a1, b1 and c1). The remaining part of the task is termed *post-discovery*. Graphs a2, b2 and c2 have the areas on either side of this separation tagged accordingly. Graphs from the second row of Fig. 2, show that discovery phases appear shorter than post-discovery phases. This observation can be generalized for other participants in the online appendix (see footnote 3).

Comparing simple tasks to those with essential complexity reveals that the discovery phase is longer for more complex tasks, as shown in Fig. 2 for P22.

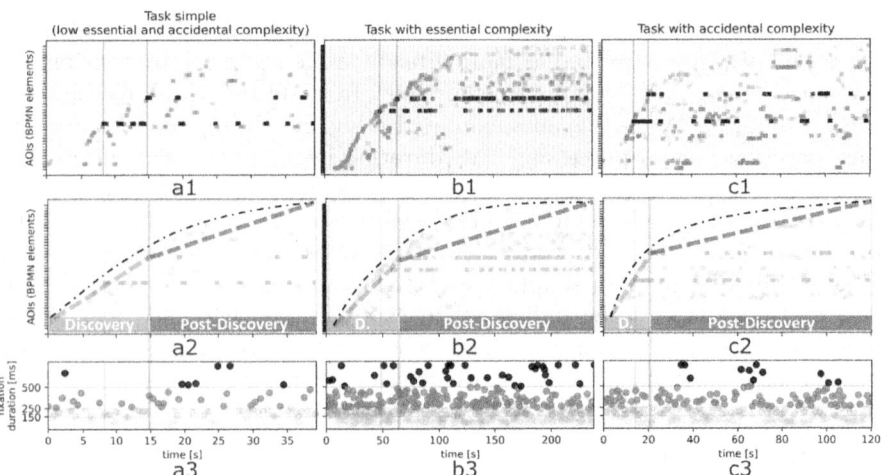

Fig. 2. Comparison of participant P22's visual behavior across three tasks: a simple task with low complexity (a1, a2, a3), a task with high essential complexity (b1, b2, b3), and a task with high accidental complexity (c1, c2, c3). The first row (a1, b1, c1) shows AOI visits over time, with vertical axis ticks indicating the order of visits. Two vertical lines mark when the two activities mentioned in the tasks' questions were visited. The second row (a2, b2, c2) overlays AOI visits with a dash-dotted *envelope* and its dashed estimations, also showing the *discovery* and *post-discovery* phases. Graphs in the third row (a3, b3, c3) plot the participant's fixations over time. Short fixations (<500 ms) are in light gray, long fixations are in black (>500 ms). For a clearer view of data comparisons, extremely long fixations are truncated at 750 ms. This figure is available in the online appendix (https://doi.org/10.5281/zenodo.15067310).

Given the time scale, the discovery phase in a2 is 14.79[s], which is shorter than 79.08[s] in b2. This trend is consistent across other participants (cf. online appendix (see footnote 3)). Additionally, still in the discovery phase, tasks with high essential complexity also involve more long fixations (duration > 500 ms), which are linked to deep mental processing. In Fig. 2, a3 presents 1 long fixations, which is less than b3 having 8 long fixations. However, when comparing simple tasks to those with accidental complexity, these differences are not clear (1 long fixation in a3 and 0 in c3). The discovery phase duration and the number of long fixations did not show notable variation in this case, and, to a greater extent, did not allow any conclusions to be drawn without further analysis.

In the post-discovery phase, the graphs a2, b2 and c2 of Fig. 2 show that complex tasks (b2 and c2, with 137.18[s] and 102.16[s], respectively) take longer to complete than simple tasks (a2, with 24.49[s]). This trend is also observable for other participants (cf. online appendix (see footnote 3)). Similarly, as shown in the third row of Fig. 2, complex tasks (b3 and c3, with 15 and 11 long fixations respectively) have more long fixations (black circles) during the post-discovery phase compared to simple tasks (a3, with 7).

Another observation shows that the revisit ratio (see Sect. 2.3) tends to be lower for the discovery phase (0.537, 0.578, 0.333 for simple, essential and accidental complexity models, respectively) compared to the post-discovery phase (0.595, 0.870, 0.759, for simple, essential and accidental complexity models, respectively). When examining visits to AOIs in the post-discovery phase, the revisit ratio indicates that accidental complexity results in more revisits to AOIs (higher ratio, 0.864) compared to essential complexity (lower ratio, 0.780). This pattern has also been observed for other participants (see online appendix (see footnote 3)).

5 Discussion

We conducted a deductive analysis to answer **RQ1**. For a comprehensive suite of metrics, each separately designed to capture specific aspects of essential and accidental complexity of artifacts (i.e. process models), the results demonstrate that (1) when the complexity between two models is clearly distinct (according to all the selected metrics), distinct estimates of cognitive load are expected for those models. Moreover, (2) the trend of specific complexity measures (i.e., whether an artifact is complex or not) appears to align with selected indicators of cognitive load (i.e., whether the load is high or low, respectively). In short, the results show that when a comprehensive suite of complexity metrics distinguishes between two models, this distinction (with the same trend) should be observed in indicators of cognitive load characterizing a task based on these models. This finding differs from those reported in the Empirical Software Engineering literature, where a relationship between complexity metrics and users' cognitive load was either not found [11] or established to a very limited degree [18,27]. In the process modeling literature, the relationship between complexity metrics and cognitive load was not extensively investigated (besides a few exceptions [2]). The existing studies investigating complexity metrics have instead established a potential correlation between the complexity of process models, user performance (in terms of comprehension and modeling errors), and perceived difficulty [8,15,22,24,24]. Compared to this literature, our findings provide additional and stronger evidence confirming the impact of essential and accidental complexity metrics on users' cognitive load using a broader set of measures delving deeper into users' behavioral and physiological responses to cognitive load.

To address **RQ2**, an inductive analysis was subsequently conducted. The envelope is a first observation at a coarse-grained level. It serves as a model to help compare tasks and visually identify the division of tasks into two phases: the discovery phase, which seems shorter (in time) with a low revisit ratio, and the post-discovery phase that is longer with a higher revisit ratio and showing higher cognitive load (deep mental processing manifested by long fixations). The discovery phase likely represents an exploration period where participants search for information relevant to the task. In the literature, this is often called the *search* phase [35]. On the other hand, the post-discovery phase likely reflects a stage where participants use reasoning to analyze the relationships between the identified information and draw new conclusions. This phase is typically referred to in the literature as the *inference* phase [21].

Comparing the model with accidental complexity and the one with essential complexity through the *revisit ratio* in the post-discovery phase, one can hypothesize that the process of mentally reorganizing the model layout yields more revisits (and thus a higher ratio) than the process of cognitively integrating different model parts. As these assumptions are based solely on observations, they require further empirical validation.

This study can be subject to validity threats. The following measures were taken to mitigate the risks threatening the internal validity of this study. As described in Sect. 3, we designed our research method and in particular the material used for the experiment, to avoid potential confounding factors. The distinct tasks were presented in a randomized order for each participant and the protocol of the experiment included a controlled environment, a uniform introduction to BPMN as well as a familiarization with the tasks. Furthermore, cognitive load was evaluated using multiple measures, allowing us to confirm our hypotheses with a high degree of confidence. Regarding external validity, our sample size may raise concerns. However, previous studies also had similar sample sizes [18,27,28], considering the challenges underlying the design and execution of eye-tracking experiments [19]. Moreover, there might be a concern about the generalizability of our findings to other process models. For this reason, we opted for popular control-flow BPMN patterns in all our models [26].

6 Conclusion and Future Work

This paper summarizes an eye-tracking experiment investigating the relationship of complexity metrics with cognitive load and visual behavior. Following a multi-granular research method, the findings demonstrate at a coarse-grained level that a thorough set of essential and accidental complexity metrics aligns well with users' cognitive load during comprehension tasks on simple and complex process models. Then, at a fine-grained level, the exploration of users' visual behavior over time yielded numerous patterns associated with users' search, inference, mental reorganization of the model layout and cognitive integration.

In future work, we plan to extend the fine-grained analysis by further investigating the dynamics of the relationship between users' behavior and cognitive load over time. Furthermore, we are planning to deepen the analysis of users' cognitive processes, particularly those associated with the search and inference behaviors, as well as the mental reorganization of the model layout and cognitive integration which are likely to occur when dealing with models having accidental and essential complexities, respectively.

References

1. Abbad-Andaloussi, A.: On the relationship between source-code metrics and cognitive load: a systematic tertiary review. J. Syst. Softw. **198**, 111619 (2023). https://doi.org/10.1016/j.jss.2023.111619
2. Abbad-Andaloussi, A., Burattin, A., Slaats, T., Kindler, E., Weber, B.: Complexity in declarative process models: Metrics and multi-modal assessment of cognitive load. Expert Syst. Appl. (2023). https://doi.org/10.1016/j.eswa.2023.120924
3. Abbad-Andaloussi, A., Lübke, D., Weber, B.: Conducting eye-tracking studies on large and interactive process models using eyemind. SoftwareX **24** (2023). https://doi.org/10.1016/j.softx.2023.101564. Article ID: 101564
4. Antinyan, V.: Evaluating essential and accidental code complexity triggers by practitioners' perception. IEEE Softw. **37**(6), 86–93 (2020). https://doi.org/10.1109/ms.2020.2976072
5. Basili, V.R., Caldiera, G., Rombach, H.D.: The goal question metric approach. In: Encyclopedia of Software Engineering, pp. 528–532. John Wiley & Sons (1994)
6. Bera, P., Soffer, P., Parsons, J.: Using eye tracking to expose cognitive processes in understanding conceptual models. MIS Q. **43**(4), 1105–1126 (2019). https://doi.org/10.25300/MISQ/2019/14163
7. Bernstein, V., Soffer, P.: Identifying and quantifying visual layout features of business process models. In: Gaaloul, K., Schmidt, R., Nurcan, S., Guerreiro, S., Ma, Q. (eds.) Enterprise, Business-Process and Information Systems Modeling, pp. 200–213. Springer, Cham (2015). https://doi.org/10.1007/978-3-319-19237-6_13
8. Burattin, A., Bernstein, V., Neurauter, M., Soffer, P., Weber, B.: Detection and quantification of flow consistency in business process models. Softw. Syst. Model. **17**(2), 633–654 (2017). https://doi.org/10.1007/s10270-017-0576-y
9. Chen, F., et al.: Robust Multimodal Cognitive Load Measurement. HIS, Springer, Cham (2016). https://doi.org/10.1007/978-3-319-31700-7
10. Cheng, C.Y.: Complexity and Usability Models for Business Process Analysis. The Pennsylvania State University (2008)
11. Couceiro, R., et al.: Spotting problematic code lines using nonintrusive programmers' biofeedback. In: 2019 IEEE 30th International Symposium on Software Reliability Engineering (ISSRE), Los Alamitos, CA, USA, pp. 93–103. IEEE Comput. Soc. Press (2019). https://doi.org/10.1109/issre.2019.00019
12. Duchowski, A.T., Krejtz, K., Gehrer, N.A., Bafna, T., Bækgaard, P.: The low/high index of pupillary activity. In: Proceedings of the 2020 CHI Conference on Human Factors in Computing Systems, CHI 2020, pp. 1–12. ACM, New York (2020). https://doi.org/10.1145/3313831.3376394
13. Dumas, M., La Rosa, M., Mendling, J., Reijers, H.A.: Fundamentals of Business Process Management. Springer, Heidelberg (2013). https://doi.org/10.1007/978-3-642-33143-5
14. Figl, K.: Comprehension of procedural visual business process models. Bus. Inf. Syst. Eng. **59**(1), 41–67 (2016). https://doi.org/10.1007/s12599-016-0460-2
15. Figl, K., Laue, R.: Cognitive complexity in business process modeling. In: Advanced Information Systems Engineering, pp. 452–466. Springer, Heidelberg (2011). https://doi.org/10.1007/978-3-642-21640-4_34

16. Glöckner, A., Herbold, A.K.: Information processing in decisions under risk: evidence for compensatory strategies based on automatic processes. SSRN Electron. J. (42) (2008). https://doi.org/10.2139/ssrn.1307664
17. Goldstine, H.H., von Neumann, J.: Planning and coding of problems for an electronic computing instrument. In: Mathematical and Logical Aspects of an Electronic Computing Instrument (1947)
18. Hao, G., et al.: On the accuracy of code complexity metrics: a neuroscience-based guideline for improvement. Front. Neurosci. **16** (2023). https://doi.org/10.3389/fnins.2022.1065366
19. Holmqvist, K., Nyström, M., Andersson, R., Dewhurst, R., Halszka, J., van de Weijer, J.: Eye Tracking: A Comprehensive Guide to Methods and Measures. Oxford University Press, Oxford (2011)
20. Just, M.A., Carpenter, P.A.: A theory of reading: from eye fixations to comprehension. Psychol. Rev. **87**(4), 329 (1980)
21. Kim, J., Hahn, J., Hahn, H.: How do we understand a system with (so) many diagrams? Cognitive integration processes in diagrammatic reasoning. Inf. Syst. Res. **11**(3), 284–303 (2000). https://doi.org/10.1287/isre.11.3.284.12206
22. Mendling, J.: Detection and prediction of errors in EPC business process models. Ph.D. thesis, Wirtschaftsuniversität Wien (2007)
23. Mendling, J., Reijers, H.A., Cardoso, J.: What makes process models understandable? In: Alonso, G., Dadam, P., Rosemann, M. (eds.) LNCS, pp. 48–63. Springer, Heidelberg (2007). https://doi.org/10.1007/978-3-540-75183-0_4
24. Mendling, J., Sánchez-González, L., García, F., Rosa, M.L.: Thresholds for error probability measures of business process models. J. Syst. Softw. **85**(5), 1188–1197 (2012). https://doi.org/10.1016/j.jss.2012.01.017
25. Moody, D.: The 'physics' of notations: toward a scientific basis for constructing visual notations in software engineering. IEEE Trans. Softw. Eng. **35**(6), 756–779 (2009). https://doi.org/10.1109/tse.2009.67
26. Muehlen, M.z., Recker, J.: How Much Language Is Enough? Theoretical and Practical Use of the Business Process Modeling Notation, pp. 465–479. Springer (2008). https://doi.org/10.1007/978-3-540-69534-9_35
27. Peitek, N.: A Neuro-Cognitive Perspective of Program Comprehension. Ph.D. thesis, Technischen Universität Chemnitz (2022). https://doi.org/10.1145/3183440.3183442
28. Petrusel, R., Mendling, J.: Eye-tracking the factors of process model comprehension tasks. In: Salinesi, C., Norrie, M.C., Pastor, Ó. (eds.) Advanced Information Systems Engineering, pp. 224–239. Springer, Heidelberg (2013). https://doi.org/10.1007/978-3-642-38709-8_15
29. Petrusel, R., Mendling, J., Reijers, H.A.: How visual cognition influences process model comprehension. Decis. Support Syst. **96**, 1–16 (2017). https://doi.org/10.1016/j.dss.2017.01.005
30. Reijers, H.A., Mendling, J.: A study into the factors that influence the understandability of business process models. IEEE Trans. Syst. Man Cybernet. Part A Syst. Hum. **41**(3), 449–462 (2011). https://doi.org/10.1109/TSMCA.2010.2087017
31. Schreiber, C., Abbad-Andaloussi, A., Weber, B.: On the cognitive effects of abstraction and fragmentation in modularized process models. In: LNCS, pp. 359–376. Springer, Cham (2023). https://doi.org/10.1007/978-3-031-41620-0_21
32. Sweller, J.: Element interactivity and intrinsic, extraneous, and germane cognitive load. Educ. Psychol. Rev. **22**(2), 123–138 (2010). https://doi.org/10.1007/s10648-010-9128-5

33. Sweller, J., Ayres, P., Kalyuga, S.: Cognitive Load Theory. Explorations in the Learning Sciences, Instructional Systems and Performance Technologies. Springer, New York (2011). https://doi.org/10.1007/978-1-4419-8126-4
34. Weber, B., Fischer, T., Riedl, R.: Brain and autonomic nervous system activity measurement in software engineering: a systematic literature review. J. Syst. Softw. **178** (2021). https://doi.org/10.1016/j.jss.2021.110946
35. Wolfe, J.M.: Guided search 2.0 a revised model of visual search. Psychon. Bull. Rev. **1**(2), 202–238 (1994). https://doi.org/10.3758/bf03200774

Event Data Extraction (BPMDS 2025)

Which Tables are Mine(able)?

Shameer K. Pradhan[1(✉)], Mieke Jans[1,2], and Niels Martin[1]

[1] UHasselt - Digital Future Lab, Wetenschapspark 2, 3590 Diepenbeek, Belgium
shameer.pradhan@uhasselt.be
[2] Maastricht University, Minderbroedersberg 4-6,
6211 LK Maastricht, The Netherlands

Abstract. Identifying relevant tables in databases to build event logs is typically a manual, error-prone task in process mining. This paper introduces TabMine, a semi-automated algorithm that identifies these tables by leveraging both the network structure of tables and their natural language descriptions. By integrating process-related business documents with table metadata, TabMine employs machine learning techniques, specifically community detection and natural language processing, to align table communities with the corresponding documents. This enables analysts to build event logs for process mining from a targeted list of tables without prior knowledge of the specific database or ERP system.

Keywords: data extraction · data preparation · event log-building · process mining · table identification

1 Introduction

Organizations are progressively dependent on information systems (IS), including Enterprise Resource Planning (ERP) systems, to effectively manage and optimize their business processes. These systems accumulate substantial volumes of process-related data, which, when analyzed proficiently through techniques such as process mining, can offer significant insights for the enhancement of operational performance [2]. Nonetheless, process mining cannot directly utilize the raw data stored within IS; it is imperative that this data be extracted and transformed into structured event logs beforehand. The construction of event logs is a multi-stage process wherein data extraction plays a pivotal role [10]. Despite the existence of various methods for data extraction [4,5,12], this procedure remains formidable and frequently necessitates considerable manual effort, especially in extensive and intricate databases [17].

The extraction of data in an efficient manner necessitates collaboration among business process experts, IS specialists, and process analysts [15]. Business process experts furnish essential insights into primary business documents and transactions, thereby establishing the groundwork for comprehending the data that requires extraction. IS specialists utilize this contextual knowledge to ascertain pertinent database tables, columns, and filters, while also interpreting timestamps to deduce significant events. Subsequently, process analysts convert the extracted data into event logs and undertake process mining analyses [15]. Nonetheless, the identification of relevant database tables represents a pivotal bottleneck within this workflow [4,10]. This phase is frequently labor-intensive and inefficient, as databases may encompass hundreds or even thousands of tables [7,17], with existing methods largely neglecting this critical component. The issue is exacerbated by the scattered nature of pertinent data across numerous tables, rendering table identification a substantial hindrance for analysts who lack database knowledge or IS expertise [13].

In this context, the study introduces TabMine, an algorithm crafted to aid process analysts in the effective identification of database tables likely associated with specific business documents. By exploiting the network structure of databases, along with community detection techniques and natural language processing (NLP), TabMine offers a semi-automated framework for table identification. This reduces dependence on extensive IS expertise and minimizes the necessity for knowledge transfer between IS specialists and process analysts, thereby improving productivity and mitigating the risk of communication errors. The algorithm is particularly advantageous for smaller organizations with constrained IS and process mining resources. Furthermore, it provides value to entities with unique processes beyond standard procedures, such as Order-to-Cash (O2C) or Procure-to-Pay (P2P), where publicly available information is often limited. By streamlining the data extraction process, TabMine renders process mining more accessible and efficient across a broad spectrum of applications.

The remainder of this paper is structured as follows: Sect. 2 provides a review of the related literature. Section 3 elaborates on the proposed solution and presents a constructed academic example. Section 4 illustrates TabMine within the context of the sales processes in the Odoo ERP system. Lastly, Sects. 5 and 6 offer a discussion and conclusion of the paper, respectively.

2 Related Work

The construction of event logs represents a crucial phase in process mining, as each process under examination necessitates an event log assembled from relevant data sources [8]. This undertaking consists of identifying the data of interest, extracting the data, and converting it into a structured event log format suited to analysis [10].

A prominent approach for the generation of event logs is the ontology-based database access (OBDA) approach, particularly instantiated through the Onprom framework [5]. Onprom facilitates the connection between high-level domain representations, such as conceptual schemas, and underlying data repositories, such as IS databases. Within this framework, analysts perform visual annotations of critical elements—cases, events, and attributes—using the Onprom interface, which allows for the specification of data extraction parameters. The erprep add-on enhances this capability by providing systematic guidance for annotation and supporting process comprehension [4]. Nonetheless, the task of mapping domain ontologies to database structures predominantly remains a manual endeavor, necessitating considerable expertise in IS and business processes, thereby making this approach reliant on specialized knowledge.

Beyond OBDA, other methodologies have been proposed to address event log-building and data extraction. Li et al. [13] developed a method to align database table attributes with task instances by employing text mining techniques on process-related documents and leveraging a lexicon derived from internal company resources and industry standards. This lexicon supports the identification of attributes in a resource-action-data format. Another notable approach to identify relevant data is the meta-model technique proposed by González López de Murillas et al. [9], which integrates process and data perspectives by linking process elements (e.g., events, cases) with data concepts such as objects and models. Stein et al. [18] introduced a method for mapping activities from an existing process model to database tables by analyzing table attributes to establish mappings. However, this method assumes the availability of a predefined process model, which might not be the case when the primary objective of process mining is to create such process models [1].

While these methods have advanced the field, they rely heavily on domain expertise for identifying relevant data, even when automation is involved. This dependency on manual effort, domain-specific resources, or predefined process models limits scalability and applicability, especially where expert knowledge is scarce. Future approaches must strike a balance by reducing manual interventions while maintaining the necessary expert input to streamline and generalize event log-building.

3 TabMine

3.1 Overview

TabMine is a semi-automatic algorithm designed to identify database tables with a high likelihood of being linked to certain business documents. It needs three crucial inputs: (i) a *database schema*; (ii) a *data dictionary* that features natural language descriptions of tables; (iii) a list of *business documents* pertinent to the process analyst, alongside potential related attributes (such as a *sales order document* with characteristics like "sales order id," "product," "quantity," and "amount"). Utilizing these inputs, TabMine pinpoints candidate tables that are most likely aligned with the identified business documents, thereby minimizing the effort and time needed for process analysts to finalize the mapping between business documents and database tables.

To demonstrate the process of TabMine, consider an academic scenario: we have a collection of business documents labeled [X, Y, Z] along with tables [A, B, ..., M] that include textual explanations. Document X's data is found in tables B, C, and D; for document Y, it is located in tables F and G; and for document Z, it is in tables H and I. Ideally, TabMine can accurately associate tables B, C,

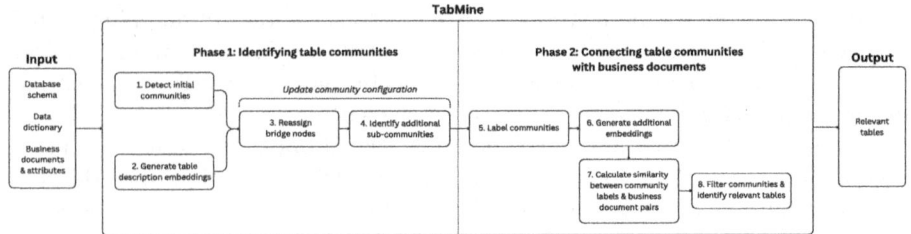

Fig. 1. TabMine workflow

and D with document X, tables F and G with document Y, and tables H and I with document Z.

Figure 1 presents an overview of TabMine, outlining its inputs, processing steps, and output. TabMine operates in two main phases: first, it identifies table communities, and second, it links these identified table communities to the corresponding business documents. Detailed explanations of these processing steps are provided in the subsequent sections. An implementation of TabMine can be found in our repository[1].

3.2 Detect Initial Communities (Start Phase 1)

In the first step of TabMine, to filter less relevant tables in the subsequent steps, communities comprising semantically analogous tables are discerned, thereby aiding in capturing the structural interrelationships among the tables. To facilitate the identification of these communities, the database schema is converted into an undirected graph, wherein each table is depicted as a node while the foreign key linkages between tables are delineated as edges. The *Louvain method* [3], a community detection algorithm, is subsequently employed on this graph to uncover communities of interconnected tables. The Louvain method functions by progressively aggregating nodes to augment modularity, which quantifies the strength of the division of a network into communities. Higher modularity indicates more concentrated connections within communities as opposed to those between them [3]. This approach is particularly suited for TabMine due to its efficiency with large networks and its ability to uncover hierarchical community structures [3]. The emergent table clusters provide baseline groups for the ensuing phases of TabMine. Within Fig. 2, the community structure exemplified in the academic scenario is depicted. Specifically, nodes A through F, nodes G through J, and nodes K, L, and M constitute Communities 1, 2, and 3, respectively.

3.3 Generate Table Description Embeddings

In the second step, textual table descriptions are converted into embeddings through the use of the *text-embedding-ada-002* large language model (LLM)

---

[1] https://github.com/shapradhan/TabMine/.

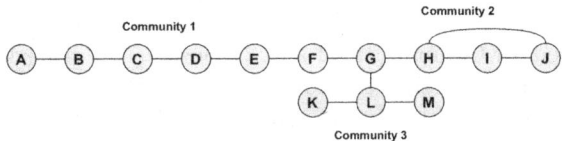

Fig. 2. Communities detected by the Louvain method (after Step 1)

offered by the *Azure OpenAI Service*. These embeddings represent the tables' semantic content, enabling a systematic comparison of their semantic similarities. Unlike traditional community detection algorithms like the Louvain method, which depend solely on graph network structure, this embedding approach integrates semantic details about the nodes. Focusing only on network topology, traditional methods can lead to suboptimal community groupings, potentially placing semantically similar nodes into different communities [11]. This embedding strategy mitigates such issues by considering semantic relationships alongside structural patterns.

3.4 Reassign Bridge Nodes

To enhance community cohesion –ensuring nodes within each community are highly similar to each other– bridge nodes that connect different communities [16] are identified and their placement reassessed (Step 3 in Fig. 1). Bridge nodes are identified by traversing the graph and identifying nodes that belong to different communities but are connected by an edge. For example, in Fig. 2, nodes F, G, and L serve as bridge nodes between two communities.

After identifying the bridge nodes, a reassessment process prioritizes those with the most neighboring communities and nodes, rather than operating in random order. This approach ensures that nodes with the greatest influence –those interacting with the most diverse and extensive graph regions– are evaluated first. By starting with these key nodes, the overall impact on community structure is maximized.

The placement of each bridge node is assessed by its impact on the cohesion of both its original and neighboring communities. This assessment involves calculating the average similarity score between the description embeddings of nodes within the bridge node's original community, considering scenarios with and without the bridge node. These calculated scores reveal whether the cohesion of the community improves or declines upon relocating the bridge node. For instance, in Community 2, a similarity score is initially determined for nodes G, H, I, and J, and then recalculated after removing bridge node G. If the absence of the bridge node leads to a better similarity score, it implies that the node may fit better in a different community. These scores are derived using cosine similarity, which effectively compares textual data like table descriptions by emphasizing the directional similarity of embeddings over their magnitude [6].

To determine the most appropriate neighboring community for a bridge node, similarity scores are calculated for each adjacent community, both with and without the inclusion of the bridge node. For instance, for bridge node G, similarity scores are assessed for Communities 1 and 3, considering both scenarios. If incorporating the bridge node increases a community's similarity score, it is reassigned to the community with the highest improvement. If no enhancement is observed, the bridge node is assigned to a new, distinct community, preserving its original community's integrity. For example, if reallocating node G results in a greater improvement for Community 1's similarity score compared to Community 3's, it is assigned to Community 1. This method of reassignment is conducted repeatedly for each bridge node.

Reassigning a bridge node can lead to its previous community splitting into smaller subgroups, which are considered new communities. For instance, reassigning bridge node L to Community 1 means nodes K and M (linked to L, but not to each other) form distinct communities. Newly formed bridge nodes, if any, are subsequently evaluated based on the same criteria as explained above. Figure 3 demonstrates the altered community structure after node G is moved from Community 2 to Community 1.

By iteratively reassessing all bridge nodes and addressing secondary effects, the process ensures a cohesive configuration of communities. This step concludes once all bridge nodes have been evaluated and reassigned to their most suitable positions.

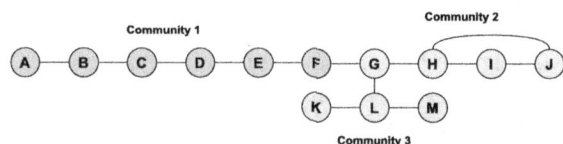

Fig. 3. Community configuration after membership of a bridge node has been updated (after Step 3)

3.5 Identify Additional Sub-communities

TabMine enhances the preliminary communities identified by the Louvain method by identifying smaller sub-communities through the inclusion of semantic meaning of the nodes, as demonstrated in Task 4 of Fig. 1. While traditional community detection methods, like Louvain, emphasize only the network structure of the graph, potentially overlooking finer substructures, TabMine accurately detects these details using node embeddings and similarity scores.

Before detecting sub-communities, the subgraph associated with each community is inspected for cycles, as TabMine does not function with cyclic graphs. If cycles are detected, they are eliminated. This elimination does not impact TabMine's functionality since it is based on similarity scores obtained from node descriptions, not the graph's edges. Cycle removal begins with the edge between the nodes exhibiting the lowest similarity and proceeds, removing additional edges between the least similar nodes until the graph becomes acyclic. This method removes cycles by targeting the weakest connections in the community. For instance, in Community 2, the cycle formed by nodes H and J is eliminated, ensuring the graph is cycle-free.

Once the graph is acyclic, the algorithm discerns sub-communities by analyzing the similarity scores between nodes connected by edges, beginning with the nodes having the least similarity within that community. This approach evaluates the least similar node pairs initially, which may lead to splitting the community at the edges with the weakest link. For instance, in Community 1, the edges connecting nodes A to B, B to C, through to G are initially sorted by increasing similarity scores. Subsequently, the structure of the graph in terms of the number of nodes on the sides of an edge determines how `TabMine` progresses. There are two primary situations, which are described below.

Single Node on One Side and Several Nodes on the Other. When a single node is on one side of an edge and several nodes are on the opposite side, whether connected directly or through other nodes, the algorithm computes the average similarity score for the larger group, both including and excluding the single node. If removing the single node increases the similarity score in its original community, the node is placed in its own sub-community. For example, in Community 1, when assessing edge BC, node A is on one side, while nodes D, E, F, and G are grouped on the other. If excluding node A results in a higher similarity score among nodes B to G, then node A becomes a separate sub-community; if not, it stays with the group.

Multiple Nodes on Both Sides of the Edge. When an edge connects multiple nodes on each side, either directly or indirectly through other nodes, `TabMine` evaluates the cohesion of these groups using similarity scores. It calculates the average similarity score for the nodes on each side separately and compares these values with the overall similarity of the combined group. If dividing the groups into separate sub-communities improves the internal similarity within each side, the groups are partitioned into separate sub-communities. For instance, examining edge DE, nodes B and C are on one side (excluding node A as it has been reassigned), and nodes F and G are on the opposite side. `TabMine` calculates the similarity score for nodes B and C alone and compares it with the similarity of all involved nodes (B through G). If the similarity of nodes B and C exceeds the overall combined similarity, they form a separate community. These activities are also performed for nodes F and G. If the independent similarity scores are lower than the overall combined similarity, the nodes remain together in the same community. This method is iterated, focusing initially on the edges with the least similarity, to progressively refine community structures.

Through iterative refinement, sub-communities emerge that reflect the fundamental semantic connections between the nodes more accurately. For instance, the ultimate structure depicted in Fig. 4 assigns node A to an individual community, whereas nodes F and G constitute a unique sub-community that is distinct from other nodes.

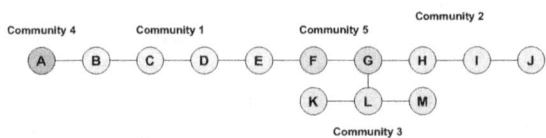

Fig. 4. Community configuration after additional nodes have been identified (after Step 4)

3.6 Label Communities (Start Phase 2)

The prior phase finalizes the community configurations. However, it remains necessary to link these communities with the business documents. Achieving this connection requires labeling the communities. As depicted in Step 5 of Fig. 1, the labeling operation uses textual table descriptions processed by the *gpt-35-turbo* large language completion model, supplied by *Azure OpenAI Service*. A customized prompt is employed to create distinct and relevant community labels.

The LLM prompt is organized into three primary sections: an initial system prompt, a customized user prompt, and a concluding system prompt. The initial system prompt sets the stage for the LLM, the user prompt provides specific table descriptions per community, and the final system prompt defines the output format and structure. This multi-tiered prompting assists the LLM in crafting precise and unique labels for every community, maintaining uniformity and pertinence among the labeled groups [14].

In our academic example, the table descriptions linked to the respective nodes within a community are provided to the LLM, which then creates a label for the community according to those descriptions. This process is repeated for all recognized communities.

3.7 Generate Additional Embeddings

At this stage, embeddings are generated for the names and attributes of business documents, as well as for database table column names and the community labels designated in the prior step, utilizing the same LLM as in Step 2. The embeddings for business document names and community labels allow for computing similarity scores between them. Concurrently, embeddings for the business document attributes and table columns are set up for application in Step 8 of `TabMine`. This procedure is demonstrated in Step 6 of Fig. 1.

Which Tables are Mine(able)? 115

3.8 Calculate Similarity Between Community Label and Business Document Pairs

TabMine utilizes the embeddings from the previous step to evaluate the similarity between business documents and community labels (Step 7 of Fig. 1). Every potential pair of business documents and community labels undergoes similarity evaluation. In the context of our example, this translates into computing similarity scores for three business documents X, Y, and Z against five community labels "Community 1" through "Community 5". This results in 15 unique similarity scores (X-1, Y-1, Z-1, X-2, ..., Y-5, Z-5). A higher similarity score indicates a higher probability that the relevant tables for a business document can be found among the tables in the corresponding community. These pairwise similarity scores serve as the initial filter for eliminating documents-community pairs with weak connections. This leads to the next stage in TabMine.

3.9 Filter Communities and Identify Relevant Tables

Once the similarity scores have been computed between community labels and business document pairs, the subsequent step is to identify the relevant tables (see Step 8 in Fig. 1). Initially, for each business document, communities are selected based on their similarity score with the document's labels. Communities that either exceed a given similarity threshold or are among the top N similar ones are chosen for further examination. This process helps to narrow the focus to specific communities rather than considering all communities. For example, for business document X, communities 1, 2, and 5 from Fig. 4 might be selected if they meet the threshold set by the process analyst.

After the communities have been chosen, TabMine identifies the tables associated with each community and extracts their columns. Using the embeddings developed in Step 6, it computes three similarity metrics to assess the alignment between business documents and database tables:

1. The **profile similarity score** gauges the overall correlation between a business document and a table. This is done by comparing the average embedding of all document attributes with the average embedding of all table columns, providing a comprehensive overview.
2. The individual **field-to-field similarity score** offers a finer assessment by calculating the average similarity between individual fields of a business document and the columns of a table. This score is determined by averaging the pairwise similarities between the embeddings of each document field and each table column, thus providing insights into field-level correspondences.
3. The **neighbor similarity score** assesses how related tables in the database schema are interconnected. Take the sales order context as an example: the central table (such as sales_order) might not include every attribute of the business document, like detailed order line information. Such details could be in a linked table, for instance, sales_order_line. To accommodate this, the score examines nearby tables associated with the central table. For each table

selected, `TabMine` computes the similarity between the business document's attributes and the columns in these adjacent tables. The table's overall score is calculated as the average of these similarity measures across its associated tables, ensuring that the table's importance is assessed in light of its related tables.

Finally, `TabMine` combines these three metrics in a weighted average. Default values have been assigned according to a 4:2:1 ratio, reflecting their relative importance in the alignment process. The field-to-field similarity is assigned the highest weight, as it directly maps document attributes to table columns and forms the core of accurate alignment. The profile similarity, which offers a broader contextual alignment, acts as a secondary refinement measure. Finally, the neighbor similarity that captures contextual relevance from related tables, is given a lower weight to prevent it from overshadowing direct matches. The default values can be adapted by the process analyst if desired.

`TabMine` generates its final output by providing a ranked list of tables pertinent to each document. This ranking is determined by the weighted average of their similarities. Process analysts can subsequently leverage this list to map and pinpoint the tables most likely to include data pertinent to the business document.

4 Evaluation

4.1 Experiment Design

We evaluated `TabMine`'s ability to map business documents to their corresponding database tables. The evaluation is based on an experiment where various sets of tables are provided to `TabMine`, along with table descriptions and a collection of business documents of interest. The table sets differ in size and degree of relevance to the business documents.

Sales-related documents within the Odoo open-source ERP system[2] are utilized for our evaluation. Documents such as *sales order*, *invoice*, *payment*, and *credit note* are used as the inputs for `TabMine`. Each document is characterized by a set of attributes that encapsulate key information relevant to its content. For instance, a sales order document features attributes like *sales order id*, *customer name*, *product*, *quantity*, and *amount*.

To evaluate the functioning of `TabMine`, the "gold standard" of mappings between sales business documents and database tables were established. This was achieved by creating specific sales documents in Odoo and observing which tables were modified during their creation. The mappings that represent the "gold standard" are presented in Table 1.

`TabMine` is applied to four different sets of database tables. The complexity of these sets rises with the increasing number of tables. Additionally, the larger the table set, the more noise is added and the more challenging the task for `TabMine` becomes. Below is a detailed account of the sets of tables:

---
[2] https://odoo.com.

Table 1. "Gold standard" mapping of business documents to the database tables for the sales process in Odoo

Business Document	Tables
Sales order	sales_order, sales_order_line
Invoice	account_move, account_move_line, sale_advance_payment_inv
Payment	account_payment, account_payment_register
Credit note	account_move_reversal

1. **Document-specific tables**: Tables directly modified when the specific sales-related documents were created or updated.
2. **All tables in the sales module**: All tables generated when the sales module is installed in Odoo.
3. **Foundational tables and sales tables**: Tables created during the initial installation of Odoo (foundational tables), combined with those from the sales module.
4. **Foundational tables, sales tables, and manufacturing tables**: Tables created during the initial installation of Odoo (foundational tables), combined with those from the sales module as well as the manufacturing module.

In addition to altering the level of noise, this study examines the sensitivity of TabMine to the similarity threshold employed in the final step of the algorithm. This parameter is anticipated to notably affect the accuracy in identifying the appropriate tables. The sensitivity analysis is conducted using four distinct similarity thresholds (75%, 80%, 85%, and 90%) between business documents and community labels. For each specific combination of similarity threshold and table set, the precision and recall metrics of TabMine's output are computed using the "gold standard". Precision is defined as the proportion of tables identified as relevant that are indeed relevant, whereas recall denotes the proportion of truly relevant tables that are accurately identified.

4.2 Evaluation Results

The evaluation results on the performance and sensitivity of TabMine are summarized in Table 2. Each cell in the table presents two metrics –precision (P) and recall (R)– for each business document of interest. For the cells without value, TabMine did not succeed in generating a list of potentially relevant tables.

The evaluation results for TabMine demonstrate significant variations in performance based on the scope of the table sets analyzed. It performs best when working with document-specific tables, where it can precisely target relevant matches with minimal interference from unrelated tables. For example, document-specific tables consistently yield high recall values across multiple similarity thresholds (often perfect score), indicating TabMine's ability to capture all relevant matches. Precision in this context is also relatively higher compared to broader table sets, as the constrained scope helps reduce false positives. On

Table 2. TabMine evaluation results (P: Precision, R: Recall)

Similarity Threshold	Business Documents	Table Sets			
		Document-specific tables	All tables in the sales module	Foundational tables and sales tables	Foundational, sales, and manufacturing tables
90%	Sales Order	-	-	P: 0 R: 0	-
	Invoice	-	-	-	-
	Payment	-	-	-	-
	Credit note	-	-	-	-
85%	Sales Order	P: 0.6667 R: 1.0000	P: 0 R: 0	P: 0 R: 0	P: 0 R: 0
	Invoice	-	-	-	-
	Payment	P: 1.0000 R: 0.5000	P: 0 R: 0	P: 0 R: 0	P: 0 R: 0
	Credit note	-	-	P: - R: 0	-
80%	Sales Order	P: 0.3333 R: 1.0000	P: 0 R: 0	P: 0 R: 0	P: 0 R: 0
	Invoice	P: 0.3333 R: 1.0000	P: 0.0488 R: 0.6667	P: 0.0380 R: 1.0000	P: 0.0303 R: 0.3333
	Payment	P: 0.2000 R: 1.0000	P: 0 R: 0	P: 0 R: 0	P: 0.0339 R: 1.0000
	Credit note	P: - R: 0	-	P: 0 R: 0	-
75%	Sales Order	P: 0.1176 R: 1.0000	P: 0.0103 R: 1.0000	P: 0.0089 R: 1.0000	P: 0.0035 R: 0.5000
	Invoice	P: 0.1765 R: 1.0000	P: 0.0116 R: 1.0000	P: 0.0085 R: 1.0000	P: 0.0095 R: 1.0000
	Payment	P: 0.1176 R: 1.0000	P: 0.0076 R: 1.0000	P: 0.0056 R: 1.0000	P: 0.0062 R: 1.0000
	Credit note	P: 0.0714 R: 1.0000	P: 0.0133 R: 1.0000	P: 0.0072 R: 1.0000	P: 0.0088 R: 1.0000

the other hand, expanding the scope to include broader sets, such as all tables in the sales module or foundational and manufacturing tables, introduces challenges. Recall remains robust and often perfect even in these broader contexts, but precision declines significantly, particularly at lower similarity thresholds, due to the algorithm's inclusion of irrelevant tables.

The impact of similarity thresholds further refines our understanding of TabMine's performance. At the highest threshold of 90%, the results are extremely limited, with successful matches identified only for the *sales order* document in the foundational and sales table set. The restrictive nature of this threshold excludes many potentially relevant tables, demonstrating that a very high similarity requirement may not be practical for most use cases. Performance tends to improve as the threshold decreases to 85% and below, especially for document-specific tables. For instance, *sales orders* achieve perfect recall (R = 1.0000) and a precision of 0.6667, reflecting a strong balance between relevance and accuracy. Similarly, recall remains consistently high at 80% and 75% across all document types and table sets, but precision progressively declines. This is particularly noticeable for broader table sets, where the algorithm struggles to filter out irrelevant tables.

Certain document types also interact uniquely with these table sets and thresholds. *Sales order*, for instance, tends to achieve relatively higher precision even at lower thresholds, suggesting that these documents may have distinct patterns or table descriptions that facilitate more accurate identification. In contrast, documents like *credit notes* show lower precision in broader table sets, possibly due to their less distinctive characteristics making it harder for the algorithm to differentiate relevant tables from irrelevant ones.

5 Discussion

The evaluation of `TabMine` reveals both strengths and limitations in identifying relevant tables across various documents, table sets, and similarity thresholds. On curated, document-specific sets, `TabMine` performs robustly, achieving high precision and recall at thresholds between 75% and 85%. This suggests strong effectiveness in narrow, well-defined contexts, making it suitable for accuracy-critical applications. However, in broader settings with more irrelevant tables, its precision deteriorates due to increased false positives, even as recall remains stable.

`TabMine`'s performance deteriorates when applied to broader table sets, such as those that integrate unrelated modules (e.g., manufacturing or foundational tables). In these cases, precision declines significantly due to increased false positives, although recall remains relatively stable. This trade-off highlights the challenges posed by more extensive sets of tables on one hand and underscores the importance of careful threshold selection on the other hand.

While lowering the similarity threshold can improve recall, it also increases the risk of irrelevant matches, requiring a balance, tailored to specific use cases. For instance, as the similarity threshold increases (e.g., 90%), the algorithm becomes, on average, overly restrictive, excluding many potentially relevant tables. This suggests that overly stringent thresholds can hinder its ability to capture meaningful relationships between tables and documents, reducing its utility in certain scenarios.

Several avenues could improve `TabMine`'s performance. First, inconsistencies in table description quality and preprocessing impact similarity results. Defining and enforcing minimal standards for descriptions could enhance robustness. Second, embedding and label generation via LLMs introduce variability. Reusing embeddings and standardizing labels (e.g., via templates) may improve consistency and reproducibility.

Handling non-transactional tables remains critical. Master data tables often interfere with relevant detection, especially in large datasets. This challenge becomes most acute when evaluating table sets across various business domains, such as the inclusion of manufacturing tables. Filtering such tables while retaining essential data appears necessary for the next version of `TabMine`.

We also observed that the algorithm's performance varies across document types, with certain documents, such as sales orders, achieving relatively higher precision even in broader contexts. This variability suggests that some documents have inherently more distinctive table patterns or descriptions, facilitating better identification. This insight could be used to design targeted optimizations, such as custom similarity thresholds or specialized preprocessing techniques, tailored to specific business documents to enhance their identification accuracy.

Community detection is used to group structurally connected tables and reduce the search space for relevant ones, as business documents often span multiple related tables. This approach assumes that foreign key relationships effectively capture table interdependencies. However, foreign key relationships reflect structural dependencies rather than document semantics and could result in potential mismatches. As a result, some relevant tables may be excluded, while unrelated ones may be included. While we incorporate semantic similarity and embeddings to enhance table relevance identification, further refinement is needed to improve alignment with business document structures. Future work could explore integrating additional domain-specific heuristics or alternative grouping strategies to enhance the accuracy of table selection.

6 Conclusion

This study introduces `TabMine`, an algorithm designed to streamline the identification of database tables associated with business documents, serving as a foundation for building event logs used in process mining. By combining database structures and table descriptions, `TabMine` presents a list of possibly relevant database tables per business document of interest to the process analyst, reducing reliance on prior knowledge of database schemas or process models. This approach enables process analysts to move towards independently extracting the required data without needing extensive input from IS experts. This enhances efficiency in process mining projects and expands the applicability of process mining across diverse domains. First evaluations in terms of `TabMine`'s functioning and sensitivity towards a critical parameter provide evidence that the current algorithm is a good baseline to continue further development. It succeeds in identifying the relevant tables in a setting without too much noise and aspects to further fine-tune the algorithm have been identified.

Future research can build on this foundation in several ways. First, a more comprehensive evaluation of `TabMine` can involve experimenting with various configurations, including adjusting similarity thresholds, similarity weights, and community detection techniques. The impact of preprocessing table descriptions—such as lemmatization and stopword removal—also needs to be assessed. Second, methods to exclude non-transaction tables from the analysis need to be explored. Third, `TabMine`'s current scope could be extended by identifying relevant timestamp fields, as they are crucial for defining activities and establishing temporal order in event logs. Finally, advanced techniques, such as fine-tuning LLMs and using retrieval-augmented generation (RAG) models, can be tested to enhance the accuracy and scalability of the algorithm. These avenues aim to refine the approach, increase its scalability, and broaden its utility across complex datasets.

References

1. van der Aalst, W.M.P: Process discovery: capturing the invisible. IEEE Comput. Intell. Mag. **5**(1), 28–41 (2010)
2. van der Aalst, W.M.P.: Process mining: a 360 degree overview. In: Process Mining Handbook, pp. 373–401. LNBIP. Springer (2022). https://doi.org/10.1007/978-3-031-08848-3_1
3. Blondel, V.D., Guillaume, J.L., Lambiotte, R., Lefebvre, E.: Fast unfolding of communities in large networks. J. Stat. Mech. Theory Exp. **2008**(10), P10008 (2008). https://doi.org/10.1088/1742-5468/2008/10/P10008
4. Calvanese, D., Jans, M., Kalayci, T.E., Montali, M.: Extracting event data from document-driven enterprise systems. In: Indulska, M., Reinhartz-Berger, I., Cetina, C., Pastor, O. (eds.) Advanced Information Systems Engineering, pp. 193–209. Springer, Cham (2023). https://doi.org/10.1007/978-3-031-34560-9_12
5. Calvanese, D., Kalayci, T.E., Montali, M., Tinella, S.: Ontology-based data access for extracting event logs from legacy data: the onprom tool and methodology. In: Abramowicz, W. (ed.) Business Information Systems, pp. 220–236. LNBIP. Springer, Cham (2017). https://doi.org/10.1007/978-3-319-59336-4_16
6. De Boom, C., Van Canneyt, S., Bohez, S., Demeester, T., Dhoedt, B.: Learning semantic similarity for very short texts. In: 2015 IEEE International Conference on Data Mining Workshop (ICDMW), pp. 1229–1234 (2015). https://doi.org/10.1109/ICDMW.2015.86. iSSN 2375-9259
7. Diba, K., Batoulis, K., Weidlich, M., Weske, M.: Extraction, correlation, and abstraction of event data for process mining. WIREs Data Min. Knowl. Discovery **10**(3), e1346 (2020). https://doi.org/10.1002/widm.1346
8. van Eck, M.L., Lu, X., Leemans, S., van der Aalst, W.M.P: PM^2: a process mining project methodology. In: Zdravkovic, J., Kirikova, M., Johannesson, P. (eds.) CAiSE 2015. LNCS, vol. 9097, pp. 297–313. Springer, Cham (2015). https://doi.org/10.1007/978-3-319-19069-3_19
9. González López de Murillas, E., Reijers, H.A., van der Aalst, W.M.P.: Connecting databases with process mining: a meta model and toolset. Softw. Syst. Model. **18**(2), 1209–1247 (2019). https://doi.org/10.1007/s10270-018-0664-7
10. Jans, M., Soffer, P., Jouck, T.: Building a valuable event log for process mining: an experimental exploration of a guided process. Enterp. Inf. Syst. **13**(5), 601–630 (2019)
11. Leskovec, J., Lang, K.J., Mahoney, M.: Empirical comparison of algorithms for network community detection. In: Proceedings of the 19th International Conference on World wide web, WWW 2010, pp. 631–640. Association for Computing Machinery, New York (2010). https://doi.org/10.1145/1772690.1772755
12. Li, G., González López de Murillas, E., de Carvalho, R.M., van der Aalst, W.M.P.: Extracting object-centric event logs to support process mining on databases. In: Mendling, J., Mouratidis, H. (eds.) CAiSE 2018. LNBIP, vol. 317, pp. 182–199. Springer, Cham (2018). https://doi.org/10.1007/978-3-319-92901-9_16
13. Li, J., Wang, H.J., Bai, X.: An intelligent approach to data extraction and task identification for process mining. Inf. Syst. Front. **17**(6), 1195–1208 (2015). https://doi.org/10.1007/s10796-015-9564-3
14. Ma, Y., Shen, X., Wu, Y., Zhang, B., Backes, M., Zhang, Y.: The death and life of great prompts: analyzing the evolution of LLM prompts from the structural perspective. In: Al-Onaizan, Y., Bansal, M., Chen, Y.N. (eds.) Proceedings of the 2024 Conference on Empirical Methods in Natural Language Processing, Miami,

Florida, USA, pp. 21990–22001. Association for Computational Linguistics (2024). https://aclanthology.org/2024.emnlp-main.1227
15. Mamudu, A., Bandara, W., Wynn, M.T., Leemans, S.J.J.: A process mining success factors model. In: Di Ciccio, C., Dijkman, R., del Río Ortega, A., Rinderle-Ma, S. (eds.) Business Process Management, pp. 143–160. Springer, Cham (2022). https://doi.org/10.1007/978-3-031-16103-2_12
16. Shu, P., Tang, M., Gong, K., Liu, Y.: Effects of weak ties on epidemic predictability on community networks. Chaos Interdisc. J. Nonlinear Sci. **22**(4), 043124 (2012). https://doi.org/10.1063/1.4767955
17. Stein Dani, V., et al.: Towards understanding the role of the human in event log extraction. In: Marrella, A., Weber, B. (eds.) Business Process Management Workshops. LNBIP, pp. 86–98. Springer, Cham (2022). https://doi.org/10.1007/978-3-030-94343-1_7
18. Stein Dani, V., Leopold, H., van der Werf, J.M.E., Reijers, H.A.: Supporting event log extraction based on matching. In: International Conference on Business Process Management, pp. 322–333. Springer, Cham (2022)

OCPM²: Extending the Process Mining Methodology for Object-Centric Event Data Extraction

Najmeh Miri[1(✉)], Shahrzad Khayatbashi[2], Jelena Zdravkovic[1], and Amin Jalali[1]

[1] Stockholm University, Stockholm, Sweden
{najmeh.miri,jelenaz,aj}@dsv.su.se
[2] Linköping University, Linköping, Sweden
shahrzad.khayatbashi@liu.se

Abstract. Object-Centric Process Mining (OCPM) enables business process analysis from multiple perspectives. For example, an educational path can be examined from the viewpoints of students, teachers, and groups. This analysis depends on Object-Centric Event Data (OCED), which captures relationships between events and object types, representing different perspectives. Unlike traditional process mining techniques, extracting OCED minimizes the need for repeated log extractions when shifting the analytical focus. However, recording these complex relationships increases the complexity of the log extraction process. To address this challenge, this paper proposes a methodology for extracting OCED based on PM², a well-established process mining framework. Our approach introduces a structured framework that guides data analysts and engineers in extracting OCED for process analysis. We validate this framework by applying it in a real-world educational setting, demonstrating its effectiveness in extracting an Object-Centric Event Log (OCEL), which serves as the standard format for recording OCED, from a learning management system and an administrative grading system.

Keywords: Object-Centric Process Mining · Methodology · Log Extraction

1 Introduction

Object-Centric Process Mining (OCPM) is a data-driven approach that enables multi-perspective process analysis, allowing for a more comprehensive understanding of complex workflows [1,22]. Unlike traditional process mining techniques that focus on a single perspective - such as analyzing the learning process from the student perspective alone - OCPM considers multiple object types simultaneously, revealing hidden dependencies and bottlenecks that might remain undetected when examining processes from a singular viewpoint [20]. For example, in an educational setting, the learning process can be analyzed not only from the perspective of students but also from that of teachers and course groups, enabling insights into instructor-student interactions, group-based collaboration, and administrative workflows.

To apply OCPM in practice, Object-Centric Event Data (OCED) [7] must be extracted to capture events in relation to multiple object types. In an educational setting, typical object types include students, teachers, and groups, each of which plays a distinct role in the learning process. Unlike traditional event logs, OCED reduces the need for repeated log extraction when shifting between analytical perspectives. Several formats exist for representing OCED, including the Object-Centric Event Log (OCEL) [1], Data-Aware Object-Centric Event Logs (DOCEL) [9], Event Knowledge Graph (EKG) [6], and Temporal Event Knowledge Graph (tEKG) [12], which can be transformed into one another [11,12]. However, extracting OCED from operational systems remains inherently complex, as it requires capturing relationships between events and all possible object types while ensuring proper data integration.

Despite recent advancements, OCED extraction from information systems continues to pose significant challenges, necessitating new methods and guidelines to support researchers and practitioners. While prior studies [2,3,24] have addressed specific challenges in OCED extraction, existing solutions are often system- or platform- dependent, tailored to particular environments such as OnProm [24] or designed for extracting logs from Enterprise Resource Planning (ERP) systems [2,3].

To bridge this gap, this study proposes a structured and system-agnostic framework for OCED extraction, addressing the complexities associated with capturing multi-perspective event data. Our approach extends PM^2 [23], a well-established process mining framework, offering a systematic framework to support data analysts and engineers in extracting event logs for process analysis. To demonstrate its practical applicability, we applied our framework in the educational domain, extracting OCEL from a learning management system and an administrative grading system. This enables the simultaneous analysis of educational paths from both the group and student perspectives, allowing for a deeper understanding of learning dynamics and collaborative processes.

The remainder of this paper is structured as follows. Section 2 elaborates on previous process mining methodologies, provides an overview of two primary OCED formats, and summarizes existing object-centric event data extraction approaches. Section 3 presents our OCED extraction method. Section 4 details the application of our method for extracting OCEL from learning management systems. Finally, Sect. 5 concludes the paper.

2 Background

This section provides an overview of existing process mining methodologies and peer-reviewed approaches for object-centric event data (OCED) extraction. In addition, it explores two primary approaches for representing OCED.

2.1 Process Mining Methodologies

Process Diagnostics Method (PDM) [4], the L* Life-Cycle Model [5], and PM^2 [23] are three well-known process mining methodologies followed by different people to apply process mining in practice. The Process Diagnostics Method (PDM) [4] focuses on rapid, high-level analysis of business processes without requiring domain-specific knowledge. It examines control flow, performance, and organizational aspects based on event logs, providing quick insights. However, PDM lacks explicit iterative refinement of the analysis [23], and is less suitable for long-term process optimization efforts [4].

In contrast, the L* Life-Cycle Model [5] follows a structured, stepwise approach that includes planning and justification, event log extraction, process model discovery, integration, and operational support. It defines three distinct project approaches: goal-driven (focusing on achieving predefined objectives), question-driven (addressing specific business queries), and data-driven (exploring available data for insights). However, this methodology is effective solely for structured processes where a single integrated process model can be developed.

To overcome the limitations of both PDM and L*, PM^2 [23] introduces an iterative process mining methodology that incorporates stakeholder involvement and a structured roadmap for continuous process improvement. Unlike L*, which primarily targets structured processes, PM^2 accommodates both structured and unstructured processes, allowing for evolving business-related questions and iterative refinements.

The PM^2 methodology consists of six key *stages* [23]: (i) *Planning*, which involves defining project goals, such as performance improvement or compliance verification, formulating research questions (we refer to as business-related questions throughout the paper), and identifying relevant business processes. This stage also involves assembling a multidisciplinary project team, including business experts, system specialists, process analysts, and business owners; (ii) *Extraction*, where event data is collected from information systems, considering data quality, scope, and process knowledge transfer; (iii) *Data Processing*, which prepares event logs by defining case notions, filtering, aggregating, and enriching event data; (iv) *Mining and Analysis*, where process discovery, conformance checking, and performance enhancement techniques are applied; (v) *Evaluation*, which includes interpreting analysis results, validating insights with domain experts, and refining business-related questions; and (vi) *Process Improvement and Support*, where process changes are implemented, or operational support is provided based on the findings.

These methodologies offer structured approaches for applying process mining in practice and are well-suited for extracting traditional event logs from source systems. However, extracting OCED presents additional complexities due to the involvement of multiple object types, each requiring the capture of different events. As a result, analysts can easily overlook some necessary relationships, leading to repeated data extraction. This redundancy creates bottlenecks in the log extraction process. To address this challenge, we extend PM^2 to enhance the efficiency of OCED extraction. Before introducing our approach in the next section, the following subsections provide an overview of OCED formats and discuss existing methodologies for OCED extraction.

2.2 Brief Overview of OCED

Object-Centric Event Data (OCED) provides a richer, more realistic representation of process event data by capturing multiple objects, their relationships, and interactions. Unlike traditional event logs, which focus on a single case notion (e.g., an order or a customer), OCED captures the relationships between different entities related to events. Figure 1 presents two metamodels for storing OCED: Object-Centric Event Logs (OCEL 2.0) [1] and Event Knowledge Graphs (EKG) [6].

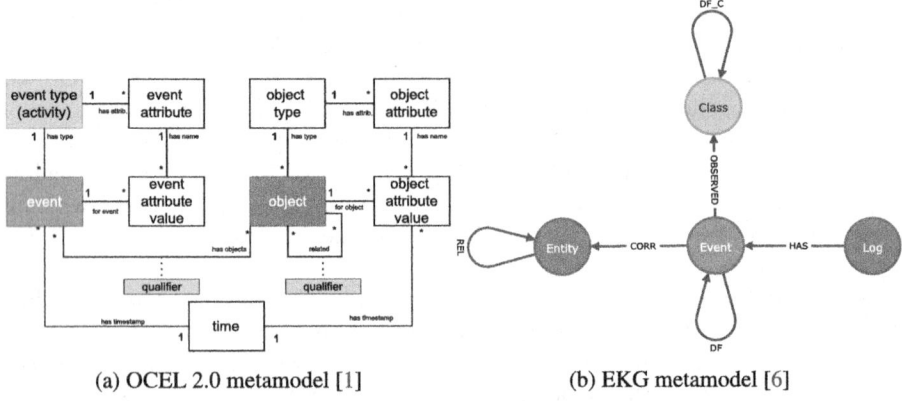

(a) OCEL 2.0 metamodel [1]   (b) EKG metamodel [6]

Fig. 1. Two metamodels for storing OCED

The OCEL 2.0 metamodel, shown on the left side of Fig. 1, defines an *event* as an atomic action that occurs in a business process, representing the execution of an *event type* (a.k.a, an *activity*), such as "place order" in Order-to-Cash process. Each event type can have multiple *event attributes*, and each event can store different *event attribute values*. OCEL records *objects* as separate entities, where each object belongs to an *object type*. For example, the "order" can be an object type with multiple instances representing different orders. Each object type can have multiple object attributes, and each object can store different values for these attributes at specific points in time. Objects can also be related to other objects through *object-to-object* relations; for example, an order can contain multiple items. As illustrated in the metamodel, events can be associated with multiple objects and vice versa through *event-to-object* relations.

EKG, on the right side of the figure, provides an alternative approach for capturing OCED by representing events, entities, logs, and classes as nodes with specific relationships among them. Events and classes in EKG correspond to events and event types in OCEL, respectively. Entities in EKG represent objects, with object types stored as a property of the entity node called *EntityType*. Object-to-object relations are captured as edges between entity nodes labeled *REL*, while event-to-object relations are represented as edges between event and entity nodes labeled *CORR*.

There are more variations capturing OCED data like temporal EKG [12], which improves EKGs by tracking how object attributes change over time so events can be analyzed using the correct object information at each point in time, and Data-aware Object-Centric Event Logs (DOCEL) [9], which extends OCEL by tracking attribute changes over time, linking attributes to objects and events, and allowing attributes to have multiple values.

2.3 OCED Extraction Initiatives

Several approaches have been developed to extract OCED from information systems, particularly Enterprise Resource Planning (ERP) systems. Here, we exclude methods that focus solely on transforming OCED formats from other formats or traditional event logs since this study focuses on proposing a method for OCED extraction directly from information systems.

Berti et al. proposed a method for extracting event data from SAP ERP systems using OCEL [3]. Their approach begins by constructing a Graph of Relations (GoR) to map relevant business process tables. Once these tables are mapped, data are extracted and stored in the OCEL format. To streamline this process, they developed a Python-based tool that identifies relevant tables and their relationships. The extracted data can subsequently be used for OCPM or converted into traditional event logs.

Building on this approach, Berti et al. conducted a case study focusing on the Purchase-to-Pay (P2P) process [2]. Similar to their previous work [3], this study employed graph-based techniques to model relationships within SAP's complex data structures. The methodology utilized an object interaction graph to visualize object relationships and applied the PM^2 framework to structure the extraction and analysis process within a well-defined methodological context.

Beyond SAP-specific solutions, Xiong et al. introduced a method for extracting OCEL from relational databases using a Virtual Knowledge Graph (VKG) approach [24]. Their method extended the OnProm framework to support both OCEL and the traditional XES format. By leveraging ontology-based data access (OBDA) and the VKG system Ontop, they defined domain ontologies and mappings, enabling event log extraction via SPARQL queries. Their approach was validated using the Dolibarr ERP system, demonstrating how relational data can be transformed into structured OCELs.

Unlike these system-specific approaches, this paper presents a generalized framework for OCED extraction that is adaptable across various information sources. Our methodology ensures broader applicability and ease of implementation across different systems by providing a step-by-step process that does not rely on platform-dependent techniques.

3 The OCPM² Methodology

This section introduces OCPM², an Object-Centric Process Mining Methodology defined as an extension of PM² [23] to facilitate the extraction of Object-Centric Event Data (OCED) [7]. We define our method by extending PM² to ensure the reuse of a well-established and previously tested methodology for event log extraction, originally designed for traditional process mining. Our approach retains the clarity and efficiency of PM² while making it suitable for extracting object-centric event data from diverse information systems. We also presented our methodology to 12 domain experts in a workshop, which helped us further confirm the OCPM² validity.

The methodology consists of twelve stages, where the related stages are grouped into phases, as indicated by dashed rectangles in Fig. 2. The process begins with the *Planning* stage, followed by the *Domain Modeling*, *Log Extraction*, and *Analysis Iteration* phases, and concludes with the *Process Improvement & Support* stage. Each stage produces specific artifacts, as outlined in the figure. The following sections elaborate on these stages, the generated artifacts, and the defined phases. The filled blue colored phases and stages are identical to those in the PM² methodology briefly described in Sect. 2 (we refer readers to the PM² [23] for further details).

3.1 Planning

The *Planning* stage follows PM², producing the following key artifacts: i) prioritized business-related questions (denoted by [?] in the Fig. 2), ii) a list of information systems ([IS]) from which data will be extracted to answer these questions. The minor difference from PM² is that the questions are prioritized, allowing for prioritizing the object type extraction later.

3.2 Domain Modeling

The *Domain Modeling* phase consists of five stages (stages 2 to 6 in Fig. 2), identifying and conceptualizing the information needed for the extraction of OCED. As OCED involves multiple object types, a domain model can act as a foundation to facilitate identifying the involved object types, their relations, activities, and the relations between object types and events. This information can be gathered through interviews with business experts, reviewing system documentation, and analyzing the underlying database schema. Without this foundation, the extraction process may result in an incomplete OCED.

The phase begins with *Object Type Identification* to determine all object types needed to address the questions elicited in the *Planing*. Because an object type may be required for multiple questions, we propose documenting this using a Question-to-Object Type Matrix (Q2OT), inspired from the bus matrix which is a widely used technique in identifying dimensions and related processes in data warehousing [16]. This matrix represents questions as rows and object types as

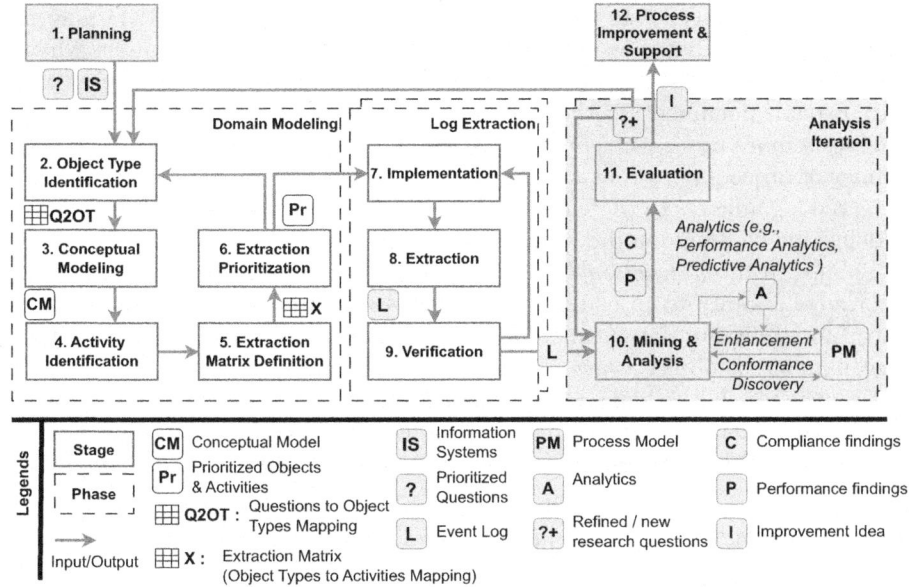

Fig. 2. An overview of the OCPM² methodology extending the PM² methodology [23]

columns, marking intersection cells to indicate the required object types for each question.

Next, in the *Conceptual Modeling* stage, process analysts and business experts collaborate to define a model (CM) that captures the relationships between object types. Business experts provide domain knowledge, while process analysts structure this information using a conceptual modeling language to represent key relationships. Among these, recognizing the "is-a" relationship- where one object type is a specialized version of another (e.g., Student is a User)- enables capturing OLAP operations such as drill-down and roll-up in OCPM based on OCEL [13,17].

The *Activity Identification* stage follows, eliciting different activities (or event types) to which the identified object types and questions are related. These activities can be identified in various ways, such as analyzing activities directly related to the formulated questions, reviewing system documentation, and consulting business experts.

The *Extraction Matrix Definition* stage defines the extraction matrix (X), where the relationships between object types and activities are documented. When an "is-a" relationship exists among object types, separate columns can specify whether an activity relates to the supertype class or a subtype class. Various documentation approaches can be adapted based on specific perspectives. From a system perspective, CRUD (Create, Read, Update, and Delete) operations are suitable for specifying the type of relationship between an activity and an object type. However, from a process perspective, CRUD may not fully capture the dynamic nature of object interactions. For example, when a user views a module such as File, CRUD cannot document the role of user properly. Instead, documenting the quantity range of objects for each object type provides a more process-oriented approach. This method captures the expected number of objects per event and supports data validation by ensuring that the extracted log adheres to these expectations. The details of these adaptations can be delegated to design and development teams.

Finally, in the *Extraction Prioritization* stage, business, process, and system experts collaborate to prioritize the extraction of objects and events based on their i) feasibility, ii) data availability, and iii) importance. Given the potentially large number of object types and activities, extracting all data at once may not be feasible due to data being fragmented across multiple sources and the need to check data quality step-by-step to catch errors early. To manage this, we propose a prioritization artifact as the output of this stage, including a set of prioritized objects and activities ($\boxed{Pr}$). Note that new object types can be identified during this phase, requiring the phase to be repeated to have a more holistic understanding of the domain.

3.3 Log Extraction

The *Log Extraction* phase in OCPM^2 consists of three stages (Stages 7 to 9 in Fig. 2) as follows:

In the *Implementation* stage, developers build pipelines to extract data from source systems, transform them into the desired OCED format, and load them into destination storage. If OCEL is the target format, objects should be processed first based on their list in the extraction matrix. When an "is-a" relationship exists among object types, we propose storing objects at the supertype level with an attribute distinguishing subtypes. This structure follows the single-table inheritance technique used in Object-Relational Mapping (ORM) [8]. This ensures referential integrity and facilitates efficient querying and aggregation, allowing drill-down operations [13,14]. Subsequently, developers implement extraction logic for object-to-object relationships, determined by the conceptual model (stage 3), in parallel with implementing extraction logic for events based on the extraction matrix. Once event extraction is complete, they implement extraction logic for event-to-object relationships. Please note that similar mapping can be done for EKG [6] and tEKG [11] as the OCED formats are transformable to each other.

The *Extraction* stage is separated from *Implementation* because it enables the development of data pipelines to extract, clean, and integrate data for process mining as well as testing the result before final extraction in a production environment.

In the *Verification* stage, correctness can automatically be checked by deriving a matrix from the extracted event data. This matrix shows the number of object types for each event type, ensuring that documented relationships in the Extraction Matrix are properly implemented.

Although the log extraction process has been adapted to extract OCED, the remaining stages remain identical to PM^2 [23] since the types of applicable process mining techniques are not based on analyzing case-centric or object-centric event logs. However, these phases may include new process mining techniques in the future as the area develops further. Additionally, one can reduce the dimensionality of OCED by converting the log to the traditional format by correlating events to only one object type, a.k.a. flattening, to enable the use of traditional process discovery techniques. The flattening can also help filter the log by identifying similar object type clusters in OCEL [10], meaning that process mining techniques can be applied to a range of case-based and object-centric event logs.

3.4 Analysis Iteration

The *Analysis Iteration* phase in PM^2 supports gaining insights from extracted event data through two stages: *Mining & Analysis* and *Evaluation*. The *Mining & Analysis* stage includes process model discovery (PM) from the input log (L), conformance checking, and process enhancement based on analytical insights (A) resulting from various analytical techniques, such as performance, and predictive analysis [21]. This can yield compliance findings (C) and performance findings (P). The *Evaluation* stage results in process improvement ideas (I) or refined/new process-related questions (?+), which may prompt further analysis or new data extraction.

3.5 Process Improvement and Support

The *Process Improvement & Support* stage applies the insights from process analysis to optimize workflows and enhance performance. It involves defining strategies, supporting implementation, and monitoring changes.

4 Case Study

This section presents the application of the OCPM^2 methodology in a process mining project conducted at the Department of Computer and Systems Sciences, Stockholm University. We elaborate on each stage and phase below. In addition, the second and last authors conducted a separate feasibility study demonstrating the applicability of this methodology in a real-world case from the insurance domain [15].

4.1 Planning

This project was initiated to explore how process mining can provide teachers with data-driven insights crucial for improving their educational content and tasks' efficiency. To determine the most important questions and their relative significance, we conducted interviews with 10 teachers. The interviews were recorded, transcribed, anonymized, and analyzed to extract key questions and assess their perceived importance. The outcome of this stage consisted of two artifacts: a set of prioritized questions compiled from the interviews (?) and a list of relevant information systems (IS). The four most important questions identified were:

- Q1: What learning paths do students typically follow when accessing educational materials, such as files, pages, and folders, throughout a course?
- Q2: How do students submit (or resubmit) individual and group assignments during the course?
- Q3: Do students who usually take the lead in submitting group assignments on behalf of the group tend to achieve higher final grades (exam and assignment grades)?
- Q4: How is students' exam success related to their frequency of accessing course materials, such as files, pages, and folders?

Students often follow different routes when accessing educational materials, influencing their engagement and performance. Thus, analyzing students' learning paths (Q1) provides insights into how these behaviors influence the outcomes while also identifying the challenging areas that affect their success [19]. Examining assignment submission patterns (Q2) helps to assess student engagement and identify potential challenges in meeting deadlines. Furthermore, analyzing whether high-achieving students demonstrate different behaviors, such as taking the lead in submitting group assignments (Q3), provides insights into collaborative learning strategies, such as encouraging role rotation. Finally, analyzing the relationship between course material access and exam performance (Q4) can help educators identify patterns that distinguish successful students from those who struggle.

Although we identified numerous questions to guide the project, we present only a subset here to illustrate the application of the methodology. The information systems identified at this stage included 1) the learning management system, Moodle [18], and 2) the platform that records students' grades.

4.2 Domain Modeling

Object Type Identification: From the questions above, we identified the following object types: *Student, File, Page, Folder, Assignment, Group, Course,* and *Exam*. These object types were identified by extracting key nouns from the questions that belong to the domain vocabulary. These object types model the domain of interest. Table 1 presents the Question-to-Object Type matrix (Q2OT), derived from the previous stage.

Table 1. Question-to-Object Type matrix supporting object type identification

	Student	File	Page	Folder	Assignment	Group	Course	Exam
Q1	*	*	*	*			*	
Q2	*				*		*	*
Q3	*				*	*	*	*
Q4	*	*	*	*			*	*

Conceptual Modeling: Figure 3 presents the conceptual model using UML notation, a de facto modeling standard widely used in the industry, illustrating the relationships between object types. Nonetheless, the methodology is modeling-language agnostic, and equivalent results can be achieved with alternative notations. This model was developed following the conceptual modeling process described in Sect. 3.2, based on stakeholder input, system documentation, and database schema analysis. The model includes additional object types beyond those represented in the Q2OT matrix, reflecting the iterative nature of our approach. For example, the object type *Teacher* was later identified by reviewing the Moodle documentation as a relevant entity within the process. Additionally, *User* was introduced as a supertype encompassing both *Teacher* and *Student* as explained in Sect. 2.

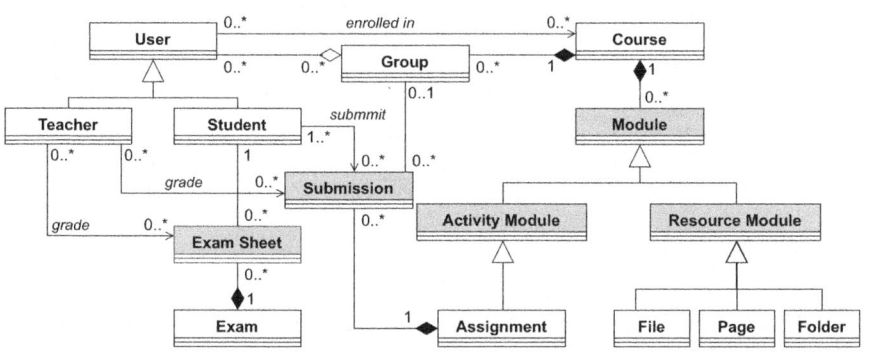

Fig. 3. The conceptual model illustrating object type relationships

Design choices also influence object type identification. For instance, *Grade* was modeled as an attribute of both *Submission* and *Exam Sheet*, though an alternative approach could define it as a separate class. The model also includes grayed-out classes, such as *Exam Sheet, Submission, Module, Activity Module,* and *Resource Module*. While some of these could be considered object types, their selection depends on modeling design choices. For example, *Exam* and *Assignment* are tightly related to *Exam Sheet* and *Submission*, respectively, due to the decomposition relation nature. Thus, we have not considered defining separate object types for *Exam Sheet* and *Submission*, which are parts of *Exam* and *Assignment*.

Activity Identification: Activities were directly identifiable from the questions by examining the leading tasks (verbs) in the questions. For example, *view file*, *view page*, and *view folder* were relevant for Q1, while *submit assignment* and *resubmit assignment* addressed Q2. Similarly, *set assignment grade*, *set exam grade*, and *submit assignment* were relevant for Q3. In addition, *set exam grade*, *view file*, *view folder*, and *view page* were relevant for Q4.

Extraction Matrix Definition: Table 2 documents relationships between identified activities and object types. In this version, we recorded the possible number of instances for each object type within the table's cells. To provide more detailed documentation, we included *User*, the supertype of *Teacher* and *Student*, as a separate column.

Table 2. The extraction matrix

	User			Exam	File	Page	Folder	Assignment	Group	Course
	User	Teacher	Student							
view file	1				1					1
view page	1					1				1
view folder	1						1			1
submit assignment			1		0..*			1	0..1	1
resubmit assignment			1		0..*			1	0..1	1
set assignment grade		1	1		0..*			1	0..1	1
set exam grade		1	1..*	1						1

Extraction Prioritization: In our study, *Assignment* was prioritized highest, followed by *File*, based on teachers' feedback, as it was the primary means of assessing student progress throughout the course before the final exam, and File was mainly used for uploading educational materials to support learning. Extraction was planned accordingly in the following sequence: *submit assignment, resubmit assignment, set assignment grade, view file, view page, view folder*, and *set exam grade*. Ultimately, we implemented all the extractions so their order does not affect the final result.

4.3 Log Extraction

Implementation: We set up development and test environments to build and validate pipelines using Python that extracted relevant data objects and events, according to the extraction matrix, from Moodle's relational database. We then transformed the extracted data into OCEL format. When transforming data into OCEL, we defined *User* as a single object type, with *Teacher* and *Student* modeled as subclasses. This approach facilitated the discovery of process models at a general level while enabling drill-down analyses to distinguish teacher- and student-specific process behaviors.

Extraction: Data extraction was performed on a single course over one year. This timeframe provided a comprehensive dataset of interactions between students, teachers, and learning materials while ensuring manageability. By focusing on one course, we captured the full lifecycle of learning activities, including assignments, submissions, grading, and resource interactions.

Verification: We developed a script to systematically verify the accuracy of the extracted event data by mapping activities to object types. The resulting dataset contained 8 object types and 607 objects, linked through 7 event types and a total of 20,100 events, as shown in Fig. 4. Since the data stems from a single course, all events are associated with this course, meaning the course column aggregates the total number of events.

Figure 4 presents this structured validation process. In this figure, the expected relationship between *Group* and *set assignment grade* is missing. This discrepancy arises because Moodle logs a separate *set assignment grade* event for each student, even when a teacher grades a group assignment collectively. Automated verification helped identify such inconsistencies, highlighting areas for improvement in future log extractions by developers. Furthermore, the relationship between *Teacher* and *Student* is not directly visible because the types of objects were recorded at the *User* level. However, drill-down analysis can reveal these relationships as needed.

In this paper, we have presented only a subset of the case study conducted to demonstrate the application of our proposed methodology. Our full study included additional questions, object types, and events, during which we encountered further challenges in the extraction of OCEL, including the lack of recorded historical temporal data and instances of incomplete data capture.

An example of such challenges is the lack of recording historical temporal data in Moodle for module sections. Moodle only captures the current section for each module, so if a module like a File has been moved, the previous section will not be recorded in the extracted OCEL. We excluded presenting the section in this paper because it was outside the scope of the questions we selected for demonstration.

Another challenge related to incomplete data capture occurs when modules, like File, are imported from one course into another. In these cases, Moodle does not accurately log the importing user's details, resulting in the user information for these imported modules being unspecified. This incomplete logging limits the completeness of the extracted OCEL.

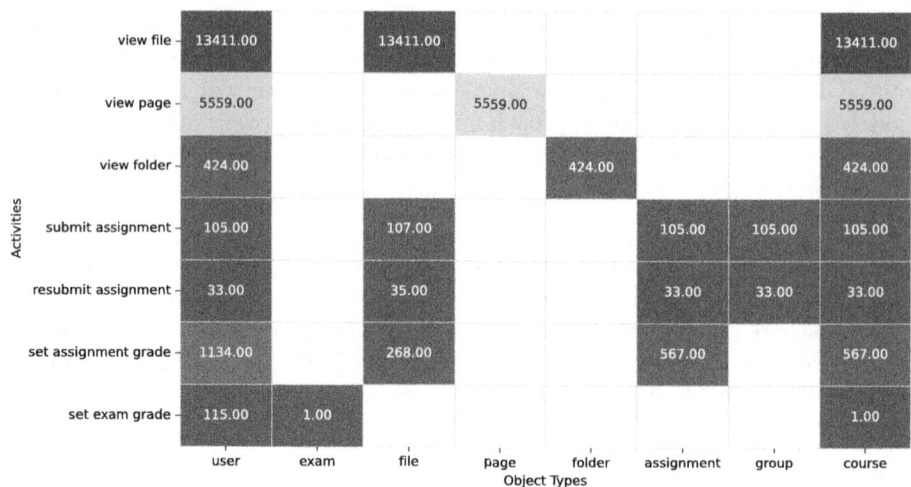

Fig. 4. The verification matrix

4.4 Analysis Iteration

We analyzed the extracted logs to answer the identified questions. The results were evaluated by the course responsible to ensure accuracy.

For Q1, Fig. 5 illustrates an Object-Centric Directly-Follows Graph (OC-DFG), discovered using the *PM4Py* library. This graph was generated by filtering the extracted log, drilling down page objects into individual page names, and unfolding *view page* events for each page using the *processmining* library [14]. The graph visualizes the sequential flow of actions during the course from the perspectives of the *User* and *Course* object types.

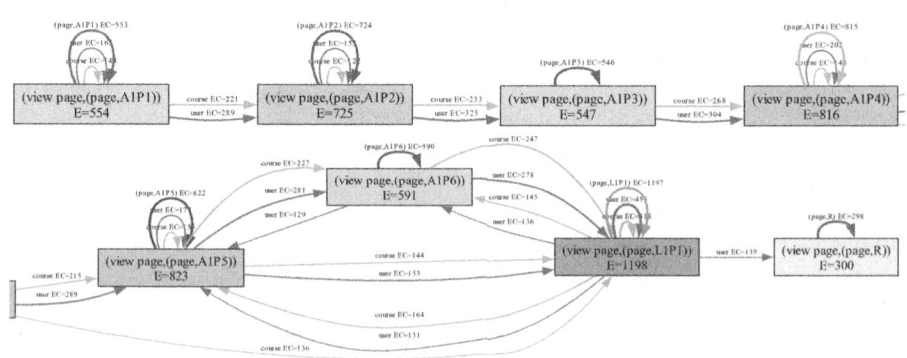

Fig. 5. Object-Centric Directly-Follows Graph (OC-DFG) illustrating how students visited some pages

In this process, the page names for given codes are as follows: *A1P1*: History of BPM, *A1P2*: Business Process Models, *A1P3*: Business Process Enactment, *A1P4*: Syntax and Semantics, *A1P5*: Control-flow Patterns, *A1P6*: Business Process Complexity, and *L1P1*: Introduction to Process Tree. The model reveals that students sequentially accessed five pages: *A1P1* to *A1P5*. Additionally, a loop between *A1P5*, *A1P6*, and *L1P1* suggests students frequently revisit these pages, indicating potential room for improvement.

As an example of an analysis related to Q2, we refer to Fig. 6, which presents an OC-DFG illustrating how individual and group assignments were submitted. The OC-DFG was discovered by filtering the log based on submission activities and events, drilling down user objects into user types (separating teachers and students) and assignments into their specific names (distinguishing different assignment object types). Additionally, the log was unfolded to include related events for these objects.

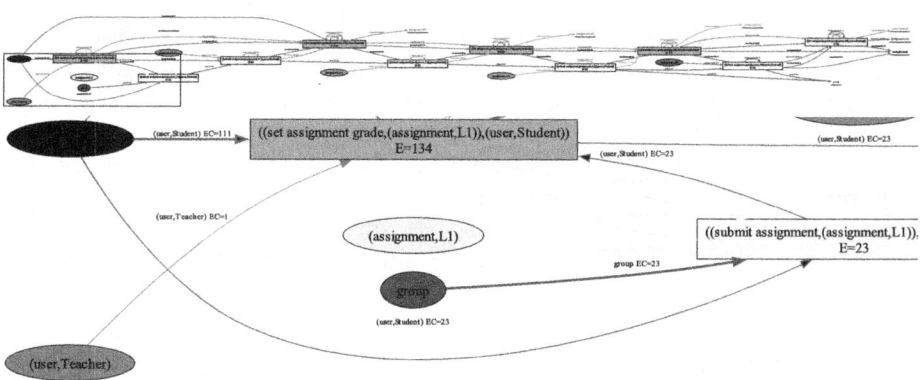

Fig. 6. OC-DFG illustrating the overall submission process for individual and group assignments in addition to a zoomed part

The upper part of the figure displays the entire process, and the lower part presents a zoomed-in version that crops the beginning of the process to enhance readability for further elaboration. The upper figure may not be easily readable (which is intentional, as we do not elaborate on details), but it effectively illustrates the sequential flow within the process. This sequence is influenced by the structured delivery of educational materials and the course setup.

In the lower part of the figure, we observe that 23 students submitted the assignment, as it was a group submission, where both the group and individual students were linked to the event. However, we also see that the grading process involved 134 students. This discrepancy highlights the issue discussed in the verification section regarding the lack of a direct relationship between *group* and *set assignment grade*.

4.5 Process Improvement and Support

Our analysis revealed that students frequently revisited pages related to control-flow perspectives, process complexity, and process trees, indicating possible challenges in comprehension or the sequence in which these topics are introduced. To address this, we propose shifting the process tree discussion to follow control-flow perspectives and introducing process complexity at the end. This adjustment may reduce unnecessary back-and-forth navigation, making the learning process more structured. Further investigation is needed to understand the underlying reasons for these recurring visits, providing insights that could help refine the course.

5 Conclusion

This paper introduced OCPM^2, an extension of the PM^2 methodology, designed to support Object-Centric Process Mining (OCPM) by providing a structured approach for Object-Centric Event Log (OCEL) extraction. Our methodology enhances existing process mining frameworks by addressing challenges associated with multi-object process modeling, ensuring compatibility with structured process analysis techniques.

By incorporating domain modeling, OCED extraction, and iterative process analysis phases, OCPM^2 provides a system-agnostic framework for object-centric process mining. The methodology reduces the complexity of extracting and analyzing multi-object event data, minimizing redundant log extraction efforts required for case-centric process mining.

To validate our approach, we applied OCPM^2 in an educational setting, extracting and analyzing OCELs from a learning management system and an administrative grading system, which cannot be shared due to privacy concerns. Our results demonstrated the practical usefulness of OCPM^2, i.e., its ability to effectively reveal student navigation patterns and assignment submission processes.

The case study exposed limitations in system logs, particularly in capturing accurate object-to-activity relationships. A key issue was the missing link between *Group* and *set assignment grade*, causing Moodle to log separate grading events per student, even for collectively graded assignments. This discrepancy resulted in a mismatch between the number of students who submitted the assignment and those involved in the grading process. Automated verification identified these inconsistencies, helping developers extract correct event logs in future extractions. Future research will focus on enhancing automated verification mechanisms, refining multi-dimensional process analysis operations, and expanding OCPM^2's applicability across other domains, such as healthcare and financial services. We also plan to develop a tool to support OCED extraction based on OCPM^2. This tool will enable organizations to document and manage OCED extraction for different projects.

References

1. Berti, A., et al.: OCEL (Object-Centric Event Log) 2.0 Specification (2023)
2. Berti, A., Jessen, U., Park, G., Rafiei, M., van der Aalst, W.M.: Analyzing interconnected processes: using object-centric process mining to analyze procurement processes. Int. J. Data Sci. Anal. **16**, 1–23 (2023)
3. Berti, A., Park, G., Rafiei, M., Aalst, W.: An event data extraction approach from SAP ERP for process mining, pp. 255–267 (2022)
4. Bozkaya, M., Gabriels, J., Van der Werf, J.M.: Process diagnostics: a method based on process mining, pp. 22–27 (2009)
5. Van der Aalst, W.M.P.: Process Mining. Discovery, conformance and enhancement of business processes. Media; Springer, Berlin/Heidelberg, Germany, vol. 136 (2011)
6. Esser, S., Fahland, D.: Multi-dimensional event data in graph databases. J. Data Semant. **10**(1), 109–141 (2021)
7. Fahland, D., et al.: Towards a simple and extensible standard for object-centric event data (OCED)–core model, design space, and lessons learned. arXiv:2410.14495 (2024)
8. Fowler, M.: Patterns of Enterprise Application Architecture. Addison-Wesley (2012)
9. Goossens, A., De Smedt, J., Vanthienen, J., van der Aalst, W.M.P.: Enhancing data-awareness of object-centric event logs. In: International Conference on Process Mining, pp. 18–30. Springer (2022)
10. Jalali, A.: Object type clustering using markov directly-follow multigraph in object-centric process mining. IEEE Access **10**, 126569–126579 (2022)
11. Khayatbashi, S., Hartig, O., Jalali, A.: Transforming event knowledge graph to object-centric event logs: a comparative study for multi-dimensional process analysis. In: International Conference on Conceptual Modeling, pp. 220–238. Springer (2023)
12. Khayatbashi, S., Hartig, O., Jalali, A.: Transforming object-centric event logs to temporal event knowledge graphs. In: International Conference on Business Process Management, pp. 300–313. Springer (2024)
13. Khayatbashi, S., Miri, N., Jalali, A.: Advancing object-centric process mining with multi-dimensional data operations. arXiv:2412.00393 (2024)
14. Khayatbashi, S., Miri, N., Jalali, A.: OLAP operations for object-centric process mining. In: Accpeted in CAiSE Forum 2025. Springer (2025)
15. Khayatbashi, S., , Anders Granåker, V., Jalali, A.: AI-enhanced business process automation: a case study in the insurance domain using object-centric process mining. arXiv:2504.17295 (2025). Accepted in BPMDS 2025
16. Kimball, R., Ross, M., Thornthwaite, W., Mundy, J., Becker, B.: The Data Warehouse Lifecycle Toolkit. John Wiley & Sons (2008)
17. Miri, N., Jalali, A.: Uncovering patterns in object-centric process mining: an approach using drill-down and roll-up techniques. In: Haghighi, P.D., Greguš, M., Kotsis, G., Khalil, I. (eds.) Information Integration and Web Intelligence, pp. 49–54. Springer Nature Switzerland, Cham (2025)
18. Moodle: Moodle Learning Management System, Version 4.4 (2024)
19. Real, E., Pimentel, E.: An educational process mining model on students' paths data from virtual learning environments. Technol. Knowl. Learn. (2025)

20. Tripathi, A., Aneesh, Shivam, Y., Pandey, S., Vyas, A., Vyas, O.P.: Exploring object centric process mining with MIMIC IV: unlocking insights in healthcare. In: International Conference on Advanced Information Systems Engineering, pp. 360–372. Springer (2024)
21. van der Aalst, W.M.P.: Process mining: a 360 degree overview, pp. 3–34. Springer International Publishing, Cham (2022)
22. Aalst, W.: Object-centric process mining: dealing with divergence and convergence in event data. In: Ölveczky, P.C., Salaün, G. (eds.) SEFM 2019. LNCS, vol. 11724, pp. 3–25. Springer, Cham (2019). https://doi.org/10.1007/978-3-030-30446-1_1
23. van Eck, M.L., Lu, X., Leemans, S.J.J., van der Aalst, W.M.P.: PM^2: a process mining project methodology. In: Zdravkovic, J., Kirikova, M., Johannesson, P. (eds.) Advanced Information Systems Engineering, pp. 297–313. Springer International Publishing, Cham (2015)
24. Xiong, J., Xiao, G., Kalayci, T., Montali, M., Gu, Z., Calvanese, D.: A virtual knowledge graph based approach for object-centric event logs extraction, pp. 466–478 (2023)

Making the Case for Process Analytics: A Use Case in Court Proceedings

Milda Aleknonytė-Resch[1(✉)], Anna-Katharina Dhungel[2], Fabian Elsaeßer[3], and Arvid Lepsien[1]

[1] Department of Computer Science, Kiel University, Kiel, Germany
{mar,ale}@cs.uni-kiel.de
[2] University of Lübeck, Lübeck, Germany
[3] Sozialgericht Kiel, Kiel, Germany

Abstract. Process mining and other forms of event data analytics have shown to be valuable tools for supporting the management and execution of business processes. For this, process recordings in the form of event logs are required. Digitalization efforts have led to an increased availability of event data for many previously paper-based processes. This has also inspired the extension of process analytics beyond classical business processes. One example of this are judicial processes, which are not necessarily bound by typical business constraints, but nonetheless face issues related to, e.g., increasing efficiency or improving resource allocation. Thus, the aim of this paper is to explore the usefulness of process analytics to judicial processes using an exemplary use case from a German social court. We show how event logs can be extracted from digitalized court files and present an approach to identify bottlenecks using these logs. The approach combines expert knowledge with data-driven analysis and process mining. Using this approach, we are able to both identify process inefficiencies and derive actionable insights for reducing case durations, showing that process analytics is a promising tool to facilitate the digitalization and optimization of judicial processes.

Keywords: Process mining · Workflow inefficiencies · Judicial processes · Use case

1 Introduction

With their process-first perspective, process mining and other forms of process analytics have shown to be valuable tools in various applications involving business processes, e.g., to identify bottlenecks in processes, detect deviations from expected workflows, and support data-driven process optimization [22]. Typically, process analytics relies on event logs, which are recordings of business processes extracted from business information systems. Due to the advancing digitalization, an increasing number of processes are supported by information systems. With this, more process-related event data is becoming available for analysis [23]. While on the one hand, this enables gaining a deeper perspective on business processes, on the other hand it has also inspired extending the scope of process analytics beyond typical business settings [4,17].

Judicial processes present a promising application, even though they differ fundamentally from business processes. While the latter prioritize typical business goals (e.g., profit, efficiency) and offer much design flexibility, judicial processes are rigid, as they are bound by procedural law, and they prioritize other objectives, i.e., their primary goal is ensuring justice, and they emphasize transparency as well as responsibility towards the affected parties. However, these types of processes also share many similarities. Both generally aim to add value to their organization [11], both are concerned with the work of people inside these organizations, and most importantly, both face similar questions: *What are the possible causes of delays in the process? Are there bottlenecks? How can we improve the duration of cases? How should resources (machines, workers, judges, ...) be allocated?*

In recent years, courts started transitioning to electronic case management, which enables the extraction of structured event logs [7]. With digital case files becoming mandatory in many countries in the near future (e.g., in January 2026 in all of Germany), an even larger availability of structured event data can be expected. Given that process analytics has successfully been used to address the above-mentioned questions in business contexts, exploring its application to judicial processes promises to provide a valuable set of tools for this domain while simultaneously extending the scope of process analytics.

Consequently, the goal of this paper is to investigate the applicability of process analytics to judicial processes. For this, we present a case study on the handling of lawsuits in a German social court, where we extracted an event log, analyzed it with an approach combining data-driven findings and expert knowledge, and generated actionable insights for process improvement. Besides demonstrating the applicability and usefulness of process analytics for judicial processes, we also give insights how to successfully conduct an analysis in this domain. Additionally, the real-world event log extracted from the court data is provided for future research.

The remainder of the paper is structured as follows. In Sect. 2, the methodology and context are summarized. Section 3 describes the dataset and outlines our exploratory analysis approach. Section 4 presents the application of this approach to the case study data. Finally, Sect. 5 summarizes our findings, discusses limitations and lessons learned from the case study, and presents directions for future research.

2 Context and Planning

2.1 Case Study Methodology

The case study was conducted based on the widely-used PM^2 methodology [12]. PM^2 divides process mining projects into six subsequent phases that may also be repeated in an iterative process if deemed necessary. Briefly summarized in terms of the PM² phases, the case study was conducted as follows: After the *planning* phase (Phase 1), which involved initial discussions to establish a basic understanding of the process and set the analysis goals, as well as a review of related literature, we *extracted* (Phase 2) and *processed* (Phase 3) an event log of the lawsuit handling process. Then, an exploratory *analysis* approach combining expert opinion with data-driven insights was designed and applied to the event log (Phase 4). The results of the analysis were *evaluated* and discussed with domain experts (Phase 5), resulting in actionable insights for *process improvement* (Phase 6). At the time of this paper's submission, Phase 6 had just begun, with domain experts leading its implementation to integrate the identified process improvements into judicial practice. In the following sections, the actions taken in each phase of the case study and their results are presented.

2.2 Anatomy of the Lawsuit Handling Process

The *planning* of the project (Phase 1) was initiated via a series of interviews and discussions with domain experts, with the aim of (1) selecting the specific process to be analyzed, (2) achieving a general understanding of the process, and (3) setting the goals of the analysis. From these discussions, it was decided that the project should focus on the process by which lawsuits are handled in the court, with the goal of identifying activities and other factors associated with process inefficiencies and increased case durations.

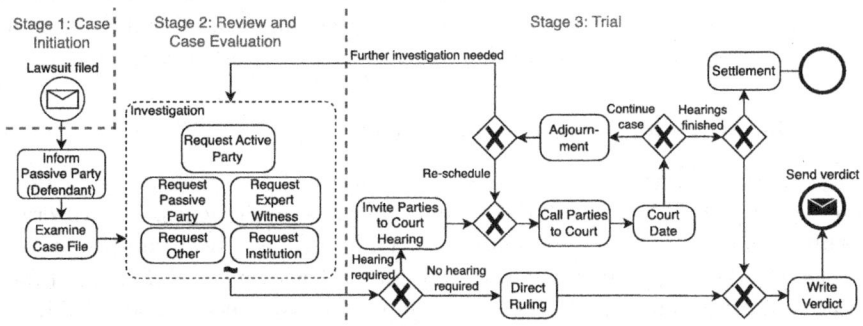

Fig. 1. BPMN model giving a high-level overview of the analyzed court process.

Figure 1 presents an abstract overview of the analyzed process. Generally, the process unfolds in three stages. The first stage, *case initiation*, encompasses all actions taken before an official lawsuit is filed, e.g., the plaintiff preparing a lawsuit individually or with assistance from a lawyer or court clerk. As this stage is executed by the plaintiff according to their personal decisions and independent of how the court handles its lawsuits, it is considered out of scope for our case study. Instead, the paper will focus on the subsequent stages, which are initiated when an official lawsuit is submitted and then executed by the court and its judges. In stage 2, *review and case evaluation*, the judge informs the defendant of the lawsuit, reviews the case and performs an investigation to collect the information necessary for a ruling. While in other fields of law, e.g., civil law, evidence is typically provided by the opposing parties, in social law the judges themselves are responsible for gathering all required evidence. This may involve requesting additional information from institutions, the active (plaintiff) and passive (defendant) parties, expert witnesses, or other sources. Based on the investigation, the judge determines whether a hearing is necessary. If no hearing is required, a direct ruling is issued, and the verdict is sent to the parties. If a hearing is required, the *trial* (stage 3) is initiated by inviting all relevant parties and scheduling a court date. At the court hearing, the case can be resolved in multiple ways. A verdict may be issued, the parties may reach a settlement, or the court may decide to adjourn the proceedings, potentially returning to the investigation phase for further evidence gathering. Furthermore, the plaintiff can withdraw their lawsuit at any point in the process.

While the trial stage is fairly structured and based on strict procedural rules, the investigation stage is highly complex and heterogeneous, mainly due to two reasons. Firstly, the constitutionally guaranteed independence of the judiciary gives judges a great deal of freedom in the way they conduct investigations. Secondly, each investigation requires case-specific steps, which might, for instance, involve concurrently and repeatedly identifying and calling witnesses, requesting expert opinions and coordinating with institutions. This poses a challenge for process mining techniques, which work best with structured processes [10]. However, process mining might still produce objective insights about the structure of the process, and together with other process analytics techniques identify patterns in procedural delays and bottlenecks that may otherwise go unnoticed.

2.3 Related Analyses and Approaches

To finalize the *planning* phase, related literature was screened for analyses conducted on similar data, and for related analysis approaches. The literature screening showed that process analytics techniques have been applied in a few case studies of civil proceedings. For example, in Italy and Brazil, where process mining and other data-driven techniques have been applied to assess the impact of digitalization on court efficacy [7], to analyze the evolution of processes over time [6], to identify activities significantly impacting process duration [6,20,23], to detect sources of process delays [5,19], to engineer features for machine learning [24], to predict the remaining duration of ongoing cases, e.g., for operational support [5,19], and to communicate analysis results to stakeholders [23]. To the best of our knowledge, there are no existing case studies that apply process mining to German court proceedings or specifically to social courts.

Identifying process inefficiencies or performance anomalies and their causes, which are also commonly called bottlenecks [15], was a common goal in papers analyzing judicial processes. Various techniques exist to detect bottlenecks, for instance using statistics or machine learning [15]. With its process-first perspective, process mining has been shown to be a viable method for bottleneck analysis. To this end, Bemthuis et al. [3] review approaches to detecting and predicting bottlenecks as well as recommending improvements using process mining. Based on this, Piest et al. [21] present a method for handling bottlenecks using process mining. In most existing approaches (see [3,21]), process mining is generally used as a supportive tool, e.g., discovered process models annotated with throughput times are inspected manually to identify bottlenecks [3,23]. Techniques using process mining for the automated detection of bottlenecks primarily exist for specific applications, for instance, in manufacturing [13].

3 Materials and Methods

3.1 Dataset

Following the PM^2 methodology [12], Phase 2 (*extraction*) involved retrieving data from the court system. Data was extracted in PDF format with personal information redacted to ensure privacy. The raw dataset consisted of 260 cases from three chambers within a single German social law court. The data originates from a single judge, who typically oversees five to six chambers, meaning that this dataset represents only a subset of the judge's total caseload. Optical Character Recognition (OCR) was used to extract the document text, which was organized into an event log according to the tabular structure of the documents. In the dataset, a single timestamp is recorded for each activity occurrence, commonly indicating only an end date rather than a precise timestamp. This limits the granularity of time-based analyses and the accuracy of calculated activity durations. Depending on the analysis goals, the occurrence of two activities on the same date might also imply uncertainty about their order [16], which might require special handling (e.g., [18]). As the analysis focuses on the overall durations of cases, which typically range from multiple months to years, the impact of the timestamp imprecisions was negligible in our use case.

After extraction, the event log was further processed in consultation with domain experts to ensure anonymity, remove noise, and raise it to an abstraction level appropriate for analysis (Phase 3). All remaining personal identifiers, such as expert witness names, were removed from the log to ensure anonymity. Additionally, timestamps were systematically perturbed to further enhance data privacy. Originally, the event log contained 22,664 recorded events and 290 unique activities. Activities that were extremely rare (i.e., occurring fewer than 30 times) were excluded to focus on frequently observed procedural steps. Furthermore, the domain experts reviewed the list of unique activity labels, based on which similar activities were merged, and terminology was standardized across cases. The refinement of the activity labels reduced the number of unique activities to 59. Finally, duplicate events were removed. These steps collectively reduced the dataset to 19,947 events. The anonymized and processed dataset with 260 cases, 19,947 events and 59 unique activities is provided online [1].

3.2 Exploratory Analysis Approach

To address the question of why some cases take significantly longer than others, we designed an exploratory approach for analyzing the event log that encompasses phases 3–5 of PM². While bottlenecks are a subset of the factors contributing to case duration, some cases may inherently require more time due to their complexity or legal requirements, which cannot be optimized. To systematically investigate the factors influencing case duration, we employed a two-fold initiation approach to further processing the log for analysis that integrates (A) a data-driven statistical analysis with (B) domain expert knowledge (see Fig. 2).

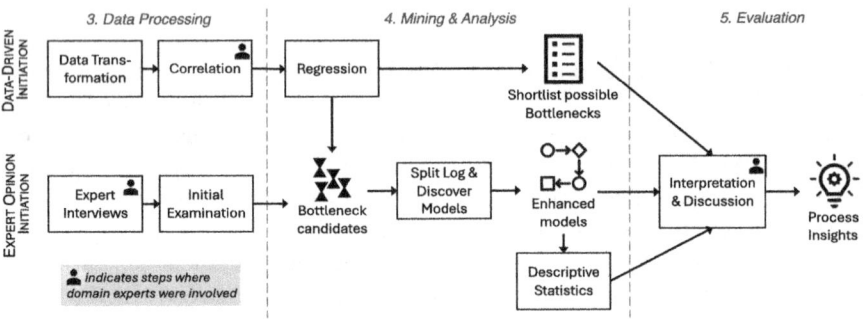

Fig. 2. Exploratory analysis approach combining expert opinions and statistical analysis, aligned to the phases of the PM² methodology.

Data Processing. The data-driven initiation (A) involved transforming the event log into a structured dataset suitable for correlation and regression analysis. To achieve this, we calculated key features for each case, including case duration, the number of unique activities per case, the total number of events per case, and a dummy variable indicating the presence of each activity class. A correlation analysis was then conducted across all variables to identify potential relationships with case duration. From this analysis, we selected the variables with the lowest p-values while ensuring that highly intercorrelated variables were excluded to avoid multicollinearity in the regression model. Meanwhile, the expert opinion initiation (B) involved interviews with judges (domain experts) from multiple different social courts. Through these interviews, we identified variables that judges perceive as bottlenecks. These variables were pre-screened with descriptive statistics to estimate their importance.

Mining and Analysis. In the mining & analysis phase, we built a regression model using the variables from the correlation analysis that had low p-values and did not exhibit high intercorrelation. A backward elimination procedure was then applied to identify the most statistically significant predictors of case duration.

This regression analysis provided a shortlist of possible bottlenecks. This list was merged with the results of the expert opinion initiation into a combined set of bottleneck candidates. Data subsets were then created by splitting cases into groups with and without these bottlenecks, allowing us to assess whether specific procedural patterns or case attributes were strongly associated with extended case durations. Additionally, the dataset was segmented based on case duration, deriving process models for the 20% fastest cases, the 20% slowest cases, and the 20% of cases closest to the mean duration. Process models were built from these subsets using Disco (Fuzzy Miner). Only cases with clear start and endpoints were included, as defined by the domain experts. Additionally, we gathered descriptive statistics on the process models, e.g. mean and median case durations, and the total number of unique activities. An initial interpretation of the results was conducted without the domain experts to prepare the discussions.

Evaluation. The evaluation phase involved comparing the descriptive statistics and the derived process models to assess differences between cases affected by bottlenecks and those that were not, aiming to identify any structural differences that may explain prolonged case durations. Additionally, metrics such as case duration, number of events per case, number of unique activities, and number of directives were analyzed to quantify the impact of identified bottlenecks. Directives are formal instructions or decisions issued by judges to advance a case. They are the primary tool judges use to manage proceedings, and their frequency reflects the judicial workload involved in a case.

The process model visualizations and statistical findings were discussed with domain experts to validate the results and ensure their practical relevance. Finally, the evaluation led to defining potential *process improvements and support measures* to optimize case handling and reduce inefficiencies in court proceedings.

4 Results

4.1 Data Processing

Initial interviews with five judges from various social courts identified several perceived bottlenecks possibly increasing case durations. These included the involvement of expert witnesses, the need to send reminders, the request for medical findings, treatment reports, and whether a court date was required.

Regarding the inclusion of expert witnesses, it was argued that it introduces a structured delay. While expert witnesses are typically given a fixed response time to submit their report, they sometimes require additional documents, which can further extend their response time. Similarly, when reminders need to be sent, judges noted this could indicate a pattern of late responses, i.e., the involved party could tend to exhaust deadlines throughout the entire process.

Additionally, requests for medical findings and treatment reports require collecting additional documents which involves multiple actors and can further delay proceedings. This is particularly tedious because the judge must wait for all requested information and can only then revisit the case file. Finally, not all cases require a court date. Judges believed that cases where a verdict could be written immediately should be resolved faster, as Stage 3 (the trial stage, see Fig. 1) would be significantly shorter without a hearing.

In the data-driven initiation branch, 22 out of 65 variables exhibited a Pearson correlation p-value less than 8×10^{-4}, indicating a possibly statistically significant relationship with case duration. However, since our analysis was exploratory, no significance threshold was set. Figure 3 shows the correlation of the case duration with these variables and their intercorrelations. A number of strong intercorrelations between certain variables can be observed. This suggests procedural dependencies. For example, a perfect correlation was found between "Request for Medical Findings and Treatment Report" and the subsequent submission of such a report. This is expected, as such a report is always submitted when the judge requests it, making this dependency structural.

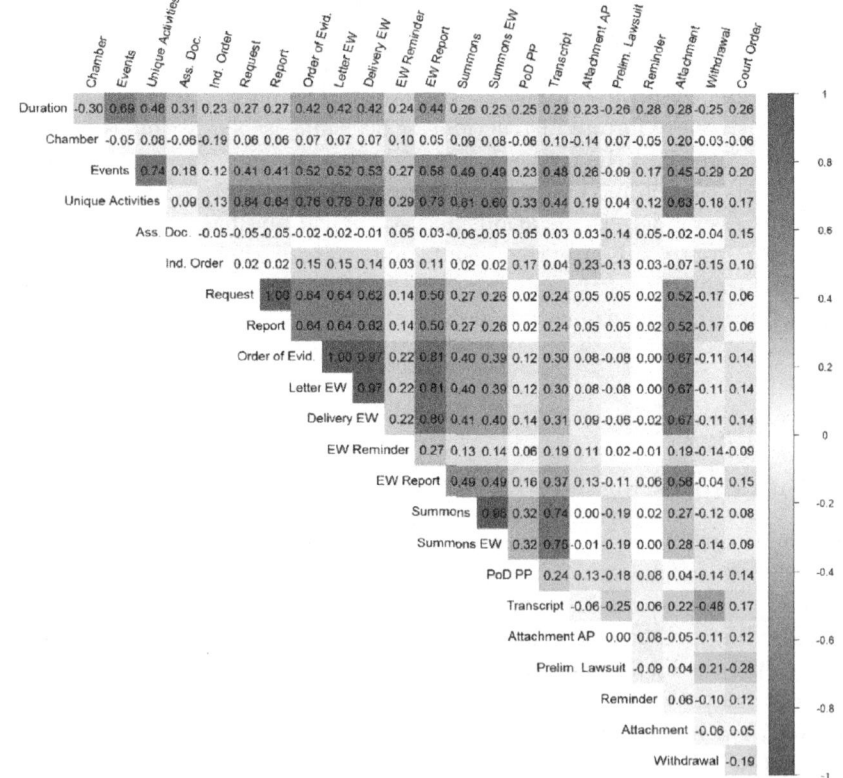

Fig. 3. Correlation with the case duration and intercorrelation of selected activities. Numerical values represent correlation coefficients.

The highest correlation coefficients with case duration were observed for the total number of events (0.69), the number of unique activities (0.48), and the presence of an expert witness report (0.44). The strong correlation with the number of events and the number of unique activities is expected, as cases with a higher number of distinct procedural steps tend to be more complex, requiring additional interactions and decisions. Similarly, the presence of an expert witness report indicates greater case complexity. Since obtaining such a report necessitates an external review, it inherently extends case duration due to dependencies on third-party availability and evaluation time.

In contrast, the lowest correlations with case duration were found for case withdrawal (−0.25), preliminary lawsuit submission (−0.26), and chamber number (−0.30). Withdrawals shorten processing time as no formal verdict is required. Withdrawal correlates with preliminary submissions, suggesting these cases (often filed by associations) could have been frequently withdrawn due to lack of merit. The correlation with chamber number is likely spurious as chamber numbers do not have a meaningful order.

Interestingly, the activity *send reminders* shows no correlation with other activities but is moderately correlated with case duration (0.28, $p = 6 \times 10^{-6}$). This suggests that parties who require reminders may tend to delay the overall process. Such findings highlight that bottlenecks may not always stem from the procedural structure itself, but from the behavior of involved parties.

4.2 Mining and Analysis

To identify key factors influencing case duration, 11 variables with low inter-correlation were selected from the correlation analysis and included in a regression model. After a backward elimination procedure, 7 variables remained nominally significant and were thus identified as possible bottlenecks. The regression results, including estimates, standard errors, and p-values, are presented in Table 1. The estimate values can be interpreted as the number of days a given factor alters the case duration on average.

The results indicate that the inclusion of an assessment document in a case file is associated with a 198-day increase in case duration. As assessment documents can be submitted at the beginning of the process alongside the lawsuit, this may indicate larger, more complex cases or cases involving legal representation. Similarly, if an expert witness report is required, the case duration is extended by 121 days, reflecting the additional time needed for the external assessment. Other factors contributing to longer case durations include individual orders (+78 days) and attachments from the plaintiff (+67 days), both suggesting more extensive case documentation and procedural steps. Conversely, certain factors were associated with shorter case durations. The submission of a preliminary lawsuit shortens case duration by 96 days, possibly due to streamlined preparation by social welfare organizations or because such cases lacked merit and were therefore more quickly resolved. Finally, case withdrawals shorten the process by 67 days, which is expected as withdrawals effectively bypass all remaining procedural steps.

Table 1. Regression after backward procedure. Adjusted R^2: 0.399, p-value of F-statistic: 2.2×10^{-16}.

	Estimate	Std. Error	$Pr(>|t|)$
(Intercept)	47.338	88.470	0.59307
No. Unique Activities	15.075	4.259	0.00048
Assessment document	198.371	38.843	6×10^{-7}
Individual Order	77.958	32.076	0.01578
Expert Witness Report	120.935	48.583	0.01345
Attachment from Plaintiff	68.671	32.891	0.03782
Submission of Preliminary Lawsuit	−96.383	29.386	0.00119
Withdrawal	−66.743	30.419	0.02915

Process models were derived from subsets of cases, where the subsets were defined based on the variables that remained nominally significant in the regression analysis above. In order to examine the impact of these factors on procedural variations, process models were visualized separately for cases with and without each significant variable. To ensure meaningful process visualization, a filter was applied in agreement with domain experts, trimming the cases to sequences beginning with a (preliminary) lawsuit filing and ending in either a court ruling, direct court ruling, or verdict, reducing the dataset to 17,819 events. Due to space constraints, we present only the process model for cases without expert witnesses. As shown in Fig. 4, it is clear and easy to interpret, unlike the complex spaghetti model observed when expert witnesses are involved.

Table 2, provides a comparison of case durations, event counts, and judicial involvement across different case subgroups. Due to space constraints, we focus on subsets based on the presence of expert witnesses, the presence of assessment documents, and case duration categories (fastest, slowest, and around the mean). Across all subgroups, mean and median case durations are very similar, suggesting that the data within each subgroup is approximately normally distributed, meaning there is no strong indication of skewness or extreme outliers.

Table 2. Descriptive statistics for case subgroups.

	Total	20% Cases that are			Expert Witness		Assessment Documents	
		Fastest	Around Mean	Slowest	Yes	No	Yes	No
Number of Cases	254	51	53	50	197	57	38	222
Mean Events per Case	70	41	73	102	80	39	90	74
Number of Activities	59	50	53	51	56	41	51	59
Median Case Duration (months)	14.8	7	16	25.7	16.6	7.6	25	16.6
Mean Case Duration (months)	15.3	6.2	16.2	23.6	17.4	8.3	25.2	17.2
Directives per Case	14.64	8.28	15.36	21.51	16.48	8.46	18.03	14.47

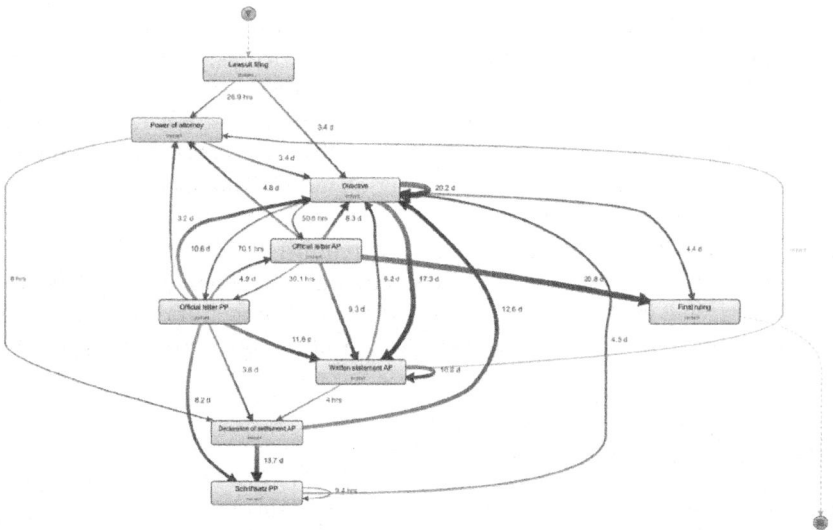

Fig. 4. Process model visualizing mean duration of the log subset containing only cases not involving expert witnesses.

The presence of an expert witness has a substantial impact on case duration. Cases without expert witnesses have a mean duration of 8.3 months, whereas cases with expert witnesses average 17.4 months. This discrepancy is further reflected in process complexity: cases without expert witnesses have fewer unique activities (41 vs. 56), total events (39 vs. 80), and directives per case (8.46 vs. 16.48). This suggests two conclusions: first, cases requiring expert witnesses tend to be more complex, as they involve additional procedural steps and evidence review. However, the higher number of directives in cases with expert witnesses indicates that further investigation might be required even after contacting an expert witness. This suggests a potential inefficiency, confirmed by domain experts: if judges could gather all necessary information for expert witnesses earlier in the process, it might be possible to reduce delays and streamline cases.

The presence of assessment documents correlates with longer case durations. Cases with assessment documents have a mean duration of 25.2 months, whereas those without take 17.2 months on average. Additionally, cases with assessment documents involve more events (90 vs. 74) and directives (18.03 vs. 14.47) (see Table 2). Assessment documents can serve as an indirect indicator of case complexity, and unlike expert witness involvement, this complexity is already apparent in Phase 1 (when the lawsuit is filed). According to domain experts, the underlying reason for increased complexity can stem either from the intrinsic nature of the case itself or from the involvement of a lawyer.

Subsequently, comparing the fastest, average and slowest 20% of cases reveals clear differences in process length and complexity. The mean case duration for the fastest cases is 6.2 months, whereas the slowest average 23.6 months, nearly four times longer. The slowest cases have more than twice as many events per case (102 vs. 41) compared to the fastest cases. This suggests that the primary reason for extended case duration is not necessarily waiting times, but rather additional procedural steps that are required. This is further supported by the number of directives per case, which reflects the level of judicial involvement. The fastest cases require significantly fewer directives per case (8.28), roughly half of the average cases (15.36), whereas slowest cases require 21.51 directives on average. This indicates that more complex cases demand substantially more input from judges. Identifying cases likely to require additional procedural steps early in the process may help courts allocate resources more effectively, potentially mitigating extensively long case durations.

4.3 Evaluation of Use Case

In Phase 5, the results were discussed with domain experts to validate their practical relevance and interpretability. The judges confirmed that the findings aligned with their professional experience and expectations, reinforcing the credibility of the analysis. The most interesting results for the domain experts were the strong effects of expert witnesses and assessment documents. While they had already observed that cases involving expert witnesses and assessment documents tended to take longer, the magnitude of these effects (123 days longer for expert witnesses and 197 days longer for assessment documents) was particularly impressive. The quantified estimate of these effects provided them with a better understanding of procedural delays. Additionally, the discussion helped clarify possible causal relationships, as some insights only became apparent after analyzing the data. For example, only through the exploratory analysis was the presence of assessment documents recognized as a strong early indicator of case complexity. Courts could potentially use this information as a predictive signal in Phase 1 to anticipate longer case durations and allocate resources accordingly.

Together with domain experts, we could derive actionable insights for improving court proceedings and reducing bottlenecks. These actionable insights include early identification of complex cases, particularly those involving expert witness reports or assessment documents, which significantly prolong case durations. By flagging such cases at the beginning of the process, courts could allocate resources more effectively and plan for necessary procedural steps in advance. Additionally, since cases requiring multiple directives, expert witnesses and extensive documentation handling tend to take longer, process efficiency could be improved by streamlining information requests and ensuring that all necessary documents are gathered as early as possible. Another insight is that cases where reminders are sent often experience systematic delays, indicating that some parties consistently exhaust deadlines, which could be addressed with stricter follow-up mechanisms or procedural adjustments.

5 Discussion and Conclusion

In this paper, we explored the applicability of process mining and process analytics in judicial processes by conducting a case study in a German social court. Our approach combined data-driven statistical analysis with expert knowledge to identify bottlenecks and variations in case duration. By extracting and analyzing event logs from digitalized court files, we demonstrated that process analytics can provide valuable insights into court proceedings. Our use case specific contributions include identifying key factors that extend case duration, such as expert witness involvement and assessment documents, and providing actionable insights to optimize judicial workflows. Through discussions with domain experts, we validated our findings and highlighted the potential of process mining to enhance transparency and efficiency in legal decision-making.

In our use case, we demonstrated that process analytics is both feasible and valuable for analyzing court proceedings data. By applying BPM techniques using our exploratory data analysis approach, we were able to gain first insights into the judicial process. Our findings were not only data-driven but also validated through discussions with judges, reinforcing the practical relevance of process analytics in the judicial domain. This collaborative approach helped to convince legal professionals of the potential benefits of process analytics, showing that process mining can enhance transparency, explain variability in case durations and identify bottlenecks in court proceedings.

Our analysis compared perceived bottlenecks (Approach B) with actual bottlenecks (Approach A), revealing that while the identified delays were expected, their magnitude was surprising. Cases involving expert witnesses and assessment documents extended case durations by 121 days and 198 days, respectively. Although assigning an expert witness is not a direct bottleneck, it alters the process flow, often prolonging cases unnecessarily. Additionally, individual orders and attachments from plaintiffs extended cases by over two months, an effect that was previously underestimated by domain experts.

By comparing the slowest and fastest cases, we found that process complexity, measured by the number of events, directives, and unique activities, could be a stronger determinant of case duration than waiting times alone. These findings, validated by domain experts, provided valuable insights into procedural inefficiencies and confirmed that certain case attributes (such as assessment documents) can serve as early indicators of complexity.

In our use case, the actionable insights derived from the analysis have proven highly valuable for domain experts. The results resonated well with judicial practitioners, who appreciated the clarity the analysis provided, especially regarding the versatility of Stage 2. While Stages 1 and 3 follow well-defined, structured workflows, Stage 2 is notably dynamic and subject to individual judicial discretion (particularly when expert witnesses are involved) resulting in a lack of a "happy path." Another key insight was the identification of specific activities, such as the inclusion of additional and assessment documents at the end of Stage 1 or the beginning of Stage 2, which are strong indicators of potential case prolongation and complexity. This finding suggests that non-judicially-binding guidelines could be developed to (1) streamline the process when expert witnesses are involved and (2) help judges recognize early signals of increased complexity, thereby enabling them to better plan and allocate their resources. Overall, these insights not only affirm that BPM can be effectively applied to court proceedings but also provide practical, data-driven strategies that can support judicial decision-making and workflow optimization.

A key limitation of this study is that the use case stems from one social law court in Germany, focusing on chambers handling specific types of cases from the same judge. While this limits generalizability across courts, regions, and legal systems, it can also be seen as a strength, as the observed differences in case duration and process structure cannot be attributed to variation between judges or jurisdictions. Nevertheless, our exploratory approach is not limited to this specific use case. Given similar structured event log data from other courts or even different countries, the methodology could be replicated and adapted to derive further insights. Furthermore, the event log available from the court system contained only end dates for activities. While certain activities, such as sending invitations, are instantaneous and the most important aspect of the event log in court proceedings is the chronological sequence of the process, the duration of activities could provide deeper insights into bottlenecks and inefficiencies.

Looking to the future, judges expect that new technologies will shorten court proceedings [9]. The introduction of the electronic case file in Germany, in conjunction with BPM, has the potential to make proceedings more efficient and to identify process slowdowns at an early stage. Future work should focus on analyzing directive types, as different directives may impact case duration differently. LLMs could help extract and categorize directive content from PDF files, enabling a more detailed process analysis. Extraction of further information, e.g., duration of activities by means of meta data would increase the quality of the event logs. For the legal domain, local LLMs are especially relevant, as they enable processing sensitive data independent of external cloud services [2]. Additionally, reducing complexity in process mining for court proceedings is essential, as legal processes are highly heterogeneous. Simplifying event logs, grouping similar process variants, and filtering non-essential steps would make BPM more effective and accessible for judicial analysis. Lastly, the increasing availability of event data might also warrant the development of sampling techniques with appropriate relevance characteristic for legal processes, which would facilitate the efficient analysis of large datasets [14]. Addressing these challenges will further optimize court processes, improve case management, and enhance transparency and interpretability [8].

Acknowledgments. This project received funding from the State of Schleswig-Holstein (SH) under the Datencampus project grant no. 220 21 016. The project ProcessPig is funded by the European Union within the framework of the European Innovation Partnership (EIP-AGRI) and the state program rural areas of the state SH (LPLR).

References

1. Aleknonyte-Resch, M., Dhungel, A.K., Elsaeßer, F., Lepsien, A.: Making the case for process analytics: a use case in court proceedings, v1. Mendeley Data (2025). https://doi.org/10.17632/3mcvbrhr7c.1
2. Apaydin, K., Zisgen, Y.: Local large language models for business process modeling. In: ICPM 2024 Workshops. LNBIP, vol. 533. Springer, Cham (2025). https://doi.org/10.1007/978-3-031-82225-4_44
3. Bemthuis, R., Van Slooten, N., Arachchige, J., Piest, J., Bukhsh, F.: A classification of process mining bottleneck analysis techniques for operational support. In: Proceedings of the 18th International Conference on e-Business. SCITEPRESS, Online Streaming (2021). https://doi.org/10.5220/0010578601270135
4. Brzychczy, E., Aleknonytė-Resch, M., Janssen, D., Koschmider, A.: Process mining on sensor data: a review of related works. Knowl. Inf. Syst. (2025). https://doi.org/10.1007/s10115-024-02297-y
5. Campi, A., Ceri, S., Dilettis, M., Pernici, B.: Variants analysis in judicial trials: challenges and initial results. In: ECML PKDD 2023 Workshops. CCIS, vol. 2133. Springer, Cham (2025). https://doi.org/10.1007/978-3-031-74630-7_30
6. Caponecchia, V., D'Agostino, B., Comandè, G., et al.: Towards visualizing and analysing legal proceedings with process mining. In: 1st International Workshop on Processes, Laws and Compliance. CEUR Workshop Proceedings, vol. 3850. CEUR-WS.org, Lyngby, Denmark (2024). https://ceur-ws.org/Vol-3850/paper5.pdf
7. Castelliano, C., Grajzl, P., Watanabe, E.: Does electronic case-processing enhance court efficacy? new quantitative evidence. Gov. Inf. Q. **40**(4) (2023). https://doi.org/10.1016/j.giq.2023.101861
8. Dhungel, A.K., Beute, E.: AI systems in the judiciary: amicus curiae? interviews with judges on acceptance and potential use of intelligent algorithms. In: ECIS 2024 Proceedings. AIS, Paphos, Cyprus (2024)
9. Dhungel, A.K., Heine, M.: Cui bono? Judicial decision-making in the era of AI: a qualitative study on the expectations of judges in Germany. TATuP **33**(1) (2024). https://doi.org/10.14512/tatup.33.1.14
10. Diamantini, C., Genga, L., Potena, D.: Behavioral process mining for unstructured processes. J. Intell. Inf. Syst. **47**(1), 5–32 (2016). https://doi.org/10.1007/s10844-016-0394-7
11. Dumas, M., Rosa, M.L., Mendling, J., Reijers, H.A.: Fundamentals of Business Process Management. Springer Berlin, Heidelberg (2018). https://doi.org/10.1007/978-3-662-56509-4
12. van Eck, M.L., Lu, X., Leemans, S., van der Aalst, W.: PM^2: a process mining project methodology. In: Zdravkovic, J., Kirikova, M., Johannesson, P. (eds.) CAiSE 2015. LNCS, vol. 9097, pp. 297–313. Springer, Cham (2015). https://doi.org/10.1007/978-3-319-19069-3_19
13. Fang, Z., Yu, C.: Bottleneck mining: a data-driven bottleneck identification method via process mining in manufacturing systems. In: 20th International Conference on Automation Science and Engineering (CASE). IEEE, Bari, Italy (2024). https://doi.org/10.1109/CASE59546.2024.10711833
14. Fonger, F., Nebelung, N., Lepsien, A., Aleknonytė-Resch, M., Koschmider, A.: Representative sampling in process mining: two novel sampling algorithms for event logs. In: ICPM 2024 Workshops. LNBIP, vol. 533. Springer, Cham (2025). https://doi.org/10.1007/978-3-031-82225-4_4

15. Ibidunmoye, O., Hernández-Rodriguez, F., Elmroth, E.: Performance anomaly detection and bottleneck identification. ACM Comput. Surv. **48**(1) (2015). https://doi.org/10.1145/2791120
16. Leemans, S.J.J., Van Zelst, S.J., Lu, X.: Partial-order-based process mining: a survey and outlook. Knowl. Inf. Syst. **65**(1) (2023). https://doi.org/10.1007/s10115-022-01777-3
17. Lepsien, A., Bosselmann, J., Melfsen, A., Koschmider, A.: Process mining on video data. In: ZEUS 2022. CEUR Workshop Proceedings, vol. 3113. CEUR-WS.org, Bamberg, Germany (2022). https://ceur-ws.org/Vol-3113/paper9.pdf
18. Lepsien, A., Pegoraro, M., Fonger, F., Langhammer, D., Aleknonytė-Resch, M., Koschmider, A.: Ranking the top-K realizations of stochastically known event logs. In: ICPM 2024 Workshops. LNBIP, vol. 533. Springer, Cham (2025). https://doi.org/10.1007/978-3-031-82225-4_26
19. Pernici, B., Bono, C.A., Piro, L., Del Treste, M., Vecchi, G.: Improving the analysis of the judiciary performance - the use of data mining techniques to assess the timeliness of civil trials. Int. J. Public Sect. Manag. **37**(1) (2024). https://doi.org/10.1108/IJPSM-02-2023-0058
20. Pernici, B., Campi, A., Dilettis, M., Gerosa, P.: Why are Italian trials taking so long? A process mining approach. In: Ital-IA 2023: 3rd National Conference on Artificial Intelligence, organized by CINI. CEUR-WS.org, Pisa, Italy (2023). https://ceur-ws.org/Vol-3486/34.pdf
21. Piest, J.P.S., Bemthuis, R.H., Cutinha, J.A., Arachchige, J.J., Bukhsh, F.A.: A method for bottleneck detection, prediction, and recommendation using process mining techniques. In: E-Business and Telecommunications, vol. 1795. Springer, Cham (2023). https://doi.org/10.1007/978-3-031-36840-0_7
22. Reinkemeyer, L. (ed.): Process Mining in Action: Principles, Use Cases and Outlook. Springer, Cham (2020). https://doi.org/10.1007/978-3-030-40172-6
23. Unger, A.J., Neto, J.F.D.S., Fantinato, M., et al.: Process mining-enabled jurimetrics: analysis of a Brazilian court's judicial performance in the business law processing. In: ICAIL '21. ACM, São Paulo, Brazil (2021). https://doi.org/10.1145/3462757.3466137
24. Vercosa, L., Silva, V., Cruz, J., et al.: Investigation of lawsuit process duration using machine learning and process mining. Discov. Anal. **2**(1) (2024). https://doi.org/10.1007/s44257-024-00015-0

Probabilistic Approaches to Uncertainty and Prediction in Process Mining (BPMDS 2025)

Predicting Unseen Process Behavior Based on Log Injection

Qian Chen[1(✉)], Karolin Winter[2], and Stefanie Rinderle-Ma[1]

[1] TUM School of Computation, Information and Technology, Technical University of Munich, Garching, Germany
{qian.chen,stefanie.rinderle-ma}@tum.de
[2] Department of Industrial Engineering and Innovation Sciences, Eindhoven University of Technology, Eindhoven, The Netherlands
k.m.winter@tue.nl

Abstract. Predictive process monitoring (PPM) offers multiple benefits for enterprises, e.g., the early planning of resources. Its efficacy depends on the quality of event data used for model training. In this work, we study the effects of unseen behavior, i.e., events that are not present in the training data, on prediction quality. Unseen behavior might occur due to infrequent traces or added compliance constraints. Existing approaches focus on predicting unseen behavior based on updating the prediction model. Another option is to inject unseen behavior into the training data based on order and temporal constraints on events. Due to the model-agnostic nature of log injection, different PPM approaches can be employed without any modification. The proposed algorithms are prototypically implemented and evaluated on real-life event logs. The results demonstrate that log injection can enhance prediction quality and is more time-efficient than state-of-the-art model update strategies.

Keywords: Predictive process monitoring · Log injection · Unseen behavior

1 Introduction

Predictive Process Monitoring (PPM) is a subfield of process mining that aims to predict the future characteristics of an ongoing process execution. Typical tasks involve the prediction of outcome [34], next activity [11], and remaining time [26] of an ongoing process execution. Predictions can help to, e.g., prevent undesired process outcomes [13]. In this paper, we focus on next event prediction.

Despite the importance of PPM, it is confronted with the problem of *unseen behavior* [9], i.e., behavior reflected by events that have not been observed in the training data, but occur in future executions due to infrequent traces or new/changing compliance constraints [15]. Compliance constraints may stem from regulatory documents such as healthcare guidelines, might change frequently (e.g., financial regulations change every 12 min[1]) and are available in

---
[1] https://thefinanser.com/2017/01/bank-regulations-change-every-12-minutes.

almost any application domain. For example, due to the pandemic, a new healthcare guideline requiring "goods must be sanitized immediately after packing" is imposed on the order to delivery process, introducing the previously unseen behavior sanitize goods in future executions. As existing PPM approaches rely on historical event data for model training [13], this might result in a possible mismatch between predicted process behavior and real-world process behavior in case of unseen behavior and subsequently in misled decisions and compliance violations. Thus, predicting unseen behavior constitutes a major challenge for next activity prediction.

Knowledge on compliance compliance and other business requirements typically arises as *context information* "outside" a process first and can then be incorporated into the process in order to avoid compliance violations. Other sources of process context information include domain knowledge provided by experts and sensor data [10,17] which both might influence the process behavior and introduce unseen behavior. In this work, we consider constraints as the source of context information.

Existing research on predicting unseen process behavior mostly relies on model generalization by presenting strategies to update the prediction model after unseen behavior has been observed at runtime in an ex-post way [7,20, 24,25,29]. In our previous work, we augmented the prediction model with order relations between activities to predict unseen behavior [9], i.e., a state transition system was used as the prediction model and augmented with order constraints. An example of an order constraint, would be sanitize goods is immediately followed by pack. We opted for model augmentation as a starting point in order to understand and explain the effects on predicting unseen behavior. By contrast to model generalization, data augmentation [30] aims at artificially modifying the original data to create new samples for model training.

In this work, we aim at studying the efficacy of *log injection* as data augmentation strategy in comparison with model update strategies. To this end, we provide algorithms for injecting order and temporal constraints (e.g., sanitize goods must be followed by pack within 2 h) into the training data resembling the occurrence of yet unknown and hence unobserved activities. The approach is evaluated in two ways. First of all, the performance of predicting unseen behavior is evaluated with and without using log injection for four existing PPM approaches with different deep learning methods, i.e., LSTM, CNN, and Transformer. Secondly, the log injection approach is compared to model generalization by updating the prediction models with unseen behavior. The results indicate that log injection technique outperforms almost all model update strategies in predicting unseen behavior while maintaining comparable overall performance. Moreover, it is more time-efficient, as it does not require model retraining.

The remainder of this paper is structured as follows. After presenting the problem statement and preliminaries in Sect. 2, the proposed *log injection* approach is introduced in Sect. 3 and evaluated in Sect. 4. Section 5 discusses related work before the conclusion in Sect. 6.

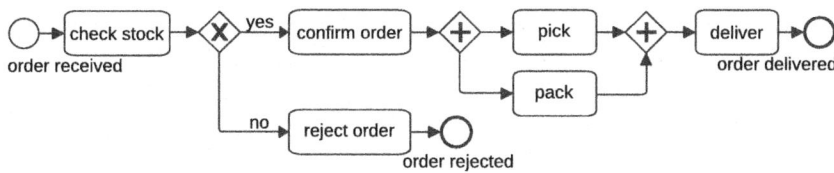

Fig. 1. Running example: Order-to-Delivery (O2D) process model

2 Problem Statement and Preliminaries

To illustrate the problem and all related preliminaries we use an Order-to-Delivery (O2D) process model, see Fig. 1. The O2D process starts with receiving an order and ends with delivering it to customers or rejecting the order. Each process execution (i.e., trace) is treated as a sequence of ordered events recorded in an event log.

Definition 1 (Event, Trace and Event Log). *Let C be the set of case identifiers, A^L the set of activities, T the set of timestamps, and D_m the set of each attribute of events in a log with $m \geq 0$. An event $e_i := (c, a, t, d_1, ..., d_m)$ is defined as a tuple consisting of a case identifier $c \in C$, an activity $a \in A^L$, a timestamp $t \in T$ and other attributes $d_i \in D_i$. Let Σ be the set of traces. A trace $\sigma \in \Sigma$ is defined as a sequence of events $\sigma := \langle e_1, e_2, ..., e_n \rangle$ of length $|\sigma|$, for which holds that $\forall e_i, e_j \in \sigma$ and $i, j \in [1, n]: j > i \land e_i.c = e_j.c \land e_j.t \geq e_i.t$. An event log is then defined as a set of traces $L := \{\sigma_1, ..., \sigma_l\}$.*

Thus, the set of unique activities for all events in the log L which is generated from our running example (cf. Fig. 1) is specified as follows:

$$A^L = \{\texttt{check stock}, \texttt{confirm order}, \texttt{reject order}, \texttt{pick}, \texttt{pack}, \texttt{deliver}\}.$$

In this work, we focus on next activity prediction, which forecasts the activity to be executed next, given its prefix from an event stream occurring at runtime.

Definition 2 (Prefix, Event Stream). *Let $\sigma \in \Sigma$ be a trace of length n. A prefix of length k of a trace is defined as $p_k(\sigma) := \langle e_1, e_2, ..., e_k \rangle$ where $k \leq n$. An event stream is defined as a set of prefixes $R := \{p_k(\sigma_1), ..., p_k(\sigma_r)\}$. The set of activities of all events in the stream R is defined as A^R.*

Definition 3 (Next Activity Prediction, [28]). *Let $p_k(\sigma)$ be a prefix of length k of a trace σ, and e' be a predicted event by a function Ω. Let π_A be a projection function that maps an event to its activity, i.e., $\pi_A(e) = a$. The next activity prediction problem is defined as learning a function Ω_A such that:*

$$\Omega_A(p_k(\sigma)) = \pi_A(e'_{k+1}) = a_{k+1}.$$

Consider prefix $p_4(\sigma) = \langle(\text{check stock}),(\text{confirm order}),(\text{pick}),(\text{pack})\rangle$ according to our O2D process (cf. Fig. 1) where other attributes of events are omitted here for simplicity. The function Ω_A would then forecast deliver as the activity to be executed next. However, the predictive model, which is trained based on L in order to learn Ω_A, can only output one of the activities that are available in A^L as the prediction for an ongoing case, e.g., deliver $\in A^L$. In other words, the prediction is restricted to activities that are seen in the training phase. Yet, at runtime, the possible next activities for an event stream A^R could contain unseen behavior, i.e., unseen activities that have not been observed in the historical event log but are occurring in reality due to the introduction or changes of constraints.

Definition 4 (Order Constraint). *Let P and S be two activities, and let $r \in \{df, ef\}$ be a sequential relation with df indicating a directly follows relation and ef an eventually follows relation. Then, an order constraint is defined as a tuple (P, S, r) meaning that P is the predecessor of S.*

Definition 5 (Temporal Constraint). *Let P and S be two activities, and let $r \in \{df, ef\}$ be a sequential relation with df indicating a directly follows relation and ef an eventually follows relation. A temporal constraint (P, S, r, r_t, g) restricts the follow relations by a temporal distance, where $r_t \in \{min, max, interval\}$ specifies the minimum, maximum or an interval between P and S and g corresponds to the granularity of time.*

Consider the COVID-19 pandemic example above in which a new order constraint requiring "goods must be sanitized immediately after packing", i.e., (pack, sanitize goods, df), is imposed on the O2D process. This introduces an unseen activity sanitize goods that is not present in A^L but occurring in future executions A^R to comply with the health guideline. The goal of this paper is to enable the prediction of such unseen activities through *log injection*.

3 Unseen Behavior Prediction Based on Log Injection

To enable the prediction of unseen behavior as presented in Sect. 2, we utilize order and temporal constraints as source of context information about future executions. Conventional PPM approaches take as input the historical event log to train the predictive model and apply this model to evolving event streams for next activity prediction. The predictive model can be either explicit or implicit, referring to model-based approaches (e.g., annotated transition systems (ATS)) or supervised learning methods (e.g., neural networks), respectively. For model-based approaches like ATS, the predictive model is constructed based on the event log and augmented with constraints to incorporate unseen behavior [9]. However, deep learning (DL) techniques have been widely applied in PPM due to their superior performance. Moreover, the superior performance of DL models over ATS has been further demonstrated in [9], particularly in terms of overall performance when dealing with unseen behavior.

Thus, in this work, we opt for DL approaches for next activity prediction. Nevertheless, neural networks are represented as an implicit model built by encoding event log information, hindering the possibility to enrich it with constraints. Therefore, we address this problem from the data perspective, i.e., *injecting* order and temporal constraints reflecting unseen behavior into the historical event log which is then used for model training and next activity prediction, see Fig. 2. Furthermore, log injection as a data augmentation strategy is preferred in order to mitigate the problem of *data scarcity* identified as one of the future directions in PPM [6].

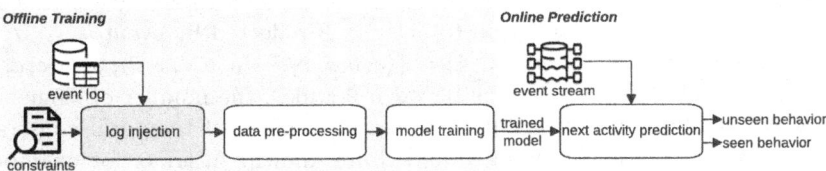

Fig. 2. Overview of the proposed approach

Log Injection: We assume that context information is provided as order relations between two activities P and S where P is the predecessor of S and S has to directly or eventually follow P. Moreover, the follow relations can be restricted by a temporal constraint (cf. Definition 5), e.g., P has to be followed eventually by S within 16 h. We also assume that an event p associated to the execution of predecessor activity P has been already observed and is hence present in traces σ in the log L, but event s related to the execution of activity S has not been seen yet and is hence not present in any σ.

Definition 6 provides the general function *inject* for augmenting a trace σ by injecting an event ϕ at either a given position or between two positions in the trace specified by the indexes of the events.

Definition 6 (Event Injection). *Let Σ be the set of all traces and ε be the set of all events. Let $\sigma = \langle e_1, e_2, \ldots, e_n \rangle \in \Sigma$ be a trace of length n and $\phi \in \varepsilon$ be an event.*

Injection function inject : $\Sigma \times \varepsilon \times \mathbb{N} \times \mathbb{N} \mapsto 2^\Sigma$ is defined as follows $(i, j \in \mathbb{N}; i \leq j)$:

$$inject(\sigma, \phi, i, j) := \begin{cases} \{\langle e_1, .., e_i, \phi, e_{i+2}, .., e_{n+1} \rangle\} & i = j \leq n \\ \{\langle e_1, .., e_i, \phi, e_{i+2}, .., e_{n+1}\rangle, \langle e_1, .., e_{i+1}, \phi, e_{i+3}, .., e_{n+1}\rangle, \\ ..\langle e_1, .., e_j, \phi, e_{j+2}, .., e_{n+1}\rangle\} & i < j \leq n \end{cases}$$

Definition 6 is used for expressing the injection of events in directly follows and eventually follows relations to an existing event in a trace in Definition 7.

Definition 7 (Injection for Directly/Eventually Follows Relations).
Let Σ be the set of all traces and ε be the set of all events. Let further $p, s \in \varepsilon$ be two events associated to activities P and S. Assume an order constraint (P, S, r) where $r \in \{df, ef\}$, see Definition 4. Then s is injected into all traces $\sigma \in \Sigma$ by using

- $r = $ **df:** $inject(\sigma, s, pos(\sigma, p), pos(\sigma, p))$
- $r = $ **ef:** $inject(\sigma, s, pos(\sigma, p), |\sigma|)$

with $pos : \Sigma \times \varepsilon \mapsto \mathbb{N}$ returns the position of an event in a trace.

Assume trace $\sigma = \langle a, b, c, d \rangle$ and event x associated to activity X that is in an eventually follows (ef) relation to activity B reflected by event $b \in \sigma$. x is injected into σ using $inject(\sigma, x, 2, 4) = \{\langle a, b, x, c, d \rangle, \langle a, b, c, x, d \rangle, \langle a, b, c, d, x \rangle\}$.

For eventually follows relations between P and S, the number of elements in the result set of the injection function can be reduced if temporal constraints imposed on the relation between P and S are known. Assume, for example, a minimum temporal distance between P and S. Based on the timestamps of events in the traces of the result set, it can be decided for which traces the temporal distance between P and S is equal or higher than the minimum distance and hence the input position i of the injection function can be determined. Analogously, for a specified maximum temporal distance, position j can be determined, and for a specified interval, i.e., a combination of minimum and maximum temporal distance, both positions i and j can be determined, see Definition 8.

Definition 8 (Injection Optimization based on Temporal Constraints).
Let Σ be the set of all traces and ε be the set of all events. Let further $p, s \in \varepsilon$ be two events associated to activities P and S respectively. Assume a temporal constraint (P, S, ef, r_t, g) where $r_t \in \{min, max, interval\}$, see Definition 5. Then s is injected into all traces $\sigma \in \Sigma$ by using

- $r_t = $ **min:** $inject(\sigma, s, i, |\sigma|)$, $pos(\sigma, p) \leq i \leq |\sigma|$ determined by Algorithm 1
- $r_t = $ **max:** $inject(\sigma, s, pos(\sigma, p), j)$, $j \leq |\sigma|$ determined by Algorithm 2
- $r_t = $ **interval:** $inject(\sigma, s, i, j)$, $pos(\sigma, p) \leq i \leq |\sigma|$ determined by Algorithm 1 and $j \leq |\sigma|$ determined by Algorithm 2 with $i \leq j$

Note here, the injected event ϕ (cf. Definition 6) or s (cf. Definition 7-8) retains the same attribute values as its previous event, except for the activity name. This is primarily because order relations are essential and consistently present across all constraints, whereas information related to other process perspectives beyond control-flow, such as resources, may not always be specified.

Algorithm 1 starts from a given event and its position in the trace and iterates over the subsequent events and their temporal distance to the event until the first one exceeding the minimum temporal distance is found or the end of the trace is reached. In the latter case, the position of the last event is returned.

Algorithm 1: Temporal Distance Checking For *min* Case

Input : A trace $\sigma = \langle e_1, \ldots, e_n \rangle$; an event e_i where $i \in \{1, 2, \ldots, n\}$; a temporal value t_{min}
Output: Position of the *first* event satisfying with the temporal limit t_{min}: p_{from}

1 **if** e_i *is the last event in* σ **then**
2   **return** $p_{from} = p_{e_i}$;
3 **else**
4   **for** $j = i + 1$ **to** n **do**
5         $temp\_dist \leftarrow$ get the temporal distance between event e_i and e_j;
6   **if** $temp\_dist < t_{min}$ **then**
7   **if** e_j *is the last event in* σ **then**
8   **return** $p_{from} = p_{e_j}$;
9   **else**
10   **return** $p_{from} = p_{e_{j-1}}$;

Algorithm 2 for $r_t = max$ works similar: once the distance between the predecessor and the subsequent events exceeds the maximum temporal limit t_{max}, the upper bound is determined at the position of the previous event. The combination of *min* and *max* specifies the lower and upper limit for $r_t = interval$.

Algorithm 2: Temporal Distance Checking For *max* Case

Input : A trace $\sigma = \langle e_1, \ldots, e_n \rangle$; an event e_i where $i \in \{1, 2, \ldots, n\}$; a temporal value t_{max}
Output: Position of the *last* event satisfying with the temporal limit t_{max}: p_{to}

1 **if** e_i *is the last event in* σ **then**
2   **return** $p_{to} = p_{e_i}$;
3 **else**
4   **for** $j = i + 1$ **to** n **do**
5         $temp\_dist \leftarrow$ get the temporal distance between event e_i and e_j;
6   **if** $temp\_dist \leq t_{max}$ **then**
7   **if** e_j *is the last event in* σ **then**
8   **return** $p_{to} = p_{e_j}$;
9   **else**
10   **return** $p_{to} = p_{e_{j-1}}$;

Consider trace $\sigma = \langle (c1, A, 8{:}00), (c1, B, 8{:}30), (c1, C, 9{:}00), (c1, D, 11{:}00) \rangle$. For example, activity B reflected by event a in case $c1$ occurred at 8:00. Assume a temporal constraint (B, X, ef, r_t, g). $r_t = min$ 1 h, results in $inject(\sigma, x, 3, 4) = \{\langle a, b, c, x, d \rangle, \langle a, b, c, d, x \rangle\}$. $r_t = max$ 2 h, results in $inject(\sigma, X, 2, 3) = \{\langle a, b, x, c, d \rangle, \langle a, b, c, x, d \rangle\}$, and $r_t = interval$ with a minimum distance of 1 and a maximum distance of 2 h results in $inject(\sigma, x, 3, 3) = \langle a, b, c, x, d \rangle$.

One challenge that is not covered yet is the *multiple occurrence of events* in a trace due to, e.g., loops. Consider $\sigma = \langle a, b, b, c, d \rangle$ with constraint (B, X, ef). This can mean that i) every occurrence of B reflected by an event b is followed by an occurrence of X reflected by event x (e.g., $\sigma = \langle a, b, x, b, x, c, d \rangle$) or ii) one occurrence of X after the last occurrence of B suffices (e.g., $\sigma = \langle a, b, b, x, c, d \rangle$). In this work, we opt for supporting case i) of "pairwise" relations through Algorithm 3, reflected by adding indexes to the events, e.g., $\sigma = \langle a, b^1, c, x^1, b^2, x^2 \rangle$. The reason is that we achieve an unambiguous assignment of events related to each other, e.g., b^1 and x^1 in the previous example.

Algorithm 3: Injection for Multiple Occurrences

Input : Trace σ; $m > 1$: number of occurrences of events reflecting the multiple execution of activity P; $r \in \{df, ef\}$ control-flow relation between P and S.
Output: Set of traces $S_{injected}$

1 **if** $r==df$ **then**
2 $\quad$ **return** $S_{injected} = \{\langle e_1, .., p^1, s^1, .., p^2, s^2, ..., p^m, s^m, .., e_n \rangle\}$;
3 **else**
4 $\quad$ $S_{injected} = \{\}$;
5 $\quad$ $\sigma_{init} = \langle e_1, .., p^1, s^1, .., p^2, s^2, ..., p^m, s^m, .., e_n \rangle$;
6 $\quad$ $S_{m+1} := \{\sigma_{init}\}$;
7 $\quad$ **for** $i = m,..,1$ **do**
8 $\quad\quad$ **for** $\sigma \in S_{i+1}$ **do**
9 $\quad\quad\quad$ split σ into $\sigma_{pre} = \langle e_1, .., p^1, s^1, .., p^{i-1}, s^{i-1} \rangle$ and σ_{suf} s.t. $\sigma_{pre} \oplus \sigma_{suf} = \sigma$;
10 $\quad\quad\quad$ remove s^i from σ_{suf};
11 $\quad\quad\quad$ $Suf_i = inject(\sigma_{suf}, s^i, pos(\sigma_{suf}, p^i), eot)$;
12 $\quad\quad\quad$ $S = \bigoplus(\sigma_{pre}, Suf_i)$;
13 $\quad\quad$ $S_i = S_i \cup S$;
14 $\quad\quad$ $S_{injected} = S_i$;
15 $\quad$ **return** $S_{injected}$

16 $\oplus : \Sigma \times \Sigma \mapsto \Sigma$ concatenates two traces into one trace;
17 $\bigoplus : \Sigma \times 2^{\Sigma} \mapsto 2^{\Sigma}$ concatenates one trace with all traces in a given set of traces into a set of traces;

Consider trace $\sigma = \langle a, b^1, c, b^2, b^3, d \rangle$ where event b occurs three times and a directly follows constraint (B, X, df). The resulting trace turns out as $\sigma = \langle a, b^1, x^1, c, b^2, x^2, b^3, x^3, d \rangle$ according to Algorithm 3. Also for multiple occurrences of events, temporal restrictions on the eventually follows relations can be exploited to optimize the injection positions. To this end, we apply Algorithms 1 and 2 as specified in Definition 8, on the pairwise occurrences of events, i.e., p^i and s^i reflecting an eventually follows relation between occurrence of activities P and S.

The augmented event log enables the use of various model-agnostic PPM techniques for next activity prediction as we work directly on the data. We keep the following steps brief since this is not the contribution of this work.

Data Pre-processing: The augmented event log after log injection is prepared into prefixes paired with the corresponding next activities, i.e., $\langle p_k(\sigma)|a_{k+1}\rangle = \langle e_1, e_2, ..., e_k|a_{k+1}\rangle$. The categorical attributes of events can be encoded with embedding or one-hot encoding, while normalization is applied to numerical values. The resulting feature vectors are taken as input for model training.

Model Training and Prediction: To learn the function Ω_A (cf. Definition 3) for next activity prediction, different neural networks, such as Long Short-Term Memory (LSTM), can be adopted as the predictive model. During online prediction, the trained model is applied to evolving event streams to forecast the activity to be executed next, whether it has been observed or remains unseen. The arg-max strategy, which selects the activity with the highest predicted probability, is the best-performing technique for next-activity prediction [5].

4 Evaluation

We evaluate *log injection* w.r.t. (i) feasibility, i.e., can unseen behavior be predicted, and (ii) performance compared to prediction model update. Moreover, we illustrate the applicability of the approach by using real-world logs. The evaluation requires event logs and associated compliance constraints as input where the latter reflect the unseen behavior to be predicted. Hence, we select three real-life event logs[2], i.e., BPIC2012w, sepsis2016, and traffic fine, together with documentation on compliance constraints. Our proposed approach is prototypically implemented and available at https://github.com/Qian915/log_injection.

Table 1 shows the compliance constraints C_1 to C_4 referring to order and temporal information. Constraint C_1 is derived by the analysis reports submitted to the BPI challenge [4]. It states that the event associated with task W_Valideren aanvraag-SCHEDULE is to be eventually followed by an event reflecting task W_Valideren aanvraag-START within a maximum of seven days. C_2 and C_3 are obtained from the medical guidelines for treating sepsis patients [1]. We adapt the original traffic fine constraint as presented in [21] to define C_4, aiming to create a dataset with medium constraint support, which will be explained later. The percentage of cases that deviate from the specified constraint in the event log is shown as violation ratio in the table.

Table 1. Constraints used for Event logs

Const.	Event log	Vio. ratio	predecessor (P)	successor (S)	r	r_t	g
C_1	BPIC2012w	45.76%	W_Valideren aanvraag -SCHEDULE	W_Valideren aanvraag -START	ef	max7	day
C_2	Sepsis2016	67.46%	ER Sepsis Triage	IV Antibiotics	ef	max1	hour
C_3		46.09%	ER Sepsis Triage	LacticAcid	ef	max3	hour
C_4	Traffic fine	27.44%	Add penalty	Send for Credit Collection	ef	max1080	day

Training log preparation is illustrated based on the process model in Fig. 3a). Input are the three original logs BPIC2012w, Sepsis2016, and Traffic_fine, together with constraints C_1 to C_4. Note here, we select $\frac{2}{3}$ of cases from the original logs for training log preparation, the remaining $\frac{1}{3}$ of traces are left out as test sets. As first step, the traces reflecting compliance violations are removed in order to evaluate the "pure" effect of log injection. Nonetheless, log injection can be used with violating traces; the performance is expected to decrease. For the resulting logs and the constraints, the base training logs are created by removing the successor events specified in the constraints from the logs, e.g., BPI12w_C_1 results from removing traces violating C_1 and all successor events reflecting task W_Valideren aanvraag from event log BPIC2012w. Figure 3b) shows the four base training logs BPIC_base to Traf_base, together with selected log characteristics. These base training logs reflect seen behavior. The ratio of

---
[2] all available at https://data.4tu.nl.

unique traces to the overall number of traces, for example, is an indicator of variability in the logs. Another set of training logs reflecting unseen behavior is created by log injection into the base training logs, resulting in augmented training logs BPIC_aug to Traf_aug.

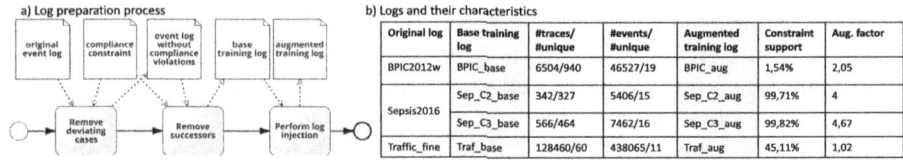

Fig. 3. Log preparation process (a) and created (training) logs (b)

For the augmented training logs, the *constraint support* reflects the percentage of traces that contain constraint-related events. For BPIC2012w, we randomly select only 100 cases relevant for C_1 to create a dataset with low constraint support. The *augmentation factor* is defined as the ratio of the number of traces after log injection. The augmentation factor is 1 for datasets with directly follows order relations. When injecting eventually follows relations into the log, the number of traces is increased as more variations are generated. For BPIC_aug, for example, an augmentation factor of 2.05 means that roughly twice as many traces are in the dataset than in the original event log. A high constraint support for eventually follows relations can lead to a high augmentation factor. However, other factors, such as excessively long traces in the dataset, multiple occurrences of predecessor events, and loose temporal restrictions imposed by the constraint, can also result in significant variations.

For evaluating the **(i) feasibility of log injection**, we adopt deep neural networks as the predictive model due to their popularity and superior performance for PPM tasks [27]. Based on [27], we select one representative approach per type of neural network for evaluation. This includes Long Short-Term Memory (Tax [32] and Bukhsh*, the latter by replacing the transformer block in [3] with two LSTM layers), Convolutional Neural Network (Mauro [22]), and Transformers (Bukhsh [3]). The baseline for each DL approach is the model trained based on the base training log, with comparison to the model trained based on the augmented log (cf. Fig. 3b). We follow the default experimental settings, such as the encoding techniques and hyperparameter configurations, as suggested in each respective work. Note that, Mauro [22] is the only approach among the selected methods that applies hyperparameter optimization, which may contribute to its superior performance.

Table 2 presents the average of three experimental runs as the final results in terms of accuracy for C_1, C_3, C_4. Due to space limitations, we omit results for the Sepsis_C_2 dataset, as its performance is comparable to that of Sepsis_C_3.

As shown in Table 2, log injection enables all approaches to predict unseen behavior. For event logs with high constraint support such as Sepsis_C_3, all

Table 2. Performance (Accuracy) of DL Approaches

Approach		BPI12w_C_1		Sepsis_C_3		Traffic_C_4	
		unseen	seen	unseen	seen	unseen	seen
Tax [32]	base	0.00	**90.05**	0.00	51.30	0.00	**92.23**
	aug.	**25.00**	83.40	**21.54**	**65.77**	**99.96**	92.12
Mauro [22]	base	0.00	**92.18**	0.00	65.38	0.00	**78.64**
	aug.	**76.92**	91.36	**44.62**	**67.26**	**100.00**	77.80
Bukhsh [3]	base	0.00	**92.15**	0.00	63.51	0.00	**78.63**
	aug.	**3.85**	87.03	**16.92**	**70.54**	**99.99**	77.87
Bukhsh*	base	0.00	**92.23**	0.00	61.35	0.00	**78.62**
	aug.	**26.92**	89.57	**16.92**	**69.89**	**99.97**	77.76

approaches show increased accuracy for predicting unseen and seen behavior. Regarding Traffic_C_4 with medium constraint support of 45.11%, prediction accuracy improves significantly for unseen behavior while maintaining comparable performance for seen behavior. This is largely due to the low augmentation factor of 1.02, which signals the accurate injection of unseen behavior without producing enormous variations to "pollute" the patterns of seen behavior. Note that the low augmentation factor might be attributed to the short case lengths in Traffic_C_4, with an average length of 3 and a maximum length of 15. The low augmentation factor also aligns with the low proportion of unique variations in the Traffic_C_4 dataset (60 unique among 128460 traces). By contrast, for BPIC2012w_C_1, which has a low constraint support of 1.54% but a relatively high augmentation factor of 2.05, the prediction performance for unseen behavior increases and decreases for seen behavior. This suggests that log injection results in approximately twice as many traces compared to the base log (as indicated by the augmentation factor), even though only a small fraction of them involve unseen behavior (as indicated by the constraint support). Thus, the large number of variations introduced with previously unseen activities may mislead the predictive model to over-weight unseen behavior, thereby obscuring the underlying patterns associated with seen behavior.

Regarding **(ii) performance compared to prediction model update**, we include all update strategies as introduced in [20] as baselines, i.e., U_1: update on new activities, U_2: update on new sequences, and U_3: update every day. Predictions are made on a daily basis across all logs. An exception is Traffic_C_4 featuring a 14-year duration, which are updated weekly in order to reduce the frequency of updates required. Prediction is made on a weekly basis accordingly.

For U_1 and U_2, if unseen activities or sequences are detected within the daily or weekly prediction window, the prediction model is updated using the past data combined with all traces observed during that window. We adopt the default settings outlined in [20], using the first 10% cases to build the initial prediction model, which features a single LSTM layer. The remaining data is reserved as a source for future incoming traces. To simulate historical data, we adjusted the timestamps of cases in the training set, ensuring that all future incoming traces occur after all cases in the training set. In this set of experiments, our approach trains the same prediction model as in [20] based on the augmented event log and evaluates its performance on the remaining 90% cases without updates. All experiments are performed on an NVIDIA GeForce RTX 4090 GPU.

The results can be seen in Table 3. In terms of unseen behavior prediction, log injection outperforms all update strategies. It is worth noting that log injection performs significantly worse regarding seen prediction than the best-performing update strategy U_2 on Sepsis_C_3 and Traffic_$C4$. This discrepancy occurs because these datasets include additional unseen activities that cannot be derived from the considered constraint. This is evidenced by the number of updates required by strategy U_1 (#updates > 1), which triggers updates when new activities are observed in the event streams.

Table 3. Results: Log Injection vs. Model Updates

Data-Approach	Accuracy		#updates	Time
	unseen	seen		
BPI12w_C_1-U_1	0.00	86.03	1	0:00:07
BPI12w_C_1-U_2	11.81	**86.54**	156	1:00:27
BPI12w_C_1-U_3	22.83	86.35	163	1:00:20
BPI12w_C_1-aug.	**37.01**	85.26	0	0:01:30
Sepsis_C_2-U_1	0.00	42.37	1	0:00:00
Sepsis_C_2-U_2	50.49	**52.99**	452	0:23:43
Sepsis_C_2-U_3	51.47	52.92	540	0:30:38
Sepsis_C_2-aug.	**67.75**	47.57	0	0:00:02
Sepsis_C_3-U_1	10.27	61.47	4	0:00:07
Sepsis_C_3-U_2	26.55	**63.61**	442	0:23:12
Sepsis_C_3-U_3	26.36	62.87	573	0:32:44
Sepsis_C_3-aug.	**31.98**	55.04	0	0:00:02
Traffic_C_4-U_1	3.99	79.27	2	0:00:46
Traffic_C_4-U_2	83.53	**79.58**	138	1:49:05
Traffic_C_4-U_3	83.86	79.57	653	9:37:33
Traffic_C_4-aug.	**99.61**	64.72	0	0:00:13

Compared to log injection, update strategies might become computationally expensive. For BPI12w_C_1-U_2, for example, the prediction model is updated each time new sequences are observed, resulting in 156 updates and the total retraining time of one hour. Moreover, model update strategies predict unseen behavior in an ex-post manner, meaning that models are updated only after unseen events have occurred. As a result, these strategies are unable to predict unseen behavior within the initial updates. This can be observed in all datasets for the best performing update strategy U_2 (cf. Fig. 4). For instance, as shown in BPI12w_C_1 (cf. (a) in Fig. 4), the accuracy for unseen predictions remains at 0 for the initial 15 updates.

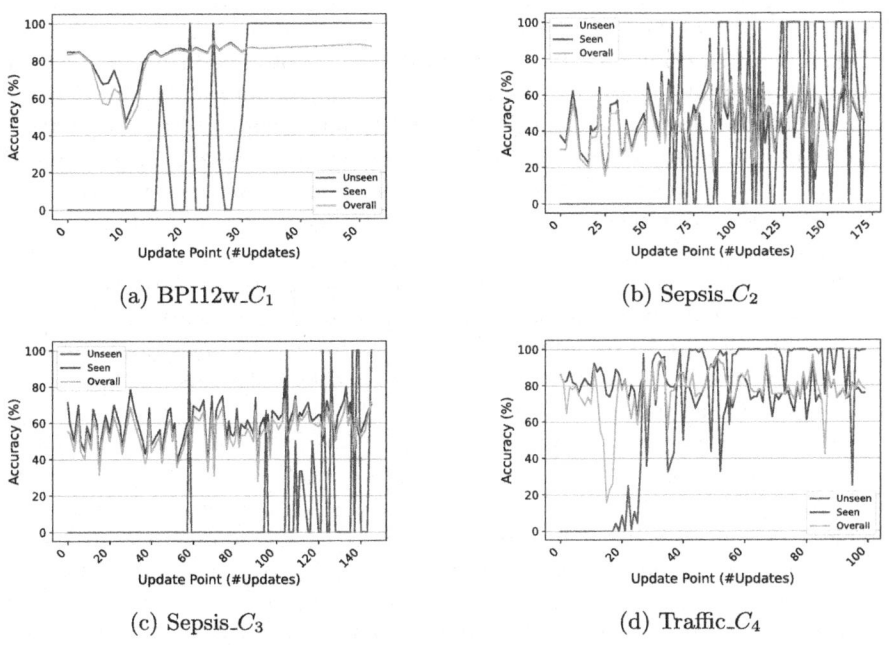

Fig. 4. Accuracy per Update Point for U_2.

Findings. In summary, log injection can significantly enhance the performance of prediction models, particularly in scenarios involving unseen behavior. The improvements are especially pronounced in datasets with strong constraint support. However, when dealing with datasets that include eventually follows relations, the augmentation factor must be carefully regularized to control the generation of excessive noise, which could "pollute" the patterns of seen behavior. By contrast, current state-of-the-art approaches, such as model update strategies, cannot predict unseen behavior in the early stage of model updates. This limitation arises from the insufficient data available for retraining. Additionally, these strategies are time-consuming, as model updates require extensive retraining, making them less efficient. By leveraging log injection, models achieve superior performance in predicting unseen behaviors while maintaining comparable overall performance. Moreover, log injection is more time-efficient than frequent model updates. Nevertheless, in situations where context information on unseen activities is limited, e.g., on Sepsis_C_3 and Traffic_$C4$, model updates may still be preferred to capture the evolving dynamics of the underlying process.

5 Related Work

Existing PPM approaches mostly update the prediction model after unseen behavior has been encountered at runtime, i.e., in an ex-post way, [7,29]. Incremental learning for predicting the outcome of a process instance has been applied by [19]. [24] use incremental learning for predicting the next activity. [20] conclude that an *"update on demand" strategy yields the best results in terms of balancing prediction quality and performance"*. [25] introduces different validation set sampling strategies to enhance the limited ability of trained models to generalize to unseen sequences. [16] apply data augmentation to solve the problem of log incompleteness in PPM, i.e., they propose several transformation techniques (e.g. randomly swap the execution order of two consecutive events) to augment the training data to predict new process variants, but not unseen activities.

The importance of context data for PPM is underpinned by the number of taxonomies for process context information, including [2,10,23]; these taxonomies differentiate its origin into internal/intrinsic (within the log) and external (outside the log) context data. In addition, [35] distinguish between structured and unstructured context information. Only few PPM approaches actually exploit context data as input. [12] discover context-aware prediction models based on internal context data. [33] include internal, textual data as unstructured context data to predict the outcome of a running case. Similarly, [18] exploit digital documents. [36] provide an approach for remaining time prediction by considering sentiments triggered by news (external context data). [8] propose an approach to identify context information for performance indicator prediction based on expert and domain knowledge. [31] exploit (external) sensor streams for predicting and explaining concept drift. [14] rank predictions based on their compliance with imposed constraints. However, for all approaches, the predictions are still based on observed behavior, i.e., they do not consider unseen behavior yet.

6 Conclusion

Despite the importance of PPM for decision making, proactively predicting unseen process behavior remains a significant challenge. Thus, in this work, we propose to inject unseen events into logs based on context information from order and temporal constraints, since they are prevalent in almost any application domain. The resulting, augmented logs are then used for model training. We evaluate the approach based on real-world logs with varying constraint support. The results show the feasibility of log injection as it enhances the model's ability to predict unseen activities. Furthermore, when compared to state-of-the-art model update strategies, log injection demonstrates superior performance in predicting unseen behavior, while the overall prediction accuracy remains comparable. Additionally, unlike model updates, which require extensive time for retraining, log injection might be preferable for scenarios requiring timely predictions.

There are limitations to acknowledge. First, log injection might introduce substantial noise, potentially obscuring patterns for seen behavior, especially in datasets with low constraint support. Second, our approach is restricted to scenarios in which context information about unseen behavior is available and traces are free of violations. Third, we focus only on augmentation with a single constraint, yet in practice, a single trace may be related to multiple constraints.

Future work will explore the inclusion of multiple, overlapping or conflicting constraints for log injection. Additionally, the applicability of log injection should be investigated across various prediction tasks, such as suffix or remaining time prediction.

Acknowledgments. This work was funded by the Deutsche Forschungsgemeinschaft (DFG, German Research Foundation) – project number 277991500.

References

1. Bakhshi, A., Hassannayebi, E., Sadeghi, A.H.: Optimizing sepsis care through heuristics methods in process mining: a trajectory analysis. CoRR **abs/2303.14328** (2023)
2. Brunk, J., Stierle, M., Papke, L., Revoredo, K., Matzner, M., Becker, J.: Cause vs. effect in context-sensitive prediction of business process instances. Inf. Syst. **95**, 101635 (2021)
3. Bukhsh, Z.A., Saeed, A., Dijkman, R.M.: ProcessTransformer: predictive business process monitoring with transformer network. CoRR **abs/2104.00721** (2021)
4. Burattin, A., Maggi, F.M., Sperduti, A.: Conformance checking based on multi-perspective declarative process models. Expert Syst. Appl. **65**, 194–211 (2016)
5. Camargo, M., Dumas, M., Rojas, O.G.: Learning accurate LSTM models of business processes. In: Business Process Management, pp. 286–302 (2019)
6. Ceravolo, P., Comuzzi, M., De Weerdt, J., Di Francescomarino, C., Maggi, F.M.: Predictive process monitoring: concepts, challenges, and future research directions. Process Sci. **1**(1), 2 (2024)
7. Chamorro, A.E.M., Nepomuceno-Chamorro, I.A., Resinas, M., Ruiz-Cortés, A.: Updating prediction models for predictive process monitoring. In: Advanced Information Systems Engineering, pp. 304–318 (2022)
8. Chamorro, A.E.M., Revoredo, K., Resinas, M., del-Río-Ortega, A., Santoro, F.M., Ruiz-Cortés, A.: Context-aware process performance indicator prediction. IEEE Access **8**, 222050–222063 (2020)
9. Chen, Q., Winter, K., Rinderle-Ma, S.: Predicting unseen process behavior based on context information from compliance constraints. In: BPM Forum, pp. 127–144 (2023)
10. Ehrendorfer, M., Mangler, J., Rinderle-Ma, S.: Assessing the impact of context data on process outcomes during runtime. In: ICSOC, pp. 3–18 (2021)
11. Evermann, J., Rehse, J., Fettke, P.: Predicting process behaviour using deep learning. Decis. Support Syst. **100**, 129–140 (2017)
12. Folino, F., Guarascio, M., Pontieri, L.: Discovering context-aware models for predicting business process performances. In: OTM, pp. 287–304 (2012)
13. Francescomarino, C.D., Ghidini, C.: Predictive process monitoring. In: van der Aalst, W.M.P., Carmona, J. (eds.) Process Mining Handbook, pp. 320–346 (2022)

14. Francescomarino, C.D., Ghidini, C., Maggi, F.M., Petrucci, G., Yeshchenko, A.: An eye into the future: leveraging a-priori knowledge in predictive business process monitoring. In: Business Process Management, pp. 252–268 (2017)
15. Hashmi, M., Governatori, G., Lam, H.-P., Wynn, M.T.: Are we done with business process compliance: state of the art and challenges ahead. Knowl. Inf. Syst. **57**(1), 79–133 (2018). https://doi.org/10.1007/s10115-017-1142-1
16. Käppel, M., Jablonski, S.: Model-agnostic event log augmentation for predictive process monitoring. In: Indulska, M., Reinhartz-Berger, I., Cetina, C., Pastor, O. (eds.) Advanced Information Systems Engineering, pp. 381–397 (2023)
17. Koschmider, A., Speidel, S.: Predictive behavior analysis for smart environments. EMISA Forum **36**(2), 68–71 (2016)
18. Levich, S., Lutz, B., Neumann, D.: Utilizing the omnipresent: incorporating digital documents into predictive process monitoring using deep neural networks. Decis. Support Syst. **175**, 114043 (2023)
19. Maisenbacher, M., Weidlich, M.: Handling concept drift in predictive process monitoring. In: Services Computing, pp. 1–8 (2017)
20. Mangat, A.S., Rinderle-Ma, S.: Next-activity prediction for non-stationary processes with unseen data variability. In: EDOC, pp. 145–161 (2022)
21. Mannhardt, F., de Leoni, M., Reijers, H.A., van der Aalst, W.: Balanced multi-perspective checking of process conformance. Computing **98**(4), 407–437 (2016)
22. Mauro, N.D., Appice, A., Basile, T.M.A.: Activity prediction of business process instances with inception CNN models. In: Advances in Artificial Intelligence, pp. 348–361 (2019)
23. Park, G., Benzin, J., van der Aalst, W.M.P.: Detecting context-aware deviations in process executions. In: Business Process Management Forum, pp. 190–206 (2022)
24. Pauwels, S., Calders, T.: Incremental predictive process monitoring: the next activity case. In: Business Process Management, pp. 123–140 (2021)
25. Peeperkorn, J., vanden Broucke, S., Weerdt, J.D.: Validation set sampling strategies for predictive process monitoring. Inf. Syst. **121**, 102330 (2024)
26. Polato, M., Sperduti, A., Burattin, A., Leoni, M.: Time and activity sequence prediction of business process instances. Computing **100**(9), 1005–1031 (2018). https://doi.org/10.1007/s00607-018-0593-x
27. Rama-Maneiro, E., Vidal, J.C., Lama, M.: Deep learning for predictive business process monitoring: review and benchmark. TSC **16**(1), 739–756 (2023)
28. Rama-Maneiro, E., Vidal, J.C., Lama, M.: Embedding graph convolutional networks in recurrent neural networks for predictive monitoring. IEEE Trans. Knowl. Data Eng. **36**(1), 137–151 (2024)
29. Rizzi, W., Francescomarino, C.D., Ghidini, C., Maggi, F.M.: How do I update my model? On the resilience of predictive process monitoring models to change. Knowl. Inf. Syst. **64**(5), 1385–1416 (2022)
30. Shorten, C., Khoshgoftaar, T.M.: A survey on image data augmentation for deep learning. J. Big Data **6**, 60 (2019)
31. Stertz, F., Rinderle-Ma, S., Mangler, J.: Analyzing process concept drifts based on sensor event streams during runtime. In: BPM, pp. 202–219 (2020)
32. Tax, N., Verenich, I., Rosa, M.L., Dumas, M.: Predictive business process monitoring with LSTM neural networks. In: CAiSE, pp. 477–492 (2017)
33. Teinemaa, I., Dumas, M., Maggi, F.M., Francescomarino, C.D.: Predictive business process monitoring with structured and unstructured data. In: BPM, pp. 401–417 (2016)
34. Teinemaa, I., Dumas, M., Rosa, M.L., Maggi, F.M.: Outcome-oriented predictive process monitoring: review and benchmark. TKDD **13**(2), 17:1–17:57 (2019)

35. Weinzierl, S., Revoredo, K., Matzner, M.: Predictive business process monitoring with context information from documents. In: ECIS (2019)
36. Yeshchenko, A., Durier, F., Revoredo, K., Mendling, J., Santoro, F.M.: Context-aware predictive process monitoring: the impact of news sentiment. In: OTM, pp. 586–603 (2018)

Toward IoT-Based Process Analytics: Extending Event Knowledge Graphs with Ambiguity

Marco Franceschetti[✉], Dominik Manuel Buchegger, Ronny Seiger, and Barbara Weber

Institute of Computer Science, University of St. Gallen, St. Gallen, Switzerland
marco.franceschetti@unisg.ch

Abstract. Digital traces of processes executed in the physical world without Information Systems (IS) support are composed of high-level events derived from low-level physical world events (e.g., from IoT). Due to this, frequently these high-level events are ambiguous, i.e., they yield multiple interpretations. As current IS lack ambiguity-awareness, ambiguity in digital traces can compromise process analytics. Motivated by this and current trends toward multi-dimensional analytics, we introduce an ambiguity-aware object-centric representation of digital traces by extending Event Knowledge Graphs with ambiguity. We integrate its construction into a framework to enable analytics for ambiguous IoT-based digital traces. A prototype implementation shows the applicability of the construction from ambiguous process event streams in online settings.

Keywords: event knowledge graphs · ambiguity · iot-based analytics

1 Introduction

Two significant emerging research directions arise in the current Business Process Management (BPM) landscape: multi-dimensional process analytics [2] and the integration of the Internet of Things with BPM for process monitoring [6,14].

On the one hand, multi-dimensional analytics represent a shift toward a more comprehensive understanding of business processes by incorporating diverse perspectives such as actor behavior, resource utilization, and entity interactions, beyond the traditional case-centric focus. This shift has led to the development of novel analysis paradigms, such as object-centric process mining [1], and advanced representation formalisms, such as Event Knowledge Graphs (EKGs) [9], able to model and analyze rich interdependencies in business processes [15,16].

On the other hand, the integration of IoT technologies into process monitoring has significantly expanded the scope of BPM. Specifically, the BPM-IoT integration enables the real-time generation of digital traces of processes executed in the physical world without Information System (IS) support [33]. This requires the observation of the physical world via sensors that generate low-level IoT events–usually without process semantics–and to abstract these IoT events into high-level events with process semantics [27]. However, this is challenged by the fact that IoT event streams are frequently characterized by noise, incomplete or missing sensor data, and limited process context-awareness [19]. This leads to uncertainty about how to interpret IoT events, i.e., to *ambiguity* [10]. Ambiguity-awareness in the event abstraction step, i.e., the ability to explicitly consider the multiple event interpretations when generating process events, is critical to avoid misrepresenting the actual process executions. Therefore, ambiguity originating from the IoT events must be explicitly propagated to the process events to avoid compromising the subsequent process analytics.

Here, we set our focus on two specific challenges posed by ambiguity. A first challenge (**C1**) arises from the ambiguity in IoT-based events during the sensing and abstraction [19]. IoT sensors often lack the process awareness or contextual information needed to clearly correlate observed events with specific process instances or entities in the situational context. This results in multiple possible interpretations of the same event and its correlations with the contextual entities [10], which can compromise process analytics outcomes [2]. A second challenge (**C2**) stems from the ambiguity in entity roles, which is also rooted in the IoT event abstraction. IoT data often provides limited information about the roles entities play in events (e.g., whether an agent is the performer or target of an activity; cf. the concept of endurants in [3]), leading to multiple possible role interpretations that also compromise process analytics outcomes [24].

To overcome these challenges with the object-centric paradigm in mind, we address the research question: *How to explicitly represent ambiguities in process events derived from the IoT-driven monitoring of processes that lead to C1–C2?*

As our overarching goal is to enable IoT-based multi-dimensional process analytics, we first set requirements and outline a software framework to support such analytics. We integrate within this framework the main contribution of this paper: an extension of EKGs *with ambiguity* (EKGAs) for the object-centric representation of digital traces with ambiguity, and an EKGA construction method. EKGAs allow modeling the uncertainty in interpreting ambiguous events and the different roles with which entities participate in events, overcoming challenges **C1–C2**. We show the applicability of EKGA construction in online settings by testing a prototype implementation on a stream of healthcare process events.

Our main contribution facilitates the creation of an object-centric representation of process executions from IoT data, explicitly modeling ambiguity that leads to uncertainty about event-entity correlations and the roles entities play in events. The EKGA bridges the current gap between object-centric digital trace representation and explicit modeling of event ambiguity. Integrating our contribution with an information system paves the way to the development of novel ambiguity-aware systems capable of performing multi-dimensional analytics of digital traces with ambiguous events. It further stimulates the development of new methods of online event disambiguation to support online process monitoring and conformance checking driven by IoT technologies.

Paper Structure. Section 2 motivates our work setting requirements. Section 3 presents a framework integrating EKGA construction. Section 4 presents a prototype implementation. Section 5 discusses related work. Section 6 concludes the paper.

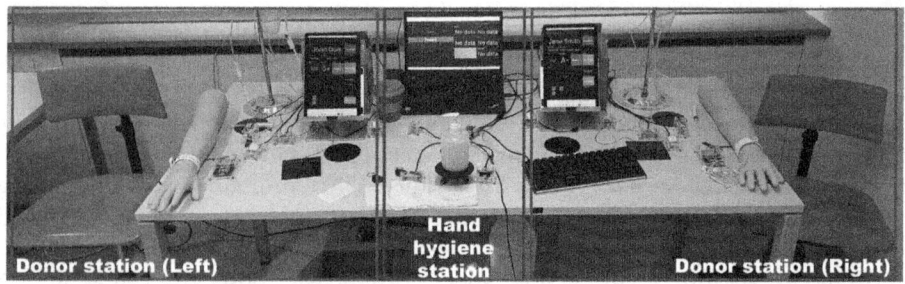

Fig. 1. Lab setup to simulate the IoT-monitored blood donation process, with two donor stations (red boxes) and one shared hand hygiene station (green box) (Color figure online)

2 Motivation and Requirements

2.1 Motivating Scenario

As a motivating scenario, we take the IoT-driven online conformance checking of a blood donation process, for which we can simulate the execution of two concurrent, co-located instances in our lab setup, shown in Fig. 1, as detailed in [11]. As a normative blueprint to check the conformance, we take the process specification extracted in [11] from the WHO guidelines in [20,26] and validated by healthcare experts. We translated the validated specification into constraints and derived the simplified process model shown in Fig. 2 as a DCR graph [13]. We assume one process instance to be associated with one *donor* (a patient donating blood), and that multiple co-located instances can run simultaneously.

The first step for the healthcare worker (HCW) is to perform a hand hygiene, then HCW proceeds with the preliminary operations (identify the donor, check the drawing machine, disinfect the injection site). Then, HCW again performs a hand hygiene, after which HCW performs the venipuncture and initiates the blood drawing. During the blood drawing, HCW closely monitors the donor. Once enough blood is drawn, HCW ends the blood drawing, removes and disposes the needle, and performs a hand hygiene. Lastly, HCW performs final operations (dismiss the donor, store the blood sample), and a hand hygiene. Any other activity performed by HCW during the process (e.g., signing a document, touching another donor) is considered as a hand contamination (cf. "Contaminate hands" in Fig. 2) and requires a hand hygiene before continuing.

Like many healthcare processes, the blood donation process is not driven by an IS and is mostly manual. To monitor its execution and check its conformance we rely on IoT technologies for sensing, aggregating, and abstracting multiple low-level IoT events into high-level process events, as proposed in [6,27], with the ultimate goal of providing online feedback about process conformance to the users. In our lab setup, we leverage sensors such as proximity, motion, and touch sensors; we deliberately do not use cameras due to privacy concerns in healthcare settings. Additionally, healthcare settings are inherently noisy environments characterized by the occurrence of unpredictable events such as medical emer-

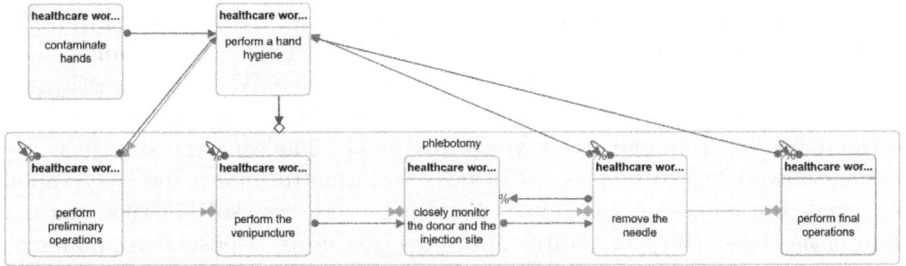

Fig. 2. Blood donation process as a DCR graph [13]. Orange arrows: condition constraints; blue arrows: response constraints; red arrows: exclusion constraints; purple arrows: milestone constraints (Color figure online)

gencies and concurrent treatments [36]. Digital traces of events generated via the IoT are likely affected by ambiguity [10], which results in uncertain event-entity correlations and uncertain entity participation roles in events. We describe examples in relation to the challenges outlined in the introduction.

*Example for Challenge **C1**.* Assume that one HCW is attending simultaneously two donors $D1$ and $D2$ in proximity of each other (cf. the two donor stations in Fig. 1). When we observe a "Perform hand hygiene" event by HCW at a hand hygiene station shared by $D1$ and $D2$, ambiguity arises regarding which donor the hand hygiene is for, i.e., which entity correlates with the event. This means that we are uncertain whether to interpret the hand hygiene as part of the blood donation by $D1$ or $D2$. This event could be retrospectively disambiguated by observing a subsequent event revealing more information. For example, if the next event is "Perform preliminary operations" on $D1$, we can confidently establish the event-entity correlation of the hand hygiene with $D1$. Still, without an explicit representation of this ambiguity, we would either treat both interpretations as certain events, or keep only one of the two, potentially discarding the correct one–in either case risking to get incorrect analysis results.

*Example for Challenge **C2**.* In healthcare processes like the blood donation process, HCW's hand hygiene is of utmost importance. Specifically, a HCW's hands must be always sanitized before treating a patient (donor); this must be done also when shifting between patients to avoid cross-contamination. So, after "Perform preliminary operations" on $D1$, HCW must perform a hand hygiene if the next step is a treatment on $D2$. As such, "Perform preliminary operations" on $D1$ is not an event in the treatment process of $D2$. However, it still has an influence on it because its occurrence adds a new precondition for the next step in $D2$'s process–executing "Perform hand hygiene". Here, we must be able to distinguish between two participation roles in treatment events: either a donor is the *target* of a treatment (the treatment is done on her as part of her process) or is *affected by* another donor's treatment (the treatment is not done on her, but it still affects her process). For the former, the event has the semantics of a normal process step; for the latter, the event has the semantics of a hand contamination. Depending on the role, the respective process instances should have different continuations. Knowing about the specific role allows us to establish how the respective instance should continue and to conclude about process conformance.

In the blood donation process, adherence of the HCW to the hand hygiene regulations is crucial to prevent infections spreading from contaminated surfaces to the donors or from one donor to another donor. The conformance of the process executions has to be checked in near real-time to inform the HCW about potential contamination and missed hand hygiene events so that they can take counter-measures through additional disinfection steps. A post-mortem analysis would only be able to reveal non-conformance but would be too late to take effective counter-measures. The conformance checking has to be aware of potential ambiguities emerging from the IoT sensor processing to identify the unclear roles of the donors in the treatment activities mentioned above, which need to be resolved in a next step to inform the HCW.

2.2 Requirements

Our overarching goal is to define a software framework enabling multi-dimensional analytics and ambiguity resolution of digital traces of processes executed without IS support and monitored via IoT. Here, we focus on a specific component of this framework: the explicit modeling of ambiguity that results in uncertain event-entity correlations and uncertain entity participation roles in events. Aligning with [12], we assume uncertainty to be known in stochastic terms.

A framework achieving this goal should meet the following functional requirements, drawn from our experience with event sensing and abstraction, ambiguity, and the IoT contexts that the system should operate in. **F1**: it should support the online sensing of low-level event data from the process environment. Our goal is to enable analytics of processes monitored via IoT; specifically in our lab setup we aim to check and provide feedback about process conformance in near real-time. Thus, we need to consider data from IoT sensors as streams of low-level events. **F2**: it should be able to abstract low-level event data into the correct high-level process events recording activity name, timestamp, and information about all entities possibly involved in each process event to facilitate the application of (online) process mining techniques in later steps. **F3**: it should emit all events when multiple interpretations of the low-level events as process events, and multiple interpretations of the entity-event correlations, are possible. **F4**: it should allow for the online translation of process events from an event stream in a data structure suitable to support multi-dimensional process analytics. This structure should include all possible interpretations of ambiguous events and correlations, allowing the explicit representation of ambiguities. We also define **N1**: performance as a non-functional requirement, as the framework should be able to handle input with latencies acceptable for online settings.

3 Framework to Enable Multi-dimensional Analytics

In this section, we outline a four-step framework (depicted in Fig. 3) that addresses the requirements listed in Sect. 2 and contextualizes our main con-

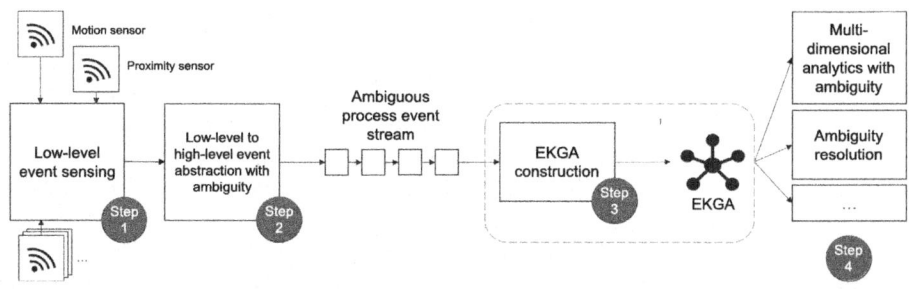

Fig. 3. Framework to enable multi-dimensional analytics of processes executed without IS support in the presence of ambiguity based on EKGAs; the focus of this paper is highlighted with the red box (Color figure online)

tribution, i.e., an extension of EKG with ambiguity and a method for its construction.

3.1 Step 1: Low-Level Event Sensing

Analyzing digital traces of physical world processes executed without IS support requires these processes to be observable. This can be achieved using IoT technologies, specifically sensors able to emit *low-level* event streams describing the events happening in the physical world [14]. Here, a challenge is selecting the right sensors to describe the physical world events that are relevant in the process, i.e., that correspond to process activity executions. Depending on the specific process, a domain expert selects and positions different sensors in the process environment to sense these physical world events (cf. requirement F1), which can then be related to process activity executions (how this is done is out of this paper scope). Still, even with the deployment of all permissible sensors within the process environment, there remains the possibility that these sensors cannot unambiguously capture and describe the targeted physical world events. Beyond the limitations posed by constrained brownfield integration scenarios, this could be attributed to the sensors' inability to provide adequate contextual information during sensing, or the insufficiency of the generated low-level events in distinguishing between physical world phenomena. Factors such as limited sensor precision, which might also be an intentional choice to safeguard user privacy [19], further contribute to this challenge. This results in multiple physical world events being represented by the same low-level events, which are undistinguishable. We assume that, when positioning the sensors, the expert is aware of which physical world events correspond to which low-level events and of any potential ambiguities. In contrast to related approaches, we leverage this awareness to explicitly model ambiguity in the following event abstraction step.

Example. In our lab setup (cf. Fig. 1), to be able to detect hand hygiene activity occurrences, we chose a proximity sensor and a scale, and positioned them in the hand hygiene station. The proximity sensor continuously emits events describing how close *something* is from the sensor at each point in time. The scale is positioned under the hand sanitizer dispenser, and it continuously emits events describing the weight it measures at each point in time. The reason is that, to perform a hand hygiene, a HCW must be in proximity of the hand hygiene station and press the sanitizer dispenser (causing an increase in the weight) to release the sanitizer, and these sensors help us to detect these events. However, the sensor configuration in the setup does not provide any contextual data about which donor is the target of the hand hygiene activity, if multiple donors are present. Thus, hand hygiene activities done for a donor in the left station and for a donor in the right station are represented by the same low-level events. Similarly, in our lab setup, we use in conjunction a motion sensor, a proximity sensor, and an ambient light sensor (sensing a donor's arm presence on the armrest) to detect three distinct process activities: *apply the tourniquet on the arm*, *disinfect the arm*, and *insert needle in the arm*. These activities are represented by the same low-level events from these sensors. Since no additional sensors can be introduced and we cannot use cameras to disambiguate, the low-level events generated by these sensors can be interpreted as either of the three activities.

3.2 Step 2: Low-Level to High-Level Event Abstraction with Ambiguity

Low-level events emitted by sensors in Step 1 do not yield process semantics. For example, events generated by a proximity sensor only state how close *something* is from the sensor, but do not specifically inform about any process activity. The event abstraction step fuses and translates low-level events into *high-level* events with process semantics (cf. requirement F2) [14]. Typically, this is achieved by matching specific low-level event patterns signifying the occurrence of a process activity. In this step, we distinguish between a design-time and a run-time phase.

At design-time, a domain expert chooses an appropriate event abstraction approach, defines patterns of low-level events (e.g., based on domain knowledge [28]), and mechanisms for matching these patterns to process events. The discussion of details on the pattern specification is out of scope of this work. Suitable approaches may involve, for instance, developing Complex Event Processing (CEP) applications, like in [27], or training Machine Learning (ML) models, like in [18]. Leveraging process and domain knowledge, each high-level event to be generated upon pattern matching is specified. Each high-level event comprises an activity name, a timestamp attribute, and additional attributes that describe the entities correlated with the event and whose values are derived from the low-level events. Current event abstraction approaches do not account for the existence of multiple high-level interpretations of a given low-level event pattern–they may either assume all interpretations as correct and generate all respective high-level events as they all occurred, or select a single interpretation and generate the respective event, e.g., [18]. To explicitly model ambiguity, we propose leveraging the ambiguity-awareness from the first step and augmenting the event abstraction procedure with a wrapper that generates each possible high-level event interpretation of a pattern, adding a representation of ambiguity

```xml
<event>
    <string key="concept:name" value="Hand hygiene"/>
    <date key="time:timestamp" value="2024-09-13T11:36:50.000+00:00"/>
    <string key="perform:hcw" value="HCW0001"/>
    <string key="location:station" value="Hygiene station"/>
    <container key="uncertainty:discrete_weak">
        <container key="uncertainty:entry">
            <string key="target:donor" value="D035"/>
            <double key="uncertainty:probability" value="0.5"/>
        </container>
        <container key="uncertainty:entry">
            <string key="target:donor" value="D036"/>
            <double key="uncertainty:probability" value="0.5"/>
        </container>
    </container>
</event>
```

Fig. 4. Ambiguous event example, with uncertainty regarding the specific correlated entity in the role of activity target. The event is represented using the XES extension for uncertain event data [23].

to it (cf. requirement F3). Specifically, we model ambiguity in terms of stochastically quantified uncertainty, i.e., a *probability* representing the confidence value of an interpretation [29]. While a domain expert can leverage domain knowledge to specify how probabilities are determined during event abstraction, a domain-agnostic naive strategy is also possible. This strategy simply distributes the probabilities equally across all interpretations of one ambiguity, for a total mass of 1. In general, however, the total probability mass for one ambiguity might be lower than 1–which is the case of indeterminate events discussed in [22].

At run-time, the event abstraction approach is deployed (e.g., as a CEP app or service, like in [27]) to fuse and analyze low-level events being produced by the sensors. Upon the detection of a defined low-level event pattern that has a single interpretation, the respective high-level event is generated. If a pattern can be interpreted as multiple high-level events, a high-level event per interpretation is generated with the respective probability attached, as defined at design-time. If a pattern can be interpreted as one high-level event but the event-entity correlations have multiple interpretations, one high-level event is generated with one attribute per interpretation with the respective probability (cf. requirement F3). Note that the run-time phase can help to inform the design-time phase by discovering low-level event patterns that unexpectedly result in multiple or incorrect high-level events. Here, an analyst can iterate between the two phases to incrementally refine event abstraction with ambiguity, for instance by defining new interpretations or re-assigning the associated probabilities.

Example. In our lab setup, we can detect the occurrence of activity *Perform hand hygiene* by observing a concurrent proximity within 20 cm from the hand hygiene station and a weight on the scale higher than 2 kg. Accordingly, we defined a low-level event pattern for a CEP service that results in the generation of a high-level event with name *Perform hand hygiene* and with an attribute specifying that the location is the hand hygiene station. However, in the presence of two donors, when generating the high-level event we are not able to determine which of the two donors is the activity target. Therefore, since in our setup we follow the naive strategy to distribute the probabilities, one high level event for the hand hygiene activity is generated with both donors indicated as target of the activity, each with a probability of 50%. Figure 4 depicts this event using the XES extension for uncertain event data [23].

3.3 Step 3: EKGA Construction

Here, we assume that the previous event abstraction step generates a stream of high-level events with ambiguity, e.g., encoded in the XES format extended with uncertain event data [23], as in our lab setup, through the near real-time fusion and analysis of low-level events. In this step, we aim to translate this stream of events with ambiguity into a representation suitable for performing multi-dimensional analytics (cf. requirement F4). To this end, we build upon the work in [9], which introduced Event Knowledge Graphs (EKGs), and extend EKGs to additionally model ambiguity. As here we focus on defining EKGs with Ambiguity (EKGAs), we refer the reader to [9] for a formal definition of EKGs.

Informally, we define an Event Knowledge Graph with Ambiguity as a Labeled Property Graph [32] in which the set of relationship labels defines directly-follows relationships and event-entity correlation types, and in which each relationship label has in addition a probability p as a property. The intuition is that a correlation type label states the specific participation role of an entity in an event, and that a probability states the likelihoods of the respective event-event or event-entity relationship. Since correlation type labels are domain-specific, we do not impose restrictions on their set of values. We specifically propose specialized correlation labels instead of reified correlations (i.e., each correlation is transformed into a new entity representing it; this new entity is correlated with the originally correlated entities by a generic relationship [5]). This is because reification introduces additional nodes and edges in the graph, increasing its size and making it more challenging in terms of cognitive demand for analysts to read and understand [35]. Additionally, in an EKGA we always specify probabilities for all relationship labels, even when their value is 1.

Formally, we define an Event Knowledge Graph with Ambiguity as follows:

Definition 1 (Event Knowledge Graph with Ambiguity). *An event knowledge graph with ambiguity is a labeled property graph $G = (N, R, \lambda, \#)$ with node labels $\{Event, Entity\} \subseteq \Lambda_N$ and relationship labels $\{df, r_{type}\}$ indicating "directly-follows" and correlation relationship types between entities and nodes, with $r_{type} \subseteq \Lambda_R$ and the following properties:*

1. *Every event node $e \in N^{Event}$ records an activity name $e.act \neq \bot$, a timestamp $e.time \neq \bot$, and records a probability $e.p \in [0,1]$.*
2. *Every entity node $n \in N^{Entity}$ has an entity type $n.type \neq \bot$ and an identifier $n.id \neq \bot$.*
3. *All correlation relationship types are subsumed by the set $R^{corr} = \bigcup R^{r_{type}}$.*

4. Every correlation relationship $r \in R^{corr}$, $\vec{r} = (e, n)$ is defined from an event node $e \in N^{Event}$ to an entity node $n \in N^{Entity}$; we write $n \in corr(e)$ and $e \in corr(n)$ as shorthand. Every $r \in R^{corr}$ records a probability $r.p \in [0, 1]$ and a type $r.type$.
5. Any directly-follows relationship $df \in R^{df}$, $\vec{df} = (e_1, e_2)$ is defined between event nodes $e_1, e_2 \in N^{Event}$, records a probability $df.p \in [0, 1]$, a pair of correlation relationship types $df.rel \in R^{rtype} \times R^{rtype}$ and refers to a specific entity $df.ent = n \in N^{Entity}$ and two correlations c_1, c_2 such that:
  (a) $c_1 = (e_1, n)$, $c_2 = (e_2, n) \in R^{corr}$;
  (b) $e_1.time < e_2.time$;
  (c) $\nexists e' \in N^{Event}$ such that $(e', n) \in R^{corr}$ and $e_1.time < e'.time < e_2.time$;
  (d) $df.p = e_1.p \times c_1.p \times e_2.p \times c_2.p$;
  (e) $df.rel = (c_1.type, c_2.type)$.

The original EKG definition in [9] states that a directly-follows relationship between two event nodes depends on the existing event-entity correlations of the nodes and their timestamp property. It can be established only if the event nodes correlate with the same entity node and there exists no other event node that correlates with the same entity node and whose timestamp is between the timestamps of the two nodes. The definition implies that an event can directly follow multiple events based on different event-entity correlations. The intuition is that a directly-follows relationship models a temporal order relation that is *local* to the entity that the events correlate with. This allows representing the behavioral information relevant to each individual entity separately from other entities' behavioral information [9]. Extending the original EKG definition, Definition 1 states that in an EKGA a directly-follows relationship is established on the basis of a correlation with a common entity node, with the additional assignment of the probability property. The probability of the directly-follows relationship is determined as the product of the probabilities of the events and of the probabilities of the correlation relationships that determine it. Note that, given an event node and an entity node, due to ambiguities there can be multiple relationships between them with a probability < 1. Therefore, in the presence of ambiguity, there can be multiple directly-follows relationships between two given event nodes due to the same entity node, with probability < 1. We denote with $\langle l, p \rangle$ a (correlation or directly-follows) relationship with label l and probability p.

The procedure we propose for the online translation of a stream of high-level events into an EKGA is similar to the one for EKG construction described in [9], with the difference that it adds additional roles and probabilities, and computes the directly-follows relations after each new event is added to the graph. For each event in the input stream, a new event node E is added to the EKGA. The new event node is created with properties activity name as node identifier, event timestamp as the node timestamp, and node probability as specified in the event or 1 if not specified. For each context attribute in the event, a new entity node N, if not preexisting, is created in the EKGA (otherwise this preexisting N is fetched from the graph), and a new correlation edge R is created between E and N, along with the role property for R as specified in the event attribute. If a probability is specified for the attribute, this is assigned to the correlation probability property, 1 otherwise. Lastly, the directly-follows relationships for the new event are computed, based on the correlation with the entity nodes. The probability of a directly-follows relationship is computed by multiplying the probabilities of the new event, of its correlation with entity N, of the most recent event correlated with N, and of its correlation with N (cf. Definition 1). In principle, the directly-follows relations can be computed after all events have been added to the graph (cf. [9]). However, when considering an event stream as input, this would mean postponing the directly-follows computation indefinitely (cf. requirement F4). Therefore, the proposed procedure computes new directly-follows relations after each new event (with its entities) is translated into the respective EKGA elements. To avoid establishing incorrect directly-follows relations, we require events to be ordered by increasing timestamp value.

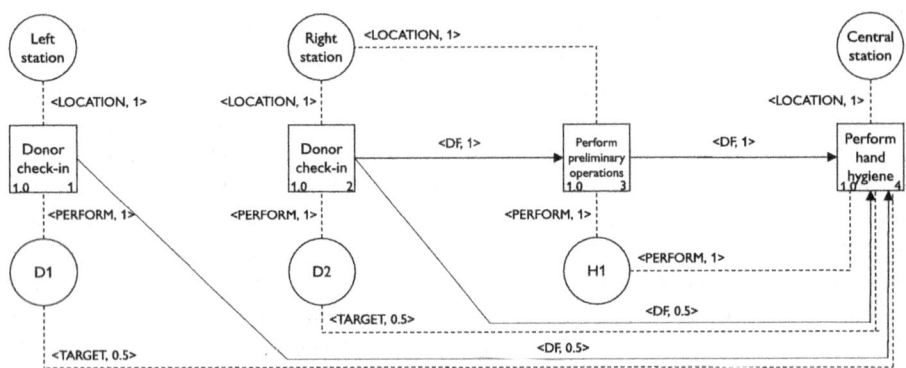

Fig. 5. Example EKGA. Squares = event nodes; circles = entity nodes; dashed lines = correlations; arrows = directly-follows relations. Event probabilities and timestamps are at each event bottom-left and bottom-right corner, respectively

Example. Figure 5 illustrates an EKGA resulting from four high-level events encoded in XES extended with uncertainty (cf. Fig. 4) from the blood donation process in our lab setup. The EKGA depicts four event nodes e_1 to e_4, all with probability 1 ($e_1.act$ = Donor check-in, $e_2.act$ = Donor check-in, $e_3.act$ = Perform preliminary operations, and $e_4.act$ = Perform hand hygiene, with $e_i.time = i$) and six entity nodes (n_1 with $n_1.type$ = Donor and $n_1.id$ = D1, n_2 with $n_2.type$ = Donor and $n_2.id$ = D2, n_3 with $n_3.type$ = HCW and $n_3.id$ = H1, n_4 with $n_4.type$ = Station and $n_4.id$ = Left station, n_5 with $n_5.type$ = Station and $n_5.id$ = Right station, and n_6 with $n_6.type$ = Station and $n_6.id$ = Central station). e_4 is correlated with n_3 with $\langle \text{perform}, 1 \rangle$, meaning that we are certain that H1 is the performer of the hand hygiene. e_4 is correlated with n_1 by $\langle \text{target}, 0.5 \rangle$ and e_4 is correlated with n_2 by $\langle \text{target}, 0.5 \rangle$, meaning that D1, resp. D2, is the donor for which e_4 occurred with probability 50%. Thus, e_4 directly follows e_1 with probability 50% due to n_1, resp. e_4 directly follows e_2 with probability 50% due to n_2, signifying that these df-relations are ambiguous.

3.4 Step 4: Multi-dimensional Analytics and Ambiguity Resolution

The EKGA representing a digital trace derived in Step 3 enables multi-dimensional analytics [9]. For example, the EKG-based deterministic analyses of actor behaviors in [16] can provide insights into the interactions between HCWs in the blood donation process (cf. Sect. 2); another example is multi-dimensional conformance checking [8], e.g., supported by the model in Fig. 2. However, to the best of our knowledge, existing approaches to multi-dimensional analytics do not contemplate the presence of stochastic event data. Developing new ambiguity-aware approaches requires considering the stochastic information associated with the event occurrence and the correlations. An option is to extend the deterministic approach in [16] to deal with stochastically known correlations between activities and the performing actors. Additionally, as interpretations of ambiguities are context-dependent [17], we foresee disambiguation methods to leverage the representation of the events situational context in terms of event-entity correlations. Specifically, knowing about event-entity correlations enables the definition of strategies to infer the admissible and most likely interpretations of ambiguous events, i.e., context-dependent ambiguity resolution. Possible strategies include unsupervised (e.g., LLM-driven) and supervised methods (i.e., domain expert-driven). We plan to investigate different ambiguity resolution approaches. On the one hand, we will leverage domain knowledge integrated with the EKGA, in analogy to the ontology-based approach in [30] to derive missing entity identifiers. On the other hand, we will use the all optimal alignments described in [25] to determine the most likely interpretations. These are only initial examples of the opportunities enabled by EKGAs for analytics and ambiguity resolution: here, an exhaustive and in-depth discussion of these opportunities is out of scope.

4 Implementation and Experiments

Having demonstrated in prior work the capabilities of event sensing and abstraction in near real-time (cf. [27]), we implemented a prototype for the EKGA construction procedure to assess its ability to process input in online settings. The prototype is able to receive in input an event stream in the MQTT-XES format [7]. To support the representation of stochastic uncertainty, we specifically consider the XES extension with uncertainty introduced in [23]. The prototype is implemented in Python; it uses the graph database Neo4j[1] to store the EKGA, with Cypher as the query language. The implementation is available at https://github.com/ics-unisg/ekga. Our execution environment is a Win Server 2025 machine with a 12-core CPU@3.80 GHz and 48 GB of memory.

To assess the applicability of the prototype to an online setting (cf. requirement N1), we measured the latency for translating each new event in an input

---

[1] https://neo4j.com/.

stream of process events (originating from a log file) into an EKGA. To the best of our knowledge, no event logs with uncertainty describing real process executions are publicly available to be used as input. Therefore, we took an event log describing 36 executions of the blood donation process conducted in our lab setup (cf. Sect. 2) in the period 11–13 September 2024 by a group of local medical students acting as HCWs[2]. Due to our lab setup being limited to two donor stations, a maximum of two blood donors treated concurrently by the same HCW is recorded in the log. The log contains a total of 800 events, of which 328 uncertain, 83 unique entities, and 39 uncertain event-entity correlations. We then artificially extended this log, generating an event log with 400800 events, of which 164328 uncertain, and 19539 uncertain event-entity correlations. In the extended log we kept the unique entities the same as in the original log without adding new ones. This is because having events that correlate with always new entities requires only local traversals of the EKGA to compute the directly-follows relationships, which is unrealistic and it would bias the latency measurement. We used this artificially extended log as the input for the prototype by streaming it using MQTT-XES and measured the latency to translate each event. The average time to process each event in the stream was 0.302 s, with a standard deviation of 0.195 s, and 95th percentile 0.645 s. Having measured the latency for each event, we observed a growth in the latency with the total number of processed events. Hypothesizing that the growth is linear, we performed a doubling test, in which we generated additional logs (all available on github) by linearly expanding the original one to measure the respective average translation latencies. With these measurements, we observed a linear trend in the average event translation times, supported by a coefficient of determination $R^2 = 0.99903$, indicating an extremely strong fit to a linear model (cf. Fig. 6).

Overall, the average latencies are below 1.0 s, therefore compatible with the online translation of an event stream into an EKGA for an application domain such as healthcare. For application domains where scalability is an additional requirement (not considered here), and safety-critical IoT systems requiring strict real-time capabilities, however, further experiments might need to be conducted.

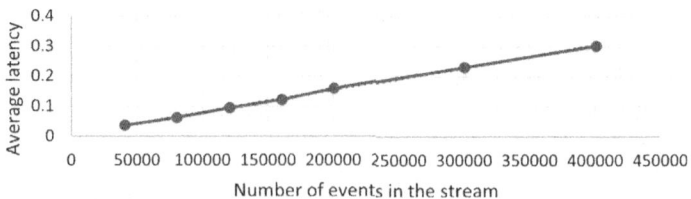

Fig. 6. Average latencies (in s) for translating events from input streams of varying size into EKGAs

---

[2] They executed a more realistic version of the process shown in Fig. 2, with a fine-grained specification of the activities: this specification is available in github.

5 Related Work

Managing ambiguity in digital traces is a recognized challenge. Ambiguity is indicated in [10] to affect multiple artifacts managed in the BPM lifecycle, among which event logs. The work in [10] analyzes sources of ambiguity in event logs such as missing and incomplete data, which frequently happen in IoT settings. The manifesto paper in [14] recognizes the necessity to deal with event log ambiguity as one of the challenges resulting from the integration of IoT and BPM. It specifically points out the problem of establishing event-instance correlations, caused by the lack of a 1:1 mapping between process events and process instances. Among the most pressing challenges in BPM indicated in [4] are challenges related to data quality and adequate data granularity for analysis. Data quality issues and inadequate data granularity are enablers of ambiguity about event-entity correlations and entity participation roles addressed here.

The work in [30] extends EKGs with entity and activity context, introducing a rule-based inference mechanism to derive missing information in an EKG derived from an event log. The proposed mechanism constitutes a potential alternative to our proposed approach and underscores the potential of ambiguity resolution in EKGAs. It assumes that at least one occurrence of each identifier appears in the original event log to be able to process the whole log at once for the inference of the missing identifiers. In contrast, we assume entity identifiers to be always present: relaxing this assumption would allow us to study how to apply the inference mechanism to our incremental EKGA construction. In [31], authors implement object-centric event data models using EKGs, while in [34], authors propose an approach for extracting object-centric event logs using knowledge graphs. We expect EKGAs to allow the extension of the set of application scenarios of these works to settings with stochastically known uncertainty.

In [21], authors studied uncertainty in event logs, proposing conformance checking methods for logs with uncertainty [22]. With the object-centric representation enabled by EKGAs, these works stimulate further research on how to transfer these methods to EKGAs. The relevance of uncertainty in log data was further highlighted in [12], focusing on challenges related to stochastically known logs. Our stochastic modeling of ambiguity further underlines the significance of these challenges and promotes developing new approaches to tackle uncertainty.

6 Conclusion

The convergence of multi-dimensional process analytics and the BPM-IoT integration brings forth the challenge of modeling ambiguity in IoT-based events to enable ambiguity-aware multi-dimensional analytics. Here, we set requirements and outlined a framework to enable the analytics of IoT-based digital traces with ambiguous events. Within the framework, we focused on the step of explicitly modeling ambiguity in process events derived from IoT data as this work main contribution. The extension of EKG with ambiguity and the definition of the EKGA online construction method are critical constituents of this step and pave the way to developing multi-dimensional ambiguity-aware analytics. Having focused on modeling ambiguity, in future work we will refine the remaining steps, develop and evaluate an end-to-end framework implementation including analytics, and evaluate its scalability. We will also conduct a user-centered study of EKGA understandability. Moreover, we plan to study ambiguity resolution methods in EKGAs based on graph transformation rules and, alternatively, optimal alignments to pinpoint the most likely interpretations of ambiguous events.

Acknowledgments. This work has received funding from the Swiss National Science Foundation under Grant No. IZSTZ0_208497 (*ProAmbitIon* project).

References

1. van der Aalst, W.: Object-centric process mining: dealing with divergence and convergence in event data. In: Ölveczky, P.C., Salaün, G. (eds.) SEFM 2019. LNCS, vol. 11724, pp. 3–25. Springer, Cham (2019). https://doi.org/10.1007/978-3-030-30446-1_1
2. van der Aalst, W.M., Carmona, J.: Process Mining Handbook. Springer Nature (2022)
3. Almeida, J., Falbo, R.A., Guizzardi, G.: Events as entities in ontology-driven conceptual modeling. In: Laender, A., Pernici, B., Lim, E.-P., de Oliveira, J. (eds.) ER 2019. LNCS, vol. 11788, pp. 469–483. Springer, Cham (2019). https://doi.org/10.1007/978-3-030-33223-5_39
4. Beerepoot, I., et al.: The biggest business process management problems to solve before we die. Comput. Ind. **146**, 103837 (2023)
5. Benelhaj-Sghaier, S., Gillet, A., Leclercq, É.: Knowledge graph multilevel abstraction: a property graph reification based approach. In: International Conference on Research Challenges in Information Science, pp. 12–19. Springer (2024)
6. Bertrand, Y., Veneruso, S., Leotta, F., Mecella, M., Serral, E.: Nice: the native IoT-centric event log model for process mining. In: International Conference on Process Mining, pp. 32–44. Springer (2023)
7. Burattin, A., Eigenmann, M., Seiger, R., Weber, B.: MQTT-XES: real-time telemetry for process event data. In: CEUR Workshop Proceedings, vol. 2673, pp. 97–101. CEUR-WS (2020)
8. Burattin, A., Maggi, F.M., Sperduti, A.: Conformance checking based on multi-perspective declarative process models. Expert Syst. Appl. **65**, 194–211 (2016)
9. Fahland, D.: Process mining over multiple behavioral dimensions with event knowledge graphs. In: Process Mining Handbook, pp. 274–319. Springer (2022)
10. Franceschetti, M., Seiger, R., López, H.A., Burattin, A., García-Bañuelos, L., Weber, B.: A characterisation of ambiguity in bpm. In: International Conference on Conceptual Modeling, pp. 277–295. Springer (2023)
11. Franceschetti, M., et al.: ProAmbition: online process conformance checking with ambiguities driven by the internet of things. In: Research Projects Exhibition at CAiSE 2023, pp. 52–59. CEUR-WS.org (2023)
12. Gal, A.: Everything there is to know about stochastically known logs. In: ICPM, pp. xvii–xxiii. IEEE (2023)

13. Hildebrandt, T., Mukkamala, R.R., Slaats, T.: Declarative modelling and safe distribution of healthcare workflows. In: Liu, Z., Wassyng, A. (eds.) FHIES 2011. LNCS, vol. 7151, pp. 39–56. Springer, Heidelberg (2012). https://doi.org/10.1007/978-3-642-32355-3_3
14. Janiesch, C., et al.: The internet of things meets business process management: a manifesto. IEEE Syst. Man Cybern. Mag. **6**(4), 34–44 (2020)
15. Klijn, E.L., Mannhardt, F., Fahland, D.: Multi-perspective concept drift detection: including the actor perspective. In: International Conference on Advanced Information Systems Engineering, pp. 141–157. Springer (2024)
16. Klijn, E.L., Tentina, I., Fahland, D., Mannhardt, F.: Decomposing process performance based on actor behavior. In: 2024 6th International Conference on Process Mining (ICPM), pp. 129–136. IEEE (2024)
17. López, H.A.: Challenges in legal process discovery. In: ITBPM@ BPM, pp. 68–73 (2021)
18. Maier, J.B., Gram, J., Weisbarth, M., Hennebold, C., Huber, M.F.: Unsupervised event abstraction for automatic process modeling of plc-controlled automation systems. Procedia CIRP **120**, 631–636 (2023)
19. Mangler, J., et al.: From internet of things data to business processes: challenges and a framework (2024). https://arxiv.org/abs/2405.08528
20. World Health Organization: Who Guidelines on Drawing Blood: Best Practices in Phlebotomy (2010)
21. Pegoraro, M., van der Aalst, W.M.: Mining uncertain event data in process mining. In: ICPM, pp. 89–96. IEEE (2019)
22. Pegoraro, M., Uysal, M.S., van der Aalst, W.M.: Conformance checking over uncertain event data. Inf. Syst. **102**, 101810 (2021)
23. Pegoraro, M., Uysal, M.S., van der Aalst, W.M.: An XES extension for uncertain event data. arXiv preprint arXiv:2204.04135 (2022)
24. Plötzky, F., Britz, K., Balke, W.T.: Shards of knowledge–modeling attributions for event-centric knowledge graphs. In: International Conference on Conceptual Modeling, pp. 259–276. Springer (2023)
25. Rivera-Partida, A., Armas-Cervantes, A., García-Bañuelos, L., Rodríguez-Flores, L.: All optimal K-bounded alignments using the FM-index. In: Cooperative Information Systems: 30th International Conference, CoopIS 2024, Proceedings (2024)
26. Safety, WHO Patient and World Health Organization, et al.: Who guidelines on hand hygiene in health care. Technical report, World Health Organization (2009)
27. Seiger, R., Franceschetti, M., Weber, B.: Data-driven generation of services for IoT-based online activity detection. In: International Conference on Service-Oriented Computing, pp. 186–194. Springer (2023)
28. Seiger, R., Franceschetti, M., Weber, B.: An interactive method for detection of process activity executions from IoT data. Future Internet **15**(2), 77 (2023)
29. Seiger, R., Zerbato, F., Burattin, A., García-Bañuelos, L., Weber, B.: Towards IoT-driven process event log generation for conformance checking in smart factories. In: 2020 IEEE 24th International Enterprise Distributed Object Computing Workshop (EDOCW), pp. 20–26. IEEE (2020)
30. Swevels, A., Dijkman, R., Fahland, D.: Inferring missing entity identifiers from context using event knowledge graphs. In: International Conference on Business Process Management, pp. 180–197. Springer (2023)
31. Swevels, A., Fahland, D., Montali, M.: Implementing object-centric event data models in event knowledge graphs. In: International Conference on Process Mining, pp. 431–443. Springer (2023)

32. Webber, J., Eifrem, E., Robinson, I.: Graph Databases. O'Reilly Media, Incorporated (2013)
33. Weber, B., Abbad-Andaloussi, A., Franceschetti, M., Seiger, R., Völzer, H., Zerbato, F.: Leveraging digital trace data to investigate and support human-centered work processes. In: International Conference on Evaluation of Novel Approaches to Software Engineering, pp. 1–23. Springer (2023)
34. Xiong, J., Xiao, G., Kalayci, T.E., Montali, M., Gu, Z., Calvanese, D.: A virtual knowledge graph based approach for object-centric event logs extraction. In: ICPM, pp. 466–478. Springer (2022)
35. Yoghourdjian, V., Yang, Y., Dwyer, T., Lawrence, L., Wybrow, M., Marriott, K.: Scalability of network visualisation from a cognitive load perspective. IEEE Trans. Visual Comput. Graphics **27**(2), 1677–1687 (2020)
36. Zavala, A.M., Day, G.E., Plummer, D., Bamford-Wade, A.: Decision-making under pressure: medical errors in uncertain and dynamic environments. Aust. Health Rev. **42**(4), 395–402 (2017)

Probabilistic Learning of Temporal Uncertainties in Business Processes

Michel Kunkler[1,2](✉) and Stefanie Rinderle-Ma[1]

[1] Technical University of Munich, Munich, Germany
{michel.kunkler,stefanie.rinderle-ma}@tum.de
[2] TUM School of Computation, Information and Technology, Technical University of Munich, Garching, Germany

Abstract. Business processes consist of process activities that must be executed to reach a business goal. The processing times of process activities, as well as the waiting times preceding them, are often influenced by inherent uncertainties, resulting in variability in the overall processing duration of the business process. Current data-driven business process simulation approaches utilize historical data of waiting and activity processing times to fit simple single-peaked probability distributions, from which samples are drawn during the simulation. Such probability distributions might be too simplistic and lead to poor simulation results. Probabilistic learning techniques enable the modeling of uncertainties as non-parametric probability distributions, whose shapes dynamically adapt to influencing factors. This work examines the applicability of a recently proposed probabilistic learner, DR-BART, to express uncertainties of activity processing and waiting times. We train multiple DR-BART models using different combinations of input features on different data sets and sample from these models in a business process simulator. We compare the simulation results with those obtained by sampling from parametric probability distributions. Our results show that DR-BART models can be used to improve business process simulation.

Keywords: Probabilistic Learning · Business Process Simulation · Business Process Management · Process Mining

1 Introduction

During their execution, business processes (processes for short) are exposed to uncertainties caused by internal and external reasons such as resource unavailabilities or compliance constraint violations [21]. Often, uncertainties are time-related, e.g., it cannot be predicted (with certainty) when an external stakeholder will deliver a part, or how long a resource will take to conduct a process activity. Quantifying such temporal uncertainties appropriately is key for different tasks of process intelligence, i.e., business process simulation (BPS) [1] and predictive process monitoring (PPM) [22]: In BPS and generative PPM approaches, processing times of activities and waiting times preceding their execution are typically modeled as probability distributions from which samples are drawn to simulate the further course of a process. Modeling the processing times of activities is challenging, especially when human resources conduct them [1]. Data-driven BPS approaches use historical data to set up simulation models. To express the uncertainty inherent to the processing time of an activity, current data-driven BPS approaches take the historical processing times of that activity to fit a simple single-peaked parametric probability distribution [15,20].

In reality, such simple probabilistic models might not fit the underlying data well. Consider a process as depicted in Fig. 1 with three activities. The first activity *waits for all parts to arrive*, which are delivered by a parcel delivery service that arrives every morning at around 9 a.m. The resulting activity completion times can be described by a multi-peaked probability distribution, as shown below the activity. Assume further that the *quality control* activity can be executed faster with every time it is executed again, e.g. because less checks have to be done in consecutive executions. Then, a fitting probability distribution would not only depend on the name of the activity but also on its previous number of executions in the running process (see distribution below the activity).

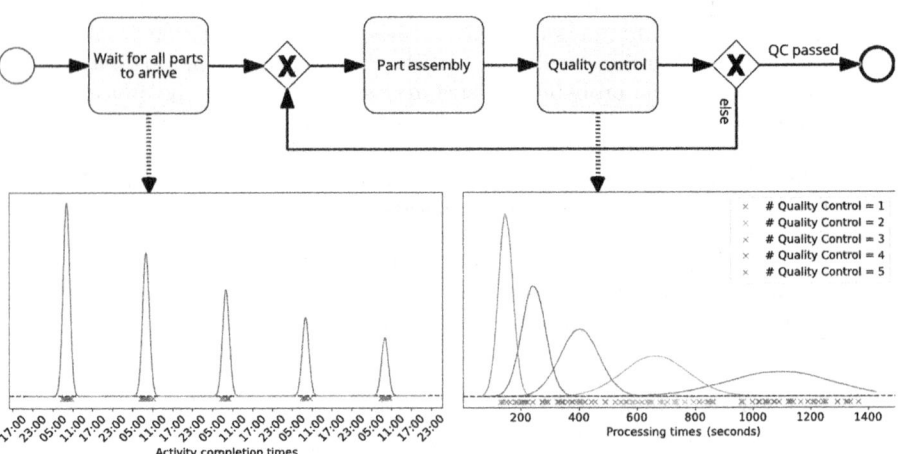

Fig. 1. Historical samples of the processing times of two activities and probability density functions

In this work, we address the learning of probability distributions for processing and waiting times of process activities on historical process data. Learning probability distributions has been addressed in statistics and machine learning as distribution(al) regression [12,13], or probabilistic learning [12]. Klein. [12] distinguishes the term probabilistic learning from distributional regression by its ability to learn higher-order dependencies inherent in the data by employing machine learning techniques.

A recently proposed probabilistic learning model is *Density Regression - Bayesian Additive Regression Trees* (DR-BART) [19]. DR-BART is a nonparametric tree-based ensemble model. For a given input, DR-BART yields a Gaussian Mixture Model (GMM), which can approximate any smooth probability density function to a desired degree. Furthermore, due to its tree-based structure, DR-BART can "capture complex, nonlinear relationships and interactions" [19] in the input data that may influence the distributions of processing or waiting times. Because DR-BART can learn multi-peaked probability distributions whose shapes can depend on context data, DR-BART has the potential to overcome the aforementioned limitations of current approaches.

However, training probabilistic DR-BART models on process data can be challenging in practice due to the following reasons: First, DR-BART requires fixed-sized input data. Traces in process event logs reflecting the execution of different process cases can be of varying length due to, e.g., alternative branchings or loop structures in the underlying process models. Hence, it is unclear how process traces should be encoded to function as input to DR-BART models. Second, because real-world event logs can consist of large numbers, e.g. millions, of events, it is unclear whether this results in intractable training times for DR-BART models. Third, because DR-BART is a non-parametric Bayesian method, i.e., it can adapt the numbers of parameters during training, it can be prone to overfitting. DR-BART utilizes regularization hyperparameters to mitigate overfitting, but the impact of these parameters has been subject to limited empirical investigation [12].

In this work, we examine the applicability of DR-BART models for sampling processing and waiting times in BPS models. We propose to apply feature encoding techniques to encode event log data to a fixed-sized input size. We then use different combinations of features from the encoded data to train multiple DR-BART models on three different event logs and apply the trained DR-BART models for sampling processing and waiting times in processes. We evaluate the application of our trained DR-BART models in a BPS model by comparing our DR-BART models with currently used (parametric models) for sampling processing times and waiting times. Our results show that DR-BART can improve the precision of a BPS model when appropriate features are encoded to DR-BART.

This work is structured as follows: In Sect. 2, we present related work and fundamentals. We present our process data encoding approach for the application of DR-BART in Sect. 3 and describe our evaluation method for examining the applicability of DR-BART in BPS in Sect. 4. Afterwards, we present our results in Sect. 5 and discuss the results and conclude our work in Sect. 6.

2 Related Work

This section discusses existing work on uncertainties, probabilistic learning, and BPS and introduces fundamentals required for the proposed approach.

Uncertainties: In machine learning, a distinction has been made between two types of uncertainties, i.e., aleatoric and epistemic uncertainties [11]. Aleatoric uncertainties are considered irreducible as the uncertainties stem from inherently random effects. In contrast, epistemic uncertainties are referred to as "uncertainty due to a lack of knowledge about the perfect predictor" [11] and hence are considered reducible uncertainties. Epistemic uncertainties can be further divided into approximation and model uncertainties. Approximation uncertainties refer to uncertainties due to a lack of data for selecting appropriate parameters for a predictor model. In general, approximation uncertainties can be reduced by obtaining more training samples. Model uncertainties refer to uncertainties due to a model's insufficient approximation capabilities. Models with high capacity allow more flexibility which can lead to disappearing model uncertainties [11]. However, approximation uncertainty can be challenging when training models with a high capacity. As models with little capacity make stronger model assumptions, i.e., stronger assumptions about the underlying data, they can require less data to fit the model. Different representations for aleatoric uncertainties exist, where probability distributions are the most general and complex representation [7].

Probabilistic Learning aims at learning aleatoric uncertainties by leveraging machine learning techniques to capture complex interactions of the input data [12]. The goal of training probabilistic models is usually to minimize a specific loss function, which is often based on proper scoring rules [11].

DR-BART is a recently proposed non-parametric tree-based ensemble learning method for training probabilistic models [19]. It yields a continuous probability distribution for a given input data. The returned continuous probability distribution of DR-BART is a GMM, which can approximate any smooth probability density function to a desired degree.

A DR-BART model combines two tree-based ensemble models: The leaves in the first tree-based ensemble model represent mean values of Normal distributions, while the leaves of the other tree-based model represent variances. DR-BART leverages a latent variable such that multiple pairs of means and variances can be returned for a given input data, which then constitute the normally distributed components in the returned GMM. In each of the two tree-based ensembles, DR-BART uses a predefined number of trees: In the implementation from Orlandi et al. [19], the default number of mean trees is set to $m_{mean} = 200$, and the number of variance trees to $m_{var} = 100$.[1]

For training a DR-BART model, the likelihood of the training samples is maximized via Gibbs sampling. At each Gibbs step, one of four possible modifications (a grow, prune, change, or swap modification) to a tree in the ensemble tree models is proposed and tested. Since maximizing the likelihood alone would quickly result in overfitting and degenerate Gaussian components where, e.g., each training sample has its distinct leaf with a matching mean value and zero variance, DR-BART regularizes the tree structure and requires a minimum amount of observations in every leaf node. In the implementation of Orlandi et al. [19], at least 5 observations are required in every leaf node. The tree structure is regularized via α and β parameters (see [5]). Orlandi et al. [19] use in default $\alpha = 0.95$ and $\beta = 2$, which rewards a "bushy" tree shape [5].

---

[1] https://github.com/vittorioorlandi/drbart/.

DR-BART itself is an extension to BART [6], which is a tree-based ensemble learning model for mean regression tasks. For BART, it is acknowledged that due to its multi-tree structure, it is robust against converging to local minima during training [6]. Therefore, running the Gibbs sampler once for sufficiently many iterations seems sufficient for training a DR-BART model.

Business Process Simulation (BPS) is considered one of the "most established analysis techniques" [2] in Business Process Management. As setting up simulation models by hand can be cumbersome, data-driven BPS approaches leverage historical process data to learn a BPS model using process mining techniques. In their seminal work on data-driven BPS, Rozinat et al. [20] consider several process perspectives separately, i.e., they discover the control-flow, decision points, roles, and processing and waiting times and integrate them into a single BPS model. In their work, they exclusively fit Normal distributions to the processing and waiting times of each activity. However, they note that it might be meaningful to train different distributions [20].

Martin et al. [16] reviewed data-driven BPS approaches: They notice that processing times in BPS models are either sampled from a parametric probability distribution or from mathematical expressions, i.e., formulas that yield a deterministic value. They suggest combining these approaches such that processing times of some components are calculated based on mathematical expressions and drawn from probability distributions for other components. Some recent data-driven BPS approaches have built upon this concept: For example, Meneghello et al. [17] propose a BPS approach in which processing and waiting times are derived from either probability distributions or obtained from mathematical expressions that take multiple input variables into account. In the simulator used in [14], mean regression is first used to predict the expected processing times of an activity. Then, a normally distributed error term is added to the prediction to account for variability.

In a recent work, López-Pintado et al. [15] build on the assumption that an activity's processing time is affected by the resource performing it. They fit multiple (single-peaked) probability distributions for each resource-activity combination and select the best-fitting one. They refer to this approach as *resource differentiation*. This differentiation approach could be adapted to other factors, e.g., case attributes or context data, but combining multiple factors would pose a challenge: Due to the curse of dimensionality, the number of observations would rapidly decrease. Furthermore, differentiation does not work directly for continuous attributes, necessitating a binning strategy and appropriately chosen bin sizes.

To the best of our knowledge, probabilistic learning has not been used to learn processing or waiting times in BPS.

3 Data Encoding

In this section, we present our approach for aggregating sequence-based data into a fixed-sized input that can be used to train DR-BART models.

3.1 Event Log Data

Table 1. Example event log

case	timestamp	label	resource
1	2024-10-31 07:00	A	Bob
1	2024-10-31 07:15	B	Alice
1	2024-10-31 08:30	B	Felix
2	2024-10-31 09:00	A	Alice
2	2024-10-31 09:15	B	Felix
1	2024-10-31 09:45	C	Bob

Historical process data is often represented in event logs [3]. In this work, we assume that an event has at least three attributes, i.e., a case identifier which links an event to a process case, a timestamp attribute which expresses the time at which an event happened, and an event label which links the event to a class of event types, such as to the start or completion of a distinct process activity. An exemplary event log can be seen in Table 1. Take the event in the first row: It occurred when executing case 1, refers to an activity with label *A*, and was processed by resource *Bob*.

3.2 Feature Engineering and Prefix Encoding

The event log data needs to be transformed for training and inferring probability distributions from DR-BART models. In particular, we derive the target data, the processing and waiting times from the event log, and apply feature engineering techniques to obtain additional features. Additionally, we apply prefix encoding techniques to encode the history of a case into the feature data.

Deriving Processing and Waiting Times: Many event logs only record the completion of activities. When only completion timestamps (or conversely, only the start timestamps) are available, it can become challenging to obtain the actual processing time of an activity and its preceding waiting time. Intuitively, the timestamp of an event and the timestamp of its preceding event from the same case can be taken to obtain a duration. Taking this duration as processing time comes with three problems: First, this approach assumes that the activities are executed in a sequential order. If activities are actually performed in parallel, the calculated duration may underestimate the actual processing time. Second, it is not possible to determine the duration of the first activity. Third, the durations may include both waiting times and actual processing times. Henceforth, special care must be taken when working with such event logs: For example, activities that run in parallel must be identified, and the duration must be taken between the activities' actual preceding activities. Other works have addressed decomposing the duration between the completion of two activities into a waiting and processing time [23].

Other event logs store each activity's internal state. Oftentimes, event logs are stored in the eXtensible Event Stream (XES) standard and use the XES lifecycle extension. The XES lifecycle extension itself implements the Business Process Analytics Format (BPAF) state model [18]. In the BPAF state model, it is, e.g., logged when an activity is ready for execution and when the execution has started and ended. When event logs use the XES lifecycle extension, we derive processing or waiting times, respectively, by calculating the time between the lifecycle transitions of an activity.

Prefix Encoding: To encode the history of a running case, but reduce the sequence-based event log data to a fixed-sized input, required for DR-BART, we use prefix encoding techniques. Verenich et al. [22] identify two prefix encoding techniques that are applicable to DR-BART: Last m-states encoding and aggregation encoding. In the last m-states encoding, the m variable specifies the number of previous events of a case that are encoded. However, [22] note that the majority of publications choose $m = 1$, i.e., do only encode the most recent event and no previous events. We also select $m = 1$ in this work, as choosing a larger m would strongly increase the input size. We provide information on previous events instead by using aggregation encoding.

Aggregation encoding adds additional attributes to the event log that aggregate information about the case's previous events. For example, information about a numerical attribute can be aggregated by adding a new attribute that represents, e.g., the sum, average, minimum, or maximum value of the previous values. For categorical attributes, for each value, an additional column can be created with the number of occurrences of the categorical attribute value. In this work, we examine count aggregations for activity and resource attributes. In Table 2, the columns `A`, `B`, `C` represent count aggregations on the activity label attribute, and the columns `Bob`, `Alice`, `Felix` count aggregations on the resource attribute.

Feature Engineering. Additionally, we apply feature engineering, i.e., obtaining new feature attributes from other features in the event log. In particular, we conduct feature engineering based on the timestamp attributes. As performances of human resources have been shown to differ over time [1], or as waiting times might also depend on the time, we added the `day of the week` and the `seconds in the day` attributes.

Table 2 shows the encoded event log from the original event log in Table 1.

Table 2. Encoded event log

case	timestamp_start	timestamp_end	label	res.	A	B	C	Bob	Alice	Felix	seconds in the day	day of week	dur.
1	2024-10-31 07:00	2024-10-31 07:15	B	Alice	1	1	0	1	1	0	25200	4	900
1	2024-10-31 07:15	2024-10-31 08:30	B	Felix	1	2	0	1	1	1	26100	4	4500
1	2024-10-31 08:30	2024-10-31 09:45	C	Bob	1	2	1	2	1	1	30600	4	4500
2	2024-10-31 09:00	2024-10-31 09:15	B	Felix	1	1	0	0	1	1	32400	4	900

4 Evaluation Method

In this section, we describe our method to evaluate the applicability of DR-BART models in BPS. First, we describe the event logs that we used for training DR-BART models and how we applied the DR-BART models for BPS. Second, we describe the metrics we used to evaluate the simulation results. We implemented our approach and the evaluation in Python, which is publicly available.[2]

4.1 Evaluation Datasets

To evaluate the applicability of DR-BART models for expressing waiting and processing times, we train DR-BART models on one artificial and two real-life data sets. Properties of the three data sets are depicted in Table 3.

The artificial data (AR)[3] set describes a sequential process with three activities, resembling a repair shop in the manufacturing domain. It has five different resources that have different properties: Some resources are faster at conducting tasks in the morning; some resources occasionally take breaks during the processing of a task that is not logged, but this increases the processing times; two resources are not able to work well with each other. If the other resource has conducted a previous activity, the resource is likely to take longer on a subsequent task. Because the data set is artificial, we can compare DR-BART to an optimal probabilistic model.

The second data set (PCR)[4] is a real-world data set of a coronavirus testing laboratory that conducts Polymerase Chain Reaction (PCR) tests. This process has been under the active control of a workflow engine, and an explicit process model exists. The resources that have conducted activities have not been tracked for this data set.

The third data set (BPIC-2017)[5] is a real-world data set from the financial domain. It is a loan application process from a Dutch bank and has been widely investigated in the Business Process Intelligence Competition (BPIC) 2017. It consists of more events, cases, and resources than the other two data sets.

Table 3. Dataset Properties

	Cases	Events	Variants	Event labels	Resources	Case Length Mean (Std.Dev.)	Case Duration Mean (Std.Dev.)
Artificial	1802	16209	1	3	5	9.00 (0.00)	12.18 (5.49) h
PCR	6166	117703	1213	8	-	19.09 (3.37)	5.52 (7.74) h
BPIC-17	31509	1202267	15930	26	159	38.16 (16.72)	21.9 (13.17) days

To examine whether DR-BART models will overfit the event log data, we conduct a train/test split based on the process case identifiers, such that 80% of

---

[2] https://github.com/ltsstar/TaskExecutionTimeMining/.
[3] AR: https://github.com/ltsstar/TaskExecutionTimeMining/blob/main/data/artificial_event_log_2.xes.
[4] PCR: https://doi.org/10.5281/zenodo.11617408.
[5] BPIC-17: https://doi.org/10.4121/uuid:5f3067df-f10b-45da-b98b-86ae4c7a310b.

the cases were assigned to the training data set and 20% to the testing data set. The evaluation was then conducted on both the test and the training data sets.

4.2 Training Probabilistic Models

The encoded training data sets are used to train DR-BART models. We train models with different combinations of attributes and two different numbers of iterations. For each data set, we select the number of training iterations such that on recent hardware, the models with few iterations could be trained within a few hours, and the models with a larger number of iterations within a few days. The number of iterations can be seen in Table 4. On the BPIC-2017 data set, some DR-BART models could not be trained: Four models ran into an error during the training due to numerical instabilities, and for the larger model, two attribute combinations were shown to be computationally infeasible, i.e., they could not be trained within a week. The long training durations for the two models are possibly due to a growing number of Gaussian components in the DR-BART models, which leads to overly long evaluation times on the training samples.

For comparison, we train resource-differentiated probabilistic models as proposed in [15], using their publicly available implementation.[6] Additionally, we use the same code to train probabilistic models for each activity, i.e., without the resource differentiation. For the AR data set, we know the underlying probabilistic model and hence also evaluated on that model for comparison.

4.3 Business Process Simulator

We apply our trained probabilistic models in a BPS model. In particular, we sample from the probabilistic models to simulate cycle times of process cases, i.e., the time from the beginning to the end of process cases. As we focus on uncertainties of processing and waiting times in this work (and do not address control flow or resource uncertainties), our simulator replays the events of a process case and samples the processing or waiting time for each event from the used probabilistic model. Similarly, when an event has a resource label, that resource is passed to the probabilistic model.

In the AR and the BPIC-2017 data set, the simulator obtains a cycle time by summing up the processing and waiting time samples of the replayed events. Since an explicit process model exists for the PCR data set, where some process activities are executed in parallel, we leverage this information to aggregate processing times: E.g., when two process activities are in parallel, processing time samples are drawn from both activities and proceed with the sample with the higher value.

---

[6] https://github.com/AutomatedProcessImprovement/pix-framework.

4.4 Monte Carlo Sampling

Deriving a probability distribution of cycle times analytically can quickly become computationally intractable. Therefore, we use Monte Carlo (MC) sampling to approximate a probability distribution of cycle times.

Because sampling sufficiently many MC trials is crucial for MC sampling, we chose to draw 10 000 MC samples for evaluating the PCR and AR data sets. On the BPIC-2017 data set, this number has proven to be computationally too expensive: Because we replay every event in a data set, choosing 10 000 MC trials on the BPIC-17 data set means sampling $1202267 \times 10000 = 12022670000$ times from each of the tested probabilistic models. For each of these samples, the individual trees of the DR-BART model have to be traversed to eventually draw a value. Therefore, we reduced the number of MC trials to 1000 for this data set.

4.5 Evaluation Metrics

We evaluate how the sampled process cases' cycle times align with the actual cycle times by using two common proper scoring rules, which "assess the quality of probabilistic forecasts, by assigning a numerical score based on the predictive distribution and on the event or value that materializes" [9]. Traditional BPS evaluation metrics compare only a single sampled outcome of a process case with its true outcome [4]. As we sample multiple scenarios for a single process case, we apply different metrics.

The first metric we use is the average log-likelihood, where higher average log-likelihood values are desirable. We obtain the average log-likelihood by averaging the log sum of the probabilities of the true cycle times on the sampled cycle times. To obtain the probability of the true cycle time x_a on the sampled cycle times $X = (x_1, ..., x_n)$, we conduct kernel density estimation on X. We use Gaussian kernels and Silverman's rule to estimate the bandwidth parameter h.

$$\hat{f}(X, x_a) = \frac{1}{n} \sum_{i=1}^{n} \mathcal{N}(x_i - x_a, h) \tag{1}$$

The second metric we used is the average continuous ranked probability score (CRPS), where a lower CRPS is desirable. Unlike the average log-likelihood metric, the CRPS is sensitive to the distance of the predicted case cycle times to the true cycle time. We adapt the notation of [10] and define the CRPS as a distance between the empirical cumulative density function $F_X(x)$ of our sampled cycle times, where $X = (x_1, ..., x_n)$ denotes our samples, and F_{x_a} as the shifted Heaviside function, shifted by the true cycle time x_a.

$$CRPS(X, x_a) := \int_{-\infty}^{\infty} [F_X(u) - F_{x_a}(u)]^2 du$$

$$F_X(x) := \frac{1}{n} \sum_{i=1}^{n} \mathbf{1}(X_i \leq x) \qquad (2)$$

$$F_{x_a}(x) := \begin{cases} 0 & \text{if } x_a > x \\ 1 & \text{if } x_a \leq x \end{cases}$$

5 Results

The evaluation results on the two metrics across the data sets and models can be seen in Table 4. The results show that the performance of simulation models that sample activity processing and waiting times from i) our herein presented DR-BART approach with different metrics; ii) the resource differentiation approach from [15]; and iii) an approach were probability distributions were fit only to activity names (without differentiating for resources) by using the PIX framework.

Not surprisingly, the performance of the DR-BART approach depends on the selected attributes: Selecting only a few attributes, e.g., only the activity label, leads to poor results for all data sets. However, selecting too many attributes also leads to degrading performances across all data sets.

AR. On the AR data set, DR-BART could achieve the best results when the right attributes were selected. While it could leverage the *seconds in day* and *resource count* information to yield better results than the *differentiated resources* approach, its performance decreases when trained for more iterations, indicating an overfitting of the models.

PCR. On the PCR data set, which does not come with resources, DR-BART could clearly outperform the approaches where only a single-peaked probability distribution was fit for each activity. Training DR-BART with the *activity count* attribute leads to degrading performances, while the *seconds in day* attribute seems to have an impact on the performances. As in the AR data set, training with more iterations decreases the performance for most DR-BART models.

BPIC 2017. The BPIC 2017 data set is the only one in which the *differentiated resources* approach consistently outperforms DR-BART. However, the difference between the *differentiated resources* and the simple activity-based probability distribution approach is only marginal, indicating that the processing and waiting times in this data set depend only little on the tested attributes. Moreover, when trained for only 750 iterations, most DR-BART models show distinctively worse results than when trained for 7500 iterations. While training for many more iterations proved computationally intractable with the current DR-BART implementation, it remains unclear whether extending training to more iterations would have yielded better results.

Table 4. Results DRB = DR-BART, PIX = PIX-Framework from [15], Opt. = Actual probabilistic model, a = activity, r = Resource, ac = activity count, rc = resource count, s = seconds in day, d = day of week, Training: (burn in iterations / kept iterations / thinning interval, Samples = Number of samples for a process case, underscored scores: best DR-BART scores, bold scores: overall best scores, - = training error due to numerical instabilities, * = training computationally infeasible

AR			Training: 100,000/100/100 Samples: 10,000				Training: 1,000,000/100/100 Samples: 10,000			
			Train		Test		Train		Test	
	a r ac rc s d		LL	CRPS	LL	CRPS	LL	CRPS	LL	CRPS
DRB	x - - - - -		−1.83	1.02E+04	0.15	9.96E+03	−0.03	1.45E+04	−0.11	1.45E+04
DRB	- x - - - -		0.06	1.43E+04	0.05	1.37E+04	−0.15	1.79E+04	−0.14	1.78E+04
DRB	x x - - - -		0.07	1.04E+04	0.30	1.00E+04	−0.00	1.30E+04	0.04	1.30E+04
DRB	x x - - x -		0.16	1.01E+04	0.33	9.65E+03	0.21	1.21E+04	0.21	1.21E+04
DRB	x x x - x -		0.09	1.34E+04	0.14	1.26E+04	−1.58	1.01E+04	−1.83	<u>1.01E+04</u>
DRB	x x - x x -		0.26	**8.25E+03**	**0.40**	**8.05E+03**	<u>0.33</u>	1.04E+04	**0.32**	1.04E+04
DRB	x x x x x -		<u>**0.36**</u>	9.69E+03	0.37	9.35E+03	0.29	1.14E+04	0.29	1.13E+04
DRB	x x - - x x		0.20	1.21E+04	0.23	1.15E+04	−1.21	<u>1.03E+04</u>	−1.28	1.03E+04
DRB	x x x x x x		0.32	9.58E+03	0.39	9.21E+03	0.28	1.16E+04	0.27	1.16E+04
PIX	x - - - - -		0.28	9.88E+03	−1.75	1.01E+04	0.28	9.88E+03	−1.75	1.01E+04
PIX	x x - - - -		0.34	9.62E+03	−0.41	9.80E+03	**0.34**	**9.62E+03**	−0.41	**9.80E+03**
Opt.	x x - x x -		*0.50*	*7.97E+03*	*0.54*	*7.97E+03*	*0.50*	*7.97E+03*	*0.54*	*7.97E+03*

PCR			Training: 10,000/100/100 Samples: 1000				Iter.: 100,000/100/100 Samples: 1000			
			Train		Test		Train		Test	
	a r ac rc s d		LL	CRPS	LL	CRPS	LL	CRPS	LL	CRPS
DRB	x - - - - -		0.66	1.25E+04	0.69	1.18E+04	0.13	1.55E+04	0.17	1.52E+04
DRB	x - - - x -		<u>**0.80**</u>	1.15E+04	0.70	1.10E+04	<u>**0.61**</u>	1.25E+04	<u>**0.63**</u>	1.20E+04
DRB	x - x - x -		0.22	1.57E+04	0.32	1.53E+04	0.54	1.42E+04	0.51	1.37E+04
DRB	x - - - x x		−3.96	**9.67E+03**	**1.20**	**8.83E+03**	−2.47	<u>1.03E+04</u>	−0.36	<u>9.79E+03</u>
PIX	x - - - - -		−8.62	1.15E+04	0.14	1.08E+04	−8.62	1.15E+04	0.14	1.08E+04

BPIC 2017			Training: 750/5/5 Samples: 1000				Training: 7500/50/50 Samples: 1000			
			Train		Test		Train		Test	
	a r ac rc s d		LL	CRPS	LL	CRPS	LL	CRPS	LL	CRPS
DRB	x - - - - -		−70.71	2.46E+64	−70.67	2.41E+64	*	*	*	*
DRB	- x - - - -		-	-	-	-	*	*	*	*
DRB	x x - - - -		-	-	-	-	-	-	-	-
DRB	x x - - x -		−20.44	5.98E+21	−20.44	5.81E+21	-	-	-	-
DRB	x x x - x -		−9.70	4.23E+13	−9.74	8.98E+13	−7.58	1.29E+13	−7.60	1.17E+11
DRB	x x - x x -		<u>−5.43</u>	4.33E+06	<u>−5.45</u>	4.32E+06	−7.07	2.54E+20	−7.06	1.45E+13
DRB	x x x x x -		n.a.	3.00E+17	n.a.	6.14E+16	−11.17	3.49E+12	−11.18	3.32E+12
DRB	x x - - x x		−16.11	2.09E+19	−16.17	1.89E+19	<u>−4.29</u>	8.56E+05	<u>**−4.26**</u>	8.55E+05
DRB	x x x x x x		−9.77	2.85E+17	−9.86	3.80E+16	−10.94	2.18E+12	−11.00	1.11E+12
PIX	x - - - - -		**−4.30**	**8.33E+05**	**−4.45**	**8.31E+05**	**−4.30**	**8.33E+05**	**−4.45**	**8.31E+05**
PIX	x x - - - -		**−4.22**	8.34E+05	−4.58	8.33E+05	**−4.22**	8.34E+05	−4.58	8.33E+05

Overall, the results show that DR-BART is able to outperform the other approaches in two of the three tested data sets when meaningful feature attributes are selected. The longer-trained models on the AR and PCR data sets show a decreasing performance. This could be due to overfitting of the DR-BART models to the individual processing and waiting times.

6 Discussion and Conclusion

In this work, we examined the applicability of a probabilistic learner, DR-BART, for learning probabilistic models that represent activity processing times and waiting times in business processes. We used feature encoding and engineering techniques to encode sequential data into fixed-sized input data required by DR-BART. We then compared the performance of sampling processing and waiting times using DR-BART models with sampling from traditional probabilistic models. Our results show that DR-BART models can contribute to better BPS models than the currently used probabilistic models.

DR-BART models were able to outperform the performance of existing approaches in two of three data sets, when meaningful feature attributes were selected. The selection of irrelevant features for DR-BART has been shown to degrade the model's predictive performance. Similarly, when only a few features were selected for training DR-BART models, the models' performance decreased in most cases when training for many iterations (e.g., for one million iterations on the AR data set). This indicates that our trained DR-BART models tend to overfit. Selecting only a few feature attributes has been shown to cause problems training DR-BART models on the BPIC 2017 data set. This issue is likely due to the model performing excessive splits on its latent variable, resulting in probability distributions that consist of many Gaussian components for each data sample. These complex distributions might then increase the computational cost for calculating the likelihood of the training samples and, at the same time, decrease the model's predictive performance due to overfitting.

Future work should address the computational issues and overfitting problems of DR-BART, which might be achievable by different means: First, the training process of DR-BART itself could be enhanced by applying hyperparameter search techniques, or implementing early stopping or restarting techniques. Second, it might be meaningful to add additional regularization to DR-BART models. For example, the number of splits on the latent variable could be regularized to avoid overly complex and overfitting models. Third, instead of training a single DR-BART model for processing and waiting times of all known activities, it might be meaningful to apply bucketing techniques [22] and, e.g., train individual DR-BART models for each activity, or one DR-BART model for waiting times and one for processing times. Fourth, the DR-BART implementation could be heavily parallelized. Currently, the DR-BART implementation uses only a single CPU core. Calculating the likelihood of the individual training samples, on which most of the time during training is spent, could be parallelized, such that, e.g., multiple CPU cores are utilized.

A future use case for DR-BART could involve testing for undesired influences of different process attributes and contextual data on processing and waiting times. For example, an organization might be interested in whether daily working hours or the time of day affect the processing times of activities. Our approach could help answer this question and assist the organization in mitigating undesired influences, such as by limiting working hours.

While we have focused on training DR-BART models in this work, future work should test the applicability of other probabilistic models. Neural network-based models, such as Bayesian Neural Networks (BNNs), or BNN approximation techniques, e.g., Monte Carlo (MC) dropout as Bayesian approximation [8], appear promising because, on the one hand, they can learn complex non-linear relationships and, on the other hand, they can approximate any probability distribution, when the neural network has sufficient capacity.

The presented results are limited to the use of a simplified business process simulator. Our simulator simulated the individual cases independently from each other, ignoring that the performances can depend on other running cases, e.g., because resources work on multiple cases simultaneously [16].

In this work, we examined the applicability of probabilistic learning for processing and waiting times in business processes using DR-BART. Our results show that DR-BART models can contribute to better BPS models than the currently used probabilistic models when meaningful feature attributes are selected.

References

1. Aalst, W.: Business process simulation revisited. In: Barjis, J. (ed.) EOMAS 2010. LNBIP, vol. 63, pp. 1–14. Springer, Heidelberg (2010). https://doi.org/10.1007/978-3-642-15723-3_1
2. Aalst, W.: Business process simulation survival guide. In: vom Brocke, J., Rosemann, M. (eds.) Handbook on Business Process Management 1. IHIS, pp. 337–370. Springer, Heidelberg (2015). https://doi.org/10.1007/978-3-642-45100-3_15
3. van der Aalst, W., et al.: Process mining manifesto. In: Daniel, F., Barkaoui, K., Dustdar, S. (eds.) BPM 2011. LNBIP, vol. 99, pp. 169–194. Springer, Heidelberg (2012). https://doi.org/10.1007/978-3-642-28108-2_19
4. Chapela-Campa, D., Benchekroun, I., Baron, O., Dumas, M., Krass, D., Senderovich, A.: A framework for measuring the quality of business process simulation models. Inf. Syst. **127**, 102447 (2025). https://doi.org/10.1016/j.is.2024.102447
5. Chipman, H.A., George, E.I., R.E.M.: Bayesian cart model search. J. Am. Stat. Assoc. **93**(443), 935–948 (1998). https://doi.org/10.1080/01621459.1998.10473750
6. Chipman, H.A., George, E.I., McCulloch, R.E.: BART: Bayesian additive regression trees. Ann. Appl. Stat. **4**(1), 266–298 (2010). https://doi.org/10.1214/09-AOAS285
7. Destercke, S., Dubois, D., Chojnacki, E.: Unifying practical uncertainty representations - I: generalized p-boxes. Int. J. Approximate Reasoning **49**(3), 649–663 (2008). https://doi.org/10.1016/j.ijar.2008.07.003

8. Gal, Y., Ghahramani, Z.: Dropout as a Bayesian approximation: representing model uncertainty in deep learning. In: Balcan, M.F., Weinberger, K.Q. (eds.) Proceedings of The 33rd International Conference on Machine Learning, Proceedings of Machine Learning Research, vol. 48, pp. 1050–1059, 20–22 June 2016
9. Gneiting, T., Raftery, A.E.: Strictly proper scoring rules, prediction, and estimation. J. Am. Stat. Assoc. **102**(477), 359–378 (2007). https://doi.org/10.1198/016214506000001437
10. Hersbach, H.: Decomposition of the continuous ranked probability score for ensemble prediction systems. Weather Forecast. **15**(5), 559–570 (2000). https://doi.org/10.1175/1520-0434(2000)015<0559:DOTCRP>2.0.CO;2
11. Hüllermeier, E., Waegeman, W.: Aleatoric and epistemic uncertainty in machine learning: an introduction to concepts and methods. Mach. Learn. **110**(3), 457–506 (2021). https://doi.org/10.1007/s10994-021-05946-3
12. Klein, N.: Distributional regression for data analysis. Ann. Rev. Stat. Appl. **11**, 321–346 (2024). https://doi.org/10.1146/annurev-statistics-040722-053607
13. Kneib, T., Silbersdorff, A., Säfken, B.: Rage against the mean - a review of distributional regression approaches. Econ. Stat. **26**, 99–123 (2023). https://doi.org/10.1016/j.ecosta.2021.07.006
14. Kunkler, M., Rinderle-Ma, S.: Online resource allocation to process tasks under uncertain resource availabilities. In: 2024 6th International Conference on Process Mining (ICPM), pp. 137–144 (2024). https://doi.org/10.1109/ICPM63005.2024.10723280
15. López-Pintado, O., Dumas, M., Berx, J.: Discovery, simulation, and optimization of business processes with differentiated resources. Inf. Syst. **120**, 102289 (2024). https://doi.org/10.1016/j.is.2023.102289
16. Martin, N., Depaire, B., Caris, A.: The use of process mining in a business process simulation context: overview and challenges. In: 2014 IEEE Symposium on Computational Intelligence and Data Mining (CIDM), pp. 381–388 (2014). https://doi.org/10.1109/CIDM.2014.7008693
17. Meneghello, F., et al.: Optimizing resource allocation policies in real-world business processes using hybrid process simulation and deep reinforcement learning. In: Marrella, A., Resinas, M., Jans, M., Rosemann, M. (eds.) Business Process Management - 22nd International Conference, BPM 2024, Krakow, Poland, 1–6 September 2024, Proceedings, LNCS, vol. 14940, pp. 167–184 (2024). https://doi.org/10.1007/978-3-031-70396-6_10
18. zur Muehlen, M., Swenson, K.D.: BPAF: a standard for the interchange of process analytics data. In: zur Muehlen, M., Su, J. (eds.) Business Process Management Workshops - BPM 2010 International Workshops and Education Track, Hoboken, NJ, USA, 13–15 September 2010, Revised Selected Papers, LNBIP, vol. 66, pp. 170–181 (2010). https://doi.org/10.1007/978-3-642-20511-8_15
19. Orlandi, V., Murray, J., Linero, A., Volfovsky, A.: Density regression with bayesian additive regression trees (2021). https://doi.org/10.48550/arXiv.2112.12259. arXiv:2112.12259 [stat]
20. Rozinat, A., Mans, R., Song, M., van der Aalst, W.: Discovering simulation models. Inf. Syst. **34**(3), 305–327 (2009). https://doi.org/10.1016/j.is.2008.09.002
21. Russell, N., van der Aalst, W., ter Hofstede, A.: Workflow exception patterns. In: Dubois, E., Pohl, K. (eds.) CAiSE 2006. LNCS, vol. 4001, pp. 288–302. Springer, Heidelberg (2006). https://doi.org/10.1007/11767138_20

22. Verenich, I., Dumas, M., Rosa, M.L., Maggi, F.M., Teinemaa, I.: Survey and cross-benchmark comparison of remaining time prediction methods in business process monitoring. ACM Trans. Intell. Syst. Technol. **10**(4), 34:1–34:34 (2019). https://doi.org/10.1145/3331449
23. Wombacher, A., Iacob, M.: Start time and duration distribution estimation in semi-structured processes. In: Shin, S.Y., Maldonado, J.C. (eds.) Proceedings of the 28th Annual ACM Symposium on Applied Computing, SAC 2013, Coimbra, Portugal, 18–22 March 2013, pp. 1403–1409 (2013).https://doi.org/10.1145/2480362.2480626

AI-Driven Modeling and Analysis (EMMSAD 2025)

Assessing the Suitability of Large Language Models in Generating UML Class Diagrams as Conceptual Models

Marco Calamo[1]((✉))[iD], Massimo Mecella[1][iD], and Monique Snoeck[2][iD]

[1] Sapienza Università di Roma, Rome, Italy
{calamo,mecella}@diag.uniroma1.it
[2] KU Leuven, Leuven, Belgium
monique.snoeck@kuleuven.be

Abstract. The breakthrough of Large Language Models (LLMs) has changed how different kinds of complex tasks are approached, including the ones that require a higher level of abstraction and critical thinking together with advanced domain-specific knowledge, like Conceptual Modeling. Several experiments on testing the modeling capabilities of LLMs have already been conducted, but the literature still lacks a structured analysis of how different LLMs and prompting techniques impact the extraction of conceptual models, as UML class diagrams, from textual specifications. In this paper, we present a comprehensive comparison of open-source and closed-source LLMs used in conjunctions with the most effective and accessible prompting techniques, on a newly crafted high-quality dataset of case specifications, implementing an automated evaluation on generated UML class diagrams. Finally, we assess how factors like model size or case complexity impact the quality of the generated models and what LLM and what prompting technique to choose for which task. The dataset and the experimental source code are made available through GitHub (https://github.com/IlKaiser/text2uml).

Keywords: Large Language Models · Conceptual Modeling · UML Class Diagrams · Prompting Technique

1 Introduction

Since the breakthrough of ChatGPT in November 2022, Large Language Models (LLMs) have been used to support several tasks that require advanced knowledge and abstraction skills, including Conceptual Modeling. This task has historically been challenging for both teachers and students [31] (later practitioners), and failing to consider the impact of LLMs in this field could lead to even greater difficulties for practitioners, students and teachers: as an example, if teachers are not aware that students can and will use LLMs to assist them in creating conceptual models during classes or exams, they will no longer be able to properly grade students' work, as it would be impossible to determine the extent of the LLM's contribution to the final solution. Passively using LLMs could also cause students to gradually lose – or fail to acquire – the necessary skills to produce conceptual models or distinguish a good conceptual model from a bad one. This, in turn, will have dramatic impact on software industry, when those students will be later practitioners and professionals.

Since stopping this phenomenon is impossible, a possible way to mitigate the problems might be thoroughly assessing the modeling capabilities of LLMs. In this work, we simulate how students might use them, identifying what part of a conceptual model can be feasibly generated with LLMs, and in which parts LLMs fail to generate conceptual models. The former also indicates where LLMs could actually help in creating better conceptual models, whereas the latter indicates where they still pose a liability. Knowing LLMs capabilities in conceptual modeling also helps understanding which skills students need to acquire to make effective use of LLMs. In the literature, different types of conceptual models and methods have been proposed, including data flow modeling (DFM) and structured systems analysis and design method (SSADM), Entity-relationship modeling (ERM), Business Process Modeling (BPM) with all variants (EPC, Petri Nets, BPMN, etc.), UML. In this work, we focus on representing the conceptual domain model (a.k.a. information model in some methods) by adopting UML class diagrams.

In this paper, we aim to answer the following general research question:

RQ: *How well do Large Language Models perform in Conceptual Modeling, and specifically in UML class diagram generation?*

The remainder of this paper is structured as follows: Sect. 2 analyzes the current state of the art regarding conceptual modeling with LLMs, Sect. 3 details the methodology of our experiments, and Sects. 4 and 5 present and discuss the obtained results. Finally, Sect. 6 concludes our work and outlines future directions. The main contributions of our work are as follows:

Contribution 1: *A comprehensive comparison of LLMs' performance on the task of Conceptual Modeling, focusing on UML class diagram generation.*

Contribution 2: *A high-quality dataset of text specifications and their UML representation of the solution of the conceptual domain model.*

2 Related Work

There have been several papers analyzing the implications of the current and potential applications of LLMs in conceptual modeling. In particular, LLMs could support the human modeler in several steps of the modeling process, from the definition of requirements [13] to the creation [27] and evaluation of conceptual models [8]. We will place the focus of our analysis on conceptual model creation, in particular on the automated generation of UML class diagrams from the textual specifications.

We analyzed the articles according to several criteria, laid down while trying to answer our original research question. We are interested in observing how LLMs are used and for what purpose, what the format of the output is, if different LLMs and prompting techniques were tested, if they considered an automated scoring mechanism, how the scoring handles different wording choices (like synonyms and partial matches). We also took into consideration the size of the test dataset and if it was publicly available.

The authors of [14] and the authors of [9] were some of the first to see the potential in using LLMs for creating UML class diagrams. Despite their results being just preliminary, they showed the potential that led to numerous follow-up research. In [10], the authors show that models like GPT-3.5 and GPT-4 combined with several prompting techniques, like few-shot and chain of thought, can successfully extract classes, attributes, and associations from text specifications with satisfactory results, with peaks of 0.76 F1 in class detection and of 0.34 F1 in association detection with their benchmark. The same authors continued their work with [37], using the same scoring function and the same dataset, but they introduced a newer, more effective extraction technique via an updated Chain of Thoughts prompts. The authors of [11] did an extensive comparison of the conceptual modeling performances of GPT-4 to the conceptual modeling performance of students, concluding that, even though the LLM performed well, the students had a clear edge over it in almost every case. The work [32] explored the capabilities of LLM to extract classes and associations from the textual specifications, not for class diagram generation but as an aid to generating Problem Frames (An approach to conceptualize requirement developed by [18]). A similar approach was used by [3], but they used GPT-3.5 with Chain of Thoughts prompting to extract class and association list for domain model generation. [30] was the only work that relied on open source LLMs for class diagram extraction. They also showed that Retrieval Augmented Generation [23] (RAG) could lead to performance improvements. Finally, the authors of [34] showed the potential of more advanced prompting techniques like Tree-of-Thoughts [38] in generating class diagrams, with near perfect results, but the test dataset was rather small. Table 1 sums up the aforementioned articles with respect to the criteria we defined earlier. What emerges from this literature review is a lot of excitement about exploiting the capabilities of LLM even for a task that still relies heavily on human abstraction skills, such as creating class diagrams. However, there is still no comprehensive comparison of how each LLM performs in similar cases and what is the most effective prompting technique. We can also see that the vast majority of work only considered closed-source LLMs. With our contribution, we want to try to fill this research gap. We now update the initial research question:

Updated RQ: *What is the most effective Large Language Model at modeling UML class diagrams and what is the most effective prompting technique?*

Table 1. Comparison of LLM Application in Literature

Article	Closed Source LLM	Open Source LLM	Prompting Techniques	Output Format	Scoring Mechanism	Ambiguity Handling	Dataset Size	Dataset Available
Chen, Kua, et al. [10]	GPT-3.5, GPT-4	X	Zero-Shot, Few-Shot (1-Shot, 2-Shot), CoT	UML class diagram, EBNF format	Custom Precision, Recall, F1	✓ (human supervised)	11 cases	✓
Yang, Yujing, et al. [37]	GPT-4	X	CoT	UML class diagram, EBNF format	Custom Precision, Recall, F1	✓ (human supervised)	11 cases	✓
De Bari, Daniele, et al. [11]	GPT-4	X	Zero-Shot	UML class diagram, PlantUML format	Manual Scoring	✓ (human supervised)	20 cases	✓ (no UML solutions)
Fill, H., P. Fettke, and J. Köpke [14]	GPT-4	X	1-Shot	UML class diagram, JSON format	X (no quantitative scoring)	X	X (no dataset used)	X
Cámara, Javier, et al. [9]	GPT-3.5	X	Zero-Shot	UML class diagram, PlantUML format	X (no quantitative scoring)	✓ (human supervised)	13 cases	✓
Ruan, Kun, Xiaohong Chen, and Zhi Jin. [32]	GPT-3.5	X	Zero-Shot	Requirement Model, custom format	X (no quantitative scoring)	X	X (no dataset used)	X
Arulmohan, S., Meurs M.J., and Mosser S. [3]	GPT-3.5	X	CoT	Domain Models from User Stories, custom format	Custom Precision, Recall, F1	✓ (human supervised)	22 Annotated User Stories	✓ (no UML solutions)
Prokop, Dominik, et al. [30]	X	Llama3-70B, Mixtal-8x7B	Zero-Shot, Few-Shot, RAG	Class, Association list, JSON format	Custom Precision, Recall, F1	✓ (human supervised)	6 cases	✓ (no UML solutions)
Silva, Jonathan, et al. [34]	GPT-4	X	Tree-of-Thoughts	UML class diagram, PlantUML format	Custom Precision, Recall, F1	✓ (human supervised)	5 cases	✓

3 Methodology

This section describes how we set up the experiments to answer *RQ*. It presents *i)* The exact task we want LLM to perform, *ii)* the dataset we created and used as a benchmark, *iii)* the different models used for comparison, *iv)* how we evaluated the results.

3.1 Task Description

The goal was to evaluate performances of LLMs generating UML diagrams from text specifications. Since generating UML is a very broad and complex task, we decided to focus our analysis on a relaxed version of the problem: generating **UML class diagrams** that contain only *i)* classes, without attributes nor methods, *ii)* associations, binary and without inheritance, and *iii)* cardinality of the association ends. Since we used textual-only LLMs to fulfill this task, the generated class diagram is outputted in plantUML[1] format. We compared several prompting techniques and different models, observing the differences and trying to obtain the most accurate technique-LLM combination. Figure 1 presents the full experimental setup, starting from the specification that is the input to the LLM-prompt combination to the plantUML output of the corresponding class diagram.

---

[1] https://plantuml.com/.

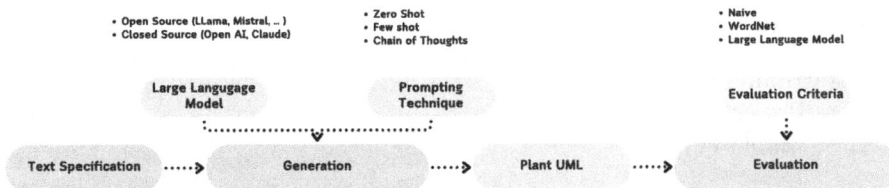

Fig. 1. Experiment Setup

3.2 Dataset Composition

To evaluate the LLM's generation performance, we needed a benchmark. However, since there is no publicly available dataset that includes both text specifications and corresponding UML class diagrams in the format we wanted, we decided to assemble our own. We therefore present the ***text2uml*** dataset, publicly available on huggingface[2]. It was obtained by manually pruning and adapting exercises that involved designing UML class diagrams from textual specification in the context the course *Architecture and Modelling of Management Information Systems* thought by prof. Monique Snoeck at KU Leuven. The dataset consists of 27 high quality cases with unique id, case name, crafted text specifications and plantUML output. The exercises have been developed over a long period of time, and address different levels of complexity. Each model solution was developed through several rounds of feedback by students and colleagues and were polished in terms of classes included, class names, associations included and chosen cardinalities. Most cases come with an elaborated explanation of choices made. The plantUML was adapted to represent classes and association in a consistent way across the dataset. The cases are of different levels of complexity, with increasing number of classes and associations. Appendix A[3] provides additional details about the format of the dataset, the cases distribution in terms of number of classes and associations and the constraints we adopted in the plantUML output. Below we present a small extract from the dataset of a simple case called *Project and Leaders*.

> **Text Specification**
>
> For each project, a number of employees are assigned as team-members, and one employee is assigned as a project-leader. A person can be a member and/or a leader of multiple projects.

---

[2] https://huggingface.co/datasets/LaserOverrider/text2uml
[3] Available online at https://osf.io/4sr5v.

PlantUML

@startuml
class Project{}
class Employee{}

Project "0..*" – "0..*" Employee : member
Project "0..*" – "1..1" Employee : leader
@enduml

3.3 Large Language Models Used and Why

We decided to pick LLMs of two main categories: closed-source and open-source. As representatives of the closed-source, we opted for several LLMs of different sizes from the GPT family from OpenAI (from smaller to bigger): **Gpt-4o-mini** [17] (about 8B, gpt-4o-mini-2024-07-18), **Gpt-3.5-turbo** [7] (175B, gpt-3.5-turbo-0125), **o3-mini** [19] (about 200B, o3-mini-2025-01-31) **Gpt-4-turbo** [2] (about 1.7T, gpt-4-turbo-2024-04-09), **Gpt-4o** [17] (about 1.7T, gpt-4o-2024-08-06). The models were interrogated via the langchain library using OpenAI API endpoints. To complete the closed-source LLM lineup, we also added **Claude 3.7**[4] (between 150B and 250B, claude-3-7-sonnet-20250219) accessed via Anthropic API and langchain, to see how good OpenAI alternatives are.

For what concerns open-source models, we focused on smaller size models, between 7B and 14B parameters, choosing some of the most recent and relevant models from the current landscape [4,22]. We picked smaller size models to make them easy to run on local machines, without resorting to external API or servers, since we observed that model size does not influence the final outcome significantly. Sometimes, to make a larger model run effectively, it was necessary to use its quantized version at 4 or 8 bits [40]. The chosen models are (from smaller to bigger): **Llama-3.2-Instruct** [12] (3B) **Phi-4** [1] (14B, 8bit), **Falcon3-Instruct** [28] (10B, 8bit), **Qwen2.5** [36] (14B, 4bit), **Mistral-Instruct-v0.3** [20] (7B, 4bit), **DeepSeek-R1-Distill-Qwen** [16] (7B, 8bit). The only exception to the smaller model policy was made for the addition of **Deepseek-V3** [24] (Deepseek chat, 671B) accessed via the Deepseek API and langchain, to include different parameter size also for open source models.

We decided to include also Deepseek R1, o3-mini and Claude 3.7, among the others, to see if models that native support reasoning and deep-thinking [29] could improve the modeling performances due to the heavy abstraction capabilities required to complete correctly the task.

All experiments were performed on a Macbook Pro M2 with 32GB of unified memory, using the huggingface[5] and langchain[6] Python libraries. For all the

---
[4] https://www.anthropic.com/news/claude-3-7-sonnet.
[5] https://huggingface.co/.
[6] https://www.langchain.com/.

open-source models, their mlx-community[7] version from huggingface was used, because they are optimized to run on Apple Silicon architecture. The source code also provides support for the Cuda architecture.

3.4 Prompting Techniques

The other crucial part of these experiments was to choose the most effective prompting technique. We decided to try several of the most effective and commonly used techniques known today [33]. We selected *Zero Shot* [21], *Chain of Thought (CoT)* [35], CoT with prompts adapted from [37] (discussed in the related work) and *Few-Shot (1-shot and 2-shots)* [7]. Other more advanced techniques like Tree-of-thoughts [38] were not included in the testing because the more advanced implementation diverges too much from our perspective of what a conceptual modeling student can achieve easily. Retrieval Augmented Generation [23] (RAG), a very common technique used in various LLM applications, was not included for the same reasons, since we assumed that students do not have easy access to a UML cases repository and the setup would be not trivial as well. In the remainder of this section we will briefly go through each technique, explaining how we adapted them for our case.

Zero Shot: It consist in generating classes, associations and cardinality in one prompt, explaining with some simple examples how the final output should be formatted.

Few-Shot (1-Shot and 2-Shots): It uses the same basis as Zero Shot for what concerns the extracting instructions, but it adds one (1-shot) or two (2-shot) examples of how plantUML is extracted from actual text specifications. Since these examples are from the dataset, the evaluation of this approach will include one or two less cases counted.

Chain of Thought (CoT): Four different prompt are used, and the results from one prompt (plus some shared context) are used as input for the next prompt. The first prompt is used only to extract class names from the specifications; the second one –given the class names and the specifications– asks to extract the associations; the third one, given the context generated thus far, extracts the cardinality for each associations; the fourth prompt assembles everything together in the final plant uml.

CoT Adapted from [37]: This CoT variant was adapted from the methodology referenced paper, changing the output format to match ours. The main difference with the previous CoT approach is the extraction of the classes. Here, a new link in the chain is introduced: the first link extracts candidate names from the text specification and then the second link of the chain extracts class names from the list of candidate names according to strict rules. The remainder of the approach is similar to the previous CoT, but associations and cardinality are jointly extracted in the same chain link. Form now on it will be referenced as *CoT-multi*, from the name of the paper.

---

[7] https://huggingface.co/mlx-community.

Appendix B[8] presents the full prompts.

3.5 Scoring Mechanism

Evaluating the correctness of the generated UML class diagram, even if they are limited to a small set of features, is no trivial task. A UML diagram can be correct even if slightly different from the reference diagram in the dataset. For example a class in the generated UML could have different name than in the reference UML and still represent the same notion, like employee and worker from our example from earlier. To properly score every generated class diagram, a human expert would be necessary. However, since the number of UML diagrams to check, including every combination of cases, LLMs and prompting techniques, well exceeds one thousand, an automated scoring mechanism was introduced. Since class identification, after having uniformed the plantUML output, was the remaining ambiguity left to address, three criteria were tested: *i)* using simple matching that considers a different word wrong, even in case of similar meaning (naïve criterion), *ii)* testing synonyms with Wordnet [26] and *iii)* assessing the correctness regarding the context with an LLM prompt (see Appendix B). For this test we have used GPT-4o as a LLM evaluator, to provide standardized performances across the board. Finally, we used the F1-score of classes (computed each time according to the three criteria). For cardinality we used a custom scoring mechanism: every association can get a max score of 5. 1 point if the association exists in the proposed solution; 1 extra point for a correct upper cardinality for each association end and 1 extra point for a correct the lower cardinality of each association end. E.g.: if the correct association in plantUML is *Project "0..*" - "0..*" Employee* and the proposed one is *Project "2..*" - "0..*" Employee*, the score would be 4/5 (+1 for existence, +1 for * as higher cardinality on Project class, +1 for 0 as lower cardinality on Employee class and +1 for * as higher cardinality on Employee class). Score results are then scaled by the total possible score ($\#Assoc \times 5$) to obtain a score percentage.

4 Results

In this section, results obtained from the experiments will be presented. We will analyze the data from different perspectives and with different aggregations, whilst in the next section we will open a critical discussion on the outcome.

4.1 Class Detection Comparison

Table 2 presents how different evaluation criteria perform compared to each other for the problem of identifying classes from the requirements. The scores are an average of all cases with all models and techniques. As expected, using other scoring techniques than strict name matching for classes is leading to a slightly

---

[8] Available online at https://osf.io/4sr5v.

higher precision and f1-score, and a significantly higher recall. It is interesting to observe that WordNet achieves the best recall. Despite this better recall, from now on, we will use LLM as a validation method because of its better overall f1-score.

We acknowledge that this kind of automated evaluation is far from perfect, especially in a field like UML modeling, characterised by hight levels of evaluative complexity, requiring nuance, discretion and critical thinking. However, choosing the best possible approximation available of a human evaluator is still quite important: by doing so, we can obtain an automated evaluation that could be as close as possible to the human sensitivity, while avoiding to settling down for trivial one-to-one correspondence to mark a class as good and enabling to compare high amount of data in a quick time. (Our evaluator based on LLM is capable of checking the grand total of 27 cases × 5 techniques × 13 LLMs = 1755 UML diagrams in about 2 min).

Table 2. Comparison of Class Scores and Percentage Differences between Criteria

Metric	Class Scores			Percentage Differences (%)		
	Naïve	WordNet	LLM	WordNet vs Naïve	LLM vs Naïve	LLM vs WordNet
Precision	0.5533	0.5537	**0.5605**	+0.07%	+1.30%	+1.23%
Recall	0.5714	**0.6050**	0.5836	+5.88%	+2.14%	-3.53%
F1	0.5449	0.5455	**0.5535**	+0.11%	+1.58%	+1.47%

4.2 Performances per Prompting Techniques

After having established the LLM-based scoring as the default approach to assessing the correctness of classes identified, we compared the different LLMs and different prompting techniques with the goal of extracting the best overall performing combination of LLM and prompting approach. Selecting a few best performing combinations will allow to conduct a deeper analysis with fewer models about how the cases' complexity impacts the performances.

The complete results, divided by category (class, association and cardinality) and aggregated ((class + association + cardinality) / 3), are presented in Fig. 2 and summed up in Table 3 and Table 4. All f1 scores are weighted to make the most difficult cases count the most in final score computation. The formula used is in Appendix A.

What emerges from results is that there is not a model that outperforms consistently the others. In Table 3 we present the best performing LLM for each scoring category, and comparing it with results from Table 4 –which presents the single best LLMs all-around–, we decided to continue our analysis considering two different paths: *i)* using a single LLM only, based on the best overall combination of LLM and prompting technique and *ii)* combining several LLMs by using the best performing model in for each sub-task. The latter path opens a perspective for the construction of a complete agent capable of offering the best in each sub-task.

4.3 Performances per Cases

For analyzing what is the variance of the model's performances in comparison to the complexity of the cases and explaining of the weight of the f1 is distributed, we have chosen to visualize each case as a bubble with a size directly proportional to the number of classes, associations or total cardinality score. With these views, we want to extract the best performing model and technique combination for the reminder of our analysis.

Figure 3 presents the results comparing the overall best performing model with the best model in each category. Since Claude 3.7 is the best overall and the best for associations and Cardinality Score, we used the runner-up, o3-mini for the comparison.

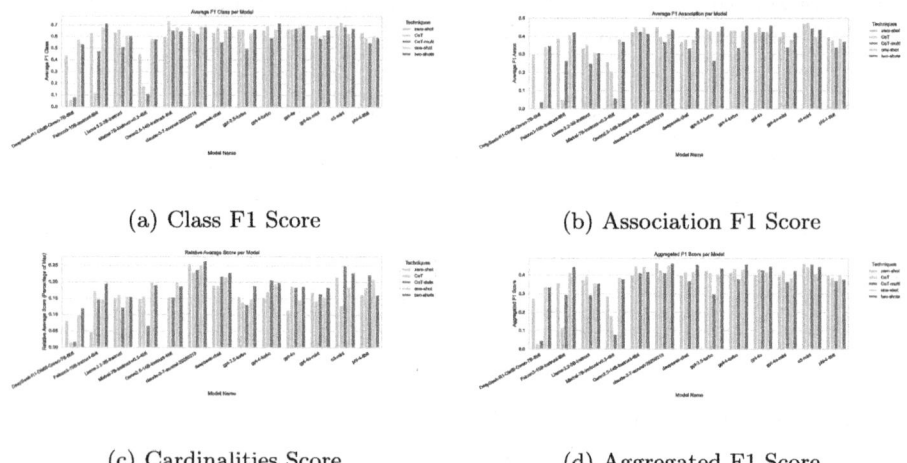

(a) Class F1 Score (b) Association F1 Score

(c) Cardinalities Score (d) Aggregated F1 Score

Fig. 2. Performance of all LLMs per prompting technique

4.4 Overall Aggregated Performances

To conclude our analysis, we present the overall performances of the absolute best LLM and the of the three best LLMs in classes, association and cardinality score together in one view. They are presented in Fig. 4.

5 Discussion and Threats to Validity

5.1 Model and Prompt Variability

The first thing that emerges by looking at the results is that there is a significant variability in model and prompt performances that is not consistent across the board. Some models achieve better performances with one prompting technique compared to another. We can observe that Few-Shot (1-shot and 2-shot) techniques obtain overall a better performances (see Fig. 2), but Chain-of-Thoughts

Table 3. Best Performing Models by Technique and Metric

Technique	Metric	Best Model	Weighted F1
zero-shot	Class F1	o3-mini	0.618
one-shot	Class F1	claude-3-7-sonnet-20250219	0.619
two-shots	Class F1	mlx-community-Falcon3-10B-Instruct-8bit	0.639
CoT	Class F1	o3-mini	**0.660**
CoT-multi	Class F1	o3-mini	0.622
zero-shot	Association F1	claude-3-7-sonnet-20250219	0.297
one-shot	Association F1	claude-3-7-sonnet-20250219	0.294
two-shots	Association F1	claude-3-7-sonnet-20250219	**0.317**
CoT	Association F1	o3-mini	0.306
CoT-multi	Association F1	o3-mini	0.290
zero-shot	Cardinality Score	claude-3-7-sonnet-20250219	0.250
one-shot	Cardinality Score	claude-3-7-sonnet-20250219	0.250
two-shots	Cardinality Score	claude-3-7-sonnet-20250219	**0.260**
CoT	Cardinality Score	claude-3-7-sonnet-20250219	0.230
CoT-multi	Cardinality Score	o3-mini	0.240

Table 4. Best Overall Result Per Model

Model Name	Technique	Weighted F1 Class	Weighted F1 Assoc	Weighted Score	Aggregated F1
claude-3-7-sonnet-20250219	two-shots	0.619	**0.317**	**0.263**	**0.400**
o3-mini	CoT-multi	*0.622*	*0.290*	*0.249*	*0.387*
deepseek-chat	two-shots	0.613	0.290	0.228	0.377
Falcon3-10B-Instruct-8bit	two-shots	**0.639**	0.279	0.196	0.371
gpt-4-turbo	two-shots	0.615	0.266	0.197	0.359

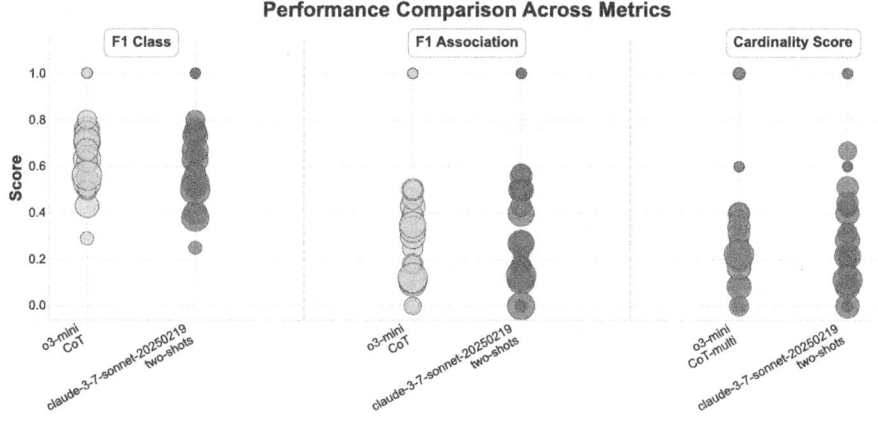

Fig. 3. Combined Metrics for Category Best LLMs o against Claude Two-Shots, the Single Best

techniques have better performances with more complex cases and thus higher weighted scores (see Table 3 and Table 4).

It seems that parameter number is not a factor in the overall performances, since smaller open-source LLMs obtained performances almost on par with bigger closed-source ones that are the state-of-the-art in a vast majority of tasks.

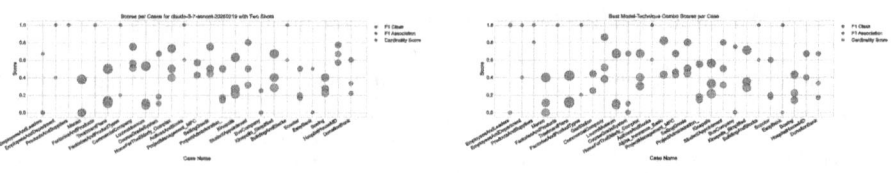

(a) Claude 3.7 Two-Shot Performance   (b) Best Model Performance

Fig. 4. Performance per Case

One decisive factor seems to be the reasoning capabilities: the two absolute best performing models, o3-mini and claude-3.7 are not the biggest LLMs, but they implement natively a deep-think and reasoning process in their prompt answering.

The leading open-source models in our benchmark is Qwen2.5, even above deepseek-chat, proving once again [15] that training on higher quality data can impact the performances of a model in a more significant way than the mere parameters size, especially in very niche tasks like UML class diagram extraction.

In some cases, the results were negatively influenced by syntax errors in the output. To further investigate this, we have gathered all information about syntax errors in the output per LLM and prompting techniques in Fig. 5. Deepseek-R1-Distilled seems the most impacted by this phenomenon, probably due to its relatively small parameter number and complex reasoning system not handling well a long prompt.

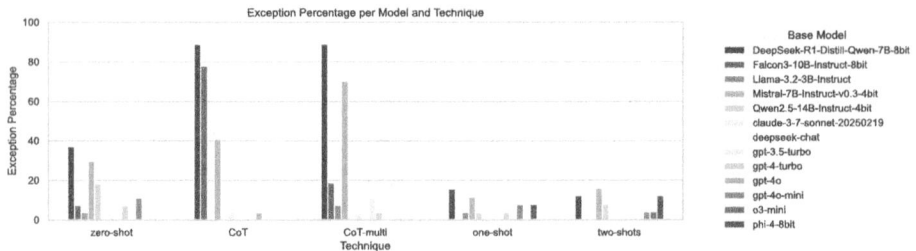

Fig. 5. Aggregated Syntax Error Rates per Technique

Finally, considering using either a single combination of LLM and prompting technique, versus an agentic approach that combines multiple LLMs and prompting techniques along the best performing per subtask, the current results seem to suggest that -apart from detecting classes- using a two-shot approach with Claude-3.7 would be the better option for a student wondering what LLM to use. Nevertheless, in view of the very low performance, the better option might still be to rely on own judgement instead of relying on an LLM's advice.

5.2 LLMs are Better at Detecting Classes

One trend recurring among all models and techniques is that the score in class detection is consistently higher than the scores for associations and cardinality, with cardinality being the least correctly detected. This can depend on a wide variety of factors, and pinpointing them all could a challenging tasks.

The first potential explanation could be that associations and cardinality detection depends directly on the class detection: if a class is not recognized correctly all associations and cardinalities involving that class will be wrong as well. However, given the relative high score for classes, this does not fully explains that much of discrepancy, especially with cardinality.

The second thing worth observing is that association and cardinality detection are a more demanding task also for an expert human modeler, requiring an increasing level of abstraction that is not there yet for LLMs. Supporting this hypothesis is that reasoning-enabled models obtain higher results.

The final observation is that UML class diagram extraction from specifications task is likely an Out-of-Domain (OOD) task [25], since there is little to no data available on the internet about this exact topic, especially in a dataset format. Arguably, the extraction of associations and cardinality is the most distant task from the widely available information extraction dataset [39], as opposed to the class extraction task, which could be reconducted to a special case of named entity recognition.

These results confirm the caution students need to observe when using LLMs: given that associations are already known as the concepts students struggle the most with [6,31], the low recall and precision is more likely to induce confusion in a student's mind than to really help out.

5.3 Case Size Dependency

Finally, a last observation is that the performance does not grow linearly with class diagram size: sometimes even a simple case in terms of number of classes and associations has a consistent low score, like the *Bus Company* case in Fig. 4. It is also hard to identify the exact cause that leads to this, but we hypothesize that the variability in the cases text description might cause variability in the LLM's performance as well.

5.4 Threats to Validity

There are two main factors that could undermine the validity of these experiments: the necessity of coming up with a rigorous scoring mechanism and the relatively small dataset size. For what concerns the first point, it was necessary to make some compromises in the scoring mechanism to enable an automated correction of the class diagrams and enable a comparison between a large number of UML class diagrams. This however inevitably introduced an unmeasurable level of uncertainty when it comes up to scoring. The second point is a well known issue in the modeling community: it is very hard to have high quality data of specifications and UML diagrams, and this forces us to limit the generalization of our results to all possible cases, since the number of cases analyzed is still too little to be considerable universal. To alleviate this issue, further research will be devote to enlarging the size of the dataset.

6 Conclusion and Future Work

This work presented a comprehensive evaluation of large language models (LLMs) for the task of generating UML class diagrams from textual specifications. Our experiments revealed that the performance of LLMs is highly variable and strongly influenced by both the choice of the model and the prompting technique used. A general observation is that LLMs are much better at detecting classes compared to finding associations and their cardinalities.

Future work will pursue several directions. First, we plan to expand the number of LLMs tested, with a particular focus on those exhibiting advanced reasoning capabilities. Second, we aim to increase the dataset size to better capture a wider range of case complexities and modeling scenarios. We also intend to explore alternative prompting techniques, such as the emerging Tree-of-Thought approach, to further enhance the quality of the generated UML diagrams. Finally, the long vision of this research is the development of the concept of smart twin (a kind of digital assistant) [5] which can help practitioners (including students and professors) to generate diagrams; the experiments of this paper show that a suitable approach is to use different LLMs specializing them to the subtask to be executed, as a pipeline.

Acknowledgments. The work of Marco Calamo, and Massimo Mecella is partially funded by MICS (Made in Italy—Circular and Sustainable) (PE00000004) Extended Partnership (CUP B53C22004130001) funded by the EU - NextGenerationEU PNRR MUR.

References

1. Abdin, M., et al.: Phi-4 technical report. arXiv preprint arXiv:2412.08905 (2024)
2. Achiam, J., et al.: GPT-4 technical report. arXiv preprint arXiv:2303.08774 (2023)
3. Arulmohan, S., Meurs, M.J., Mosser, S.: Extracting domain models from textual requirements in the era of large language models. In: 2023 ACM/IEEE International Conference on Model Driven Engineering Languages and Systems Companion (MODELS-C), pp. 580–587. IEEE (2023)
4. Bi, X., et al.: DeepSeek LLM: scaling open-source language models with longtermism. arXiv preprint arXiv:2401.02954 (2024)
5. Bianchini, F., et al.: Engineering information systems with LLMs and AI- based techniques, June 2024. https://doi.org/10.5281/zenodo.11489177
6. Bogdanova, D., Snoeck, M.: Learning from errors: error-based exercises in domain modelling pedagogy. In: Buchmann, R.A., Karagiannis, D., Kirikova, M. (eds.) The Practice of Enterprise Modeling, pp. 321–334. Springer International Publishing, Cham (2018)
7. Brown, T., et al.: Language models are few-shot learners. In: Advances in Neural Information Processing Systems, vol. 33, pp. 1877–1901 (2020)

8. Cámara, J., Burgueño, L., Troya, J.: Towards standarized benchmarks of LLMs in software modeling tasks: a conceptual framework. Softw. Syst. Model., 1–10 (2024)
9. Cámara, J., Troya, J., Burgueño, L., Vallecillo, A.: On the assessment of generative AI in modeling tasks: an experience report with ChatGPT and UML. Softw. Syst. Model. **22**(3), 781–793 (2023)
10. Chen, K., Yang, Y., Chen, B., López, J.A.H., Mussbacher, G., Varró, D.: Automated domain modeling with large language models: a comparative study. In: 2023 ACM/IEEE 26th International Conference on Model Driven Engineering Languages and Systems (MODELS), pp. 162–172. IEEE (2023)
11. De Bari, D., Garaccione, G., Coppola, R., Torchiano, M., Ardito, L.: Evaluating large language models in exercises of UML class diagram modeling. In: Proceedings of the 18th ACM/IEEE International Symposium on Empirical Software Engineering and Measurement, pp. 393–399 (2024)
12. Dubey, A., et al.: The Llama 3 herd of models. arXiv preprint arXiv:2407.21783 (2024)
13. Ferrari, A., Spoletini, P.: Formal requirements engineering and large language models: a two-way roadmap. Inf. Softw. Technol., 107697 (2025)
14. Fill, H.G., Fettke, P., Köpke, J.: Conceptual modeling and large language models: impressions from first experiments with ChatGPT. Enterp. Modell. Inf. Syst. Architectures (EMISAJ) **18**, 1–15 (2023)
15. Gunasekar, S., et al.: Textbooks are all You need. arXiv preprint arXiv:2306.11644 (2023)
16. Guo, D., et al.: DeepSeek-R1: incentivizing reasoning capability in LLMs via reinforcement learning. arXiv preprint arXiv:2501.12948 (2025)
17. Hurst, A., et al.: GPT-4o system card. arXiv preprint arXiv:2410.21276 (2024)
18. Jackson, M.: Problem Frames: Analyzing and Structuring Software Development Problems. Addison-Wesley Longman Publishing Co., Inc. (2000)
19. Jaech, A., et al.: OpenAI o1 system card. arXiv preprint arXiv:2412.16720 (2024)
20. Jiang, A.Q., et al.: Mistral 7B (2023). https://arxiv.org/abs/2310.06825
21. Kojima, T., Gu, S.S., Reid, M., Matsuo, Y., Iwasawa, Y.: Large language models are zero-shot reasoners. In: Advances in Neural Information Processing Systems, vol. 35, pp. 22199–22213 (2022)
22. Kukreja, S., Kumar, T., Purohit, A., Dasgupta, A., Guha, D.: A literature survey on open source large language models. In: Proceedings of the 2024 7th International Conference on Computers in Management and Business, pp. 133–143 (2024)
23. Lewis, P., et al.: Retrieval-augmented generation for knowledge-intensive NLP tasks. In: Advances in Neural Information Processing Systems, vol. 33, pp. 9459–9474 (2020)
24. Liu, A., et al.: DeepSeek-V3 technical report. arXiv preprint arXiv:2412.19437 (2024)
25. Liu, B., Zhan, L.M., Lu, Z., Feng, Y., Xue, L., Wu, X.M.: How good are LLMs at out-of-distribution detection? In: Proceedings of the 2024 Joint International Conference on Computational Linguistics, Language Resources and Evaluation (LREC-COLING 2024), pp. 8211–8222 (2024)
26. Miller, G.A.: WordNet: a lexical database for English. Commun. ACM **38**(11), 39–41 (1995)
27. Mosquera, D., Ruiz, M., Pastor, O., Spielberger, J.: Understanding the landscape of software modelling assistants for MDSE tools: a systematic mapping. Inf. Softw. Technol., 107492 (2024)
28. Penedo, G., et al.: The RefinedWeb dataset for falcon LLM: outperforming curated corpora with web data, and web data only. arXiv preprint arXiv:2306.01116 (2023)

29. Plaat, A., Wong, A., Verberne, S., Broekens, J., van Stein, N., Back, T.: Reasoning with large language models, a survey. arXiv preprint arXiv:2407.11511 (2024)
30. Prokop, D., Stenchlák, Š., Škoda, P., Klímek, J., Nečaský, M.: Enhancing domain modeling with pre-trained large language models: an automated assistant for domain modelers. In: International Conference on Conceptual Modeling, pp. 235–253. Springer (2024)
31. Rosenthal, K., Strecker, S., Snoeck, M.: Modeling difficulties in creating conceptual data models. Softw. Syst. Model. **22**(3), 1005–1030 (2023). https://doi.org/10.1007/s10270-022-01051-8
32. Ruan, K., Chen, X., Jin, Z.: Requirements modeling aided by ChatGPT: an experience in embedded systems. In: 2023 IEEE 31st International Requirements Engineering Conference Workshops (REW), pp. 170–177. IEEE (2023)
33. Sahoo, P., Singh, A.K., Saha, S., Jain, V., Mondal, S., Chadha, A.: A systematic survey of prompt engineering in large language models: techniques and applications. arXiv preprint arXiv:2402.07927 (2024)
34. Silva, J., Ma, Q., Cabot, J., Kelsen, P., Proper, H.A.: Application of the tree-of-thoughts framework to LLM-enabled domain modeling. In: International Conference on Conceptual Modeling, pp. 94–111. Springer (2024)
35. Wei, J., et al.: Chain-of-thought prompting elicits reasoning in large language models. In: Advances in Neural Information Processing Systems, vol. 35, pp. 24824–24837 (2022)
36. Yang, A., et al.: Qwen2. 5 technical report. arXiv preprint arXiv:2412.15115 (2024)
37. Yang, Y., Chen, B., Chen, K., Mussbacher, G., Varró, D.: Multi-step iterative automated domain modeling with large language models. In: Proceedings of the ACM/IEEE 27th International Conference on Model Driven Engineering Languages and Systems, pp. 587–595 (2024)
38. Yao, S., et al.: Tree of thoughts: deliberate problem solving with large language models. In: Advances in Neural Information Processing Systems, vol. 36, pp. 11809–11822 (2023)
39. Zhang, Z., You, W., Wu, T., Wang, X., Li, J., Zhang, M.: A survey of generative information extraction. In: Proceedings of the 31st International Conference on Computational Linguistics, pp. 4840–4870 (2025)
40. Zhou, Z., et al.: A survey on efficient inference for large language models. arXiv preprint arXiv:2404.14294 (2024)

Exploring the Influence of Data Characteristics on Machine Learning Outcomes

Camilla Sancricca(✉)📷, Pasquale Castiglione, and Cinzia Cappiello📷

Politecnico di Milano, Piazza Leonardo da Vinci 32, 20133 Milan, Italy
{camilla.sancricca,cinzia.cappiello}@polimi.it,
pasquale.castiglione@mail.polimi.it

Abstract. Data-centric AI highlights the importance of high-quality input data in machine learning, as it is essential for achieving reliable and accurate results. To this purpose, traditional data quality assessment and improvement systems might help detect and address data errors, inconsistencies, or missing values. However, recent literature has demonstrated that other factors, besides standard data quality issues, could compromise the performance of machine-learning applications. These factors are related to the characteristics of the considered datasets, such as their structure or statistical and ethical aspects (e.g., possible biases or unfairness). This paper aims to present the results of a literature survey and propose a quality model for data-centric AI. Such a model includes all the possible data characteristics that may undermine the execution of a machine-learning pipeline together with their related metrics. Validation experiments demonstrate how these characteristics affect the performance of various classification algorithms, highlighting the model's relevance and applicability. We believe the proposed model can support the development of novel AI systems, helping data scientists to assess the suitability of input data for specific machine-learning-based analyses.

Keywords: Data-centric AI · Data Quality · Machine Learning

1 Introduction

The emerging concept of Data-centric Artificial Intelligence (DCAI) [13] promotes the importance of feeding AI systems with high-quality data to guarantee dependable analytics results. The focus is now on improving the data quality (DQ) rather than only selecting effective machine-learning (ML) models and optimizing hyperparameters. The DQ research area focuses on traditional issues such as outliers, inconsistencies, or missing values. However, recent contributions (see Sect. 2) have emphasized that other data-related factors can impact the results of an ML-based analysis, such as the structure of the datasets or the statistical properties of their attributes. Furthermore, ethical aspects and fairness of the input data must be considered when applying AI systems, especially in sensitive contexts such as healthcare, finance, or school admissions. For this reason, traditional DQ models (such as [5,6]) are no longer sufficient to represent and cover all the issues that can undermine the reliability of ML-based tools' execution and outcomes.

This paper introduces a novel quality model designed to support the development of DCAI-based systems. Assessing the presented metrics will help data scientists evaluate the suitability of datasets for specific analytical purposes. The model has been defined for tabular datasets considering the results of (a) a literature survey investigating the data characteristics that can influence the performance of ML models and (b) a set of experiments designed to confirm such an impact. In analyzing the existing literature, we searched for contributions discussing factors that can compromise the performance of an ML-based analysis. Such factors include all the data-related aspects that traditional DQ may overlook, including those related to data profiling characteristics and data ethics, e.g., bias. For each factor, we searched for metrics that could be employed to measure it effectively. To validate the model, we conducted a series of experiments to evaluate the practical impact of the identified factors on the performance of several classification algorithms.

The paper is structured as follows: Section 2 describes (i) existing literature on data-centric approaches, especially those aimed at capturing the data aspects that impact the success of ML-based analyses and (ii) highlights the limitations of traditional DQ dimensions in capturing those aspects. The quality model is detailed in Sect. 3. Section 4 discusses the experiments we performed to validate the proposed model. Section 5 discusses conclusions and future work.

2 Literature Contributions

This section presents (a) an analysis of the recent state-of-the-art that emphasizes the crucial role of data characteristics in AI-based pipelines and (b) a set of research efforts for DQ assessment and improvement in DCAI in Sect. 2.1. Moreover, Sect. 2.2 (c) highlights the identified literature gaps and how we aim to address them. Table 1 summarizes the findings of our literature review, highlighting the discussed papers and the data aspects they identify as significantly influencing ML analysis outcomes.

2.1 State-of-the-Art Analysis

Methodology. We performed a keyword search on Google Scholar[1], considering the papers published in the last ten years (from 2015). The first round search was based on a set of keywords (Data-centric, Data errors, Data quality, Data problems) combined with the contexts we were interested in (AI, machine learning, classification, regression, clustering); the first search was based on the following prompt:

---

[1] https://scholar.google.com/.

(Data-centric OR Data errors OR Data quality OR Data problems) AND (AI OR machine learning OR classification OR regression OR clustering).

Then, we identified the names of the data characteristics reported in the papers (the ones listed in the following subsection), and considering one name (`name_characteristic`) at a time, we performed a second search as follows:

`name_characteristic` AND (AI OR machine learning OR classification OR regression OR clustering).

We considered all the papers in Google Scholar's results as long as they remained relevant. Finally, we examined the papers and selected relevant contributions that described data issues influencing the results of ML-based analyses. They are detailed in the following subsections. Note that works published on arXiv were excluded.

Table 1. Related work mapping with DQ dimensions and data characteristics

	Accuracy	Completeness	Consistency	Uniqueness	Dimensionality	Data Types	Correlation	Feature Relevance	Imbalance	Normalization	Homogeneity	Class Noise	Class Imbalance	Class Overlap
Ajiboye et al. 2015 [1]					X									
Ali et al. 2019 [2]									X					
Althnian et al. 2021 [3]					X									
Bailly et al. 2022 [4]					X	X								
Chen et al. 2021 [8]										X				
Emmert-Streib et al. 2020 [9]					X	X								
Foroni et al. 2021 [11]		X												
Gupta et al. 2019 [12]	X											X		
Li et al. 2021 [14]	X	X	X	X										
Luca et al. 2022 [15]					X	X								
Ma et al. 2018 [16]					X						X			
Osisanwo et al. 2017 [19]	X	X					X	X	X					
Patel et al. 2022 [20]	X	X		X			X	X				X	X	X
Patel et al. 2023 [21]												X		X
Sen et al. 2023 [27]						X			X					
Qi et al. [23, 24]	X	X	X											
Sancricca et al. 2022 [25]	X	X	X											
Sancricca et al. 2024 [26]	X	X												
Singh and B. Singh 2020 [28]										X				
Vuttipittayamongkol et al. 2021 [31]									X					X
Zhao et al. 2021 [33]				X										

Traditional DQ Models. It is well-known that incorrect, incomplete, inconsistent, and duplicated values (related to `accuracy`, `completeness`, `consistency` and `uniqueness` DQ dimensions) can impact ML results. [11,23,24] demonstrate such an impact by showing experiments in which they injected DQ errors (e.g., missing values, different formats, inconsistencies, etc.) in datasets and investigated the effect of such errors on the prediction outcome of different ML applications. They show that it depends on the datasets and the ML model used. [33] focuses instead on data duplication issues in the domain of malware detection using ML. The authors found that de-duplication has minimal impact on the performance of supervised malware classification models. In contrast, [14] investigated the impact of data cleaning techniques (e.g., data imputation, outlier detection, duplicates, and inconsistencies detection) on ML classification models, which, again, can change depending on the dataset and model used for analysis. Similarly, our previous works [25,26] demonstrate the different impacts that DQ errors (e.g., missing values, outliers, and inconsistencies) and cleaning techniques (e.g., data imputation and outlier detection) can have depending on the dataset and the ML model used.

Impact of Data Characteristics. In addition to the traditional DQ issues, several recent literature contributions highlighted the relationships between other data characteristics and the results of different ML models. Such characteristics are listed and described as follows.

`Dimensionality` and `data types` are two of the analyzed aspects. A high number of features (i.e., columns) can potentially result in overfitting or cause the *curse of dimensionality*, i.e., phenomena that might emerge when analyzing data in a high-dimensional space and discovering things that do not occur in low-dimensional settings. This happens when we start feeding the model with an exaggerated number of useless features: the model suffers from information overload, reducing its accuracy. Moreover, larger datasets require more computational costs and longer training time. Other issues arise with data types as most ML models do not deal with categorical variables during training, and choosing the proper encoding technique can be challenging: label encoding could affect the weights the model assigns to the features, while one-hot encoding could exaggerate the volume of data. Moreover, encoding categorical variables with many distinct values can lead to sparse feature representations and affect the model's performance. Data types and dimensionality issues in deep learning are discussed in [9,15]. [1,3] evaluate the effect of the dataset size on the performance of ML models, implementing different size reduction scenarios on diverse datasets; These articles highlight that ML model performance depends more on dataset representativity than size, though higher dimensionality can improve generalization. They also emphasize that the minimum sample size needed for optimal performance varies based on the dataset and model used.

Redundant or highly `correlated` features can increase computational complexity, slowing the training time and causing overfitting. High correlation levels can also cause the problem of *multicollinearity* [7]: many ML models assume input features are linearly independent, so highly correlated features can violate this assumption and lead to unreliable results. [4] investigates how different training dataset sizes and correlation levels affect the performance of logistic regression and deep learning models. This study showed no significant impact of dimensionality for these models; moreover, all tested algorithms perform quite well at different correlation degrees. Finally, [19] evaluates supervised learning algorithms, highlighting their strengths and weaknesses based on dataset characteristics like missing values, noise, redundancy, and data types. Experimental results show that algorithms like Support Vector Machines, Naive Bayes, and Random Forest are less affected by dataset dimensionality than others.

Data imbalance, which is related to the presence of unbalanced value distributions, can introduce bias in the ML model and worsen the performance. This problem is discussed in [31], which compares pre-processing, algorithmic, and hybrid approaches for handling data imbalance and implements experiments for different data distributions and analysis applications. This problem can also be related only to the targeted class in ML classification: [2] focuses on the class imbalance problem and discusses the difficulties in handling this problem in ML classification. Usually, data normalization approaches are implemented to mitigate data imbalance: [28] examines the impact of fourteen data normalization methods on the performance of classification models in different settings, such as complete feature set, feature selection, and feature weighting.

Other issues can be related to the targeted label in ML classification tasks: if the targeted class contains noise, it can worsen performance and affect the prediction; [12] presents a systematic literature review of several studies that show the impact of attribute noise, i.e., erroneous values for one or more attributes and class noise (such as contradictory or mislabeled instances) on ML analysis. They review for detecting and managing noisy features and labels in tabular data, noting that highly overlapping classes can hinder predictors like Support Vector Machines from effectively separating them in feature space. Finally, [31] performs an experimental comparison of class overlap and class imbalance problems. They also comprehensively review existing strategies to handle imbalanced data classification.

Data-Centric AI Approaches. Instead of evaluating the impact, some papers propose strategies to measure and improve DQ. [20] groups several tools for DQ analysis in the context of ML (e.g., Pandas Profilers, Amazon Deepqu, IBM's Data Quality for AI), discussing their strengths and similarities. They also discuss potential factors that can affect classification performance, such as missing data, homogeneity, outliers, duplication, correlation, feature relevance, and label purity (i.e., class noise), parity (i.e., class imbalance), and overlap. In addition to the contribution mentioned before, the work described in [21] proposes a framework for data exploration and DQ for DCAI. They propose and validate four novel algorithms for assessing the label purity and class overlap metrics. In the deep learning context, [27] proposes a model to improve data imbalance for high-dimensional datasets; [16] implements a dimensionality-driven approach to deal with noisy labels; finally, [8] develops a transfer-learning-based strategy for DQ and performance improvement. The authors exploit quality problems to build a system to normalize medical concepts in a social media text.

2.2 Literature Gaps

Looking at the literature, it emerges that current research on AI is moving towards data-centric approaches. Contributions highlight several data aspects that, besides DQ traditional issues, can directly impact the outcome of a machine-learning analysis pipeline. However, a comprehensive quality model that includes data-related characteristics and helps understand whether the data are suitable for specific AI-based analyses is missing. There is also a noticeable lack of metrics that effectively quantify the aspects mentioned above. Finally, experimental studies on the impact of those features on ML need to be implemented and translated into suitable guidelines.

To bridge those open issues, in this paper, we propose a quality model that includes all the data-related aspects that impact ML performance. In particular, we extended the traditional DQ model, inheriting the well-known issues related to completeness, accuracy, consistency, uniqueness, etc., with aspects related to the data profiling characteristics, such as dimensionality, data types, correlation and feature relevance (in our model, dependency), data imbalance, normalization, and homogeneity (in our model, imbalance), and class noise, imbalance (in our model, purity and balance) and overlap. Moreover, we also identified and included ethical aspects of data such as coverage, disparity, density, and diversity. The model has been (i) extended with metrics to guarantee the measurability of the identified characteristics and (ii) validated with experiments to verify if and how those aspects influence ML performance.

3 Extending the Quality Model for Data-Centric AI

This section describes the DCAI quality model we designed. As already explained in Sect. 2, the newly introduced data characteristics (a) will enrich traditional DQ models (presented below) and (b) aim to quantify additional aspects that could enhance or worsen ML outcomes. Note that the presented metrics already exist in the literature, but they were used in different contexts. Moreover, as highlighted in Sect. 1, we introduced the assessment of ethical aspects that are fundamental for ensuring the reliability and fairness of AI outputs. In our model, these aspects are related to the early identification and measurement of potential biases that can affect the data (i.e., when the data distribution is not representative of the real world). The model is tailored to support evaluating the tabular datasets' suitability for AI analyses.

The data characteristics have been classified into *Profile-related* and *Bias-related* data characteristics. The former describes the profiling characteristics that can be automatically extracted from a dataset through data profiling operations. The latter aims to capture ethical aspects of data. In particular, they aim to detect and measure the presence of bias in the training data. Bias-related data characteristics can be particularly useful in sensitive contexts when early bias detection is crucial for ethical decision-making.

Figure 1 provides an overview of the DCAI quality model specifying the granularity at which each data characteristic can be measured, i.e., at the dataset level (`dataset`), attribute level (`feature`), and, when applicable, the targeted class level (`class`). It is important to note that the measures defined for the targeted class are relevant only for ML classification tasks.

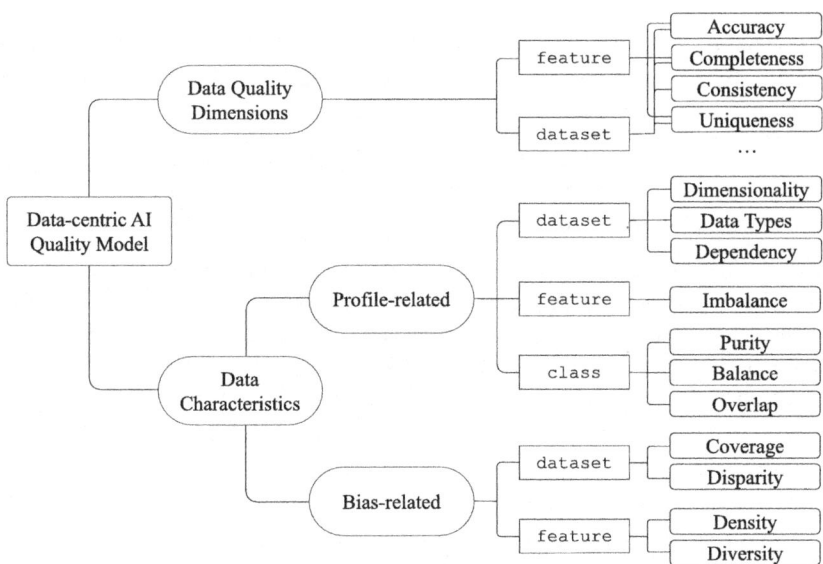

Fig. 1. Data-centric AI Quality Model

Traditional DQ Dimensions. Traditional DQ models often include multiple data dimensions to identify and resolve issues from different perspectives. Such perspectives commonly refer to values, schema, and usage [32]. However, the most commonly used DQ dimensions are Accuracy, Completeness, Consistency, and Uniqueness [6]. ***Accuracy*** is defined as the closeness between a data value v and a data value v', considered as the correct representation of the real-life phenomenon that the data value v aims to represent [6]. Accuracy is measured as the number of accurate values with respect to the total number of not-null values. ***Completeness*** characterizes the extent to which a dataset represents the corresponding real-world [6]. A simple way to assess the completeness of a table is to calculate the ratio between the number of non-null values and the number of cells in a table. ***Consistency*** relates to the capability of the information to comply without contradictions to all properties of the reality of interest, e.g., integrity constraints, data edits, business rules, and other formalism [6]. A way to assess it is to compute the number of violations of semantic rules defined over (a set of) data items. Rules can be both functional dependencies or business rules. ***Uniqueness*** is related to the level of duplication of rows [5]. A simple way to measure it is to compute the number of duplicated rows in a dataset.

Our model inherits the above-described dimensions and extends them for proper use in DCAI with the data characteristics described below. However, as stated above, there are a multitude of other DQ dimensions that can be used in specific contexts [5,32].

Profile-Related Data Characteristics. *Dimensionality* refers to the size (i.e., the number of features and instances) of a dataset. It can be easily assessed as the number of rows and columns of a dataset.

Data Types represent the count of numerical, categorical, or boolean variables in a dataset. It can be assessed as the proportion of numerical/categorical/boolean features relative to the total number of features.

Dependency is related to the presence of redundant or highly correlated features within a dataset. Using a correlation coefficient (e.g., Pearson, Spearman, etc.) and a predefined threshold to identify high correlation (e.g., Pearson's correlation coefficient greater than 0.7), it can be assessed as the ratio of the number of highly correlated features to the total number of features.

Imbalance is the deviation of the values distribution of a feature from an "ideal" distribution. For simplicity, we considered the Gaussian distribution as baseline (aware that it does not always reflect real-world distributions). It can be assessed by first calculating the mean and standard deviation of an ideal Gaussian fit derived from the original distribution. The ideal distribution is then compared to the original one using standard approaches from the literature for comparing value distributions, such as:

- *Intersection Over Union* is a metric that evaluates the distance between two distributions. It quantifies the overlap between the original data and the ideal Gaussian distribution.
- *Normalized Mean Squared Error* (NMSE) is an estimator of the deviation between the original data and the ideal Gaussian distribution. The NMSE is computed as the ratio of the Mean Square Error (MSE) to the variance of the original distribution.
- *Wasserstein distance*, also called the optimal transport distance, is a distance function between probability distributions; it calculates the effort required to transform a distribution into another one [30]. Given two probability distributions, P and Q, we need to calculate the cost of an optimal transport plan to transform P into Q. In the context of the continuous probability domain, the distance is assessed as follows:

$$Imbalance = \inf_{\gamma \sim \Pi(P,Q)} \mathbb{E}_{(x,y) \sim \gamma}[||x-y||]$$

where $\Pi(P,Q)$ is the set of all possible joint probability distributions between P and Q; one joint probability distribution $\gamma \in \Pi(P,Q)$ describes a plan of adjustments to transform P into Q in the continuous probability space. $\gamma(x,y)$ indicates the portion of probability that should be transferred from point x to y to make x follows the same probability distribution of y. The inf (infimum, i.e., the greatest lower bound) indicates that the goal is to minimize the transportation cost. We employ this metric to assess Imbalance in the experiments shown in Sect. 4.

Class Purity quantifies the presence of label errors or inconsistencies within the targeted class, estimating the degree to which the labels of a dataset represent the intended class assignments. To assess this data characteristic, we propose a metric based on the k-means clustering algorithm. The k-means algorithm is applied to the dataset, excluding the class label, with the number of clusters k set equal to the number of classes in the dataset. After clustering, a confusion matrix is used to compute the degree of misclassification. Class Purity measures the extent to which clusters contain a single class and can be computed as the proportion of correctly classified instances relative to the total number of points.

Class Balance assesses the degree to which the values of the targeted class are equally distributed [20]. Once we identified the majority class, i.e., the label assigned to the largest number of data points, and the minority classes, i.e., the labels assigned to fewer data points, we propose two assessment metrics:

- *Absolute Class Balance* is the ratio of the number of data points in the least populated class to the number of data points in the majority class.
- *Average Class Balance* is the ratio of the average number of data points in the minority classes to the number of points of the majority class:

$$Class\ Balance = \frac{\frac{1}{|N|} \sum_{i \in N} n_i}{|M|}$$

where $|M|$ is the number of data points of the majority class, and $[n_1, .., n_i] \in N$ is the set of the minority classes. We employ this metric to assess class Balance in the experiments of Sect. 4.

Class Overlap measures the similarity of data points with different labels based on their proximity in the feature space. To compute the class Overlap of a targeted class, we propose a metric that employs a classifier that can be either an SVM or Logistic Regression. We train the classifier on the dataset and extract its decision function, which assigns the points to the different labels on the basis of a decision boundary. Next, a threshold is set to define an overlapping region: data points whose closeness to the decision boundary is below the defined threshold are considered part of the overlapping region. Using the decision function generated by the classifier, the points in the overlapping region are identified, and the class Overlap metric is assessed as the ratio of the number of points in the overlapping region to the total number of points in the dataset.

Bias-Related Data Characteristics. *Coverage* represents the degree to which a dataset is representative of the real world. It is defined and calculated as "the proportion of entities represented in the dataset relative to the number of real-world entities" [18]. Note that the total size of the real-world entities is ground truth information and, if known, must be provided by the user.

Disparity aims to assess whether there is a disparity in the label distribution among different demographic groups. To assess the bias in a dataset, we considered the group fairness concept [17], which is commonly used in the literature to assess the fairness of the prediction during the post-processing phase. However, in our model, we propose a metric to be used in pre-processing that can be computed on the training dataset. Once established, for a protected attribute (e.g., sex, age, etc.), the characteristics of the protected group PG (e.g., female, younger than 25, etc.), Disparity can be computed as the ratio between the cardinalities of the sets $|P|$ and $|NP|$, where $P = \{x \mid y(x) = 1, x \in PG\}$ contains the samples x belonging to the protected group that have a favorable outcome in the training dataset and $NP = \{x \mid y(x) = 1, x \notin PG\}$ contains the samples x belonging to any group that have a favorable outcome.

Density is a measure of how densely concentrated certain values are within a feature; it is defined as "a measure of appropriate numerosity and intensity between different real-world entities available in the data" [18]. It can be assessed as the ratio of the number of occurrences of a specific value of a feature to the total number of distinct values.

Diversity is a measure of the value heterogeneity within a feature; it is defined as "the degree to which different kinds of objects are represented in a dataset" [10]. It is closely linked to the concept of entropy, which measures the amount of information contained within a dataset or a specific attribute. It can be evaluated using well-established metrics such as (1) Shannon's entropy and (2) the Gini index.

$$Diversity\ (1) = -\sum_{i=1}^{n} p(x_i) * log(p(x_i)) \qquad Diversity\ (2) = 1 - \sum_{i=1}^{n} (p(x_i))^2$$

where $p(x_i)$ is the relative frequency of the element i in a specific column.

4 Impact on Machine Learning Performance

This section describes the experiments conducted to investigate the impact of the proposed data characteristics on ML, i.e., whether variations in the characteristics values of the training data influence ML model performance and, in the case of the Disparity characteristic, the fairness of the results.

Section 4.1 presents the experimental pipeline and explains the setup choices that guided our implementation. Then, Sect. 4.2 presents and discusses the key findings, considering that only a representative subset of the results is shown. An example of the computation of the assessment metrics defined in Sect. 3 and the complete list of all the conducted experiments are available in a shared folder[2].

---

[2] https://github.com/camillasancricca/influence-data-characteristics.git

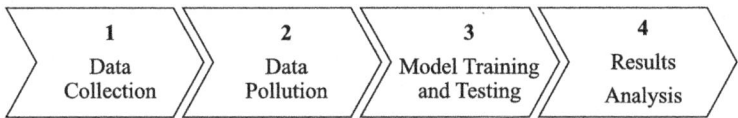

Fig. 2. Pipeline of the experiments

4.1 Experimental Pipeline and Setup

Pipeline. We followed the steps depicted in Fig. 2. We collected and analyzed several datasets to encompass a comprehensive range of heterogeneous characteristics in the **Data Collection** phase.

In the subsequent **Data Preparation** phase, we clean the datasets to make them suitable for analysis: missing values were handled by applying imputation methods (e.g., forward fill), for smaller datasets, while for bigger datasets, we removed the rows containing missing values; categorical features were converted to numerical form using label encoding, and we eliminated redundant features, such as IDs or those with minimal variability.

Next, we defined, for each analyzed characteristic, a **Data Pollution** function to simulate variations in the dataset content. This function creates three to five modified versions of the original dataset, each corresponding to a different pollution level. A detailed description of each pollution function is provided in Sect. 4.2.

During the **Model Training and Testing** phase, we split each perturbed dataset using 70% of instances for training the model and the remaining 30% for testing it. During testing, a set of performance evaluation metrics was extracted and saved. To control the randomness introduced by the pollution function, we applied a five-fold cross-validation strategy, each time considering splits with different samples and averaging the results.

Finally, in the **Results Analysis** phase, we analyzed how variations in data characteristics affected model performance. Experimental results were investigated to identify correlations between variations in metrics and the quality of the results.

Setup Datasets. Heterogeneous datasets were gathered from the UCI ML Repository[3] and Kaggle[4]. Datasets were chosen by selecting well-known datasets from the literature that are suitable for machine learning classification. Moreover, we selected different datasets for each experiment, as the data characteristics under investigation required us to consider different aspects. The list of datasets used for each characteristics-related experiment is reported in Table 2. For the majority of the data characteristics, we used the following state-of-the-art datasets: Airline Passenger Satisfaction, Heart Attack, Heart Failure, Marketing Campaign, and Stroke. For some Profile-related data characteristics, we

---

[3] https://archive.ics.uci.edu/.
[4] https://www.kaggle.com/.

Table 2. Experimental setup: datasets used for each data characteristic

	Airline Passenger Satisfaction	Heart Attack	Heart Failure	Marketing Campaign	Stroke	Synthetic Dataset	Cruise Ship	Customer Churn	KC House Data	Adult	COMPAS	German Credit	Bank	Law School	NLSY
Dimensionality	X	X	X	X	X	X				X					
Data Types						X									
Dependency						X	X	X	X						
Imbalance						X									
Purity	X	X	X	X	X										
Balance	X	X	X	X	X										
Overlap	X	X	X	X	X	X									
Coverage	X	X	X	X	X										
Disparity										X	X	X	X	X	X
Density	X	X	X	X	X										
Diversity	X	X	X	X	X										

also generated synthetic data using the `make_classification` function of the *scikit-learn* library [22]. For Dependency, we needed datasets with different correlation levels; thus, we chose Cruise Ship, Customer Churn, and Kansas City (KC) House Data. For Disparity, we considered famous datasets that contain sensible attributes and biases: Adult, Correctional Offender Management Profiling for Alternative Sanctions (COMPAS), Statlog German Credit (German Credit), Bank Marketing (Bank), Law School, National Longitudinal Survey (NLSY). Additional details on the main datasets' characteristics are provided in the shared folder.

Data Characteristics' Metrics. The data characteristics after the pollution were measured using the metrics described in Sect. 3.

Models. We focused on binary classification. For each experiment, we used a variety of models: Decision Tree, Gradient Boosting, k-Nearest Neighbors, Logistic Regression, Naive Bayes, Random Forest, and Support Vector Machine implemented by the *scikit-learn* library [22].

Performance Evaluation Metrics. We extracted the Accuracy, Precision, Recall, and F1 score metrics to evaluate the performance of the selected binary classification tasks. We compute Group Fairness, Predictive Parity, Predictive Equality, Equal Opportunity, Equalized Odds, and Conditional Use Accuracy Equality [29] to assess fairness in the Disparity-related experiment.

4.2 Results and Discussion

In this section, we show the most representative results of all the experiments (see Table 2). Figures 3 and 4 show the effect of varying data characteristics on the performance of the results. The x-axis represents the different levels of the data characteristic metric, while the y-axis shows the corresponding performance or fairness metric (only the F1 score and Group Fairness are displayed). Each colored line reflects the performance of a specific model, while the dashed line summarizes the overall trend of all the models.

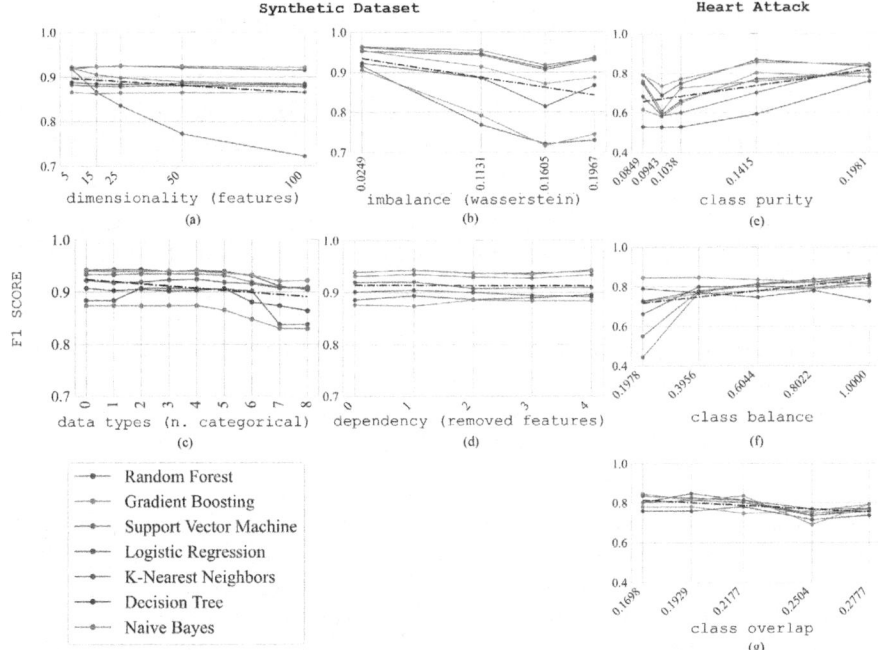

Fig. 3. Profile-related data characteristics impact on ML performance

Dimensionality. *Pollution.* The number of features was manipulated by changing the n_features parameter of the make_classification function, while the size of the data was manipulated by progressively removing rows from the selected datasets. We tested 5, 15, 25, 50, and 100 features and kept the 10%, 20%, 40%, 80%, and 100% of the training set size.

Results. Figure 3 (a) shows that varying the number of features, the performance does not change, except for the k-Nearest Neighbors, where the performance declines as the number of features increases. This is justified by the curse of dimensionality, as the distance between data points in high-dimensional spaces may not be significant in a low-dimensional setting (see Sect. 3). For the other algorithms, the performance is always the same since the number of significant features (the parameter n_informative) never changed in our experiment; thus, redundant features have no positive or negative impact on performance. The experiment revealed that models can improve their generalization capabilities with a larger number of rows.

Imbalance. *Pollution.* Imbalanced distributions were generated by varying the `n_clusters_per_class` (from 1 to 4) parameters of the `make_classification` function. Imbalance was calculated using the Wasserstein distance.

Results. The experiment shown in Fig. 3 (b) reveals that higher levels of imbalance worsened the performance. This demonstrates that non-uniform distributions can compromise the learning process of the underrepresented samples.

Data Types. *Pollution.* The dataset was modified with discretization, with which we converted an increasing number of continuous attributes (from 0 to 8) to nominal features.

Results. Figure 3 (c) shows that the performance remains almost unchanged until around five features are discretized; then, it decreases: since continuous variables provide more discriminative information than categorical ones, some information in the data may be lost in the discretization process.

Dependency. *Pollution.* To produce datasets with varying numbers of highly correlated features, we proceeded as follows: (1) we computed the correlation matrix, ignoring the self-correlations; (2) we sorted all feature pairs in descending order based on their correlation values; (3) we systematically removed one feature from the most highly correlated pairs (removing from one to four features).

Results. Variations in the number of highly correlated features did not significantly affect performance (see Fig. 3 (d)). This suggests that the models are not sensitive to the redundant information added by these correlated features.

Class Purity. *Pollution.* Different values of Purity were obtained by randomly flipping an increasing percentage of class labels.

Results. The experiments confirmed that (i) the proposed metric (see Sect. 3) effectively estimates class Purity and (ii) higher class Purity improves performance (see Fig. 3 (e)).

Class Balance. *Pollution.* Varying levels of class Balance were introduced by removing a percentage of data points (from 20% to 100% with an increasing step of 20%) belonging to the majority class or the minority class.

Results. Results in Fig. 3 (f) show that class Balance significantly impacts the model performance, as balanced class distributions increase the performance. This impact becomes more pronounced in datasets with lower dimensionality, such as the Heart Attack dataset: as stated in the Dimensionality experiment, a model trained on fewer samples is less capable of generalizing across the different classes; very unbalanced classes may compromise its predictions, and worsen the performance.

Class Overlap. *Pollution.* To introduce different class Overlap levels, we first identified the data points in the overlapping region. Then, we created synthetic data points (from 0% to 80% with an increasing step of 20%) in the overlapping region using *SMOTE* (Synthetic Minority Over-sampling Technique) and *ADASYN* (Adaptive Synthetic Sampling) oversampling methods.

Results. Figure 3 (g) demonstrates (i) the effectiveness of the proposed metrics in capturing class Overlap and (ii) a negative correlation between class Overlap and performance. For smaller datasets, this characteristic has a more significant impact; as stated above, training a model on fewer samples reduces its generalization capabilities; thus, very overlapping classes may worsen the predictions.

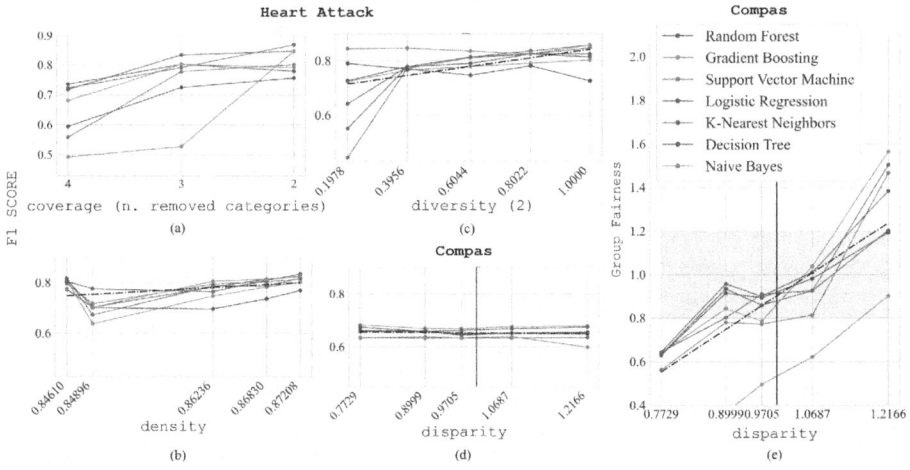

Fig. 4. Bias-related data characteristics impact on ML performance and fairness

Coverage, Density, and Diversity. *Pollution.* To vary the Coverage, we systematically removed a decreasing number of categories, i.e., distinct values (from 4 to 2) for each feature, replacing them with null values. Then, missing data were imputed using mode imputation before feeding the model. Variations of Density and Diversity were simulated by removing an increasing percentage of rows (from

0% to 50% with an increasing step of 10%) containing the second-most frequent attribute value. This process was applied to all categorical features.

Results. As shown in Fig. 4, (a) higher Coverage levels can improve the models' performance. Figure 4 (b) demonstrates that datasets with greater Density provide more balanced and varied information, thus enhancing performance. Finally, Fig. 4 (c) confirmed that increasing Diversity provides more valuable information, positively affecting performance.

Disparity. *Pollution.* To obtain different Disparity values, datasets were edited by removing an increasing percentage of rows (0%, 30%, 40%, 50%, and 60%) not belonging to protected groups (e.g., male, older than 25, etc.) and with favorable outcome (e.g., high income, loan granted, etc.).

Results. Figure 4 (d) reveals that changes in the Disparity levels of the training dataset do not influence ML performance. However, Fig. 4 (e) shows a clear correlation between pre-processing bias measurement and outcome fairness. Specifically, datasets with Disparity values close to 1 produce models with fairer predictions while, when Disparity values deviate substantially from 1, the classifiers produce less equitable results. These findings underscore the potential utility of the proposed Bias-related data characteristics as early indicators for performing fair ML.

5 Conclusions and Future Work

This paper aims to discuss the limitations of traditional DQ models in capturing all the key aspects that can affect the results of AI systems. We define a quality model for DCAI, enriching traditional DQ dimensions with data characteristics and related metrics to support the development of systems that help users understand the suitability of data for ML.

Experimental results demonstrate that the identified metrics can effectively measure the presence of the data characteristics of our model, as the metrics computed on the modified datasets reflected the amount of injected data pollution.

We analyze the impact of the identified data characteristics on the results of different classification models. Imbalance, class Purity, Balance, Coverage, Density, and Diversity influence the performance of the tested algorithms significantly. Therefore, data scientists should measure whether their datasets are characterized by a proper level of these metrics (or implement strategies to improve them) to ensure that such datasets are suitable for an ML-based analysis. Moreover, Dimensionality, Data Types, and Dependency have very small or even no impact. However, the presence of high levels of Dimensionality, Dependency, or many categorical features can significantly increase the time and the number of resources required for computation, which is why we also decided to maintain this aspect in our model. Finally, the proposed Disparity metric has a significant impact on fairness, which underscores the potential utility of the metric as an early indicator of bias in fair machine learning.

In future work, we will refine the model to consider different sources, such as unstructured data. Moreover, we plan to extend the impact analysis to more complex algorithms, such as deep learning models.

Acknowledgments. This research was supported by EU Horizon Framework grant agreement 101069543 (CS-AWARE-NEXT).

References

1. Ajiboye, A., Abdullah-Arshah, R., Hongwu, Q.: Evaluating the effect of dataset size on predictive model using supervised learning technique (2015)
2. Ali, H., Salleh, M.M., Saedudin, R., Hussain, K., Mushtaq, M.F.: Imbalance class problems in data mining: a review. Indonesian J. Electric. Eng. Comput. Sci. **14**(3), 1560–1571 (2019)
3. Althnian, A., et al.: Impact of dataset size on classification performance: an empirical evaluation in the medical domain. Appl. Sci. **11**(2), 796 (2021)
4. Bailly, A., et al.: Effects of dataset size and interactions on the prediction performance of logistic regression and deep learning models. Comput. Methods Programs Biomed. **213**, 106504 (2022)
5. Batini, C., Cappiello, C., Francalanci, C., Maurino, A.: Methodologies for data quality assessment and improvement. ACM Comput. Surv. **41**(3), 16:1–16:52 (2009)
6. Batini, C., Scannapieco, M.: Data and Information Quality - Dimensions, Principles and Techniques. Data-Centric Systems and Applications. Springer (2016)
7. Chan, J.Y.L., et al.: Mitigating the multicollinearity problem and its machine learning approach: a review. Mathematics **10** (2022)
8. Chen, H., Chen, J., Ding, J.: Data evaluation and enhancement for quality improvement of machine learning. IEEE Trans. Reliab. **70**(2), 831–847 (2021)
9. Emmert-Streib, F., Yang, Z., Feng, H., Tripathi, S., Dehmer, M.: An introductory review of deep learning for prediction models with big data. Front. Artif. Intell. **3**, 4 (2020)
10. Firmani, D., Tanca, L., Torlone, R.: Ethical dimensions for data quality. ACM J. Data Inf. Qual. **12**(1), 2:1–2:5 (2020)
11. Foroni, D., Lissandrini, M., Velegrakis, Y.: Estimating the extent of the effects of data quality through observations. In: ICDE 2021, pp. 1913–1918. IEEE (2021)
12. Gupta, S., Gupta, A.: Dealing with noise problem in machine learning data-sets: a systematic review. Procedia Comput. Sci. **161**, 466–474 (2019)
13. Jarrahi, M.H., Memariani, A., Guha, S.: The principles of data-centric AI. Commun. ACM **66**(8), 84–92 (2023)
14. Li, P., Rao, X., Blase, J., Zhang, Y., Chu, X., Zhang, C.: CleanML: a study for evaluating the impact of data cleaning on ML classification tasks. In: ICDE 2021, pp. 13–24. IEEE (2021)
15. Luca, A.R., et al.: Impact of quality, type and volume of data used by deep learning models in the analysis of medical images. Inf. Med. Unlocked **29**, 100911 (2022)
16. Ma, X., et al.: Dimensionality-driven learning with noisy labels. In: ICML. Proceedings of Machine Learning Research, vol. 80, pp. 3361–3370. PMLR (2018)

17. Mehrabi, N., Morstatter, F., Saxena, N., Lerman, K., Galstyan, A.: A survey on bias and fairness in machine learning. ACM Comput. Surv. **54**(6), 115:1–115:35 (2022)
18. Naumann, F., Freytag, J.C., Leser, U.: Completeness of integrated information sources. Inf. Syst. **29**(7), 583–615 (2004)
19. Osisanwo, F., et al.: Supervised machine learning algorithms: classification and comparison. Int. J. Comput. Trends Technol. (IJCTT) **48**(3), 128–138 (2017)
20. Patel, H., et al.: Automatic assessment of quality of your data for AI. In: COMAD/CODS, pp. 354–357. ACM (2022)
21. Patel, H., Guttula, S.C., Gupta, N., Hans, S., Mittal, R.S., Nagalapatti, L.: A datacentric AI framework for automating exploratory data analysis and data quality tasks. ACM J. Data Inf. Qual. **15**(4), 44:1–44:26 (2023)
22. Pedregosa, F., et al.: Scikit-learn: machine learning in Python. J. Mach. Learn. Res. **12**, 2825–2830 (2011)
23. Qi, Z., Wang, H., Wang, A.: Impacts of dirty data on classification and clustering models: an experimental evaluation. J. Comput. Sci. Technol. **36**(4), 806–821 (2021)
24. Qi, Z., Wang, H.: Dirty-data impacts on regression models: an experimental evaluation. In: Jensen, C.S., et al. (eds.) DASFAA 2021. LNCS, vol. 12681, pp. 88–95. Springer, Cham (2021). https://doi.org/10.1007/978-3-030-73194-6_6
25. Sancricca, C., Cappiello, C.: Supporting the design of data preparation pipelines. In: Proceedings of SEBD 2022. CEUR Workshop Proceedings, vol. 3194, pp. 149–158. CEUR-WS.org (2022)
26. Sancricca, C., Siracusa, G., Cappiello, C.: Enhancing data preparation: insights from a time series case study. J. Intell. Inf. Syst., 1–28 (2024)
27. Sen, S., Singh, K.P., Chakraborty, P.: Dealing with imbalanced regression problem for large dataset using scalable artificial neural network. New Astron. **99**, 101959 (2023)
28. Singh, D., Singh, B.: Investigating the impact of data normalization on classification performance. Appl. Soft Comput. **97**(Part B), 105524 (2020)
29. Verma, S., Rubin, J.: Fairness definitions explained. In: Brun, Y., Johnson, B., Meliou, A. (eds.) Proceedings of the International Workshop on Software Fairness, FairWare@ICSE 2018, Gothenburg, Sweden, 29 May 2018, pp. 1–7. ACM (2018)
30. Virtanen, P., et al.: SciPy 1.0 contributors: SciPy 1.0: fundamental algorithms for scientific computing in Python. Nat. Methods (2020)
31. Vuttipittayamongkol, P., Elyan, E., Petrovski, A.: On the class overlap problem in imbalanced data classification. Knowl. Based Syst. **212**, 106631 (2021)
32. Wang, R.Y., Strong, D.M.: Beyond accuracy: what data quality means to data consumers. J. Manag. Inf. Syst. **12**(4), 5–33 (1996)
33. Zhao, Y., et al.: On the impact of sample duplication in machine-learning-based android malware detection. ACM Trans. Softw. Eng. Methodol. **30**(3), 40:1–40:38 (2021)

Can an LLM Use Work System Axioms When Describing Work Systems for Requirements Analysis?

Steven Alter

University of San Francisco, 2130 Fulton Street, San Francisco 94117, USA
alter@usfca.edu

Abstract. This research-in-progress paper presents part of an ongoing project related to using LLMs for describing, analyzing, and designing work systems (including information systems). General axioms that apply to any non-trivial WS or IS might provide a path toward new tools and methods. This paper identifies 24 work system axioms that extend earlier research. They are organized in five categories: 1) system in context, 2) system operation, 3) system goals and goal attainment, 4) system uncertainties, and 5) system-related change. The axioms potentially address the challenge of helping business and IS/IT professionals understand and collaborate around systems in organization. This preliminary research hints at the potential value of the axioms based on results when an LLM applied them to two case studies.

Keywords: Requirements Analysis · Large Language Model · Systems Analysis and Design · Work System Axioms

1 Reasons for Pursuing a Set of Axioms for Understanding and Analyzing Systems in Organizational Settings

Axioms are statements assumed to be true for all instances within a given domain. Thus, they differ from generalizations such as theories, models, principles, and rules of thumb that typically are assumed not to be true for at least some instances within the domain. Axioms appear in mathematics, systems theory, economics, accounting, natural science, marketing, and computer science, but thus far have been largely invisible in the IS discipline except in discussions about whether many IS theories seem to be obvious (and hence axiomatic) and hence not valuable or informative in practice.

This paper proposes a set of axioms that apply to typical WSs designed and operated to support goal achievement in organizations. Those axioms apply to ISs, which are a special case of WS (Alter, 2013, 2025). Axioms are assumed true for all instances in a domain or a specific subdomain. In contrast, most theories discussed in the IS discipline, such as TAM (Davis, 1989) and UTAUT (Venkatesh et al., 2003) are stated in terms of relationships between variables and are tested based on statistical calculations that may or may not reveal their practical strength or value. The axioms proposed here concern WSs themselves and not perceptions, intentions, psychological phenomena, organizational change or other topics not specifically about WSs per se.

The proposed axioms aim to help business and IS/IT professionals understand and collaborate around systems in organizations. A readily accessible set of system-related axioms stated in understandable terms or expressed through easily used analysis tools or templates could focus attention on topics and issues that otherwise might be taken for granted or ignored, especially in discussions between people with different work experiences, skill sets, professional interests, and goals. Axioms made accessible through tools or templates could help business and IS/IT professionals visualize and understand systems for their own purposes and could help them communicate about topics and issues that are mutually understandable.

Goal. This paper presents progress-to-date related to producing a set of axioms and testing their value by using an LLM that applies them to WSs and ISs to help in creating, understanding, and/or improving those systems. This paper makes no claim that the proposed axioms are the best possible axioms. To the contrary, it treats a proposed set of system-related axioms as a potentially useful step toward new systems analysis tools and methods.

Organization. Section 2 summarizes how the set of axioms was developed. Section 3 identifies 24 axioms that are relevant to all sociotechnical and totally automated work systems. Section 4 explains how an LLM applied the axioms to two case studies. Section 5 presents implications. An Online Supplement provides a complete transcript of the results when an LLM used the 24 axioms to describe each of two case studies. It also includes parts of an unpublished draft aimed at developing an axiomatic basis for IS. It includes background, literature, and useful analysis questions related to each axiom, and previously published ideas about work systems. It can be accessed at: https://www.dropbox.com/scl/fo/q8c0l5hwmfx8zfweo1akh/AAswjJyDi EnbLOmyCaX0czg?rlkey=t3ft78bqsa5j8n8xa7xn5wc0z&dl=0.

Limitation. The axioms are presented as statements that describe WSs (and hence ISs) in organizational settings. Each axiom suggests related questions for managers, analysts, and researchers trying to understand, analyze, design, or evaluate a WS or IS. The axioms are not presented as a systems analysis method even though they might be incorporated into systems analysis methods that could be developed in the future.

2 Background Concerning the Set of Axioms Presented Here

The initial impetus for developing the axioms was an informal discussion at ICIS 2015 with Prof. Carson Woo, who had used work system ideas in his systems analysis courses. Prof. Woo asked whether work system theory (WST) could be derived from more basic ideas. Sociotechnical principles (Cherns, 1976, 1987; Clegg, 2000) were too focused on social issues to describe automated work systems. Ideas associated with general systems theory (Bertanalffy, 1950; Skyttner, 1996; 2005) seemed too general.

A paper for the ICIS track on Methodological and Philosophical Foundations of IS (Alter, 2016) identified 20 "intrinsic principles" and seven "observability principles."

Informal discussions at AMCIS 2016 and ICIS 2016 and presentations and discussions at seven major universities in Europe and Australia generated many comments and criticisms. The general topic seemed interesting, but the axioms needed to be organized into categories so they would be less overwhelming. Also, there was no way to justify a particular number of axioms – 14 or 20 or 38 – although clear criteria for including or excluding any candidate axiom could be proposed. The ICIS 2017 track on Service Science and IS provided a nudge to think about axioms again. That led to 25 proposed service system axioms in an ICIS 2017 paper (Alter, 2017). 24 of those axioms emerged again seven years later as a starting point for proposing the work system axioms presented next, which also apply to sociotechnical and totally automated ISs.

3 The Nature of Work System Axioms

All 24 work system axioms presented here apply to every nontrivial sociotechnical and totally automated WS that I am familiar with. All are revisions of service system axioms in Alter (2017). Most use the acronym WS/IS as a reminder that they apply to WSs and to ISs. Each axiom satisfies the following set of qualifying conditions:

- A WS axiom is a generalization assumed true for every WS within the domain of small-to-medium-to-large WSs operated to achieve organizational goals over a duration of weeks, months, or years. (This excludes WSs that are tiny or that operate briefly and then disappear).
- Any proposed WS axiom can be challenged by providing at least one example of a nontrivial WS that does not conform to the proposed axiom.
- A WS axiom should express an idea that is not expressed directly by other WS axioms and that seems useful for describing, analyzing, designing, or evaluating WSs.
- WS axioms differ from principles, frameworks, models, and theories and other types of generalizations meant to describe aspects of some WSs but not other WSs.
- Work system axioms are meant to apply to work systems but not to other systems, such as abstract systems "all of whose elements are concepts" (Ackoff, 1971, p. 662). Thus, they exclude computational axioms that specify relationships within computational ontologies and also exclude natural systems.

4 Proposed Work System Axioms

The following list identifies axioms in each of five categories: 1) system in context, 2) system operation, 3) goal attainment, 4) system uncertainties, and 5) system-related change. Iterations of different sets of categories led to concluding that this grouping was more effective for organizing the axioms than other possible groupings that were considered. The Online Supplement (see above) includes a discussion of each axiom in the context of related literature.

Given the 8-page length maximum for this research-in-progress paper, the Online Supplement provides a discussion of each axiom followed by two or more "useful questions" that could be applied for describing, analyzing, or evaluating many WS/ISs. The questions are indented and numbered. Inclusion of those questions demonstrates that the axioms point to issues and concerns that are often relevant when analyzing or designing operational systems. The questions are meant to be straightforward for a manager, analyst, or researcher who is using the axioms as an aid when trying to describe, analyze, or design a work system. In many cases those questions point to concerns and issues that might otherwise be overlooked.

4.1 Axioms Related to Systems in Context

A1: **Open system axiom.** A WS/IS is an open system that receives inputs from the external environment outside of its boundary and generates outputs that affect external entities and/or aspects of its external environment.
A2: **Purposeful system axiom.** A WS/IS operates with the intention of facilitating or producing beneficial outcomes for at least one beneficiary.
A3: **Stakeholders axiom.** A WS/IS's stakeholders include its beneficiaries and others who care about its operation and outputs.
A4: **Externalities axiom.** A WS/IS is affected by direct and/or indirect interactions with the environment within which it operates. Specific interactions may have positive or negative impacts.

4.2 Axioms Related to System Operation

A5: **Purposeful activities axiom.** A WS/IS performs activities or actions that contribute to achieving its purposes.
A6: **Resources axiom.** Execution of a WS/IS's activities requires resources in one or more of the following categories: time, informational resources, physical resources, human and automated actors, and other organizational, technical, or societal resources (such as culture, policies, regulations, and standards).
A7: **Regulation axiom.** A WS/IS's activities are guided or controlled by implicit or explicit regulation activities and/or rules, norms, or guidelines.
A8. **Internal interactions axiom.** A WS/IS operates through direct and indirect interactions between its various subsystems or components and in some cases interactions within the WS/IS that involve beneficiaries or external resources.
A9: **External interactions axiom.** A WS/IS interacts with beneficiaries, suppliers, and other external entities through a variety of means including co-production activities within the WS/IS, transfer of information and product/services to entities outside of the WS/IS, accessibility of boundary objects that are used jointly with external entities, and/or creation of conditions that affect beneficiaries or other external entities.
A10: **Maintenance axiom.** Maintenance of a WS/IS uses and/or consumes resources.
A11: **System of systems axiom.** A nontrivial WS/IS contains smaller WS/ISs that individually conform to the other axioms.

4.3 Axioms Related to Goal Attainment

A12: **Goal variety axiom.** The structure, characteristics, operation, and interactions of a WS/IS's subsystems or components affect attainment of multiple goals related to the WS/IS as a whole, related to its subsystems or components, and related to whatever it produces for its beneficiaries.

A13: **Internal alignment axiom.** Achieving a WS/IS's various goals depends at least partly on how well those goals are mutually aligned and how well goals of subsystems are mutually aligned and are aligned with WS/IS goals.
A14: **Internal/external alignment axiom.** Achieving a WS/IS's goals related to serving its beneficiaries depends at least partly on how well its internal goals are aligned with goals of value-creating activities of beneficiaries.
A15: **Trade-offs axiom.** Conflicts between internal WS/IS goals and goals of various beneficiaries and stakeholders lead to implicit or explicit trade-offs.
A16: **Operational fit axiom.** Operational fit between the structure, logic, and details of a WS/IS component (or an entire WS/IS) and the structure, logic, and details of complementary components (or complementary WS/ISs) facilitates goal achievement.
A17: **Adaptability and resilience axiom.** Goal attainment depends partly on a WS/IS's capabilities for recognizing and responding to the diversity of situations that it will encounter.

4.4 Axioms Related to Operational Variability

A18: **Agency axiom.** Both human participants and totally automated entities that perform actor roles in a WS/IS may or may not pursue the WS/IS's stated goals.
A19: **Compliance/noncompliance axiom.** Although compliance to well-designed WS/IS specifications and/or routines is usually beneficial, noncompliance may be beneficial in some situations and strict compliance may be detrimental in other situations.
A20: **Performance uncertainty axiom.** It is not possible to predict exactly how a WS/IS will operate or what outcomes it will produce.

4.5 Axioms Related to System Change

A21: **Design incompletion axiom.** The design of a WS/IS tends to evolve over a span of months or years based on adaptations related to insights from performing the work, changes in the organization, and/or demands and constraints related to resource availability, changes in wants and needs of beneficiaries, and changes in the surrounding environment.
A22: **Planned and unplanned change axiom.** A WS/IS that operates over a span of months or years evolves through planned and/or unplanned change (unless it is terminated).
A23: **Path dependence axiom.** The feasibility of future changes in a WS/IS depends partly on the path of planned and unplanned changes that brought it to its current state.
A24: **Absorptive capacity axiom.** The amount of change that a WS/IS can absorb during a period when it continues to operate is limited by its structure, history, human and technical resources, and other factors.

5 How an LLM Might Apply the Axioms to Support Requirements Analysis

This section shows how the axioms could be the basis of automated support for human deliberations based on combining questions based on the axioms in Sect. 4 with capabilities of an LLM. The Online Supplement mentioned earlier includes a complete transcript of the results from the following steps:

1) A Word document was produced containing the definition of work system and the 24 axioms. The Word document was converted to a PDF called BASIS2. That arbitrary name was chosen to simplify a prompt instructing an LLM to use that PDF.
2) Two test cases were used. The first was a 3385-word case study constructed based on excerpts from an article in *Organization Science* (Cameron & Rahman, 2022) that explored resistance versus control in ride hailing and in gig work. The excerpt focused on ride hailing and eliminated all references to gig work, sociological theory, and literature references. The second was the entirety of a famous surgeon's 9,248-word non-research article "The Update: Why Doctors Hate Their Computers" (Gawande, 2018) that was published in *New Yorker Magazine*.
3) A ChatGPT-4o prompt said that ChatGPT-4o would serve as an assistant for a manager trying to improve a work system described in a PDF (either RDH403 for ride hailing or EMR588 for the medical example) while referring to the definition of work system and the 24 axioms in another PDF called BASIS2. The prompt contained a single question for each of the 24 axioms. Most of the questions repeated or were constructed from the "useful questions" listed in the Online Supplement following the comments about each axiom. The questions asked for descriptions related to a work system's current operation and did not ask for suggestions for improvement due to the widely recognized inability of current LLMs to understand contexts (e.g., see Alter (2024a), p. 7) for a series of impractical suggestions generated by LLMs for RDH403 and two other cases). The prompt instructed ChatGPT-4o to use factual details related to the case being analyzed, to avoid making suggestions or fabricating hypothetical comments, and to avoid repeating the axioms.

The Online Supplement shows the full prompts and the answers that ChatGPT-4O produced for both cases. Most of the answers make sense and reflect important aspects of the cases. In combination those answers provide a meaningful summary impression of the context, operation, goals, and key sources of variability for both work systems. An implication is that an LLM-enabled tool that uses the proposed set of axioms might contribute to initial phases of requirements analysis by summarizing important topics and issues that could be found in documentation, interview notes, and other documents generated during early phases of requirements analysis. That could save time and effort, although it obviously would not replace careful consideration by human analysts and managers who are able to understand the context. Users would have to check answers for errors and omissions and also would need to add situation-specific details. They would need to be careful about LLM responses that are vague or generic or that do not mention direct evidence from the case even though they touch on axiom-related issues. Those common issues stem from the token-based operation of LLMs (e.g., Bender et al., 2021; Borji, 2023; Dutta & Chakraborty, 2023; Teubner et al., 2023), which do not understand anything about the world despite their proficiency in producing grammatical sentences.

The overarching implication is that an integrated set of axioms related to systems in organizations might be useful to business and IS/IT professionals engaged in requirements analysis. It is possible, but certainly debatable, that business and IS/IT professionals would find them more useful than most of the widely cited IS-related theories that are tested based on covariances involving multiple independent, moderating, and dependent variables. In addition, note that ongoing research in industry may produce advanced LLMs that could overcome some of the key limitations of current LLMs that have become available only recently.

6 Conclusion

The idea of axiom is almost invisible in today's IS discipline except in relation to computational ontologies. This research-in-progress aims to contribute to IS research and practice by illustrating a largely untapped opportunity to identify and codify knowledge that is useful in practice. It demonstrates the practicality of that approach by identifying an internally consistent set of 24 axioms that apply to sociotechnical or totally automated WS/ISs.

I am not aware of any comparable sets of axioms designed to support WS/IS description, analysis, design, and evaluation other than earlier versions of those ideas. The closest comparable set of axioms that I could find is a set of seven axioms presented as a basis for systems theory (Adams et al., 2014).

In combination, the 24 axioms potentially contribute to a discussion of what is genuinely fundamental for describing and understanding WS/ISs. The approach of proposing axioms and exposing them to clarification and criticism could lead to a better set of axioms and to other progress. Pursuit of that approach would raise questions about why the IS discipline seems to favor variance theories that express the influence of independent and moderating variables on dependent variables when most variance theories of that type are difficult to apply in real world practice, as noted by Ramiller & Pentland (2009). An organized set of axioms, axiomatic theories, or principles (statements about paths that typically should be pursued in specific types of situations, although with exceptions) would express fundamental ideas more directly and could be more useful in practice, especially if embedded in templates or interactive tools.

Each of the 24 axioms presented in Sect. 3 can be evaluated using the eight criteria for evaluating generalizations that were presented in Alter (2024b).

- **Conceptual clarity**. The ideas in each of the axioms seem sufficiently clear.
- **Domain clarity**. The domain is typical WS/ISs that may be sociotechnical (with human participants) or may be totally automated.
- **Parsimony**. The 24 axioms are mutually independent, although it is possible that some smaller or larger set of axioms might serve the same purpose.
- **Examples**. The transcript in the Online Supplement shows results from applying an LLM analysis of two separate cases based on a question for each axiom.
- **Omissions**. The proposed axioms focus on operational systems in organizational settings. They do not attempt to cover other IS-related topics involving perceptions, intentions, psychological phenomena, organizational change processes, and so on.
- **Time span clarity**. The axioms are meant to be equally relevant to WS/ISs in the past and in the near-term future. Axioms related to system change and possibly other topics may become obsolete due to future developments that are difficult to foresee.
- **Justification**. Each axiom is justified based on the author's inability to identify counterexamples within the relevant domain. That form of justification is weak for obvious reasons. On the other hand, it raises the interesting challenge of demonstrating that specific proposed axioms do not apply to identifiable instances within the domain.

- **Value.** The Online Supplement's transcript in the application of the LLM illustrates the potential value of the axioms for supporting systems analysis.

6.1 Limitations and Next Steps

This paper presents new ideas and argues for a new approach. Its most fundamental limitation is that it does not test the usefulness of its proposed axioms in teaching or practice. Other limitations start with the fact that ideas discussed here remain largely peripheral to widely cited IS theories and research approaches even though they are rooted in a work system perspective that emerged from IS textbooks produced in the 1990s. Also, the iterative research that generated the axioms was not performed as a formal DSR project (identify a problem, gather information, produce artifacts, get feedback, iterate, and articulate and communicate the results). Therefore, it might seem unscientific to some IS researchers, especially those who strongly prefer anchoring research in existing methods or theoretical frameworks, such as activity theory, actor-network theory, and so on.

Possible next steps in this research start with testing the axioms in teaching. This can be done in many ways, such as a simple comparison of the type used in Bolloju et al. (2017) to test the usefulness of "work system snapshots" as a starting point for producing use cases in a software engineering course. Ideally, the axioms should be tested in practice, which probably would require collaboration with a firm's IT group or training group. The set of axioms presented here surely might be extended further, perhaps with the help of an LLM that is prompted to identify 10 or 20 generalizations related to the main ideas underlying each of the axioms. That might generate "axiom candidates" that could be evaluated for conceptual clarity, domain relevance (sociotechnical WSs? totally automated ISs?), ease of application to real world systems, and so on. That type of research would call for an atypical research method that intentionally pursued multiple iterations of candidate generation, evaluation, and revision.

Finally, the LLM application discussed here is part of a project for developing new systems analysis tools that might be presented to users in templates or in other forms. Various versions of the questions associated with the axioms (shown in the Online Supplement) could be built into some of those tools. Similar use could apply to additional axioms that focus on specific special cases or on specific components such activities related to capturing information or storing information.

References

Ackoff, R.L.: Towards a system of systems concepts. Manage. Sci. **17**(11), 661–671 (1971)

Adams, J., Hester, P., Bradley, J., Meyers, T., Keating, C.: Systems theory as the foundation for understanding systems. Syst. Eng. **17**(1), 112–123 (2014)

Alter, S.: Work system theory: overview of core concepts, extensions, and challenges for the future. J. Assoc. Inf. Syst. **14**(2), 72–121 (2013)

Alter, S.: Principles for "purposefully constructed activity systems" – a step toward a body of knowledge for information systems. In: Proceedings of ICIS 2016 (2016)

Alter, S.: Service system axioms that accept positive and negative outcomes and impacts of service systems. In: Proceedings of ICIS 2017 (2017)

Alter, S.: Could a large language model contribute significantly to requirements analysis? In: Proceedings of EMMSAD 2024 (2024)

Alter, S.: Vanquishing theory as king by focusing instead on rigorous generalizations. In: European Conference on Information Systems 2024 (2024)

Alter, S.: Making cyber-human systems smarter. Inf. Syst. **127**, 102428 (2025)

Bender, E.M., Gebru, T., McMillan-Major, A., Shmitchell, S.: On the dangers of stochastic parrots: Can language models be too big? In: Proceedings of the 2021 ACM Conference on Fairness, Accountability, and Transparency, pp. 610–623 (2021)

Bertalanffy, L.V.: An outline of general system theory. Br. J. Philos. Sci. **1**(2), 134–165 (1950)

Bolloju, N., Alter, S., Gupta, A., Gupta, S., Jain, S.: Improving scrum user stories and product backlog using work system snapshots. In: Proceedings of AMCIS 2017 (2017)

Borji, A.: A categorical archive of chatgpt failures (2023). arXiv:2302.03494

Cameron, L.D., Rahman, H.: Expanding the locus of resistance: Understanding the co-constitution of control and resistance in the gig economy. Organ. Sci. **33**(1), 38–58 (2022)

Cherns, A.: Principles of socio-technical design. Hum. Relat. **2**(9), 783–792 (1976)

Cherns, A.: Principles of sociotechnical design revisited. Hum. Relat. **40**(3), 153–161 (1987)

Clegg, C.W.: Sociotechnical principles for system design. Appl. Ergon. **31**(5), 463–477 (2000)

Davis, F.D.: Perceived usefulness, perceived ease of use, and user acceptance of information technology. MIS Q. **13**(3), 319–340 (1989)

Dutta, S., Chakraborty, T.: Thus Spake ChatGPT. Commun. ACM **66**(12), 16–19 (2023)

Gawande, A.: Why doctors hate their computers. New Yorker (2018). https://www.newyorker.com/magazine/2018/11/12/why-doctors-hate-their-computers

Ramiller, N.C., Pentland, B.T.: Management implications in information systems research: the untold story. J. Assoc. Inf. Syst. **10**(6), 474–494 (2009)

Skyttner, L.: General systems theory: origin and hallmarks. Kybernetes **25**(6), 16–22 (1996)

Skyttner, L.: General Systems Theory: Problems, Perspectives, Practice. World Scientific Publishing, Singapore (2005)

Teubner, T., et al.: Welcome to the era of chatgpt et al.: the prospects of large language models. Bus. Inf. Syst. Eng. **65**(2), 95–101 (2023)

Venkatesh, V., Morris, M.G., Davis, G.B., Davis, F.D.: User acceptance of information technology: toward a unified view. MIS Q. **27**, 425–478 (2003)

Security (EMMSAD 2025)

Forensic Readiness and Privacy: Towards Resolving Software Goal Conflict

Lukas Daubner[1](✉)[iD], Jakub Harašta[2][iD], and Raimundas Matulevičius[1][iD]

[1] University of Tartu, Tartu, Estonia
{lukas.daubner,raimundas.matulevicius}@ut.ee
[2] Masaryk University, Brno, Czechia
harasta@muni.cz

Abstract. Forensic readiness focuses on systematic preparation for an investigation. In the context of software systems (i.e., forensic-ready systems), it revolves around gathering and processing potential digital evidence. While such endeavours significantly impact privacy, the exact nature of the conflict between forensic readiness and privacy has been unaddressed. Thus, a goal modelling approach is utilised to gain understanding and explore the conflict. Specifically, a GDPR goal model for privacy and Rowlingson's guide model for forensic readiness are created and compared. The conflict patterns are formulated based on the comparisons, outlining a resolution strategy. The patterns are utilised in a forensic-ready design process to establish effective forensic readiness while ensuring compliance with GDPR in a car-sharing system.

Keywords: Goal Modelling · Forensic Readiness · Forensic-Ready System · GDPR · Requirements Engineering

1 Introduction

Digital forensic investigation is launched in response to an incident (e.g., information security incident) to reliably answer queries about its causes and circumstances based on evidence from the systems. However, it is often a costly endeavour with uncertain success. Forensic readiness is employed as a proactive measure [31] to improve the odds of having useful evidence with minimal costs.

Forensic readiness can be integrated into software system design, giving rise to forensic-ready systems. These integrated qualities lower the costs of forensic processes and produce sound evidence [27]. While often overlapping with logging and auditing, forensic readiness is also concerned with the data quality, targeted and systematic collection, and the ability to present the data to third parties.

Thus, such a systematic data processing for a potential future forensic investigation impacts privacy as it often includes personal data (PD) and might aim to identify the subject [7]. Especially considering the appropriateness of infringing privacy due to pre-emptive collection of potential evidence. Consequently, a trade-off between privacy and forensic readiness requirements is recognised [27].

The motivation for forensic readiness stems from addressing risks or proving due diligence [8], privacy is often mandated by user expectations [29] or regulations akin to GDPR [15]. Although trends in forensic readiness becoming mandatory [26] appear, it is not a far-reaching compulsory obligation akin to GDPR. Still, a realistic and secure system should satisfy both qualities. The first step is then to explicitly formulate the objectives. While the general principles are recognised, they must be clarified on "how" and "how else" they are reflected in the software. Only then can the arising conflicts lead to the actionable requirements for the software.

This paper tackles the question of *"How to resolve the conflicts between the goals of forensic readiness and the goals of privacy?"*. To that end, goal modelling [21] is utilised to capture the objectives of forensic-ready and GDPR-compliant software. The models enable goal conflict analysis to point out relationships between the two qualities. Based on the results, conflict patterns are outlined, encapsulating acceptable resolution strategies. These are then demonstrated in a specific case concerning a car-sharing system.

2 Background and Related Work

Forensic-Ready Software: Forensic readiness presents a vital add-on to secure systems, addressing residual and low-probability risks. Thus, a risk-based approach eliciting requirements for forensic-ready software was developed [8]. The risks were also used to orchestrate evidence collection [4]. Some of the non-risk approaches use model-based constraints of activities [33].

Digital Forensics and Privacy: Several approaches were proposed to address the tension between the two. A framework was formulated for privacy-preserving investigations [16]. Searchable encryption [2] and privacy-preserving imaging [14] were proposed to allow investigation while ensuring privacy. In contrast, anti-forensic measures prioritising privacy were also proposed [34]. The conflict remains challenging in the context of software engineering.

Goal Modelling: It captures the objectives that system should meet [21]. It guides goal refinement towards specific requirements, examining why a functionality needs to be implemented, how it can be implemented, and its alternatives. The analysis allows for goal organisation and helps uncover potential conflicts. Goal modelling languages support the analysis by providing visual syntax for the goal models [22]. We use it to outline the existing conflicts and alignments.

Goal-oriented approaches were indeed utilised to resolve compliance conflicts. LEGA-URN framework [17] aims at capturing the regulations into goals and resolving conflicts between them. Another approach aims to detect regulatory violations and their resolutions via patterns [24].

Privacy-Preserving Software: In privacy compliance, GDPR especially resonated, leading to requirements elicitation approaches [3,18]. Further proposals suggested modelling GDPR in UML [23,36], resulting in a compliance-checking tool used in this paper. Goal modelling specifically is well-utilised for legal and regulatory compliance [1]. An example focused on GDPR used an extension of

STS-ml [30] and GRL [28]. To our knowledge, forensic readiness has not yet been approached from a goal modelling perspective. We contribute to filling this gap.

3 Goal Analysis

To analyse the conflicts between the implementation of privacy and forensic readiness, we created two goal models[1]. The privacy goal model is based on achieving compliance with GDPR [15], while the forensic readiness model is based on Rowlingson's ten-step implementation guideline [31]. The models allow for structuring the key objectives and analysing the relationships between goals.

3.1 GDPR Goal Model

GDPR is a complex legislation with a total of 99 articles spanning across 11 chapters, covering a wide array of data protection requirements [15]. Thus, we scoped the analysis to chapters 2 (Art. 5–11) and 3 (Art. 12–23), covering the basic principles and rights of data subjects, where we expect the main conflicts.

The goals were formulated through a combination of top-down and bottom-up approaches. Initially, the articles were taken as they were, and the initial goals, representing the satisfaction of an article, were formulated. As the GDPR articles are rather complex and dependent on each other, we followed an iterative top-down refinement. Each goal (article) was dissected into components of "how" to satisfy it. Then, the goals were compared to see if the satisfaction of one contributes to the satisfaction of another. Afterwards, the goals were inspected bottom-up, whether they contribute to a common "why" and grouped into super-goals, ultimately leading to the "Compliant with GDPR" goal.

We opted to limit the refinement of goals up to the sub-paragraph level to keep them on a high level, avoiding the enumeration of possible implementation directions. Thus, we selected the super-goals in Table 1 for the conflict analysis.

3.2 Forensic Readiness Goal Model

In contrast, forensic readiness is missing such a high-impact regulation. While several guidelines exist [6,20,31,33], they are typically conceptual or focus on a specific area. Thus, for the goal analysis, we opted for Rowlingson's ten-step guideline [31] due to its scope, maturity, and wide use by others [32].

As with the GDPR, we first formulated a goal for every step. Then, following a top-down approach, we decomposed the goals based on the steps' contents. The resulting goals were further inspected in the bottom-up approach and grouped when they relate to a common "why" within the step. Finally, the goals (steps) were grouped into super-goals, ultimately contributing to satisfying the "Forensic Readiness Established" goal. Table 2 shows super-goals and their goals (steps).

---

[1] Models available in the supplement: https://doi.org/10.5281/zenodo.14740582.

Table 1. Mapping of GDPR Super-Goals

Basic Principles Implemented	Personal Data Processing Basis Determined	Rights of Data Subject Respected
PD Processed Lawfully, Fairly, and Transparently	PD Processed on Consent	Provide Requested Information
PD Processed with Limited Purpose	PD Processed on Contract Necessity	Respond without Undue Delay
Minimal PD Processed	PD Processed on Legal Obligation	Information Provided on Request
Accurate PD Processed	PD Processed to Protect Vital Interest	Identify Requestor
PD Processed for a Limited Time Period	PD Processed for Public Interest	Provide Information Clearly
PD is Secured	PD Processed for Legitimate Interest	Right to Rectify PD Supported
Compliance is Accountable and Demonstrable	PD of Special Category Processed	Right to Restriction of Processing Supported
	PD of Criminal Convictions Processed	Right to Be Forgotten Supported
	PD Not Requiring Identification Processed	Right to Portable PD Supported
		Purpose Objected
		Automated Individual Decision-Making and Profiling Limited

Table 2. Mapping of Forensic Readiness Super-Goals

	Scenarios Requiring Digital Evidence Defined
Deficiencies Identified	Available Potential Evidence Identified
Implementation Planned	Evidence Collection Requirement Determined
Controls Implemented	Capability for Evidence Gathering Established
	Policy for Evidence Storage and Handling Established
Incident Response Planned	Targeted Monitoring for Incidents Ensured
	Escalation Policy Established
	Staff Training Undertaken
Investigation Execution Prepared	Evidence-Based Case Presentable
	Legal Review of Actions Ensured

3.3 Goal Model Conflict Analysis

With both goal models established, the bottom-level goals are selected for conflict analysis through cross-comparison between the qualities. The goals are projected into a matrix, and we individually examine each cell for the type of relationship between the pairs of goals. Those are conflicts (satisfaction of one contradicts another), alignments (satisfaction of one supports another), or no relationship. The simplified matrix[2] is visualised in Fig. 1.

Based on the resulting relationship matrix, several patterns emerged. These are then described in detail, and the conceptual resolution strategy is outlined. The patterns and resolutions are then scrutinised from a legal perspective. Notably, this paper focuses solely on conflict patterns. While the identified alignments could also be utilised in the design process, they are out of the scope.

---

[2] Details available in the supplement: https://doi.org/10.5281/zenodo.14740582.

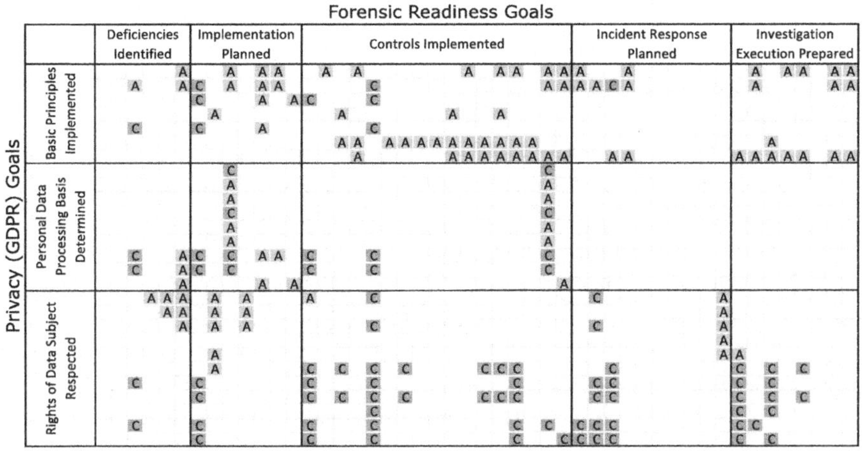

Fig. 1. Goal Conflict (C) and Alignment (A) Heatmap

3.4 Conflicts

The identified conflict patterns are described based on their cause from the perspective of the GDPR article that is affected. Then, a general conflict resolution is outlined. A specific resolution would be instantiated on the designed system.

Purpose (Art. 5.1.b): Conflict may manifest while defining the purpose of processing. Retaining data for general incident response is not justifiable by itself. Forensic readiness motivates the definition of the desired benefits (Step 1), which are proportional to an incident (Step 3), suspicious activities to monitor (Step 6) and escalation criteria. *Resolution:* Narrowing down the scenarios based on risk assessment outcomes, which, in turn, narrows down the purpose to specifically formulated incident response.

Basis (Art. 6): Some data processing bases are unsuitable for forensic readiness purposes. Consent (Art. 6.1.a, 7) allows withdrawal at any time, invalidating the use of potential evidence. Vital interest (Art. 6.1.d) cannot be argued, as the evidence might be used against the data subject. *Resolution*: The suitable bases for processing of personal data include performance of a contract (Art. 6.1.b) related to business processes; legal obligation (Art. 6.1.c) for compliance with personal data protection, cybersecurity or other laws (must be explicitly stated); public interest (Art. 6.1.e), which may be available to organisations exercising public authority; and legitimate interest (Art. 6.1.f), which must be based on, and appropriate to, risks, and requires documented balancing test.

Limited Retention (Art. 5.1.e): The related data would have to be stored indefinitely to allow for unlimited forensic investigation of the incidents. However, this is neither practical (associated costs) nor justifiable (GDPR requirements). Additionally, the longer the incident goes unnoticed or uninvestigated, the more the eventual forensic investigation loses purpose. The data retention period must be set based on risk assessment and forensic strategy. *Resolution:* Establish the period for the investigation within specific scenarios. After the period passes, the data must be deleted. If data must be retained for a significant portion of time, their aggregation or anonymization is advisable (e.g., to disallow identification of data subjects but allow the establishment of indicators of compromise).

Processing Minimal Data (Art. 5.1.c): GDPR requires only the minimal possible scope of personal data to be processed. That includes forensic readiness as well. *Resolution:* Identify the minimal scope of data required for each risk scenario. Additionally, high data volumes lead to higher processing costs. Besides compliance, data minimization promotes cost efficiency.

Processing of Special Categories of Data (Art. 9, 10): Utilizing data of special categories (Art. 9) and data related to criminal convictions (Art. 10) can be challenging to justify for forensic readiness purposes. Directly processing or inferring these data from existing data raises significant compliance issues. In forensic readiness, special categories of data might be second-order consequences of data processing. For example, CCTV records of the hospital, collected for physical security, might reveal the medical conditions of some of the data subjects (e.g., by capturing them entering the oncology ward), or patterns of car usage might reveal information regarding the data subject's political views or sex life. *Resolution:* Assess whether the data collected falls within the special categories of data. Avoid their collection or further processing with prejudice whenever possible, as they can significantly raise compliance costs and complexity of related processes. Otherwise, seek if an exception would apply through the regular business use (e.g., foreground evidence).

Providing Information to Data Subject (Art. 12, 13, 14, 15): GDPR mandates transparency about processed personal data and allows data subjects to exercise the right of access. While it may not be in the organisation's interest to disclose the information to data subjects, ignoring these requirements presents a clear risk of forensic readiness becoming a liability instead of an asset. The related articles provide the scope of the information to be communicated. Additionally, the required information outlines the logic and the extent of data processing. General descriptions and processing policies can be disclosed without revealing precise forensic readiness policies. *Resolution:* Prepare scenario for personal data release, including compulsory transparency information and copy of the personal data. Ensure the information is truthful and not detrimental to the forensic readiness goal. Focus on outlining factors and criteria guiding the logic of processing. Unfounded or excessive requests can be rejected, but a valid reason must be demonstrated (e.g., unreasonably requesting low-level data).

Right to Rectification (Art. 16): The data subject has a right to rectification of incorrect or incomplete data. However, directly changing the already collected potential evidence weakens its authenticity and integrity. Some data integrity controls do not support data change (e.g., blockchain). Furthermore, incorrect or incomplete data must be accounted for as an error for the soundness of the investigation. Therefore, the rectification should be done without changing the original data. *Resolution:* Decouple personal data from the evidence whenever possible. Support indirect rectification records (e.g., change as a reference). Track changes with timestamps to ensure integrity. Unfounded or excessive requests can be rejected, but a valid reason must be demonstrated (e.g., unreasonably requesting large-scale rectifications with the intent to cause disruption).

Right to be Forgotten (Art. 17): Data erasure has a detrimental effect on forensic readiness, impacting the availability of evidence for investigation. The data subject might demand erasure if the processing is no longer necessary or unlawful, consent is withdrawn, or there is a general legal obligation for erasure. The right to be forgotten does not apply if a legal obligation to process exists or if the data are necessary to exercise legal claims. *Resolution:* Ensure basis for processing rules out erasure. Ensure documentation or processes are readily available to truthfully establish the need for data in the exercise of legal claims. If the right to erasure is exercised, its scope and contextual information must be documented. Unfounded or excessive requests can be rejected, but a valid reason must be demonstrated (e.g., requesting data erasure with the intent to cause disruption).

Restriction of Processing (Art. 18) and Purpose Objection (Art. 21): Restriction of processing has a detrimental effect on forensic readiness as it directly impacts the availability of potential evidence. The right to restriction of processing can be applied only in specific situations outlined by the GDPR, and the risk can be mitigated by having robust processes in place (e.g., verification of the accuracy of the personal data). Additionally, the data subject has a right to object to personal data processing based on public interest (Art. 6.1.e) and legitimate interest (Art. 6.1.f). *Resolution:* The legal basis for processing must be well-documented and demonstrable. Additionally, processes must be in place to demonstrate the accuracy of data. Unfounded or excessive requests can be rejected, but a valid reason must be demonstrated (e.g., unreasonably objecting with the intent to cause disruption).

Right to Data Portability (Art. 20): Personal data processing based on consent (Art. 6.1.a) or on a contract (Art. 6.1.b), which are processed by automated means, can be subjected to a request for data portability. Exercise of such a right is detrimental to forensic readiness, as it would mean disclosure of potential evidence. *Resolution:* Ensure basis for processing rules out data portability. If alternate bases are impossible to use, prepare a scenario for personal data release. Unfounded or excessive requests can be rejected, but a valid reason must be demonstrated (e.g., repetitive requests intended to cause disruption).

Limitation of Automated Decision-Making and Profiling (Art. 22): GDPR grants the right to protect data subjects from profiling and decision-making based solely on automated means, which produces legal effects or significantly affects the data subject. As automated analysis may play a role in the implemented forensic readiness controls due to the volume of data, any decision must be subjected to human oversight and meaningfully reviewed. *Resolution:* If automated decision-making is implemented, analyse the potential effect on the data subject. If the effect is significant, the processing must be subjected to specific legal bases (Art. 6.1.a, 6.1.b, 6.1.c) or accompanied by robust human oversight (e.g., avoiding formal review blindly following automation results). Documentation of all the steps is necessary.

4 Car-Sharing Scenario

The conflict patterns are meant to be used by designers in the software design process to facilitate the implementation of forensic readiness while being GDPR-compliant. The design process and contribution of the patterns are demonstrated in the scenario of a car-sharing system [13].

This paper uses an excerpt of the scenario with three actors. **User** represents the car-sharing service user and their device. A **Service Provider** is an application allowing users to book a car and manage their booking. And **Car** representing the onboard hardware and software. These actors collaborate to provide a verified user with a shared car ride. The process is illustrated in Fig. 2. It consists of three sub-parts: **Booking** (2.1–2.2), **Car Access** (3.1–3.5), **Ride** (4.1–4.4). The preceding **User Authentication** (1.1–1.4) sub-part is omitted from the paper, with the full model available in the supplementary material[3].

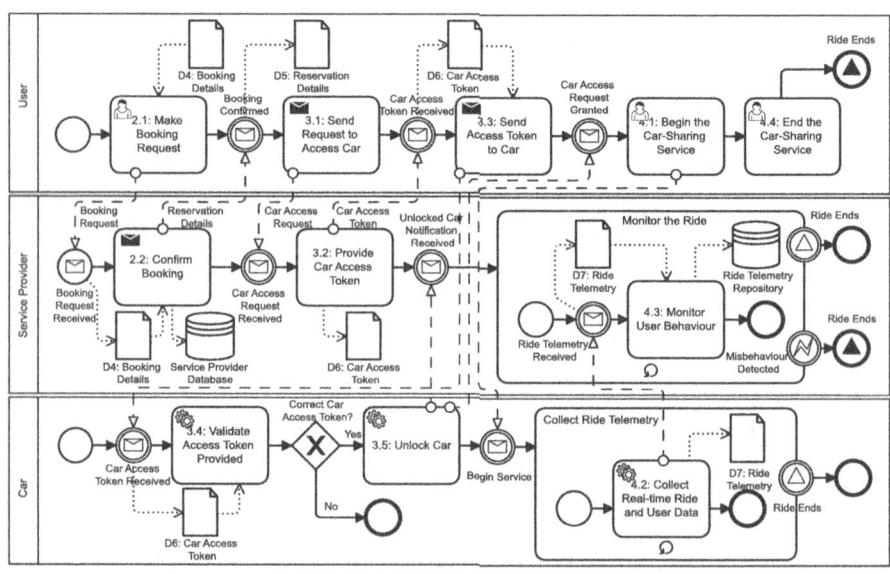

Fig. 2. Car-Sharing System: Business Model (excerpt)

First and foremost, the system needs to be secured. It is both a prerequisite of forensic-ready design and a component of GDPR compliance. The security risks connected to car-sharing were identified in [13] through STRIDE threat modelling [19]. Table 3 contains an excerpt of risks for Information Disclosure threat.

---

[3] Full scenario available in the supplement: https://doi.org/10.5281/zenodo.14740582.

Then, following the information systems security risk management (ISSRM), the risk mitigations were outlined, focusing primarily on secure channels and access control. It also mentions data minimisation, anonymisation, and audit trail collection, typical privacy and forensic readiness controls.

Table 3. Car-Sharing System: Risks (excerpt) [13]

Threat	Vulnerability	Impact
Information Disclosure: The attacker gains unauthorised access to sensitive data	1) Ride telemetry (D7) is attributable to a user 2) Injectable *Ride Telemetry Repository* queries	1) Loss of D7 confidentiality, leading to the loss of D4 (incl. personal data) confidentiality 2) Reputation damage 3) Operational cost due to breach investigation

4.1 Design Plan

The goal is to introduce forensic readiness as a security complement to system design due to the substantial risks identified during security risk management. Thus, the system would, by design, account for the risk occurrence and subsequent investigation. Furthermore, since the system would operate in the EU, it must comply with GDPR, including forensic readiness.

However, the sequence of forensic readiness and privacy (GDPR compliance) design steps substantially impacts the outcome. There are two possibilities:

- **Forensic Readiness ⇒ Privacy** – The privacy step might require redesigning or restricting the forensic readiness, weakening it in the process. However, the step would end with achieving privacy compliance.
- **Privacy ⇒ Forensic Readiness** – The forensic readiness design, without any restrictions, might break privacy compliance. Thus, the privacy step would need to be repeated to ensure compliance.

We opt to follow the former for the higher risks and costs associated with non-compliance (fines) compared to forensic readiness (residual security risks, heightened investigation costs). Thus, the design first follows the Forensic-Ready Information Systems Security Risk Management (FR-ISSRM) [8] approach, eliciting requirements specific to enhancing forensic readiness in the system. Then, compliance with GDPR is checked utilising a DPO tool [5], supplemented with a manual review of the forensic readiness enhancements. Found issues are compared with conflict patterns, and a resolution is instanced based on them.

4.2 Forensic Readiness Design

The first step in designing a forensic-ready system is to set goals with the stakeholders and security analysts. They capture the incentives *why* forensic readiness should be implemented in the system, formulated as a claim towards an asset [8]. Based on the existing risks [13], the following goals are formulated:

- **FRG1**: Enable reliable investigation of car theft: Car theft severely impacts the business goal of the car-sharing service. It should account for car access token (D6) replays and jamming attacks [25].
- **FRG2**: Prove misuse of car access token (D6): The token could be stolen or used to unlock and use a car without payment.
- **FRG3**: Enable evidence release of car ride-related data (D6, D7): Car data are provided to law enforcement in case of accident or dispute [35]. Discussed as mitigation for Information Disclosure threats.
- **FRG4**: Ensure access auditing of ride telemetry (D7): Telemetry contains sensitive user behaviour traces, so access to it should be limited. Discussed as mitigation for Information Disclosure threats.

Subsequently, the forensic readiness goals are related to the risks. Thus, they describe how exactly the goal is addressed, using the assets as potential evidence and the risk it covers. The considered scenarios are listed in Table 4. They serve as a bridge to elicit known potential evidence currently present in the system.

Table 4. Car-Sharing System: Forensic Readiness Scenarios

FR Scenario 1	FR Scenario 2	FR Scenario 3
FRG1: Enable reliable investigation of car theft		**FRG2**: Prove misuse of the car access token
Risk: A malicious actor steals the car access token (D6) by intercepting the communication between the service provider and the user. Then, they use the car access token to access the car and steal the car.	**Risk**: A malicious actor borrows the shared car and jams its geolocation sensors, which leads to the loss of data integrity and availability of Ride Telemetry (D7). Then, they proceed to steal the car.	**Risk**: A malicious actor forges the car access token, leading to the loss of the car access token (D6) integrity. Then, they use it to access and ride the car without paying for the service.
Evidence: D5, D6, D7	Evidence: D5, D6, D7	Evidence: D5, D6, D7, D8
FR Scenario 4	**FR Scenario 5**	**FR Scenario 6**
FRG3: Enable evidence release of car ride-related data	**FRG4**: Ensure access auditing of user behaviour data	
Risk: A service user gets into a car accident, resulting in injuries and material damage. The law enforcement agency requests ride-related data (D4, D5, D6, D7) to investigate the accident.	**Risk**: A malicious actor accesses the Ride Telemetry (D7) stored in the car due to physical tampering, leading to the loss of confidentiality.	**Risk**: A malicious actor accesses the Ride Telemetry (D7) stored in the service provider due to database vulnerability, leading to the loss of confidentiality.
Evidence: D4, D5, D6, D7	Evidence: -	Evidence: -

In the FR-ISSRM process, the scenarios are assessed for weaknesses, akin to risk assessment. Possible assessment techniques include a manual review [8], metrics [10], scenario simulation [11], and tool-supported analysis [9]. The general goal is to identify missing or weak (e.g., unreliable) potential evidence. For example, the context of car access token creation, delivery, and usage is not recorded except indirectly from ride telemetry. Thus, it is hard to draw conclusions about theft (FR Scenario 1) or forgery (FR Scenario 3). These issues are mitigated by enhancing the scenarios, primarily by introducing new potential evidence to fill the gaps. The enhancements are as follows:

- **FRE1: Auditing of D6** (FR Scenario 1, 2, 3, 4): Added record of creation and utilisation of Car Access Token (D6). The token ID and the communicating party identification (IP, transaction ID) are recorded for context.
- **FRE2: Enriching of D7 context** (FR Scenario 2, 3, 4): The beginning and end of the ride are recorded, including the used Car Access Token (D6), which is traceable to the reservation.
- **FRE3: Remote car data storage** (FR Scenario 1, 2, 4, 5): Audit records are, like telemetry (D7), transmitted from the Car to the Service Provider.
- **FRE4: Car data backup** (FR Scenario 4): Data also persisted in the car.
- **FRE5: Auditing of D7** (FR Scenario 6): Audit the usage of the Ride Telemetry Repository. The audit records are transferred to a remote location.

Additionally, enhancements are modelled using BPMN4FRSS [12] notation in Fig. 3. It extends BPMN with constructs for potential evidence (specialised data object), its source (magnifying glass), and its storage (specialised data store). Thus, it complements the model-based security approach of ISSRM and enables further analysis utilising the process model.

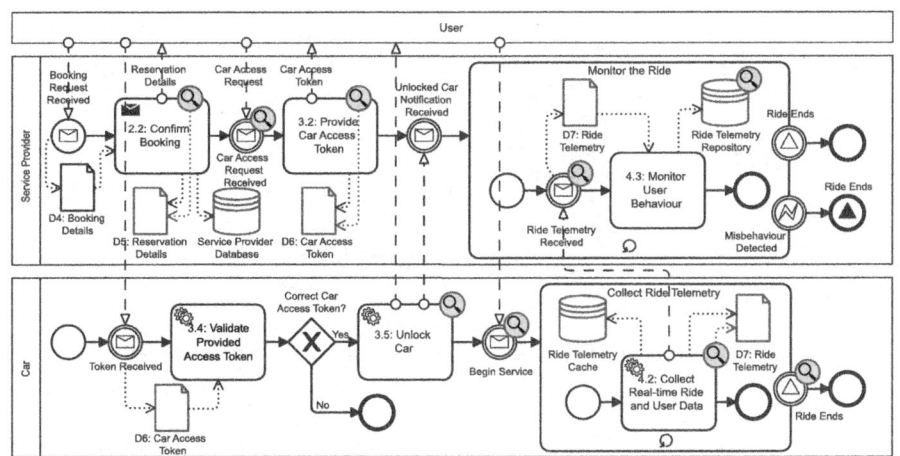

Fig. 3. Car-Sharing System: Forensic-Ready Model (excerpt, collapsed evid. sources)

Implementing the enhancements addresses the weaknesses. While it is a step in the right direction, the improvement should be measured for proper assessment [10]. However, a precise assessment of forensic readiness and cost-effectiveness falls outside this paper's scope as it focuses on the goal conflict.

4.3 Privacy Design

The system with applied enhancements is now considered to be sufficiently forensic-ready. As a next step, the enhanced process is checked for privacy issues stemming from GDPR non-compliance. To that end, the DPO tool[4] is used. The tool is a prototype implementation of a model-based approach for checking GDPR compliance of business processes [5].

The forensic-ready model is supplied to the DPO tool. However, due to the limitations of the tool, the BPMN4FRSS evidence and evidence sources were transformed to output data objects and the internal processes flattened[5]. Furthermore, the model does not contain any GDPR-related annotations; instead, they are assigned during the check. Specifically, the focus is on *D7: Ride Telemetry* processed by *4.3: Monitor User Behaviour* task, in which the *User* is the data subject and the *Service Provider* is both the data controller and processor.

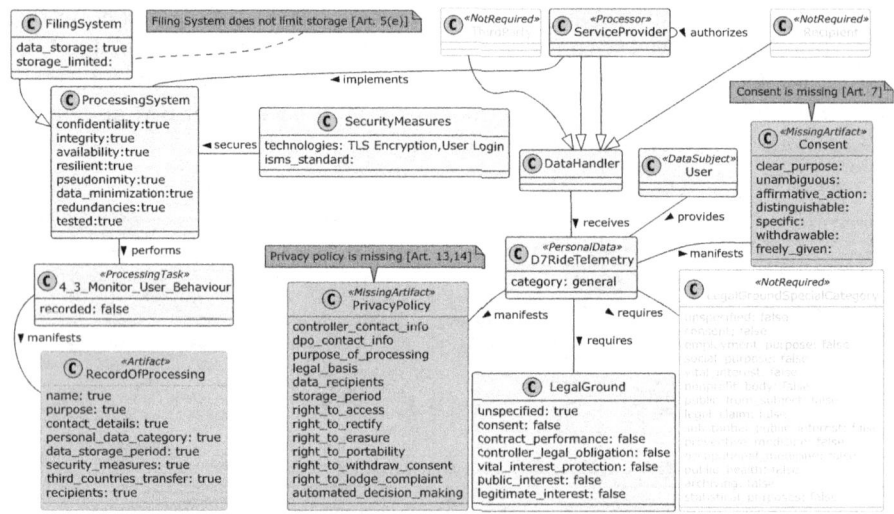

Fig. 4. Output of the DPO Tool: Instantiated GDPR Model

As a result of the DPO tool compliance check, the instantiated GDPR model is received and visualised in Fig. 4. It points out several compliance issues:

- **PI1: Missing basis and consent (Art. 6, 7):** The basis for processing is not specified; thus, consent is required as part of the business process.
- **PI2: Missing privacy policy (Art. 13, 14):** Privacy policy is not specified as part of the business process; thus, it is assumed that it is not given out.

---

[4] Available at: https://dpotool.cs.ut.ee/.
[5] Models are available in the supplement: https://doi.org/10.5281/zenodo.14740582.

- **PI3: Data storage is not limited (Art. 5.1.e):** Retention is not defined.

While valuable, the DPO tool only supports partial privacy assessment. Thus, the following privacy issues are pointed out through further manual assessment:

- **PI4: User tracing:** The enhancement FRE2 essentially enables the profiling of the users. In extreme cases, the full behavioural data might uncover highly sensitive details in a special category (Art. 9).
- **PI5: Telemetry leakage risk:** The enhancement FRE4 increases the risk of traceable ride telemetry leakage, as it persists within the car.

Resolving the privacy issues in isolation is likely to invalidate the forensic readiness enhancements. E.g., by processing based on consent. Thus, the conflict patterns are used to guide the resolution while maintaining forensic readiness.

4.4 Conflict Resolution

First, all the identified privacy issues are compared whether they fit to the conflict patterns (Sect. 3.4). The comparison is made based on the articles the issue offends. If the articles are not specified, a resolution is drafted, and the comparison is made manually based on the draft.

Then, the conflicts are resolved by manifesting the general resolution specified in the pattern within the system context. As the pattern restricts the resolution, the designer is guided towards the option that preserves the forensic readiness. E.g., to resolve PI3, the designer is guided to introduce a data retention period, based on the risk and forensic strategy. If there is no applicable pattern, the designer is not limited. Still, all resolutions need to be internally consistent. Table 5 covers the resolution of the issues for the car-sharing system.

5 Discussion and Conclusion

To answer the question *"How to resolve the conflicts between the goals of forensic readiness and the goals of privacy?"*, we utilised goal modelling to express the goals and analyse their relationships. Based on the models, we outlined patterns that encapsulate the principal conflicts and resolutions. The patterns are meant to be used in the design process of a system with both forensic readiness and privacy qualities. First, they help to identify the instances of conflict in the system. Second, they provide guardrails to formulate acceptable resolutions. The way it can be achieved was demonstrated in a car-sharing system case.

Beyond the design, other uses for the conflict patterns are envisioned. The patterns might be used to develop organisational measures of forensic readiness, as they need to consider privacy as well. Tackling the privacy concerns connected to forensic readiness and contributing to a more transparent but secure environment. Further use is in the education domain in GDPR compliance training.

Threats to Validity: The primary threat to external validity is the choice of the subset of GDPR articles to represent privacy, and Rowlingson's guide for

Table 5. Car-Sharing System: Conflicts and Resolution

PI1: Missing basis and consent (Art. 6, 7)
Conflict Pattern: Basis (Art. 6)
The process model does not specify the basis for processing. From the limited choice of applicable bases, the processing of Ride Telemetry (D7) shall be based on a legitimate interest (Art. 6.1.f) in protecting the leased property (car) proportionate to the explicitly formulated risks. However, additional processing safeguards should be introduced to avoid breaching the context (e.g., reusing the data for marketing). Alternatively, a legal obligation (Art. 6.1.c) might be chosen in the light of cybersecurity incident reporting obligations, but the appropriateness regarding other security controls must be shown. On the other hand, contract necessity is inappropriate as the data are not mandatory when car-sharing. Neither is the public interest, as collecting the data in case of a police investigation does not present enough of a reason. As a result, the model shall be updated with the basis specification.
PI2: Missing privacy policy (Art. 13, 14)
Conflict Pattern: –
As with the basis, the privacy policy is not specified in the process model. Thus, the model shall be updated accordingly, including the specified basis.
PI3: Data storage is not limited (Art. 5.e)
Conflict Pattern: Limited Retention (Art. 5.1.e)
The data retention must reflect the basis and risks. Instances of car theft (FR Scenario 1, 2) or accidents (FR Scenario 4) are most likely detected rather quickly. Forensic readiness focuses on providing rich contextual information and sound evidence handling. For misuse of a Car Access Token (D6) (FR Scenario 3), the implemented forensic readiness controls provide contextual information to quickly detect discrepancies in the process. Thus, the data retention is limited to one year, after which the Ride Telemetry (D7) data are anonymised and aggregated.
PI4: User Tracing
Conflict Pattern: Processing of Special Categories of Data (Art. 9, 10)
Ride telemetry (D7) data does not fall under a special data category (Art. 9). However, it could, especially in larger volumes, be used to reveal behavioural patterns about users, including political views or sex life. The aforementioned one-year storage limitation minimises the risk.
PI5: Telemetry Leakage Risk
Conflict Pattern: Limited Retention.(Art. 5.1.e)
Keeping a copy of Ride Telemetry (D7) data on the Car serves as a redundancy measure, beneficial for forensic readiness (non-disputability). However, due to the possibility of physical access to the storage, the risk of data leakage is higher, thus requiring re-evaluation. One possibility is to delete the data after each ride, or accept the risk based on the Car Access Token (D6) pseudonymity. We chose the former, as the attacker needs to compromise both the Car and the Service Provider to impact privacy.

forensic readiness. While we consider both good representatives of their respective domains, the results are not generalisable to privacy and forensic readiness as a whole. Additionally, the choice of broad, high-level goals also translates to the patterns. On the other hand, the internal validity is threatened by errors in the decomposition of goals. It was mitigated through a review from an engineering and legal point of view. Still, a further systematic review is appropriate. Lastly, the conflict patterns were applied to a single scenario. While it shows their utility and viability, there are low guarantees of generalisability.

Limitations and Future Work: The general privacy and forensic readiness goals go beyond GDPR and Rowlingson's guide. However, in the current iteration, the patterns are tied to those contexts. Thus, the next step is to expand and generalise the goals and patterns with further GDPR articles, other regulations, and guidelines. At the same time, the goals shall be further decomposed, as currently they are on a relatively broad level. This decomposition should lead to more specific and nuanced resolution guidelines. Additionally, further validation beyond the running scenario from both the engineering and legal points of view would enhance the generalisability. A similar approach could also be utilised for other qualitative factors like security and reliability. Lastly, the analysis uncovered aligned goals, which could be investigated for further insights.

Acknowledgments. This research was co-founded by the European Union under Grant Agreement No. 101087529. Views and opinions expressed are however those of the author(s) only and do not necessarily reflect those of the European Union or European Research Executive Agency. Neither the European Union nor the granting authority can be held responsible for them. Additionally, it was supported by the Grant Agency of Masaryk University (GAMU) project "Forensic Support for Building Trust in Smart Software Ecosystems" (no. MUNI/G/1142/2022).

Disclosure of Interests. The authors have no competing interests declare that are relevant to the content of this article.

References

1. Akhigbe, O., Amyot, D., Richards, G.: A systematic literature mapping of goal and non-goal modelling methods for legal and regulatory compliance. Requirements Eng. **24**(4), 459–481 (2019)
2. Armknecht, F., Dewald, A.: Privacy-preserving email forensics. Digit. Inv. **14**, S127–S136 (2015)
3. Ayala-Rivera, V., Pasquale, L.: The grace period has ended: an approach to operationalize GDPR requirements. In: IEEE 26th International Requirements Engineering Conference, pp. 136–146 (2018)
4. Azzam, M., Pasquale, L., Provan, G., Nuseibeh, B.: Forensic readiness of industrial control systems under stealthy attacks. Comput. Secur. **125**, 103010 (2023)
5. Bakhtina, M., Matulevičius, R., Seeba, M.: Tool-supported method for privacy analysis of a business process model. J. Inf. Secur. Appl. **76**, 103525 (2023)
6. CESG: Good Practice Guide No. 18: Forensic Readiness. Guideline, National Technical Authority for Information Assurance, United Kingdom (2015)
7. Daubner, L., Buhnova, B., Pitner, T.: Forensic experts' view of forensic-ready software systems: a qualitative study. J. Softw. Evol. Process **e2598** (2023)
8. Daubner, L., Macak, M., Matulevičius, R., Buhnova, B., Maksović, S., Pitner, T.: Addressing insider attacks via forensic-ready risk management. J. Inf. Secur. Appl. **73**, 103433 (2023)
9. Daubner, L., Maksović, S., Matulevičius, R., Buhnova, B., Sedláček, T.: Forensic-ready analysis suite: a tool support for forensic-ready software systems design. In: Araújo, J., de la Vara, J.L., Santos, M.Y., Assar, S. (eds.) Research Challenges in Information Science: 18th International Conference, RCIS 2024, Guimarães, Portugal, May 14–17, 2024, Proceedings, Part II, pp. 47–55. Springer Nature Switzerland, Cham (2024). https://doi.org/10.1007/978-3-031-59468-7_6
10. Daubner, L., Matulevičius, R., Buhnova, B.: A model of qualitative factors in forensic-ready software systems. In: Nurcan, S., Opdahl, A.L., Mouratidis, H., Tsohou, A. (eds.) Research Challenges in Information Science: Information Science and the Connected World: 17th International Conference, RCIS 2023, Corfu, Greece, May 23–26, 2023, Proceedings, pp. 308–324. Springer Nature Switzerland, Cham (2023). https://doi.org/10.1007/978-3-031-33080-3_19
11. Daubner, L., Matulevičius, R., Buhnova, B., Antol, M., Růžička, M., Pitner, T.: A case study on the impact of forensic-ready information systems on the security posture. In: Indulska, M., Reinhartz-Berger, I., Cetina, C., Pastor, O. (eds) Advanced Information Systems Engineering, pp. 522–538. Springer, Cham (2023). https://doi.org/10.1007/978-3-031-34560-9_31

12. Daubner, L., Matulevičius, R., Buhnova, B., Pitner, T.: BPMN4FRSS: an BPMN extension to support risk-based development of forensic-ready software systems. In: Kaindl, H., Mannion, M., Maciaszek, L.A. (eds) Evaluation of Novel Approaches to Software Engineering, pp. 20–43. Springer, Cham (2023). https://doi.org/10.1007/978-3-031-36597-3_2
13. Ekeh, I.F.: A Recommendation Model for Security Risk Management in Car-Sharing Scenarios. Master's thesis, University of Tartu (2024)
14. Englbrecht, L., Pernul, G.: A privacy-aware digital forensics investigation in enterprises. In: Proceedings of the 15th International Conference on Availability, Reliability and Security. ACM (2020)
15. European Parliament, Council of the European Union: Regulation (EU) 2016/679 of the European Parliament and of the Council
16. Ferguson, R.I., Renaud, K., Wilford, S., Irons, A.: Precept: a framework for ethical digital forensics investigations. J. Intellect. Cap. **21**(2), 257–290 (2020)
17. Ghanavati, S., Rifaut, A., Dubois, E., Amyot, D.: Goal-oriented compliance with multiple regulations. In: IEEE 22nd International Requirements Engineering Conference (RE), pp. 73–82 (2014)
18. Hjerppe, K., Ruohonen, J., Leppänen, V.: The general data protection regulation: requirements, architectures, and constraints. In: IEEE 27th International Requirements Engineering Conference, pp. 265–275 (2019)
19. Howard, M.: The Security Development Lifecycle. Microsoft Press (2006)
20. ISO/IEC: Information technology - Security techniques - Incident investigation principles and processes. Standard, International Organization for Standardization, Switzerland (2015)
21. Lamsweerde, A.V.: Requirements engineering: from system goals to UML models to software specifications. Wiley (2009)
22. Matulevičius, R., Heymans, P.: Comparing goal modelling languages: an experiment. In: Sawyer, P., Paech, B., Heymans, P. (eds.) Requirements Engineering: Foundation for Software Quality, pp. 18–32. Springer Berlin Heidelberg, Berlin, Heidelberg (2007). https://doi.org/10.1007/978-3-540-73031-6_2
23. Matulevičius, R., Tom, J., Kala, K., Sing, E.: A method for managing GDPR compliance in business processes. In: Herbaut, N., La Rosa, M. (eds) Advanced Information Systems Engineering: CAiSE Forum 2020, Grenoble, France, June 8–12, 2020, Proceedings, pp. 100–112. Springer International Publishing, Cham (2020). https://doi.org/10.1007/978-3-030-58135-0_9
24. Negishi, Y., Hayashi, S., Saeki, M.: Establishing regulatory compliance in goal-oriented requirements analysis. In: IEEE 19th Conference on Business Informatics (CBI), vol. 01, pp. 434–443 (2017)
25. Oligeri, G., Sciancalepore, S., Ibrahim, O.A., Di Pietro, R.: GPS spoofing detection via crowd-sourced information for connected vehicles. Comput. Netw. **216**, 109230 (2022)
26. Park, S., et al.: A comparative study on data protection legislations and government standards to implement digital forensic readiness as mandatory requirement. Digit. Inv. **24**, S93–S100 (2018)
27. Pasquale, L., Alrajeh, D., Peersman, C., Tun, T., Nuseibeh, B., Rashid, A.: Towards forensic-ready software systems. In: Proceedings of the 40th International Conference on Software Engineering: NIER, pp. 9–12. ACM (2018)
28. Rabinia, A., Ghanavati, S.: The FOL-based legal-GRL (FLG) framework: towards an automated goal modeling approach for regulations. In: IEEE 8th International Model-Driven Requirements Engineering Workshop (MoDRE), pp. 58–67 (2018)

29. Rao, A., Pfeffer, J.: Types of privacy expectations. Front. Big Data (2020)
30. Robol, M., Salnitri, M., Giorgini, P.: Toward GDPR-compliant socio-technical systems: modeling language and reasoning framework. In: Poels, G., Gailly, F., Serral Asensio, E., Snoeck, M. (eds.) The Practice of Enterprise Modeling: 10th IFIP WG 8.1. Working Conference, PoEM 2017, Leuven, Belgium, November 22-24, 2017, Proceedings, pp. 236–250. Springer International Publishing, Cham (2017). https://doi.org/10.1007/978-3-319-70241-4_16
31. Rowlingson, R.: A ten step process for forensic readiness. Int. J. Digit. Evid. **2** (2004)
32. Sachowski, J.: Implementing digital forensic readiness: from reactive to proactive process. CRC Press (2019)
33. Simou, S., Kalloniatis, C., Gritzalis, S., Katos, V.: A framework for designing cloud forensic-enabled services (CFeS). Requirements Eng. **24**(3), 403–430 (2019)
34. Stahlberg, P., Miklau, G., Levine, B.N.: Threats to privacy in the forensic analysis of database systems. In: Proceedings of the 2007 ACM SIGMOD International Conference on Management of Data, pp. 91–102. ACM (2007)
35. Symeonidis, I., Aly, A., Mustafa, M.A., Mennink, B., Dhooghe, S., Preneel, B.: SePCAR: a secure and privacy-enhancing protocol for car access provision. In: Foley, S.N., Gollmann, D., Snekkenes, E. (eds.) ESORICS 2017. LNCS, vol. 10493, pp. 475–493. Springer, Cham (2017). https://doi.org/10.1007/978-3-319-66399-9_26
36. Torre, D., Soltana, G., Sabetzadeh, M., Briand, L.C., Auffinger, Y., Goes, P.: Using models to enable compliance checking against the GDPR: an experience report. In: ACM/IEEE 22nd International Conference on Model Driven Engineering Languages and Systems, pp. 1–11 (2019)

An Ontological Model of the Phishing Attack Process

Ítalo Oliveira[1(✉)], Gerd Wagner[2], Glenda Amaral[1],
Tiago Prince Sales[1], Jan-Willem Bullée[3], Marianne Junger[3],
Dipti K. Sarmah[1], Maya Daneva[1], and Giancarlo Guizzardi[1]

[1] Semantics, Cybersecurity, and Services Group, University of Twente, Enschede, The Netherlands
{i.j.dasilvaoliveira,g.c.mouraamaral,t.princesales,d.k.sarmah, m.daneva,g.guizzardi}@utwente.nl

[2] Chair of Internet Technology Institute of Informatics, Brandenburg University of Technology, Cottbus, Germany
wagnerg@b-tu.de

[3] Industrial Engineering and Business Information Systems Group, University of Twente, Enschede, The Netherlands
{j.h.bullee,m.junger}@utwente.nl

Abstract. Phishing attacks are common social engineering cyber attacks in which threat actors masquerade as reputable entities to mislead recipients into performing specific actions, such as revealing financial information, system login credentials, or installing malware. Grasping the phishing attack process is crucial to prevent and counteract this type of scam. Although useful, current conceptual models describing phishing attacks do not provide an unambiguous characterization to support human understanding, communication, and computational tasks. They are informal drawings, diagrams, data models, or schemata of application-focused RDF/OWL ontologies. Instead, we approach the problem by leveraging the Unified Foundational Ontology (UFO) and OntoUML modeling language to propose a Phishing Attack Process Ontology (PAPO), making ontological commitments explicit. We show that this ontological model supports risk identification, according to ISO 31000, and satisfies important quality requirements, including domain adequacy, transparency, logical and ontological coherence, generality, as well as the FAIR principles. By providing ontological foundations for the investigation and fight against phishing attacks, PAPO paves the way for rigorous representation of corresponding real-world scenarios and enhanced applications, such as systems interoperability, data modeling, knowledge-based systems, discrete event simulations, design of phishing detection systems, and evaluation of security mechanisms' effectiveness.

Keywords: phishing attack · phishing attack process ontology · unified foundational ontology · OntoUML

1 Introduction

Social engineering is a type of cyberattack through which threat agents exploit *human vulnerabilities* to breach security goals, such as confidentiality, integrity, and availability of sensitive data [36]. Phishing is a common social engineering attack in which threat actors masquerade as reputable entities to mislead targets into performing specific actions, such as revealing financial information, system login credentials, or installing malware.

Because phishing attacks are scams that enable other crimes, such as extortion and identity theft, they lead to multiple negative impacts, namely direct damage from phishing scams (e.g. financial loss, loss of intellectual property, and sensitive customer information), impact on employee productivity, costs of business disruption, costs of business email compromise, costs of ransomware, damage to the company reputation and brand value, drop in the stock price, general weakening trust, and even compromise to national security [3,10,28].

To understand the complex dynamics of phishing attacks and design suitable preventive and control measures, such as phishing awareness training and phishing detection systems, researchers have proposed several domain conceptual models, lightweight ontologies, and informal descriptions of phishing. Although these attempts provide vocabularies and applications, they have limitations. For example, because the most detailed descriptions of phishing attacks are in natural language plain texts, drawings, informal diagrams, and schemata, they lack formal semantics, upper ontological distinctions (e.g., objects, intrinsic properties, events), serialization in multiple formats, and the capacity of being computationally queried. The phishing attack process is yet to be explicitly structured for human and machine understanding and communication.

To address this gap, we approach the problem by leveraging the *Unified Foundational Ontology* (UFO) [14] and the UFO-based OntoUML modeling language (ibid.) to propose a Phishing Attack Process Ontology (PAPO) making ontological commitments explicit. We show that this ontological model supports risk identification, according to ISO 31000 [17], and satisfies important quality requirements, including domain adequacy, transparency, logical and ontological coherence, generality, and FAIR principles. By providing ontological foundations for the investigation and fight against phishing attacks, PAPO paves the way for rigorous representation of corresponding real-world scenarios and enhanced applications, such as systems interoperability, data modeling, knowledge-based systems, discrete event simulations, design of phishing detection systems, and evaluation of security mechanisms' effectiveness.

In what follows, Sect. 2 discusses related works and their limitations, considering descriptions of the phishing attack process. After defining ontology requirements, Sect. 3 presents our main contribution: a well-founded ontological model of the phishing process, summarizing domain-specific knowledge, and accounting for the role of trust. Section 4 discusses the ontology evaluation according to the requirements described in Sect. 3. Section 5 concludes with final considerations, limitations, and future work.

2 Related Work

Numerous works describe the phishing attack process and propose definitions. We discuss part of this related literature to ground our ontological analysis and identify their shortcomings. The word "phishing" is a variation of the term "fishing" because the act of phishing resembles that of fishing: the attacker lures a victim by employing some bait, then fishes for certain assets from the victim [10]. A 2014 study examines 113 different definitions to propose that phishing is a "scalable act of deception whereby impersonation is used to obtain information from a target" [22]. In 2021, researchers claimed that *tricking the recipient into taking the attacker's desired action* is the *de facto* definition of phishing attacks [4]. Based on that, they define phishing as a "socio-technical attack, in which the attacker targets specific valuables by exploiting an existing vulnerability to pass a specific threat via a selected medium into the victim's system, utilizing social engineering tricks or some other techniques to convince the victim into taking a specific action that causes various types of damages" [4]. The attacker can utilize different communication channels (emails, instant messages, voice calls, social networks, etc.) to either deceive the victim directly by a scam or to deliver a payload through an indirect manner, such as by using steganography techniques to hide malicious code within seemingly harmless files, to obtain personal or confidential information (login, passwords, bank account number, etc.) from the victim.

According to Jakobsson [20], the most representative form of phishing displays three key elements: the *lure*, the *hook*, and the *catch*. The lure consists of a phisher spamming many users with an email message that appears to be from a legitimate institution. The message frequently employs a convincing story to encourage the user to follow a hyperlink embedded in the email to a website controlled by the phisher and to provide it with certain requested information. The hook often consists of a website that emulates the appearance of a reputable agent, such as Microsoft's login website. The goal of the hook is for victims to be directed to it via the lure message and for the victims to disclose confidential information in it. The catch involves the phisher exploiting the collected sensitive data for illegal purposes, such as fraud or identity theft.

In the phishing literature, conceptual models describing the step-by-step attack process are called "anatomy of phishing attacks" [4,38], "phishing attack processes" [3], "phishing attack lifecycle" [10,19,24], root causes analysis [1], and "information flow of phishing attacks" [20]. All these models consist of an informal mixture of natural language texts, drawings, diagrams, and tables. Therefore, they neither possess formal semantics nor a computational representation for software applications.

Current phishing attack ontologies are represented in RDF, OWL, frames, and description logics, focusing on taxonomies and narrow applications, such as detecting phishing emails [8,21,27,33,34], designing warning interfaces [39], and enhanced automatic extraction of hidden semantic information in texts [29]. All these ontologies do not follow upper ontology guidelines, hiding their ontological commitments and making interoperability difficult [13]. Moreover, their respective artifacts seem publicly unavailable, which hinders any evaluation effort (for example, checking logical consistency and possible unintended instances). These artifacts fail to comply with the FAIR principle [18] because they are not findable or accessible. An initial attempt to propose a well-founded phishing attack ontology [25] was a work-in-progress with no validation. That work does not consider the different compound phases of the phishing attack process, including planning and preparation, nor does it address trust elements. Our work builds upon all these previous initiatives to overcome their limitations.

3 A Phishing Attack Process Ontology

As there is no consensus among researchers on the exact divisions of the phishing attack process, which also depends on the type of attack, we propose an original synthesis to be represented by the Phishing Attack Process Ontology (PAPO). In our view, the following elements characterize most, if not all, forms of phishing attacks (not only phishing emails) as compound events: *(1) a phisher impersonates a reputable agent, (2) exploiting the target's trust in this agent, (3) aiming to trick the target into taking the attacker's desired action, (4) offering supposedly plausible reasons for this behavior.* The PAPO ontologically unfolds this understanding revealing which entities are involved and how they hang together. The ontology core presents the phishing process as a sequence of events and its participants. These events refer to different phases of the phishing attack from planning and preparation to execution and post-attack phase. We explain the role of trust in phishing attacks by leveraging a UFO-based reference ontology of trust [7]. All files related to PAPO are publicly available under the Apache 2.0 license:[1]

3.1 Ontology Requirements

The functional requirement sets out the scope of PAPO. Quality requirements are domain-independent but desirable as they prescribe attributes that enable or strengthen the ontology functionalities.

The purpose of PAPO is to serve as a reference artifact for activities related to risk assessment regarding phishing attacks, particularly *risk identification*. The ISO 31000 [17] describes risk assessment as a process that includes (a) risk identification, (b) risk analysis, and (c) risk evaluation, which informs risk treatment decisions. Risk identification aims to identify and describe risks that might prevent an organization from achieving its objectives. Risk identification should consider factors such as tangible and intangible sources of risk, causes and events, vulnerabilities and capabilities, changes in the external and internal context, indicators of emerging risks, the nature and value of assets and resources, consequences and their impact on objectives, time-related factors, among others. Considering this understanding of risk identification, we define the following

---

[1] Permanent link to the repository of the Phishing Attack Process Ontology (PAPO) http://w3id.org/phishing-process-ontology/git.

functional requirement for our proposed artifact: *PAPO must model the phishing attack process for risk identification, according to ISO 31000*.

The ontology engineering literature discusses many quality criteria for ontologies [35]. Based on that, we define the following *quality requirements* for PAPO: (1) *Domain adequacy* (appropriateness, accuracy): PAPO shall correctly represent shared real-world conceptual elements in the phishing attack process. This requirement is a necessary condition for the functional requirement satisfaction. Moreover, it is essential to enable interoperability among systems or data in the phishing domain [13]; (2) *Transparency* (intelligibility, clarity): PAPO shall contain explicit definitions for all its concepts and count with corresponding publicly available documentation; (3) *Ontological coherence*: PAPO shall comply with upper ontological distinctions; (4) *Logical consistency*: PAPO shall be free from logical contradictions, that is, it shall be consistent and satisfiable; (5) *Generality*: PAPO shall represent multiple forms of phishing (not only phishing emails, for example), meaning phishing must be characterized in a general way; (6) *FAIR principles* [18]: PAPO shall be findable, accessible, interoperable, and reusable, according to the *International Conference on Formal Ontology in Information Systems*'s guidelines for ontology research artifacts [31].

3.2 Phishing-Related Events and Their Participants

In UFO, events always exist in the past and, consequently, cannot change [9]. Therefore, phishing-related events correspond to phishing incidents or related previous or posterior occurrences— for example, respectively, preparation and post-attack events. In OntoUML language, an event *b depends historically on* an event *a* whenever: (i) *a* (or one of its parts) brings about the situation that triggers *b* (or one of its parts); (ii) *a* (or one of its parts) brings about a situation that is necessary– but not sufficient– to trigger *b* (or one of its parts); (iii) *a* (or one of its parts) brings about a situation that is necessary– and more than sufficient– to trigger *b* (or one of its parts); or (iv) *b* depends historically on an event *z* that depends historically on *a* [6]. We employ this framework to represent the phishing attack process as a succession of orderly events. When used between objects, e.g., object A historically depends on object B, this relation means that the latter must have existed before A, i.e., B's life either *precedes*, *meets* or *overlaps* with A's life - in the sense of Allen's Algebra [6,11].

PAPO describes a PHISHING ATTACK PROCESS as a complex event necessarily composed of PHISHING ATTACK PLANNING, followed by PHISHING ATTACK PREPARATION, then PHISHING ATTACK EXECUTION with optional subsequent FRAUD and POST-ATTACK PHASE.[2] The PHISHING ATTACK PREPARATION is historically dependent on PHISHING ATTACK PLANNING, and PHISHING ATTACK EXECUTION is historically dependent on PHISHING ATTACK PREPARATION. Due to the transitivity of the historical dependence relation, a PHISHING ATTACK EXECUTION must be historically dependent on a PHISHING ATTACK PLANNING.

---

[2] In this paper, expressions in small caps font, such as PHISHER and PHISHING ATTACK PROCESS, refer to explicit ontology classes.

Although FRAUD and POST-ATTACK PHASE may not occur as part of a PHISHING ATTACK PROCESS, they are historically dependent on PHISHING ATTACK EXECUTION. This represents the expected causal temporal order of the phishing incident events, displayed in Fig. 1. Besides this overview, PAPO has three views of the model: (a) Fig. 2 detailing planning and preparation, (b) Fig. 3 describing the attack execution, and (c) Fig. 4 accounting for the role of trust in phishing attacks. Some entities participate throughout the phases of a PHISHING ATTACK PROCESS, for example, a PHISHER. Other participants join in only some events, depending on the type of incident and its particular outcomes, for example, a PHISHING TARGET does not participate in the PHISHING ATTACK PLANNING and a HOOK (for instance, a malicious webpage) may not participate at all due to the attack type.

A PHISHER is a historical role [6] played by an AGENT (an individual person or a criminal organization, hence classified as Mixin), which means an AGENT is a PHISHER *in virtue of having participated in* a PHISHING ATTACK PROCESS or one of its parts. The IMPERSONATED REPUTABLE AGENT does not directly participate in the PHISHING ATTACK PROCESS but via the impersonation performed by a PHISHER. The latter can impersonate a person trusted by the PHISHING TARGET, such as a family member or colleague, or a known organization, such as Microsoft. The PHISHER can also impersonate a made-up AGENT (say, a supposed millionaire) and persuade the PHISHING TARGET to trust it.

A PHISHING TARGET is a historical role and needs to participate in the PHISHING ATTACK PROCESS (or one of its parts). Although possibly a member of a targeted organization, a PHISHING TARGET can only be a PERSON because the attack aims to exploit human vulnerabilities related to trust, beliefs, and intentions. PHISHING ENABLERS are ancillary entities contributing to the PHISHING ATTACK EXECUTION, such as HOOK website or a malicious code embedded into an attachment.

The PHISHING ATTACK PLANNING (depicted in Fig. 2), performed by a PHISHER, is an event that creates a PHISHING PLAN. This plan involves multiple decisions made by the PHISHER about whom to attack, how to attack, and for what purpose: (a) the selection of the ATTACK METHOD, which can be a malware-based attack (for example, via keylogger or ransomware embedded into PDF files sent by emails), a webpage-based attack (typically, via a redirected HOOK webpage requesting for sensitive information), a direct request (for instance, in-person or online solicitations), among others; (b) the choice of MESSAGE MEDIUM TYPE, which can be SMS, email, social network, in-person direct communication, etc.; (c) the decision about the FRAUD TYPE to be enabled by the PHISHING ATTACK EXECUTION, such as extortion or identity theft. The PHISHING PLAN also establishes the AGENTS to be impersonated by the PHISHER, the AGENTS to be tricked (who will turn into PHISHING TARGETS once they participate in the attack process), the aimed TARGET ASSETS (for example, login credentials, money, or sensitive bank information), and it

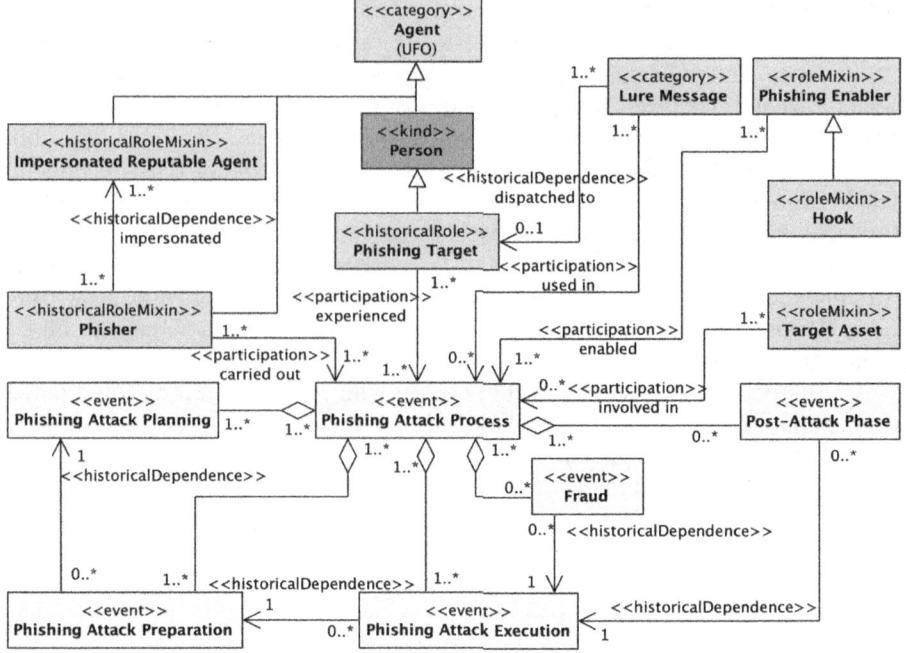

Fig. 1. Phishing attack process overview. The OntoUML stereotypes connect types and relations in these models to ontological categories of monadic and relational universals in UFO, respectively. [14] The colors in these diagrams represent a convention used by the OntoUML community: object types are represented in pinkish, intrinsic aspect types in blue, and event types in yellow, truth-makers of material relations in green, and higher-order types in darker blue

considers relevant PHISHING ENABLERS. The PHISHING PLAN specifies what is known as a "phishing campaign" in the cybersecurity community.[3]

The next phase is the PHISHING ATTACK PREPARATION (also depicted in Fig. 2). The preparation consists of events wherein the PHISHER acquires the needed PHISHING ATTACK CAPABILITIES for the PHISHING ATTACK EXECUTION. These include gathering hacking knowledge and target information (email addresses, for example), spotting vulnerabilities, setting up HOOK webpages and malware, creating LURE MESSAGES, purchasing phishing kits, etc. The PHISHING ATTACK EXECUTION is the manifestation of those PHISHING ATTACK CAPABILITIES.

The PHISHING ATTACK EXECUTION is what we usually recognize as a phishing attack. In this phase, shown in Fig. 3, the ultimate attack's goal is to mislead PHISHING TARGETS into performing specific actions according to the PHISHING

---

[3] "(...) the MITRE ATT&CK team uses the term Campaign to describe any grouping of intrusion activity conducted over a specific period of time with common targets and objectives." (https://attack.mitre.org/campaigns/).

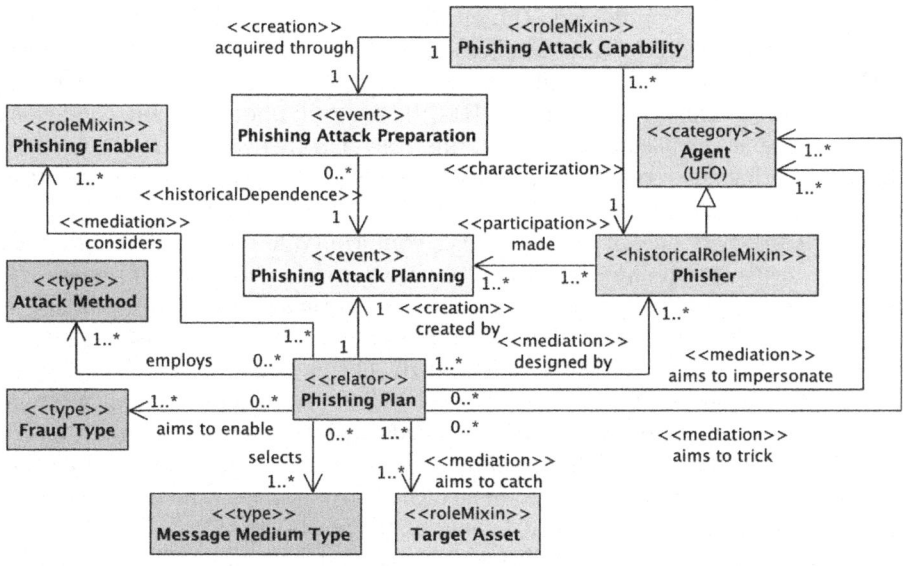

Fig. 2. Phishing planning and preparation

PLAN devised by the PHISHER. The PHISHING ATTACK EXECUTION is a complex event composed of several others that occur in succession, varying according to the employed ATTACK METHOD. However, PAPO is designed to capture the essence of this attack execution, that is, what is shared by different forms of phishing. So, a single PHISHING ATTACK EXECUTION is necessarily composed of a single LURE MESSAGE DISPATCH and, contingently, a LURE MESSAGE ARRIVAL event, a LURE MESSAGE PERCEPTION event, and a FULFILLMENT OF PHISHER'S REQUEST event, all of which are temporally ordered by historical dependence relations. For each PHISHING PLAN there may be (and often there is) a large number of PHISHING ATTACK EXECUTION events as manifestations of the PHISHER's PHISHING ATTACK CAPABILITIES.[4]

In the common case of a phishing email attack, each PHISHING ATTACK EXECUTION corresponds to a single email addressed to a single PHISHING TARGET. It starts when the PHISHER dispatches an email LURE MESSAGE addressed to a PHISHING TARGET's email address. The arrival of this email may be prevented by some security measures like spam filters or due to the wrong email address. A possible automatic system reply would be an event historically dependent on the email dispatch and may be a useful piece of information for PHISHERS. The email arrival in the target's inbox is a LURE MESSAGE ARRIVAL. For some reason, the email may never be seen by the user. The event wherein the PHISHING

---

[4] In general, there is a trade-off between scalability and effectiveness of a phishing attack because personalized LURE MESSAGES tend to be more effective, though are harder to scale [23]. However, by leveraging generative artificial intelligence techniques, attackers can produce personalized lure messages at scale [15].

TARGET sees, opens, and reads the email corresponds to the LURE MESSAGE PERCEPTION event. If for whatever reason the PHISHING TARGET clicks the link in the email and downloads malware (PHISHING ENABLER), they are performing a FULFILLMENT OF PHISHER'S REQUEST event under certain conditions. These represent the situations where PHISHING TARGETS are prone to fall for a phish answering the requests. This effect happens due to the presence of certain TARGET FRAGILITIES, which are various kinds of VULNERABILITIES including ignorance, inexperience, prejudice or bias, conformity, hurry, intuitive judgment, laziness, curiosity, tiredness, fear, habits, anger, excitement, tension, happiness, sadness, disgust, guilt, surprise, greed, lust, neuroticism, and many others [37]. The FULFILLMENT OF PHISHER'S REQUEST event may be composed of several sub-events, depending on ATTACK METHOD. For example, in a webpage-based attack, the PHISHING TARGET firstly clicks the link inside the email message, visits a HOOK webpage, and, finally, proceeds with sending the data via it.

A FULFILLMENT OF PHISHER'S REQUEST event concludes a PHISHING ATTACK EXECUTION. What comes next is the FRAUD phase, which involves committing a *different crime* enabled by successful phishing attacks. The PHISHER can commit criminal identity theft (posing as another person when apprehended for a crime), financial identity theft (using another's identity to obtain credit, goods, and services), identity cloning (using another's information to assume his or her identity in daily life), medical identity theft (using another's identity to obtain medical care or drugs), among other crimes. Before, in parallel, or after the FRAUD phase, the PHISHER can proceed with the *Post-attack* phase by taking measures to protect themselves and assessing the results. This includes deleting HOOK websites, shutting down attack machinery, tracking hunters, money laundering, etc.

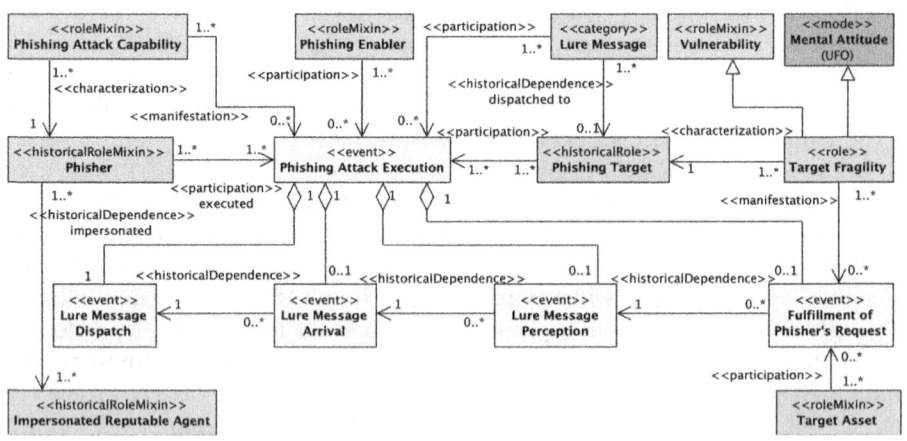

Fig. 3. Phishing attack execution

3.3 Phishing and Trust

To succeed, a PHISHING ATTACK EXECUTION requires existing trust relations between the PHISHING TARGET (TRUSTOR) and IMPERSONATED REPUTABLE AGENTS (TRUSTEE). Victims trust people or organizations to satisfy a particular objective. Different entities play the role of TRUSTEE, for example, the IMPERSONATED REPUTABLE AGENTS, the LURE MESSAGE, and the HOOK WEBPAGE. To represent these relations suitably, we employ the *Reference Ontology of Trust* (ROT) [2], a UFO-based ontology. Figure 4 describes the role of trust in phishing attacks by leveraging ROT's concepts.

ROT defines TRUST as a complex mental state of a TRUSTOR agent, composed of an INTENTION related to a goal, for the achievement of which she counts upon the TRUSTEE, and a set of BELIEFS about the TRUSTEE and its behavior. A TRUSTOR is necessarily an "intentional entity', that is, a cognitive agent, an agent endowed with goals and beliefs. As for the TRUSTEE, it is an entity capable of impacting ones intentions by the outcome of its behavior. The TRUST mental state of a TRUSTOR regarding a TRUSTEE and its behavior is composed of (i) an intention of the TRUSTOR; (ii) a set of beliefs about the TRUSTEE's capabilities, vulnerabilities, and commitments; and (iii) if the TRUSTEE is an agent, beliefs that the TRUSTEE intends to exhibit the expected behavior. Another ontological commitment of ROT is that TRUST implies risks. By trusting, the TRUSTOR becomes vulnerable to the TRUSTEE in terms of potential failure of the expected behavior or outcome.

ROT also provides an ontological account of the factors that can influence TRUST. The ontology categorizes influence relations according to the ontological nature of the factors that explain them, namely: (F1) other TRUST relations; (F2) mental biases; (F3) TRUST CALIBRATION SIGNALS; and (F4) TRUSTWORTHINESS EVIDENCE. F1 represents the situation in which TRUST is influenced by other trust relations. F2 represents situations in which TRUST is influenced by MENTAL MOMENTS. Examples of MENTAL MOMENTS include PERCEPTIONS, BELIEFS, DESIRES and INTENTIONS. F3 categorizes situations in which TRUST can be influenced by trust signals purposefully emitted by the TRUSTEE, to indicate trustworthy behavior. Some examples are uniforms and established brands to create visual identities. In F4, the influence comes from shreds of evidence suggesting that a TRUSTEE could be trusted. They result from TRUSTEES' trustworthy actions. Examples include third-party certifications and credentials, performance history, track record, recommendations, reputation records, and past successful experiences.

Several factors can influence trust: (i) other trust relations; (ii) TRUSTOR's mental biases and mental states (perceptions, beliefs, desires, and intentions); (iii) trust signals emitted by the TRUSTEE, such as uniforms, logotypes, and speech style; and (iv) trustworthiness evidence that demonstrates trustworthy behavior on the part of the TRUSTEE. In the case of phishing attacks, trust signals correspond to fake signals emitted by, for example, a HOOK WEBPAGE and LURE MESSAGE, while trustworthiness evidence can be either fake evidence produced by the attacker or true evidence about IMPERSONATED REPUTABLE

AGENTS, such as past successful experiences, performance history, recommendations, and certifications by trusted parties. Because the PHISHING TARGETS trust both a IMPERSONATED REPUTABLE AGENT and a LURE MESSAGE, they follow the instructions in the LURE MESSAGE, according to the PHISHER's expectations.

Consider the example in which the PHISHER sends an email (LURE MESSAGE) to Mary (PHISHING TARGET) impersonating a trusted airline company X (IMPERSONATED REPUTABLE AGENT). The LURE MESSAGE offers discounted flight tickets to attractive destinations. Airline X is a traditional trusted company and thus Mary trusts X to purchase flight tickets (TRUSTOR's INTENTIONS). She believes that (1) Airline X is capable of taking her to the desired destination if she buys the tickets; (2) the airline will provide her with tickets for the trip after she makes the payment; and (3) Airline X has the INTENTION to do (1) and (2). Mary's trust in Airline X influences her to trust the email. Other factors that can positively influence Mary's trust in the email are her excitement and desire to travel, the email's design according to airline X visual identity (TRUST CALIBRATION SIGNAL), and TRUSTWORTHINESS EVIDENCE about Airline X, such as Mary's past successful experiences flying with them. Based on her trust in the email, Mary clicks on the link to access Airline X's (fake) website (HOOK webpage) to buy the tickets. Mary's trust in the airline along with the TRUST CALIBRATION SIGNALS emitted by the fake website positively influenced her to trust the HOOK WEBPAGE too, leading her to provide her credit card data to pay for the tickets. At this point, the PHISHER has reached his goal, accomplishing a successful phishing attack.

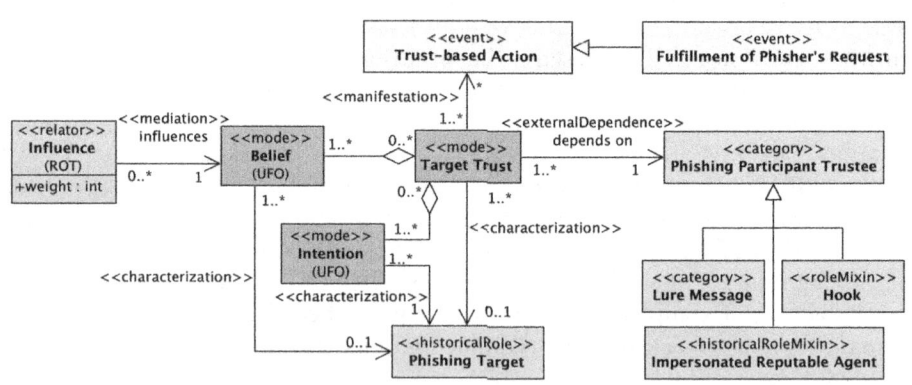

Fig. 4. Trust elements involved in Target answering phisher's requests

4 Ontology Evaluation

To show that PAPO can support risk identification activities defined in ISO 31000, explained in Sect. 3.1, we illustrate a phishing incident through a UML Object diagram that instantiates PAPO, as shown in Fig. 5. Incidents are realized instances of risks. Because of this, risk analysis and incident analysis are similar activities. The former investigates possible occurrences, whereas the latter looks into past events, but both share the goal of informing risk treatment decisions.

Our illustration describes a realistic incident wherein the APT16[5] executes a successful spear phishing attack, that is, a personalized phishing attack directed to a PHISHING TARGET, namely, the SoftBank CTO.[6] The Spear Phishing Campaign is the PHISHING PLAN, which employs the Hookpage-based Spear Phishing as its ATTACK METHOD, aims to enable Espionage as its Fraud Type, selects Email as its Message Medium Type, to catch SoftBank Secret Information on Cutting-Edge Technology (TARGET ASSET). This campaign also specifies the impersonation of the Japanese Financial Services Agency as its IMPERSONATED REPUTABLE AGENT to trick the SoftBank CTO by exploiting his trust in this authority. The PHISHING ATTACK PREPARATION involves the Set up Hookpage 1 event. The Spear Phishing Execution is composed of Spear Phishing Email Dispatch on day X at time Y, followed by SoftBank CTO submits data on Hookpage 1 (FULFILLMENT OF PHISHER'S REQUEST). This event is the manifestation of the SoftBank CTO's Fatigue at a given moment and his Trust in Email 1, which is composed of his Belief in the authenticity of the Email 1 and Intention to answer that Japanese authority requests.

Furthermore, we can leverage the *Common Ontology of Value and Risk* (COVER) [30] to expand this analysis. For example, by creating event types for certain events of PHISHING ATTACK PROCESS, we can assign CAUSAL LIKELIHOOD values to these event types and update the assignments according to real or simulated phishing incidents. The interoperability between COVER and PAPO is facilitated by the fact that both are UFO-based reference ontologies. For instance, PHISHING ATTACK EXECUTION can be seen as a subtype of COVER's RISK EVENT, where LURE MESSAGE DISPATCH is a THREAT EVENT and FULFILLMENT OF PHISHER'S REQUEST is a LOSS EVENT, just like FRAUD. Naturally, these LOSS EVENTS positively impact the PHISHER'S INTENTIONS (objectives), at the same time that they hurt PHISHING TARGET's INTENTIONS. These considerations show that PAPO can cover all major elements of risk identification related to phishing attacks, according to ISO 31000, as described in Sect. 3.1, including tangible and intangible sources of risk, causes and events, vulnerabilities and capabilities, assets, consequences and their impact on objectives, time-related factors, etc.

---

[5] "APT16 is a China-based threat group that has launched spearphishing campaigns targeting Japanese and Taiwanese organizations". (https://attack.mitre.org/groups/G0023/).

[6] We use expressions in LaTeX teletype font, such as APT16 and SoftBank CTO, to denote individuals of the UML Object diagram.

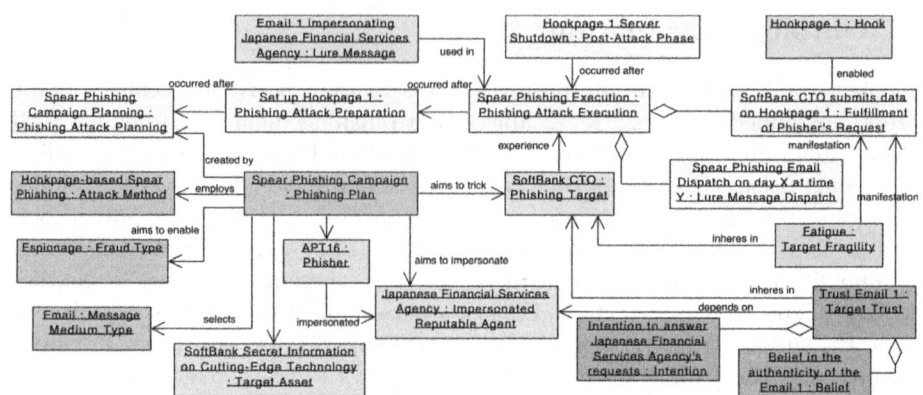

Fig. 5. An illustration of a phishing incident

Let us now consider each quality requirement (QR). The above illustration is evidence of PAPO's domain adequacy (QR1). The consideration of phishing dataset schemata is also a factor that favors domain appropriateness.[7] In fact, common phishing dataset features are easily mapped into PAPO concepts, such as the impersonated brand (IMPERSONATED REPUTABLE AGENT), URL and its status (active/inactive) as attributes of a HOOK webpage, and email content as an attribute of LURE MESSAGE.

PAPO accomplishes QR2 (transparency) because every concept is defined and documented in multiple formats (VPP, JSON, TTL, and HTML). Ontological coherence (QR3) is obtained by complying with UFO and OntoUML, verified by a service of the OntoUML plugin [12]. Logical consistency (QR4) has been checked for the TTL version of PAPO, which is automatically generated via the plugin from an OWL implementation of UFO [5]. This verification has been performed in Protégé [32] using the HermiT reasoner. Generality (QR5) has already been shown as our very definition of phishing, captured by PAPO, includes multiple forms of phishing attacks, unlike other models in the literature. Finally, PAPO is publicly available following FAIR principles (QR6): stably findable and accessible in multiple formats, including metadata, reusable, and interoperable with other ontologies, powered by *explicit* ontological commitments– a key requirement for interoperability [13].

5 Conclusion

Phishing attacks involve intricate relations among physical, social, technical, and psychological entities. They have manifold negative impacts on people and

---

[7] Examples of phishing datasets include: (a) https://www.phishtank.com/developer_info.php, the Anti-Phishing Working Group (APWG)'s datasets, datasets on Kaggle (for instance, https://www.kaggle.com/datasets/arnavs19/phishing-websites-dataset), a dataset for web page phishing detection [16], and many others.

organizations and are hard to manage and fight against. Understanding and modeling phishing attacks is crucial in this context. However, current models are mostly drawings, informal diagrams, data models, or schemas of application-focused RDF/OWL ontologies. This imposes limitations on what they can do as information tools for human understanding and communication, and supporting machine tasks. We addressed this gap by proposing a well-founded Phishing Attack Process Ontology (PAPO), grounded in the Unified Foundational Ontology (UFO). The resulting artifact is a model described in the OntoUML language, accounting for the phishing attack process, divided into planning, preparation, execution, fraud, and post-attack. This model ontologically unpacks our characterization of the phishing attack process as a complex event wherein: (1) a phisher impersonates a reputable agent, (2) exploits the target's trust in this agent, (3) aims to trick the target into taking the attacker's desired action, (4) offering supposedly plausible reasons for this behavior.

This is the first model of the phishing attack process that satisfies several important quality requirements (detailed in Sect. 3.1). PAPO stands out for complying with FAIR principles for scientific artifacts and a level of generality that allows the representation of different forms of phishing (email, SMS, social network, in-person communication, etc.). Moreover, it accounts for the role of trust and human vulnerabilities in the attack process.

PAPO, however, is limited to the overall attack description. It does *not* include security elements, which can be placed to counteract each phase of the phishing attack process. Moreover, a detailed taxonomy of phishing attacks is not included in PAPO by default, but can be added by subtyping PAPO's classes.

Once we have established ontological foundations of phishing attacks, we intend to employ them to support risk treatment activities (the design and evaluation of security mechanisms) and phishing research, including experiments, empirical phishing research, simulations, and RDF knowledge graph construction (for example, via phishing dataset integrations). The natural next steps are modeling security aspects via alignment with the Reference Ontology of Security Engineering (ROSE) [26].

References

1. Abroshan, H., Devos, J., Poels, G., Laermans, E.: Phishing attacks root causes. In: Cuppens, N., Cuppens, F., Lanet, J.-L., Legay, A., Garcia-Alfaro, J. (eds.) Risks and Security of Internet and Systems, pp. 187–202. Springer International Publishing, Cham (2018). https://doi.org/10.1007/978-3-319-76687-4_13
2. Akbar, N.: Analysing Persuasion Principles in Phishing Emails. Master's thesis, University of Twente (2014). https://purl.utwente.nl/essays/66177
3. Aleroud, A., Zhou, L.: Phishing environments, techniques, and countermeasures: a survey. Comput. Secur. **68**, 160–196 (2017)
4. Alkhalil, Z., Hewage, C., Nawaf, L., Khan, I.: Phishing attacks: a recent comprehensive study and a new anatomy. Front. Comput. Sci. **3**, 563060 (2021)
5. Almeida, J.P.A., Guizzardi, G., Sales, T.P., Falbo, R.A.: gUFO: a lightweight implementation of the unified foundational ontology (UFO) (2019). http://purl.org/nemo/doc/gufo

6. Almeida, J., Falbo, R.A., Guizzardi, G.: Events as entities in ontology-driven conceptual modeling. In: Laender, A., Pernici, B., Lim, E.-P., de Oliveira, J. (eds.) ER 2019. LNCS, vol. 11788, pp. 469–483. Springer, Cham (2019). https://doi.org/10.1007/978-3-030-33223-5_39
7. Amaral, G., Sales, T.P., Guizzardi, G., Porello, D.: Towards a reference ontology of trust. In: Panetto, H., Debruyne, C., Hepp, M., Lewis, D., Ardagna, C., Meersman, R. (eds) On the Move to Meaningful Internet Systems: OTM 2019 Conferences: Confederated International Conferences: CoopIS, ODBASE, C&TC 2019, Rhodes, Greece, October 21–25, 2019, Proceedings, pp. 3–21. Springer (2019). https://doi.org/10.1007/978-3-030-33246-4_1
8. Bazarganigilani, M.: Phishing e-mail detection using ontology concept and Naive Bayes algorithm. Int. J. Res. Rev. Comput. Sci. 2(2), 249 (2011)
9. Benevides, A.B., et al.: Representing a reference foundational ontology of events in SROIQ. Appl. Ontol. 14(3), 293–334 (2019)
10. Chiew, K.L., Yong, K., Tan, C.L.: A survey of phishing attacks: their types, vectors and technical approaches. Expert Syst. Appl. 106, 1–20 (2018)
11. Fonseca, C.M., Porello, D., Guizzardi, G., Almeida, J., Guarino, N.: Relations in ontology-driven conceptual modeling. In: Laender, A., Pernici, B., Lim, E.-P., de Oliveira, J. (eds.) ER 2019. LNCS, vol. 11788, pp. 28–42. Springer, Cham (2019). https://doi.org/10.1007/978-3-030-33223-5_4
12. Fonseca, C.M., Sales, T.P., Viola, V., Da Fonseca, L.B., Guizzardi, G., Almeida, J.P.A.: Ontology-driven conceptual modeling as a service. In: CEUR workshop proceedings, vol. 2969. Rheinisch Westfälische Technische Hochschule (2021)
13. Guizzardi, G.: Ontology, ontologies and the "I" of FAIR. Data Intell. 2(1–2), 181–191 (2020)
14. Guizzardi, G., Botti Benevides, A., Fonseca, C.M., Porello, D., Almeida, J.P.A., Sales, T.P.: UFO: Unified foundational ontology. Appl. Ontol. 17(1), 1–44 (2022)
15. Gupta, M., Akiri, C., Aryal, K., Parker, E., Praharaj, L.: From ChatGPT to ThreatGPT: impact of generative AI in cybersecurity and privacy. IEEE Access (2023)
16. Hannousse, A., Yahiouche, S.: Web page phishing detection (2021). https://doi.org/10.17632/c2gw7fy2j4.3
17. ISO: ISO 31000:2018 - Risk management – Guidelines (2018)
18. Jacobsen, A., et al.: FAIR principles: interpretations and implementation considerations. Data Intell. 2(1–2), 10–29 (2020)
19. Jain, A.K., Gupta, B.: A survey of phishing attack techniques, defence mechanisms and open research challenges. Enterp. Inf. Syst. 16(4), 527–565 (2022)
20. Jakobsson, M., Myers, S.: Phishing and countermeasures: understanding the increasing problem of electronic identity theft. John Wiley & Sons (2006)
21. Kerremans, K., Tang, Y., Temmerman, R., Zhao, G.: Towards ontology-based e-mail fraud detection. In: 2005 Portuguese Conference on Artificial Intelligence, pp. 106–111. IEEE (2005)
22. Lastdrager, E.: Achieving a consensual definition of phishing based on a systematic review of the literature. Crime Sci. 3(1), 1–10 (2014). https://doi.org/10.1186/s40163-014-0009-y
23. Lastdrager, E.E.H.: From fishing to phishing. PhD thesis, University of Twente, Enschede, Netherlands (2018). https://doi.org/10.3990/1.9789036544795
24. Mohammad, R.M., Thabtah, F., McCluskey, L.: Tutorial and critical analysis of phishing websites methods. Comput. Sci. Rev. 17, 1–24 (2015)

25. Oliveira, Í., Calhau, R.F., Guizzardi, G.: Toward a phishing attack ontology. In: ER-Companion 2023: ER Forum, 7th SCME, Project Exhibitions, Posters and Demos, and Doctoral Consortium, pp. 10–21. No. 3618 in CEUR Workshop Proceedings, Aachen (2023). https://ceur-ws.org/Vol-3618/forum_paper_25.pdf
26. Oliveira, Í., Sales, T.P., Baratella, R., Fumagalli, M., Guizzardi, G.: An ontology of security from a risk treatment perspective. In: Ralyté, J., Chakravarthy, S., Mohania, M., Jeusfeld, M.A., Karlapalem, K. (eds.) Conceptual Modeling: 41st International Conference, ER 2022, Hyderabad, India, October 17–20, 2022, Proceedings, pp. 365–379. Springer International Publishing, Cham (2022). https://doi.org/10.1007/978-3-031-17995-2_26
27. Park, G., Rayz, J.: Ontological detection of phishing emails. In: 2018 IEEE International Conference on Systems, Man, and Cybernetics (SMC), pp. 2858–2863. IEEE (2018)
28. Ponemon Institute LLC: The 2021 Cost of Phishing Study. Tech. rep., Ponemon Institute LLC (2021). https://www.proofpoint.com/au/resources/analyst-reports/ponemon-cost-of-phishing-study
29. Raskin, V., Taylor, J.M., Hempelmann, C.F.: Ontological semantic technology for detecting insider threat and social engineering. In: Proceedings of the 2010 New Security Paradigms Workshop, pp. 115–128 (2010)
30. Sales, T.P., Baião, F., Guizzardi, G., Almeida, J., Guarino, N., Mylopoulos, J.: The common ontology of value and risk. In: Trujillo, J.C., et al. (eds.) ER 2018. LNCS, vol. 11157, pp. 121–135. Springer, Cham (2018). https://doi.org/10.1007/978-3-030-00847-5_11
31. Bonino da Silva Santos, L.O., dos Santos Vieira, B., Bernabé, C.H.: FAIR FOR FOIS. https://w3id.org/FAIR-academic/fair4fois (2024). Accessed May 2024
32. Stanford Center for Biomedical Informatics Research: Protégé (2024). https://protege.stanford.edu/
33. Tchakounté, F., Molengar, D., Ngossaha, J.M.: A description logic ontology for email phishing. Int. J. Inf. Secur. Sci. **9**(1), 44–63 (2020)
34. Tseng, S.S., Ku, C.H., Lee, T.J., Geng, G.G., Wang, Y.J.: Building a frame-based anti-phishing model based on phishing ontology. In: International Conference on Advances in Information Technology (2013)
35. Vrandečić, D.: Ontology evaluation. In: Staab, S., Studer, R. (eds.) Handbook on Ontologies, pp. 293–313. Springer, Berlin, Heidelberg (2009). https://doi.org/10.1007/978-3-540-92673-3_13
36. Wang, Z., Sun, L., Zhu, H.: Defining social engineering in cybersecurity. IEEE Access **8**, 85094–85115 (2020)
37. Wang, Z., Zhu, H., Sun, L.: Social engineering in cybersecurity: effect mechanisms, human vulnerabilities and attack methods. IEEE Access **9**, 11895–11910 (2021)
38. Wetzel, R.: Tackling phishing. Bus. Commun. Rev. **35**(2), 46–49 (2005)
39. Zahedi, F.M., Chen, Y., Zhao, H.: Ontology-based intelligent interface personalization for protection against phishing attacks. Inf. Syst. Res. (2023)

HarborLang: Enhancing Maritime Operational Safety Through Cyber Threat Simulation and Assessment

Diana Malakhova[1(✉)], Simon Hacks[1], Anna Alexeeva[2], and Thomas Ricardo Pathe[1]

[1] Stockholm University, Stockholm, Sweden
{diana.malakhova,simon.hacks,thomas.pathe}@dsv.su.se
[2] Sunet, Stockholm, Sweden
anna@sunet.com

Abstract. Maritime operations, crucial for global trade, increasingly rely on digital navigation and communication systems, making them vulnerable to cyber threats such as Global Positioning System (GPS) jamming, Automatic Identification System (AIS) spoofing, and multi-vector attacks. These threats compromise vessel safety, disrupt port logistics, and challenge maritime security.

This paper introduces harborLang, a domain-specific language (DSL) for modeling and analyzing maritime cybersecurity risks. Built on the Meta Attack Language (MAL) framework, harborLang provides a structured approach to representing maritime assets, their interdependencies, and cyberattack propagation pathways. By enabling systematic risk assessment, it supports the secure digitalization of maritime operations. The evaluation demonstrates harborLang's ability to model real-world cyber threats, highlighting its potential for enhancing maritime cybersecurity. Future extensions will expand its applicability to multi-vessel interactions and port-wide threat modeling, further strengthening maritime resilience against cyber risks.

Keywords: harborLang · Domain-Specific Language (DSL) · Maritime Cybersecurity · Attack Simulation · GPS Jamming · AIS Spoofing · Maritime Operations

1 Introduction

The maritime industry, responsible for over 80% of global trade [1], is undergoing rapid digitalization, integrating advanced navigation, communication, and logistics technologies. While these innovations enhance efficiency, they also expose vessels and port infrastructure to increasing cyber threats [2]. The growing interconnectivity between critical systems has led to a 900% surge in maritime cybersecurity incidents [3], with attackers exploiting vulnerabilities in systems such as the Global Positioning System (GPS), Automatic Identification System (AIS), and vessel traffic management.

Cyberattacks targeting maritime operations include GPS jamming, which disrupts vessel positioning, and AIS spoofing, which manipulates ship identity and location data. The Automatic Identification System (AIS), as defined by the International Maritime Organization, is "designed to be capable of providing information about the ship to other ships and to coastal authorities automatically" [4]. Despite its operational importance, AIS suffers from serious vulnerabilities. As highlighted by Androjna et al., unprotected AIS transmissions can be spoofed or manipulated, which opens the possibility for cyber attackers to mislead traffic coordination and vessel navigation [5]. These threats can significantly impact maritime safety by disrupting port logistics and increasing the risk of collisions.

This paper presents harborLang, a domain-specific language (DSL) built on the Meta Attack Language (MAL) [6,7], designed to systematically model and analyze maritime cybersecurity threats. Previous research introduced conceptual maritime cybersecurity models but lacked executable implementations for attack simulation. This work bridges that gap by formalizing maritime-specific attack propagation pathways in a structured, machine-readable format.

To support practical assessment of cyber risks, harborLang integrates with MAL GUI for model visualization and Neo4j for attack graph analysis. The language enables structured modeling of cyber-physical interactions, demonstrating how cyberattacks can escalate into operational disruptions. This approach supports risk assessment and security planning, aligning with the cybersecurity objectives of the Maritime Integrated Software-based Solution for Interoperable Networks (MISSION) Project, which promotes secure digitalization in maritime transport.

The remainder of this paper is structured as follows: Sect. 2 reviews existing research on maritime cybersecurity modeling and structured threat assessment approaches. Section 3 outlines the research objectives. Section 4 details the design and implementation of harborLang. Section 5 presents an attack simulation focusing on GPS jamming and AIS spoofing. Section 6 discusses limitations and future research directions, and Conclusion 7.

2 Related Work

Cybersecurity modeling and risk assessment in critical infrastructure domains have been extensively studied, leading to several domain-specific languages built upon the MAL framework. Notably, coreLang [8] addresses cybersecurity threats in generic ICT infrastructures, while powerLang [9] focuses on attack propagation in energy systems. These languages use inheritance-based structures to represent domain-specific attack pathways and countermeasures. However, they do not address the unique threats and operational characteristics of maritime environments.

Beyond DSL development, several researchers have proposed tailored maritime cybersecurity solutions. Tatar [10] presents a fuzzy decision support model to assess maritime cyber risks under uncertainty. Hossain et al. [11] introduce a federated learning-based intrusion detection system designed for maritime radar networks, demonstrating an AI-driven approach to maritime security. These contributions improve detection and evaluation capabilities but lack a structured modeling framework for asset-level propagation and simulation of threats.

Initial work on harborLang introduced a conceptual asset-centric framework for modeling maritime cybersecurity [12], identifying core components such as GPS, AIS, and vessel control systems. However, earlier versions were not formally encoded within MAL and lacked automated simulation capabilities.

This work extends harborLang by delivering a fully operational MAL-based language with executable attack semantics. It explicitly defines maritime-specific assets, interdependencies, and cyberattack propagation patterns. The model integrates with the MISSION Project, supporting digital coordination tools with a structured approach to threat modeling and risk assessment.

3 Objectives

The development of harborLang addresses the growing need for a domain-specific modeling language tailored to the cybersecurity challenges of maritime systems. While existing threat modeling approaches focus on generic ICT or industrial control systems [8,9], they do not capture the domain-specific nuances of maritime navigation, communication, and port infrastructure. Cyber threats such as GPS jamming, AIS spoofing, ransomware, and targeted attacks on port operations [13] require specialized modeling frameworks to enable realistic risk analysis and mitigation.

O1: Structured Asset-Centric Modeling. Cyber threats in maritime systems propagate across interconnected assets, impacting navigation, communication, and operational technologies [13]. harborLang introduces a layered architecture that defines a hierarchical representation of maritime assets-including vessels, communication systems, and infrastructure-enabling inherited attack steps and systematic defense modeling. This structure promotes scalability and allows for comprehensive system-wide risk assessments, in line with methodologies applied in critical infrastructure modeling [14].

O2: Maritime-Specific Threat Representation. harborLang explicitly models threats unique to the maritime domain, such as GPS interference, AIS manipulation, and traffic management disruptions. Recent incidents involving vessel traffic management and port logistics [15] illustrate how localized attacks can have system-wide implications. By embedding these threat patterns into its meta-model, harborLang enables more realistic simulation and predictive cybersecurity assessments [16].

O3: Alignment with the MISSION Project. The MISSION Project focuses on enhancing efficiency and interoperability in maritime transport through digital optimization. However, this shift increases the attack surface. harborLang contributes to MISSION's cybersecurity dimension by offering a risk assessment tool that models how digital threats can impact operational coordination. Its structured design ensures that vulnerabilities in communication, navigation, or port systems are traceable and mitigatable, aligning with the project's goals for secure digital transformation.

By addressing these three objectives, `harborLang` provides a structured, realistic, and operationally relevant language for assessing and mitigating maritime cybersecurity risks.

4 Engineering HarborLang

`harborLang` is implemented using the MAL framework to represent cybersecurity threats in maritime systems. It encodes cyber-physical attack pathways and shows how vulnerabilities in navigation, communication, and control systems propagate into operational disruptions. The modeling process is supported by MAL GUI for interactive construction and Neo4j for generating and analyzing attack graphs. The implementation follows a systematic approach to developing MAL-based languages as outlined by Hacks et al. [17].

The model defines key maritime assets and their interdependencies. GPS is vulnerable to jamming and spoofing, both of which compromise vessel positioning. In the event of jamming, INS takes over navigation but gradually accumulates errors, leading to navigational drift. Spoofed AIS signals can mislead the Traffic Management System, resulting in false vessel tracking and incorrect routing decisions. These cascading failures often require manual intervention, but human misinterpretation of AIS data may lead to incorrect course corrections, worsening the situation.

`harborLang` formally encodes attack steps and inter-asset relationships in its metamodel. AIS spoofing initiates false tracking in Traffic Management, which in turn causes incorrect routing and vessel deviation. Simultaneously, GPS jamming triggers reliance on INS, where drift accumulates and contributes to navigational errors. These interactions are visualized and analyzed through the integration with Neo4j and the MAL GUI interface.

The following excerpt illustrates a subset of `harborLang`'s syntax used to model GPS jamming and AIS spoofing:

```
// Cyber Layer: Navigation and Communication
category CyberLayer {
  asset GPS extends NavigationSystem {
    | gpsJamming -> ins.coordinatesDrifting
    | gpsSpoofing -> ins.adjustmentToFalseCoordinates
  }
  asset AIS extends CommunicationSystem {
    | aisSpoofing -> trafficManagement.falseVesselTracking
    | aisDataManipulation -> vessel.receivedFalseAIS
  }
  asset TrafficManagement extends CommunicationSystem {
    | falseVesselTracking -> incorrectFleetRouting
    | incorrectFleetRouting -> vessel.routeDeviation
```

```
  }
}

// Asset Relationships
associations {
  GPS [gps] 1 <-- CommunicatesWith --> 1 [ins] INS
  AIS [ais] 1 <-- CommunicatesWith -->
      1 [trafficManagement] TrafficManagement
  TrafficManagement [trafficManagement] 1 <-- Manages -->
      1 [vessel] Vessel
}
```

The full implementation is available at: [1]

This structured modeling approach is well aligned with existing cybersecurity risk assessment methodologies, such as YACRAF [18]. YACRAF offers a metamodel-driven framework for assessing vulnerabilities, threat propagation, and business impact across complex systems. By integrating harborLang with that framework, maritime cybersecurity modeling can benefit from more systematic evaluations, scenario-based analysis, and data-driven mitigation planning.

5 Demonstration

To assess the expressiveness and utility of harborLang, we conducted a simulation using the MAL toolbox, integrating both MAL GUI for interactive model configuration and Neo4j for attack graph visualization. The simulation illustrates how GPS jamming and AIS spoofing-two well-documented maritime cyber threats-affect navigation systems and operational decisions.

The scenario focuses on a single vessel navigating a congested port environment. The vessel depends on GPS for accurate geolocation, INS as a fallback, and AIS to communicate its identity and position to nearby ships and the port traffic management system. The attacker initiates a multi-vector cyberattack comprising two simultaneous actions:

- **GPS jamming** disables satellite-based navigation. The vessel switches to INS, which accumulates drift over time, leading to gradual deviation from the intended route.
- **AIS spoofing** injects falsified location and identity data, which is received by the traffic management system and surrounding vessels, leading to misinformation about the ship's position.

These manipulations result in false tracking data within the traffic management system, which then issues incorrect routing instructions. The affected vessel drifts off course, increasing the risk of collision. Human operators may intervene, but their corrective actions are constrained by their reliance on compromised

---

[1] https://github.com/DizzyFizzDi/harborLang.

data. As such, the attack illustrates not only technological vulnerabilities but also the limits of manual override under uncertainty.

Figure 1 presents the attack graph generated from the `harborLang` model. It visualizes the sequence of compromised components and the propagation of risk across interconnected systems-from compromised GPS and AIS data to navigational failures and potential operational disruptions at the port.

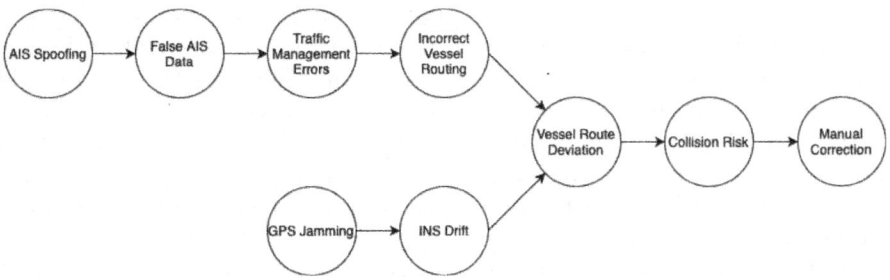

Fig. 1. Attack path generated from harborLang showing GPS jamming and AIS spoofing propagation

The simulation confirms that `harborLang` effectively models cyber-physical dependencies and supports structured reasoning about attack propagation. By tracing how local cyber incidents lead to system-wide disruptions, the language enables proactive risk identification and mitigation strategy design.

This demonstration focuses on a targeted scenario involving a single vessel; however, `harborLang` is scalable. Future applications may explore broader attack surfaces involving multi-vessel coordination, shore-to-ship communication, and port infrastructure interdependencies. These aspects are planned as part of our roadmap toward port-wide threat modeling and probabilistic risk assessment.

6 Discussions

This work introduced `harborLang` as a structured approach to modeling cyber threats in maritime navigation and communication systems. The results confirm that it effectively captures cyber-physical attack propagation, illustrating how localized incidents, such as GPS jamming and AIS spoofing, escalate into vessel misnavigation and operational disruptions.

The study successfully fulfills its primary objectives. First, it implements a structured asset-centric modeling approach (O1), ensuring an inheritance-based framework that captures interconnected cyber risks. The attack paths demonstrate how threats propagate between navigation, communication, and operational systems. Second, it explicitly represents maritime-specific threats (O2), integrating GPS and AIS manipulation, vessel misrouting, and traffic management errors into a unified threat model. Lastly, it aligns with the security objectives of the MISSION Project (O3) by providing a systematic methodology for assessing digital vulnerabilities in maritime operations.

The development of `harborLang` followed an iterative and problem-driven design process consistent with the principles of Action Design Research (ADR) [19], allowing the language to evolve in response to real-world modeling challenges and stakeholder needs. This methodology helped ensure that the tool not only addressed theoretical modeling requirements but also remained practically applicable to maritime cybersecurity scenarios.

Although the model is based on established cybersecurity and maritime risk principles, certain limitations should be considered. The current implementation primarily focuses on individual vessel cybersecurity, whereas real-world maritime operations involve interactions between multiple vessels and port-wide infrastructures. Additionally, attack propagation is modeled deterministically, whereas actual cyber threats often involve probabilistic uncertainties. These aspects impact both internal validity (the correctness of the model in capturing realistic attack paths) and external validity (its applicability to broader maritime cybersecurity challenges).

Future work should extend `harborLang` beyond single-vessel modeling to capture multi-vessel interactions and cyber threats targeting port ecosystems. Probabilistic modeling will further enhance realism by reflecting uncertainty in attack execution and human response. Integration of empirical incident data into simulation processes will improve the external validity of assessments and foster trust among maritime cybersecurity stakeholders.

By refining scalability and incorporating empirical validation, `harborLang` has the potential to evolve into a robust tool for securing maritime operations against emerging cyber threats.

7 Conclusion

This paper presented `harborLang`, a modeling language for analyzing maritime cybersecurity threats through structured simulation of cyber-physical interactions. By explicitly representing navigation, communication, and operational systems, `harborLang` supports the systematic assessment of cyberattack propagation and risk evaluation. Implemented within the MAL framework and supported by MAL GUI and Neo4j, the approach enables both model visualization and graph-based analysis.

The attack simulation focused on GPS jamming and AIS spoofing demonstrated how localized incidents can lead to navigational failures and traffic miscoordination. The results also emphasized the influence of human intervention-whether corrective or erroneous-in the escalation or mitigation of cyber-induced risks.

Future work will extend `harborLang` to address multi-vessel dynamics, port-wide infrastructures, and probabilistic modeling of uncertain threat behaviors. As the maritime sector continues to digitalize, structured tools such as `harborLang` will be critical for ensuring resilient and secure maritime operations.

Acknowledgement. This work has received funding from European Union's HORIZON research and innovation programme under the Grant Agreement no. 101138583.

References

1. UNCTAD: review of maritime transport (2024). https://unctad.org/publication/review-maritime-transport-2024. Accessed 15 Jan 2025
2. Alcaide, J.I., Garcia Llave, R.: Critical infrastructures cybersecurity and the maritime sector. Transp. Res. Procedia **45**, 547–554. Elsevier (2020). https://doi.org/10.1016/j.trpro.2020.03.058
3. Akpan, F., Bendiab, G., Shiaeles, S., Karamperidis, S., Michaloliakos, M.: Cybersecurity challenges in the maritime sector. In: Network 2022, vol. 2, pp. 123–138. Springer (2022). https://doi.org/10.3390/network2010009
4. International Maritime Organization: Automatic Identification Systems (AIS). https://www.imo.org/en/OurWork/Safety/Pages/AIS.aspx. Accessed 15 Jan 2025
5. Androjna, A., Brcko, T., Pavic, I., Greidanus, H.: Assessing Cyber Challenges of Maritime Navigation. J. Marine Sci. Eng. **8**(10), 776 (2020). https://www.mdpi.com/2077-1312/8/10/776
6. Johnson, P., Lagerström, R., Ekstedt, M.: A meta language for threat modeling and attack simulations. In: Proceedings of the 13th International Conference on Availability, Reliability and Security, p. 38. ACM (2018)
7. Wideł, W., Hacks, S., Ekstedt, M., Johnson, P., Lagerström, R.: The meta attack language - a formal description. Comput. Secur. **130**, 103284. Elsevier (2023). https://doi.org/10.1016/j.cose.2021.103284
8. Katsikeas, S., Buhaiu, A., Ekstedt, M., Afzal, Z., Hacks, S., Mukherjee, P.: Development and validation of coreLang: a threat modeling language for the ICT domain. Comput. Secur. **146**, 104057 (2024). https://doi.org/10.1016/j.cose.2024.104057
9. Hacks, S., Katsikeas, S., Ling, E., Lagerström, R., Ekstedt, M.: powerLang: a probabilistic attack simulation language for the power domain. Energy Inform. **3**(1), 1–17 (2020). https://doi.org/10.1186/s42162-020-00134-4
10. Tatar, U.: A decision support model for assessing cybersecurity risks in maritime transportation using spherical fuzzy information. Expert Syst. Appl. **237**, 121308. Elsevier (2024). https://doi.org/10.1016/j.eswa.2023.121308
11. Hossain, M.A., Hossain, M.D., Choupani, R. et al.: MRS-PFIDS: federated learning driven detection of network intrusions in maritime radar systems. Int. J. Inf. Secur. **24**, 92 (2025). https://doi.org/10.1007/s10207-025-01008-0
12. Malakhova, D., Hacks, S., Alexeeva, A.: Securing digital maritime operations: defense against signal manipulation in vessel navigation systems integration through harborLang. In: Companion Proceedings of the 17th IFIP WG 8.1 Working Conference on the Practice of Enterprise Modeling Forum. Paper presented at PoEM 2024, Stockholm, Sweden, Dec 3-5 (2024)
13. Clavijo Mesa, M.V., Patino-Rodriguez, C.E., Guevara Carazas, F.J.: Cybersecurity at sea: a literature review of cyber-attack impacts and defenses in maritime supply chains. Information **15**, 710 (2024). https://doi.org/10.3390/info15110710
14. Frøseth, H.: Threat modeling for satellite communications in maritime operations. Ocean Eng. 285 (2024). https://doi.org/10.1016/j.oceaneng.2023.116901
15. Pyykkö, H., Kuusijärvi, J., Silverajan, B., et al.: The cyber threat preparedness in the maritime logistics industry. In: Proceedings of the 8th Transport Research Arena (TRA), pp. 1–12 (2020)

16. Ali, A., et al.: Federated cybersecurity framework for shipboard microgrids. IEEE Trans. Industr. Inf. **20**(2), 3071–3085 (2024). https://doi.org/10.1109/TII.2023.3339470
17. Hacks, S., Katsikeas, S., Rencelj Ling, E., Xiong, W., Pfeiffer, J., Wortmann, A.: Towards a systematic method for developing meta attack language instances. In: Augusto, A., Gill, A., Bork, D., Nurcan, S., Reinhartz-Berger, I., Schmidt, R. (eds.) Enterprise, Business-Process and Information Systems Modeling: 23rd International Conference, BPMDS 2022 and 27th International Conference, EMMSAD 2022, Held at CAiSE 2022, Leuven, Belgium, June 6–7, 2022, Proceedings, pp. 139–154. Springer International Publishing, Cham (2022). https://doi.org/10.1007/978-3-031-07475-2_10
18. Ekstedt, M., Afzal, Z., Mukherjee, P., Hacks, S., Lagerström, R.: Yet another cybersecurity risk assessment framework. Int. J. Inf. Secur. **22**, 1–17 (2023). https://doi.org/10.1007/s10207-023-00713-y
19. Sein, M.K., Henfridsson, O., Purao, S., Rossi, M., Lindgren, R.: Action design research. MIS Q., 37–56 (2011)

Evaluation of Modeling Practices (EMMSAD 2025)

Learning Analytics Dashboard with Peer Comparison for Student Feedback in Conceptual Modeling Education

Elena Tiukhova[1(✉)], Charlotte Verbruggen[1,4], Tinne De Laet[2], Bart Baesens[1,3], and Monique Snoeck[1]

[1] LIRIS, KU Leuven, Leuven, Belgium
elena.tiukhova@kuleuven.be
[2] Tutorial Services, Faculty of Engineering Science, KU Leuven, Leuven, Belgium
[3] Department of Decision Analytics and Risk, University of Southampton, Southampton, UK
[4] Business Informatics Group, TU Wien, Vienna, Austria
charlotte.verbruggen@tuwien.ac.at

Abstract. Conceptual modeling education benefits from technological support due to the complex nature of the learning processes required to master modeling skills. Along with existing modeling and prototyping tools, providing feedback to students using Learning Analytics Dashboards (LADs) can enhance their learning experience. To interpret LADs, students are provided with a frame of reference, often peer comparison, although its effectiveness is debated. This study presents two LADs used to provide feedback to students from diverse backgrounds enrolled in a conceptual modeling course: a default-LAD with mastery and progress reference frames, and an extended peer-LAD that also includes a performance reference frame. We examine students' preferences for LAD visuals, the relationship between their study activity and performance, and the relationship between the use patterns of different LAD versions and student activity and performance. The results show that most of the relationships are significant only for the peer-enhanced LAD and are stronger for students with less modeling experience, underscoring the value of peer LADs for novice modelers.

Keywords: Learning Analytics Dashboards · Conceptual Modeling Education · Social Comparison

1 Introduction

Conceptual modeling (CM) is a cognitively demanding task that involves creating high-level symbolic representations of reality. Due to its complexity, effective teaching of CM requires a carefully designed instructional approach that includes providing learning tools, applying learning theories, offering feedback, and fostering the development of problem solving skills [26]. From the learner's perspective, it is important to spread learning effort throughout the course because complex cognitive modeling skills require time to develop: it is not a good study strategy to binge on all the course material just before the exam [40].

As learners engage with learning tools and materials, they generate data that can be used to perform learning analytics (LA) aimed at improving learning experiences [33]. Existing research at the intersection of LA and CM leverages usage data from modeling tools [4,27,32] as well as learners' interactions with course materials [40]. According to [45], this data represents motivated learning choices made to achieve learning goals and move from a current state of knowledge to a desired state [17]. To support these self-regulated learning processes, insights from LA can be presented to learners via Learning Analytics Dashboards (LADs) that present this data in a user-friendly way, by consolidating multiple visualizations into a single, comprehensive display [29].

To correctly interpret data visualized in a LAD, learners need a reference frame. There exist several possible frames, including social frames (e.g., comparison with class peers or top peers), achievement frames (comparison with learning goals/outcomes), and progress frames (self-comparison) [16]. We believe that social comparison is particularly important in the context of CM education (CME), where continuous effort is required to develop complex modeling skills, and peer comparison could potentially help stimulate the students self-regulation. The findings of existing research on LADs that include social reference frames reveal both positive and negative student perceptions [18,23]. These mixed perceptions may be explained by differences between learners [11], such as differences in prior educational background or learning approaches.

With technology support already integrated into CME, incorporating LADs into CME offers new ways to provide valuable learning feedback. Moreover, it is essential to ensure that LA is conducted ethically, upholding the principles of transparency and learner autonomy, respecting the learner's right to opt in/out of LA systems and ensuring that they are informed about their progress [41]. LAD solutions should therefore be both voluntary and accessible to all learners.

This paper presents a LAD for a CM course at KU Leuven, catering to two study programs with different background requirements, to provide learners with feedback on study activity, performance, and progress. The LAD is available in two versions: a default-LAD, which has achievement (learning goals) and progress (past activity) reference frames, and a peer-LAD, which adds a social (peer-comparison) frame to the default-LAD. The goals of this study are to (1) examine student preferences for LAD visualizations in order to select appropriate visualizations for the final LAD; (2) understand the relationship between study activity and performance to ensure that feedback is meaningful; (3) examine the relationships between use patterns of different LAD versions and study activity and (4) between use patterns and performance. Objectives (2)-(4) will be examined for two study programs with different background characteristics to investigate if these differences generalize across different groups of students.

The rest of the paper is organized as follows: Sect. 2 reviews related work and research gaps; Sect. 3 outlines the methodology; Sects. 4 and 5 present and discuss the results, while Sect. 6 summarizes key findings.

2 Related Work

Social comparison is common in daily life, helping individuals evaluate themselves relative to others. Various theories explain social comparison, including the achievement goal orientation theory [5]. It identifies two distinct approaches that learners adopt in achievement contexts: mastery goal orientation, which emphasizes task completion and personal growth, and performance goal orientation, which focuses on outperforming others. Jivet et al. explicitly examined the reference frames used in existing LADs, including a social frame such as peer comparison. The findings revealed mixed perceptions of the social frame, showing both positive and negative effects on student motivation, behavior, and performance [18]. Matcha et al. conducted a systematic literature review on LADs, focusing primarily on self-regulated learning and examining the types of feedback provided by LADs, including various reference frames. Their findings revealed that feedback is predominantly focused on individual learning activities, with peer comparison being the second most common type [23].

To account for LADs studies with a social comparison component published after 2019, we conducted forward snowballing on the reviews [18,23] (see Online Appendix A [38]). Most of the reported LADs are designed for STEM (Science, Technology, Engineering and Mathematics) courses offered by Computer Science or Engineering faculties, typically in blended/online learning environments [8,10,12,13,15,21,28,35–37,42]. The visualizations in these LADs primarily rely on data from LMS while the most commonly used evaluation techniques are questionnaires/surveys, followed by controlled experiments, interviews, and log data analysis. Feedback on study activity and academic performance is the most commonly featured topic. These studies have reported peer-comparison effects as positive, mixed, or negative, depending on the context. According to [11], this phenomenon can be explained by differences between learners. Six studies [6,12,13,24,25,36] discuss the background differences and how they might influence the LAD effects, including the peer comparison effects. These differences appear in different backgrounds of learners, including cultural differences [6], prior education and knowledge [25,36], or learning orientation [12].

Research Gap. While previous research has examined peer effects in LADs, it has not done so in the context of conceptual modeling education. In addition, we make a comparison between student populations with different backgrounds to address a gap in understanding how such characteristics may influence the relationships between LAD use, study activity and performance. In our course, prerequisite knowledge is defined, but its coverage varies across programs, resulting in different student perceptions of the course's difficulty.

3 Methodology

This paper investigates the following research questions in the context of CME:

RQ1 What types of visualizations (e.g., bar charts, line graphs, texts, tables) do students prefer in the LAD and what is the preferred order of different sources of information in the LAD?

RQ2 What is the relationship between *study activity* and *academic achievement*?

RQ3 How do students with varying levels of *study activity* differ in their frequency of use of the LAD versions?

RQ4 How do students with varying levels of *academic achievement* differ in their frequency of use of the LAD versions?

3.1 Study Context and Data

The LAD has been developed and used in a master-level CM course "Architecture and Modelling of Management Information Systems" offered at KU Leuven for the Master of Information Management (MInfM) and Master of Business (and IS) Engineering (MBISE) programs (Table 1). The course teaches artifact-centric domain modeling, where students learn to create a domain model consisting of a conceptual data model and a set of state charts that define the lifecycle of domain object types. The modeling approach is supported with an online modelling tool, and a prototyping tool that automatically transforms models to code.

Table 1. Program details. Grades are the final exam grades (including retakes)

Program	ECTS	Admission requirements	#stud.	Pass. rate	Avg. grade
MBISE	120	Accessible to applicants with an academic Bachelor's degree with a strong quantitative and technological focus and with sufficient knowledge of economics and management science	48	89.5%	12.2/20
MInfM	60	Accessible to applicants with a Bachelor's or Master's degree awarded by a university	103	78.6%	10.7/20

The course is taught in a blended learning format: (1) an online part on the edX Edge platform (https://edge.edx.org/) with the course material (video lectures, slides, exercises with automated grading) and a website containing the cases and their solutions; (2) an offline part with several live lectures and eight on-campus exercise sessions (ES). These sessions give the students an opportunity to solve large modeling cases and receive immediate feedback. To stimulate attendance, students are requested to register for these sessions.

To provide students with insightful feedback on learning goal achievement, following the CM Taxonomy of Learning Objectives [3], online quizzes on the edX Edge platform are classified according to Bloom's Taxonomy [20], based on the cognitive skills required to complete each task. These range from basic memorization of modeling notations to more complex tasks such as evaluating models against requirements and creating models. Aligning activities with Bloom's Taxonomy helps address a key gap in current CM courses - namely, the lack of assessment of modeling skills at lower cognitive levels [2].

The final exam is structured according to Bloom's Taxonomy and consists of two parts, with a joint passing grade of 10/20. Part 1 (8/20 points) assesses a range of cognitive levels up to and including the "evaluate" level. Part 1.A evaluates students' knowledge and comprehension of course fundamentals, while Part 1.B tests more advanced skills of applying learned concepts, analyzing requirements, and evaluating existing models. Part 2 (12/20 points) focuses on the ability to design a conceptual model based on given requirements. Students can only attempt Part 2 if they have successfully passed Part 1. Given the importance of passing Part 1 of the exam, students receive an online multiple-choice formative test to check their readiness for the exam.

3.2 LAD Design

The general purpose of the LAD is to provide students with feedback on their learning activities, progress, and performance. The LAD design is based on several educational theories, i.e., the achievement goal orientation [5] and self-regulated learning [45] theories, and Bloom's taxonomy [20]. Achievement goal orientation theory supports the purpose of providing feedback on learning activity and performance and is applied by incorporating mastery learning goals into both LAD versions (e.g., expected progress on assignments and quizzes) and performance learning goals (peer progress) in the peer-LAD. Bloom's taxonomy is used by breaking down mastery goals into different cognitive levels, to keep students updated on their progress according to different levels of material difficulty. The use of Bloom's taxonomy is well established in the field of LAD [1, 19]. Some LAD visualizations also display past activity, allowing learners to reflect on their transitions between learning states as they pursue study goals, thereby supporting their self-regulation and providing feedback on study progress.

While developing the LAD, we followed the design science research methodology [14], which is based on rapid prototyping and iterative evaluation, an approach successfully adopted in the LAD domain [28]. The *first iteration* of the LAD development included the brainstorming sessions with the instructor team to decide on which data sources were available for visualization and what types of meaningful visualizations could be offered to the students.

Given the differences between students and their potential influence on feedback preferences, it is crucial to consider students' perspectives when designing effective LA solutions. In other words, students should be involved as primary stakeholders in the development of LA solutions [43], which can be achieved by incorporating their preferences into the LAD development. In the *second iteration*, we developed two potential visualizations for each data source (eight sources in total) identified in the first iteration, and students were asked to choose a preferred visualization from two options given in the questionnaire distributed during the first exercise session. The details of the given options can be found in Online Appendix C [38]. The visualization types offered to students were based on Schwendimann et al. [30], selecting the most commonly used types: bar charts, line graphs, tables, pie charts, gauge charts, text, and traffic lights (ordered by frequency of use [30]). Following an approach of Santos et al. [28], the students were also asked to rank the visualization categories according to their preference. Because each visualization is generic, the LAD design can be applied to other skill-based courses, particularly those structured around Bloom's taxonomy.

Building on the insights from the first and second iterations, two final LAD versions were developed and made available via two links on the LMS page. The default-LAD provided visualizations that focused solely on an individual student's progress, along with mastery goals (i.e., the best possible performance) shown in each visualization. The peer-LAD also included performance goals (i.e., peer comparison), which were represented by the average performance of all active students to highlight general learning trends. In the latest LAD updates, the trends for the passing/failing student groups were also added. We followed a widely used approach of updating the LAD weekly [6,8,42], with announcements posted to inform students of each update. The LMS collected weekly log data on LAD use, with access statistics compiled weekly before the LAD update.

Despite their widespread popularity in LAD studies, controlled experiments that withhold feedback from one group of students raise ethical concerns [41]. Therefore, it is essential to ensure that students are not compelled to use a particular type of feedback or to use none at all, as this could lead to adverse outcomes. Hence, the LAD usage remained entirely voluntary, with no incentives or penalties for participation, aligning with the principle of transparency [41] that ensures students could make informed decisions about opting in/out. Students also had the freedom to choose between the versions, as both links were published on the LMS page that every enrolled student had access to, giving them considerable control over the type of feedback they receive - a factor shown to positively influence learner performance [7]. The feedback provided by the LAD was purely informative and did not suggest any specific actions.

3.3 Log Data Analysis

While the course defines prerequisite knowledge (Table 1), the level to which it is addressed in prior education varies across the programs in which the course is offered, resulting in the course being perceived as harder or easier by the students from different backgrounds. Moreover, historical data shows significantly higher average exam grades in the MBISE program than in MInfM (Table 1, see Online Appendix B, Table 2 [38] for more details). We believe that in this setting, students' educational background plays an important role in LAD use and the type of feedback desired (= LAD version). Therefore, we analyze the relationships between study activity, academic performance and LAD frequency of use separately for each program.

We used the K-means clustering algorithm, a widely used technique for behavioral profiling [9], to create activity profiles (representations of a learner's engagement with the course) of both groups. To provide the most complete view of student activity, the clustering analysis used activity data from the last week of the course before Part 2 of the exam. To interpret the clustering solution, a decision tree was constructed using cluster labels as the target and Gini impurity as the splitting criterion.

Box plots were used to visually compare the distribution of numerical variables across groups (e.g., activity or academic achievement profiles). To determine whether the observed differences between groups were statistically significant, the non-parametric Mann-Whitney U test was applied. This test evaluates the null hypothesis that the underlying distributions of the two samples are identical [22]. The Pearson correlation coefficient was used to measure the strength of the relationship between the numerical variables.

4 Results

4.1 RQ1: LAD as an Artifact

Table 2 shows the data sources identified during the first iteration and the visualization types that were possible for those sources. It also presents the results of the visualization questionnaire, showing the students' preferred visualizations and their order of preference (more details in Online Appendix C [38]).

Table 2. Data sources and visualizations: first and second iterations

Data source	Visuals offered	Preferred visual	Rank
ES attendance	Traffic light vs. Table	Traffic light	8
Modeling tool activity	Bar chart vs. Line chart	Line chart	7
Home assignments grades	Gauge vs. Text	Text	1
Practice test grade	Gauge vs. Text	Text	2
edX online activity: #exercise sessions	Bar chart vs. Line chart	Bar chart	6
edX online activity: #quizzes	Line chart & Pie chart vs. Stacked bar chart	Bar chart	5
edX online activity : score on exercise sessions	Bar chart vs. Line chart	Bar chart	3
edX online activity : score on quizzes	Line chart & Table vs. Bar chart	Bar chart	4

The chosen visualizations were then placed in the LAD (Fig. 1a - 1d).[1] The activity visualizations (e.g., attendance) displayed retrospective information from previous weeks, while performance (i.e., grades) visualizations reflected the most recent information.

4.2 RQ2: Study Activity vs. Performance

Figure 2a shows the clustering solution for the **MInfM** students, where the clusters correspond to: (1) students who are highly active in both online and offline course components (green), (2) students who exhibit moderate activity, i.e., active online but inactive offline (yellow), and (3) students who are generally inactive (red), confirming the study profiles reported by the previous research on student profiling [39,40]. Examination of a decision tree built on the basis of these clusters (Fig. 2b) shows that the average score achieved by a student in online quizzes is the most informative feature. This underlines the importance for learners to engage with part-task practices (quizzes) aimed at training "mechanical" skills [40]. When mapping activity to performance (Fig. 2b), we see that most students from highly and moderately active clusters pass the exam, while most students from the inactive cluster fail the exam, confirming the relationships reported by [40].

The optimal clustering solution for the **MBISE** students returns three activity clusters with the same interpretation as for the MInfM program (Fig. 3a). The decision tree reveals similar patterns: the only difference is that the most informative feature here is the average score obtained on online exercise sessions (Fig. 3b). The distribution of exam scores within clusters also shows differences with the MInfM program: regardless of the activity cluster, the majority of MBISE students (89.5%) pass the exam.

---

[1] The LAD demo can be found at https://youtu.be/xJXFmNO25oA.

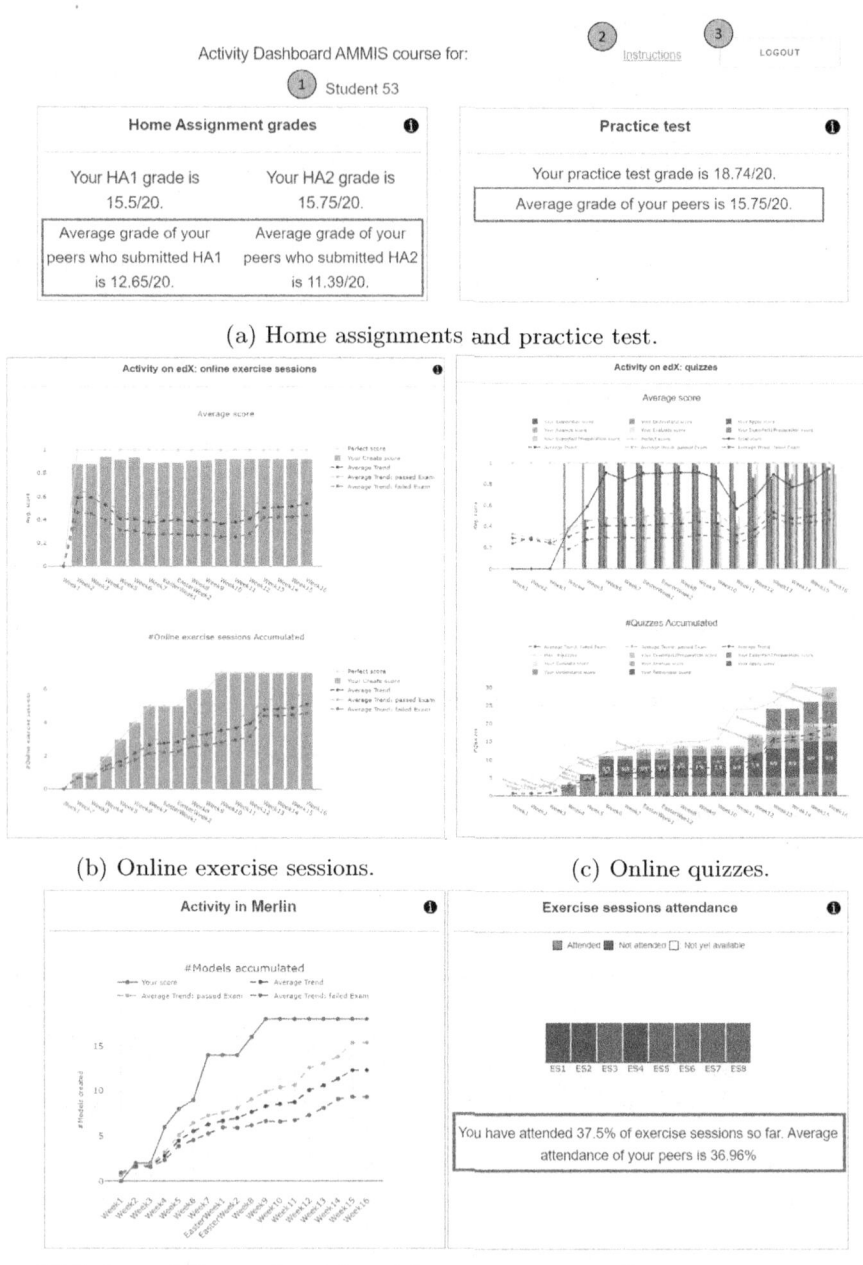

Fig. 1. LAD. Peer-LAD-specific features include highlighted text and trend lines

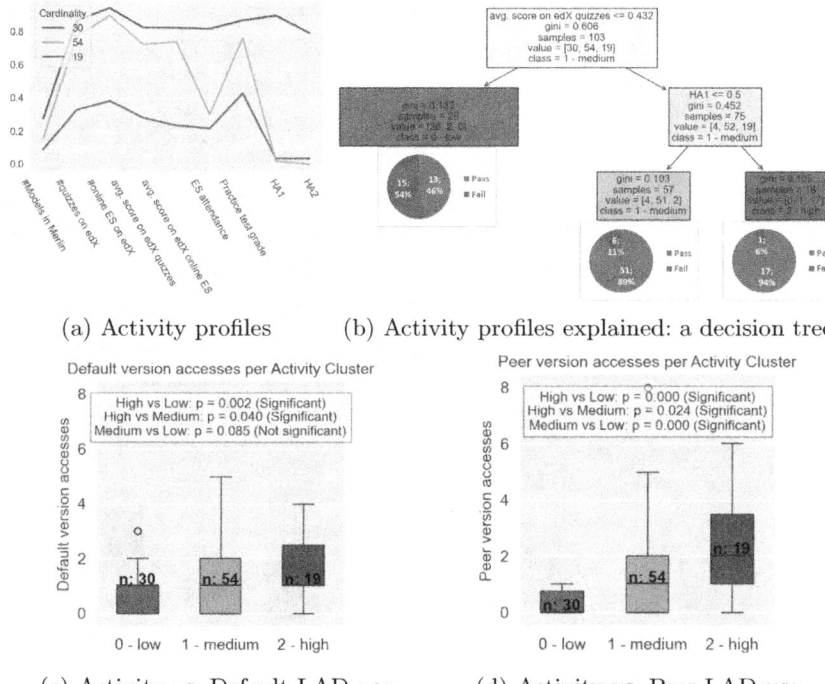

Fig. 2. RQ2 & RQ3: MInfM

4.3 RQ3: Study Activity vs. LAD Usage

To explore the relationship between study activity and LAD usage for **MInfM** students, we examine the boxplots that use the identified activity clusters as groups to display the distribution of LAD accesses (Fig. 2c-2d). The usage patterns of the peer-LAD show a stronger relationship with the activity patterns: the Mann-Whitney U test shows that all comparisons are statistically significant at the 0.05 significance level (Fig. 2d). The usage patterns of the default-LAD show statistically significant differences when highly active students are compared with medium or low active students, but only marginally statistically significant differences between medium and low active students (Fig. 2c).

The relationship between student activity and LAD usage for the **MBISE** students (Fig. 3c - 3d) is less pronounced than for the MInfM program, with more pairwise comparisons not being statistically significant. Statistically significant differences between the LAD accesses by different activity profiles are detected for the peer-LAD, with highly active students accessing the LAD significantly more often than those in the medium or low activity clusters (Fig. 3d). Accesses to the default-LAD differ significantly only between highly active and medium active students, leaving other comparisons insignificant (Fig. 3c).

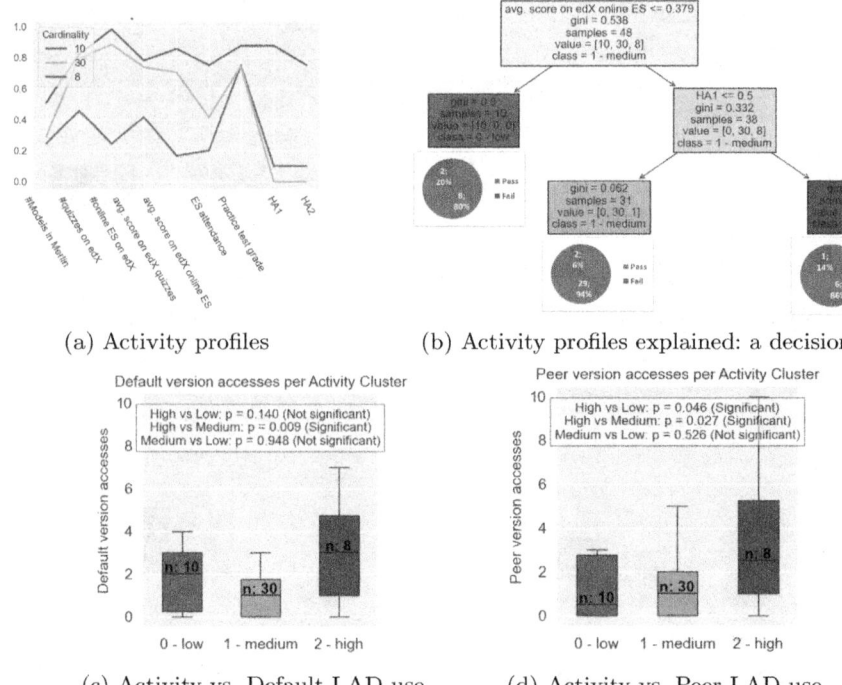

Fig. 3. RQ2 & RQ3: MBISE

4.4 RQ4: Academic Performance vs. LAD Usage

To examine the relationship between academic performance and LAD usage, we examine the boxplots using performance clusters (passing and failing based on the final exam grade) as groups to display the distribution of LAD accesses. For the **MInfM** students, Fig. 4a shows that the differences between LAD usage by passing and failing students are statistically significant for the peer-LAD only, with passing students using the LAD more often compared to failing students. The Pearson correlation between a final grade and LAD accesses is relatively high and statistically significant for the peer-LAD and low and insignificant for the default-LAD. For the **MBISE** students, Fig. 4b shows that there are no significant differences between the usage patterns of both LAD versions by passing and failing students, with the Pearson correlation coefficients being relatively low and insignificant.

To further explore the relationship between LAD usage and academic performance, we introduce the concept of "LAD preference". Specifically, a student is considered to have a "Default preference" if they have accessed the default-LAD at least once, and the number of accesses to the default-LAD exceeds the number of accesses to the peer-LAD. Similarly, a "Peer preference" is defined when a student has accessed the peer-LAD at least once, and the number of accesses to the peer-LAD exceeds the number of accesses to the default-LAD. The cases where both LAD versions are accessed the same number of times or not accessed at all are excluded for this analysis. The preference specification helps differentiate students based on their goal orientation [5]. Students with performance orientation are expected to prefer the peer-LAD, while those who are not performance-oriented are more likely to have the default preference.

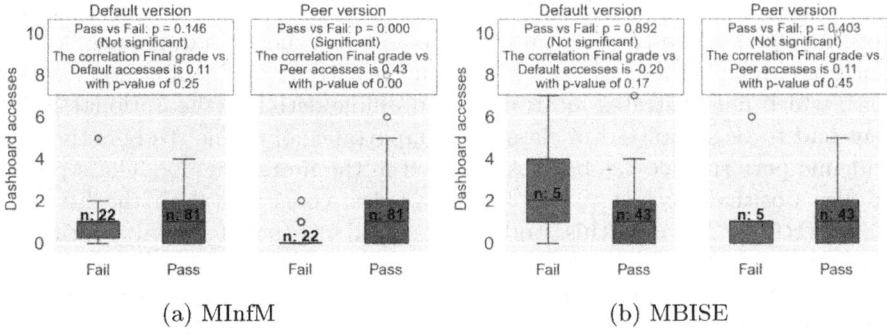

Fig. 4. RQ4: Student performance vs. LAD usage

The boxplots in Fig. 5 illustrate the statistically significant differences in final grades between the peer and default preferences, with the first being superior for both the MBISE and MInfM programs. The LAD users with a peer preference always pass the final exam (minimal grade ≥ 10), with the median grades of 13 and 14 for the MInfM and MBISE groups, respectively.

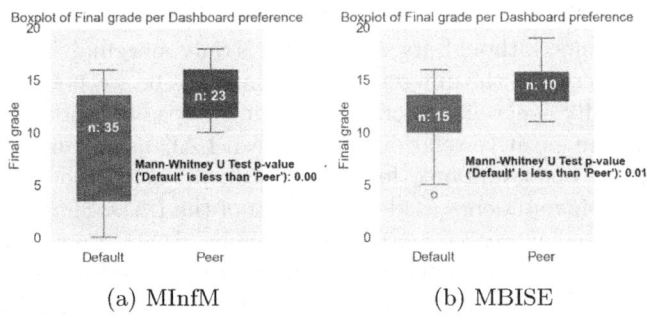

Fig. 5. RQ4: LAD preference vs. Final grade

5 Discussion

In terms of the LAD design (**RQ1**), students showed a preference for simpler visualizations over more complex ones - favoring text over gauges and single-diagram visuals over multiple-diagram formats. Consistent with the literature on visualization preferences [29], bar charts emerged as the favored choice among students. Additionally, students preferred receiving direct feedback on their performance (e.g., grades for assignments and tests) rather than broader feedback on their activity and progress. This preference contrasts with the mastery-oriented approach advocated in CME [34], underscoring the need to further promote mastery goals through improved instructional design.

In line with previous research [39,40], the identified study activity profiles exhibit low, medium, and high levels of engagement on the LMS and learning tools. As the decision trees reveal (Figs. 2b and 3b), the main difference between a medium and a highly active profile lies in the activity for the first home assignment, which demonstrates motivation and offline activity (the optional assignment had to be submitted in class): the importance of offline study activity for academic performance has been established in the literature [40]. These profiles are also positively correlated with final grades, consistent with the literature [39,40] (**RQ2**). Notably, this study only considers student activity during the semester, while the final grade also takes into account retakes. This suggests that consistent engagement throughout the semester is crucial for success, as last-minute efforts during the summer retake period do not compensate for inactivity during the semester. However, this pattern is only observed among MInfM students, as MBISE students tend to pass the final exam regardless of their activity level. This distinction may be explained by differences in their academic background, as MBISE students are required to have completed undergraduate CS courses prior to enrolling in the program. Hence, they have enough knowledge to pass the exam even without extensively studying for it. Exploring the statistical significance of these differences is a potential avenue for future research.

When examining the relationship between study activity and the *peer* LAD usage (**RQ3**), we found a positive and statistically significant correlation for both study programs. Notably, for *both* LAD versions, the correlation is stronger for the MInfM students, although its significance is only marginal for some pairwise comparisons. Therefore, the difference in relationships between activity and LAD use cannot be fully generalized across different groups of students.

The significant positive relationship between LAD usage and academic performance (**RQ4**) was found only for MInfM students using the peer-LAD: more than 50% of passing students used this version of the LAD. Similarly, Somyurek et al. [36] reported increased performance among LAD users who followed a course that required prior knowledge compared to another course that required no prior knowledge. This prior knowledge requirement can be challenging for students who have not had the opportunity to acquire this knowledge in their previous education, as in the case of the MInfM program in our study. However, the majority of MBISE students pass the exam, and this fact may also explain the difficulty in obtaining significant LAD effects for this group. Another possible explanation for the significant relationship found for the peer LAD can be attributed to the fact that students who feel they are doing better than their peers are more likely to seek out the comparison data in the LAD than students who feel they are doing worse than their peers. This is consistent with downward comparison theory [44], which states that "exposure to a less fortunate other (i.e., a downward target) boosts subjective well-being." Examining LAD preferences, we find that performance-oriented students who prefer the peer-LAD tend to achieve higher final exam grades than students who prefer the standard LAD. This finding reinforces the importance of peer reference points in the CME domain. Based on the different results found for both groups, the difference in relationships between performance and LAD use cannot be fully generalized across different groups of students.

The differences in findings between the MInfM and MBISE programs may be attributed to students' familiarity with university teaching and grading practices. MBISE students, having prior academic experience at KU Leuven, may feel more confident about their progress and performance. This could explain the weaker relationships between study activity, academic performance and LAD usage. Similar patterns were reported by Rets et al. [25]: their "distinction" students felt more skeptical about using the LAD, while students with lower scores found the LAD more informative. Despite these differences, some findings hold for both programs. Regarding the association between LAD preference and performance, we observed that among students who used the LAD at least once, those who preferred the peer-LAD (=who are considered performance-oriented) were consistently among those who passed in both the MBISE and MInfM programs.

Overall, our findings illustrate the importance of including the peer component in LADs, especially for programs where students lack background in CM and require more sophisticated learning feedback. Similar to modeling tool support [31], the peer-LAD can facilitate self-regulated learning processes in CME.

Threads to Validity and Future Research. Our study has several limitations. While controlled experiments are a powerful tool for identifying causal relationships, we chose not to employ them in order to remain ethically fair, ensuring that everyone had an equal opportunity to receive progress feedback. We acknowledge that correlation does not imply causation and leave the task of designing fair controlled experiments to assess the impact of LADs in CME to future research. Additionally, other analytical techniques such as interviews or surveys can be explored to provide better insights into the mechanisms behind the observed relationships. The reliance on traditional educational theories, such as Bloom's Taxonomy, may constrain the adoption of more contemporary frameworks, which can be further investigated in future research. Conducting the experiment over a single semester at one institution limits the study's generalizability and highlights the need for future validation across diverse contexts. Additionally, future research can focus on exploring statistical significance of differences of LAD use patterns between MBISE and MInfM students.

6 Conclusion

CME benefits from technological support due to the complex nature of the learning processes required to master modeling skills. Along with existing modeling and prototyping tools, providing feedback to students using LADs can enhance the learning experience and increase student motivation. Social comparison is often used in LADs to provide learners with a reference frame for interpreting data correctly, which is especially important for novice modelers who need to know if they are progressing in the right direction. This paper presented two versions of the LAD used in the context of a CM course taught at several study programs with diverse background requirements: a default-LAD with only mastery and progress reference frames, and a peer-LAD that adds a performance reference frame to the default-LAD. We examined students' preferences for LAD visualizations, the relationship between their study activity and performance, the usage patterns of different LAD versions, and their relationship with student activity, performance, and academic background.

First, simpler visualizations, such as text and bar charts, were the most desirable and students preferred to receive feedback on their performance first. Second, we confirmed the findings of existing studies on the positive relationship between study activity and academic performance. Although ethical considerations did not allow us to conduct a causal analysis through a controlled experiment, our findings remain important for advising students: staying active (both online and offline) has historically been associated with better performance. Third, we discovered a significant relationship between LAD usage and study activity for the students enrolled in the MInfM study program, which has no prior knowledge requirements. This relationship was significant for both the default-LAD and peer-LAD, with the latter being the strongest. Active usage of the peer-LAD was also positively correlated with the study activity of the more experienced MBISE students, although some comparisons were only marginally significant. Finally, a positive relationship was discovered between usage of the peer-LAD and academic performance for the MInfM students, with the peer-LAD preferences being associated with higher and always passing grades for both study programs.

References

1. Aljohani, N.R., Davis, H.C.: Learning analytics and formative assessment to provide immediate detailed feedback using a student centered mobile dashboard. In: 2013 Seventh International Conference on Next Generation Mobile Apps, Services and Technologies, pp. 262–267. IEEE (2013)
2. Bogdanova, D., Snoeck, M.: Domain modelling in bloom: deciphering how we teach it. In: Poels, G., Gailly, F., Serral Asensio, E., Snoeck, M. (eds.) The Practice of Enterprise Modeling, pp. 3–17. Springer International Publishing, Cham (2017)
3. Bogdanova, D., Snoeck, M.: Camelot: an educational framework for conceptual data modelling. Inf. Softw. Technol. **110**, 92–107 (2019)
4. Claes, J., Vanderfeesten, I., Pinggera, J., Reijers, H.A., Weber, B., Poels, G.: A visual analysis of the process of process modeling. ISEB **13**, 147–190 (2015)
5. Covington, M.V.: Goal theory, motivation, and school achievement: an integrative review. Annu. Rev. Psychol. **51**(1), 171–200 (2000)

6. Davis, D., Jivet, I., Kizilcec, R.F., Chen, G., Hauff, C., Houben, G.J.: Follow the successful crowd: raising mooc completion rates through social comparison at scale. In: Proceedings of the LAK Conference, pp. 454–463 (2017)
7. Deeva, G., Bogdanova, D., Serral, E., Snoeck, M., De Weerdt, J.: A review of automated feedback systems for learners: classification framework, challenges and opportunities. Comput. Educ. **162**, 104094 (2021)
8. Duan, X., Wang, C., Rouamba, G.: Designing a learning analytics dashboard to provide students with actionable feedback and evaluating its impacts. In: Proceedings of International Conference on Computer Supported Education (2022)
9. Dutt, A., Ismail, M.A., Herawan, T.: A systematic review on educational data mining. IEEE Access **5**, 15991–16005 (2017)
10. Fleur, D.S., van den Bos, W., Bredeweg, B.: Social comparison in learning analytics dashboard supporting motivation and academic achievement. Comput. Educ. Open **4**, 100130 (2023)
11. Gallagher, T., Slof, B., van der Schaaf, M., Arztmann, M., Fracaro, S.G., Kester, L.: Learning analytics dashboard design: workplace learner preferences for reference frames in immersive training in practice. J. Comput. Assist. Learn. (2024)
12. Guerra, J., Hosseini, R., Somyürek, S., Brusilovsky, P.: An intelligent interface for learning content: combining an open learner model and social comparison to support self-regulated learning and engagement. In: Proceedings of the UIU Conference, pp. 152–163 (2016)
13. Günther, S.A.: The impact of social norms on students' online learning behavior: insights from two randomized controlled trials. In: Proceedings of the LAK Conference, pp. 12–21 (2021)
14. Hevner, A.R., March, S.T., Park, J., Ram, S.: Design science in information systems research. Manag. Inf. Syst. Q. **28**(1), 6 (2008)
15. Jayashanka, R., Hettiarachchi, E., Hewagamage, K.: Technology enhanced learning analytics dashboard in higher education. Electron. J. e-Learn. **20**(2), 151–170 (2022)
16. Jivet, I., Scheffel, M., Drachsler, H., Specht, M.: Awareness is not enough: Pitfalls of learning analytics dashboards in the educational practice. In: Proceedings of the EC-TEL Conference, pp. 82–96. Springer (2017)
17. Jivet, I., Scheffel, M., Schmitz, M., Robbers, S., Specht, M., Drachsler, H.: From students with love: an empirical study on learner goals, self-regulated learning and sense-making of learning analytics in higher education. Internet High. Educ. **47**, 100758 (2020)
18. Jivet, I., Scheffel, M., Specht, M., Drachsler, H.: License to evaluate: preparing learning analytics dashboards for educational practice. In: Proceedings of the LAK Conference, pp. 31–40 (2018)
19. Konert, J., Bohr, C., Bellhäuser, H., Rensing, C.: Peerla-assistant for individual learning goals and self-regulation competency improvement in online learning scenarios. In: 2016 IEEE 16th International Conference on Advanced Learning Technologies (ICALT), pp. 52–56. IEEE (2016)
20. Krathwohl, D.R.: A revision of bloom's taxonomy: an overview. Theory Pract. **41**(4), 212–218 (2002)
21. Loboda, T.D., Guerra, J., Hosseini, R., Brusilovsky, P.: Mastery grids: an open source social educational progress visualization. In: Proceedings of the EC-TEL Conference, pp. 235–248. Springer (2014)
22. Mann, H.B., Whitney, D.R.: On a test of whether one of two random variables is stochastically larger than the other. Ann. Math. Stat. 50–60 (1947)

23. Matcha, W., Gašević, D., Pardo, A., et al.: A systematic review of empirical studies on learning analytics dashboards: a self-regulated learning perspective. IEEE Trans. Learn. Technol. **13**(2), 226–245 (2019)
24. de Quincey, E., Briggs, C., Kyriacou, T., Waller, R.: Student centred design of a learning analytics system. In: Proceedings of the LAK Conference, pp. 353–362 (2019)
25. Rets, I., Herodotou, C., Bayer, V., Hlosta, M., Rienties, B.: Exploring critical factors of the perceived usefulness of a learning analytics dashboard for distance university students. Int. J. Educ. Technol. High. Educ. **18**(1), 1–23 (2021). https://doi.org/10.1186/s41239-021-00284-9
26. Rosenthal, K., Strecker, S., Asensio, E.S., Snoeck, M.: Guest editorial to the special issue on teaching and learning conceptual modeling (2023)
27. Rosenthal, K., Strecker, S., Snoeck, M.: Modeling difficulties in creating conceptual data models: multimodal studies on individual modeling processes. Softw. Syst. Model. **22**(3), 1005–1030 (2023)
28. Santos, J.L., Govaerts, S., Verbert, K., Duval, E.: Goal-oriented visualizations of activity tracking: a case study with engineering students. In: Proceedings of the LAK Conference, pp. 143–152 (2012)
29. Schwendimann, B.A., et al.: Perceiving learning at a glance: a systematic literature review of learning dashboard research. IEEE Trans. Learn. Technol. **10**(1), 30–41 (2016)
30. Schwendimann, B.A., et al.: Perceiving learning at a glance: a systematic literature review of learning dashboard research. IEEE Trans. Learn. Technol. **10**(1), 30–41 (2017)
31. Sedrakyan, G., Snoeck, M.: Technology-enhanced support for learning conceptual modeling. In: International Workshop on Business Process Modeling, Development and Support, pp. 435–449. Springer (2012)
32. Sedrakyan, G., Snoeck, M., De Weerdt, J.: Process mining analysis of conceptual modeling behavior of novices-empirical study using jmermaid modeling and experimental logging environment. Comput. Hum. Behav. **41**, 486–503 (2014)
33. Siemens, G., Long, P.: Penetrating the fog: analytics in learning and education. EDUCAUSE Rev. **46**(5), 30 (2011)
34. Sins, P.H., van Joolingen, W.R., Savelsbergh, E.R., van Hout-Wolters, B.: Motivation and performance within a collaborative computer-based modeling task: relations between students' achievement goal orientation, self-efficacy, cognitive processing, and achievement. Contemp. Educ. Psychol. **33**(1), 58–77 (2008)
35. Somyürek, S., Brusilovsky, P., Çebi, A., Akhüseyinoğlu, K., Güyer, T.: How do students perceive their own and their peers' progress in e-learning? Int. J. Inf. Learn. Technol. **38**(1), 49–74 (2020)
36. Somyürek, S., Brusilovsky, P., Guerra, J.: Supporting knowledge monitoring ability: open learner modeling vs. open social learner modeling. Res. Pract. Technol. Enhanc. Learn. **15**(1), 1–24 (2020). https://doi.org/10.1186/s41039-020-00137-5
37. Taniguchi, Y., Owatari, T., Minematsu, T., Okubo, F., Shimada, A.: Live sharing of learning activities on e-books for enhanced learning in online classes. Sustainability **14**(12), 6946 (2022)
38. Tiukhova, E., Verbruggen, C., De Laet, T., Baesens, B., Snoeck, M.: Learning analytics dashboard with peer comparison for student feedback in conceptual modeling education: online appendices (2025). https://doi.org/10.5281/zenodo.15007566
39. Tiukhova, E., Vemuri, P., Óskarsdóttir, M., Poelmans, S., Baesens, B., Snoeck, M.: Discovering unusual study patterns using anomaly detection and XAI. In: Proceedings of the HICSS (2024)

40. Tiukhova, E., Verbruggen, C., Baesens, B., Snoeck, M.: Learning analytics tells: know your basics and go to class. In: CEUR Workshop Proceedings, vol. 3618. CEUR Workshop Proceedings (2024)
41. Tzimas, D., Demetriadis, S.: Ethical issues in learning analytics: a review of the field. Educ. Tech. Res. Dev. **69**, 1101–1133 (2021)
42. Valle, N., et al.: Predict or describe? how learning analytics dashboard design influences motivation and statistics anxiety in an online statistics course. Educ. Technol. Res. Dev. **69**(3), 1405–1431 (2021)
43. West, D., Luzeckyj, A., Toohey, D., Vanderlelie, J., Searle, B.: Do academics and university administrators really know better? the ethics of positioning student perspectives in learning analytics. Australas. J. Educ. Technol. **36**(2), 60–70 (2020)
44. Wills, T.A.: Downward comparison principles in social psychology. Psychol. Bull. **90**(2), 245–271 (1981). https://doi.org/10.1037/0033-2909.90.2.245
45. Winne, P.H., Baker, R.S., et al.: The potentials of educational data mining for researching metacognition, motivation and self-regulated learning. J. Educ. Data Min. **5**(1), 1–8 (2013)

Are Code and Design Models Similarly Effective in Understanding Software Structure and Behavior?

Iris Reinhartz-Berger[1](✉) and Monique Snoeck[2]

[1] Department of Information Systems, University of Haifa, Haifa, Israel
iris@is.haifa.ac.il
[2] Research Center for Information System Engineering (LIRIS), KU Leuven, Leuven, Belgium
monique.snoeck@kuleuven.be

Abstract. Developers dedicate an average of 58% of their time to software comprehension, highlighting its critical role in software maintenance and evolution. This significant investment underscores the need of tools and methods that facilitate effective understanding. While prior research has primarily explored the use of models as complementary aids for understanding code, limited evidence exists regarding their standalone effectiveness in conveying software's structural and behavioral aspects. This gap is particularly relevant in contexts such as Model-Driven Engineering (MDE), low-code, and no-code approaches, where models often serve as the primary or sole representation of software.

In this paper, we report on a controlled experiment evaluating the effectiveness of understanding software structure and behavior through detailed design models compared to code. The study involved undergraduate IS students who completed comprehension tasks (designed along Bloom's taxonomy) using either code or model, based on their preference.

The results indicated no statistically significant differences in correctness between participants using models and those using code. However, participants working with code completed tasks related to software behavior significantly faster. These findings highlight the need for further research into enhancing the use of models as standalone artifacts for software comprehension, particularly in situations where access to code is limited or impossible.

Keywords: Software Comprehension · Code Comprehension · Model Comprehension · Controlled Experiment · Bloom's Taxonomy

1 Introduction

Around 80% of software lifecycle costs are devoted to system maintenance [1]. On average, developers spend 58% of their time on program comprehension [2]. Therefore, effective understanding is crucial for any software development or maintenance task. The costs associated with projects involving extensive software reuse and updates are heavily affected by factors related to software comprehension. These factors include understanding the software's structure and behavior, the clarity and the self-descriptiveness of its

© The Author(s), under exclusive license to Springer Nature Switzerland AG 2025
R. Guizzardi et al. (Eds.): BPMDS 2025/EMMSAD 2025, LNBIP 558, pp. 318–334, 2025.
https://doi.org/10.1007/978-3-031-95397-2_20

artifacts, the developer's level of (un)familiarity with the domain, and the effort required for assessment and assimilation, which can range from basic reading to comprehensive test and evaluation [1].

To facilitate software comprehension, models are often used as abstract representations of systems. At design time, models assist in transforming requirements into conceptual designs and documenting system architecture [3]. They are particularly useful for analyzing architectural decisions and identifying potential defects early [4]. During maintenance, models are used as complementary aids for understanding code. However, methodologies such as Agile, which emphasize iterative development and rapid delivery, often limit the extensive use of models. As a result, domain models are often overlooked or underutilized [5, 6]. Furthermore, as software evolves, discrepancies between initial models and actual implementations frequently lead to inadequate documentation and outdated representations of the code [7, 8]. This problem is exacerbated by local practices and time constraints, which hinder effective documentation efforts.

Consequently, software understanding may need to be based on code alone. However, in the context of Model-Driven Engineering (MDE), modern integrated development environments, such as Visual Paradigm and Eclipse, support roundtrip engineering between models and code. Unlike conceptual models, which abstract away technical details, these models are highly detailed and accurately reflect the current state of the code. Since abstraction is intended to facilitate communication and understanding by omitting details, it raises the question of whether design models – offering detailed graphical representations of structural and behavioral aspects of the software – are more effective for software comprehension than simply the code itself.

With the growing adoption of low-code and no-code development platforms [9], organizations increasingly face situations where models serve as the primary or sole representation of software, with the underlying code inaccessible (e.g., Flutterflow, Bubble.io) or available only at additional costs (e.g., Mendix, Outsystems). These scenarios raise broader questions about the costs and benefits of model-based maintenance. Specifically, it remains unclear whether understanding software through its model representation alone is more or less effective – or leads to better or worse comprehension – compared to the code itself. To the best of our knowledge, no rigorous studies have systematically addressed the standalone comprehension of software models versus code, particularly using a cognitive framework. Given the prevalence of situations where access to code is limited or costly, this paper examined the correctness, efficiency and productivity of understanding software structure and behavior through design models versus code using Bloom's Taxonomy [10, 11].

The rest of the paper is structured as follows. Section 2 provides related work and the needed background; Sect. 3 describes the experimental design; Sect. 4 presents the results; and Sect. 5 discusses implications and threats to validity. Finally, Sect. 6 concludes and refers to future directions.

2 Related Work and Background

Model and Code Comprehension. Model comprehension has been studied extensively (e.g., [12–16]), but these studies primarily focus on understanding conceptual models per se, without considering their corresponding code artifacts. More importantly, the models used in such research are typically highly abstract and omit design details important for understanding software structure or behavior.

A review of 40 years of research on code comprehension experiments shows that comprehension support (e.g., through models) has received far less attention compared to factors such as semantic cues, developer characteristics, and code structure [17]. When models are considered in these studies, they are generally used as supplementary artifacts alongside the code, rather than as standalone artifacts [18, 19]. This leaves a critical gap in investigating the effectiveness of models as primary instruments for software comprehension. The research in [20], for example, investigates the use of UML documentation on software maintenance tasks. While UML documentation does not reduce completion time, it does improve the correctness and quality of solutions for complex tasks. The authors attribute this improvement to a learning effect: as participants advance to more complex tasks, they better appreciate the benefits of using the diagrams. The research in [21] found that participants using UML diagrams consistently performed as well as, or better than, those not using them, where the no-UML group encountered greater difficulties in understanding the most complex part of the system. Here again differences in completion time were not statistically significant, but the UML group was slightly faster on average.

The longitudinal study in [18] presents a meta-analysis of 12 experiments, with mixed results across the individual studies. Out of the 12 experiments, four provided statistically significant findings: three in favor of using models for code comprehension, and one indicating better comprehension when models are not used. Comprehension time was measured in only four of the experiments, with two statistically significant but contradictory results. The authors considered the type of models used in the experiment, and the meta-analysis suggests that UML models affect code comprehension in two opposing ways: the models produced during the *analysis phase* can reduce code comprehension and increase the time to complete the tasks; Conversely, models produced during the *design phase* improve code comprehension and reduce completion time. These findings suggest that the closer a model is to the code, the more effective it may be for comprehension. The study in [19] recommends the use of UML class diagrams created during the *design phase*. These diagrams were found to improve understanding more effectively than reverse engineered diagrams, which participants deemed less helpful. Nevertheless, design diagrams are not always available. In our study, we use reverse engineered models, in order to assure information equivalence to the code. Such detailed models can also be used for generating code in MDE environments or creating applications in no-code or low-code approaches.

Bloom's Taxonomy. The challenges associated with model or code comprehension are not unique; many disciplines face similar issues, including a lack of systematic resources, diverse approaches, and the absence of universally accepted learning objectives. To address these challenges, various classification frameworks have been suggested, with Bloom's taxonomy [10, 11] being one of the most widely recognized foundations for creating structured educational frameworks and assessment tools. Its influence extends across a wide variety of fields including biology [22–24], anatomy [25], as well as software engineering [26], and in particular modeling [27, 28].

Bloom's taxonomy [11] presents a matrix that categorizes six levels of cognitive processes (Remember, Understand, Apply, Analyze, Evaluate, Create) alongside four different types of knowledge (Factual, Conceptual, Procedural, Metacognitive). For the specific purpose of this research, we focus on the cognitive process level of "Understanding", which involves explaining ideas and concepts, and "Conceptual" knowledge type, which emphasizes notions and the relationships among the fundamental elements.

Table 1 presents the sub-categories of "Understanding" in Bloom's taxonomy, with their descriptions and examples focusing on conceptual knowledge. These skills collectively contribute to a deeper comprehension of the software, enabling developers to navigate complex codebases, make informed decisions, and foster effective collaboration within development teams.

Table 1. Sub-categories of Understanding in Bloom's Taxonomy

Sub-category	Description	Software Comprehension Example
Interpreting	Converting information from one form to another (e.g., paraphrasing, translating)	Interpreting a sequence diagram to describe the interaction between different components
Exemplifying	Providing examples or illustrations of a concept	Providing an example of a recursive function to illustrate the concept of recursion
Classifying	Categorizing or organizing information into groups	Classifying different types of software bugs (e.g., logic, syntax, and runtime errors) based on their causes
Summarizing	Condensing information into a concise statement	Summarizing the purpose of a software function after reading its code
Inferring	Drawing logical conclusions from evidence or data	Inferring the likely behavior of a program by analyzing the flow of control structures in the code

3 The Experimental Design

This study aims to explore whether detailed design models (hereafter referred to as models), such as reverse-engineered models or those used for code generation, are as comprehensible and effective for understanding software as the code itself. To achieve this, we conducted a controlled experiment whose main elements are summarized in Table 2. Following the guidelines of Wohlin et al. [29], this section describes the experimental design, including goals, settings, tasks, participants and related procedures.

3.1 Goals, Hypotheses and Variables

The *goal* of the study is to analyze the understanding of software structure and behavior, with the *purpose* of identifying the software artifact that facilitates the most correct understanding while minimizing the time needed. The *researchers' perspective* concentrates on examining how the use of *either* code or model – specifically class and sequence diagrams – affects both correctness and efficiency (i.e., completion time). Acknowledging the potential trade-off between correctness and efficiency, we introduced a third dependent variable: productivity, which is calculated as a combined measure of correctness and efficiency.

Table 2. Overview of the experimental study

Goal	To analyze the understanding of software structure and behavior
Context	A controlled experiment with 18 questions – 9 on structural aspects and 9 on behavioral aspects; Overall, the responses of 46 participants were analyzed
Independent variables	• Artifact type (code vs. model)
Additional experimental factors	• Software aspect (structure vs. behavior) • Understanding sub-category (classification, comparison, exemplification, explanation, inference, interpretation, summarization)
Dependent variables	• Correctness (score ranged between 0 and 1) • Efficiency (completion time in seconds) • Productivity (the number of correct answers per time unit)
Hypotheses	H_{01}: There is no significant difference in overall correctness, efficiency, or productivity between participants using models and those using code to understand software H_{02}: There is no significant difference in correctness, efficiency, or productivity across software aspects (structural vs. behavioral), regardless of whether models or code are used H_{03}: There is no significant difference in correctness, efficiency, or productivity across different understanding sub-categories, regardless of whether models or code are used

Accordingly, we formulated the following research questions:

RQ1: Which type of *software artifact* – code or model – leads to better overall understanding of software in terms of correctness, efficiency, and productivity?

RQ2: To what extent does understanding *software aspects* – structure versus behavior – vary in correctness, efficiency, and productivity when using models vs. code?

RQ3: How do different *understanding sub-categories* – classification, comparison, exemplification, explanation, inference, interpretation, summarization – vary in correctness, efficiency, and productivity when using models vs. code?

As shown in Table 2, the null hypotheses suggest that the artifact type (code or model) does not influence correctness, efficiency and productivity. The independent variable is the *artifact type*, which can be either *code* or its *model*; The additional experimental factors are the *software aspect*, which can focus on *structure* or *behavior*, and the *understanding sub-category*, which, according to Bloom's taxonomy, can involve *classification, comparison, exemplification, explanation, inference, interpretation,* or *summarization*. The study's dependent variables, representing the observed outcomes, include *correctness* – scored between 0 and 1; *efficiency*, completion time measured in seconds; and *productivity*, as the number of correct answers per time unit.

3.2 Settings

The study followed a between-subject experimental design. The software we used is of a simple elevator system, taken from [30] and implemented in Java. The system is structured into four packages: ui, sim, model, and controller. The *ui* package manages the user interface components, including the main window, while the *sim* package is responsible for simulation-related functionality. The *model* package represents the core domain logic, including the *Elevator* class, and, finally, the *controller* package governs the coordination and execution of system operations through a control unit.

The objects of the study were the code of this system and a UML model that was created by reverse engineering[1] the code into class and sequence diagrams, which capture structure and behavior, respectively. For behavioral aspects, we concentrated on the functionality of the *control unit* which includes operations such as running the system, calculating an elevator's next state, listening to tick events, and more (overall five non-trivial operations). Each operation was represented in a separate sequence diagram; five sequence diagrams overall. However, the questions specifically targeted the *run* operation, as its logic is particularly interesting and more complex.[2]

To reduce variability, all participants were required to use the same tools – Eclipse[3] for the code artifacts and Visual Paradigm[4] for the model artifacts – both of which they were expected to have prior experience with.

To assign participants to experimental groups, we used a pre-experiment questionnaire to assess their self-perceived knowledge and experience in software modeling and object-oriented programming. Randomly distributing the participants could have resulted in individuals working with artifacts they are less familiar with, potentially introducing bias. To mitigate this, we aimed to measure the participants' proficiency in coding and modeling. Unfortunately, no standardized and validated instruments exist for this purpose. Given that people are likely to prefer working with the artifact they feel most comfortable with, we opted to let the participants work with the artifact they felt most confident using. A few days before the experiment took place, the participants were asked to complete a pre-experiment questionnaire[5] assessing their perceived knowledge and experience in Java, UML, Eclipse and Visual Paradigm. Based on the responses, participants were divided into two groups: those feeling more familiar and experienced

---

[1] The code was reverse-engineered using a well-known modeling tool – Visual Paradigm.
[2] The experimental material can be found at: https://zenodo.org/records/15252652.
[3] https://eclipseide.org/
[4] https://www.visual-paradigm.com/
[5] The pre-experiment questionnaire is included in the experimental material.

in programming were assigned to the *code* group, while those feeling more familiar and experienced in modeling were assigned to the *model* group.

3.3 Tasks

In line with the proposed terminology in [17], and assuming that the participants are unfamiliar with the domain of elevator controllers, we characterize the assignment as a bottom-up understanding task rather than (top-down) mapping pre-existing knowledge to software pieces. Furthermore, according to the classification in [31], the tasks can be characterized as inference-based understanding as opposed to expectation-based comprehension. In other words, the given artifacts are very detailed and the tasks do not assume existing knowledge of the participants on the domain or the software.

Participants were instructed to first explore the provided software artifact (code or model) in the designated tool (Eclipse or Visual Paradigm) before answering 18 questions, ensuring that the time spent on exploring the artifact did not contribute to the completion times of the initial questions. Table 3 lists the questions, their software aspects and understanding sub-categories. Note that the questions were all close-ended, with answers available in the experimental material (See Footnote 2). The participants used their computers to explore the artifacts via the tools and their mobile phones to view and respond to the questions. Each question was presented individually and in a random order, with no option to revisit previously answered questions. All questions related to structural aspects were presented before those related to behavioral aspects, to first establish a foundational understanding of software structure, upon which the behavior is built.

After completing all the questions, participants were asked to fill out a post-experiment questionnaire. This questionnaire, also included in the experimental materials, assessed their perceived confidence and opinions on the effectiveness of the artifacts and tools used for performing the tasks.

3.4 Participants

The experiment was conducted during a mandatory annual project course in the third (final) year of an undergraduate (B.Sc.) Information Systems program. Throughout their studies, students complete a range of courses, including procedural programming in C, object-oriented programming in Java, information systems design and implementation using UML and Java, and information systems analysis with UML and BPMN. In the annual project course, students are required to analyze, design, implement, and deploy an IT solution for a "real" client from industry or academia. The course includes several enrichment lectures, one of which covered roundtrip engineering, where our experiment was conducted.

64 students participated in the enrichment lecture, but only 49 completed the pre-experiment questionnaire on time and answered the questions according to the artifact type assigned to them before the experiment. Of those, 48 provided informed consent[6] to use their responses for this research, so we analyzed only their answers.

---

[6] This research was approved by the Institutional Review Board (IRB) at the University of Haifa, Israel; Application no. 233/24.

Table 3. The comprehension questions

Software Aspect	#	Question	Understanding Sub-Category
Structure	Q01	How are the **ui** and **sim** packages related, if at all?	Interpretation
	Q02	How do the **core** and **sim** packages compare in terms of their responsibilities and interactions?	Comparison
	Q03	Which of the following exemplifies the dependencies between the **core** and **ui** packages?	Exemplification
	Q04	What are the **top-level** packages of the Elevator software?	Classification
	Q05	What can be inferred about the indirect relationship between the **SimulationUnit** and **FloorComposite** classes?	Inference
	Q06	What are the purposes of the **core** package, in terms of the MVC pattern?	Summarization
	Q07	What is the functional role of the **FloorComposite** class?	Interpretation
	Q08	Which of the following sentences explains the role of the **Elevator** class?	Explanation
	Q09	For calculating the next state of the elevator, what information can the **control unit** base its decision on?	Inference
Behavior	Q10	For how long does the **run** method of the **control unit** wait before the next moving cycle?	Interpretation
	Q11	Which of the following exemplifies a situation in which the **triggerOnTick** method is called when the **control unit** is running?	Exemplification
	Q12	Which of the following sentences explains the role of the **Thread** object when the **control unit** is running?	Explanation
	Q13	What happens when the **control unit** is running and the elevator state is **MOVING_UP**?	Summarization

(*continued*)

Table 3. (*continued*)

Software Aspect	#	Question	Understanding Sub-Category
	Q14	How do handling **FLOORING** and **MOVING_UP/ MOVING_DOWN** differ when the **control unit** is running?	Comparison
	Q15	How long does the **run** method of the **control unit** run?	Inference
	Q16	How many **different** methods of the **Elevator** class are used when the **control unit** is running?	Classification
	Q17	What is the **third** method executed when the **control unit** is given the instruction to **run**, assuming that the elevator state is **MOVING_DOWN**?	Interpretation
	Q18	What does **TIME_DELAY** simulate when the **control unit** is running?	Inference

3.5 Instrumentation, Data Collection and Cleaning

The experiment was conducted during an online enrichment lecture as part of the annual project course. Participants began with a 20-min introduction to roundtrip engineering, which included examples and a discussion of its strengths and limitations. They then performed the experiment tasks and filled out a post-experiment questionnaire. Responses to the understanding questions and the post-experiment feedback were collected via LimeSurvey. The final 15 min of the session were devoted to summarizing the experiment and presenting the initial results.

Correctness of a question was measured as a score between 0 to 1. Single-value questions, which required participants to select one correct answer from a list of options, were assessed based on whether the participant chose the correct option (1) or not (0). Multi-value questions, on the other hand, could get partial scores, evaluating whether participants identified all relevant correct answers while avoiding incorrect selections. For example, if a question had two correct answers out of four, and a participant selected both correct answers but also included one incorrect answer, they would receive a score of 0.75. We summed up the scores for structure, behavior, and overall, as well as for each understanding sub-category, and presented them in percentages.

The completion time of each question was recorded by LimeSurvey in seconds, with the constraint that participants could not revisit answered questions. During the analysis, we observed a few instances where the completion times for specific questions and participants were very long, possibly indicating breaks or other interruptions during the experiment. To address these anomalies, we used the z-score measure to identify and account for outliers: following the advice in [32], long completion times with z-scores beyond the thresholds of +3 were adjusted to the maximal allowed deviation (+3) from the mean. Two observations of extremely short completion times (164.41 and 90.82 s overall, compared to at least 500 s for all other participants) were excluded, resulting in a final count of 46 participants.

Finally, we examine productivity, defined as the number of correct answers per time unit. Formally expressed: $\frac{CorretnessScore}{CompletionTime/MaximalCompletionTime}$, where the maximal completion time represents the longest completion time taken by a participant across both groups (model or code). Since both numerator and denominator represent values between 0 and 1, a "standard" productivity score is 1.0 (e.g., 80% correctness in 80% of the time). A score above 1.0 indicates greater productivity, where higher correctness is achieved in less time (e.g., 80% correctness in 40% of the time). Conversely, a score below 1.0 reflects lower productivity, with fewer correct answers requiring more time (e.g., 80% correctness in 100% of the time).

3.6 Analysis Procedure

We used boxplots to summarize succinctly the outcomes. In all our statistical tests, we decided to accept a probability of 5% of committing a Type-I-error. Normality was assessed using the one-sample Kolmogorov-Smirnov test, which indicated that most metrics, including both correctness and efficiency, deviated from the normal distribution. As a result, we applied non-parametric tests for all analyses, considering both p-value and adjusted p-value (Bonferroni correction).

4 Results

4.1 Results for Correctness

Figure 1 presents the correctness score distributions for all three research questions. The Wilcoxon rank sums test, used to assess differences in the overall correctness between the code and model groups (RQ1), revealed no statistically significant differences (p-value of 0.938 for structure, 0.370 for behavior, and 0.527 overall).

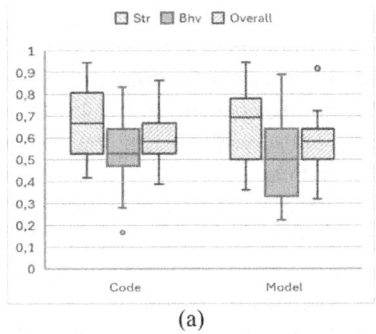
(a)

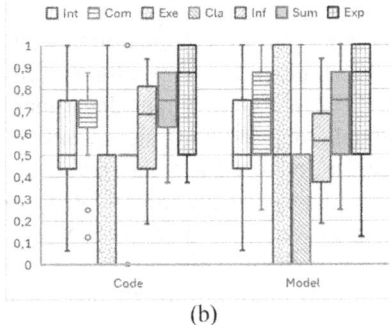
(b)

Fig. 1. Correctness score distributions: (a) structure (str) vs. behavior (bhv) vs. overall. (b) understanding sub-categories

Nevertheless, participants in both groups performed significantly better on structure-related questions than on behavior-related questions (RQ2). For the code group, the Wilcoxon signed ranks test revealed significant differences in correctness between the two aspects (Z = −3.03, p-value = 0.002), with median scores of 0.6667 for structure and 0.5278 for behavior. Similarly, for the model group, the Wilcoxon signed ranks test showed significant differences (Z = −2.59, p-value = 0.010), indicating a significant structure-behavior comprehension gap, with median scores of 0.6944 for structure and 0.5000 for behavior. These results highlight a clear trend where participants, regardless of the artifact type, demonstrated a stronger understanding of structural aspects compared to behavioral ones.

A deeper analysis of correctness across specific understanding sub-categories (see Fig. 1(b), RQ3) revealed significant variations, particularly within the code group. The Friedman's two-way ANOVA test for the code group showed a p-value < 0.001 ($\chi^2(6)$ = 42.4), prompting post-hoc tests with Bonferroni correction. The results indicated significant differences between multiple sub-categories, including exemplification (Exe) versus explanation (Exp; adjusted p-value < 0.001), summarization (Sum; adjusted p-value = 0.001) and comparison (Com; adjusted p-value = 0.004), as well as classification (Cla) versus both explanation (Exp; adjusted p-value < 0.001) and summarization (Sum; adjusted p-value = 0.011). Similarly, significant differences among sub-categories were found in the model group (p-value < 0.001, $\chi^2(6) = 29.8$): classification (Cla) versus both explanation (Exp; adjusted p-value = 0.004) and summarization (Sum; adjusted p-value = 0.009) and exemplification (Exe) versus explanation (Exp; adjusted p-value = 0.23) and summarization (Sum; adjusted p-value = 0.049). For both groups, exemplification stood out as the weakest area and classification was worse than explanation and summarization. These results are further discussed in Sect. 5.

> In summary, with respect to correctness, H_{01} can be accepted, while H_{02} and H_{03} can be rejected. In other words, for novice developers, code and design models are similarly effective for correct understanding, but differences exist in comprehension of various aspects.

4.2 Results for Efficiency

Figure 2 presents the completion time distributions for all three research questions. The Wilcoxon rank sums test reveals no significant differences in overall completion times (p-value = 0.226, RQ1), with median times of 347.03 s for the code group and 453.35 s for the model group. While no significant differences were observed in the completion times of structure-related questions (p-value = 0.842), significant differences were found in completion times of questions related to behavior (p-value = 0.016). Notably, significant differences were identified for questions Q10–Q12 with p-values of 0.024, 0.019 and 0.031, respectively.

Across both groups, participants demonstrated statistically significant faster completion times for behavior-related questions compared to structure-related ones (RQ2). The Wilcoxon signed-rank test showed highly significant results for both the code group (Z = −4.52, p-value < 0.001) and the model group (Z = −3.54, p-value < 0.001).

Figure 2(b) presents the distribution of completion times along the understanding sub-categories (RQ3). The Friedman's two-way ANOVA test revealed significant differences in both groups (p-value $= 0.027$, $\chi^2(6) = 14.3$ for the code group and p-value $= 0.021$, $\chi^2(6) = 14.9$ for the model group). The only significant pairwise differences found in post-hoc Wilcoxon signed-rank tests after applying the Bonferroni correction are: classification (Cla) vs. inference (Inf; adjusted p-value $= 0.034$) for the code group and classification (Cla) vs. comparison (Com; adjusted p-value $= 0.034$). The median times suggest high values for comparison and inference tasks in both groups. Interestingly, the code group exhibited greater variability in completion times for structure-related tasks, with outliers more pronounced compared to behavior-related tasks.

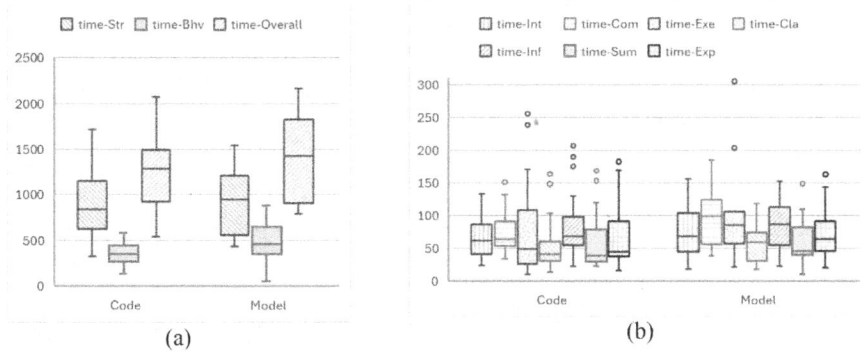

Fig. 2. Completion time distributions: (a) structure (str) vs. behavior (bhv) vs. overall. (b) understanding sub-categories

---

To summarize, with respect to efficiency, H_{01} can be accepted, while H_{02} and H_{03} can be rejected. In other words, for novice developers, code and design models are similar in the overall time needed for understanding different aspects of software, but the understanding of behavior-related aspects takes significantly more time with design models. Also, differences exist in the time needed to address various tasks for each software artifact.

4.3 Results for Productivity

As can be seen in Fig. 3, the productivity of the code group is better in terms of structure, behavior and overall (RQ1). However, the Wilcoxon rank sums test shows significant differences only for behavior-related questions (p-value $= 0.007$): the model group is much less productive when it comes to behavior. The productivity of answering structure-related questions was significantly better than that of behavior-related questions only in the model group (p-value $= 0.010$, $Z = 2.58$; RQ2).

Figure 3(b) presents the distribution of productivity along the understanding sub-categories (RQ3). The Friedman's two-way ANOVA test revealed significant differences in both groups (p-value = 0.006, $\chi^2(6)$ = 18.1 for the code group and p-value = 0.011, $\chi^2(6)$ = 16.5 for the model group). The only significant pairwise differences found in the post-hoc Wilcoxon signed-rank tests after applying the Bonferroni correction is exemplification (Exe) vs. summarization (Sum) for the code group (adjusted p-value = 0.031).

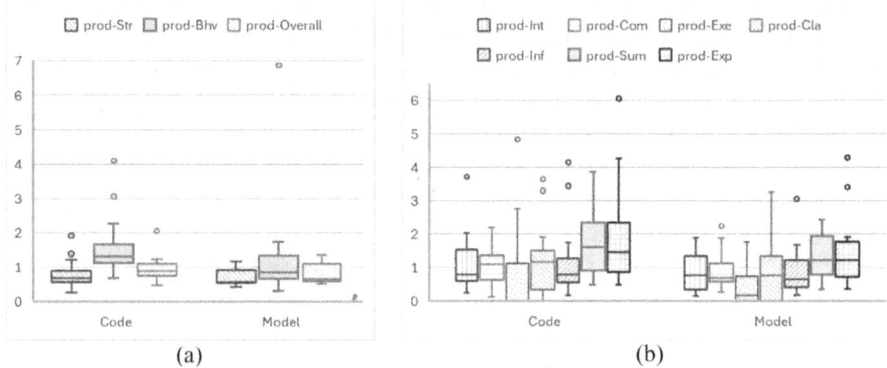

Fig. 3. Productivity distribution: (a) structure (str) vs. behavior (bhv) vs. overall. (b) understanding sub-categories

---

To summarize, with respect to productivity, H01 can be accepted, H02 can be accepted for the code group and rejected for the model group, and H03 can be rejected for both groups. In other words, for novice developers, code and design models demonstrate overall similar effectiveness in terms of productivity. However, productivity in understanding behavior-related aspects is significantly higher with code (due to greater efficiency in achieving a similar level of correctness). Also, productivity differences exist with respect to various tasks for each group.

5 Discussion and Threats to Validity

While prior research on model comprehension has often reported mixed benefits [17], models are being used more and more frequently as the primary or sole representation of software in contemporary approaches. Our results show that (at least for novices) detailed design models can be effectively used to a wide extent to understand different structural and behavioral aspects of software, even when the code is not accessible. Although this understanding may sometimes be less accurate and require more time, the lack of statistically significant differences in correctness and the overall efficiency highlights the comparable utility of both artifact for software comprehension tasks.

As opposed to previous research, our experiment allows a finer granular analysis along software aspects and understanding sub-categories. Consistent with previous studies, our participants demonstrated higher correctness for structural aspects over behavioral ones, reaffirming the findings in [16], where students' understanding of UML class diagrams shows relatively better results than their understanding of system behavior modelled by means of parallel statecharts.

We further observed some significant differences among understanding subcategories that persisted across both groups. First, *exemplification* emerged as the weakest area, potentially since the questions required a deeper level of understanding, as participants needed to not only identify and comprehend a given exemplar but also relate it to broader concepts and constructs within the software. Second, *classification* questions were answered less correctly than *explanation* and *summarization* questions. Unlike tasks that involve explaining or summarizing, which focus on utilizing or describing existing knowledge, classification requires both abstraction and reasoning and demands a higher level of cognitive engagement. This suggests that more targeted training or support may be needed to help participants develop the necessary skills for abstract thinking and classification, which could improve overall performance in complex tasks.

Regardless of the artifact type, participants responded faster to behavior-related than to structure-related questions. The larger variability in completion times for structure-related questions suggests that some of these posed greater challenges, requiring more time for participants to explore different parts of the artifact and synthesize the needed information. In contrast, the shorter completion times for behavior-related tasks may be attributed to their focus on a specific scenario – the *run* operation of the *control unit*. This focused scope required understanding a single operation within one class, which might have been more straightforward than grasping behavior spread across multiple interacting classes. Prior research indeed indicates that students tend to perform better on structure-related tasks [15] than on tasks involving behavioral understanding across multiple interacting components [16]. This calls for further research with more intricate scenarios. Additionally, the significantly more time needed to answer the behavior-related questions in the model group, which also led to significantly lower productivity of that group, may originate from the selection of the sequence diagram notation to represent behavior. The impact of choosing other notations (e.g. statecharts) on efficiency and productivity of behavior comprehension is to be further explored.

Next, we list the main validity threats of our study, according to Wohlin et al.'s categorization [29], and the actions taken to mitigate them. ***Conclusion validity***: The use of non-parametric tests was required due to the small number of participants and the deviations from normality. Despite this, the analysis yielded consistent trends across groups and tasks, supporting the reliability of the conclusions. ***Internal validity***: The experiment's structure may have introduced learning effects, as structure-related questions preceded behavior-related ones, potentially enhancing participants' comprehension of behavior or shortening completion times. Yet, as the same order was applied to all participants, its impact on the comparative results is likely minimal. Another concern was the deviation of some participants from their pre-assigned groups, leading to their exclusion and resulting in imbalanced group sizes (27 in the code group, 19 in the model group). Despite this, the sample sizes in both groups were comparable to those used in similar studies and were deemed sufficient for meaningful statistical analysis. ***Construct validity***: The tasks were designed to evaluate both structure and behavior comprehension, but behavior-related tasks were restricted to a single class. While this simplification ensured feasibility within the experimental timeframe, it limits the generalizability of findings and requires further investigation of more complex scenarios. Additionally, the experience level of participants was assessed through a pre-survey questionnaire based on self-perception. While this approach aimed to respect participants' preferences and mitigate discomfort with unfamiliar tools, relying solely on self-assessment introduces a potential threat. Self-perceptions may not accurately reflect actual proficiency, which could affect the balance between groups. Incorporating an objective test could help strengthen the accuracy of group assignments in future replications. *External validity*: The relatively small size of the system and the student-based participant pool also constrain the generalizability of our findings. Nevertheless, the system used was realistic for educational contexts, and students have been shown to serve as reliable proxies for early-career professionals in empirical studies [33]. Further research is needed to validate these findings in professional settings, using larger and more complex systems. Additionally, while UML [7, 34] and Java[7] are widely used, future studies should explore a broader range of modeling languages (including other types of UML diagrams) and assess environments aligned with no-code and low-code approaches.

6 Conclusions and Future Work

The research presented in this paper compared the effectiveness of code and detailed design models (in particular reverse-engineered models) for understanding software structure and behavior. The tasks included questions across all understanding categories of Bloom's taxonomy. While the results suggest that code generally outperforms models in terms of correctness, efficiency and productivity, most differences are not statistically significant. These findings support scenarios where models serve as the primary or sole representation of software, such as in MDE, no-code and low-code approaches. However, the results also highlight the challenges in comprehending software behavior in general and particularly when using models, as evidenced by significantly lower efficiency and productivity. This calls for further research to improve comprehension in such contexts. Additionally, exemplification emerged as the weakest area of understanding, and classification was found to be less effective than explanation and summarization when using both code and models.

Given the limited scope of this study in terms of participant numbers and system complexity, further research is needed to generalize the findings to other settings and enhance their robustness. In particular, including a third group of participants exposed to both code and diagrams can provide valuable insights into how the combination of representations influences comprehension. Nonetheless, the results suggest potential challenges for organizations where the code is not readily available, particularly regarding maintenance. Moreover, the setting of the experiment, specifically in terms of project size and participant profile (i.e., students vs. practitioners), should be extended to support generalizability of the findings. Future research should also investigate software comprehension within particular MDE, low-code and no-code tools, which commonly describe behavior through workflow diagrams.

---

[7] https://spectrum.ieee.org/top-programming-languages-2024.

Disclosure of Interests. The authors have no competing interests to declare that are relevant to the content of this article.

References

1. Boehm, B.W., et al.: Software Cost Estimation with COCOMO II, 1st edn. Prentice Hall Press, USA (2009)
2. Xia, X., Bao, L., Lo, D., Xing, Z., Hassan, A.E., Li, S.: Measuring program comprehension: a large-scale field study with professionals. In 2018 IEEE/ACM 40th International Conference on Software Engineering (ICSE), p. 584 (2018). https://doi.org/10.1145/3180155.3182538
3. Ludewig, J.: Models in software engineering – an introduction. Softw. Syst. Model. **2**(1), 5–14 (2003). https://doi.org/10.1007/s10270-003-0020-3
4. Ardagna, D., Ghezzi, C., Mirandola, R.: Rethinking the use of models in software architecture. In: Becker, S., Plasil, F., Reussner, R. (eds.) Quality of Software Architectures. Models and Architectures, pp. 1–27. Springer Berlin Heidelberg (2008)
5. Rios, N., Mendonça, M., Seaman, C., Spínola, R.: Causes and Effects of the Presence of Technical Debt in Agile Software Projects (2019)
6. Alfraihi, H.A.A., Lano, K.C.: The Integration of Agile Development and Model Driven Development: A Systematic Literature Review, Portugal (2017)
7. Verbruggen, C., Snoeck, M.: Practitioners' experiences with model-driven engineering: a meta-review. Softw. Syst. Model. (2022). https://doi.org/10.1007/s10270-022-01020-1
8. Ulziit, B., Warraich, Z.A., Gencel, C., Petersen, K.: A conceptual framework of challenges and solutions for managing global software maintenance. J. Softw. Evol. Process **27**(10), 763–792 (2015). https://doi.org/10.1002/smr.1720
9. Gartner. Gartner Forecasts Worldwide Low-Code Development Technologies Market to Grow 20% in 2023. https://www.gartner.com/en/newsroom/press-releases/2022-12-13-gartner-forecasts-worldwide-low-code-development-technologies-market-to-grow-20-percent-in-2023. Accessed 04 October 2024
10. B. S. Bloom and C. of C. and U. Examiners, Taxonomy of Educational Objectives, vol. 2. Longmans, Green New York (1964)
11. Krathwohl, D.R.: A revision of bloom's taxonomy: an overview. Theory Pract. **41**(4), 212–218 (2002). https://doi.org/10.1207/s15430421tip4104_2
12. Figl, K.: Comprehension of procedural visual business process models: a literature review. Bus. Inf. Syst. Eng. **59**(1), 41–67 (2017). https://doi.org/10.1007/s12599-016-0460-2
13. Weitlaner, D., Guettinger, A., Kohlbacher, M.: Intuitive comprehensibility of process models. In: Communications in Computer and Information Science (2013). https://doi.org/10.1007/978-3-642-36754-0_4
14. Recker, J., Reijers, H.A., van de Wouw, S.G.: Process model comprehension: the effects of cognitive abilities, learning style, and strategy. Commun. Assoc. Inf. Syst. **34**(1) (2014)
15. Sedrakyan, G., Snoeck, M., Poelmans, S.: Assessing the effectiveness of feedback enabled simulation in teaching conceptual modeling. Comput. Educ. **78**, 367–382 (2014). https://doi.org/10.1016/j.compedu.2014.06.014
16. Sedrakyan, G., Poelmans, S., Snoeck, M.: Assessing the influence of feedback-inclusive rapid prototyping on understanding the semantics of parallel UML statecharts by novice modellers. Inf. Softw. Technol. **82** (2017). https://doi.org/10.1016/j.infsof.2016.11.001
17. Wyrich, M., Bogner, J., Wagner, S.: 40 years of designing code comprehension experiments: a systematic mapping study. ACM Comput. Surv. **56**(4) (2023). https://doi.org/10.1145/3626522

18. Scanniello, G., et al.: Do software models based on the UML aid in source-code comprehensibility? Aggregating evidence from 12 controlled experiments. Empir. Softw. Engg. **23**(5), 2695–2733 (2018). https://doi.org/10.1007/s10664-017-9591-4
19. Fernández-Sáez, A.M., Genero, M., Chaudron, M.R.V., Caivano, D., Ramos, I.: Are forward designed or reverse-engineered UML diagrams more helpful for code maintenance? A family of experiments. Inf. Softw. Technol. **57**, 644–663 (2015). https://doi.org/10.1016/j.infsof.2014.05.014
20. Arisholm, E., Briand, L.C., Hove, S.E., Labiche, Y.: The impact of UML documentation on software maintenance: an experimental evaluation. IEEE Trans. Softw. Eng. **32**(6), 365–381 (2006). https://doi.org/10.1109/TSE.2006.59
21. Dzidek, W.J., Arisholm, E., Briand, L.C.: A realistic empirical evaluation of the costs and benefits of UML in software maintenance. IEEE Trans. Softw. Eng. **34**(3), 407–432 (2008). https://doi.org/10.1109/TSE.2008.15
22. Crowe, A., Dirks, C., Wenderoth, M.P.: Biology in bloom: implementing bloom's taxonomy to enhance student learning in biology. CBE – Life Sci. Educ. **7**(4), 368–381 (2008). https://doi.org/10.1187/cbe.08-05-0024
23. Zheng, A.Y., Lawhorn, J.K., Lumley, T., Freeman, S.: Application of bloom's taxonomy debunks the 'MCAT Myth'. Science (1979) **319**(5862), 414–415 (2008). https://doi.org/10.1126/science.1147852
24. Zaidi, N.B., Hwang, C., Scott, S., Stallard, S., Purkiss, J., Hortsch, M.: Climbing Bloom's taxonomy pyramid: lessons from a graduate histology course. Anat. Sci. Educ. **10**(5), 456–464 (2017). https://doi.org/10.1002/ase.1685
25. Thompson, A.R., O'Loughlin, V.D.: The Blooming Anatomy Tool (BAT): a discipline-specific rubric for utilizing Bloom's taxonomy in the design and evaluation of assessments in the anatomical sciences. Anat. Sci. Educ. **8**(6), 493–501 (2015). https://doi.org/10.1002/ase.1507
26. Starr, C.W., Manaris, B., Stalvey, R.H.: Bloom's taxonomy revisited: specifying assessable learning objectives in computer science. SIGCSE Bull. **40**(1), 261–265 (2008). https://doi.org/10.1145/1352322.1352227
27. Bogdanova, D., Snoeck, M.: CaMeLOT: an educational framework for conceptual data modelling. Inf. Softw. Technol. **110**(June), 92–107 (2019). https://doi.org/10.1016/j.infsof.2019.02.006
28. Biggs, J.: Enhancing teaching through constructive alignment. High. Educ. (Dordr.) **32**(3), 347–364 (1996). https://doi.org/10.1007/BF00138871
29. Wohlin, C., Runeson, P., Höst, M., Ohlsonn, M.C., Regnell, B., Wesslén, A.: Experimentation in Software Engineering. Springer Science & Business Media (2012)
30. Meinicke, J., Thm, T., Schrter, R., Benduhn, F., Leich, T., Saake, G.: Mastering Software Variability with FeatureIDE, 1st edn. Springer Publishing Company Incorporated (2017)
31. O'Brien, M.P., Buckley, J., Shaft, T.M.: Expectation-based, inference-based, and bottom-up software comprehension: research Articles. J. Softw. Maint. Evol. **16**(6), 427–447 (2004)
32. Baesens, B.: Analytics in a Big Data World: The Essential Guide to Data Science and Its Applications. John Wiley & Sons (2014)
33. Falessi, D., et al.: Empirical software engineering experts on the use of students and professionals in experiments. Empir. Softw. Eng. **23**(1), 452–489 (2018). https://doi.org/10.1007/s10664-017-9523-3
34. van der Linden, D., Hadar, I., Zamansky, A.: What practitioners really want: requirements for visual notations in conceptual modeling. Softw. Syst. Model. **18**(3), 1813–1831 (2019). https://doi.org/10.1007/s10270-018-0667-4

Towards a Maturity Assessment Framework for MBSE Adoption: Results from a Meta-synthesis

Tobias Henoeckl, Charlotte Verbruggen(✉)[ID], and Dominik Bork[ID]

Business Informatics Group, TU Wien, Austria
{charlotte.verbruggen,dominik.bork}@tuwien.ac.at

Abstract. As engineering systems become increasingly complex, organizations must adopt strategic approaches to manage the interdependencies of their processes, tools, and teams. Model-Based Systems Engineering (MBSE) offers a promising solution, but transitioning from a traditional SE approach to MBSE is a complex endeavor that requires significant organizational change. This paper addresses the need for structured guidance in this process by proposing a maturity assessment framework that supports organizations in navigating this transition. The proposed framework is developed using a design science based approach and identifies key challenges, pitfalls, and best practices that are organized into several maturity levels of MBSE adoption. This structured, high-level approach provides organizations with the tools to understand their current maturity level, prioritize efforts, and avoid common missteps. The framework allows organizations to tailor the insights to their unique context, ensuring practical applicability. It emphasizes the importance of leadership, cultural readiness, technical tools, workforce development, and modeling practices for successful MBSE implementation.

Keywords: MBSE adoption · maturity assessment · framework · design science

1 Introduction

MBSE is often suggested as a solution when facing challenges during the development of complex systems [6,14]. Its effectiveness during product development has been proven in numerous studies in academia as well as in industry, with advantages of improved system understanding, reduction of development time, reduction of errors, increased consistency, and traceability, improved communication, and others [36]. Although the benefits that come with the transition to MBSE are manifold, so are the challenges faced during the adoption phase [11,21]. Breaking up the traditional way of working in a company is not an easy task and the path of this transition is not clearly defined. Several surveys and studies have been conducted with varying outcomes and different best practices that have to be taken into consideration, making it difficult for practitioners and researchers alike to prioritize among them [46]. Currently the research is lacking a holistic perspective on MBSE adoption, bringing together all the mentioned aspects, challenges faced, potential pitfalls, and best practices as well as a form of contextual prioritization. The aim of this paper is to investigate the adoption of MBSE in companies and provide an overview of the associated challenges, pitfalls, and best practices during the transition from a traditional approach of Systems Engineering to a model-based approach. While the current literature covers various aspects with regard to MBSE adoption, the challenges and difficulties encountered, the lessons learned and best practices discovered, this information remains fragmented across numerous sources. In this paper, we conduct a meta-synthesis of literature on challenges, pitfalls, and best practices for MBSE adoption. The result of this meta-synthesis is a prescriptive and comprehensive maturity assessment framework that addresses this fragmentation and is populated with the identified challenges, pitfalls, and best practices. The challenges should highlight potential issues that the organization should actively aim to resolve, while pitfalls should highlight issues that should be avoided. The best practices should fulfill the prescriptive nature of the proposed maturity framework, by providing actionable advice on overcoming challenges and pitfalls. Given that challenges, pitfalls, and best practices can be seen as different perspectives on the same underlying issue, the framework might contain some redundancies. However, we chose these categories to preserve the viewpoints expressed in the literature and ensure the prescriptive quality of the framework. The research question we address is the following:

RQ What challenges, pitfalls, and best practices have been identified in the literature on MBSE adoption, and how do they relate to the maturity of MBSE adoption in an organization?

In the remainder of this paper, Sect. 2 presents related work, followed by the methodology in Sect. 3. The resulting framework is presented in Sect. 4. Section 5 consists of an initial evaluation and critical reflection, followed by a conclusion in Sect. 6.

2 Related Work

To the best of our knowledge, there is no research on maturity assessment frameworks that provide prescriptive guidance for navigating the changes required for successful MBSE adoption. To identify related work, we first searched for publications on maturity assessment frameworks in the domain of IS engineering by considering the proceedings of CAISE, EMMSAD/BPMDS, and POEM. Korsten et al. [31] developed a maturity model for organizational capabilities. Anwar et al. [5] developed a maturity model in the domain of information security audit processes. Haidar et al. [19] proposed a maturity assessment for agile development adoption in the domain of software product lines. They organize agile practices in a two-dimensional framework consisting of maturity levels and categories. van Zwienen et al. [57] propose a method for tailoring a generic maturity model for enterprise architecture to a specific domain. They apply their proposed method to develop an enterprise architecture maturity model for hospitals. These publications all apply design science research approaches and evaluate their results using illustrative examples and/or feedback from practitioners.

As further discussed in Sect. 3, we also conduct a literature review on MBSE adoption in organizations. Two reviewed publications address research gaps comparable to our research question. The INCOSE MBSE initiative [27] presents a descriptive maturity assessment model that assesses an organization's current state of MBSE adoption and offers benchmarking against competitors or industry averages. While this paper provides clear assessment criteria for concerns such as managing requirements, modeling efforts and technical issues, it does not address other criteria such as the organization's culture and leadership buy-in. It also does not provide prescriptive guidelines for a company to advance their adoption of MBSE. Amorim et al. [3] provides no assessment, but valuable decision support for prioritizing tasks and capabilities during MBSE adoption. They introduce a framework used to calculate which capabilities to prioritize for optimizing the ROI. While this publication offers a valuable method for prioritizing specific capabilities during MBSE adoption, it focuses on task-level decisions rather than a holistic maturity assessment of the entire transition process.

3 Methodology

To answer the research question, we aim to develop a high-level overview for organizations to understand their MBSE adoption level and receive actionable steps tailored to each maturity level. In this way, the maturity assessment serves as an applied synthesis, transforming dispersed knowledge from the literature into a structured framework that aims to help practitioners navigate MBSE adoption with greater clarity and direction. In developing our maturity assessment, we adhere to the research methodology for maturity assessment design outlined by [13] and [30], who build on principles of design science research. In [13], the six phases of developing a maturity assessment model are (1) determining the scope; (2) designing the framework, (3) populating the framework, (4) testing the framework, (5) deploying the framework and (6) maintaining the framework. This paper follows phases 1–4. The phases 5–6 are considered future work.

Scope. Our maturity assessment is not focused on a specific domain but serves as a general guidance for any organization interested in adopting or transitioning to MBSE. It is meant for academia as a novel synthesized baseline of knowledge as well as for practitioners during their MBSE journey.

Design. In our framework, challenges, pitfalls, and best practices of MBSE adoption are categorized in cumulative maturity levels, meaning that challenges, pitfalls, and best practices from lower levels are a prerequisite for higher maturity levels. These levels were determined based on the context provided in the literature. Based on a recommendation from [13], we developed four to five targeted questions per level that practitioners can use to determine the maturity level of MBSE adoption: if all questions for a level are answered with a Yes, they continue to the next level. Once a No is encountered, that level is assigned as their current maturity level. This approach balances comprehensive assessment with ease of use, enabling a practical evaluation without an overwhelming number of questions.

Populate. The next step in the development of a maturity assessment is to identify the information necessary for a deeper understanding of maturity and how this can be measured. The goal is to gather input that, when organized across defined maturity levels, remains mutually exclusive and collectively exhaustive on the topic of interest. For established domains, this is often achieved through a comprehensive literature review [13,30]. We conducted a systematic literature review aimed at identifying the challenges, pitfalls, and best practices in MBSE adoption following the guidelines by Kitchenham [29]. We searched four scientific databases (ACM Digital Library, IEEE, Scopus, and Wiley Online Library) with the following query:

$$\text{Query} = (\bigvee MBSE_i) \wedge (\bigvee ADOPTION_j) \; \textbf{where}$$
$MBSE_i \in \{$"mbse" $\vee$ "model-based system* engineering" $\vee$ "document-cent* system* engineering" $\vee$ "dbse" $\vee$ "digital engineering" $\vee$ "digital model-based engineering"$\}$

and

$ADOPTION_j \in \{$"adoption" $\vee$ "implementation" $\vee$ "transition" $\vee$ "switch*" $\vee$ "experience*" $\vee$ "challenge*" $\vee$ "strateg*" $\vee$ "best practice*"$\}$

Our initial search was performed on the 5th of March 2024 and resulted in 1,295 potentially relevant publications (1,672 before removing duplicates). After applying six exclusion criteria (Publications only reporting on MBSE, DBSE or Digital Engineering in general but not on its adoption in practice; Publications not written in English; Publications where the full text is not accessible; Non-Peer-reviewed and non-scientific publications; Publications with less than 5 or more than 60 pages; Publications that are published before 2014), the selection was further reduced to 346 publications. From the remaining publications, 102 were selected to be included in the literature review based on their abstract. Another 7 publications were excluded as the full text was not accessible. As a final step, we conducted a backward and forward search in Google Scholar to identify additional relevant research. This resulted in 19 additional publications bringing the selection to 114 publications. These papers were analyzed in full. Of the 114 read papers, 44 contributed challenges, pitfalls, and best practices to the framework.

For all eventually selected papers, the reported challenges, pitfalls, and best practices for MBSE adoption were extracted to populate the maturity assessment framework. The process followed to identify and organize the challenges, pitfalls, and best practices adheres to principles from grounded theory; first, codes were assigned to relevant concepts and memos were created to document insights and support the synthesis of the identified codes. Additionally, four maturity levels for MBSE adoption were derived based on literature on maturity assessment frameworks. The synthesis of codes resulted in the final set of challenges, pitfalls,

Table 1. References for each Challenge (C) in MBSE Adoption

C	References	C	References
C1	[9] [20] [11] [26] [28] [10] [54] [53] [1]	C9	[54] [11] [4] [21] [2] [28] [50] [49]
C2	[26] [40] [41] [46] [21] [2] [10] [47] [38] [54] [53] [1]	C10	[20] [28]
C3	[9] [26] [46] [21] [37] [28] [1]	C11	[40] [11] [41]
C4	[9] [21] [28] [47] [53] [48] [1]	C12	[11] [21] [2] [54]
C5	[26] [44] [21] [37] [2] [38] [49] [54]	C13	[44]
C6	[26] [40] [41] [46] [52] [37] [11] [28] [53]	C14	[20] [2] [15] [1]
C7	[21] [37] [11] [54]	C15	[40] [41]
C8	[20] [37] [11] [28] [54] [1]	C16	[11] [47] [54]

and best practices that could then be grouped in the identified maturity levels. We found limited guidance in the existing literature on how to prioritize challenges, pitfalls, and best practices within maturity levels. While [46] offers some direction by analyzing how contextual factors influence best practices, their conclusion remains that all best practices are generally relevant and context affects the order of priority rather than the applicability of practices themselves. This insight aligns with our structured approach, as our maturity levels naturally prioritize practices according to the general level of MBSE readiness. Furthermore, some topics identified in the literature keep repeating across challenges, pitfalls, and best practices, reflecting their relevance in different contexts. As an effort to improve visual clarity and overall structure within each level, we categorize challenges, pitfalls, and best practices into the following five categories: *Knowledge and Skills*; *Work Culture*; *Management*; *Methodology, Language, and Tools*; and *Modeling*.

Evaluation. To test and evaluate the maturity model, we conduct an initial validation survey aimed at domain experts investigating the respondents' MBSE background, their level of agreement with the assessment, and potential areas for improvement. In future work, a full evaluation would ideally involve extensive case studies to assess the accuracy of maturity assignments and the utility of our recommendations.

4 Results

In this section, we present the four levels of maturity for MBSE adoption and the challenges (C), pitfalls (P), and best practices (BP) for each level. Tables 1, 2 and 3 list the sources for each Challenge, Pitfall, and Best Practice respectively.

Each organization is unique, with distinct characteristics, goals, and constraints that only its management fully understands. However, for a transition as complex and context-dependent as MBSE, providing precise instructions that are applicable in any organizational context is neither practical nor achievable. Therefore, the assessment intentionally focuses on a holistic, high-level approach, enabling companies to identify critical areas for attention while ensuring that no key aspect of the adoption process is overlooked.

Table 2. References for each Pitfall (P) in MBSE Adoption

P	References	P	References
P1	[55] [56]	P7	[55] [21] [7] [56]
P2	[55]	P8	[44] [21] [32] [42] [56]
P3	[44]	P9	[44] [55]
P4	[40]	P10	[55]
P5	[7]	P11	[44]
P6	[55] [21] [32] [7] [56]		

Table 3. References for each Best Practice (BP) in MBSE Adoption

BP	References	BP	References	BP	References
BP1	[20] [4] [46] [21] [39] [16] [1]	BP12	[10] [37] [34] [7] [49] [53]	BP23	[10] [44] [7]
BP2	[10] [4] [46] [21] [39] [16] [49] [45]	BP13	[9] [44] [37] [21]	BP24	[4] [40] [41] [37] [21] [54]
BP3	[4] [8] [12] [46] [37] [21] [47] [7] [54]	BP14	[4] [21] [38] [49]	BP25	[9] [8] [21] [35] [38] [51]
BP4	[20] [10] [4] [40] [41] [8] [46] [37] [21] [39] [7] [16] [45] [53]	BP15	[4] [40] [46] [55] [21] [39]	BP26	[40] [4] [41] [7] [54] [9]
BP5	[9] [20] [12] [7] [46] [37] [21] [54] [53]	BP16	[20] [12] [46] [37] [21] [49]	BP27	[40] [41] [21]
BP6	[20] [4] [8] [25] [46] [37] [21] [49] [45] [53] [51]	BP17	[40] [41] [20]	BP28	[40] [41] [44] [37]
BP7	[20] [4] [12] [46] [21] [39] [7] [53]	BP18	[10] [4] [55] [21]	BP29	[40] [41] [21] [43]
BP8	[10] [8] [18] [46] [23] [37] [21] [38] [7] [49] [54] [45] [53]	BP19	[20] [10] [40] [41] [7] [16]	BP30	[10] [44] [21] [2] [35] [54] [43]
BP9	[12] [37] [47] [33]	BP20	[40] [41] [34] [53] [8]	BP31	[20] [21] [2] [49] [17] [51]
BP10	[10] [40] [41] [46] [37] [21] [35] [22] [7]	BP21	[20] [23] [21] [7] [10] [40] [44] [37] [2] [35] [34] [38]		
BP11	[4] [8] [12] [37] [21]	BP22	[4] [46]		

This approach empowers management to derive tailored, lower-level instructions and actionable steps from the holistic framework specific to their organization's needs. For example, while the assessment emphasizes the importance of selecting tools that integrate effectively with existing infrastructure, the specific tool choice depends on the organization's unique technical and operational requirements. Similarly, while it highlights the need to address knowledge gaps and align divergent understandings of MBSE, the exact methods and content of training to achieve this must be determined by the organization itself. The maturity assessment outlined in this section provides a structured and comprehensive collection of challenges, pitfalls, and best practices. In the literature, 16 challenges, 11 pitfalls, and 31 best practices were identified. A complete list with descriptions for each challenge, pitfall and best practice can be found in the online appendix [24]. Table 4 shows how they are distributed over the maturity levels and categories. The identified challenges are distributed fairly evenly over the four maturity levels, while most best practices are reported in the second maturity level and most pitfalls are reported in the third maturity level. However, the distribution over categories shows a shift in focus; challenges, pitfalls, and best practices belonging to the more people-centric categories "Knowledge and Skills" and "Work Culture" are only represented in the lower maturity levels. On the other hand, challenges, pitfalls, and best practices related to "Methodology, Language, and Tools" occur in the second and third maturity level while elements related to "Modeling" occur in the third and fourth maturity level. The only category that is represented across all levels is "Management".

Table 4. Overview of all in the literature identified Challenges (C), Pitfalls (P), and Best Practices (BP) in MBSE Adoption

Category	Maturity level			
	Level 1 C P BP	Level 2 C P BP	Level 3 C P BP	Level 4 C P BP
Work Culture	1 – –	– – –	– – –	– – –
Knowledge and Skills	3 – –	1 – –	– – –	– – –
Management	– – 3	3 3 9	– 2 2	2 2 1
Methodologies, Languages and Tools	– – –	1 – 3	1 – 1	– – –
Modeling	– – –	– – –	2 4 6	2 – 6

The categories "Management" and "Modeling" are by far the most populated categories, with 27 and 20 elements, respectively.

4.1 Maturity Level 1: Initial Preparation

This maturity level marks the foundational phase of any organization's transition toward MBSE. It focuses primarily on preparing the workforce and management for upcoming changes, establishing a shared understanding, and addressing early challenges. This level sets essential prerequisites for a successful MBSE adoption.

There are no specific pitfalls mentioned in the literature that could be classified into Level 1 of this maturity assessment. We attribute this absence to the nature of the term itself. Pitfalls are defined as avoidable mistakes or traps that teams may fall into during the process of MBSE adoption. However, at this early level, the focus is on establishing a common ground and building the correct understanding, rendering it more about addressing fundamental challenges rather than avoiding missteps. These foundational aspects, like ensuring a mutual understanding of terms, goals, and reasons, are so critical that they tend to be classified as challenges or best practices, rather than pitfalls (Fig. 1).

To demonstrate the use of the framework, we include an example for Level 1 (detailed descriptions of each challenge and best practice can be found in the online appendix [24]). A challenge for Level 1 is cultural resistance to change (C1). This challenge rises from the fact that engineers and stakeholders are traditionally accustomed to working with and reviewing documents, making the transition to models as primary artifacts a substantial shift in established workflows. A lack of training and time to adapt can lead to a deficiency in understanding MBSE's value and processes (see also C2). Such gaps not only foster skepticism but can create a belief among employees that their systems are too large or complex to be effectively integrated into an MBSE framework, leading to cultural resistance to change. This challenge can be mitigated by fostering an understanding of the value of MBSE (BP3). This Best Practice states that it is essential that employees not only understand the theoretical benefits of MBSE,

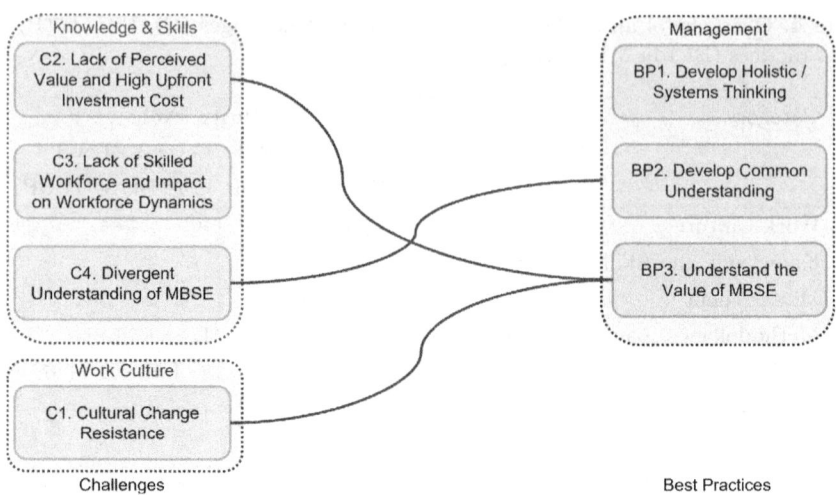

Fig. 1. Simplified overview of Maturity Assessment Level 1: Initial Preparation

but also recognize how it can improve their own work, such as enhancing efficiency, quality, and reducing effort. This understanding helps build a unified workforce that supports the transition. Targeted presentations and demonstrations of successful project experiences can further reinforce the value proposition and motivate engineers to collaborate toward successful adoption. This is crucial for fostering commitment and overcoming the inertia often encountered with organizational change (C1).

4.2 Maturity Level 2: Planning and Structure

Once initial preparation is completed, this maturity level emphasizes strategic planning and structural decisions. Key actions include defining clear goals and scope, implementing progress metrics, managing expectations, and establishing the necessary infrastructure and teams. This sets a solid foundation for subsequent modeling efforts and enables the launch of MBSE in pilot projects (Fig. 2).

For example, a Challenge at Level 2 is the need to define a clear scope and goals (C8). Without a well-defined scope, there is a risk of over-enthusiasm to model the whole organization (or a large part of it) from the start. This challenge leads to the Pitfall of having a fast false start (P1) with too many initiatives, causing skepticism within the organization, reinforcing the belief that modeling doesn't work. To avoid this Pitfall, organizations should think big, start small, and evolve (BP6). A strategic MBSE approach should begin by identifying clear, long-term goals, but manage the uncertainty and complexity of the transition by introducing small, manageable steps. Starting with a small, highly motivated group or a pilot project allows the organization to experiment in a controlled environment, learning from the specific challenges of the involved

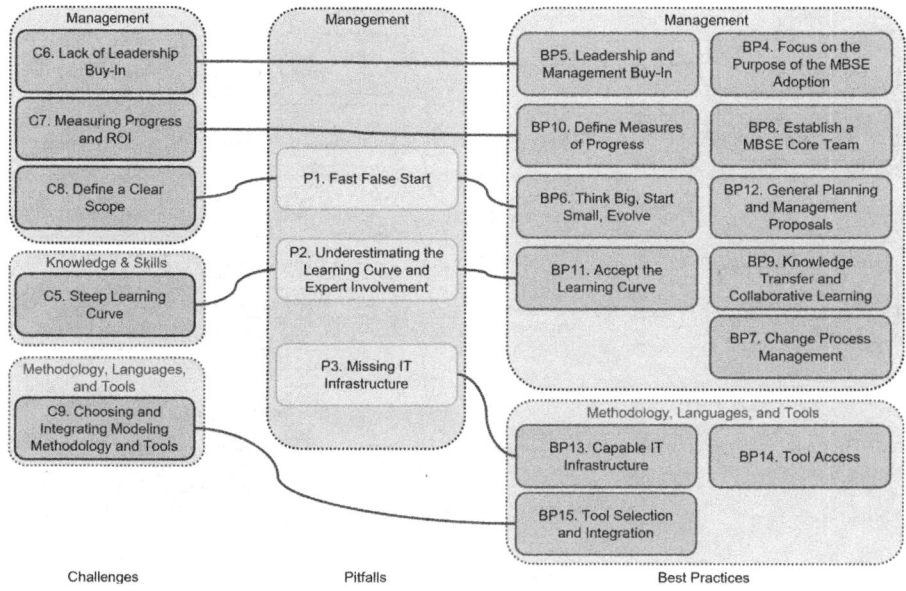

Fig. 2. Simplified overview of Maturity Assessment Level 2: Planning and Structure

processes, domains, and tools. This approach helps to identify and resolve issues early, creating a foundation for broader adoption.

4.3 Maturity Level 3: Pilot Projects

At this maturity level, organizations are applying MBSE to specific pilot projects. This is the first level to involve active modeling, requiring strategic decisions and preparatory steps to avoid early missteps. Key objectives include maximizing the return on pilot efforts, ensuring best practices in modeling, and building a foundation for sustainable MBSE use across future projects (Fig. 3).

For example, a Challenge at Level 3 is a lack of a clear modeling purpose (C11). While high-level MBSE goals are clear, many struggle to ensure that individual models are tailored to answer well-defined questions or meet specific project needs. Without this clarity, there is a risk of overmodeling (P7) or creating models for the sake of modeling (P6), which can lead to inefficiencies and models that are not as effective or communicative as they could be. Therefore, it is essential to clearly define the model's purpose when embarking on any modeling initiative (BP19). These purposes should be articulated as specific questions that the model is intended to answer. This way the model is clearly finished when all relevant questions can be answered. By aligning each model with specific, measurable outcomes and reducing unnecessary maintenance efforts, organizations can ensure that MBSE drives meaningful results and supports business objectives effectively.

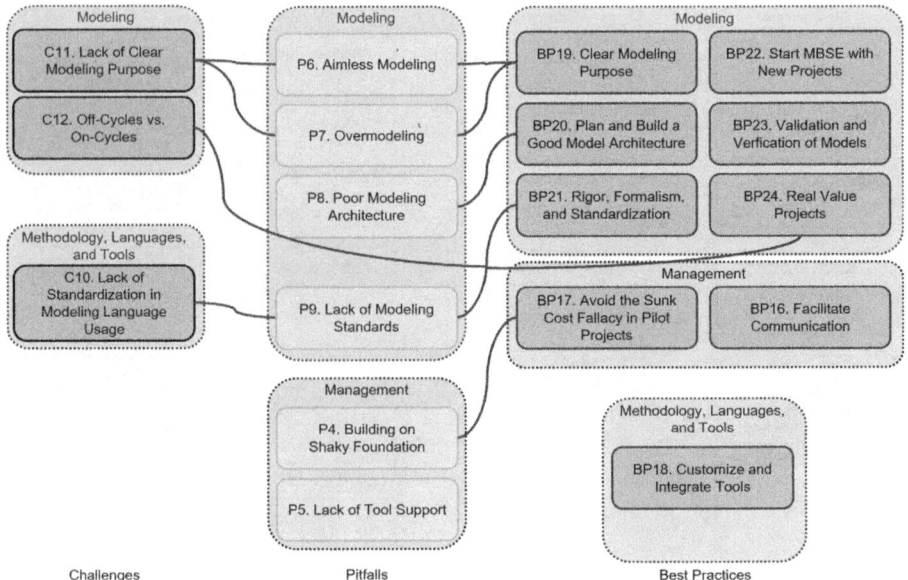

Fig. 3. Simplified overview of Maturity Assessment Level 3: Pilot Projects

4.4 Maturity Level 4: Scaling MBSE Adoption

After pilot projects have been completed, the final maturity level focuses on scaling MBSE adoption across the organization. Here, the focus is on expanding the MBSE application, improving modeling efficiency, and establishing robust maintenance and long-term management of models. This level aims to secure the long-term value and success of the MBSE approach by fully integrating it within organizational processes (Fig. 4).

For example, a Challenge at Level 4 is the need for reusability and model libraries (C16). Establishing modularity and reusability requires careful planning to ensure consistency and efficiency across the system models. The Pitfall of poor management and enforcement of reuse libraries (P11) occurs when libraries of reusable models are not properly maintained or consistently enforced. Without clear guidelines, teams may fail to use existing models effectively, leading to duplication of effort, inconsistencies, and wasted time. A key best practice when scaling MBSE adoption is to start developing and utilizing libraries of reusable model elements (BP30). As organizations gain experience through pilot projects, the creation of libraries for interfaces, components, and other reusable system elements becomes essential for accelerating future projects. Establishing modular and reusable libraries like interface-, component-, or unit-libraries, enables teams to avoid starting from scratch for each project, streamlining model development and fostering consistency across efforts. By making reusable models and modularity a cornerstone of the MBSE process, organizations can significantly accelerate project timelines and drive the successful scaling of MBSE across the enterprise.

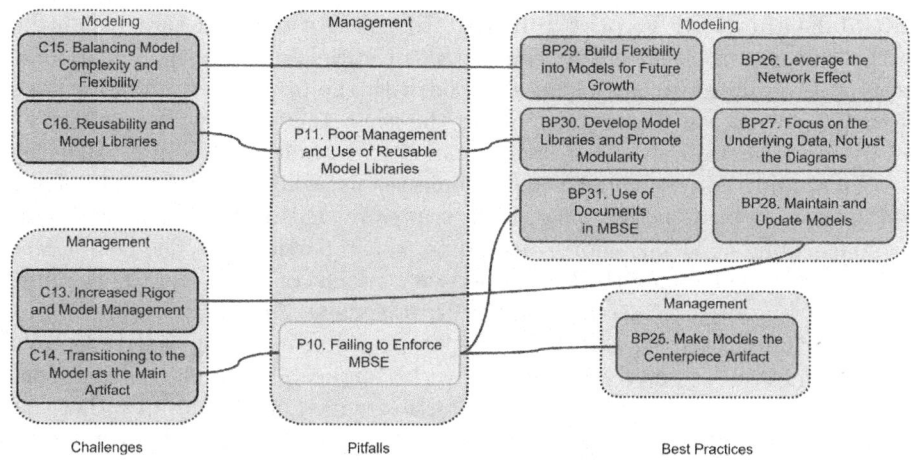

Fig. 4. Simplified overview of Maturity Assessment Level 4: Scaling MBSE adoption

4.5 Self-assessment Questionnaire

The main goal of this questionnaire is to provide a pragmatic tool for organizations to easily identify at which maturity level of MBSE adoption they are. As stated in Sect. 2, we found limited guidance in the literature on developing such a questionnaire. Therefore, we formulated 3–5 questions per level covering the key aspects of that level. As long as all questions for a level can be answered with a "Yes", the organization progresses to the next level. The full set of questions can be found in the online appendix [24]. As an illustrative example, we include the self-assessment questions for Level 1:

1. Is there a shared understanding of MBSE across all involved teams and disciplines?
2. Is the workforce familiar with SE or the systems thinking approach? Do they understand thinking holistically about the system - understanding interactions and interdependencies between subsystems?
3. Have you already taken steps to clearly communicate the value of MBSE to relevant stakeholders?
4. Have you considered potential resistance from (senior) employees and provided training or developed plans to address skepticism and reluctance to change?

5 Discussion

In this paper, we investigated the literature on challenges, pitfalls, and best practices for MBSE adoption. Challenges, pitfalls, and best practices were identified through a meta-synthesis of the literature and organized in a maturity assessment framework with four maturity levels, thus answering the research question. The framework also provides a self-assessment questionnaire that allows practitioners to identify at what level their organization is situated.

Initial Evaluation: Expert Survey. To validate the structure and utility of the maturity assessment, we conducted an initial survey with eight domain experts. Overall, most participants agreed with the proposed framework. Most of their feedback can be summarized in the sense that they would prefer more detailed information. Another suggestion is to include a fifth level such that Level 4 would represent adoption by some teams, while Level 5 would signify widespread adoption across most of the company. This might better reflect the gradual scaling of MBSE efforts, according to one participant. The respondents also suggested enhancing the framework with a focus on tools and toy examples in the first two levels to increase employee involvement. Another recommendation was to include "applying MBSE to existing projects" as an alternative for pilot projects in Level 3, to increase the framework's applicability. Finally, respondents noted that currently, MBSE adoption efforts often begin bottom-up rather than top-down. This indicates that the adoption is typically initiated by employees with technical skills. With this framework, we hope to provide a useful tool for managers who want to adopt MBSE to improve their organization's SE processes.

The final overall feedback on the maturity assessment was largely positive, with six respondents agreeing that the maturity framework is meaningful. Additionally, they indicated they would consider using the maturity assessment professionally. The feedback emphasized the relevance and value of the maturity assessment. Comments included praise for its applicability, with one respondent specifically mentioning its alignment with their current MBSE program and another calling the work "very important".

Limitations and Future Work. While this paper provides a comprehensive framework for guiding organizations through the MBSE adoption process, it is not without limitations. The methodology relies on existing literature, which inherently reflects the biases, scope, and limitations of previous studies. As such, while the findings are rooted in established research, they may not capture emerging practices or innovations in rapidly evolving industries. We mitigated this limitation by conducting a survey with domain experts to collect feedback and suggestions rooted in current practice. Additionally, the high-level nature of the maturity assessment prioritizes generalizability over specificity. This leaves the task of deriving detailed, actionable steps to individual organizations; however, it ensures the broad applicability of the framework as a starting point across diverse organizations. The survey format was chosen to maximize accessibility and reach within the professional community, allowing participants to efficiently provide feedback. While it was recognized that this method might not yield the depth of insight possible through dedicated expert interviews, it enabled a broader and more time-efficient collection of initial feedback.

The feedback gathered from the survey offers specific possibilities for refinement. Future research could focus on validating and refining the maturity assessment framework through empirical studies and real-world case applications. Testing the tool's effectiveness in diverse organizational settings would not only provide valuable feedback for improvement but also enhance its credibility and practical relevance. Another suggestion from the survey participants is incorporating a fifth level into the framework and adjusting the focus of certain levels to align with earlier phases. As suggested by the respondents, this could better reflect the nuanced progression of MBSE adoption. Finally, as MBSE and the fields around it continue to evolve, ongoing research should aim to keep the framework up-to-date. Incorporating advancements will ensure the maturity assessment remains a relevant and effective resource for organizations navigating MBSE transitions. However, the proposed framework and self-assessment already provide significant added value by synthesizing an extensive set of findings from literature. The usefulness and applicability of the framework were confirmed by domain experts.

6 Conclusion

This paper presents a maturity assessment model for the adoption of MBSE in organizations. The framework synthesizes reported challenges, pitfalls, and best practices of MBSE adoption from 44 publications by means of a systematic literature review and organizes them into four cumulative maturity levels and five topic categories. The framework demonstrates that the focus of the challenges, pitfalls, and best practices shifts from more people-oriented categories ("Work Culture" and "Knowledge and Skills") to more technical categories "Methodologies, Language and Tools" and "Modeling") as the maturity level of MBSE adoption increases. This approach balances the complexity of MBSE transitions with actionable steps specific to the maturity level, naturally prioritizing and focusing on key areas that past projects highlighted as critical. The framework was evaluated by means of a survey with experts from the MBSE community. The overall reception was positive with six out of eight respondents agreeing that the assessment is meaningful for supporting MBSE adoption, while specific feedback was given on possible refinements and further research opportunities.

References

1. Akundi, A., Ankobiah, W.: Mapping industry workforce needs to academic curricula - a workforce development effort in model-based systems engineering. Syst. Eng. **27**(4), 685–698 (2024). https://doi.org/10.1002/sys.21745
2. Alvarez, J.L., de Koning, H.P., Fischer, D., Wallum, M., Metselaar, H., Kretzenbacher, M.: Best practices for model based systems engineering in ESA projects. In: 2018 AIAA SPACE and Astronautics Forum and Exposition (2018)
3. Amorim, T., Vogelsang, A., Canedo, E.D.: Decision support for process maturity improvement in model-based systems engineering. In: Proceedings of the International Conference on Software and System Processes and International Conference on Global Software Engineering, pp. 13–23. Association for Computing Machinery, New York, NY, USA (2022). https://doi.org/10.1145/3529320.3529322
4. Amorim, T., Vogelsang, A., Pudlitz, F., Gersing, P., Philipps, J.: Strategies and best practices for model-based systems engineering adoption in embedded systems industry. In: 2019 IEEE/ACM 41st International Conference on Software Engineering: Software Engineering in Practice (ICSE-SEIP), pp. 203–212 (2019)
5. Anwar, M., Gill, A., Proper, H.: A conceptual model to assess the maturity of information security audit process. In: Practice of Enterprise Modelling 2022 Workshops and Models at Work. CEUR (2022)

6. Beihoff, B., et al.: A World in Motion - Systems Engineering Vision 2025 (2014)
7. Bonnet, S., Voirin, J.L., Normand, V., Exertier, D.: Implementing the MBSE cultural change: Organization, coaching and lessons learned. In: INCOSE International Symposium, vol. 25, no. 1, pp. 508–523 (2015)
8. Call, D.R., Herber, D.R.: Applicability of the diffusion of innovation theory to accelerate model-based systems engineering adoption. Syst. Eng. **25**(6), 574–583 (2022). https://doi.org/10.1002/sys.21638
9. Carroll, E.R., Malins, R.J.: Systematic literature review: how is model-based systems engineering justified? (2016). https://doi.org/10.2172/1561164
10. Chami, M., Aleksandraviciene, A., Morkevicius, A., Bruel, J.M.: Towards solving MBSE adoption challenges: the D3 MBSE adoption toolbox. In: INCOSE International Symposium, vol. 28, no. 1, pp. 1463–1477 (2018)
11. Chami, M., Bruel, J.M.: A survey on MBSE adoption challenges. In: INCOSE EMEA Sector Systems Engineering Conference (INCOSE EMEASEC 2018), pp. 1–16. Berlin, Germany (2018)
12. Dawson, S., Batchelor, A.: Empowering engineers in a digital engineering transition: applying organizational psychology and systems thinking approaches to define the problem and to develop recommended actions. In: INCOSE International Symposium, vol. 32, no. 1, pp. 594–607 (2022). https://doi.org/10.1002/iis2.12951
13. de Bruin, T., Rosemann, M., Freeze, R., Kulkarni, U.: Understanding the main phases of developing a maturity assessment model. In: ACIS 2005 Proceedings - 16th Australasian Conference on Information Systems (2005)
14. Delligatti, L.: SysML Distilled: A Brief Guide to the Systems Modeling Language, 1st edn. Addison-Wesley Professional (2013)
15. Dubos, G., Schreiner, S., Wagner, D.A., Jones, G., Kerzhner, A.A., Kaderka, J.: Architecture modeling on the Europa project. In: AIAA SPACE 2016 (2016)
16. Faudou, R., Bruel, J.M.: An industrial feedback on model-based requirements engineering in systems engineering context. In: 2016 IEEE 24th International Requirements Engineering Conference Workshops (REW), pp. 190–199 (2016)
17. Ferguson, R., Marshall, J., Guzman, M.: Adapting progressive MBSE development to document based contracts. In: 2020 IEEE Aerospace Conference, pp. 1–11 (2020)
18. Gustavsson, H., Enoiu, E.P., Carlson, J.: Model-based system engineering adoption in the vehicular systems domain. In: 2022 17th Conference on Computer Science and Intelligence Systems (FedCSIS), pp. 907–911 (2022)
19. Haidar, H., Kolp, M., Wautelet, Y.: Assessing the adoption level of agile development within software product lines: the AgiPL-AM model. In: The Practice of Enterprise Modeling, pp. 134–148. Springer International Publishing, Cham (2019)
20. Hallqvist, J., Larsson, J.: Introducing MBSE by using systems engineering principles. In: INCOSE International Symposium, vol. 26, no. 1, pp. 512–525 (2016)
21. Henderson, K., McDermott, T., Salado, A.: MBSE adoption experiences in organizations: lessons learned. Syst. Eng. **27**(1), 214–239 (2024)
22. Henderson, K., McDermott, T., Van Aken, E., Salado, A.: Towards developing metrics to evaluate digital engineering. Syst. Eng. **26**(1), 3–31 (2023)
23. Henderson, K., Salado, A.: The effects of organizational structure on MBSE adoption in industry: insights from practitioners. Eng. Manag. J. **36**(1), 117–143 (2024). https://doi.org/10.1080/10429247.2023.2210494
24. Henoeckl, T., Verbruggen, C., Bork, D.: Towards a maturity assessment framework for MBSE adoption: results from a meta-synthesis - supplementary material (2025). https://doi.org/10.5281/zenodo.15224260

25. Holladay, J.B., Knizhnik, J., Weiland, K.J., Stein, A., Sanders, T., Schwindt, P.: MBSE infusion and modernization initiative (MIAMI): "hot" benefits for real NASA applications. In: 2019 IEEE Aerospace Conference, pp. 1–14 (2019)
26. Huldt, T., Stenius, I.: State-of-practice survey of model-based systems engineering. Syst. Eng. **22**(2), 134–145 (2019)
27. INCOSE MBSE Initiative: Systems engineering your MBSE implementation: where are you on your MBSE journey? In: INCOSE International Symposium, vol. 32, no. 1, pp. 249–261 (2022). https://doi.org/10.1002/iis2.12929
28. Khandoker, A., et al.: Towards a logical framework for ideal MBSE tool selection based on discipline specific requirements. J. Syst. Softw. **189**, 111306 (2022). https://doi.org/10.1016/j.jss.2022.111306
29. Kitchenham, B., Charters, S.: Guidelines for performing systematic literature reviews in software engineering **2** (2007)
30. Knackstedt, R., Pöppelbuß, J., Becker, J.: Vorgehensmodell zur entwicklung von reifegradmodellen. In: Wirtschaftsinformatik (2009)
31. Korsten, G., Ozkan, B., Aysolmaz, B., Mul, D., Turetken, O.: Understanding capability progression: a model for defining maturity levels for organizational capabilities. In: Enterprise. Business-Process and Information Systems Modeling, pp. 355–371. Springer Nature Switzerland, Cham (2024)
32. Lerat, J.P.: 5.5.2 three reasons why document-based se (usually) works better than (most of) MBSE. In: INCOSE International Symposium, vol. 20, no. 1, pp. 723–738 (2010)
33. Li, T., et al.: Learning MBSE online: a tale of two professional cohorts. Systems **11**(5) (2023). https://doi.org/10.3390/systems11050224
34. Mancin, E.: How model based systems engineering streamlines the development of complex systems. In: INCOSE Italia Conference on Systems Engineering (2014)
35. McDermott, T., Henderson, K., Van Aken, E., Salado, A., Bradley, J.: Measuring the roi of digital engineering: it's a journey, not a number. AIRC Perspectives 1–8 (2022)
36. McDermott, T.A., Hutchison, N., Clifford, M., Van Aken, E., Salado, A., Henderson, K.: Benchmarking the benefits and current maturity of model-based systems engineering across the enterprise. Syst. Eng. Res. Center (2020)
37. McDermott, T., Henderson, K., Van Aken, E., Salado, A.: Framework for and progress of adoption of digital and model-based systems engineering into engineering enterprises. In: The Proceedings of the 2023 Conference on Systems Engineering Research, pp. 69–82. Springer Nature Switzerland (2024)
38. Mitchell, S.W.: Transitioning the SWFTS program combat system product family from traditional document-centric to model-based systems engineering. Syst. Eng. **17**(3), 313–329 (2014). https://doi.org/10.1002/sys.21271
39. Nanfuka, J.G., Oosthuizen, R.: MBSE-lite: a framework for adopting model-based systems engineering in small and medium-sized enterprises in South Africa. Bus. Manag. Econ. Eng. **21**, 218–236 (2023)
40. Noguchi, R.A.: Recommended best practices based on MBSE pilot projects. In: INCOSE International Symposium, vol. 29, no. 1, pp. 753–770 (2019)
41. Noguchi, R.A., Minnichelli, R.J., Wheaton, M.J.: Architecting success in model based systems engineering pilot projects. In: 2019 IEEE International Conference on Systems, Man and Cybernetics (SMC), pp. 755–760 (2019)
42. Orosz, M., Duffy, B., Charlton, C., Saunders, H., Thomas, E.: Unique challenges in mission engineering and technology integration. In: Systems Engineering for the Digital Age, pp. 665–681. John Wiley and Sons, Ltd. (2023)

43. Papke, B., Hause, M., Hetherington, D.: Fuse agility as a foundation for sound MBSE lifecycle management. Insight **26**(2), 34–38 (2023)
44. Papke, B., Hause, M., Hetherington, D., McGervey, S., Rodriguez, S.: MBSE model management pain points - wait, this looks familiar! In: INCOSE International Symposium, vol. 33, no. 1, pp. 273–289 (2023). https://doi.org/10.1002/iis2.13021
45. Papke, B.L., Wang, G., Kratzke, R., Schreiber, C.: Implementing MBSE - an enterprise approach to an enterprise problem. In: INCOSE International Symposium, vol. 30, no. 1, pp. 1550–1567 (2020). https://doi.org/10.1002/j.2334-5837.2020.00803.x
46. Ploeg, C., Lai, K., Olechowski, A.: Prioritization of best practices in the implementation of model-based systems engineering. In: INCOSE International Symposium, vol. 32, no. 1, pp. 961–975 (2022)
47. Pratt, M., Dabkowski, M.: Analyzing the integration of MBSE approaches within the aerospace industry according to utaut. Ind. Syst. Eng. Rev. **10**(2), 127–134 (2022)
48. Schumacher, T., Ammersdörfer, T., Inkermann, D.: Development and application of simulation games to introduce model-based systems engineering. In: Towards a New Future in Engineering Education, New Scenarios that European Alliances of Tech Universities Open Up, pp. 702–709. Universitat Politècnica de Catalunya (2022)
49. Sindiy, O., Mozafari, T., Budney, C.: Application of model-based systems engineering for the development of the asteroid redirect robotic mission. In: AIAA SPACE 2016 (2016). https://doi.org/10.2514/6.2016-5312
50. Suryadevara, J., Tiwari, S.: Adopting MBSE in construction equipment industry: an experience report. In: 2018 25th Asia-Pacific Software Engineering Conference (APSEC), pp. 512–521 (2018). https://doi.org/10.1109/APSEC.2018.00066
51. Vasenev, A., Suermondt, W.T., Behl, A., Lukkien, J.: Step-wise MBSE introduction into a company: an interface-centric case study. In: 2023 18th Annual System of Systems Engineering Conference (SoSe), pp. 1–6 (2023)
52. Vogelsang, A., Amorim, T., Pudlitz, F., Gersing, P., Philipps, J.: Should i stay or should i go? on forces that drive and prevent MBSE adoption in the embedded systems industry. arXiv:1709.00266 (2017)
53. Wang, G.: Implementing a model-based, digital engineering enterprise for a defense systems integrator - an ongoing journey. In: INCOSE International Symposium, vol. 30, no. 1, pp. 783–798 (2020). https://doi.org/10.1002/j.2334-5837.2020.00755.x
54. Wang, L., Izygon, M., Okon, S., Wagner, H., Garner, L.: Effort to accelerate MBSE adoption and usage at JSC. In: AIAA SPACE 2016 (2016)
55. Weilkiens, T.: Adoption of MBSE in an organization. In: Handbook of Model-Based Systems Engineering, pp. 1–19. Springer International Publishing (2020). https://doi.org/10.1007/978-3-030-27486-3_18-1
56. Zhu, H., McDermott, A.: Optimal architecting strategy for partially developed products: challenges and solutions. In: 2023 IEEE International Systems Conference, pp. 1–6 (2023). https://doi.org/10.1109/SysCon53073.2023.10131213
57. van Zwienen, M., Ruiz, M., van Steenbergen, M., Burriel, V.: A process for tailoring domain-specific enterprise architecture maturity models. In: Enterprise. Business-Process and Information Systems Modeling, pp. 196–211. Springer International Publishing, Cham (2019)

Modeling of and within Organizations (EMMSAD 2025)

Enhancing C2-Systems: Validation of Goal and Concept Models with Stakeholders

Jan Lundberg[1,2](✉) [iD], Kent Andersson[1] [iD], and Janis Stirna[2] [iD]

[1] Swedish Defence University, Drottning Kristinas väg 37, 114 28 Stockholm, Sweden
jan.lundberg@dsv.su.se
[2] Department of Computer and Systems Sciences, Stockholm University, Borgarfjordsgatan 12, 164 55 Kista, Sweden

Abstract. The increasing complexity of military command and control systems (C2-systems) requires a robust framework for integrating emerging technologies effectively. This article is part of a research project employing Design Science Research Methodology (DSRM) with the primary objective of developing a conceptual framework, including models and methods, designed to assist designers and military commanders in assessing and understanding C2-systems from a socio-technical perspective. Additionally, the research aims to provide guidance on analyzing how individual sub-systems in a C2-system influence the entire system. In previous publications, the authors have explored the challenges associated with the integration of emerging technologies into C2-systems, and have also outlined an initial iteration of a concepts model and a goal model. This article addresses the refinement and stakeholder validation of these models, and outlines an in-depth exploration of the decomposition process from high-level goals to specific sub-goals and requirements. Following the DSRM, the authors have engaged stakeholders from the military, research and acquisition domains in a series of workshops. These were designed to extract feedback and insights, ensuring that the models are both accurate and relevant. Data elicited during these sessions were analyzed to validate the coherence of the overall structure as well as the semantic quality of proposed models. The findings indicate that combining goal models with a concepts model, enhances the understanding of, and the requirements on, C2-systems. Moreover, the validation through stakeholder engagement not only refines the goal and concepts model but also fosters a shared understanding among stakeholders regarding the objectives and challenges associated with integration of emerging technologies. The results presented in this article provide actionable insights for practitioners seeking to understand and improve military C2-systems. The results also highlight the importance of both conceptual and goal-oriented frameworks in guiding the understanding and integration of emerging technologies, ultimately contributing to more effective C2-systems.

Keywords: Command- and control systems (C2-systems) · capability development · System of Systems (SoS) · validation

1 Introduction

The integration of emerging technologies into military capabilities has become increasingly important for maintaining tactical advantages. Military command and control systems (C2-systems), vital for decision-making, coordination, and execution of operations, are no exception. New and emerging technologies, such as Robotics and Autonomous Systems (RAS) and Artificial Intelligence (AI), are poised to transform warfare, making traditional approaches to C2-system design insufficient. At the same time, C2-systems must evolve to meet the demands of future warfare, characterized by Multi-Domain Operations (MDO) that require coordination and synchronization across all military domains, air, land, sea, cyber and space. As technologies and warfare evolve, the complexity of C2-systems increases, heightening the need for relevant frameworks that can guide the design and understanding of these systems. However, the integration of these technologies into future C2-systems, alongside legacy subsystems, is a complex challenge that requires a systematic approach.

This challenge has been explored in various frameworks, e.g., the NATO Architecture Framework (NAF) [1]. NAF provides guidelines for, among other things, interoperability and integration challenges within systems, including C2-systems. NAF should be recognized as a foundation for understanding the challenges of integrating new technologies into C2-systems. However, these challenges also underscore the need for further development of frameworks that can guide the design and understanding of future C2-systems.

The necessity of such a framework is driven by the nature of the future military environment, which requires C2-systems that can adapt and integrate across multiple domains. C2-systems must not only coordinate a wide array of technological elements but also synchronize with human operators in a way that is seamless and intuitive. This calls for a holistic view of C2-systems that highlights the interaction between human operators, technology, the organizational structures, and the processes involved. Existing frameworks, such as NAF, primarily focus on the technical aspects of a C2-system, addressing issues like technical requirements. Nevertheless, these frameworks do not fully adopt a holistic approach to C2-systems, often overlooking the human, organizational, and methodological dimensions. As emerging technologies such as AI and autonomous systems become more integrated into military operations, it is increasingly important to consider how these technologies interact with human operators and fit within broader organizational structures. Effective C2-system design requires ensuring that human operators can manage and control advanced technologies in ways that align with organizational processes and objectives. That aspect has not been thoroughly explored in existing frameworks, and this research seeks to fill that gap.

This paper contributes to a research project focused on developing a conceptual framework to facilitate the integration of emerging technologies into military command and control (C2) systems. The framework identifies models and methods designed to help designers and commanders analyse and validate C2 systems through a socio-technical lens.

We aim for a comprehensive approach that considers both the technological, procedural, and organizational dimensions of C2-systems, and thereby offer a clearer view of how various subsystems interact within the larger system. This approach recognizes that a successful C2-system is not only about technology, but instead the combination of a complex network of people, processes, and technology that operate cohesively. In previous papers [2–6] we have explored the challenges associated with integrating emerging technologies into C2-systems, and introduced initial models, including a concept model and a goal model. However, these models are preliminary and have not yet been validated. To this end, the goal of this paper is to validate and refine these models, thereby contributing to the overall objectives of the research project.

The rest of this paper is structured as follows. In Sect. 2, we provide a background to and an overview of related work. Section 3 describes the research approach, design science research methodology [7] (DSRM), and the principles of model validation and refinement. Section 4 presents the findings, Sect. 5 provides a discussion, and finally Sect. 6 includes conclusions and directions for future work.

2 Background and Related Work

This article focuses specifically on the validation of the goal- and concept-based models outlined in earlier research [4, 6] which aim to support the understanding and design of military C2-systems. These systems should be understood as Systems of Systems (SoS), composed of multiple conceptual components, including people, processes, communications networks, and command post constellations [8]. A SoS is typically defined as an arrangement of individual and independent systems that are integrated to form a more complex whole, with the goal of achieving greater functionality and performance than the individual systems can provide on their own [9].

The research approach is grounded in three core areas of study: (i) capability development frameworks, such as NAF, (ii) modeling, particularly goal- and concept-based models as described in Enterprise Modeling (4EM) [10], and (iii) the validation of these models in real-world contexts.

NAF is a cornerstone in military capability development, particularly in providing a standardized approach for defining system components and their interrelations. However, as C2-systems grow more complex and agile, the static nature of NAF becomes increasingly limiting. The requirement for flexibility and adaptability in future C2-systems, combined with a dynamic tactical environment, has led to a call for more agile frameworks. This is highlighted in [11], where the authors argue for a shift from the rigid, hierarchical understanding of C2-systems to a more flexible and adaptable approach. When C2-systems grow in complexity, so must the development frameworks that support the design of these C2-systems. While NAF focuses on standardization, there is a growing need for a more holistic and agile development approach that allows C2-systems to evolve in response to real-time tactical needs. Adopting this approach will make C2-systems more relevant in unpredictable contexts where emerging technology plays an important role.

Consequently, there is a need for effective modeling. In C2-system development, we argue that the core role of modeling is to enhance the understanding of the relationships and dynamics between technical advancements and practical applications. Specifically, there is a need for models that not only represent the structure of C2-systems but also capture their dynamic behavior as they adapt to real-time tactical needs. Accordingly, concept modeling plays a key role in abstracting and identifying the key components of a C2-system and their interrelations. Due to the complexity of C2-systems, these are difficult to capture using traditional system representations. In [12], the authors argue that by using conceptual models, decision-makers can identify key relationships and dependencies between system components, thereby improving both system design and operational planning.

As a complement to concepts models, we also use goal modeling. In C2-system development, goal modeling is central to ensure that high- and low-level goals and requirements align with the overarching purpose of the C2-system [6]. As outlined in [13], goal models assist in translating broad tactical goals into specific, actionable tasks.

While this article focuses on validation of goal- and concept models for military command and control, much of the existing literature has concentrated on developing relevant models within the Information Systems (IS) domain, and with less attention paid to how these models are validated. However, in [14], the authors employed focus group studies (FGS), closely related to the Exploratory Focus Groups (EFG) used in this study, to validate a model by collecting qualitative feedback from stakeholders with relevant expertise. Your authors argue that qualitative validation methods can complement a quantitative approach by providing a deeper understanding of how models perform.

3 Method

This research project follows the DSRM [7], aimed at developing a framework with models and methods to support practitioners in the understanding, use, and design of military C2-systems. This paper focuses on the validation and refinement of our initial iteration of a goal model [4] and of a concepts model [6], using Enterprise Modeling (EM) [10] as a theoretical baseline. By grounding our models in EM principles, we ensure that the decomposition of high-level goals into sub-goals and requirements aligns with established EM and analysis practices, thereby enhancing both the theoretical rigor and practical applicability of our framework.

The research strategy is a case study [15], focusing specifically on the development and operation of C2-systems within the Swedish Armed Forces. In this ongoing case, the models developed in the project are presented as potential solutions to stakeholder needs and are validated based on their alignment with these requirements. This approach allows us to assess the models' coherence and semantic quality [16]. By assessing coherence, we address the refinement of the models' structure and relationships, as well as analyze the decomposition of high-level goals into sub-goals and into specific requirements. Semantic quality addresses how well the developed model represents real-world concepts and its logical consistency.

For data generation, we employed Exploratory Focus Groups (EFGs), as outlined in [17, 18], to gather qualitative feedback that could inform potential design changes. The EFGs were particularly useful in gathering deep, qualitative insights from a diverse group of stakeholders [19], including military commanders and personnel involved in research, development, and acquisition. The stakeholders were selected following the guidelines in [18] to ensure a comprehensive representation of different roles and perspectives. Each EFG session consisted of seven participants and lasted 86–98 min, with one of the authors acting as the moderator. Key questions posed during the sessions included: *what aspects of the conceptual/goal model do you find useful?* and, *how should the models be adjusted to better meet their intended purposes?* The question guide to EFGs is found in [20]. These discussions were recorded and transcribed for analysis.

The data generated from the EFGs, and interviews were transcribed[1] and subjected to thematic analysis [21], using systematic coding to identify themes and patterns. This helped capture the contextual nuances in the stakeholder feedback, providing a clearer understanding of necessary refinements regarding the proposed models.

The finalized guide for EFGs, including the validated goal model, the full list of questions, and a detailed description of the thematic coding framework has been made available in a separate supplementary report [20]. Specific goals referenced has been denoted with "G" followed by a position number in the decomposition, like "1.1", for traceability reasons.

4 Findings

We engaged a total of fourteen participants (Table 1) in two sessions with the purpose of validating the goal model. By employing thematic analysis, we systematically coded the data and structured it into themes. A detailed description of the coding framework, including the mapping of codes to themes, is described in detail in [20]. This section presents the general and specific feedback on the goal model and resulting themes, including suggestions for potential improvements to the goal model.

4.1 General Feedback on the Goal Model

The stakeholders recognized the value of the model, especially the hierarchy of goals and sub-goals that logically connect to requirements. However, they also found specific areas requiring further refinement, including the need for clearly defined feedback loops and adaptability mechanisms that address both short-term tactical needs, such as responding to rapidly changing battlefield conditions, and long-term strategic objectives, like the incremental development of new technologies. See the following example statements:

> *"Goals G4 and G6 focus on development from a backward and forward perspective, respectively. I believe one of the biggest benefits is considering them together. Even though you're focused on developing something forward, I think the backward perspective also brings valuable insights, even if it's not a completely new system."* Participant L.

> *"The feedback loop comes up very often in this one (G2, author remark). It struck me when I looked at the others as well. It keeps recurring in the sub-goals. So, the question is how much of this is being emphasized redundantly."* Participant G.

The general opinion of the goal model is that while the model provides a structured framework, it could benefit from enhanced flexibility and comprehensiveness to handle both technical and human factors more thoroughly. This could potentially address the

---

[1] https://www.amberscript.com/en/

Table 1. Participants

Stakeholder/Position	Group
A/Swedish Defense Materiel Administration	Expert & designer
B/Swedish Defense University	Researcher
C/Army Headquarter	Problem owner
D/SWE Military Headquarters	Expert & designer
E/Swedish Defense Materiel Administration	Expert & designer
F/SWE Military Headquarters	Expert & designer
G/Army Headquarter	Problem owner
H/Army Headquarter	Problem owner
I/Defense Research Agency	Researcher
J/Swedish Defense Materiel Administration	Expert & designer
K/Army Headquarter	Expert & designer
L/Army Headquarter	Expert & designer
M/Army Headquarter	Expert & designer
N/ Defense Research Agency	Researcher

contradictory and often unpredictable requirements experienced in a real-world military context, as expressed in the following example statements.

> "I embrace the idea of trying to create a shared understanding. That there is a language to be able to communicate with each other in the first place." Participant E.

> "It is technology focused. Both incremental and disruptive development can, of course, come from factors other than technology. And it doesn't take the sociological aspects into account." Participant F.

Some participants also expressed a need for a clearer separation between high-level goals and requirements. This is to ensure that the model stays relevant and usable. The overarching subject of this feedback is a call for balance between the model's holistic ambitions and the actual needs of users, highlighting adaptability, real-time responsiveness, and modularity as essential improvements. This is an example of such a statement.

> "If a disruptive technology emerges, it could mean that this goal (G4 – integration, author remark) is absolutely unattainable. This is because the disruptive element is transformative. It doesn't fit, and it might not be integrable with anything. It means we must do things in a different way. Then it becomes a decision point in the integration process. We say, for example: scrap these because they don't work. And that must be incorporated into the process. It needs to be clear that we're saying: this is outdated now. Otherwise, we tend to integrate a lot of things

just because we decide that everything should be system-integrated at all levels." Participant M.

The feedback on the goal model also highlights complexity and rigidity, which some participants stated may hinder its practical applicability in a rapidly evolving context. One participant especially noted the overarching complexity of managing all parts of the system, suggesting that while a holistic approach is valuable, it also requires clearer boundaries to prevent overwhelming users with an expansive scope that may not always be practical in real-time decision-making situations.

"...all parts of a system are a very large entity. Perhaps it's too much, a bit overwhelming." Participant B.

One participant argued that certain rigidities in the model, such as predefined scenario goals and requirements (R8.8, *the scenario repository should include a wide variety of predefined realistic scenarios*, and G3.1.1, *Establish tools for developing realistic scenarios, author remark*) might constrain creativity, particularly when trying to innovate or adapt to new tactics.

"There is one thing I don't like in the model. It's R8.8. That it should include predefined realistic scenarios. I think that could kill the whole purpose here. For me, it's painful to be stuck in such a rigid framework. It also depends on your personality, but it stifles my creativity." Participant F.

Lastly, several participants underlined the importance of standardizing the formulation of requirements. They argued that inconsistencies in how requirements are expressed could lead to misunderstandings.

4.2 Specific Feedback on the Goal Model

One participant (B) argued that some goals and effects are insufficiently described, especially G1.1, *develop an overarching SoS framework*. He states that this must be refined as it is an important component, especially as it is a design task. Consequently, the boundaries of each component must be described more precisely (goals and requirements) to avoid redundancies. The same participant expressed concerns regarding the scope and complexity of the goal model, particularly the high-level goals and especially G1, *be able to be levering from a high system level to a lower*. He highlighted the challenge of analyzing *"all parts of a system"* with a holistic approach, noting that this broad scope creates a perhaps too large entity. The participant also underlined the need to represent change effectively within the model.

Participant G highlighted the importance of considering the cultural dimensions as well as the organizational aspect in G2, *be able to evaluate holistic*. He argues that it is essential to have a culture that accepts the need to change the organization when introducing new technology. This means that certain positions within military units will be replaced by digital, AI-based applications. However, he states that it will take some time before we, as a collective, fully understand and embrace the impact that AI and digitalization will have on the organization.

"It is not just about materiel, technology, and methods, it also involves organization. One may also need to consider the culture." Participant G.

One participant emphasized the importance of simulating not only the interoperability capability (G3.2) but also requirements for new and legacy systems.

Participants K and M called for clearly defined protocols regarding system integration (G4) and the need to establish relevance criteria, especially with legacy and disruptive new technologies.

"We must start asking the question: What is it that we actually want to interact with? I recognize a gap in the process when it comes to assessing – Is this a relevant integration? Is it a rational effort to ensure that this integration will function? What are the associated risks? This would allow for an evaluation whether it is worth it." Participant M.

Participant G argued for creating Integrated Project Teams (IPTs) to address identified challenges effectively. These must consist of diverse expertise from the research agencies, military, and acquisitions agency.

One participant (B) argued to refine G10, *be able to evaluate the synergies between different domains*, and here consider domain-specific requirements within the C2-system, when the different domains have specific needs. This should be done to refrain from a one-size-fits-all approach.

"I believe the domains differ significantly, depending on which domain you are operating in." Participant I.

4.3 Identified Themes

This thematic analysis captures participant feedback and provides a precise understanding of the goal model's strengths and areas for improvements. By addressing these themes, our aim is for the model to evolve into a more adaptable, integrated, and practically applicable tool within military C2-system development and understanding.

Theme 1 – Structure. The stakeholders' feedback highlights a recognition of the model's structure, particularly the hierarchy of goals and sub-goals that logically connect to requirements. This hierarchical organization is appreciated by stakeholders as it aligns tactical needs with broader strategic objectives, providing a clear path from high-level goals down to operational requirements. However, some stakeholders also highlighted the need for clearer boundaries within this structure to avoid over-complication and to ensure that the model remains relevant and actionable. Several participants pointed out that an expansive scope, attempting to cover "all parts of a system," can be overwhelming. This feedback reflects an understanding that while a holistic approach is valuable, practical limitations should guide the model's focus to maintain its real-time applicability.

Theme 2 – Feedback and Evaluation Mechanisms. The feedback mechanisms within the model were a recurring topic among participants, who acknowledged the importance of continuous evaluation but suggested that some feedback loops might be redundant. The data reveals that participants appreciate the role of feedback in aligning goals with evolving operational needs. However, there was a suggestion to streamline these mechanisms to prevent unnecessary overlaps. This highlights the need for a consolidated feedback structure that remains adaptable without compromising clarity or efficiency. By reducing repetitive and overlapping feedback loops, the model could be reduced in complexity, allowing it to better support both immediate and long-term strategic decision-making.

Theme 3 – Cultural and Organizational Aspects. Some stakeholders stressed that while the model's technical focus is essential, it must also incorporate cultural and organizational aspects to be effective within a military context. This indicates an awareness of the impact that organizational culture has, especially in environments that are changing and adaptive. This in turn reflects a broader understanding of organizational congruence, that technical systems must work within an established organizational framework, which includes norms, values, and adaptability to change. By integrating these human-centered factors, the model would better reflect the complexities of real-world operations and thereby support a framework that underpins both technological and cultural integration.

Theme 4 – Adaptability for Tactical and Strategic Needs. Feedback from several participants accentuate the importance of adaptability within the model to address both short-term tactical demands and long-term strategic goals. The participants recognize this flexibility as essential when navigating a rapidly evolving battlefield and supporting incremental technological advancements. The feedback highlights the need for adaptability mechanisms that enable the model to respond effectively to unexpected changes while maintaining alignment with strategic objectives. Participants also recognized the benefit of considering incremental development alongside disruptive innovation to maintain operational relevance, especially in military contexts where technology and tactics can shift unexpectedly.

4.4 Refinement of the Goal Model

The refinement of the goal model is based on the feedback provided in Sect. 4.1 (*General feedback on the goal model*) and Sect. 4.2 (*Specific feedback on the goal model*). These two sections summarize the insights from the focus group participants, which were central to the iterative development of the model. In addition to the critique outlined in these sections, participants also submitted their own notes regarding additional suggestions. These contributions improved the refinement process and provided additional depth to the understanding of the model.

The goal model, even in its initial iteration, is extensive. The validation process, outlined in this article, has resulted in a model containing 85 low-level goals and 114 requirements. This provides a strong base for further development and refinement. Due to space constraints, we have had to present the refined goal model in a separate supplementary report [20]. Interested readers are encouraged to read it alongside this article to gain a comprehensive perspective on the model's refinement. In Fig. 1, we illustrate the refinement of the goal model with changes in the first goal.

The validation reported in this study highlights the need for a control function for G4, *be able to integrate earlier version and interact with higher and lower level*, to guide the integration process. This function will assess the *necessity* of integration based on three primary criteria: (i) operational/tactical necessity, the integration supports with tactical and operational goals, (ii) resource soundness, evaluating the economic feasibility, including efforts and man-hours required, and (iii) time, accounting for time constraints and urgency. The design and implementation of this control function are beyond the scope of this article. However, it will be a central focus of future research.

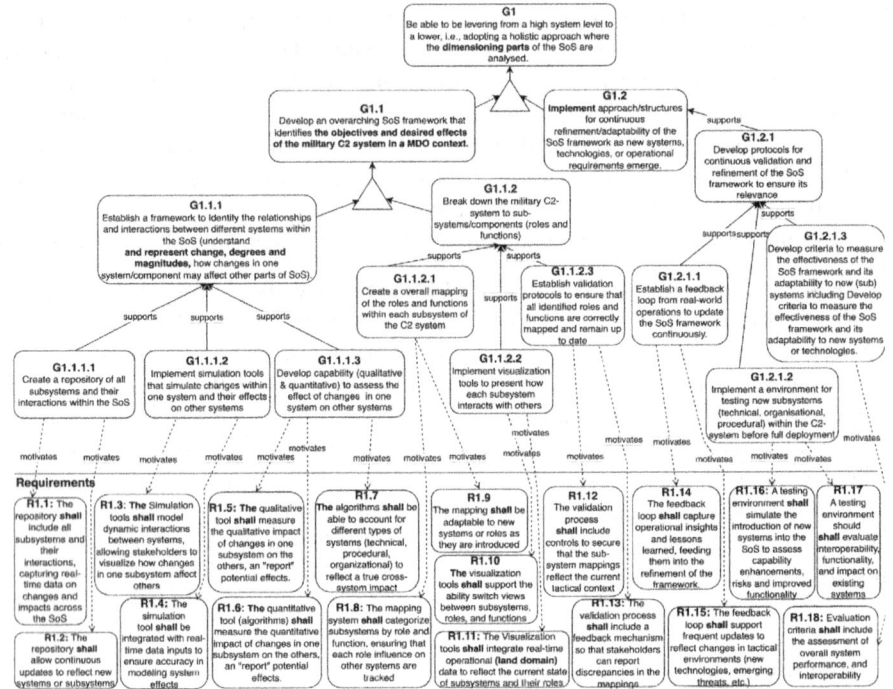

Fig. 1. The Figure shows the decomposition of the first goal, G1, to illustrate the goal model after refinement. In RED, are the refinements suggested by stakeholders. (Color figure online)

4.5 Refinement of the Concepts Model

To clarify the domain of C2-systems a concepts model was created, see Fig. 2. It presents three aspects of our research project: (i) the domain concepts of the C2 systems originating from the theory of C2, (ii) key concepts raised by the domain experts and stakeholders presented in the goals model, as well as (iii) constructs of Method Engineering (ME) needed to propose the initial architecture of the envisioned framework.

The domain concepts reflect the key conceptual components of C2 systems as well as aspects of command and control. The envisioned framework needs to support a holistic and interdisciplinary approach, integrating insights from military science, C2 theory, and IS development to improve understanding and, consequently, functionality of C2-systems. Therefore, the envisioned framework needs to support the elaboration of these

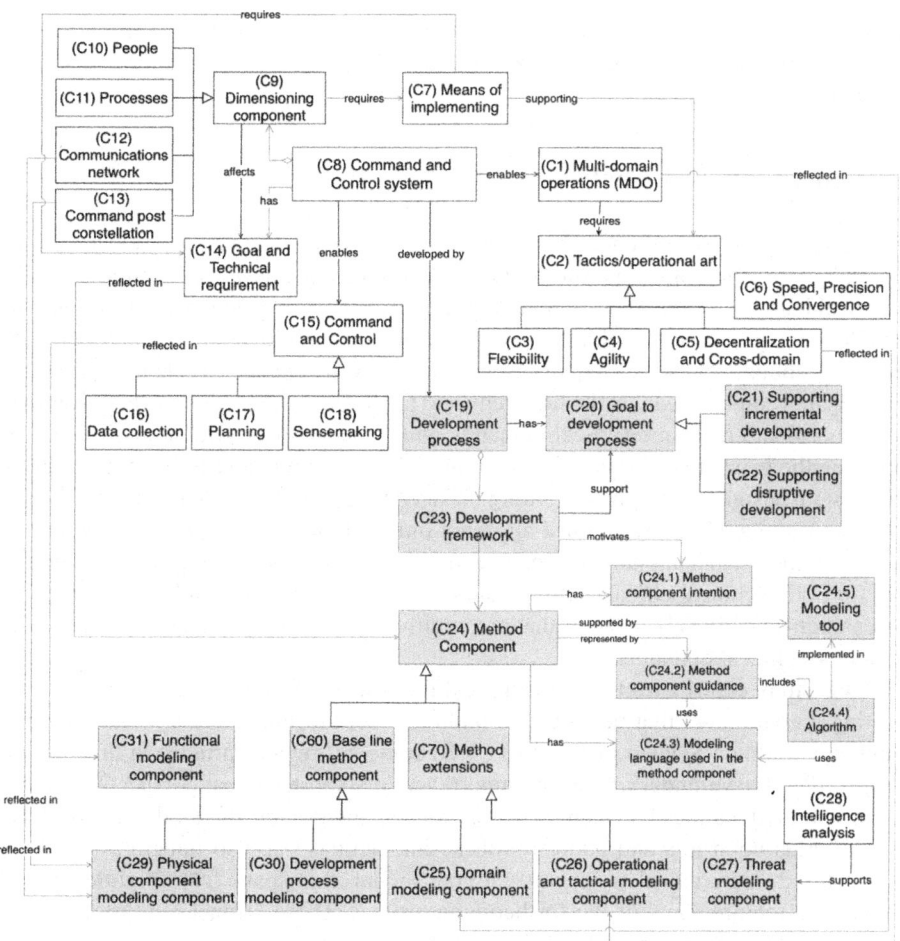

Fig. 2. A figure describing the refined concepts model.

concepts in accordance with the goals of the framework. We currently envision that the framework will consist of method components expressed in the form of method chunks, cf. [22], following the principles of ME as presented in [23]. The purpose of this concepts model is to document the initial set of the domain concepts (in white) and how they are linked to the concepts of ME and parts of the resulting framework. A detailed meta-model of method chunks, as defined in [22] is outside the scope of this paper. However, we recognize that each method component (chunk) to be developed will consist of a modeling product part defining the modeling language and a modeling process part providing the way of working, as well as the intention of use for the modeling component. There will be two kinds of components – (C60) baseline method components supporting the main tasks of C2 system development, such as the ones exemplified by the subcomponents of C60, and (C70) method extensions that would contribute to C2-system design or redesign but that are externally developed and would provide input to the baseline components.

5 Discussion and Analysis

This case study's findings underscore the role of the goal model in guiding the integration of emerging technologies within military C2-systems, and at the same time providing practical insights for military commanders, researchers, and system designers. For commanders, the goal model highlights a way to achieve operational flexibility by enabling the understanding of and consequences of adaptability in dynamic and changing contexts. Participants emphasized that the hierarchy and feedback mechanisms can help commanders coordinate real-time tactical demands with broader long-term strategic goals, by bridging the gap between immediate operational needs and longer-term strategic needs. For system designers, insights regarding the need for cultural and organizational integration suggest that C2-systems must align not only with technological specifications but also with the organizational culture. The model underscores the importance of designing for both technical efficacy and human-centric functionality, enabling designers and researchers to define C2-systems that are intuitive for military personnel and responsive to socio-technical demands.

This study contributes to the theoretical framework of military C2-systems by presenting a goal model that holistically combines socio-technical theory with enterprise modeling within a System of Systems (SoS) context. Previous articles in this research project [2, 5] have underscored the importance of socio-technical perspectives, which highlight the dynamics between the technological and organizational dimensions. This study builds upon this and addresses these interactions but also integrates them into a structured, hierarchical framework, a goal model, that spans from high-level goals to specific requirements of the forthcoming artifact. These artifact requirements contribute by offering an approach that is adaptable across both tactical and strategic levels. Furthermore, the goal model provides a framework to balance incremental and disruptive innovations, indicating how emerging technologies can be systematically integrated while maintaining long-term stability.

Earlier work within the overarching project to develop a framework for guiding the design of military command and control (C2) systems resulted in a concepts model [24]. This model defines the key components, functions, relationships, and dynamics within a military C2 system and supports its development. We argue that refining the goal model to address the shortcomings identified earlier and combining it with the concepts model, will create a robust foundation for supporting the design of military C2 systems. First, the goal model assists in prioritizing features and functionalities that align with overarching development objectives, while the conceptual model provides designers with a shared vocabulary and structural framework. Together, these models bridge the gap between abstract objectives and tangible framework design. Both models facilitate communication and collaboration throughout the design process. Second, given the dynamic nature of the operational environment, C2 systems must continuously adapt to changing conditions. The goal model ensures that designers remain focused on high-level, enduring objectives, while the conceptual model supports flexibility in how these goals are operationalized and identifies the key components of the framework.

From the perspectives of Enterprise Modeling, this paper presents a case in which a large goal model is validated with a group of stakeholders representing several large groups of potential end-product users. This contrasts with more typical modeling projects where the initial models are developed in a participatory manner and then refined and validated with the same group in subsequent participatory modeling sessions. That would not have been possible in our case, as the stakeholders would have difficulty allocating the sufficient time required for participatory modeling of a model of this scale.

5.1 Limitations

This study has several limitations that will guide future work. First, the stakeholder group was limited to Swedish Armed Forces, defence researchers, and acquisition personnel. This may affect the generalizability of findings, and calls for broader involvement, including international, in future stages. Second, the validation relied on two structured workshops, providing useful insights but limited in scope. Additional engagements will be necessary to evaluate the artefact across roles and contexts. Lastly, in line with the iterative nature of DSRM some feedback has been deferred to future design cycles, where the artefact will continue to evolve through demonstration and evaluation.

6 Conclusions and Future Work

The overarching project aims to develop a framework for guiding the evolution of future military command and control systems, driven by the rapid advancements in AI, ICT, and autonomous weapon systems. The goal of the research presented in this article is to validate the initial iteration of the goal model and the concepts model, developed for the framework using Enterprise Modeling principles within the broader context of the DSRM framework.

The goal model was validated through EFGs comprising a diverse range of military C2-system stakeholders. The concepts model was validated by examining how it integrates its core elements, such as domain concepts, expert insights, and ME constructs, into the proposed framework. The models validated in this paper represent the domain needs and stakeholder goals and requirements for the envisioned framework. We have validated them with a group of stakeholders different from the initial group that participated in the elicitation phase. The refined goal model has been updated based on feedback, reaching a level of maturity that allows it to be used in identifying framework components for the next phase of the overarching project. The stakeholders represent the organizations involved in the design, procurement, and use of C2-systems, and they have the competence profiles similar to those of the intended users of the framework. This validation step supported the development of a reasonably complete and stable set of goals and requirements, against which future development iterations will be validated.

To summarize, the key findings are as follows: First, stakeholders appreciated the goal model's hierarchical structure, which links tactical needs to strategic objectives and aligns high-level goals with operational requirements. Second, they emphasized the importance of incorporating practical constraints to maintain the model's relevance in real-time, dynamic scenarios. Third, stakeholders suggested streamlining the model to reduce redundant feedback loops, making it more effective for both immediate and long-term strategic decision-making. Fourth, they highlighted the need to integrate cultural and organizational factors to ensure the model aligns technical systems with military values and adaptability. Finally, the combination of the goal model with the concepts model was seen as a key enhancement, fostering better communication among the stakeholders and between stakeholders and developers, all of which contributes to increasing adaptability in dynamic operational environments.

As part of the DSRM, future work in the overarching research project will involve developing the modeling components and method extensions found missing in current C2-system development frameworks, and demonstrating their practical utility. Specifically, considering the improvements suggested by stakeholders in this study, we will explore and integrate the framework of Anticipatory Ethics for Emerging Technologies (AET) [25] into our envisioned conceptual framework. AET emphasizes the integration of ethical dimensions into the design process to ensure that C2-systems design aligns with ethical principles. This approach enables designers to proactively identify and address potential ethical challenges.

All data, for instance, transcriptions and participants' personal notes, are securely stored by the first author and will remain accessible for potential future review and use in future research.

References

1. NATO. NATO Architecture Framework Version 4 Acknowledgments for NAFv4 Publication (2020)
2. Lundberg, J.: Towards a conceptual framework for system of systems. In: CEUR Workshop Proceedings (2023). https://ceur-ws.org/Vol-3407/paper3.pdf. Accessed 01 May 2024
3. Andersson, K., Lundberg, J., Stirna, J.: Emerging technology calls for a systemic view on military capability. In: Poels, G., Van Riel, J., Fernandes Calhau, R. (eds.) CEUR-WS.org, Vienna (2023). https://ceur-ws.org/Vol-3645/facete2.pdf. Accessed 04 April 2024
4. Lundberg, J., Stirna, J., Zdravkovic, J., Andersson, K.: Beyond technology: goal-oriented analysis for integrating emerging technologies into military command and control systems. In: 29th International Command and Control Research and Technology Symposium, London (2024)
5. Lundberg, J., Stirna, J., Andersson, K.: Designing military command and control systems as system of systems – an analysis of stakeholder needs and challenges. In: Advanced Information Systems Engineering, pp. 336–351 (2024). https://doi.org/10.1007/978-3-031-61057-8_20
6. Lundberg, J., Hacks, S., Andersson, K.: Refinement of a conceptual model of a military C2-system through low-level goal decomposition. In: Companion Proceedings of the 17th IFIP WG 8.1 Working Conference on the Practice of Enterprise Modeling Forum, 2024. https://ceur-ws.org/Vol-3855/forum9.pdf. Accessed 04 December 2024
7. Hevner, March, Park, Ram: Design science in information systems research. MIS Q. **28**(1), 75 (2004). https://doi.org/10.2307/25148625
8. US Army – Army Futures Command. Army Futures Command Concept for Command and Control 2028: Pursuing Decision Dominance (2021)

9. Boardman, J., Sauser, B.: System of systems – the meaning of of. In: Proceedings 2006 IEEE/SMC International Conference on System of Systems Engineering, pp. 118–123 (2006). https://doi.org/10.1109/sysose.2006.1652284
10. Sandkuhl, K., Stirna, J., Persson, A., Wißotzki, M.: Enterprise Modeling Tackling Business Challenges with the 4EM Method (2014). https://doi.org/10.1007/978-3-662-43725-4
11. Alberts, D.S.: Agility, focus, and convergence: the future of command and control. Int. C2 J. (2007)
12. Nato Research and Technology Organization. Conceptual Modeling (CM) for Military Modeling and Simulation (M&S) (2012). https://apps.dtic.mil/sti/citations/ADA569241. Accessed 02 December 2024
13. Gil, E.B., Rodrigues, G.N., Pelliccione, P., Calinescu, R.: Mission specification and decomposition for multi-robot systems. Rob. Auton. Syst. **163**, 104386 (2023). https://doi.org/10.1016/J.ROBOT.2023.104386
14. Subiyakto, A., Ahlan, A.R., Putra, S.J., Kartiwi, M.: Validation of information system project success model: a focus group study. SAGE Open **5**(2), 1–14 (2015). https://doi.org/10.1177/2158244015581650/ASSET/IMAGES/LARGE/10.1177_2158244015581650-FIG5.JPEG
15. Denscombe, M.: The Good Research Guide for Small-Scale Social Research Projects, 4th ed. Open University Press (2010)
16. Krogstie, J., Krogstie, J.: SEQUAL as a Framework for Understanding and Assessing Quality of Models and Modeling Languages, pp. 1611–1620. https://doi.org/10.4018/978-1-4666-5888-2.CH154
17. Stewart, D.W., Shamdasani, P.N., Rook, D.W.: Focus Groups: Theory and Practice (2007). https://doi.org/10.4135/9781412991841
18. Tremblay, M.C., Hevner, A.R., Berndt, D.J.: Focus groups for artifact refinement and evaluation in design research. In: Communications of the Association for Information Systems, vol. 26 (2010). https://doi.org/10.17705/1CAIS.02627
19. Deverka, P.A., et al.: Stakeholder participation in comparative effectiveness research: defining a framework for effective engagement. J. Comp. Eff. Res. **1**(2), 181 (2012). https://doi.org/10.2217/CER.12.7
20. Lundberg, J., Stirna, J., Andersson, K.: Operationalizing Military Insights – A Second Report on C2-System Development. https://www.researchgate.net/publication/386328609_Operationalizing_military_insights_-A_second_report_on_C2-System_development. Accessed 02 December 2024
21. Braun, V., Clarke, V.: Using thematic analysis in psychology. Qual. Res. Psychol. **3**(2), 77–101 (2006). https://doi.org/10.1191/1478088706qp063oa
22. Ralyté, J., Rolland, C.: An approach for method reengineering. In: Lecture Notes in Computer Science (including subseries Lecture Notes in Artificial Intelligence and Lecture Notes in Bioinformatics), vol. 2224, pp. 471–484 (2001).https://doi.org/10.1007/3-540-45581-7_35
23. Henderson-Sellers, B., Ralyté, J., Ågerfalk, P.J., Rossi, M.: Situational Method Engineering, pp. 1–310 (2014). https://doi.org/10.1007/978-3-642-41467-1
24. Lundberg, J., Stirna, J., Andersson, K., Zdravkovic, J.: Beyond technology: goal-oriented analysis for integrating emerging technologies into military command and control systems. In: International Command and Control Research and Technology Symposium, London (2024)
25. Brey, P.A.E.: Anticipatory ethics for emerging technologies. NanoEthics **6**(1), 1–13 (2012). https://doi.org/10.1007/S11569-012-0141-7/TABLES/1

Supporting Collaborative Design by Diagram Briefs in the Early Stage of Innovation Projects

Tobias Kautz[✉] [ID] and Robert Winter [ID]

University of St. Gallen, Institute of Information Systems and Digital Business, 9000 St. Gallen, Switzerland
{tobias.kautz,robert.winter}@unisg.ch

Abstract. Methods, incl. modeling methods, are important for designing innovations. They (should) provide hands-on guidance for creating outcomes in a systematic way using certain techniques. These techniques need to be understood, (correctly) applied, and possibly also selected as well as arranged. Previous research called for more studies on the 'presentation formats' supporting these tasks, specifically for practitioners. This is especially relevant for the early stage of innovation projects. Here, business stakeholders with different disciplinary backgrounds engage in collaborative design who are not accustomed to, e.g., formalized notations. For this context, we develop support for understanding, selecting, arranging, and applying modeling techniques. Following the design science research paradigm, we develop the presentation format of a two-page diagram brief. The development of this artifact is informed by the established format of design cards as well as knowledge from research in enterprise modeling and situational method engineering. A brief is centered around one or few closely related diagrams and provides information structured along nine categories which are identical for all briefs. For example, briefs provide outcome creation and usage instructions, excerpts from a stakeholder perspective catalog, and quality criteria. The brief design is demonstrated through 18 briefs for strategy, organization, and high-level information technology design and evaluated with survey data (n = 88). Our research contributes a template for researchers, instructors, and practitioners to support lightweight, collaborative modeling by non-experts (i.e., grass-roots modeling) in the early stage of innovation projects.

Keywords: Innovation · Collaborative Design · Collaborative Modeling

1 Introduction

Innovations are highly relevant for companies [1]. Often, innovations involve information technology (IT), either as an enabler or at their core [1]. Thus, the integrated design of business and IT aspects [2] is the key concern of these projects. If business and IT aspects should be designed systematically, designers need to draw on methods [3, 4]. On the one hand, methods add value through structuring (design) activities in a systematic, consistent form [5]. On the other, they (should) provide 'hands-on' support for activities by means of techniques, i.e., detailed instructions to create results [5]. To fulfill the 'promise' of systematically created results, designers must (correctly) *apply* techniques and, as a precondition, *understand* them in the first place [6]. If a suitable method is not available, designers also need to *select* and *arrange* suitable techniques [4, 6, 7]. To support these tasks, considering the 'presentation formats' of methodical guidance is relevant [8]. Yet, presentation formats specifically for practitioners are an under-researched field [8]. This is especially relevant for the early stage of innovation projects, where we also have stakeholders not accustomed to, e.g., formalized notations (for examples cf. [7]). Briefs – in other words, two-paged handouts – have been found promising for presenting methodical guidance to practitioners [9]. However, the existing proposal for the conceptual design of such briefs does not consider the importance of modeling for design [2–4, 10] and of (situational) method engineering [4]. Following a design science research approach [11], we ask: *How can we support practitioners in an early stage of innovation projects in understanding, selecting, arranging, and applying modeling techniques?*

The remainder of the paper is structured as follows: First, we present the research background in Sect. 2, clarifying relevant design terminology incl. the notions of 'systematic' and 'collaborative' (Sect. 2.1) as well as the research gap (Sect. 2.2). Then, the approach to fill this gap and the solution objectives follow in Sect. 3. Thereafter, we outline our research methodology in Sect. 4. The brief design is elaborated in Sect. 5, before its demonstration is described in Sect. 6 and its evaluation in Sect. 7. The discussion and conclusion in Sect. 8 wrap up the paper.

2 Research Background

2.1 Design

Systematic Design through Artifacts. *Design* can be defined as "devis[ing] courses of action aimed at changing existing situations into preferred ones" [12, p. 111]. Note that such a definition views design as an overarching type of activity, covering other types like 'analysis' some authors [e.g., 13] see separate to design. Consequently, it is not restricted to – but covers – design as a phase as used in systems development [2]. If design should be approached systematically, practitioners can seek guidance from design *methods* [3, 4]. A method provides a set of suitable *techniques*, alongside an overall *procedure model*, *results* (i.e., outcomes) to be created/used, *roles*, and a *meta-model* [5]. Especially in the early stage of innovation projects, where limited 'real', material changes are made, *models* are an important type of results. Based on [14], a model can be defined as "a social artifact that is acknowledged by an observer to represent ... some domain for a particular purpose" [p. 60, emphases removed] in a more abstract manner. The 'tangible' form of the model is often a *diagram* [14], which provides a view (i.e., an excerpt) of the model [15]. Modeling is an important part of design [2–4, 10]. Broader definitions of an (enterprise) *modeling method* [e.g., 16] propose similar constituents as mentioned above. However, researchers acknowledge that design goes beyond modeling, e.g., if working out/deciding how something should be – which is central to design as defined above – and not 'just' documenting these decisions [10]. In other words, while having similar constituents, the 'scope' or 'nature' of activities relevant for design methods is wider than the one for modeling methods.

Yet, without guidance, created models may be neither coherent (i.e., forming an integral whole [17]) nor consistent (i.e., free from contradictions [17]). Again, methods can help to realize these properties through integrating the results with a meta-model [5]. Methods also provide techniques to support the hands-on creation of results [5]. In the case of models, these are *modeling techniques*. They consist of a *modeling language* (i.e., notation, syntax, and semantics) and a *modeling procedure* (i.e., activities and (sub-)results) [18]. Modeling languages used in an early, exploratory stage of business and IT design projects are often custom and potentially less expressive [19]. This fits well to the notion of "light-weight models [that] usually only . . . [have] less type and entity or relationship categories than [models created with] conventional modeling languages" [20, p. 78].

Technique Utilization Tasks. Evidently, designers need to *apply*, i.e., "to put into operation" [21], each technique to create the desired results. As a necessary pre-condition – which is especially important for non-experts – they need to have *understood* a technique before, i.e., they need "to know or realize how . . . something happens, how it works or why it is important" [22]. As explained above, the concrete techniques designers need to apply (and understand) can be prescribed by a design method. Yet, it might be that no method for the design problem exists at all. Or it might be that certain characteristics of the design problem (e.g., what exactly needs to be designed) and/or the problem context (e.g., industry) are so specific that no 'optimal' method exists [23]. Then, designers also need to *select* as well as *arrange*, i.e., "to put into a proper order or into a correct or suitable sequence, relationship, or adjustment" [24], suitable techniques [4, 7]. In these cases, situational method engineering (SME) helps to construct methods fitting to the situation, i.e., ones that are situational [4, 7, 23]. Thus, the aforementioned four *technique utilization tasks* (TUTs) were defined in analogy to the activities of (assembly-based) situational method construction [7, 25]. The relevance of similar tasks is also recognized by other researchers [e.g., 6].

Collaboration in Innovation Design. As with any design effort that integrates business and IT aspects [2], innovation projects actively involve stakeholders from various disciplines. Given that interdisciplinary stakeholders working jointly on a unified whole is known as *collaborative design* [26], we can view innovation design as an instance of collaborative design. Given the relevance of both modeling and collaboration for innovation design, one might also consider their intersection, i.e., *collaborative modeling* [2], which can be defined as "the joint creation of a shared graphical representation of a system" [27, p. 249].

2.2 Presentation Formats for Methodical Guidance to Support the Technique Utilization Tasks

Relevance. As elaborated in Sect. 2.1, designers need to be supported by means of methods and techniques. As also explained, even if potentially suitable techniques are available, designers still are confronted with the TUTs. In other words, 'just' having – and from a research perspective supplying – suitable design methods/techniques is necessary, but not sufficient [8]. To support the TUTs, it is important to consider adequate presentation formats, i.e., the way methodical guidance is conveyed to users [8]. Note that, as described in Sect. 2.1, methods can also provide support in the sense that they relieve designers from selecting and arranging techniques – yet not from understanding and applying them. In other words, even if a suitable method is available, the presentation format of a method is still relevant.

Examples. Examples for typical presentation formats in academic publications are, for instance, free text (already identified by [8]; e.g., [13]), tables (e.g., [28]), or maps (e.g., [28]). Software-based formats are, for example, templates for digital whiteboards (e.g., [29–31]), digital repositories (cf. the examples in Table 3 in Sect. 5), workflow-supporting software (already identified by [8]; e.g., [6, 31]), augmented reality (e.g., [32]) or artificial intelligence (e.g., [31, 33]). In design literature, cards are a popular presentation format [34]. Going beyond the 'over the fence' logic of the other formats, one might consider consulting/facilitation [cf. 6], which is in a modeling context known as participatory modeling [35].

Research Gap. An in-depth presentation of each format's potential to support the TUTs goes beyond the page limits of this paper. Summing up, some formats are not suitable for the context at hand (i.e., practitioners and non-experts in design/modeling) and/or show other disadvantages (e.g., regarding development effort, costs, or maturity). Moreover, several formats appear to be most suitable for specific TUTs. Though possibly providing 'worse' support for each individual task, a presentation format providing comprehensive support for all TUTs might be more easily usable, e.g., through avoiding media breaks when switching between presentation formats and 'translation/mappings' between the respective structures for presenting information. This easy usability might be especially relevant for individuals who are unfamiliar with techniques as such (i.e., beginners) [36] and/or with the documentation of techniques (e.g., practitioners).

Similar observations are made by other researchers. In an investigation of methods in a smart service context, Heinz and Anke [8] call for more research on adequate presentation formats for practitioners. The need for more application support is also recognized in the SME and modeling literature. There, the lack manifests in too technical formalizations [7] or an overly focus on the modeling language [35], respectively. The next section presents briefs, the presentation format we chose to close the gap.

3 Support Approach and Solution Objectives

Support Approach. As an example for the presentation format of briefs, the "InnoDeck" [9, p. 83] inter alia provides briefs for mainstream innovation methods (e.g., design thinking) or associated techniques (e.g., for data collection). Despite the referenced authors' usage of the term 'card', we prefer the term 'brief', given the artifact's rather large size of maximum two DIN-A4 pages [9]. As shown in Table 1 below, briefs have promising characteristics for providing comprehensive support for all TUTs.

Besides the potential to provide comprehensive support, particularly the low-tech character of briefs [9] appears promising. Unlike a software-based solution approach which could also provide comprehensive support [8], briefs allow for a quick research

Table 1. Characteristics of briefs (based on [9]) matched to TUTs.

TUT	Characteristics of briefs
Understanding	Conveying content easily and quickly
Selection	Short
Arrangement	Self-contained, having only optional references to other briefs
Application	• Highly memorable • Quickly readable at time of application

prototype to gain first insights. Yet, the shortcoming regarding the arrangement task requires further elaboration. It can be extended to the argument that the existing brief design proposal 'ignores' the role of modeling for design, i.e., its scope appears not to cover modeling techniques, and modeling and SME research have not informed its development [9]. In turn, this means that if briefs are 'infused' with knowledge from these areas, we believe that they can also support the arrangement task.

Solution Objectives. Based on the elaborations so far, we derive the following solution objectives: A generic, conceptual brief design should provide comprehensive support for understanding, selecting, arranging, and applying modeling techniques from a pre-defined set. Briefs should be usable in the early stage of innovation projects by heterogeneous stakeholders that are often non-experts in modeling – if not design – to create lightweight diagrams. Given the necessity of being trained before using briefs [9], having experienced training before usage is assumed. The next section summarizes the training users received in our case and the followed research methodology in general.

4 Research Methodology

Overall, we followed the process model by Peffers et al. [11]. The problem was identified, and solution objectives were derived based on the authors' experience in teaching innovation design, validated through the literature presented in the previous sections. For the design/development, literature on SME, enterprise modeling, and design cards as well as existing technique repositories provided inspiration (cf. Sect. 5, especially Table 3). The information to be included onto the briefs were then determined and graphically allocated. It should be noted that the development of the briefs was conducted in parallel to the development of another, complementary artifact. Changes to the briefs' conceptual design and to the created ('instantiated') briefs (incl. which ones are contained in the set) were made after each evaluation, i.e., then a new iteration started [11]. Given the seven evaluations (cf. Sect. 7), this implies seven iterations.

The research team's involvement in teaching innovation design provided the opportunity to demonstrate and evaluate the briefs efficiently in a setting coming close to the situation outlined in Sect. 2. In concrete, this was an Executive MBA course focusing on the early stage of innovation projects. For the exam, groups of executives were charged to present a design associated to a real-life case from their professional background, either a current/future one or a past one in retrospect. For that purpose, executives had to *understand* the techniques presented on the lecture slides (based on [4], cf. Section 6 for examples), *select* the ones best fitting to their case, *arrange* them, and of course *apply* them. Yet, for the first, fourth and seventh evaluations (cf. Section 7), the same case was given to all groups and/or the techniques were to a larger degree pre-selected. Inter alia, this was a consequence of the course content (incl. the set of briefs, while overlaps existed) being split into two modules (i.e., teaching blocks), where executives participated once in each module. The cases comprised various types of innovations and transformations. The design (result) were several diagrams, mostly based on sticky notes created with the online whiteboard *miro* (www.miro.com) recommended and trained in the course – another facet of lightweight modeling [cf. 37].

Executives came from different industries and had at least five years of job experience. They worked in business, IT, and 'interfacing' roles and often had no dedicated modeling experience. Usually, in the beginning of the modules, the briefs as a support artifact were introduced, alongside some 'disclaimers' (e.g., regarding completeness) and an overview about the briefs available for the individual design tasks was given (incl. a rough sequence for the design tasks within the enterprise architecture layers referenced in the next section). Depending on the module and the concrete run of the course (i.e., a conducted module), sometimes the executives were reminded of this overview, or the availability of a brief was mentioned on the lecture slides for the respective modeling technique. The executives were provided with the briefs on the course's online learning platform. Noteworthy, engaging with the briefs was in the executives' responsibility, i.e., the lecturer did not go through the individual briefs.

For the most runs, evaluation began after one course week, in which a presentation of the – depending on the module intermediate or final – groupwork results had taken place. Given the 'straightforward' (i.e., from a usage perspective non-complex) nature of the artifact, we opted for an anonymous survey. Due to the development parallel to the other artifact (incl. its evaluation) and the constraint of not asking 'too many' questions, we focused on the understanding and application tasks. We also concentrated on the most important evaluation criteria, which we considered to be – quite evidently – the effectiveness/objective achievement and comprehensibility of the instantiated contents (i.e., not to be confused with how the format as such supports understanding) [38]. We also asked for usage intensity (i.e., for control purposes) as well as for the appropriateness of the information on the briefs and any other feedback. The survey instrument is provided under https://doi.org/10.6084/m9.figshare.28823507.

5 Design of the Briefs

In the following, we outline our design decisions regarding two major aspects. First, the scope, i.e., subject or type of content shown on the briefs. Second, the choice of the categories through which the information is structured. More information on these aspects and an overview of other ones to consider is provided, e.g., in [9, 34, 39].

Scope. Given the relevance of modeling for design, briefs are 'centered' around a diagram – or, more precisely, a diagram type [4, 15] – as a 'core result', sometimes also several closely related diagrams. Each diagram refers to a 'theme' of innovation design (e.g., value proposition, business processes) [4, 15]. Among others, briefs then contain information on components of the modeling technique associated to the respective diagram [15]. For example, information on the modeling procedure [18] is provided in the category 'Procedure' of a brief. Yet, in line with other researchers, we believe that the understanding of and ease of application in a real business environment increases if the diagram is put into an end-to-end context [13, 30]. Thus, depending on the space

Table 2. Description of information categories.

Information category	Contents (based on prescriptions from literature, if applicable)
Design Layer Allocation	Allocates a diagram onto a **design layer** [2, 15] **adopted from enterprise architecture** layers [3, 4, 40]
Purpose	Comprises two parts: 1) Statement on **'what the diagram does'** • Uses verbs such as 'show', 'describe' – or, referring to more specific operations – 'aggregate', 'relate', etc. • Mentions the concepts (cf. respective row below) that are used in the diagram, in some cases these are used to explain how an overarching concept (e.g., a business model, value proposition) is decomposed 2) List of analytical, sometimes also 'social' **tasks a diagram supports** [cf. 41], where the most important are picked up in the category 'Procedure'
Addressed Stakeholders	• Oriented at a **stakeholder perspective catalog**, which aims to make the value of models for certain stakeholders explicit [42] • Concretely, a **stakeholder** (i.e., a business-related role), one or few important (business-related) **goals** of her/him, and **how the diagram can help** achieving a respective goal is shown (referring to the actor, need, and consequence in [42], respectively) • Mostly, the help relates to **satisfying information requirements**
Input/Output-Relationships	• Shows the **input-** (i.e., dependency) and **output-relationships**, mainly to **other diagrams** • Relationships are considered **content-wise**, often based on the relations between concepts of the respective diagrams, i.e., they are similar to "semantic linkages" [43, p. 10] (cf. to row for the category 'Concept') • Concretely, the **name of the other diagram** is mentioned, and the **relationship** is **shortly described**, possibly referencing relevant shared concepts • Sometimes the relationships also regard a **group of diagrams** (with a specified commonality), **representations in other forms** than diagrams [cf. 14], or **processes** that deliver required results for which however no common diagram (group) is established (and thus recognizable by users)

(*continued*)

Table 2. (*continued*)

Information category	Contents (based on prescriptions from literature, if applicable)
Alternatives	• Shows (some) **alternatives** (possibly with a hyperlinked reference) in terms of **diagrams/modeling languages** or **briefs**, sometimes also **'design paradigms'** [cf. 25] (e.g., agile vs 'traditional') • Sometimes also **explicitly states** that there is **no alternative**, together with a **rationale** and/or **specific diagrams/modeling languages** that are explicitly **no alternatives** (but might wrongly be seen as such) • Especially important for non-experts, often also the **differences** between the **diagram** and the **alternatives** are summarized in terms of **'constructional'**, superficial differences (e.g., related to concepts, degree of formality, the kind of diagram, other beneficial properties) or **'functional'**, **effect-related** differences (e.g., associated to the suitability for a specific problem context, supported tasks from the category 'Purpose', possibilities to be combined with other techniques, (non-)beneficial results that can be achieved from a business perspective)
Concepts	• Are **constructs** in a (brief-specific) **meta-model** (i.e., the syntax [18]) • Yet, **'concepts'** is used to be **more easily understandable** for practitioners • Mostly, the concepts are the ones that are **'visibly' instantiated** in the respective **diagram** • Sometimes, concepts are also relevant for, e.g., **understanding another concept**, **activities** in the category 'Procedure', or a **diagram's scope** (e.g., customer segment for which a value proposition is designed) • **Integration** between the brief-specific meta-models is achieved by **"interlinked metamodels"** [43, p. 10], where linkages were made explicit for the user through the category 'Input/Output-Relationships' • **Each concept** is introduced as a **term followed by a short explanation** (i.e., the semantics [18]) • Depending on the difficulty of the concept, sometimes also **examples** were provided for promoting comprehensibility

(*continued*)

Table 2. (*continued*)

Information category	Contents (based on prescriptions from literature, if applicable)
Procedure	Basic content: • Lists the **activities** that are necessary **for creating the diagram** (i.e., modeling procedure [18] in the narrower sense) as well as **preparatory** activities and activities **'post-processing'** the diagram (cf. explanations at the beginning of Sect. 5) • Given space constraints, activities are described at **different levels of detail** and/or **hyperlinked references** are provided to more detailed descriptions • If available, also hyperlinks to **questions triggering ideas** for the **instantiation of the concepts** are shown [30, 35] Provides information relevant for **situational design approaches**, which comprise: • **Situation-related characteristics** regarding the **problem context** (e.g., related to organizational characteristics, focal 'design object'/domain [cf. 25], involved stakeholders, available software tools) and **design problem** (e.g., related to existing/intermediate results and supported tasks from the category 'Purpose') • **Adaptions** (often) based on these characteristics especially regarding **activities** (e.g., additional/alternative ones, other sequence, scoping) or the **diagram directly** (e.g., versions, contents) • **Options**, either similar to a **"strategy"** [7, p. 100] (e.g., possible information sources, techniques, briefs) or regarding the **actual modeling** (e.g., possible visualizations for intermediate results, modeling languages, adaptions while modeling [cf. 44])
Example	• Comprises an **exemplary instance** of the diagram for **illustration purposes** • **Chosen** based on its **degree of difficulty**, e.g., in some cases a textbook example was preferred over a real-life one • Sometimes showing only **excerpts** of the diagram or **exemplary instances of concepts** • Sometimes complemented by **textual explanations** (e.g., as speech bubbles) • Included as a **high-resolution graphic** and offering a **hyperlink to a digital whiteboard** providing a maximally zoomable view
Quality Criteria	• Lists the most important **quality criteria** [35], sometimes also considering **common mistakes**, which are relevant for a **content-wise** and **'technically clean'** diagram (and therefore must be kept in mind to fulfill the purpose [41]) • Sometimes also refers to the **activities as such** (e.g., that customers need to be involved in the creation of a diagram)

available, briefs also shortly outline other activities relevant before or after the diagram is created, potentially with an explicit reference to a technique (e.g., for data collection).

Information Categories. To enable comparability, information categories should be identical for all created briefs [9, 25]. Table 2 provides a description of each information category, also referencing relevant concepts from modeling research. Due to the two-page space limit, only the most relevant category candidates were included on the briefs, as shown in Table 3. Additionally, Table 3 compares a category to common concepts from SME as well as categories found in the investigated technique repositories, as these provided inspiration. The concepts from SME are mainly based on the comprehensive

Table 3. Relevance of the information categories. In the first column, categories that can similarly be found in the brief design proposal by [9] are indicated with an asterisk (*). For the last column, please note that not all items in a repository were investigated, so the matching might be incomplete.

Information category	Conceptual rationale for inclusion (based on prescriptions from literature, if applicable)	Inspired by…	
		Concepts from SME	Investigated repositories
Design Layer Allocation	• Provides overview [45], given the temporal implications (see next bullet) • Provides rough indication of logical and temporal allocation [3, 4, 40]	Other layering used, e.g., logical/ technical [25]	[46, 47]
Purpose*	Considers that models are defined through their purpose [14]	Goal, definition [25]	[46–49]
Addressed Stakeholders	Shows satisfiable information requirements, which are highly relevant for change [50]	Destination [25]	*Only involved roles* [33, 46, 47]
Input/Output-Relationships	• Informs about dependencies, which are important for sequence [25] • Must be 'kept in mind' for realizing coherency/consistency	Association [25]	[46, 47, 49] (yet without specifying how other items are related)
Alternatives	Makes design approaches situational	*Inherent*	[33]
Concepts	• Shows satisfiable information requirements (fine-grained) • Relevant for realizing coherency/consistency of results [5]	Root [25]	[48, 49] (yet partially just implicitly defined through questions)

(*continued*)

Table 3. (*continued*)

Information category	Conceptual rationale for inclusion (based on prescriptions from literature, if applicable)	Inspired by...	
		Concepts from SME	Investigated repositories
Procedure*	*Evidently relevant for application*	Process aspects [7]	[48, 49]
Example*	• Makes the other categories more tangible • Provides orientation	*Not explicitly found*	[48, 49]
Quality Criteria	Guides application [35]	Rules [25]	[47, 49]

list of elements for selecting and assembling method building blocks proposed in [25]. Exemplary content is illustrated in the next section.

6 Demonstration

The final, relevant set comprises 18 created briefs on three design layers [3, 4, 40]: Briefs on the *strategy* layer cover the design of the (1) business environment, (2) business ecosystem, (3) business model, (4) value proposition, (5) customer journey, and (6) goal system. On the *organization* layer, briefs cover the design of the (7) process architecture, (8) end-to-end processes, (9) process outputs, and processes, both for processes (10) with high customer involvement and (11) without high customer involvement. Moreover, briefs exist for (12) an institutionalized project/program organization as well as the information structure, both (13) analytical and (14) transactional. On the *alignment* layer, high-level IT design is covered by briefs for (15) capability mapping and (16) application landscape design. Other briefs relate to (17) visually highly attractive diagrams especially for communication purposes and (18) an instrument for project portfolio management. Figure 1 shows an exemplary brief for a (5) customer journey diagram. An additional example for a (11) process diagram can be found under https://doi.org/10.6084/m9.figshare.28823393.

7 Evaluation

Table 4 below summarizes the results of the evaluations (i.e., mean values, rounded) conducted along multiple runs of the course.

Much qualitative feedback relates to the category 'Example' (i.e., the number of examples provided, their content and format) and not to the actual, conceptual design of the briefs. One respondent also recognized the need to instantiate the contents and that this is not always directly possible but might be facilitated by providing reference models (e.g., showing common processes). Other feedback selectively occurring during almost all evaluations concerns the graphical design (e.g., density of text and information

Supporting Collaborative Design by Diagram Briefs 379

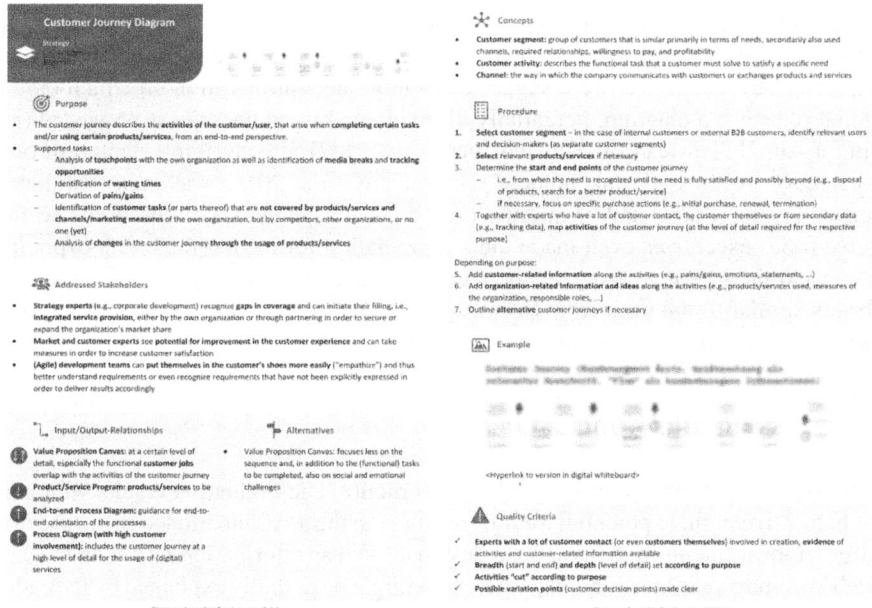

Fig. 1. Exemplary brief for a (5) customer journey diagram, translated into English (first/front and second/back page). Slight content and color/font adaptations were made for comprehensibility and anonymity, respectively.

Table 4. Evaluation results. Scales range from 1 to 5 (the higher the better). Evaluations 1/4/7 and 2/3/5/6 were conducted in each module (cf. Sect. 4), respectively. Thus, the 'n'-row refers to respondents, not unique executives. Specifically for evaluation no. 7, only 15 (not 16) responses were received for the comprehensibility criterion.

Evaluation number (i.e., one for each run of the course)	1	2	3	4	5	6	7
n	26	8	10	11	14	3	16
Usage intensity (e.g., in terms of frequency, duration)	3.69	3.88	4.30	3.27	3.93	4.00	3.69
Effectiveness (for supporting understanding task)	4.27	4.38	4.50	4.09	4.36	5.00	4.00
Effectiveness (for supporting application task)	3.69	4.38	4.30	4.09	4.29	5.00	3.88
Comprehensibility (of contents)	3.81	4.13	4.10	4.00	4.21	4.33	4.07

in general), the explanations within the categories (e.g., level of detail), and the desire for more references to further information. Other occasional feedback from the first and fourth evaluation is the desire to have more concrete and detailed application instructions in the category 'Procedure'. One respondent criticized the briefs for being too theoretical and not having helped much for the practical application. One participant also demanded diagram 'templates' for each design task relevant for the exam. No category is considered superfluous, and the categories are judged rather exhaustive (given that nearly no completely new categories were suggested). Only once, information on which organizational roles use a diagram, potentially differentiated by industry, was requested (i.e., taking a 'supply' instead of 'demand' perspective [42] already implemented through the category 'Addressed Stakeholders'). Frequently (n = 20), it was indicated that no category is superfluous and/or missing (based on engagement with the briefs so far). Twelve times executives even made their appreciation for having the briefs explicit in the free text fields of the survey. Respondents also selectively mentioned useful features of briefs similar to the ones from Sect. 3, i.e., being compact and logically structured, containing important facts, as well as giving an overview.

8 Discussion and Conclusion

Evaluation-Indicated Potential for Improvement. The evaluation results with averages below five point to potential for improvement in the areas mentioned in the previous section. Improvements of the graphical design as well as information related to the category 'Procedure', explanations, and references might be partially explained by individual differences. These are, e.g., visual preferences as well as pre-experience, perceptive ability, and interest in a topic, respectively. Moreover, all improvement areas might require attention every time briefs are revised, e.g., when identifying new potential for references. The areas of information related to the category 'Procedure' and explanations also point to a more fundamental issue, i.e., that the space for providing information is limited. Together with the intention to provide end-to-end information on the procedure – in contrast to the course contents and exam requirements focusing on the final designs – this might be one factor explaining why the potential to support the application task is rated (slightly) lower in evaluations one, three, five, and seven.

Contribution. This research has enhanced a presentation format, i.e., a brief, to support modeling/design non-experts in understanding, selecting, arranging, and applying (lightweight) modeling techniques in the early stage of innovation projects. The linkage to SME and enterprise modeling has made it possible to close the gap between the more formal aspects of modularizing and the rather informal way of presenting methodical guidance in the brief design proposal in [9]. Against this backdrop, researchers – or method experts in companies – can draw on the presentation format of a diagram brief to create briefs for other lightweight modeling techniques. Analogously, instructors might adopt this format as a template for their own modeling techniques or methods. Specifically for the latter, the briefs might be used as a complementary artifact to facilitate understanding and applying the respective techniques. Thus, overall, this research also answers to the call for "work . . . on how grass-roots model creation and use can be supported and stimulated" [20, p. 75].

Limitations. Yet, some limitations exist. The first concerns the investigation of existing solutions. While keyword-based and selective forward searches were performed, no dedicated systematic search was conducted. Related to that, for the understanding task we have not considered technique teaching or more cognitive aspects of understanding and visualization [cf. 8]. For the selection task, our focus on lightweight models/diagrams might have overlooked projectable categories from, e.g., classifications/comparisons or selection approaches for conventional [20] enterprise modeling techniques. For example, in [51], a "fact sheet" [p. 277] is used – yet without further details on its 'shape' or creation – as a research instrument to discuss reviewed modeling languages for industrial product service systems with practitioners. After a first comparison of their proposed categories with the ones of the briefs, while overlaps exist, several of the proposed categories also appear less relevant. In concrete, these are the number of concepts, symbols, standardization, and software support [51]. For the arrangement task, our focus on the dominant approaches to SME (as documented in [7]) has, e.g., not in detail considered method engineering based on multi-level modeling [15]. Last, for the application task, we did not cover more detailed aspects of application such as group dynamics/interactions [e.g., 2], "ways-of-working" [52, p. 337], and (projectable) insights from modelling session setup and facilitation [e.g., 16, 29, 30, 35]. Regarding the final design, the scope of briefs, their 'ideal type', and the features making modeling with briefs 'lightweight' has been rather emergent over the iterations. For the demonstration, we relied on a rather small set of diagrams. If the number of relevant diagrams significantly increases, it may be necessary to introduce further (sub-)categories. Several limitations also arose due to the possibly to 'easily' chosen evaluation setting in an education and no corporate context, especially regarding long-term usage and existing ways of presenting models. For example, in an empirical study of model usage in design projects that integrate business and IT aspects [19], the authors find that practitioners already use a "method for phenomena" [p. 1310], i.e., a short description about the content of a model in relation to the real-world, managerial phenomenon (i.e., similar to the category 'Purpose') – which appears to be, however, not standardized like the briefs. Back to the course, evaluation results might be biased through respondents 'intermingling' what should have been evaluated (i.e., presentation format of a brief in principle vs. created briefs vs. overall course contents), an evaluation relative to how well the modeling techniques have been initially conveyed in the lecture, and the possibility to take the survey two times with a different set of briefs. This was also selectively indicated by 'the briefs have been better last time' comments in the survey. Also sporadically mentioned in the survey, time to engage with the briefs was limited. In general, the evaluations might have been conducted too early. Last, not having evaluated support for selection and arrangement as well as not having collected data about the executives' prior experience with modeling (incl. software tools) are limitations.

Future Research Opportunities. Besides addressing the limitations, we see future research opportunities in the following areas: One could explore how the brief design might also facilitate a basic understanding of conventional [20] modeling techniques by non-experts, especially from business, through omitting certain information/categories (cf. the comparison with fact sheets above) and focusing on the ones relevant for a brief. In other words and similar to [20], a notion of 'lightweight' is created through replacing 'traditional' aspects of modeling through new ones more relevant in the context of (non-expert) business stakeholders. This could also be relevant for participatory modeling, where for certain purposes (slightly) more complex modeling techniques might be selected, arranged, and applied by the modeling experts but where stakeholders still need to understand them [35]. Regarding the contents, one might identify necessary briefs more systematically and create briefs for results other than diagrams. Concerning the format, the briefs might additionally be 'translated' into templates for digital whiteboards (cf. Sect. 2.2), keeping the volume of information similarly compact and using the same categories. Specifically, these categories, that are conceptually (cf. Sect. 5) and empirically (cf. Sect. 7) validated for their relevance, might complement existing templates such as the one in [29], which focuses on procedural and notational information. Given a sufficiently high number of created briefs, types (e.g., for relationships in the category 'Input/Output-Relationships') or patterns of brief usage per design problem can be identified [8, 9, 13]. These patterns could also provide a basis for developing briefs into a situational method. This may inter alia also require further adaptations to the briefs' conceptual design, e.g., additional categories from the different types of method building blocks known in SME [7]. Last, one might use the presentation format of a brief for diagrams with a design focus other than IT/business alignment, such as sustainability.

Acknowledgments. We thank the participants of the *1st European Workshop on Research for Impact in Digital Innovation* for their comments on an early version of the brief design, the guest lecturers for their collaboration on the creation of briefs, and the reviewers for their feedback.

Disclosure of Interests. The authors have no competing interests to declare that are relevant to the content of this article.

Transparency on Usage of GenAI. The translation tool DeepL (www.deepl.com) was used to improve some passages in this article (incl. tables and figures).

References

1. Teo, T.S.H., Ranganathan, C., Srivastava, S.C., Loo, J.W.K.: Fostering IT-enabled business innovation at YCH group. MIS Q. Exec. **6**(4), 75–81 (2007)
2. Rittgen, P.: Collaborative business and information systems design. Int. J. e-Collab. **5**(4), 1–15 (2009)
3. Winter, R.: Organisational design and engineering – proposal of a conceptual framework and comparison of business engineering with other approaches. Int. J. Org. Des. Eng. **1**(1–2), 126–147 (2010)
4. Winter, R.: Business Engineering Navigator – Gestaltung und Analyse von Geschäftslösungen "Business-to-IT." Springer, Berlin, Heidelberg (2011)
5. Braun, C., Wortmann, F., Hafner, M., Winter, R.: Method construction – a core approach to organizational engineering. In: ACM Symposium on Applied Computing, pp. 1295–1299. ACM, Santa Fe (2005)
6. Steffen, B., Moller, F.: Linking multi-perspectives to enable educated decision making in digital platform design. In: Annual Computers Software, and Applications Conference, pp. 1135–1140. IEEE, Los Alamitos (2022)
7. Henderson-Sellers, B., Ralyté, J., Ågerfalk, P.J., Rossi, M.: Situational Method Engineering. Springer, Berlin, Heidelberg (2014)

8. Heinz, D., Anke, J.: Empowering practitioners: a conceptual framework for value co-creation through smart service innovation methodologies. In: European Conference on Information Systems, pp. 1–18. Kristiansand (2023)
9. Kasper, H., Pohl, V., Kochanowski, M.: InnoDeck: card based innovation support – a modular human-centered approach to facilitate innovation workshops. In: International Joint Conference on Knowledge Discovery, Knowledge Engineering and Knowledge Management, pp. 83–91. SciTePress, Vienna (2019)
10. Kannengiesser, U., Gero, J.S.: Modelling the design of models: an example using CRISP-DM. In: International Conference on Engineering Design, pp. 2705–2714. Cambridge University Press, Bordeaux (2023)
11. Peffers, K., Tuunanen, T., Rothenberger, M.A., Chatterjee, S.: A design science research methodology for information systems research. J. Manag. Inf. Syst. **24**(3), 45–77 (2007)
12. Simon, H.A.: The Sciences of the Artificial, 3rd edn. MIT Press, Cambridge, London (1996)
13. Alter, S., Bork, D.: Systems analysis and design toolkit based on work system theory and its extensions. J. Database Manage. **31**(3), 1–13 (2020)
14. Proper, H.A., Guizzardi, G.: On domain conceptualization. In: Aveiro, D., Guizzardi, G., Pergl, R., Proper, H.A. (eds.) Advances in Enterprise Engineering XIV, LNBIP, vol. 411, pp. 49–69. Springer, Cham (2021)
15. Frank, U.: Multi-perspective enterprise modeling: foundational concepts, prospects and future research challenges. Softw. Syst. Model. **13**(3), 941–962 (2014)
16. Sandkuhl, K., Stirna, J., Persson, A., Wißotzki, M.: Enterprise Modeling: Tackling Business Challenges within the 4EM Method. Springer, Berlin, Heidelberg (2014)
17. Dietz, J.L.G., Mulder, H.B.F.: Enterprise Ontology, 2nd edn. Springer, Cham (2024)
18. Karagiannis, D., Kühn, H.: Metamodelling platforms. In: Bauknecht, K., Min Tjoa, A., Quirchmayer, G. (eds.) EC Web 2002: E-Commerce and Web Technologies, LNCS, vol. 2455. Springer, Berlin, Heidelberg (2002)
19. Anaby-Tavor, A., et al.: Insights into enterprise conceptual modeling. Data Knowl. Eng. **69**(12), 1302–1318 (2010)
20. Sandkuhl, K., et al.: From expert discipline to common practice: a vision and research agenda for extending the reach of enterprise modeling. Bus. Inf. Syst. Eng. **60**(1), 69–80 (2018)
21. apply verb. https://www.merriam-webster.com/dictionary/apply. Accessed 04 January 2025
22. understand verb. https://www.oxfordlearnersdictionaries.com/definition/english/understand. Accessed 04 January 2025
23. Bucher, T., Klesse, M., Kurpjuweit, S., Winter, R.: Situational method engineering. In: Ralyté, J., Brinkkemper, S., Henderson-Sellers, A. (eds.) Situational Method Engineering: Fundamentals and Experiences, IFIP – The International Federation for Information Processing, vol. 244, pp. 33–48. Springer, Boston, MA (2007)
24. arrange verb. https://www.merriam-webster.com/dictionary/arrange. Accessed 04 January 2025
25. Harmsen, A.F.: Situational Method Engineering [Dissertation]. University of Twente (1997)
26. Tessier, V.: Insights on collaborative design research: a scoping review. Des. J. **23**(5), 655–675 (2020)
27. Renger, M., Kolfschoten, G.L., Vreede, G.J.D.: Challenges in collaborative modelling: a literature review and research agenda. Int. J. Simul. Process Model. **4**(3/4) (2008)
28. Tsai, C.H., Zdravkovic, J., Stirna, J.: Model-based digital business ecosystems: a method design. In: Hinkelmann, K., López-Pellicer, F.J., Polini, A. (eds.) Perspectives in Business Informatics Research, LNBIP, vol. 493, pp. 214–228. Springer, Cham (2023)
29. de Vries, M., Opperman, P.: Improving active participation during enterprise operations modeling with an extended story-card-method and participative modeling software. Softw. Syst. Model. **22**(4), 1341–1368 (2023)

30. Venter, A., de Vries, M.: Evaluating the usability of online tools during participatory enterprise modelling, using the business model canvas. In: Nah, F.F.-H., Siau, K.L. (eds.) HCI in Business, Government and Organizations, Lecture Notes in Computer Science, vol. 14721, pp. 96–114. Springer, Cham (2024)
31. Kudryavtsev, D.: AI-driven digital business design assistant: a prototype demo. In: International Conference on Software Business, pp. 1–4. CEUR-WS.org, Lahti (2023)
32. Fill, H.-G., Muff, F.: Bridging the mental and the physical world: conceptual modeling and augmented reality. In: Strecker, S., Jung, J. (eds.) Informing Possible Future Worlds: Essays in Honour of Ulrich Frank, pp. 197–212. Logos Verlag, Berlin (2024)
33. Liu, X., He, S., Maedche, A.: Designing an AI-based advisory platform for design techniques. In: European Conference on Information Systems, pp. 1–16. Stockholm-Uppsala (2019)
34. Aarts, T., et al.: Design card sets. In: Designing Interactive Systems Conference, pp. 419–428. ACM, Eindhoven (2020)
35. Stirna, J., Persson, A.: Enterprise Modeling: Facilitating the Process and the People. Springer, Cham (2018)
36. Liu, X., Werder, K., Maedche, A.: Novice digital service designers' decision-making with decision aids – a comparison of taxonomy and tags. Decis. Support Syst. **137**, Article 113367 (2020)
37. Kautz, T., Winter, R.: Digital transformation designer: towards a comprehensive, collaborative and easy-to-use modeling support for enterprise-wide change programs. Enterp. Model. Inf. Syst. Architect. J. **19**(4), 1–31 (2024)
38. Prat, N., Comyn-Wattiau, I., Akoka, J.: A taxonomy of evaluation methods for information systems artifacts. J. Manag. Inf. Syst. **32**(3), 229–267 (2015)
39. Zagel, C., Grimm, L., Luo, X.: Method cards – a new concept for teaching in academia and to innovate in SMEs. In: Ahram, T.Z. (ed.) Advances in Artificial Intelligence, Software and Systems Engineering, Advances in Intelligent Systems and Computing, vol. 787, pp. 230–241. Springer, Cham (2019)
40. Winter, R., Fischer, R.: Essential layers, artifacts, and dependencies of enterprise architecture. J. Enterpr. Architect. **3**(2), 1–12 (2007)
41. Guizzardi, G., Proper, E.: On understanding the value of domain modeling. In: International Workshop on Value Modelling and Business Ontologies, pp. 1–12. CEUR-WS.org, Virtual Conference (2021)
42. de Kinderen, S.: Model bundling: componential language engineering. In: Proper, H.A., Winter, R., Aier, S., de Kinderen, S. (eds.) Architectural Coordination of Enterprise Transformation, The Enterprise Engineering Series, pp. 221–233. Springer, Cham (2017)
43. Bork, D., Alter, S.: Satisfying four requirements for more flexible modeling methods: theory and test case. Enterpr. Model. Inf. Syst. Architect. J. **15**(3), 1–25 (2020)
44. Bork, D., Alter, S.: Relaxing modeling criteria to produce genuinely flexible, controllable, and usable enterprise modeling methods. In: International Workshop on Enterprise Modeling and Information Systems Architectures, pp. 121–125. De Gruyter, Rostock (2018)
45. Liu, X., Werder, K., Maedche, A.: A taxonomy of digital service design techniques. In: International Conference on Information Systems, pp. 1–12. Dublin (2016)
46. Roschuni, C., Kramer, J., Zhang, Q., Zakskorn, L., Agogino, A.: Design talking: an ontology of design methods to support a common language of design. In: International Conference on Engineering Design, pp. 1–10. Milano (2015)
47. Business Model Canvas. https://servicedesigntools.org/tools/business-model-canvas. Accessed 19 July 2024
48. Business Model Canvas, https://bmtoolbox.net/tools/business-model-canvas. Accessed 19 July 2024
49. Business Model Canvas, https://www.designabetterbusiness.tools/tools/business-model-canvas. Accessed 19 July 2024

50. Labusch, N.: Information requirements for enterprise transformation. In: Proper, H.A., Winter, R., Aier, S., de Kinderen, S. (eds.) Architectural Coordination of Enterprise Transformation, The Enterprise Engineering Series, pp. 111–121. Springer, Cham (2017)
51. Hagen, S., Schoormann, T., Jannaber, S., Knackstedt, R., Thomas, O.: Towards an integrated approach for modelling product-service systems: status quo and future challenges. In: Workshops der INFORMATIK, pp. 274–279. Köllen Druck+Verlag GmbH, Berlin (2018)
52. Rolland, C., Souveyet, C., Moreno, M.: An approach for defining ways-of-working. Inf. Syst. **20**(4), 337–359 (1995)

A Metamodel for Applying Green BPM Approaches with the EU Taxonomy

Ilona Bogatinovska[1](✉), Finn Klessascheck[1,2], Kerstin Andree[1], and Luise Pufahl[1,2]

[1] Technical University of Munich, School of CIT, Heilbronn, Germany
{Ilona.Bogatinovska,Finn.Klessascheck,Kerstin.Andree,Luise.Pufahl}@tum.de
[2] Weizenbaum Institute, Berlin, Germany

Abstract. Increasingly, companies are obliged and incentivized to consider the impact of their business processes on the environment, to promote *sustainable* business practices. In particular, the *EU Taxonomy for Sustainable Activities* outlines criteria for when business practices contribute towards a sustainable future. However, it is unclear in how far existing methods for identifying, analysing, and improving business practices, in particular those of the disciplines of *Business Process Management* (BPM) and *Green BPM* (that is, a variant of BPM with a focus on environmental sustainability) can relate to those criteria and the concepts contained therein. Therefore, we develop and propose a metamodel that combines concepts of the EU taxonomy and Green BPM, and clarifies the relationship of the two frameworks. This metamodel increases conceptual clarity and allows practitioners to apply Green BPM approaches in light of the EU taxonomy, and researchers and tool providers to further explore technical solutions in light of the EU taxonomy. It provides a clear overview of how the gap between sustainability regulations and approaches for sustainable business practices can be bridged. We evaluate the semantics and pragmatics of our metamodel, and sketch potential applications with an illustrative example.

Keywords: Green BPM · EU Taxonomy · Metamodel · Sustainability

1 Introduction

Organizations and businesses, particularly in industrial sectors, usually consume natural resources, leading to habitat destruction and resource scarcity, climate change and waste that pollutes ecosystems and harms communities. Global supply chains extend these environmental impacts between regions [3,14,18]. In response to these significant environmental challenges, the notion of *sustainability* outlines "adopting practices that meet present needs without compromising the ability of future generations to meet their own" as a solution [13]. Recognizing the importance of this, bodies such as the *European Union* (EU) have developed frameworks and incentives to help and to incentivize companies to integrate sustainability into their business practices and strategies. One of the frameworks

---

F. Klessascheck and I. Bogatinovska—Equal contribution.

© The Author(s), under exclusive license to Springer Nature Switzerland AG 2025
R. Guizzardi et al. (Eds.): BPMDS 2025/EMMSAD 2025, LNBIP 558, pp. 386–402, 2025.
https://doi.org/10.1007/978-3-031-95397-2_24

is the EU's *taxonomy for sustainable activities*, subsequently referred to as *EU taxonomy* [7,26]. An overarching goal of the EU taxonomy lies in providing clear criteria for when business practices contribute to sustainability objectives, and when not [20].

As a relevant viewpoint for managing and improving business practices, and specifically business processes, *Business Process Management* (BPM) is a discipline commonly used within organizations. The underlying notion of BPM is that each product or service an organization offers results from various activities performed in a coordinated manner, i.e. a business process [39]. *Green BPM* extends this concept by integrating environmental sustainability into all phases of the process management lifecycle [5,17]. Given this, it therefore is prudent to examine in how far the EU taxonomy aligns with a Green BPM "perspective"— doing so will offer the potential for making business processes more sustainable by providing a structured methodology for analysing and improving them in light of the EU taxonomy.

However, integrating Green BPM with the EU taxonomy is challenging due to different points of view: BPM, the foundation upon which Green BPM is built, is concerned with managing activities and processes w.r.t. business goals [39], whereas the EU taxonomy formulates criteria for when business practices contribute towards specific sustainability goals [20]. Bridging this gap by conceptually linking Green BPM approaches to the EU taxonomy would help organizations in increasing regulatory compliance and meeting potential reporting obligations on the one hand, and in implementing sustainable business practices on the other [20]. Further, it would allow Green BPM practitioners, researchers, and vendors to orient Green BPM approaches towards the EU taxonomy. In this study, we therefore explore how, conceptually, Green BPM and the EU taxonomy could be aligned and jointly used to assess and improve business processes w.r.t. sustainability criteria. To achieve this, we here propose a *metamodel* that explicates the conceptual relationships between Green BPM and the EU taxonomy; in doing so, we aim to address the following research objective:

RO1: Constructing a metamodel that represents aligned concepts between Green BPM and the EU taxonomy.

The remainder of this work is organized as follows: In Sect. 2, we provide the necessary background and discuss related work. In Sect. 3, we describe the methodology used to develop the metamodel. Section 4 presents the main result of our study, which is evaluated and applied to an illustrative example in Sect. 5. Finally, we discuss our findings and conclude the article in Sect. 6, in addition to suggesting directions for future work.

2 Theoretical Background

In the following, we summarize the general concept and aims of the EU taxonomy, and provide an overview of existing Green BPM approaches; we also discuss existing work relating to our study.

EU Taxonomy. The EU taxonomy is a framework established to drive sustainable *economic activities* (i.e. families of *business processes* involving the production, distribution, or consumption of goods and services [10,20]) by offering a clear and standardized system for classifying environmentally sustainable practices. It aims to assist investors, businesses, and regulators in determining which economic activities contribute to environmental sustainability. The primary objective of the taxonomy is to aid the European Union in its goal of achieving climate neutrality by 2050 [9,36]. By establishing clear criteria for what constitutes a sustainable activity, the EU taxonomy contributes to 1) establishing clear indicators to differentiate between sustainable and non-sustainable business activities, thereby preventing greenwashing; 2) motivating businesses to prioritize sustainable practices; and 3) encouraging financial investments in companies that contribute to sustainability [7,20].

To classify and identify sustainable activities, the EU taxonomy uses *Nomenclature of Economic Activities* (NACE) codes, a standard classification system for economic activities within the EU. Each economic activity is assigned one or more NACE codes, which provides a detailed categorization based on the type of activity being performed. These codes are essential in the context of the EU taxonomy because they allow businesses and regulators to identify which activities are subject to the sustainability criteria outlined by the EU taxonomy [15]. Further, the definition of NACE codes and economic activities (see [12]) is closely aligned with the definition of business processes (see [39])—in line with Klessascheck et al. [20], we understand economic activities to provide "families" or "classes" of business processes and business practices.

For making a contribution towards sustainability goals, those economic activities that can theoretically do so (i.e. *taxonomy-eligible* economic activities) must meet four requirements [15]: First, *Substantial Contributions*: Economic activities must significantly contribute to environmental objectives, such as climate change mitigation, adaptation, water and marine resource protection, circular economy transition, pollution prevention, or biodiversity restoration [38]. Second, *Do No Significant Harm* (DNSH): Economic activities must not harm other environmental objectives [16,38]. Third, *Minimum Safeguards*: Economic activities must adhere to social safeguards, including human rights and ethical practices [19,29–31]. Fourth, *Technical Screening Criteria*: Economic activities must fulfil specific technical standards to ensure adherence to the requirements above. Notably, taxonomy-eligible economic activities identified as potentially contributing to environmental objectives become *taxonomy-aligned* only when all criteria are satisfied [6]. For another useful conceptual overview of the EU taxonomy, we refer to a previous study of ours [20].

Green BPM. An area of BPM that is well-situated to integrate concepts of the EU taxonomy is Green BPM: This field has emerged as a response to an increasing awareness of environmental concerns and a need to integrate a perspective on environmental sustainability into the management of business processes [33,37]. To this end, Green BPM offers various techniques and approaches to model, deploy, manage, and improve business processes regarding their environmental performance [5]. These include: 1) *Modelling* approaches (e.g., modelling guidelines for modelling business processes that can be optimized for the environmental impact of corresponding process executions [25], or extended notions for representing environmental impact or resource consumption in process models) [5,17]; 2) *Deployment* approaches (e.g., for measuring and controlling emissions) [5,17]; 3) *Optimization* approaches (e.g., for benchmarking process redesigns for their environmental impact) [5,17]; and 4) *Management* approaches (e.g., extensions of the business process lifecycle with concepts of sustainability) [17]. Further, in a previous study, we have proposed the applicability of *compliance monitoring*, in extension to existing deployment approaches, with which various constraints of the EU taxonomy might be monitored for violations during business process execution [20].

Related Work. In this paper, we investigate to what extent and where concretely the EU taxonomy aligns with Green BPM concepts, to outline fruitful avenues for operationalizing constraints from the taxonomy with Green BPM approaches. In that sense, our study is related to other contributions that deal with conceptual overviews of the (Green) BPM "perspective" on organizations and processes, or propose conceptual integrations of sustainability into BPM or organizational practice.

Several studies formally capture entities that make up business processes and organizations from the BPM discipline's standpoint. For example, Annane et al. [2] present a *BPMN-based ontology* (BBO) for business representation, aiming to provide a formal and structured representation of business processes using ontologies to improve the analysis, simulation, and automation of business processes. Vom Brocke et al. [4] emphasize the role of context in BPM initiatives, which influences through various factors the concrete application of BPM practices; they also propose a framework to systematically identify and analyse them. Andree and Pufahl [1] address the role of context in business process redesign by presenting a metamodel that captures relevant contextual information to assess change operations. Rosemann et al. [34] focus on addressing the flexibility of business process; they propose a framework and metamodel for identifying and integrating these contextual factors into business process modelling.

In addition, various studies have engaged with integrating sustainability concepts into business practice, particularly in the research stream of Green BPM [5,17]. However, only some studies, which we found via a literature search, provide conceptual models of the entities and relationships involved in this. For example, Medini et al. [27] provide a metamodel that combines components of enterprises and their processes with entities regarding sustainability. Reiter et al. [32] present a conceptual model for integrating IT components, applications, and business processes, for reducing the energy consumption of business processes. Further, [23] present a sequential approach for process analysis in Green BPM, and provide a metamodel that relates business processes with sustainability concepts. Finally, while not providing a conceptual model, Roohy Gohar and Indulska [33] describe concepts and indicators for incorporating environmental sustainability into BPM. In a previous study [22], we provide an approach for data-driven holistic assessments of the environmental impact of business processes; most relevant here being a metamodel that provides a conceptual overview of processes, activities, instances thereof, and instantiations of environmental impact.

In a similar vein as the previous group of related work, our study converses with contributions that conceptually address the complexities of multiple reporting standards and the ambiguity of informal textual descriptions of sustainability indicators. As a particular example, Zhou and Perzylo [40] propose the *OntoSustain* model and provide a conceptual overview of how small and medium-sized enterprises can benefit in navigating sustainability reporting challenges. While also providing a conceptual model, their contribution does not directly align with BPM practices, nor the EU taxonomy and the concept of EU taxonomy alignment.

Currently, there are only initial and exploratory approaches that investigate in how far companies can be supported in aligning Green BPM approaches and practices with sustainability regulations, without clear and generalized guidance [35]; only some attention has been paid to understand how business processes can be viewed from the EU taxonomy perspective: In a previous study [20], we investigated whether the constraints of the EU taxonomy could be used for regulatory compliance monitoring with process mining techniques. What is still missing, however, is a generalized notion of the conceptual alignment between Green BPM and the EU taxonomy. Although existing contributions and their conceptualizations of sustainability reporting or business processes (e.g., [2,40]) can provide a point of departure, the specific alignment of Green BPM with the EU taxonomy remains unaddressed. We therefore see the need to provide a conceptual foundation for investigating and using this relation.

3 Research Method

So far, Green BPM and the EU taxonomy regulation have largely been treated separately. To bridge the gap between these domains and their concepts, we develop a metamodel in the following, thereby integrating both domains and identifying common concepts. In this, we follow the methodology for conceptual model development presented by Naeem et al. [28]; Fig. 1 provides a graphical overview of our research method.

For developing the metamodel, we selected relevant statements from literature and abstracted and summarized them into keywords. We assigned these keywords to representative codes that better reflect the core entities of the EU

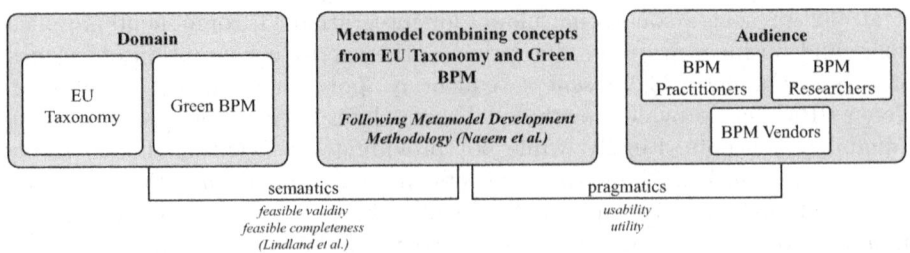

Fig. 1. Methodological overview, adapted from [24]

taxonomy or the Green BPM domain, respectively, and organized them in meaningful themes that match our research objectives and embodied patterns of the regulations.

For conceptualizing the identified themes, we used *Unified Modeling Language* (UML) class diagrams, since it allows for detailed modelling of relationships between entities. Its widespread and standardized nature ensures clear communication and consistent modelling. In short, we create a metamodel for each domain to determine the relevant concepts. By comparing both models, we identify commonalities and differences, merging them into a unified metamodel.

For evaluation, we follow the methodology for conceptual modelling according to Lindland et al. [24]. As shown in Fig. 1, we focus on *semantics* to assess the feasible validity and completeness of the model and on *pragmatics* to evaluate usability and utility. The audience of the aligned metamodel includes BPM practitioners wanting to align business practices with the EU taxonomy, BPM researchers wanting to make sense of the EU taxonomy to research novel techniques and approaches in this field, and BPM vendors wanting to make use of concepts from the EU taxonomy in their tools. Correct syntax of the model is already given, since we strictly follow the UML standard for modelling. In the following, we provide an overview of the sources being used for statement selection for each model. Moreover, we explain how the aligned metamodel was derived.

EU Taxonomy Model Development. Following Naeem et al. [28], we manually extracted relevant statements from the EU taxonomy regulation [15] by thoroughly exploring the specific sustainability criteria and compliance requirements. For this extraction step, we used the *taxonomy navigator* [8] and the *official journal* [15], both providing identification and classification of economic activities aligned with sustainability objectives. In addition, the ontology presented in Zhou and Perzylo [40] was particularly useful for extracting sustainability entities. It captures key sustainability aspects and indicators relevant to corporate reporting, thus helping us in better conceptualizing the sustainability perspective for companies and how sustainability indicators relate to the business domain entities. However, due to the specific focus of the OntoSustain model on corporate sustainability reporting, it does not deal with all the elements covered by the EU taxonomy. Therefore, we added further statements directly from the EU taxonomy regulation [15]. We then abstracted and summarized the collected statements into keywords. We assigned these keywords to representative codes that better reflect the core entities of the EU taxonomy, and organized them into meaningful themes that match our research objectives and embody patterns of the regulations. We then arranged the extracted entities into a schematic model. This schematic model was iteratively improved with additional relationships between the entities.

Green BPM Model Development. Relevant statements within the BPM domain were selected by screening various related work, in line with Naeem et al. [28]. We incorporated the foundations of BPM presented in [22,39], in particular the BPM lifecycle, business-relevant works, such as [2,4,34] to bridge the gap between process and different business perspectives, and principles of the Green BPM field [5,17] to include environmental objectives, sustainability practices, and compliance requirements. Similarly to the metamodel derived from the EU taxonomy, we applied the methodological framework of Naeem et al. [28] to conceptualize the identified statements.

Aligned Metamodel Development. Having established the two metamodels for the EU taxonomy and the Green BPM domain, we analysed their similarities and differences to determine areas of alignment. Overlapping concepts were identified by comparing entities from both models. Common elements such as economic activities, compliance requirements, and sustainability indicators were assessed. Elements from BPM were mapped to corresponding regulatory components from the EU taxonomy, with economic activities in the taxonomy aligning with processes in BPM. Shared concepts, including environmental impact assessments, sustainability reporting, and regulatory compliance were also counted in the alignment. At the same time, certain elements remained unique to each framework, such as BPM's business goal structuring and the EU taxonomy's legal enforcement criteria. These differences were carefully considered to determine whether they should be incorporated or omitted in the final aligned metamodel. The decision-making process was guided by the principle of maintaining relevance to the core objective of our study (i.e. conceptually aligning business processes with sustainability regulations) and discussed between all authors. The final step involved synthesizing the identified overlaps into a single aligned metamodel. Redundant elements were removed, to present the model without sacrificing important details. This led to the synthesis of the two developed metamodels on Green BPM and the EU taxonomy into a third model that represents their conceptual alignments.

4 Results

In the following, we present the results of applying the metamodel development methodology on the EU taxonomy and Green BPM.[1]

EU Taxonomy Model. The EU taxonomy metamodel outlines the regulatory framework for sustainable economic activities. *Economic Activities or Business Practices* as the core entity of the EU taxonomy metamodel are classified according to the *NACE* code classification [26]. We differentiate between *transitional* and *enabling* economic activities, indicating whether they are moving towards sustainability or facilitating sustainable business practices directly.

Assessing whether an economic activity aligns with the EU taxonomy is represented via the *Taxonomy Alignment* entity. Relevant for this is whether activities meet *Technical Screening Criteria*, i.e. specific requirements they must satisfy to be considered sustainable. Additionally, activities are linked to *Environmental Objectives*, such as mitigation, adaptation, and biodiversity protection,

---

[1] Due to limitations in length, we provide the intermediate metamodels and further illustration of the conceptual model development via supplementary material available online at https://doi.org/10.6084/m9.figshare.28554260.

complying with *DNSH* criteria. *Key Performance Indicators* such as turnover, *operational expenditure* (OpEx), and *capital expenditure* (CapEx) are used to measure the performance and financial implications of sustainability initiatives. These KPIs, along with other reporting values, feed into *Sustainability Reports*, which document the organization's efforts to align with the EU taxonomy.

To realize a *Product* or *Service*, *Resources* are required and, thus, considered as *Input*. Resources include humans, finances, materials, and data. They contribute to the *Environmental impact* of the organization's *Operations*, which can be tracked using the model. *Information and Traceability of Substances* maintain transparency and ensure compliance with sustainability standards, particularly in monitoring the environmental footprint of materials used within processes. Plants, vehicles, and machinery are listed as the organization's assets. They are managed via the *Equipment Restrictions*. Environmental impact is caused by *Outputs*, e.g., *Emissions* (such as Greenhouse Gas (GHG) and others) and *Waste*.

Green BPM Model. The developed Green BPM metamodel presents a conceptual view on Green BPM. A *Business Process* is a collection of related, structured activities that are performed in coordination to produce a service or product serving a particular business goal [39]. A *Process Instance* contains multiple *Activity Instances* representing the real-time execution of individual process activities. These instances are critical for generating operational data and *Key Performance Indicators* (KPIs) measuring efficiency, effectiveness, and alignment with business goals.

The extended Green BPM model incorporates a broader set of entities to represent the internal and external dynamics of an enterprise. *Resources*, e.g., *Data, Material, Software*, are the inputs necessary to execute *Activity Instances*. We differentiate between *Raw* materials, *Energy, Equipment,* and *Technology* [2,27]. Furthermore, *Environmental Resources* include resources related to *Air, Water, Land*, and *Mined resources* [27]. *Enterprise Objects* are functional units or assets within the organization that interact with or are impacted by the *Process Model* [27]. The *Enterprise* entity represents the organization as a whole, incorporating all *Enterprise Objects, Business Processes*, and *Compliance Requirements*. *Compliance Requirements* ensure that business operations meet legal, environmental, and quality standards. *Business Goals* drive the design and execution of processes and are categorized into *Hard, Soft*, and *Environmental* goals, taken from [34]. *Market* represents the external environment composed of customers, governments, and local communities [27]. *Organization Policy* guides the strategic direction and operational standards within the organization. It includes policies that support environmental sustainability.

In the context of Green BPM, KPIs continue to play a central role in measuring the performance of activities and process instances. However, in an environmentally conscious approach, these KPIs are extended to include *Environmental Performance Indicators* (EPIs) and specifically measure environmental impacts such as emissions, waste, energy consumption, and water usage [33]. The more sustainably *Resources* are used, the better the environmental impact of business

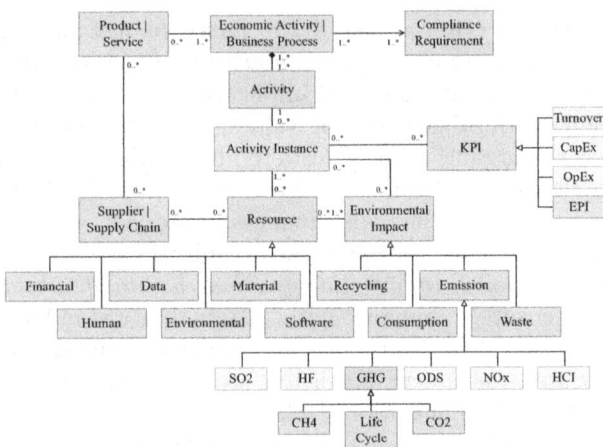

Fig. 2. Metamodel displaying concepts from Green BPM (in green), the EU taxonomy (in yellow), and their relationships; aligned concepts shown in purple (Color figure online)

processes. *Resources* are linked to the execution of activities and are essential for achieving the desired outcomes of the processes. The concept of *Green Supplier Monitoring* emphasizes the importance of sustainable sourcing by ensuring suppliers meet environmental standards [5].

Green Behaviour captures environmentally conscious actions within the organization, such as recycling, energy conservation, and emission reductions. *Stakeholders*, which include customers, employees, and suppliers, play a significant role in influencing business goals and processes. In this, their *Green Behaviour* is important [5]. *Environmental* goals (i.e. goals stemming from the *environment* of a process) [34] are particularly relevant in the context of *EU taxonomy*, as they motivate adopting sustainable practices within business operations.

Aligned Metamodel. The aligned metamodel that is the result of synthesising the two previous models into one, shown in Fig. 2, integrates concepts from Green BPM and the EU taxonomy framework to create a unified (*"aligned"*) model. The entities highlighted in purple represent aligned concepts that bridge the gap between Green BPM and the EU taxonomy. Green entities originate exclusively from the Green BPM discipline, while yellow entities are drawn exclusively from the EU taxonomy.

At the centre of the aligned metamodel is the *Economic Activity — Business Process* entity, which serves as the bridge between Green BPM and the EU taxonomy. A business process is subject to *Compliance Requirements*, which are concerned with regulatory, legal, and environmental constraints. The *Activity* entity represents the individual tasks or steps that comprise a business process or economic activity. Each activity contributes to the overall objective of the business process or economic activity, and is necessary for realizing a *Product* or *Service*. A specific execution of an *Activity* leads to an *Activity Instance*. *Activity Instances* also interact with *Resources*, drawing from financial, material, human, and other input forms (such as resources that can be "taken" directly from the environment, e.g. sunlight, or air) to execute specific tasks. External partners are represented by *Supplier — Supply Chain*. Suppliers provide the *Resources* necessary for processes to operate effectively. In this aligned view, the supply chain is important to achieve business goals and ensure that sustainability criteria are met through the inclusion of Green Supplier Monitoring [33].

In the aligned view, the sustainability of products ties directly to compliance with environmental regulations. The quality, lifecycle, and environmental footprints of products are influenced by the activities and resources used in their production. The impact of these business processes/economic activities on the environment is captured by *Environmental Impact*. An *Environmental Impact* can be divided into a range of subcategories, such as *Recycling, Emissions, Consumption*, and *Waste*. Although some of them align and are covered by both views, there are more specific types of *Emissions* and *Waste* from the EU taxonomy view, which is why purple highlighting was not used for them. Subcategories under *Resource* and *Environmental Impact* (e.g., emission types, material inputs) are included to reflect established sustainability standards and enable domain-specific granularity where needed. Another area of overlap is that both *Economic Activities* and *Business Processes* are evaluated using performance indicators. However, while the EU taxonomy prescribes financial metrics (shown in yellow) for reporting alignment, Green BPM introduces process-level and environmental indicators to support operational sustainability. Finally, the *Compliance Requirement* entity ensures that all economic activities or processes adhere to relevant legal, environmental, and regulatory standards.

5 Evaluation

In the following, we will evaluate the aligned metamodel. For this, we draw on the framework for systematically addressing different aspects of model quality provided by Lindland et al. [24]. Concretely, we will evaluate the metamodel for 1) *semantic* validity and completeness and 2) *pragmatic* usability and utility.

Semantics. For semantic evaluation, we examine the model's validity and completeness, considering feasibility [24].

Feasible Validity. A *valid* model only contains correct statements regarding its domain. Thus, we systematically assess each *relation* in the model and verify whether it accurately reflects the domain (i.e. EU Taxonomy Regulation (EU) 2020/852 [15], or Green BPM) to be considered correct. Table 1 presents all explicitly modelled relations included in the aligned metamodel model shown in Fig. 2 and their origin, proving its validity.

For example, the relationship between *Economic Activity* and *Compliance Requirement* is directly validated by the EU taxonomy's regulatory requirements, while relationships such as those between *Activity Instances, Resources*, and *KPIs* are part of the Green BPM domain. The model is considered valid for both domains.

Table 1. Overview of relations included in the aligned metamodel and their origins (**EU T**axonomy, **G**reen **BPM**)

Relationship	EUT	G-BPM
KPI - Taxonomy Alignment Metrics	x	
Emissions - Types of Emissions	x	
Product — Service - Supply Chain and Environmental Management	x	
Business Process - Activity	x	[39]
Activity Instance - Activity		[39]
Activity Instance - KPI		[39]
Resource - Resource Types		[2, 27]
KPI - EPI		[33]
Resource - Green Supplier Monitoring		[5]
Resources - Activity Instance		[39]
Resources - Environmental Impact	x	[5]
Business Process - Product — Service		[39]
Supplier - Resource		[39]
Economic Activity - Compliance Requirement	x	[20]

Feasible Completeness. A *complete* model contains all relevant statements defined by the domain. *Feasible* completeness ensures that the model accurately represents the domain while only focussing on significant statements. Thus, we review each statement defined by the domain and assess whether it is already included in the respective metamodel and whether it adds value to it. If not, it is excluded from the model to reduce complexity. This is done for each metamodel separately. If the two models of the individual domains (i.e. Green BPM and the EU taxonomy) are complete regarding their respective domains, the aligned metamodel representing the intersections of the two models is complete regarding the intersection of their domains.

Statements made by the EU taxonomy were derived from official sources and related work, including [11–13, 15, 20, 40]. In line with the methodology of Naeem et al. [28], only relevant concepts have been incorporated into the EU taxonomy metamodel, which is why we consider it to be feasible *complete*. Significant but missing statements would have been identified by the methodological process we followed. Thus, we conclude that there are no missing statements that would provide additional value to the metamodel. For including concepts of Green BPM, we also followed the predefined and systematic approach by Naeem at al. [28], thereby ensuring that all key components and key statements of Green BPM are included. Section 4 explains each concept included in the model in detail, and provides a rationale for why it is relevant to the metamodel. This shows the significance of the statements made by the Green BPM metamodel. Therefore, this metamodel is considered feasible *complete* regarding Green BPM.

Now we further consider the completeness of the aligned metamodel: The decision to include only the overlapping concepts from both metamodels was made to maintain focus on the main objective, i.e. aligning Green BPM with sustainability goals as outlined by the EU taxonomy, while ensuring feasible completeness. The majority of concepts that appeared in only one of the two metamodels was excluded intentionally, as they were not necessary for the primary goal of this alignment. Including additional concepts from only one domain would have introduced complexity without adding value to the model. Notably, some entities, while not mutual between both metamodels, were still considered in the aligned metamodel. These include *Activity Instance*, *Types of Emissions*, and *KPIs*. *Activity Instance* was added to represent the execution of a business process or economic activity. The different types of *KPI* represent how both Green BPM and the EU taxonomy measure business processes or economic activities. While both perspectives use KPIs, it is important to emphasize that the specific KPIs are not the same. *Types of Emissions* and *Waste* were also included. Although the EU taxonomy covers a broader range of emissions and waste types compared to Green BPM, which focuses on some overarching categories [17], both perspectives deal with these environmental outputs. Thus, including these entities reinforces the model's completeness because it covers both perspectives without introducing unnecessary or invalid elements.

The aligned metamodel is considered feasible *complete* because all relevant concepts from the EU taxonomy and the Green BPM metamodels that are necessary to address both the business process execution and the compliance with sustainability goals have been incorporated. Removing any of the existing elements would compromise the model's ability to address key questions of sustainability and Green BPM alignment, as already demonstrated above, where each concept is justified in detail.

Pragmatics. For evaluating the pragmatics of the aligned metamodel, we employ a business process for *battery manufacturing* as an illustrating example. The business process, shown in Fig. 3, consists of four sequential stages, being 1) electrode manufacturing, 2) cell assembly, 3) formation, and 4) pack production, with various subordinate activities, and results in a single battery pack. We iteratively developed the business process model (provided here as a BPMN diagram) based on a description of battery manufacturing of lithium-iron batteries provided by a large battery manufacturing company[2] and the description of the economic activity "Manufacture of batteries" (NACE code C27.2). Thereby, we ensure that the illustrating example corresponds to an economic activity covered by the EU taxonomy. A full-size version is provided in the supplementary material available online.

For evaluating the aligned metamodel regarding its usability (i.e. can the model's audience apply it to real-world settings) and utility (i.e. does it help the model's audience to identify the conceptual alignment between Green BPM and the EU taxonomy), we *first* identify and summarize constraints formulated in the taxonomy [8] for the battery manufacturing process (i.e. the technical screening criteria), and identify entities of the aligned metamodel that relate to these constraints. *Second*, based on the constraints and their corresponding metamodel entities, we identify potential types of Green BPM approaches with

---

[2] See https://inside.lgensol.com/en/2023/06/infographics-3-battery-making-at-a-glance/.

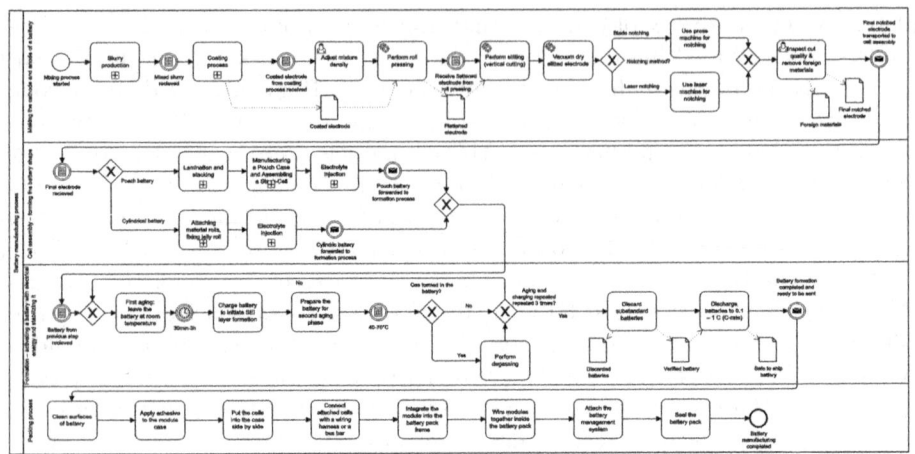

Fig. 3. A BPMN diagram of a battery manufacturing business process, covered by the EU taxonomy. A full-size version is available as supplementary material online.

which the constraints formulated for the metamodel entities can be assessed, improved, or made use of.

We find, as shown in the first two columns of Table 2, that all concepts of the aligned metamodel are covered by our illustrating business process. For example, the *Economic Activity* concept maps the entire business process of battery manufacturing. An obligation to report financial KPIs relates to the *KPI* concept. The requirement for the business process to produce rechargeable batteries is covered by the *Product* concept, as is the requirement for the product to be durable, recyclable, disassemblable, and adaptable. The requirement to recycle at least 70% of non-hazardous materials maps to the *Environmental Impact - Recycling* concept, whereas the requirement to use software systems to aid in resource efficiency, emission management, and compliance aligns to the *Resource - Software* concept. Finally, the requirement to recycle end-of-life batteries maps to the *Activity* concept, as this requires that the process contains an activity in which the recycling is done (for which then also an *Activity Instance* must exist).

Based on the mapping of taxonomy constraints to the aligned metamodel, we can better reason about potential applications of Green BPM approaches to assess or improve taxonomy alignment of our illustrative process. Due to limitations in length, we can only provide an *intuition* of how such a mapping could work, and plan to further investigate the alignment between entities and techniques in the future. This intuition is illustrated in the third column of Table 2.

For example, we could use modelling approaches to make sure that recycling end of-life batteries is part of the business process (since so far, no such activity is part of Fig. 3), and use compliance monitoring approaches to ensure that recycling actually takes place. We can implement deployment and optimization

A Metamodel for Applying Green BPM Approaches with the EU Taxonomy

Table 2. Summarized constraints from the EU taxonomy for the example process, with relating concepts from the aligned metamodel (AM) and potential Green BPM approaches

EU Taxonomy Constraints	AM Concepts	GBPM Approaches
Battery Manufacturing	Economic Activity	Modelling
Report turnover, CapEx, and OpEx to show alignment with sustainable activities	KPIs	Compliance Monitoring
Rechargeable batteries, battery packs, accumulators	Product	Modelling, Management
Recycle end-of-life batteries	Activity	Modelling, Compliance Monitoring
Design products for high durability, recyclability, easy disassembly, and adaptability	Product	Modelling, Management
Materials must be sourced responsibly, incorporating secondary raw materials	Material, Supplier	Management, Compliance Monitoring
Substantial GHG emission reductions in transport	Environmental Impact - Emission - GHG	Deployment, Optimization
Recycling at least 70% of non-hazardous materials	Environmental Impact - Recycling	Optimization
Support GHG reduction, comply with EU waste laws, implement sorting systems, and ensure at least 70% recycling of non-hazardous construction waste	Environmental Impact - Waste	Deployment, Optimization
Information on and traceability of substances of concern throughout the lifecycle of manufactured products	Environmental Impact - Consumption	Deployment, Management
Minimize use of hazardous substances	Resource - Material	Modelling, Deployment
Environmental impact assessment has been conducted, and the necessary measures have been implemented	Resource - Environmental	Compliance Monitoring
Adherence to EU labour laws and standards	Resource - Human	Management, Compliance Monitoring
Software systems aid in resource efficiency, emissions management, and compliance	Resource - Software	Deployment, Optimization
Report on sust. metrics as part of disclosure obligations	Compliance Requirement	Compliance Monitoring

approaches for addressing various constraints that require GHG emission reductions. With management approaches, we can make sure that information on the traceability of specific substances is collected, and use deployment approaches for collecting adequate data. While the implementation of all approaches requires further understanding of the constraints at hand, we can now nonetheless better understand how they relate to entities known from a Green BPM point-of-view and reason about the kinds of Green BPM approaches that might be relevant.

6 Discussion and Conclusion

In this work, we have designed and evaluated a metamodel that conceptualizes the alignment between concepts of the EU taxonomy and Green BPM, thereby having addressed RO1. Besides showing the semantic quality of the model, we have also shown its usability and utility via an exemplary case. By making the involved concepts and relations explicit, we have contributed towards 1) empowering practitioners to apply Green BPM approaches for assessing and improving taxonomy alignment of business practices, 2) enabling research to develop novel Green BPM approaches in light of the EU taxonomy, and 3) allowing Green BPM tool providers to align their systems with the EU taxonomy.

Threats to Validity. There are several limitations to the validity of our study that we need to acknowledge. Firstly, the way the intermediate and final models were developed and statements were selected was subjective in nature. However, we aimed to counter potential biases by continuously discussing among the author team each decision during model development and evaluation and resolving any arising conflict. Further, the EU taxonomy as a *political* project may be subject to change in its implementation. However, we have shown that this *type* of regulation, making requirements for economic activities and outlining criteria for when they contribute to certain environmental objectives can be integrated into, and used for, Green BPM. Finally, the evaluation was limited to semantics and pragmatics, and a real-world case study for usability regarding Green BPM practitioners and vendors is, so far, missing. Nonetheless, we show the feasibility and usability/utility of the developed metamodel with a real-world-*adjacent* scenario.

Potential *future work* may include empirical evaluations of our conceptual perspective on alignments between the EU taxonomy and Green BPM concepts—concrete applications of approaches after having identified them via the metamodel could strengthen the validity of our findings further. We also believe that it would be beneficial to provide more concrete guidance on how, based on identified entities of the aligned metamodel for a specific business process, concrete Green BPM approaches can be chosen and implemented. As diagnosed in a previous study [21], we see substantial potential for technical (in particular, automated or semi-automated) support for checking conformance of specific business processes regarding regulations; we believe that the metamodel developed herein can form the basis of such an approach, at least regarding the EU taxonomy.

Acknowldegment. This work was funded by the Deutsche Forschungsgemeinschaft (DFG, German Research Foundation) - Grant no. 465904964.

Data Availability. Supplementary material, including all figures, is made available via an online repository at https://doi.org/10.6084/m9.figshare.28554260.

Disclosure of Interests. The authors have no competing interests to declare.

References

1. Andree, K., Pufahl, L.: Am I allowed to change an activity relationship?-a metamodel for behavioral business process redesign. In: EDOC Forum 2024 (2025)
2. Annane, A., Aussenac-Gilles, N., Kamel, M.: BBO: BPMN 2.0 based ontology for business process representation. In: ECKM 2019, vol. 1 (2019)
3. Bocken, N., Short, S.: Unsustainable business models - recognising and resolving institutionalised social and environmental harm. J. Clean Prod. **312** (2021)

4. vom Brocke, J., Zelt, S., Schmiedel, T.: On the role of context in business process management. Int. J. Inf. Manag. **36**(3) (2016)
5. Couckuyt, D., Van Looy, A.: A systematic review of green business process management. BPMJ **26**(2) (2019)
6. European Comission: FAQ: what is the EU taxonomy and how will it work in practice? https://finance.ec.europa.eu/system/files/2021-04/sustainable-finance-taxonomy-faq_en.pdf
7. European Commission: Eu taxonomy for sustainable activities. https://finance.ec.europa.eu/sustainable-finance/tools-and-standards/eu-taxonomy-sustainable-activities_en
8. European Commission: Eu taxonomy navigator. https://ec.europa.eu/sustainable-finance-taxonomy
9. European Commission: The European green deal: priorities 2019-2024. https://commission.europa.eu/strategy-and-policy/priorities-2019-2024/european-green-deal_en
10. European Commission: Glossary: economic activity. https://ec.europa.eu/eurostat/statistics-explained/index.php?title=Glossary:Economic_activity
11. European Commission: Green deal action plan. https://op.europa.eu/en/publication-detail/-/publication/629b90ab-367f-11ea-ba6e-01aa75ed71a1/language-en
12. European Commission: Nace rev. 2: statistical classification of economic activities in the European community (2008)
13. European Commission: Summary for sustainable development (2024). https://eur-lex.europa.eu/EN/legal-content/glossary/sustainable-development.html
14. European Environment Agency (EEA): Resource extraction (2022). https://www.eea.europa.eu/publications/zero-pollution/production-consumption/resource-extraction
15. European Parliament and Council of the European Union: Regulation (eu) 2020/852 on the establishment of a framework to facilitate sustainable investment and amending regulation (eu) 2019/2088. https://eur-lex.europa.eu/eli/reg/2020/852/oj (2020)
16. European Securities and Markets Authority (ESMA): DNSH definitions and criteria across the eu sustainable finance framework. https://www.esma.europa.eu/sites/default/files/2023-11/ESMA30-379-2281_Note_DNSH_definitions_and_criteria_across_the_EU_Sustainable_Finance_framework.pdf (2023)
17. Fritsch, A., von Hammerstein, J., Schreiber, C., Betz, S., Oberweis, A.: Pathways to greener pastures: research opportunities to integrate life cycle assessment and sustainable business process management based on a systematic tertiary literature review. Sustainability **14**(18) (2022)
18. Gani, A., Sharma, B.: The effect of the business environment on pollution. In: International Trade and Finance Association Conference Papers. Be Press (2009)
19. International Labour Organization (ILO): International labour standards. https://www.ilo.org/international-labour-standards
20. Klessascheck, F., Fahrenkrog-Petersen, S.A., Mendling, J., Pufahl, L.: Unlocking sustainability compliance: characterizing the EU taxonomy for business process management. In: EDOC 2024. Springer (2025)
21. Klessascheck, F., Knoche, T., Pufahl, L.: Reviewing conformance checking uses for run-time regulatory compliance. In: Enterprise, Business-Process and Information Systems Modeling. Springer (2024)

22. Klessascheck, F., Weber, I., Pufahl, L.: SOPA: a framework for sustainability-oriented process analysis and re-design in business process management. Inf. Syst. e-Bus. Manage. (2025)
23. Larsch, S., Betz, S., Duboc, L., Magdaleno, A.M., Bomfim, C.: Integrating sustainability aspects in business process management. In: BPM Workhops. Springer (2017)
24. Lindland, O., Sindre, G., Solvberg, A.: Understanding quality in conceptual modeling. IEEE Softw. **11**(2) (1994)
25. Lübbecke, P., Fettke, P., Loos, P.: Towards guidelines of modeling for ecology-aware process design. In: Teniente, E., Weidlich, M. (eds.) BPM 2017. LNBIP, vol. 308, pp. 510–519. Springer, Cham (2018). https://doi.org/10.1007/978-3-319-74030-0_40
26. Maier, C., Wilhelm, A.: Eu taxonomy in practice: what companies should know (2023). https://www.roedl.com/insights/nachhaltigkeit-csr/eu-taxonomy-2022-green-deal-action-plan-climate-neutrality
27. Medini, K., Da-Cunha, C., Bernard, A.: An enterprise meta model for the assessment and improvement of sustainability and mass customization performance. In: MOSIM'12 (2012)
28. Naeem, M., Ozuem, W., Howell, K., Ranfagni, S.: A step-by-step process of thematic analysis to develop a conceptual model in qualitative research. Int. J. Qual. Methods **22** (2023)
29. Office of the United Nations High Commissioner for Human Rights: Guiding principles on business and human rights (2011). https://www.ohchr.org/sites/default/files/documents/publications/guidingprinciplesbusinesshr_en.pdf
30. Office of the United Nations High Commissioner for Human Rights (OHCHR): International bill of human rights. https://www.ohchr.org/en/what-are-human-rights/international-bill-human-rights
31. Organisation for Economic Co-operation and Development (OECD): OECD guidelines for multinational enterprises on responsible business conduct (2023)
32. Reiter, M., Fettke, P., Loos, P.: Towards green business process management: concept and implementation of an artifact to reduce the energy consumption of business processes. In: HICSS 2024 (2014)
33. Roohy Gohar, S., Indulska, M.: Environmental sustainability through green business process management. Australas. J. Inf. Syst. **24** (2020)
34. Rosemann, M., Recker, J., Flender, C.: Contextualisation of business processes. Int. J. Bus. Process Integration Manag. **3**(1) (2008)
35. Schoormann, T., Di Maria, M.: Business process pattern for improving social sustainability. Australas. J. Inf. Syst. **28** (2024)
36. Schütze, F., Stede, J.: The EU sustainable finance taxonomy and its contribution to climate neutrality. J Sustain. Financ. Inv. **14**(1) (2024)
37. Seidel, S., Recker, J., vom Brocke, J.: Green Business Process Management, pp. 3–13. Springer (2012)
38. Viridad: The EU taxonomy regulation: in-depth insights. https://www.viridad.eu/eu-taxonomy
39. Weske, M.: Business Process Management: Concepts, Languages, Architectures, 2nd edn. Springer (2012)
40. Zhou, Y., Perzylo, A.: Ontosustain: towards an ontology for corporate sustainability reporting. In: ISWC (2023)

Experience Report: Applying a Capability Heat Map in a Government Organization

Evelien Groenendal[1] and Ben Roelens[1,2]

[1] Open Universiteit, Valkenburgerweg 177, 6419 AT, Heerlen, The Netherlands
ben.roelens@ou.nl
[2] Ghent University, Tweekerkenstraat 2, 9000, Ghent, Belgium
ben.roelens@ugent.be

Abstract. Government organizations must operate in a complex and unpredictable environment, driven by rapid technological advancements, shifting regulations, and evolving stakeholder expectations. To cope with these challenges, they must balance adaptability with structural consistency. Capability heat maps serve as a conceptual foundation to preserve this stability by enabling organizations to evolve while maintaining coherence, even as implementation strategies shift. The capability heat map provides a structured overview of an organization's capabilities, focusing on what the organization does or can do to achieve business goals. Previous research indicates that there is a research gap on the use of these models. Therefore, this report examines the application of a capability heat map in a government organization using a case study, in which the model is developed and subsequently evaluated. The results show that stakeholders find it useful to model business capabilities in a heat map. However, supporting elements such as guidance from a modeling expert, a legend, a reading guide, a supporting explanation, and the necessity of a clear modeling purpose are essential prerequisites.

Keywords: Experience Report · Capability Heat Map · Case Study

1 Introduction

Government organizations face unpredictable and sudden circumstances that trigger change processes, such as technological advancements, shifting regulations, and evolving stakeholder needs and expectations. Failing to respond to these circumstances negatively impacts organizational performance [1]. Therefore, it is crucial for organizations to react quickly and efficiently to these dynamic developments, while preserving their structural consistency [3,4]. This can be addressed by mapping capabilities [3,4] and managing the organization based on these capabilities [6]. In particular, a capability heat map represents at a high level of abstraction what the organization does to achieve business goals by making abstraction of the actual implementation [7,14,16]. In this respect, capabilities are defined as *the ability and capacity that enable an enterprise to achieve a business goal in a certain context* [2, p.16]. The current state of the organization can be assessed using a capability heat map, as well as the necessary changes needed to achieve the desired state [13,14]. These models also enable collaboration with various stakeholders to communicate about capabilities and ultimately achieve alignment between business and IT [13].

Sandkuhl et al. [10] developed a research agenda that shows that achieving broadly applicable enterprise models is an important challenge. They indicate that further research is needed on how models can be embedded in daily work, applied with less technical knowledge, and made more flexible in terms of completeness, coherence, and accuracy [10]. This is necessary to ensure that business stakeholders use and understand the models effectively [10]. In particular, this research aligns with their vision by focusing on enterprise modeling using capability heat maps. This heat map is applied and evaluated based on case study research performed in the context of a real-life governmental organization. A case study methodology is particularly useful as it provides information on the practical applicability of the capability heat map in a real-world context [15]. In this experience report, we will describe the methods and theories used, the organizational context, and the insights that we gained from this application.

This report is structured as follows. Section 2 discusses Capability Modeling as relevant background literature and Sect. 3 explains the case study methodology for applying and evaluating the capability heat map. Section 4 shows the results of the application, while the evaluation and lessons learned are presented in Sect. 5. The conclusions and options for future research are discussed in Sect. 6.

2 Capability Modeling

Capability modeling languages identify relationships between capabilities and various business architecture concepts, such as goal [4], process [4,7], organization [4,7,16], value [7,16], etc. In contrast, a capability heat map represents what the organization does to achieve business goals by making an abstraction of the actual implementation [7,14,16]. Capability heat maps can be realized by modeling standards as the Value Delivery Modeling Language (VDML) [7], ArchiMate [11] and TOGAF (i.e. The Open Group Architecture Framework) [12].

The capability heat map can serve multiple purposes, such as incorporating parameters to assess the strategic importance, performance, or profitability of a capability [7,14]. It presents a hierarchical structure of capabilities using color to highlight specific capabilities [12]. As such, it provides insight into opportunities to reach the desired state of an organization [14]. In the modeling standards, multiple levels of capabilities are identified. VDML [7] refers to parent and child capabilities. In contrast, ArchiMate [11] identifies two or three levels, while TOGAF [12] describes three to six levels of capabilities and applies layers to discriminate between strategic, core, and supporting capabilities. ArchiMate and TOGAF specify that the description of capabilities should consist of a noun-verb combination [11,12]. Furthermore, TOGAF emphasizes the terminology used when defining capabilities to ensure that they are understandable for relevant stakeholders in the organization [12]. The VDML specification is more extensive than ArchiMate and TOGAF regarding the relationships with various other elements, such as CapabilityLibrary, CapabilityDependency, and

Characteristics [7]. In this research, TOGAF is applied as it offers a clear and structured model for modeling capabilities, in combination with ArchiMate as modeling language. The advantage of using TOGAF is that it provides a concrete description for capability modeling by means of clear instructions and examples on how capabilities should be defined. Additionally, capabilities are also divided into layers, providing a better structure for the organization.

3 Methodology

The case study is elaborated according to Yin [15]: research question and hypothesis (Sect. 3.1), unit of analysis (Sect. 3.2), the logic linking the data to the hypotheses (Sect. 3.3) and the criteria for interpreting the findings (Sect. 3.4).

3.1 Research Question and Hypothesis

The case study focuses on both the application and evaluation of the capability heat map in a governmental context. Hence, the research question relevant to the case study is: 'How applicable is the capability heat map in a real-world government organization and to what extent does the developed model meet relevant evaluation criteria of the stakeholders?' The hypothesis that is examined in this study is that capabilities can be modeled within a governmental context using TOGAF and ArchiMate (see Sect. 2).

3.2 Unit of Analysis

Case Organization. This research is a single case study in one government organization. Furthermore, a holistic design is applied, as the case study focuses on the organization as a whole rather than specific departments [15]. The case organization is facing upcoming budget cuts due to a government decision, which will affect its service delivery. Although the organization has documentation outlining its structure and business model, the organization currently lacks a comprehensive overview of its capabilities. The case organization employs over 2,000 staff members and is a shared services organization providing support related to human resources and organizational management. To address the budget cuts, the case study uses a capability heat map to examine the organization's capabilities and assess their strategic importance in supporting core service provisioning. Therefore, participation is required from executives working at the strategic (i.e. CEO (R1) and Director of Strategy (R2)), core (i.e. Director of Service Delivery (R3)), and supporting levels (i.e. Director of Information Management (R4) and Business Operations (R5)). These participants are relevant as they have a high-level view of the organization's operations to ensure a comprehensive understanding of the business capabilities.

Modeling Approach. The authors act as modeling experts and follow a top-down approach [12]. An initial version of the capability map is created based on an analysis of internal documents, including the organizational structure, business model, strategy, and financial plan. An inductive thematic analysis is conducted to systematically identify the capabilities. This means that the authors code the relevant data, search for themes and relationships, and further refine them. In this study, the focus is on identifying capabilities, sub-capabilities, and the TOGAF layers to which they belong (i.e. strategic, core, or supporting). Based on this analysis, a first draft of the capability heat map is created. To complete the model, the Analytic Hierarchy Process (AHP) methodology is applied to determine the strategic importance of the capabilities [9]. Each respondent receives an anonymous questionnaire that asks to indicate the importance of a capability using a 9-point Likert scale. To determine consensus among the AHP scores of the respondents, a decision tree was developed (see Fig. 1). In the first step, it is determined whether at least 80% of the respondents provides a strategic importance score within the same category. In this respect, the 9-point Likert scale is divided into three categories: low/moderate (i.e. score 1 to 3), high (i.e. score 4 to 6), and very high/extreme (i.e. score 7 to 9). If consensus is established, the median value is calculated across the respondents. The second step of the decision tree involves calculating the range between the lowest and highest strategic importance score for the capabilities that did not reach quantitative consensus in step 1. If this range is less than 4, the consensus score can be calculated as the median value. For the remaining capabilities, step 3 of the decision tree calculates the interquartile range between the 25th and 75th percentiles. If this interquartile range is less than 2, consensus can be calculated based on the median value. A plenary modeling session is finally conducted to address capabilities for which no quantitative consensus was reached. Prioritization is determined through a qualitative discussion with the respondents and integrated into the capability heat map.

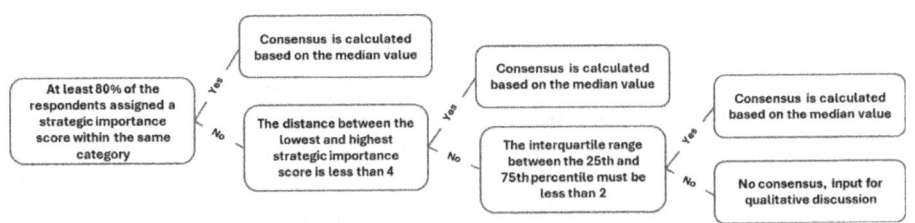

Fig. 1. Decision tree for AHP consensus, adapted from [8]

3.3 Logic Linking the Data to the Hypotheses

The evaluation includes a statistically validated questionnaire, which focuses on the quality of conceptual models based on the perception of end-users [5]. This method is relevant as it enables to assess how the end-user perceives the quality of the capability heat map by measuring four constructs [5]: (i) perceived ease of understanding (PEOU), (ii) perceived semantic quality (PSQ), (iii) perceived usefulness (PU), and (iv) user satisfaction (US). The evaluation questionnaire collects quantitative data from the executives who provided input for the capability heat map about the practical applicability of the resulting model. A 7-point Likert scale, ranging from strongly disagree to strongly agree, is used by the participants to indicate their level of agreement or disagreement with a statement. The evaluation questionnaire that was used, can be found in Appendix A.

3.4 Criteria for Interpreting the Findings

Due to the limited number of respondents, significance of the quantitative data cannot be statistically examined. Therefore, the quantitative data of the evaluation questionnaire [5] are supplemented by semi-structured interviews to gather additional lessons learned. For the interview, the questions are derived from the items in the questionnaire with emphasis on the high (agree/strongly agree) and low (disagree/strongly disagree) scores. These scores are particularly interesting as they may reveal explaining factors or suggestions to improve the practical applicability of the capability heat map. The online interviews are conducted individually, and recordings are made with participants' consent.

4 Capability Heat Map

The case study was conducted during October and November 2024. The first step involved an inductive thematic analysis of internal company documents. As a result, 65 capabilities were identified across two decomposition levels (i.e. 27 at level 1 and 38 at level 2), comprising 7 strategic, 46 core, and 12 supporting capabilities. These capabilities were included in an A4-sized capability map using ArchiMate, which was further refined by incorporating the strategic, core, and supporting layers of TOGAF. In addition, all capabilities received an explicit definition. Afterwards, the five executives completed the AHP questionnaire and the decision tree was used to determine whether consensus between the respondents was achieved (see Fig. 1). Consensus was confirmed for 17 capabilities in the first step, for 26 capabilities in the second step and for 14 more capabilities in the final step of the decision tree. For these capabilities, the median value (i.e. decimal values were rounded up) determined the category of strategic importance and the capabilities received a corresponding color in the heat map (red for low/moderate, yellow for high, and green for very high/extreme importance [12]). For eight capabilities, no quantitative consensus was reached, so these were discussed with the respondents in the plenary modeling session to reach an agreement on their strategic importance and to complete the heat map.

The anonymized excerpt of the capability heat map in Fig. 2 provides an overview of a sample of (i) strategic, (ii) core, and (iii) supporting capabilities. At the strategic level, a very important ability of the organization is *policy-making and strategy*, ensuring alignment with stakeholders, including clients, owners, and other governmental organizations. Additionally, it has a significant focus on *performance management*, assessing key performance indicators, and implementing measures to enhance effectiveness. Another critical strategic capability is *planning and control*, which involves creating optimal conditions for executing core functions while ensuring internal governance and control. The core capabilities of the organization center around *customer support* functions, enabling it to maintain relationships with clients and users at both tactical and operational levels. Customer support can be expanded in sub-capabilities, including (very) important support functions such as *recruitment and selection support*, *absence support*, *career support*, and *diversity and inclusion support*, ensuring that client organizations receive guidance and assistance in various aspects of human resource management. Additionally, the organization offers nonessential *financial support* to guide clients with budgetary questions (e.g. assessing the financial impact of retirement) and crucial *legal support* for civil and administrative procedures. The organization also maintains several supporting capabilities. *Security and privacy management* is of very high importance as it ensures compliance with relevant security and privacy laws. Besides, *facility management* covers a broad range of important operational needs, including administrative support, housing, cleaning, catering, and security services. Finally, *quality management* is a crucial function, which ensures that internal organizational standards are maintained and improved while complying with regulatory requirements.

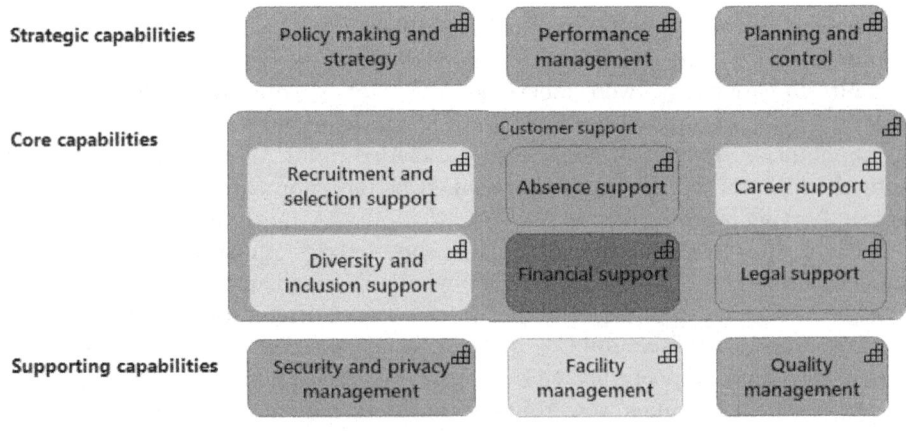

Fig. 2. Excerpt of the capability heat map of the case organization

5 Quantitative Evaluation and Lessons Learned

The PEOU was evaluated positively by an average score of 4.8. The scores per respondent (see Appendix B) show that four of them either 'somewhat agree' or 'agree' with the statements. However, one respondent (i.e. R1) gave an average score of 'disagree'. Most respondents found the model understandable, especially with guidance during the modeling session to overcome varying levels of comprehension (cfr. $PEOU_1$). Improvement suggestions included providing an example case, a guide, or a short description. Familiarity with models contributed to easier understanding, though some struggled due to differences in thinking styles. One respondent found the use of the model frustrating due to its complexity and preferred alternative tools like checklists or mind maps (cfr. $PEOU_2$). However, three others did not agree, attributing this to familiarity with similar models, structured guidance, and a logical layout. Four respondents emphasized the importance of guidance during the modeling session for effective use (cfr. $PEOU_3$). While some required explanations to engage with the model, others found it intuitive. One respondent highlighted the need to keep the model updated for continued usability. Most respondents found the model visually clear and easy to read (cfr. $PEOU_4$). Some suggested adding a legend, clearer color distinctions, or bold headings to improve readability. While most understood the term "capability," a few found it confusing, leading to a language gap. Color use was effective, but issues were raised with respect to readability for color-blind users.

The PSQ has also been rated positively with an average score of 5.1. Three respondents stated that the model accurately represents the capabilities, aligning with their perception of the organization (cfr. PSQ_1). Some respondents suggested minor refinements, such as further detailing or restructuring capabilities. Four respondents agreed that the model provides a realistic and complete depiction of capabilities (cfr. PSQ_2). The model's structure and grouping of capabilities are familiar, and its design aligns with existing architectural representations. Four respondents found no contradictory elements in the model, stating that it appeared logical and consistent (cfr. PSQ_3). One respondent commented on the relevance of the elements, stating that they accurately represent the capabilities (cfr. PSQ_4). One respondent felt that the model was complete, covering strategic, core, and supporting capabilities, providing a full overview (cfr. PSQ_5). Two respondents suggested adding more depth to the weighting of capabilities, as they currently appeared equally important. Finally, four respondents felt the model's level of abstraction met the balance of detail and accessibility. However, opinions differed on whether a further breakdown of level-2 capabilities is necessary.

The PU is evaluated with an average score of 5.3. The PU average per respondent shows that four respondents 'somewhat agree' to 'agree' with the statements, while respondent R1 gave an average score of 'neither agree nor disagree' (see Appendix B). Four respondents find the model useful as it provides structure and shows relationships, making it an improvement over textual descriptions (cfr. PU_1). However, one respondent prefers textual descriptions, such as a mind map or checklist. All respondents find the capability heat map useful, especially for management, as it provides quick insights and supports strategic discussions (cfr. PU_2). In particular, the heat map is seen as a tool rather than an end goal. Four respondents noted that the model can provide insights to support analyses such as SWOT assessments and risk evaluations. Three respondents believe the model helps in understanding capabilities by providing structure and four respondents stated that the model enables zooming in on specific capabilities (cfr. PU_3). One respondent mentioned that reaching a consensus on capabilities is challenging, but the model facilitates the discussions.

The US was evaluated with an average score of 5.4. While one respondent would delegate the use of the capability heat map, two respondents found the model helpful for structuring information (cfr. US_1). The model facilitated systematic thinking and resolving differing perspectives. Three respondents found the model efficient as it presents relevant information in a single visualization (cfr. US_2). Two respondents found the model effective, though one emphasized that its effectiveness depends on the supporting explanation (cfr. US_3). Another respondent believed effectiveness came from the discussions it facilitated rather than the model itself. Three respondents were satisfied, seeing the model as a fresh perspective to support managerial discussions (cfr. US_4). One respondent, however, preferred textual formats as a means of information delivery.

6 Conclusion

This experience report discusses the results of a case study to investigate the application of a capability heat map in a government organization. We can conclude that the model could be developed according to the approach that was set up in the case study design (see Sect. 3.2). This resulted in a heat map, including 65 capabilities and their corresponding strategic importance. The stakeholder evaluation shows that the structure of the model, the depth and layers of the capabilities, the strategic discussion, and the use of the model as an analysis tool contribute to its practical applicability. However, respondents consider the guidance of a modeling expert as a prerequisite for using and understanding the model. Additionally, a legend, reading guide, and/or brief description of the model are essential. Finally, the usefulness of the capability heat map is only recognized when there is a clear purpose to use the model's insights.

The developed capability map was manageable in an A4-sized format. However, future research could explore how the size of a capability map influences the effectiveness of various textual formats for communication between end-users. A limitation of this study is that it is a single, holistic case study, so replicating this research in other practical contexts will enhance the generalizability of the results. In particular, the developed decision tree for AHP consensus requires further testing to enhance its practical applicability. Additionally, executives were used as participants to provide insights into the practical applicability of the model. Future research could focus on the needs of other stakeholder groups to gain a broader perspective on the applicability of the capability heat map and to integrate it into the daily operations of the entire organization [10]. Finally, the respondents consider the guidance of a modeling expert as a prerequisite for understanding and using the model. A longitudinal study could explore which type of guidance is needed once respondents become familiar with the model and what is needed to use it independently.

A Evaluation Questionnaire

Item	Question
$PEOU_1$	It was easy for me to understand what the capability model was trying to model.
$PEOU_2$	Using the capability model was often frustrating.
$PEOU_3$	Overall, the capability model was easy to use.
$PEOU_4$	Learning how to read the capability model was easy.
PSQ_1	The capability model represents the capabilities correctly.
PSQ_2	The capability model is a realistic representation of the capabilities.
PSQ_3	The capability model contains contradictory elements.
PSQ_4	All the elements in the capability model are relevant for the representation of the capabilities.
PSQ_5	The capability model gives a complete representation of the capabilities.
PU_1	Overall, I think the capability model would be an improvement to a textual description of the capabilities.
PU_2	Overall, I found the capability model useful for understanding the capabilities.
PU_3	Overall, I think the capability model improves my performance when understanding the capabilities.
US_1	The capability model adequately met the information needs I was asked to support.
US_2	The capability model was not efficient in providing the information I needed.
US_3	The capability model was effective in providing the information I needed.
US_4	Overall, I am satisfied with the capability model for providing the information I needed.

B Quantitative Evaluation of the Capability Heat Map

Quality construct	R1	R2	R3	R4	R5
Perceived ease of understanding	2.0	5.8	5.0	5.5	5.8
Perceived semantic quality	4.6	5.0	5.0	5.0	5.8
Perceived usefulness	3.7	5.3	6.0	5.3	6.0
User satisfaction	5.3	5.8	5.5	4.8	5.8

References

1. Azevedo, C.L., Iacob, M.E., Almeida, J.P.A., van Sinderen, M., Pires, L.F., Guizzardi, G.: An ontology-based well-founded proposal for modeling resources and capabilities in archimate. In: 2013 17th IEEE International Enterprise Distributed Object Computing Conference, pp. 39–48. IEEE (2013). https://doi.org/10.1109/EDOC.2013.14

2. Bērziša, S., et al.: Capability driven development: an approach to designing digital enterprises. Bus. Inf. Syst. Eng. **57**(1), 15–25 (2015). https://doi.org/10.1007/s12599-014-0362-0
3. Koç, H.: Methods in designing and developing capabilities: a systematic mapping study. In: Ralyté, J., España, S., Pastor, Ó. (eds.) The Practice of Enterprise Modeling, pp. 209–222. Springer International Publishing, Cham (2015). https://doi.org/10.1007/978-3-319-25897-3_14
4. Koutsopoulos, G., Henkel, M., Stirna, J.: An analysis of capability meta-models for expressing dynamic business transformation. Softw. Syst. Model. **20**(1), 147–174 (2020). https://doi.org/10.1007/s10270-020-00843-0
5. Maes, A., Poels, G.: Evaluating quality of conceptual modelling scripts based on user perceptions. Data Knowl. Eng. **63**(3), 701–724 (2007). https://doi.org/10.1016/j.datak.2007.04.008
6. Offerman, T., Stettina, C.J., Plaat, A.: Business capabilities: a systematic literature review and a research agenda. In: 2017 International Conference on Engineering, Technology and Innovation (ICE/ITMC), pp. 383–393 (2017). https://doi.org/10.1109/ICE.2017.8279911
7. OMG: Value Delivery Modeling Language (VDML) 1.1 (2018)
8. Roelens, B.: PGA 2.0: a modeling technique for the alignment of the organizational strategy and processes. In: Domain-Specific Conceptual Modeling: Concepts, Methods and ADOxx Tools, pp. 121–139. Springer (2021)
9. Saaty, T.L.: Decision making with the analytic hierarchy process. Int. J. Serv. Sci. **1**(1), 83–98 (2008). https://doi.org/10.1504/IJSSCI.2008.017590
10. Sandkuhl, K., et al.: From expert discipline to common practice: a vision and research agenda for extending the reach of enterprise modeling. Bus. Inf. Syst. Eng. **60**(1), 69–80 (2018). https://doi.org/10.1007/s12599-017-0516-y
11. The Open Group: ArchiMate®3.2 Specification (2022)
12. The Open Group: TOGAF v10.0 (2022)
13. Ulrich, W., Rosen, M.: The business capability map: the "rosetta stone" of business/it alignment. Enterp. Archit. **14**(2), 1–23 (2011)
14. Van Riel, J., Poels, G.: A method for developing generic capability maps: a design science study in the professional sport industry. Bus. Inf. Syst. Eng. **65**(4), 403–424 (2023). https://doi.org/10.1007/s12599-023-00793-z
15. Yin, R.: Case Study Research and Applications: Design and Methods. SAGE Publications, Inc, 6 edn. (2017)
16. Zdravkovic, J., Stirna, J., Grabis, J.: A comparative analysis of using the capability notion for congruent business and information systems engineering. Complex Syst. Inform. Model. Q. **10**, 1–20 (2017). https://doi.org/10.7250/csimq.2017-10.01

Domain Modeling (EMMSAD 2025)

State of the Art and Research Directions for Visual Conceptual Modeling in Robotics

Daniel Borcard(✉)[iD] and Hans-Georg Fill[iD]

University of Fribourg, Digitalization and Information Systems Research Group,
Fribourg, Switzerland
{daniel.borcard,hans-georg.fill}@unifr.ch
https://www.unifr.ch/inf/digits/en/

Abstract. Visual Conceptual Modeling plays a critical role in advancing robotics by enhancing expressiveness and facilitating collaboration through intuitive visual representations. This paper presents an exploratory literature review of 47 relevant papers, systematically analyzing the application of visual modeling techniques in robotics. The papers are analyzed along seven key criteria to give a comprehensive assessment of their characteristics. Our study shows that despite the increasing adoption of visual modeling techniques, there are still significant gaps in the use of advanced visualization features such as 3D representations and orientation differentiation. The findings thus highlight the potential for enhanced expressiveness through the integration of 3D representations, which could bridge the gap between simulation models and conceptual models. Finally, we propose future directions for the development of more effective visual modeling solutions tailored to robotics.

Keywords: Visual Conceptual Modeling · Robotics · Domain Specific Languages · Standardized Modeling Languages · Visual Representation

1 Introduction

In the field of robotics, visual conceptual modeling can be used to provide intuitive and accessible visual representations to enhance the understandability of complex robotic systems [3,8]. This concerns for example the interaction of different components such as sensors, actuators, microcontrollers and algorithms, as well as the flow of data, dependencies between components, and potential impacts of changes, thus making it easier to develop efficient and effective robotic systems [8]. Furthermore, the use of visual models can facilitate the collaboration among researchers and engineers by providing a shared framework for communication and problem-solving, ensuring that everyone is aligned on the system's architecture and functionality [13]. In contrast to sequential, text-based programming languages, visual models allow to more easily discover relations between concepts. This may be particularly beneficial in robotics, where the integration of diverse technologies demands a holistic understanding of how different parts function together.

In this research-in-progress paper we investigate the state-of-the-art in the field of visual modeling applied to robotics. Through an exploratory literature review we have identified the most relevant papers combining these two fields. We provide a detailed analysis and derive a roadmap for future research in this field.

The paper is structured as follows: in Sect. 2 we discuss foundations in terms of previous approaches for conceptual modeling in robotics and visual properties of modeling languages. In Sect. 3 we describe the data collection and analysis process of the study. In Sect. 4 we present the results of the analysis, followed by a discussion in Sect. 5. Section 6 concludes the paper with an outlook on further work.

2 Foundations

In this section we briefly revisit previous work on standardized and domain-specific modeling languages in the field of robotics, as well as visual properties of modeling languages that will be the foundation for our subsequent analysis.

2.1 Standardized Modeling Languages for Robotics

Modeling languages based on international standards and issued by organizations such as OMG, e.g. BPMN or UML, or which are considered as de-facto standard in some domains have been previously applied to robotics. For example, Wiesmayr et al. [14] use the combination of BPMN and SysML to orchestrate multi-agent robotic systems dynamically. Daun et al. [5] leverage the goal oriented requirements language (GRL) to assess secure behaviors of human-robot collaboration. While on a more technical level, uncertain measurements were added to OCL and UML by Bertoa et al. [2]. They demonstrate how this concept could be applied to a robotic battle system.

The systematic mapping study by Casalaro et al. from 2022 [3] investigated the application of model-driven engineering (MDE) to the sub-field of mobile robots. Their analysis encompassed 97 publications from 2004 to 2018. They found that UML has a large share among model-driven engineering approaches for mobile robots, including several profiles such as SysML, RobotML, or MechatronicUML. However, the larger share of approaches reverts to domain-specific languages (DSL) for robotics.

2.2 Domain-Specific Languages for Robotics

In 2014, Nordmann et al. [12] surveyed DSLs in robotics, analyzing 41 publications from 1986 to 2013. Based on the categories in the *Handbook of Robotics* [1], they derived nine subdomains to classify papers: Robot Structure, Coordinate Representations and Transformations, Perception, Reasoning and Planning, Manipulation and Grasping, Coordination, Motion Control, Architecture and Components. The survey revealed that effective DSLs require accessibility, comprehensive documentation, and illustrative examples/tutorials. Artifact generation (e.g., code, visualizations) is particularly impactful when integrated within a tool-chain utilizing model-to-model or model-to-text transformations. Notably, the authors observed a relative lack of explanation regarding abstraction strategies employed in DSL design. Their work focused on DSLs in general and not on visual aspects of modeling languages. The above mentioned study of Casalaro et al. [3] found in addition, that there seems to be a trend to re-use UML profiles in combination with newly created DSLs. The languages and workbenches used for creating such DSLs included mostly EMF, Xtext, MontiCore, AToM, and MPS. They neither investigated the role of visual aspects in these approaches and only focused on the domain of mobile robots.

2.3 Visual Properties of Modeling Languages

The visual representation of concepts in a modeling language can take many different forms. For this purpose, Costagliola et al. [4] proposed a classification using five categories: *Graph*, *Plex*, *Box*, *Iconic* and *Hybrid*. The *Graph* category consists of nodes and edges. In the *Plex* category, graphical objects have a fixed and predefined number of attaching points, interconnected by links, which are visualized as polylines or structured connections. This category is particularly suited for visual languages with strict connectivity rules. The *Box* category emphasizes containment, nesting, spatial arrangement, and block-based representations, particularly suitable for interface languages, spatial queries, and structured program visualizations. The *Iconic* category represents visual modeling languages where meaning is primarily conveyed through the arrangement, spatial positioning, or composition of graphical symbols called icons. Such iconic languages emphasize visual recognition and intuitive meaning, relying on predefined spatial grammar and syntax rules to construct meaningful visual sentences. The *Hybrid* category is obtained by combining the features of multiple visual language categories, particularly box and graph. Hybrid visual modeling languages possess attributes of both geometric (spatial) arrangements and explicit connectivity rules.

In the well-known paper by Moody et al. [10], the classification of visual notations of modeling languages is further detailed. They analyze each element through eight aspects: *shape, size, color, brightness, orientation, texture, horizontal position, vertical position*. The choice of visual variables to represent a specific concept can greatly affect its effectiveness to convey information. Based on the analysis of the variables, each element can have a level of expressiveness ranging from 0 (no visual elements) to 8 (all variables present).

With these foundations we establish the context for our research by exploring visual properties of standardized and domain-specific modeling languages in robotics. While previous surveys have investigated modeling languages in robotics in general, we will place in the following an emphasis on *visual* modeling languages.

3 Data Collection and Analysis Process

For our review of visual modeling languages in robotics, we first present our data collection and analysis process. This includes the choice of outlets that have been selected for the data collection as well as the search queries that have been used to retrieve the papers.

3.1 Data Collection

At first, we identified the venues that are relevant for the field. For conceptual modeling and model-driven engineering in general, Härer et al. [9] identified nine outlets that are considered relevant by the community. The field of robotics is however much broader. In the study by Casalaro et al. on model-driven engineering in mobile robotics they identified in addition ten relevant outlets [3] and the study from Nordmann et al. in 2014 reverted to six outlets [12]. Merging these three lists is relevant, indeed each venue has already been judged relevant by at least one prior systematic survey, avoiding adhoc additions. Combining modeling-centric and robotics-centric channels prevents bias toward either discipline and captures work published at their intersection. This final venue set maximises expected recall while keeping the screening effort manageable. We therefore decided to search first in all 19 outlets that were used previously for discovering visual modeling approaches in robotics. From these, 11 outlets remained that contained relevant papers after 2015 as will be described in the following - see Table 1 and Fig. 9.

Initial Selection. For identifying relevant papers from the initial outlets we used the following search string: *Robot** **AND** (Visual language **OR** Visual model **OR** Graphical language **OR** Graphical model). This includes variations such as '*robotic*' and '*robots*'. The actual formulation of the search string was adapted for the digital libraries IEEE Xplore Digital Library, ACM Digital Library, and Elsevier ScienceDirect. This broad search led however to the inclusion of papers that mentioned robotics-related terms incidentally, such as in authors' academic CVs or unrelated contexts. Following the initial identification of candidate papers, we thus applied rigorous selection criteria to filter out non-relevant or low-quality contributions. Our inclusion criteria were set as follows: studies demonstrating a visual modeling language (e.g., a BPMN profile with new elements), research applying such languages to robotics or processes involving robotics, publications written in English, and those with accessible full texts. Our study excludes papers where robotics was not a core concept, did not occur at least in a demonstration, or in a proof-of-concept. Thereby we omitted papers merely mentioning robotics in introductory or discussion sections. Further, we excluded publications prior to 2015, surveys or reviews, works that did not focus on domain-specific languages or conceptual models, and non-peer reviewed papers. We limited our search to publications between January 2015 and March 2025 for two complementary reasons: Two comprehensive reviews of DSL for robotics cover work up to 2013 and 2018, respectively [3,12]. Starting in 2015 therefore guarantees an overlap with the later survey while avoiding duplication of material that has already been systematically assessed. While conceptual modeling is a well known topic that is mature and well researched, robotic and modeldriven engineering toolchains have evolved rapidly over the

Table 1. The table contains the selected outlets with the number of papers after the selection process

Outlet Name (Short name)	Σ	References
ACM Southeast Conference (ACM SE)	1	[R1]
Workshop on Domain-Specific Languages and Models for Robotic Systems (DSLRob)	4	[R36, R28, R27, R26]
International Conference on Conceptual Modeling (ER)	2	[R40, R8]
IEEE International Conference on Robotics and Automation (ICRA)	1	[R24]
International Conference on Robotic Computing (IRC)	1	[R7]
IEEE/RSJ International Conference on Intelligent Robots and Systems (IROS)	5	[R35, R34, R31, R29, R30]
ACM/IEEE International Conference on Model Driven Engineering Languages and Systems (MODELS)	15	[R45, R38, R37, R17, R43, R42, R25, R21, R11, R44, R2, R13, R9, R5, R19]
IFIP Working Conference on the Practice of Enterprise Modeling (POEM)	1	[R46]
International Workshop on Robotics Software Engineering (RoSE)	1	[R20]
International Conference on Simulation, Modeling, and Programming for Autonomous Robots (SIMPAR)	3	[R14, R33, R32]
International Journal on Software and Systems Modeling (SOSYM)	13	[R15, R6, R18, R12, R47, R16, R41, R4, R23, R22, R3, R39, R10]
Total	47	

past decade (e.g., widespread adoption of ROS 2, deep-learning-based integrations, and digital twining concepts). Focusing on the last ten years ensures that the visual languages we analyses reflect current practice rather than legacy platforms. Taken together, these considerations make the 2015–2025 window a defensible compromise between completeness and relevance. Applying these inclusion and exclusion criteria led to 47 relevant papers from an original corpus of 71'430 papers across all investigated outlets - see Fig. 9. To mitigate potential biases, both authors were involved in the filtering process.

3.2 Analysis Process

In the next step we specified the following criteria for analyzing the relevant papers. The criteria relate to descriptive aspects, considering the metadata of the papers as well as the content of the papers:

- **Number of papers per year**: Based on the publication date of each paper we can track the evolution of popularity of visual modeling languages in robotics.
- **Abstraction Level**: This category refers to the technical level of the visual models discussed in the papers. The abstraction level is thereby evaluated on a discrete scale: *Technical* papers that focus on deep technical topics such as the Architecture Analysis and Design Language (AADL) profile shown in Fig. 1, which focuses on analyzing robot operating system (ROS); *Mixed* papers that

combine both technical details about robot operations and higher-level concepts like business processes or coordination. For example, the model provided in Fig. 2a blends technical aspects (e.g., sensor readings) with strategic elements (e.g., "Robotic platform," "Controllers") without a clear predominance of either; and *strategical* papers including broader concepts, such as how robot coordinates or fit with a system, without delving into technical aspects. The BPMN model shown in Fig. 2b is an example for this category as the purpose of the visual modeling language is to represent how autonomous robots interact with each other.

- **Expressiveness**: This category evaluates how a modeling language is adapted to align with specific domain requirements. We distinguish three levels: *Standard* approaches that use a standardized modeling language without profiles - e.g., the BPMN model shown in Fig. 2b. *Mixed* approaches that extend a standard language, e.g., using profiles, by incorporating specialized elements while maintaining the original structure. An example would be the AADL profile from [R42] shown in Fig. 1, which is classified as "Mixed" due to its inclusion of robotic-specific concepts like ROS nodes while keeping a significant portion of standard AADL. And finally, *domain-specific* approaches that create a DSL tailored to some field of robotics. For example, the Robochart model from [R22], illustrated in Fig. 2a, is designed specifically for robotic applications, incorporating domain-specific elements such as meta-modeling constructs.
- **Purpose**: This category reflects the application of a visual modeling language. It is based on the categories proposed by Casalaro et al. [3]: *Code Generation, Transformation,* and *Analysis*. In addition, we slightly extended the last category to *Analysis/Simulation* to account for simulation capabilities, which are crucial in robotics contexts.
- **Role of robotics**: In this category we distinguish between *core papers* that develop a language or framework specifically designed for robotics, *demonstration papers* that do not have robotics as their core concept but demonstrate an application using robotics, and *proof-of-concept papers* that use robotics to prove the potential of a concept in a robotics context.
- **Base Language**: In this category we identify the base language that is either directly used, extended, or referenced within the paper. For instance, in the work cited in [R25], the base language is the SysML UML profile and thus classified as "SysML" since it serves as the primary modeling foundation. Whereas, the research presented in [R22] creates a new DSL based on UML and is thus categorized as both "New DSL" and "UML," reflecting its derivative nature from this established language.
- **Main Robotics Topics**: This category stands for the key robotics concepts a paper addresses, based on the categorization in the *Handbook of Robotics* [1]. For example, the study mentioned in [R21] can be categorized under "Robotic Systems Architectures and Programming" because it introduces a novel method to integrate knowledge into model-based engineering tools. Additionally, the work includes coverage of the topic "Flying Robots" due to its focus on drones and extends further into topic "Modeling and Control

State of the Art in Visual Conceptual Modeling in Robotics   421

of Aerial Robots" by incorporating an ontology-specific approach for drone systems.
- **Visual Properties**: In this category we focus on the classes of visual modeling languages proposed by Costagliola et al. [4] and the visual variables by Moody et al. [10]. We will only apply this category to newly created domain-specific languages to highlight how language designers make use of these aspects for creating new languages and due to the fact that existing languages have already been analyzed for these aspects.

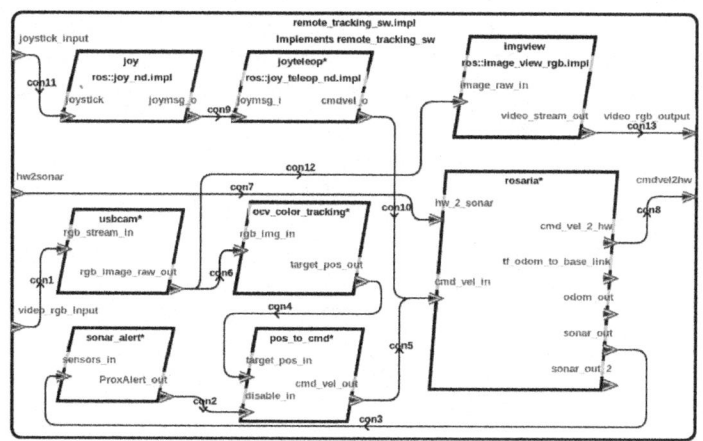

Fig. 1. Example for a Visual Model based on the AADL profile [R42]

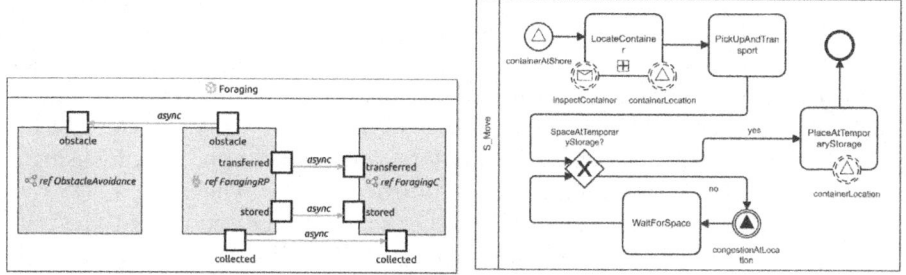

(a) Example of a Robochart model [R22]   (b) Example of a BPMN model [R45]

Fig. 2. Examples for Visual Coneptual Models in Robotics

4 Results

Based on the categories defines above we can now advance to present results of our analysis. This concerns the descriptive analysis focusing on the evolution of the number of papers over time and a content-based analysis based on reading each paper and manually classifying it according to the categories.

Number of Papers Per Year: The distribution of the number of papers over the time span 2015–2025 is shown in Fig. 3. The number of papers published per venue has been shown previously in Table 1. We can observe that the number of publications remains relatively low across the analyzed period, with at most eight papers per year in 2016, 2020, and 2022. Thus, while the topic seems to be continuously investigated, it can be viewed as a niche topic compared to the high number of publications in robotic-specific outlets and even conceptual modeling and model-driven engineering - see Fig. 9.

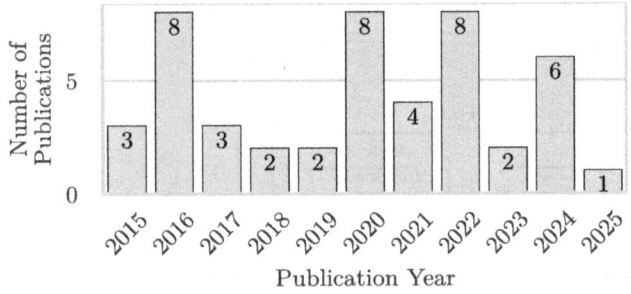

Fig. 3. Number of publications per year

Abstraction Level: Concerning the level of abstraction, 24 papers are categorized as "Mixed," reflecting a holistic approach and not focusing on a specific level - see Fig. 4. The paper of Fend et al. [R25] demonstrates this approach by developing a modeling language that allows system architects to analyze and model the robotic system to be used. This high level strategic model includes technical concepts in the metamodel such as sensors and actuators making it also technically oriented. The next highest category, with 15 papers, is the "Technical" category. These papers have adopted a more applied approach, focusing on practical solutions without addressing strategic matters. The category "Strategic" only contains 8 papers. This low number suggests that models with a strategic perspective on robotics remain underexplored within the field. It may also indicate that researchers are either hesitant to develop high-level strategic models or find it challenging to translate such ideas into suitable modeling languages.

Expressiveness: As shown in Fig. 4 (b), the majority of papers fall into the "Standard" and "Mixed" categories regarding expressiveness, with 22 and 19 papers respectively, while only six papers exhibit domain-specific approaches. This distribution may be attributed to the fact that developing new profiles within existing languages is less time-intensive and resource-consuming than creating entirely new domain-specific languages such as the Robochart visual

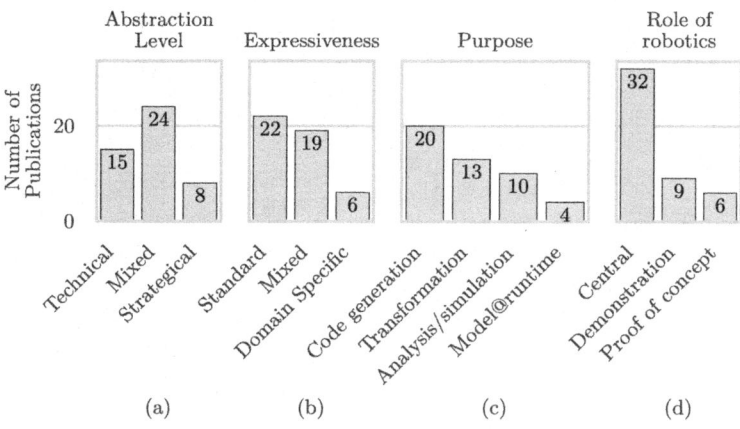

Fig. 4. Number of papers per abstraction level (a), expressiveness (b), purpose (c) and role (d)

modeling language [R22]. The effort involved in developing such languages might deter researchers unless there is a clear necessity or benefit. Standard languages offer a wide range of tools and methodologies, allowing researchers to focus on incremental improvements rather than starting from scratch. Furthermore, the "Mixed" category represents efforts to profile languages or adapt existing tools for specific purposes without fully committing to a new domain-specific solution.

Purpose: In terms of purpose of an approach, the majority of papers (20) focuses on code generation - see Fig. 4 (c). This serves various purposes such as: controlling robots physically or autonomously [R2, R20,R27,R1], creating dynamic interfaces that interact with humans or other systems [R7, R25], simulating and analyzing robot behavior, aiding in planning and testing without physical implementation [R44, R13, R30, R33]. The underexplored area of "Models@runtime" (4 papers) indicates that real-time model deployment and adaptability have not yet been a major research focus. This could be an area of future interest, as dynamically updating visual models during runtime could enhance understanding of the robotic systems' behavior.

Role of Robotics: We observed that a large majority of 32 papers explicitly incorporates robotics as their core topic, while only nine revert to the domain of robotics for demonstration purposes only and six employ robotic systems as proof-of-concept studies - see Fig. 4 (d). Papers that focus on proof-of-concept are either highly strategical, meaning that an asset may be a robot or another system because the language is very abstract (e.g., [R17, R43]), an early-stage analysis that will focus on robotics later (e.g. [R23]) or a deep technical concept that can be applied to various systems, including robotics (e.g. [R4]).

Base Language: Our analysis revealed that only nine out of 47 papers focus on the creation of new domain-specific languages - see Fig. 5. These languages serve specific purposes, as demonstrated by Nordmann et al. [R24] for movement modeling, Paulius et al. [R29] for representing relationships between objects to

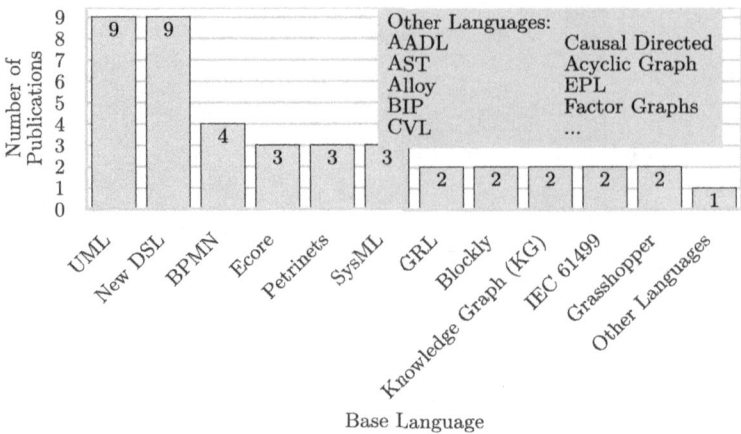

Fig. 5. Number of publications per base language

improve manipulation of them, RoboChart [R22] that aims to represent robot behavior independently of their type complexity or purpose, [R16] for model verification through ROS package models generation or [R9] to model discrete and continuous behaviors in cobotic cells based on hGALS Petri nets.

Profiling or utilizing plain UML is equally important with nine papers. This finding is not unexpected, as UML serves as the foundation for many existing DSLs. Furthermore, high-level modeling languages such as BPMN and SysML are well-represented in our corpus, with four [R45, R46, R6, R41] and 3 [R45, R23, R11] papers respectively. This indicates that the research community makes an effort to adapt these general-purpose languages to meet the specific technical requirements of robotics applications.

Main Robotics Topics: The main robotics topics covered in this corpus were derived from the *Handbook of Robotics* [1]. As shown in Fig. 6, the distribution of papers per main robotic topic reveals that most papers - 33 out of 47 - focus on implementing interaction methods or frameworks, making "12. Robotic Systems Architectures and Programming" the dominant topic.

Industrial robots are the most popular covered by 17 papers and include robots such as 6dof robotic arms [R8, R44, R9] or CNC machines [R12, R13]. Wheeled robots are covered in 13 papers making it the second most popular type of robot after industrial robots. Notably, only 3 of these papers address "Intelligent Vehicles" [R5, R18, R10]. Surprisingly, flying robots such as drones received minimal attention in terms of visual modeling approaches so far, covered in only three papers [R1, R6, R21].

This shows a focus on more mature robotics types, particularly industrial robots. This preference aligns with the structured architectures and processes present in industrial environments, which lower the entry barriers for research in these fields. In contrast, domestic robotics remains underexplored, with only five papers addressing this topic with a relation to visual modeling [R24, R25, R16, R31, R34], despite it's broad range of applications, such as

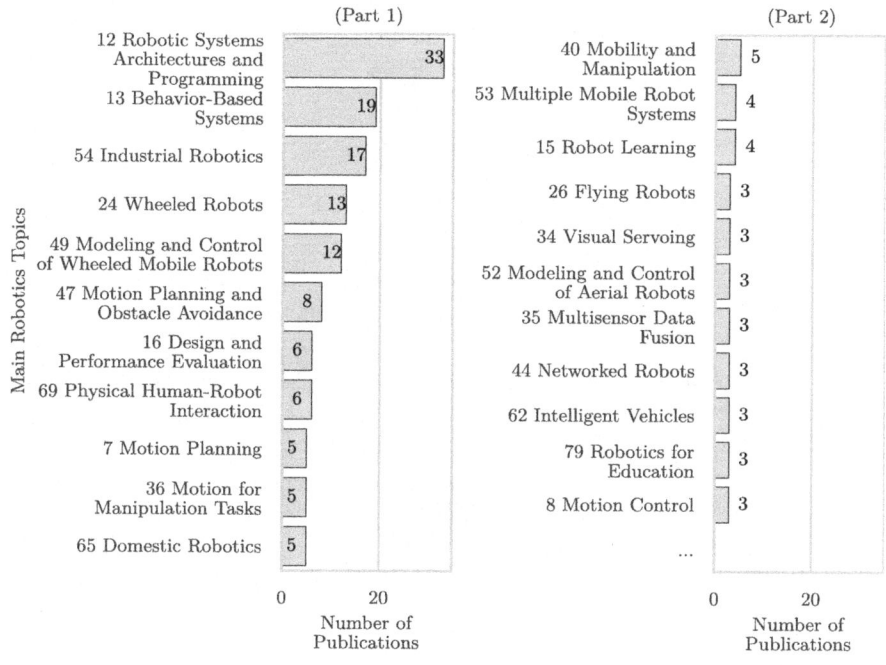

Fig. 6. Number of papers per main robotics topics

the Roomba case study by Fend et al. [R25], the multipurpose Care-O-bot4 by Hammoudeh et al. [R16], and Nordmann et al.'s proposal for an industrial 6DoF robotic arm (KUKA LWR IV) in a collaborative domestic context. Collaborative robotics, which involves human interaction within the same working space, is covered in seven papers (i.e. 69 Physical Human-Robot Interaction).

Cross-Analysis of Expressiveness, Abstraction Level, and Purpose: We further analyzed the relations between abstraction level and purpose in a cross-analysis. It became evident that papers with expressiveness level 'mixed' also exhibit a mixed abstraction level - see Fig. 7. This indicates that the languages profiled in these papers often address both technical and strategic aspects of robotics. Notably, while many technical papers utilize standard languages (8), there is a lack of domain-specific languages designed specifically for strategic purposes, with only two papers addressing this area [R36,R32].

When contrasting the categories expressiveness and purpose - as shown in Fig. 8, we see that domain-specific visual modeling languages are mainly used for code generation and are not represented in Analysis/Simulation and Models@runtime categories so far. Profiled visual modeling languages, on the other hand, are also heavily employed for code generation, with 11 papers dedicated to this purpose. Standard, un-profiled languages seem to be primarily used for model transformation tasks.

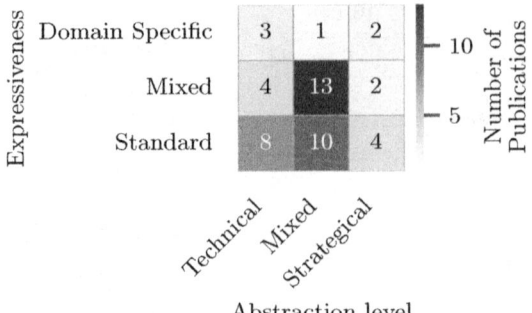

Fig. 7. Number of papers per expressiveness and abstraction level

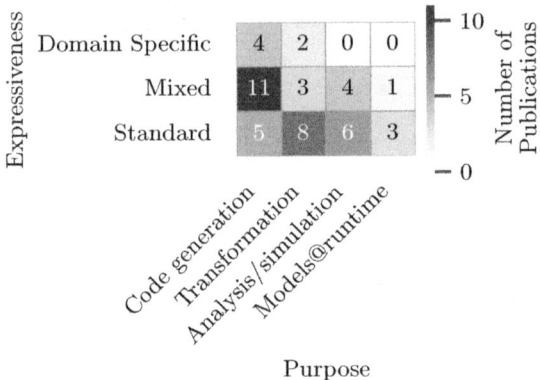

Fig. 8. Number of papers per expressiveness and purpose

These findings underscore the need for a more comprehensive exploration of new domain-specific visual modeling languages to address strategical requirements and goals. Furthermore, visual modeling languages applied to Analysis/Simulation and Models@runtime could represent a stepping stone in robotics as well as in modeling-related research.

Visual Properties of New Domain Specific Languages: When inspecting the visual properties of newly created visual domain-specific languages in robotics, we observe that all of the languages except one include some form of shape differentiation. Similarly, color plays a central role in several languages to enhance readability and represent complex robotic models. For example, in Robochart [R22], a blue robotics icon signifies a "Robotic Platform Reference," while a black-and-white version represents a "Robotic Platform Definition". Different texture are mostly present in connecting objects such as the difference between a solid arrow and a dashed arrow. However, the absence of brightness and orientation differentiation in these languages may be attributed to their foundation in classical 2D visual systems, which traditionally prioritize shape, color, texture, horizontal and vertical position over spatial orientation. In terms of the classes of visual modeling languages, as presented in the Table 2, four out nine belong to the class *hybrid*, three to *graph* and two to *plex*. For example, the graph model of Paulius et al. [R29] is a "directed semi-acyclic graph" meaning that one node can have any number of input and output edges. This ensure the flexibility of the produced knowledge graph. Types of the hybrid class are well represented among the new DSLs. For example, the approach by Zhang et al. [R34] belongs to the iconic and plex classes. It defines multiple icons representing concepts such as "Robot Model", "VmModel" or "Web service", while the metamodel defines strict connection rules as defined for the Plex class.

The hybrid approach seems to be the most effective method to conceive a visual language because it combine the advantages of several other class while minimizing the constraints. The concept of container (i.e. an element represented inside another) from the box class, paired with icon representations may reduce the amount of textual information on screen while keeping the hierarchical structure.

Table 2. Table of visual variables expressed and visual class for the New DSL.

Visual Variables	[R16]	[R24]	[R22]	[R12]	[R27]	[R36]	[R29]	[R33]	[R32]
Shape	X	X	X	X	X	X	X	X	
Size					X	X		X	
Colour	X	X	X		X		X	X	
Brightness									
Orientation									
Texture			X	X				X	
Horizontal position	X		X		X	X		X	
Vertical position	X		X		X	X		X	
Σ	4	3	5	1	5	4	2	6	0
Visual Class	Graph	Graph	Hybrid: Plex, Box, Iconic	Plex	Hybrid: Plex, Box, Iconic	Hybrid: Plex, Box, Iconic	Graph	Hybrid: Plex, Box, Iconic	Plex

5 Discussion

The findings of this exploratory literature analysis showed the role of visual conceptual modeling in robotics research, particularly through the development and application of domain-specific and standardized modeling languages. The analysis reveals that the majority of studies relies on well-established standardized modeling languages like UML [R4,R21], BPMN [R45,R46,R6,R41] and SysML [R45,R23, R11], which are frequently extended through profiling (e.g., blockly profile [R1,R20]). Standardized visual modeling languages act as foundations for robotics research due to their broad acceptance and existing tool support. However, creating specialized visual domain-specific modeling languages tailored to specific robotic subdomains remain a less-explored area with only nine papers out of the 47 analysed. While standardized languages are valuable, the creation of specialized languages for specific robotic subdomains (e.g., industrial robotics, flying robots, domestic robotics) remains promising for future research. Such new domain-specific visual modeling languages could significantly improve the design and understanding of the behavior of service robots and others where human interaction is central. Indeed, service robots are becoming more and more complex and capable [7]. As demonstrated by Hammoudeh et al. [R16], the Care-O-bot4 full robot has a omnidirectional base to move around it's environment, two 7DoF arms to manipulate objects and a 15 touchscreen to interact with users. Visual models could lower the entry barrier to develop such complex robots.

The under-utilization of orientation, brightness, and 3D representations in current domain-specific modeling languages may pose a limit to their expressiveness. The results suggest that future research could explore the integration of 3D visualizations in these languages to enhance realism and representativeness. For example the Movement architecture modeling of Nordmann et al. [R24] could thus represent the different positions of the 6DoF arm in a 3D environment to add more intuitive understanding of the actions. Addressing these gaps could involve integrating 3D visualization techniques, offering a more realistic bridge between simulation models and conceptual models as had been proposed recently in the area of spatial conceptual modeling [6,11].

The findings also highlight underexplored areas such as modeling for simulation/analysis and Models@runtime capabilities. These capabilities are essential for developing adaptive and efficient robotic systems capable of dynamic responses in real-world environments.

While technical and mixed abstraction-level models are prevalent, the development of domain-specific modeling languages for higher-level strategic purposes remained limited so far. For example, Zhang et al. [R36] tackle the management and optimization of Cloud robotics' architecture through a new visual DSL. A more general robotic behavior and process modeling solution could be explored as future research.

This analysis has several limitations that should be considered when interpreting its findings. The review focuses exclusively on studies published from 2015 onwards, potentially excluding valuable research conducted before this period. Additionally, the study focused on a predefined set of venues rather than conducting a comprehensive search across all relevant science databases using keywords. This narrow focus may have excluded valuable studies published in outlets not included in the initial selection. The absence of a backward-forward search method means that not all relevant studies might have been captured.

6 Conclusion and Outlook

This paper provides an overview of the state of visual conceptual modeling in robotics, highlighting key findings, gaps, and opportunities for future research. The results demonstrate that while significant progress has been made in applying visual modeling languages to robotics, there remain important areas that require further exploration. By addressing these gaps and leveraging advanced visualization techniques, researchers can develop more effective tools for creating and analysing robotic systems, ultimately advancing the field of robotics and visual conceptual modeling.

A Dataset of the Review Process

The list of all the selected papers (R1-R47) and the classification for this analysis are available online at https://neptuniux.github.io/VDSL_Robotics_2025.

B Additional Figure

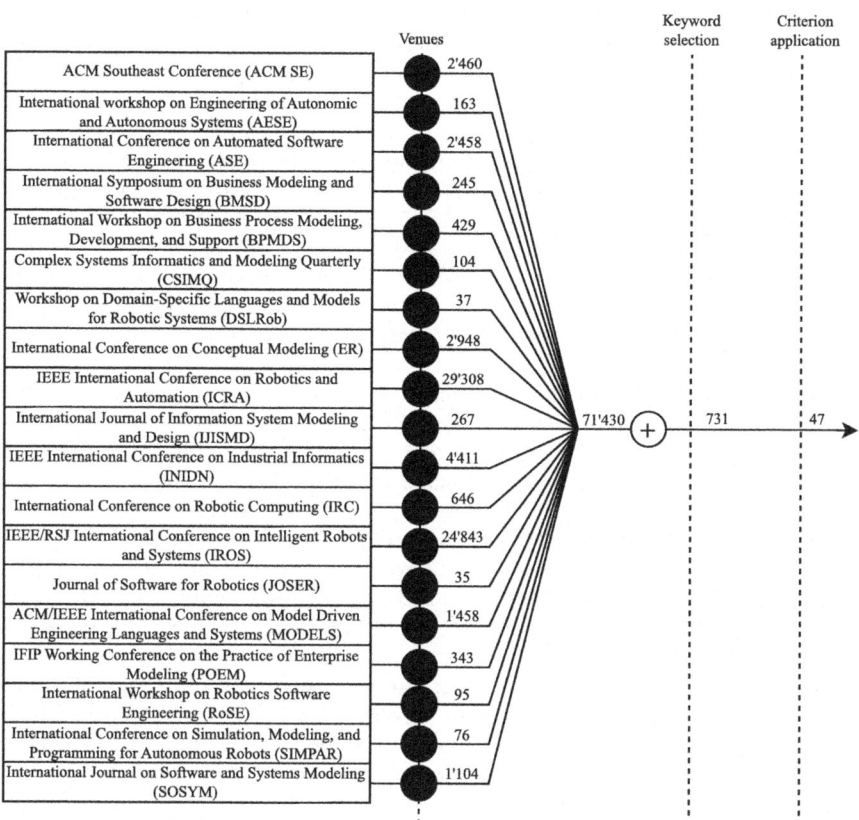

Fig. 9. Selection process based on the original 19 outlets

References

1. Siciliano, B., Khatib, O. (eds.): Springer Handbook of Robotics. Springer, Cham (2016). https://doi.org/10.1007/978-3-319-32552-1
2. Bertoa, M.F., Burgueño, L., Moreno, N., Vallecillo, A.: Incorporating measurement uncertainty into OCL/UML primitive datatypes. Softw. Syst. Model. **19**(5), 1163–1189 (2019). https://doi.org/10.1007/s10270-019-00741-0
3. Casalaro, G.L., Cattivera, G., Ciccozzi, F., Malavolta, I., Wortmann, A., Pelliccione, P.: Model-driven engineering for mobile robotic systems: a systematic mapping study. Softw. Syst. Model. (5), 1–31 (2021). https://doi.org/10.1007/s10270-021-00908-8
4. Costagliola, G., Delucia, A., Orefice, S., Polese, G.: A classification framework to support the design of visual languages. J. Vis. Lang. Comput. **13**(6), 573–600 (2002). https://doi.org/10.1006/jvlc.2002.0234
5. Daun, M., Manjunath, M., Jesus Raja, J.: Safety analysis of human robot collaborations with GRL goal models. In: Conceptual Modeling, pp. 317–333 (2023)
6. Fill, H.G.: Spatial Conceptual Modeling: Anchoring Knowledge in the Real World, pp. 35–50. Springer Nature Switzerland (2024). https://doi.org/10.1007/978-3-031-56862-6_3
7. Gonzalez-Aguirre, J.A., et al.: Service robots: trends and technology. Appl. Sci. **11**(22), 10702 (2021). https://doi.org/10.3390/app112210702
8. Hammoudeh García, N., Deshpande, H., Santos, A., Kahl, B., Bordignon, M.: Bootstrapping MDE development from ROS manual code: Part 2—model generation and leveraging models at runtime. Softw. Syst. Model. **20**(6), 2047–2070 (2021). https://doi.org/10.1007/s10270-021-00873-2
9. Härer, F., Fill, H.G.: Past trends and future prospects in conceptual modeling - a bibliometric analysis. In: Conceptual Modeling, vol. 12400, pp. 34–47. Springer International Publishing, Cham (2020). https://doi.org/10.1007/978-3-030-62522-1_3
10. Moody, D.: The "Physics" of notations: toward a scientific basis for constructing visual notations in software engineering. IEEE Trans. Software Eng. **35**(6), 756–779 (2009). https://doi.org/10.1109/TSE.2009.67
11. Muff, F., Fill, H.G.: A domain-specific visual modeling language for augmented reality applications using WebXR, vol. 14320, pp. 334–353. Springer Nature Switzerland (2023). https://doi.org/10.1007/978-3-031-47262-6_18
12. Nordmann, A., Hochgeschwender, N., Wrede, S.: A survey on domain-specific languages in robotics. In: Simulation, Modeling, and Programming for Autonomous Robots, pp. 195–206. Springer International Publishing, Cham (2014). https://doi.org/10.1007/978-3-319-11900-7_17
13. Senn, E., Bourdon, L.W.J., Blouin, D.: Multi-paradigm modeling for early analysis of ROS-based robotic applications using a library of AADL models. In: Proceedings of the 25th International Conference on Model Driven Engineering Languages and Systems: Companion Proceedings, pp. 677–683. MODELS '22, Association for Computing Machinery, New York, NY, USA (2022). https://doi.org/10.1145/3550356.3563129
14. Wiesmayr, B., Zoitl, A., Hästbacka, D.: Modeling service choreographies and collaborative tasks for autonomous mixed-fleet systems. In: International Conference on Model Driven Engineering Languages and Systems, pp. 234–244. ACM (2024). https://doi.org/10.1145/3652620.3686244

A Domain-Specific Modeling Method for Designing Conversational Agents for Coaching: A Case from Health Coaching

Charuta Pande[1,2(✉)], Hans-Georg Fill[1], and Knut Hinkelmann[2]

[1] University of Fribourg, Research Group Digitalization and Information Systems, Bd de Pérolles 90, 1700 Fribourg, Switzerland
{charuta.pande,hans-georg.fill}@unifr.ch
[2] FHNW University of Applied Sciences and Arts Northwestern Switzerland, Intelligent Information Systems Research Group, Riggenbachstrasse 16, 4600 Olten, Switzerland
{charuta.pande,knut.hinkelmann}@fhnw.ch

Abstract. Conversational agents offer possibilities to effectively support scenarios like health coaching to promote awareness and behavioral change. However, the process of designing conversational agents requires technical knowledge, posing challenges in onboarding domain experts such as health coaches and counselors, healthcare educators, etc. We propose a metamodeling-based domain-specific language for designing health coaching agents and conversations. Our modeling method provides elements specialized for health coaching while remaining adaptable for other coaching domains. We demonstrate the modeling language through the use case of an HIV health coaching agent. Through a feature comparison with existing model-driven approaches for chatbot development, we highlight the technology-neutral and application domain-focused contribution of our visual modeling method. Initial feedback from HIV domain experts substantiates its feasibility and relevance.

Keywords: Metamodeling · Modeling Language · Conversational AI · Chatbots · Conversational Agents · Health Coaching · Domain-specific Models

1 Introduction

The benefits, effectiveness, and usability of conversational agents or chatbots in health-related coaching have been researched in several studies [2,3,17]. Common motivations for technology-assisted coaching through conversational agents (CA) are the round-the-clock availability and the ability to support human coaches, especially in a high-demand field like healthcare.

The design and development of a domain-specific CA is an elaborate process and involves collaborative communication between domain experts and Conversational AI experts to define requirements, goals, and technical implementation [2,9]. Most existing conversation design tools include technical configurations and focus more on chatbot development than on domain-specific agent and conversation design. This limits usability for domain experts with limited or no experience with programming. While past works in model-driven development for chatbots abstract from technical details, they still build upon familiarity with chatbot development technology. We propose a technology-neutral, domain-specific modeling language to simplify and enhance the design of agents and conversations, especially in high-demand fields like health coaching. We aim to leverage features of domain-specific modeling languages like "expressiveness" and "abstraction" to make chatbot design and development more intuitive for domain experts.

We derive the requirements of our modeling method from a research project on a health coaching chatbot for people living with HIV. Our contributions are (1) a metamodel and modeling elements for designing requirements of a health coaching agent and (2) a metamodel and modeling elements for designing conversations with a focus on health coaching. The paper is structured as follows: foundational concepts in Sect. 2, related work in Sect. 3, the HIV health coaching case in Sect. 4, our modeling method in Sect. 5, a use case to demonstrate the modeling method in Sect. 6, evaluation in Sect. 7, concluding with limitations and future work.

2 Foundations

The design and development of a CA is a multidisciplinary activity and involves concepts from various fields like UX Design, Natural Language Processing (NLP), and Web Engineering. We refer to this multidisciplinary field as 'Hybrid Conversational AI' and explain the involved concepts.

2.1 Conversation Design

Conversation design is a user-centric approach, starting by defining the target user personas, their demographics, motivations, challenges, and needs. Tools like customer journey or empathy mapping help understand user pain points. One or more *bot personas* are then defined to ensure a consistent tone in user interactions. For example, service bots are designed to be attentive and helpful, whereas companion bots are designed to be empathetic, sensitive, and supportive [12]. Finally, conversations are designed as turn-taking sequences of *bot and user utterances*, capturing common (happy) paths and alternative (unhappy) paths, with human handoff for edge cases. Moore and Arar [18] define Conversational UX design patterns to guide the process of conversation design based on (a) main activities supported by the bot, (b) users' goals, (c) interactions and decisions at the conversation level, e.g., when to end or continue a conversation, and (d) interactions and decisions at the agent level, e.g., opening or closing a user session. Although conversation design does not focus on technical implementation, some technical concepts like variables and NLP components (described in Sect. 2.2) are identified and integrated early into the design. Thus, conversation designers are expected to be familiar with relevant UX and Conversational AI concepts. In our work, we aim to support domain experts in agent and conversation design by minimizing technical complexity.

2.2 Hybrid Conversational AI

A CA's architecture, as suggested by Adamopoulu et al. [1], consists of components for understanding user input (*Natural Language Understanding - NLU*), managing context and dialog (*Dialog Management - DM*), generating responses (*Natural Language Generation - NLG*), and integration with *data sources* for information retrieval. The DM component may apply strategies like handcrafted (or rule-based) or probabilistic (or data-driven) approaches [10,11]. In rule-based dialog management, user-CA interactions follow a predefined path, with user input restricted to selectable options, typically via buttons. In probabilistic dialog management, however, users interact freely via text or voice. The NLU component identifies *intents* and *entities*, DM remembers the *state* of the conversation, and predicts the next *action*. Often, NLU models are fine-tuned with custom training data.

Recently, pre-trained generative large language models (LLMs) with Retrieval Augmented Generation (RAG) have been used to create simple chatbots. However, these chatbots do not follow the architecture explained above, nor do they have a predefined dialog structure. The responses are generated by providing *input prompts* to trained dialog models. Such chatbots may generate false or misleading responses, a known problem with generative LLMs. Integrating *knowledge sources* using RAG minimizes the risk of misinformation.

Bot responses (NLG) may be predefined, LLM-generated, or defined as templates with runtime *slot-filling* from user input [11]. Domain knowledge can be integrated into the dialogs via websites, databases, or knowledge graphs. Finally, CAs are deployed on cloud-based platforms and accessed through websites, chat apps, or social media channels. Most platforms provide mechanisms to continuously test and optimize CAs. Thus, *Hybrid Conversational AI* can be categorized as a field that combines multiple approaches for interpreting user input, dialog management, response generation, and domain knowledge integration, depending on the goals and requirements of a CA.

2.3 Implementation Tools and Platforms

Many tools and platforms support CA design, development, and deployment. General diagramming or mockup tools like Draw.io, Adobe XD, etc., can be used for conversation design, while chatbot-specific tools like Botframe, Mockitt, Landbot focus on prototyping. Conversational AI platforms like Google Dialogflow, Rasa, IBM Watson, Botpress, Voiceflow, etc. support the entire chatbot development lifecycle and include features like multi-language support, integration with external sources and channels, deployment, versioning, analytics, and NLP configuration. Some tools like Dialogflow CX, Botpress, and Voiceflow include graphical or node-based design capabilities for users to visualize and design conversations, but users still require technical knowledge. Despite low-code features in these tools, separating design from technical components remains challenging.

3 Related Work

Martínez-Gárate et al. [16] have reviewed model-driven approaches for chatbot development. These include metamodeling, domain-specific languages (DSL) [8], model-driven development (MDD) [26], and model-driven architecture[1] (MDA). A DSL specifies an abstract syntax, a concrete syntax, and semantics. MDD uses models as an artifact to develop software and tools to transform models into executable code, whereas MDA defines three abstractions for development and transformation between them: business logic (Computation Independent Model - CIM), technology-independent functionality (Platform Independent Model - PIM), and technology-specific functionality (Platform Specific Model - PSM).

MDD for chatbots has been explored in several approaches. Daniel and Cabot [4,5] define Xatkit; a set of domain-specific languages for platform-independent definition of chatbots using MDD that can help in reducing technology-related complexity. The main problem they address is reducing the dependency on intent-recognition providers. Pérez et al. [23] present Conga, an approach for forward and reverse chatbot engineering with Dialogflow and Rasa platforms. Ouaddi et al. [19] define a DSL metamodel for abstracting bot creation using the Rasa framework, and in [20] they define a graphical DSL. Planas et al. [24] define a DSL for designing conversational UIs for multi-experience platforms. A DSL for open-source virtual assistants is presented in [13].

Vahdati and Ramsin [28] define a four-phase methodology for chatbot development and a metamodel for each phase based on MDA; however, they do not describe a concrete syntax for the metamodels. The methodology applies phases of the software development lifecycle (SDLC) to chatbot development. The methodology we followed [14] has similar phases and, in addition, includes customer (coachee)-centric phases like user persona design, customer journey mapping, etc.

All these approaches provide an abstraction of the technical implementation but do not provide abstractions or specializations specific to the application domain, which is the area most familiar to domain experts. In [22], the authors propose an automatic synthesis of chatbots by combining a metamodel for the application domain with Xatkit DSL. Garcia et al. [9] propose a model-driven approach for developing chatbots for triage in healthcare systems. Their metamodel combines elements from the application domain and elements to develop a simple chatbot that collects responses to triage questions.

Our approach differentiates itself from the above approaches by focusing on the application domain and conversation design, enabling a holistic design of

---

[1] https://www.omg.org/mda/mda_files/Cephas_MDA_Fast_Guide.pdf.

health coaching CAs. We separate agent and conversation design from chatbot development by defining abstract and technology-neutral concrete syntax tailored to health coaching.

4 Motivation: Case of HIV Health Coaching Agent

"Researching Intelligent Chatbots as Health Coaches" is an ongoing research project developing a chatbot based on *Hybrid Conversational AI* to coach young people with HIV in Nigeria on educational topics and behavioral change. The chatbot development followed the steps outlined in [14], which applies SDLC phases to Conversational AI as described in Sect. 2.2. To define the scope and specify the requirements of the chatbot, a collaborative workshop of five days was carried out with experts from relevant fields - HIV care and counseling experts from Nigeria, who contributed to domain-specific aspects of chatbot development including the socio-economic, cultural, and religious background of the end users, and Conversational AI experts from Switzerland. These included two nurses, two HIV counselors, five researchers in public health, one researcher in behavioral sciences, and three experts in Conversational AI. The workshop defined topics, tools, and technical requirements of the chatbot. Feedback was collected from twenty-three test users (young people between 18 and 25 years of age living in Nigeria) on the bot's name, persona, language, interaction style, etc., and was used to refine the final design. Domain experts designed the content of the conversations, while Conversational AI experts handled the technical implementation of the chatbot; these activities were continued after the workshop for several months to develop the chatbot iteratively [15,21].

Since most domain experts had no or limited experience with technology and chatbot development, they received training on tool usage, Conversational AI concepts, and conversation design principles. We used Voiceflow, a low-code model-driven tool, to create graphical conversation models. The following observations from the project (O1-O6) contributed to the requirements of the modeling language and serve as the motivation for the current work:

O1: *Domain experts found conversation design intuitive with 'drag-and-drop' blocks for creating conversation flows.* **O2**: *Voiceflow lacks domain-specific block specializations for an intuitive conversation design.* To address this, we used color-coding and labels to highlight specific blocks and paths, enhancing clarity for domain experts. **O3**: *Domain experts struggled with technical configurations in Voiceflow, such as using variables and including intents and entities (described in Sect. 2.2), as these technical aspects were closely tied to conversation design.* These elements were integrated into the chatbot by Conversational AI experts. **O4**: *The available blocks (palette) in Voiceflow do not differentiate between those needed for conversation design and those integrating technical components.* It was challenging to onboard domain experts in designing conversations directly using the tool, as users require prior knowledge of Conversational AI concepts. **O5**: *Designing a health coaching chatbot requires a top-down approach that integrates various conversation design and chatbot development methods* [21]. Guidelines for conversation design were derived from multiple sources, and a custom methodology was developed to identify bot persona(s), user personas, conversation topics, and navigation strategies between topics. **O6**: *Domain experts prefer working with templates, guidelines, and examples that help in converting implicit knowledge into explicit knowledge.* A custom template was designed to help them identify the goal of the conversation, cite official or scientific resources, and specify conversation turns.

Despite the training, the domain experts required significant support from Conversational AI experts, as the tool lacked a clear separation between conversation design and technical configuration elements. Based on these observations, we propose that a DSL can enhance the process of designing health coaching chatbots. We outline a set of requirements in Sect. 5.1.

5 Modeling Method for Agent and Conversation Design

We propose a modeling method based on metamodeling that conforms to requirements derived from literature and observations from the HIV health coaching case described in Sect. 4. We followed the macro process proposed by Frank [8], which consists of the following seven steps (Fig. 1):

Fig. 1. Process for Domain-Specific Language Development [8]

The target users of the modeling language are healthcare experts with little or no experience in programming or chatbot development, e.g., health coaches, public health counselors, healthcare educators, researchers, etc., as identified by Scandiffio et al. [25] in their study on technology adoption in healthcare. The HIV health coaching case described in 4 served as the primary basis for defining the scope and purpose of the modeling language. Additional insights were drawn from literature, e.g., common conversation topics in health coaching [27], mapping between coaching concepts and Conversational AI strategies [6], etc., and limitations in existing Conversational AI tools (see Sect. 2.3).

5.1 Requirements

As proposed by Frank [8], we have formulated the requirements of our modeling method into two categories: generic and specific. The generic requirements capture levels of abstraction, expressiveness, and understandability from the point of view of different stakeholders, for which we use the concepts from MDA (see Sect. 5.2). We also take into account the interoperability between existing tools and frameworks. Thus, we have identified the following seven generic requirements:

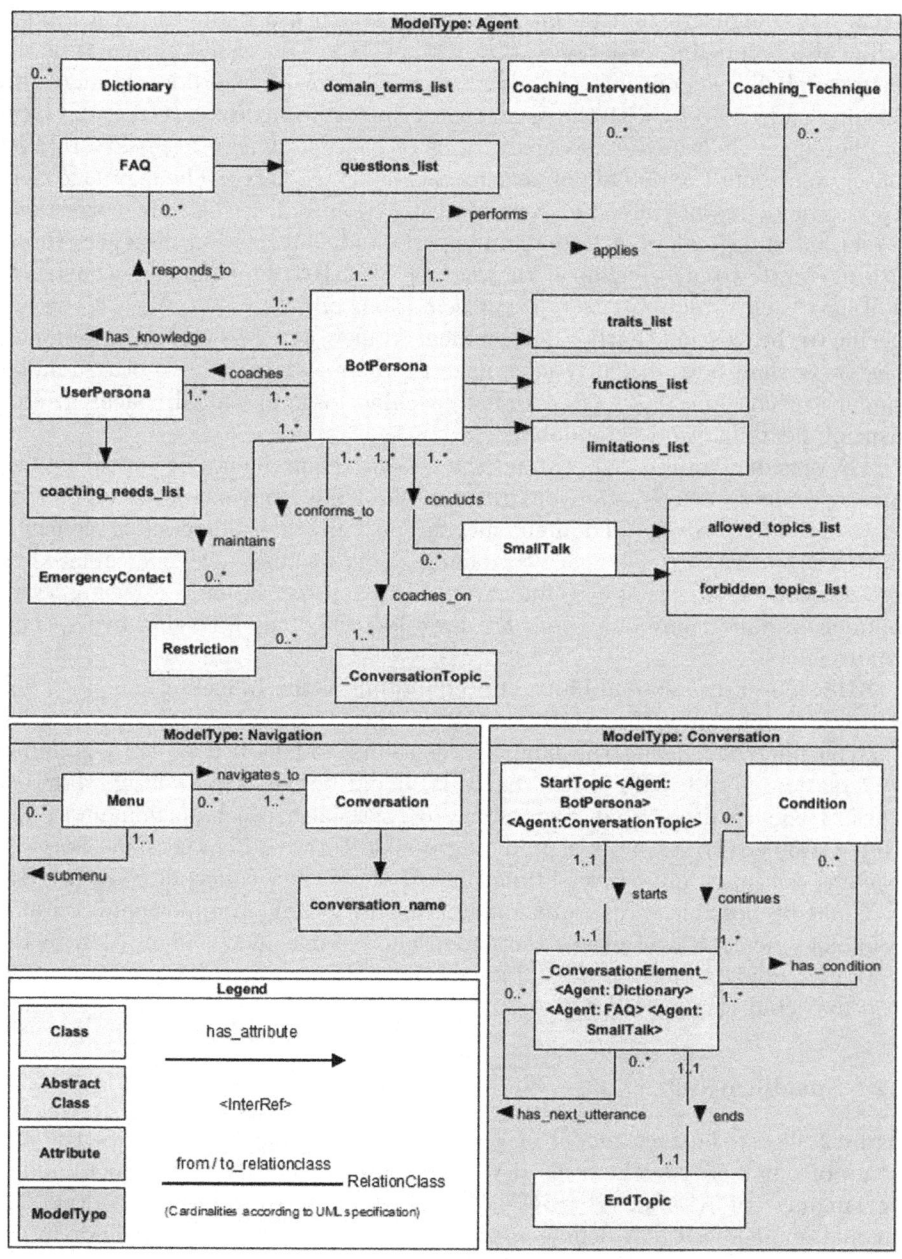

Fig. 2. Metamodel of the DSL for Designing Health Coaching Agents

GR1: The modeling language shall support the configuration and specification of elements required for designing health coaching conversational agents (O2).

GR2: The language shall be intuitive and easy to use for users with limited technical or modeling experience (O1, O3). **GR3**: The visual elements of the language shall use concepts that align specifically with the domain of health coaching and generally with the principles of conversation design (O1, O5). **GR4**: The language shall include specializations of concepts where necessary to adequately represent the domain of health coaching (O2). **GR5**: The language shall support modeling at different levels of abstraction and details that correspond to relevant stakeholders, e.g., domain experts and conversation designers (users with moderate to high technical knowledge) [8]. **GR6**: The language constructs shall have a clear mapping to the representations of target concepts, i.e., details specific to the existing chatbot development frameworks [8]. **GR7**: The language constructs shall be sufficiently generalized to allow adaptation to other similar domains of coaching, e.g., educational coaching, organizational coaching, etc., ensuring flexibility and extendability [8].

The specific requirements extend the generic requirements by capturing features specific to conversation design, e.g., modeling conversations, navigation between conversations, and domain-specific specializations of modeling elements. At this level, we also take care to include some technical elements related to conversation design using a technology-neutral representation, i.e., using terms common in daily communication. We have identified the following five specific requirements:

SR1: To ensure extendibility and adaptability, the modeling language will be based on meta-modeling (GR7). **SR2**: It should be possible to design a modular coaching plan using the language concepts and map it to corresponding conversations (GR3, GR5, GR7). **SR3**: It should be possible to design different types of conversations that correspond to the health coaching domain (GR1, GR2, GR3, GR4). **SR4**: It should be possible to create connections between coaching concepts and conversational (chatbot-specific) concepts (GR6). **SR5**: It should be possible to capture some details of technical implementation at a technology-neutral level of abstraction to allow reuse and configuration in the PSM, e.g., domain data, sources of knowledge, NLU training data, variables and their expected values, etc. (GR6).

5.2 Specification

Figure 2 shows the metamodel of our modeling language. To specify the elements of our metamodel, we used the convention followed by the metamodeling language of ADOxx [7] (SR1). We use the following ADOxx concepts in our metamodel - a *Class* defines *attributes* with specific data types and can be instantiated with a graphical notation. An *AbstractClass* cannot be instantiated but defines a structure that can be inherited by classes. *Relation classes* define relationships, including cardinalities, between source and target classes. *InterRef* specifies relationships between classes from different models. A *ModelType* is a meaningful collection of concrete classes and relationships.

In our modeling language, we define three model types - *Agent*, *Conversation*, and *Navigation*.

Model Type *Agent*: The *Agent* model defines the domain of a health coaching agent, capturing its scope, requirements, and constraints that influence the design and development of a CA as a health coach. Following MDA, the model type *Agent* serves as a CIM, focusing on domain-specific aspects rather than system structure or implementation (SR2).

The mandatory elements of this model include at least one *BotPersona*, *UserPersona*, and *ConversationTopic*; other elements are optional. Bot personas influence the style of conversation with the user. Defining user personas - a key UX practice - helps tailor conversations to target users.

Domain knowledge can be configured as a dictionary or FAQ sources, which can be linked to elements in *Conversation* models. These may further be integrated with generative AI or used for fine-tuning NLU models (SR5).

Elements like coaching interventions and coaching techniques help in applying coaching models to the agent. Defining these elements early ensures that conversation design follows relevant coaching styles and addresses specific coaching goals.

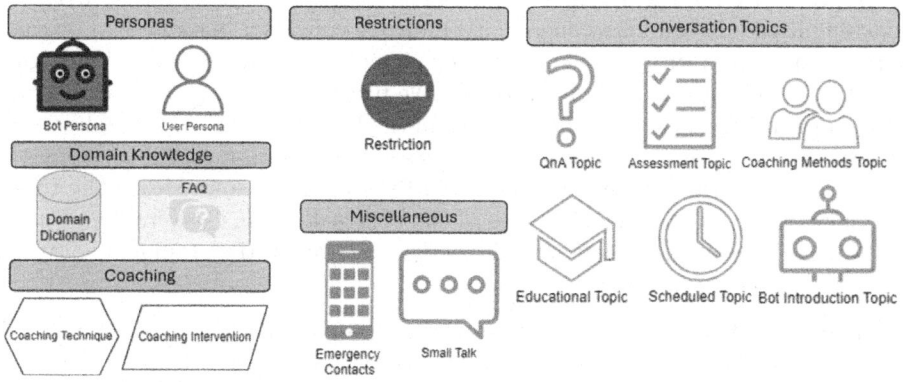

Fig. 3. Graphical Modeling Elements for Agent Model

Small talk or chitchat is a function of CAs that imparts to them a touch of friendliness. However, it is important to define the scope and boundary of small talk by configuring topics that the agent should avoid talking about, e.g., politics, religion, medical advice, etc. Further legal, privacy-related, or ethical restrictions may be configured using the *Restriction* element. Some miscellaneous details, like emergency contacts, which are commonly required in health-related situations, can also be configured in the agent design. Figure 3 gives an overview of all elements in the *Agent* model.

Model Type *Conversation*: The model type *Conversation* defines the logical structure and the behavior of the conversational system and conforms to the abstraction PIM of MDA (SR3). As in human conversations, agentic conversations involve two entities-the human and the agent. The *ConversationElement* is an abstraction to represent two main types of conversational elements: bot utterances and user utterances. A *Condition* element may be used to introduce branches in a conversation using which a tree-like conversation structure can be designed (see Sect. 5.2). The *StartTopic* element signifies the beginning of a conversation and defines the type of topic (see Sect. 5.2). The *EndTopic* element denotes the end of a conversation. Currently, a rule-based design is envisioned for most conversations in health coaching, as also identified in [27]. A more flexible conversation design needs knowledge of NLU components and dialog management approaches, which can be achieved more effectively in a PSM using one of the Conversational AI tools. To enable such a translation from a rule-based design using our metamodel to a flexible implementation of conversations, a mapping between relevant elements of PIM and PSM will be defined.

Model Type *Navigation*: This model focuses on the design of menu and submenu options and the navigation between conversations. The *Navigation* model is a PIM, as it models the behavior of the system concerning switching between different conversations.

Conversation Topics: Designing a health coaching agent is a process driven by coaching needs [21] and may encompass multiple conversations that can be categorized into topics with specific goals. Beinema et al. [27] have grouped dialogues in health coaching into a "Topic Model". We further abstracted from this model and supplemented it with our findings from the literature and the case described in Sect. 4. Thus, we identified *six* categories of conversation topics based on the dialog structure they follow and the goal of the conversation (SR3). The topics are represented as specialized classes of the abstract class $\_ConversationTopic\_$[2] and can be used in the model type *Agent*. Figure 3 shows the graphical notations for each conversation topic.

Educational Topic: This category includes all topics on the "what", the "how", and the "why" of a coaching domain. It corresponds to the "Health education" topic in the topic model by Beinema et al. [27]. Examples include conversations that educate users on medication adherence, HIV basics, medication storage, etc. In educational topics, the conversation design focuses mainly on bot utterances, and the user interaction is limited to either confirmation of knowledge or asking for further explanation.

Bot Introduction Topic: This category includes all miscellaneous conversations that give information about the chatbot, its personality, functions, etc. E.g., "Bot Introduction", "How to use the system", and "Discuss Coaching Approach" in the topic model by Beinema et al. [27] can be mapped to this category.

Assessment Topic: Conversations that involve an assessment of users' knowledge or skills as a numeric score may fall in this category. Examples are: "Do an exercise" in the topic model by Beinema et al. [27], quizzes, assessment of wellness score, etc.

---

[2] Due to space limitations, specializations are not shown in the metamodel.

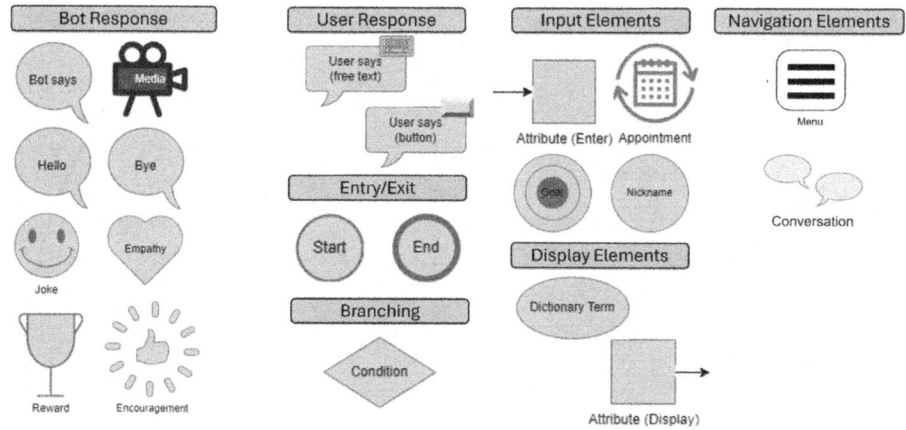

Fig. 4. Graphical Modeling Elements for Conversation and Navigation Model

Scheduled Topic: This category includes conversations that are triggered at a predefined frequency, e.g., "Medication Reminder", "Schedule Appointment", "Task Follow-up", etc., mapped to "Reminders" in the topic model by Beinema et al. [27].

QnA Topic: This category focuses on designing short conversations to facilitate multiple question-answer loops. These topics focus on allowing users to repeatedly ask questions, e.g., conversations on Frequently Asked Questions [15].

Coaching Methods Topic: This topic category deals with conversations that correspond to various coaching-related activities and interventions. The topics "Goals and planning", "Monitoring", "Feedback", and "Gather information" in the Topic Model by Beinema et al. [27] can be grouped in this category. To ensure the success of an intervention, it is important to involve domain experts to identify suitable intervention types and adapt them, if necessary, such that they can be conducted effectively through a chatbot.

Conversation Elements: In our metamodel, we represent elements for modeling conversations as an abstract class _ConversationElement_[2]. Since conversations are between two participants, the bot and the user, the *Conversation* model defines two main types of conversation elements: *Bot says* and *User says*. The *Bot says* element is further specialized to represent domain-specific utterances, e.g., *Empathy, Reward, Encouragement*, etc.; see Fig. 4 (SR4). User responses can be captured either through predefined options (buttons) or as free-text inputs, modeled as specializations of the *User says* element. The *condition* element allows for modeling branches in a conversation. The elements *Enter Attribute* and *Display Attribute* allow the integration of dynamic attributes in conversations, e.g., nickname of the user, dates, goals (represented as specializations of *Enter Attribute*), or other custom variables (SR5). The element *Dictionary Term*

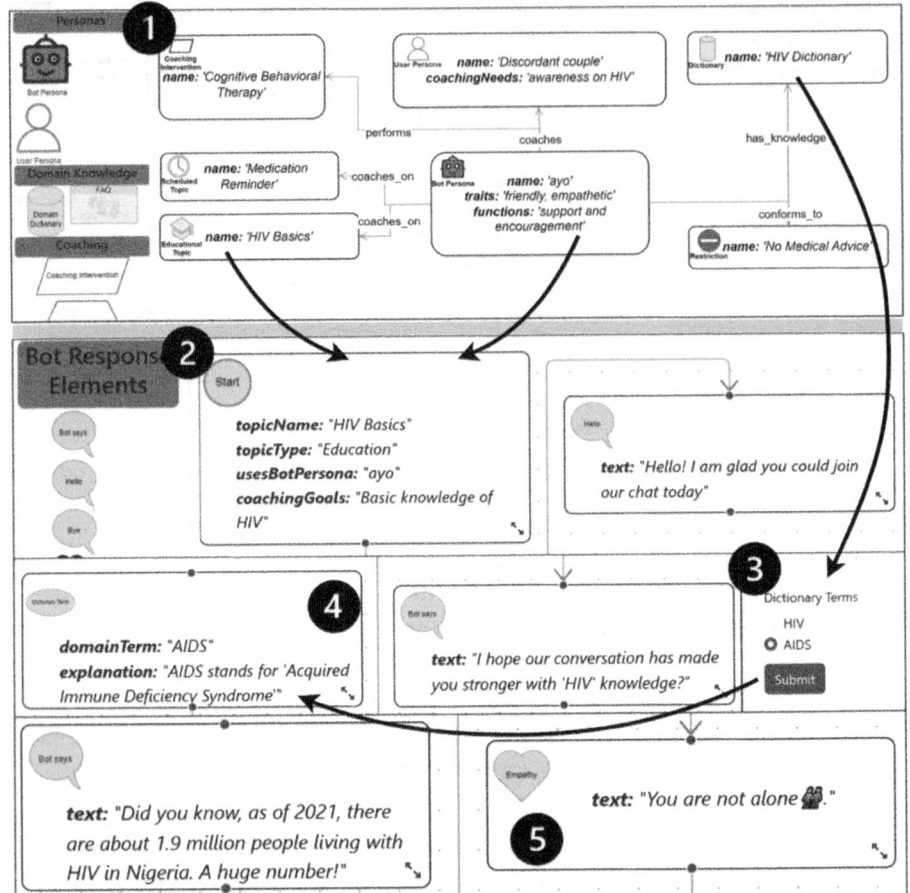

Fig. 5. HIV Health Coaching Agent Use Case showing 1. Simplified *Agent* model 2. Snippets of *Conversation* model for Educational Topic 'HIV Basics' 3. Property pane showing available Dictionary Elements configured in the *Agent* model 4. Element to integrate domain knowledge in conversation design 5. Specialized element for empathetic bot utterances. Arrows show inter-connection between *Agent* and *Conversation* models

allows integration of concepts from the Domain Dictionary (model type *Agent*) into conversations.

The graphical notations for the modeling elements described above were chosen pragmatically: (a) borrowed from existing modeling languages, e.g., *Start*, *End*, *Condition*, or (b) denoted using common concepts from daily communication, e.g., *Appointment*, *Media*, *Bot Persona*, *User Persona*, etc. However, since the target users most likely will not be experienced in modeling, we include a label for each element for more clarity.

We limit our work to modeling CIM and PIM for health coaching chatbots. Existing approaches and Conversational AI tools will be used to create PSMs. To allow transformation between PIMs created with our approach and existing tools, a mapping between the modeling elements and elements of one or more Conversational AI tools will be defined.

6 Use Case Models for an HIV Health Coaching Agent

We demonstrate the application of our modeling method using simplified examples from the HIV health coaching case described in Sect. 4. The upper part of Fig. 5 shows how the requirements of designing an HIV health coaching agent can be captured in an *Agent* model (1). The agent has a *botPersona* named Ayo with traits 'friendly and empathetic' and functions of providing 'support and encouragement'. The agent coaches one user persona, 'Discordant Couple'[3] that seeks 'awareness on HIV', and maintains domain knowledge in the form of an HIV dictionary including terms and definitions related to HIV. It performs the coaching intervention 'Cognitive Behavioral Therapy' and has a restriction to exclude medical advice during user interactions. Furthermore, the agent is designed to coach users on two topics - an educational topic on 'HIV Basics' and one scheduled topic on 'Medication Reminder'. These topics will be designed as *Conversation* models.

The bottom part of Fig. 5 shows snippets of the *Conversation* model for the educational topic 'HIV Basics' designed using our modeling method (2). The topic uses the persona 'ayo' and addresses the coaching goal of providing basic knowledge on HIV. Figure 5 further demonstrates the usage of specialized elements for bot utterances - *Hello*, and *Empathy* (5). It also demonstrates how domain knowledge configured in the *Agent* model can be integrated into a conversation using the element *Dictionary Term* and its property pane (3 and 4). The arrows show references between the *Agent* model and the *Conversation* model.

7 Evaluation

We evaluate our modeling method by comparing it with six approaches that propose DSLs for chatbot development, as discussed in Sect. 3. Approaches that do not define a concrete syntax are not included. The comparison is based on the five specific requirements and two additional criteria - dialog design support and type of modeling. The approaches chosen for the comparison are by Daniel et al. [4,5], Pérez-Soler et al. [23], Planas et al. [24], Malamas et al. [13], Ouaddi et al. [19], and Garcia et al. [9].

A detailed comparison is shown in Fig. 6. It can be seen that our approach supports domain experts in designing a CIM and a PIM that are technology-neutral, whereas other approaches contribute to abstracting technology concepts

---
[3] For better understanding, we use the representative target user group here instead of the persona name, e.g., Sisi and Bobo (Discordant Couple).

Requirements	Approaches						
	Daniel et al. 2020, 2024	P'erez-Soler et al. 2020	Planas et al. 2021	Malamas et al. 2023	Ouaddi et al. 2024	Garcia et al. 2024	Our modeling method
SR1 - Metamodelling	Y	Y	Y	Y	Y	Y	Y
SR2 - Domain-specific elements							
Application Domain Related							
Specialized elements	N	N	N	N	N	Y	Y
Agent Design elements	N	N	N	N	N	N	Y
Chatbot Development Related							
NLU - intents, entities, training examples	Y	Y	Y	Y	Y	N	(-)
API/External Service	Y	Y	Y	Y	Y	N	(-)
Knowledge source	N	N	N	N	N	N	Y
Variables	Y	Y	Y	Y	Y	N	Y
SR3 - Domain-specific Conversation Design							
Specialized conversation topics	N	N	N	N	N	N	Y
Conversation Design elements							
Chatbot and user utterances	(-)	(-)	Y	Y	Y	Y	Y
Conditions and Branching	(-)	(-)	(-)	(-)	(-)	Y	Y
Navigation	(-)	(-)	(-)	(-)	(-)	Y	Y
SR4 - Connection between models and elements							
Interconnection between models	Y	Y	Y	Y	Y	Y	Y
SR5 - Technology-neutral terminology	N	N	N	N	N	N	Y
Dialog Design Support							
Rule-based	N	N	N	N	Y	Y	Y
NLU-based	Y	Y	Y	Y	Y	N	(-)
Modelling - Graphical (G)/Textual (T)	T	T	T	T	G, T	G	G

Fig. 6. Feature comparison of our modeling method based on five specific requirements SR1-5 Y: Requirement met, N: Requirement not met, (-): Requirement partially met or difference in implementation

aligned with chatbot development. Some requirements, like metamodeling (SR1) and providing interconnections between various models (SR4), are common to all approaches, including ours. On the other hand, no approach besides ours supports a holistic design of a CA or defines domain-specific data as a source of knowledge that can be integrated into conversations or potentially with generative AI approaches. Most existing approaches provide an abstraction for NLU-based dialog management; hence, conversation design is implicitly handled. Our approach provides an abstraction of rule-based dialog design and defines conversation design elements but hides details of technology-specific elements like intents, entities, variables, external services, etc. Only one approach [9] defines elements that capture the application domain; however, the elements are limited to a specific task of collecting responses to triage questions.

In addition to a feature comparison, we did an empirical evaluation with *four* domain experts involved in the HIV health coaching case to collect initial feedback on the understandability and relevance of the concrete syntax. Two experts had experience with Voiceflow and, thus, visual modeling of conversations. They were asked to model a simplified conversation on the topic of 'HIV Basics', using the modeling elements of the *Conversation* model. The other two experts were involved in agent and conversation design but did not use Voiceflow. These experts were asked to briefly ideate agents for similar use cases in health coaching using the modeling elements of the *Agent* model, e.g., an agent to support prenatal healthcare. The evaluation did not focus on designing a complete solution but on validating the feasibility of our approach with short examples and exercises. The experts provided a few suggestions to make the visual representation of elements like *Domain Dictionary* and *Restriction* more intuitive. Overall, the domain experts found most elements understandable and very relevant. This initial feedback gives us a positive indication of the usefulness and relevance of our approach.

8 Conclusion and Future Work

In this work, we presented a DSL for designing health coaching CAs. The modeling method allows to 1. *design and capture the requirements of health coaching agents*, and 2. *design conversations that address the coaching needs in healthcare*. Our approach supports domain experts having limited or no experience in chatbot development. It allows augmenting the ideation and design of health coaching agents by capturing domain knowledge.

There are some limitations to our work. The modeling elements supported by our DSL may not be exhaustive. The first feedback from experts, however, shows that the defined elements sufficiently capture the requirements for modeling an HIV health coaching agent and its conversations. Further evaluation with additional health coaching use cases and domain experts is required to ensure the adaptability of our approach. Besides conducting additional evaluations, in our future work, we will define reference models for each conversation topic to allow easy onboarding of domain experts. Finally, transformation rules will be defined to translate the models generated using our DSL to an existing Conversational AI framework.

Acknowldegement. The case in this work has been derived from the research project "Researching intelligent chatbots as healthcare coaches" funded by the Swiss National Science Foundation (SNSF) under grant IZSTZ0_202602 within the Swiss Programme for International Research by Scientific Investigation Teams (SPIRIT).

References

1. Adamopoulou, E., Moussiades, L.: An overview of chatbot technology. In: Maglogiannis, I., Iliadis, L., Pimenidis, E. (eds.) AIAI 2020. IAICT, vol. 584, pp. 373–383. Springer, Cham (2020). https://doi.org/10.1007/978-3-030-49186-4_31
2. Beaudry, J., Consigli, A., Clark, C., Robinson, K.J.: Getting ready for adult healthcare: designing a chatbot to coach adolescents with special health needs through the transitions of care. J. Pediatr. Nurs. **49**, 85–91 (2019). https://doi.org/10.1016/j.pedn.2019.09.004
3. Boucher, E.M., et al.: Artificially intelligent chatbots in digital mental health interventions: a review. Expert Rev. Med. Dev. **18**(sup1), 37–49 (2021). https://doi.org/10.1080/17434440.2021.2013200

4. Daniel, G., Cabot, J.: Applying model-driven engineering to the domain of chatbots: the xatkit experience. Sci. Comput. Program. **232**, 103032 (2024). https://doi.org/10.1016/j.scico.2023.103032
5. Daniel, G., Cabot, J., Deruelle, L., Derras, M.: Xatkit: a multimodal low-code chatbot development framework. IEEE Access **8**, 15332–15346 (2020). https://doi.org/10.1109/ACCESS.2020.2966919
6. Duhan, R., Pande, C., Martin, A.: A flexible, extendable and adaptable model to support AI coaching. In: Hinkelmann, K., López-Pellicer, F.J., Polini, A. (eds.) Perspectives in Business Informatics Research, pp. 172–187. Springer Nature Switzerland, Cham (2023). https://doi.org/10.1007/978-3-031-43126-5_13
7. Fill, H., Karagiannis, D.: On the conceptualisation of modelling methods using the ADOxx meta modelling platform. Enterp. Model. Inf. Syst. Archit. Int. J. Concept. Model. **8**(1), 4–25 (2013). https://doi.org/10.18417/EMISA.8.1.1
8. Frank, U.: Domain-specific modeling languages: requirements analysis and design guidelines. Domain engineering: product lines, languages, and conceptual models, pp. 133–157 (2013). https://doi.org/10.1007/978-3-642-36654-3_6
9. García-García, J.A., Sánchez-Gómez, N., Escalona, M.J., Ruiz, M.: COTriage: applying a model-driven proposal for improving the development of health information systems with chatbots. IT Professional **26**(3), 22–31 (2024). https://doi.org/10.1109/MITP.2024.3380916
10. Harms, J.G., Kucherbaev, P., Bozzon, A., Houben, G.J.: Approaches for dialog management in conversational agents. IEEE Internet Comput. **23**(2), 13–22 (2019). https://doi.org/10.1109/MIC.2018.2881519
11. Jurafsky, D., Martin, J.H.: Chatbots and dialogue systems. In: Jurafsky, D., Martin, J.H. (eds.) Speech and Language Processing, chap. 15. Stanford and Colorado at Boulder, draft 3rd edn. (2023). https://web.stanford.edu/~jurafsky/slp3/
12. Lessio, N., Morris, A.: Toward design archetypes for conversational agent personality. In: 2020 IEEE International Conference on Systems, Man, and Cybernetics (SMC), pp. 3221–3228 (2020). https://doi.org/10.1109/SMC42975.2020.9283254
13. Malamas, N., Panayiotou, K., Symeonidis, A.L.: dFlow: a domain specific language for the rapid development of open-source virtual assistants. arXiv preprint arXiv:2310.02102 (2023). https://doi.org/10.48550/arXiv.2310.02102
14. Martin, A.: The conversational AI life-cycle - version 2 (2023). https://doi.org/10.5281/zenodo.7992227
15. Martin, A., Pande, C., Schwander, S., Ajuwon, A.J., Pimmer, C.: Domain-specific embeddings for question-answering systems: FAQS for health coaching. In: Proceedings of the AAAI Symposium Series, vol. 3, pp. 175–179 (2024). https://doi.org/10.1609/aaaiss.v3i1.31197
16. Martínez-Gárate, Á.A., Aguilar-Calderón, J.A., Tripp-Barba, C., Zaldívar-Colado, A.: Model-driven approaches for conversational agents development: a systematic mapping study. IEEE Access **11**, 73088–73103 (2023). https://doi.org/10.1109/ACCESS.2023.3293849
17. Mitchell, E.G., et al.: Automated vs. human health coaching: exploring participant and practitioner experiences. Proc. ACM Hum. Comput. Interact. **5**(CSCW1), 1–37 (2021). https://doi.org/10.1145/3449173
18. Moore, R.J., Arar, R.: Conversational UX Design: A Practitioner's Guide to the Natural Conversation Framework. Morgan & Claypool (2019). https://doi.org/10.1145/3304087
19. Ouaddi, C., Benaddi, L., Jakimi, A., Chehri, A., Saadane, R., et al.: A sketch of DSL and code generator for accelerating chatbot development. Procedia Comput. Sci. **246**, 3585–3594 (2024)

20. Ouaddi, C., Benaddi, L., Naimi, L., Bouziane, E.M., Jakimi, A.: A graphical DSL for accelerating chatbot development. In: 2024 7th International Conference on Advanced Communication Technologies and Networking (CommNet), pp. 1–6 (2024). https://doi.org/10.1109/CommNet63022.2024.10793369
21. Pande, C., Martin, A., Pimmer, C.: Towards hybrid dialog management strategies for a health coach chatbot. In: Proceedings of the AAAI 2023 Spring Symposium on Challenges Requiring the Combination of Machine Learning and Knowledge Engineering (AAAI-MAKE 2023), vol. 3433. CEUR-WS.org (2023). https://ceur-ws.org/Vol-3433/paper11.pdf
22. Pérez-Soler, S., Daniel, G., Cabot, J., Guerra, E., de Lara, J.: Towards automating the synthesis of chatbots for conversational model query. In: Nurcan, S., Reinhartz-Berger, I., Soffer, P., Zdravkovic, J. (eds.) Enterprise, Business-Process and Information Systems Modeling, pp. 257–265. Springer International Publishing, Cham (2020). https://doi.org/10.1007/978-3-030-49418-6_17
23. Pérez-Soler, S., Guerra, E., de Lara, J.: Model-driven chatbot development. In: Dobbie, G., Frank, U., Kappel, G., Liddle, S.W., Mayr, H.C. (eds.) Conceptual Modeling, pp. 207–222. Springer International Publishing, Cham (2020). https://doi.org/10.1007/978-3-030-62522-1_15
24. Planas, E., Daniel, G., Brambilla, M., Cabot, J.: Towards a model-driven approach for multiexperience AI-based user interfaces. Softw. Syst. Model. **20**(4), 997–1009 (2021). https://doi.org/10.1007/s10270-021-00904-y
25. Scandiffio, J., et al.: The role of mentoring and coaching of healthcare professionals for digital technology adoption and implementation: a scoping review. Digit. Health **10**, 20552076241238075 (2024). https://doi.org/10.1177/20552076241238075
26. Selic, B.: The pragmatics of model-driven development. IEEE Softw. **20**(5), 19–25 (2003). https://doi.org/10.1109/MS.2003.1231146
27. Beinema, T., Op den Akker, H., Hermens, H.J., van Velsen, L.: What to discuss?- A blueprint topic model for health coaching dialogues with conversational agents. Int. J. Hum. Comput. Interact. **39**(1), 164–182 (2023). https://doi.org/10.1080/10447318.2022.2041884
28. Vahdati, A., Ramsin, R.: Model-driven methodology for developing chatbots based on microservice architecture. In: MODELSWARD, pp. 247–254 (2024). https://doi.org/10.5220/0012433700003645

Designing Decision Support Systems for Rural Mobility Enhancement

Sabine Janzen[1], Hannah Stein[1,2(✉)], Lotfy Abdel Khaliq[1], Florian Hergert[1], and Wolfgang Maass[1,2]

[1] German Research Center for Artificial Intelligence, Stuhlsatzenhausweg 3, 66123 Saarbruecken, Germany
{sabine.janzen,hannah.stein,wolfgang.maass}@dfki.de
[2] Saarland University, Campus, 66123 Saarbruecken, Germany

Abstract. Mobility in rural regions is critical for ensuring access to essential services such as education, healthcare, and employment. However, rural mobility remains largely individualized, with heavy reliance on private cars-leading to environmental, social, and infrastructural challenges. Despite increasing data availability from GPS, mobile devices, and public transport applications, data-driven approaches for generating integrated mobility insights tailored to specific rural areas remain underdeveloped. This paper addresses this gap by investigating how decision support systems (DSS) can be designed to provide actionable, region-specific mobility insights for policymakers, businesses, and public transport providers. Following a Design Science Research (DSR) methodology, we identified factors of mobility mode choice. From this, we derived meta-requirements and proposed a set of design principles for data-driven DSS in rural mobility contexts. These principles were implemented in a DSS for the Saarland region of Germany and evaluated with policymakers and public transport planners. Our findings contribute both conceptual design knowledge and practical guidance, demonstrating how DSS can foster more efficient, inclusive, and sustainable rural mobility planning.

Keywords: Rural mobility · Decision Support Systems · Design principles · Mobility mode choice · Design Science Research

1 Introduction

Mobility, particularly in rural regions, is fundamental to contemporary life and significantly influences the accessibility of critical services such as education, healthcare, and employment [34]. However, mobility in rural areas is predominantly individual-based, mainly using private cars [9]. This leads to various challenges, such as increased traffic, environmental degradation, and restricted mobility for socially or physically disadvantaged people [21,26]. There is a notable lack of transparency about the factors of this strong individualization and the role of public transport in specific rural areas. This hinders the creation of effective data-driven decision support systems (DSS) that policymakers, enterprises, and public transportation authorities could use to improve transportation infrastructure [2,8]. Related work analyzed influential factors for mode choice in rural mobility through qualitative interviews, literature reviews, or empirical studies [4,16]. However, until now, open data analytical approaches that support mobility insights for *specific rural regions* are missing, contrary to the increasing availability of data sets on human movements [3], GPS sources, social media [20], and public transport applications [22]. This work investigates data-driven DSS for policymakers, businesses, and public transport in specific rural areas. The objective is to optimize traffic flows, enhance efficiency and sustainability of mobility, and boost social and cultural engagement of citizens [32]. In this context, prerequisites are actual insights into factors and their correlations, influencing the decision for and against individual and public transport by citizens of these regions, extending prior work that focused on general approaches for rural mobility [23,25,35]. Thus, we defined the following research question (RQ):

RQ: How to design decision support systems for policymakers, businesses, and public transport providing data-driven mobility insights for specific regions?

We applied a DSR approach [24] instantiated in a first iteration (cf. Fig. 1). To identify and motivate the problem, we combined the framework of modal choice determinants [7] with qualitative expert interviews [6]. Based on this, meta-requirements, i.e., high-level, generalized requirements, and design principles [11,15] were deduced to define objectives of DSS supporting mobility insights for specific rural regions. Subsequently, an architecture for such DSS was developed, representing the conceptual and technical framework of the solution (cf. Fig. 1). By means of this how-to knowledge, a prototype of a DSS was created and applied to a specific real-world scenario, the mobility in German Saarland region. The final step covered the qualitative evaluation of the DSS. The contribution of this paper is two-fold. First, we propose a **set of design principles** for answering the research question. The design principles were evaluated in real-word scenario by implementing them into an architecture and instantiating a DSS prototype for a specific rural region. The resulting prototype was evaluated in collaboration with relevant stakeholders, i.e., users, including policymakers and public transport planners, validating both the practical applicability of the DSS and thereby relevance of the underlying design principles. Second, the specified design principles address the issue of determining **data that are relevant** in DSS for rural mobility enhancement. Therefore, factors for mobility mode choice were analyzed and mirrored with experts from practice. As a result, design principles list a set of relevant factors that DSS should capture data for. Findings demonstrate that DSS developed by means of the specified design principles can provide valuable mobility insights, improve planning decisions, and support sustainable and inclusive mobility solutions in specific rural areas.

The paper is structured as follows. Section 2 gives an overview of existing research on the design of information systems for decision support in enhancing rural mobility. Next, we identify and motivate the problem (Sect. 3). In Sect. 4, meta-requirements and design principles for data-driven DSS supporting mobility insights are derived for defining objectives of the intended solution. Based on this, an architecture for this class of DSS is introduced in Sect. 5, before the instantiation of a DSS and its application in a real-world scenario is described

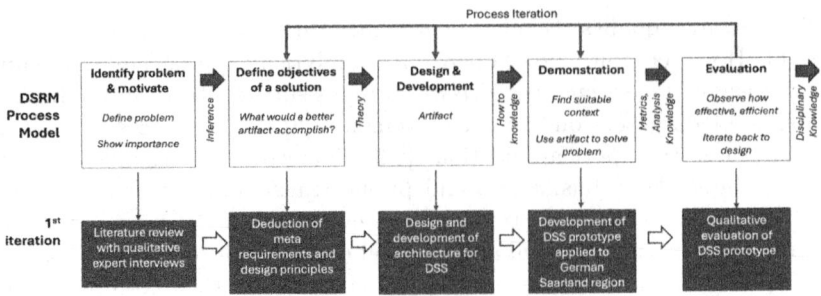

Fig. 1. Applied research approach according to Design Science Research Methodology (DSRM) by Peffers et al. [24].

(Sect. 6). The DSS was evaluated through expert interviews (Sect. 7). Results are interpreted, including a discussion of implications for designing DSS for policymakers, businesses, and public transport, as well as limitations of this work (Sect. 8). Last, the paper is concluded in Sect. 9.

2 Related Work

The design of information systems (IS) for decision support in enhancing rural mobility has gathered attention in various disciplines, including transportation planning, information technology, community development, and data science [31]. Effective decision-support systems rely heavily on robust data collection methods. Surveys and sensor data have been widely used to understand travel patterns and mobility needs in rural areas, e.g., GPS tracking to analyze travel behavior for informing transport policies [29]. Geographic Information Systems have been employed to visualize transport routes and identify service gaps [1]. Techniques range from traffic data visualization [5] and interactive maps for real-time network analysis [28] to analysis frameworks for public transport mobility [36] and urban mobility patterns [30]. Further research integrates environmental, IoT, and smart mobility factors to optimize rural transportation networks [12,26]. Existing related work highlights the multifaceted nature of designing DSS for rural mobility enhancement, but there is a gap in clear design principles and generalizable requirements for developing DSS that provide data-driven mobility insights for specific rural regions that can support decision-makers in enhancing rural mobility on site.

3 Identification and Motivation of Problem

To identify and motivate the problem, we applied an integrative research approach combining the framework of modal choice determinants by DeWitte et al. [7] with qualitative expert interviews [6]. The 26 modal choice determinants divided into the categories socio-demographic, spatial, journey characteristics, and socio-psychological served as a basis for identifying factors influencing transport mode choice in rural areas, while expert interviews were used to reflect on these by incorporating professional insights and practical experience. Table 1 shows 19 determinants that were selected for the discussion with experts. The journey characteristics travel motive, departure time, weather conditions and information were aggregated by the factor *comfort* [7]. As the determinant interchange had conceptual overlappings with *trip chaining*, only the latter was selected for the subset. In the context of socio-pyschological determinants, experiences, familiarity (with means of travel), and lifestyle were skipped as according to [7] they have a strong relation with the socio-demographic determinants education, occupation, income and car availability (cf. Table 1). Next, we interviewed three experts in mobility (interviewee A), public transport (interviewee B), and land management (interviewee C). They were selected based on their expertise and professional experience (3, 9 and 21 years). The qualitative interviews with an average duration of 31 min were conducted via video conference. During the interviews, the selected socio-demographic, spatial, journey characteristics, and socio-psychological factors (cf. Table 1) were discussed with respect to their practical relevance. We therefore applied a semi-structured questionnaire [19] based on the categories and factors (cf. Table 1). After the interviews, the conversations were transcribed and analyzed using qualitative content analysis [18]. For the coding process, we used the categories socio-demographic, spatial, journey characteristics, and socio-psychological as a priori codes. In addition, we allowed emerging codes based on the interview transcripts during the analysis. Ethical considerations were considered, with informed consent obtained from all participants, ensuring anonymity and data handling following privacy laws. After triangulating the results from literature and expert interviews, we ended up with 15 factors (F) relevant to transport mode choice in rural areas. In case interviewees classified factors as not relevant, they were removed from the set. In the category **socio-demographic**, the factors age, education, occupation, household composition, and car availability were specified to influence mode of choice in rural areas. The interviews confirmed these factors. They additionally highlighted the need for alternative solutions and tailored public transport for the aging population (cf. age) as well as for public transportation to align with occupational needs (cf. occupation). Furthermore, flexible solutions for families need to be found (cf. household composition) and alternatives need to be found for cars as the dominant transportation mode (cf. car availability). "Gender" and "income" were not described as currently "borderline factors" that might or might not influence the choice of transport mode in Saarland currently; nevertheless, they might in other rural areas. For the category **spatial**, the factors density, diversity, frequency of public transport and proximity to infrastructure and services were considered relevant. Low population densities often result in limited public transport availability and higher car use. Interviewees A and C highlighted the issue of economic challenges in implementing efficient public transport in rural areas. The same accounts for scattered diversity in contrast to mixed land-use in terms of diverse patterns of residence, industry etc. [7], according to interviewee

B. Due to isolated farms and small units, a cost-effective and efficient design of public transportation services is aggravated. The factor proximity to infrastructure and services was supported by all interviewees as relevant. In addition, they reflected the necessity of a balanced approach to tailor frequency of public transport to local lifestyles and mobility needs. The factor "Parking", i.e., availability of parking at train stations or Park-and-Ride spaces, was removed as contradictory factor that sometimes even leads to more car usage. Distance, travel time, comfort as well as trip chaining are vital factors within **journey characteristics**. The interviews confirmed them, emphasizing the challenge for public transport to compete with speed and convenience of cars (cf. travel time). Furthermore, a lack of comfort in terms of bad weather conditions, high effort in getting information on public transport options or departure times beyond the peak times could lead travelers to prefer using a car. Although these factors play a role, they are rather considered secondary in rural areas, compared to more practical considerations like availability and frequency. All interviewees undermined efficient trip chaining and direct routes as pivotal for public transport choice in rural areas. The factor of travel costs was discarded as less relevant according to the interviewees. Within **socio-psychological factors**, habits and perceptions are considered as influencing factors for mobility mode choice. Interviewee B noted that strong car orientation in rural areas is habitual (cf. habits), making other means of transport less present in people's minds. In addition, emotional attachment to cars and habitual use represent barriers to switch to public transport. Furthermore, people's preferences and perceptions, e.g. with respect to reliability, influence the use and loyalty towards public transport.

Table 1. Selection of socio-demographic, spatial, journey characteristics, and socio-psychological factors influencing mobility mode choice according to framework of modal choice determinants by [7]. In case interviewees classified factors as not relevant, they are visualized as crossed out.

Socio-demographic	Spatial	Journey characteristics	Socio-psychological
Age	~~Parking~~	Travel time	Habits
~~Gender~~	Diversity	Comfort	Perceptions
Education	Density	Distance	
Occupation	Proximity to infrastructure and services	~~Travel cost~~	
~~Income~~	Frequency of public transport	Trip chaining	
Household composition			
Car availability			

4 Deduction of Meta-requirements and Design Principles

Based on the determined 15 factors (F), seven meta-requirements (MR) were formulated, and three design principles (DP) were proposed (cf. Fig. 2) [11]. In

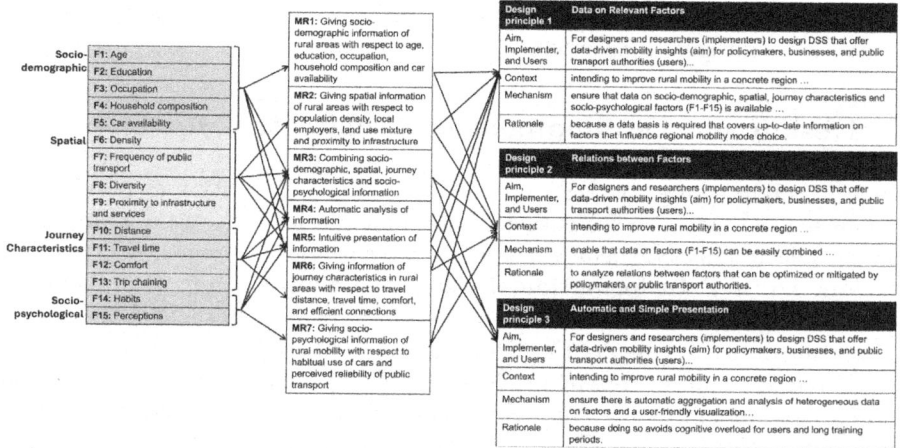

Fig. 2. Factors (F), meta-requirements (MR), and design principles (DP) for specifying objectives of the intended DSS. According to Gregor et al. [11], the schematic presentation of design principles consists of aim, implementers, and users; context; mechanism; and rationale.

combination, they represent the objectives of the intended artifact, i.e., an initial description of the design of DSS providing data-driven mobility insights for specific regions to policymakers, businesses, and public transport. Each DP is described by adopting the schema proposed by [11] covering aim, implementers and users as well as context, the mechanism, i.e., actions, and a rationale giving a justification that the mechanism will help to achieve the aim (cf. Fig. 2). As the derived factors represent entities of mobility, we applied meta-requirements (MR) as helper concepts to enable causal relations from domain-specific knowledge to design knowledge. As factors F1-F15 influence mobility mode choices of citizens in rural areas, giving socio-demographic, spatial, journey characteristics and socio-psychological information forms MR1, MR2, MR6 and MR7 (cf. Fig. 2). To provide an integrated view, information on factors should be combined (MR3). In addition to an intuitive presentation (MR5), an automatic analysis of this heterogeneous information (MR4) is required. The requirements to present information on relevant factors in such an intuitive, i.e. easy-to-use way, is reflected by DP 3 focusing on automatic and simple presentation of data by a DSS (cf. Fig. 2). The requirements to integrate socio-demographic (MR1), spatial (MR2), journey characteristics (MR6), and socio-psychological information (MR7) on F1 - F15 lead to DP1, which states that implementers have to ensure that data on all the relevant factors with respect to the specific rural region focused by the DSS is available (cf. Fig. 2). Users should be able to combine the available data on factors as they like. Thus, the meta-requirements MR3, MR1, MR2, MR6, and MR7 are culminating in DP2 that address that users should be able to combine data on F1-F15 in an easy ways as this helps policymakers or public transport authorities to analyze relations between factors that can be optimized or mitigated for enhancing rural mobility.

5 Design and Development of Architecture for DSS

Next, an architecture for DSS supporting mobility insights for specific rural regions was developed representing the technical framework of the solution (cf. Fig. 1). The architecture defines a pipeline covering four components: **Data Collection, Data Transformation, Interactive Map Generation** and **Analyzer** (cf. Fig. 3). The Data Collection component instantiates DP1 (cf. Fig. 2) by integrating data according to the determined socio-demographic, spatial, journey characteristics, and socio-psychological factors, e.g., geographic data on districts and cities or mobility app requests by users, by means of web scrapers, parsers and APIs. Task of the Data Transformation component is to transform this data into formats usable for instantiating DP3 (cf. Fig. 2) by means of position localization of data, track filtering and track reduction algorithms as well as district assignment and district aggregation methods (cf. Fig. 3). The Interactive Map Generation component performs a cyclic layer projection process to integrate the transformed heterogeneous data onto a base empty map (cf. Fig. 3) until all layers are added, resulting in a dynamic and multi-layered map representation that can be controlled and combined by users (cf. DP2, Fig. 2). Derived factors frame the interface structure of the DSS, displaying controls for data on factors as well as check-boxes for detailed views (cf. DP1 and DP3, Fig. 2). The Analyzer component instantiates DP2 and DP3 by enabling users to stack and visualize data for the analysis of correlations between factors that affect individuals' mobility mode choices in a specific rural region.

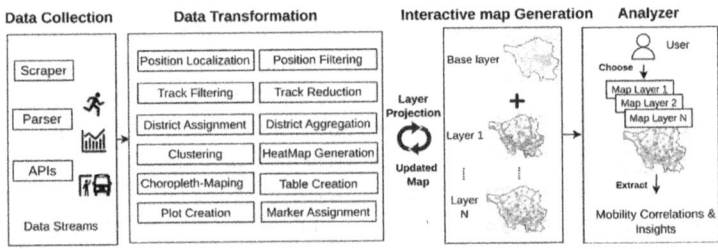

Fig. 3. Architecture for decision support systems supporting data-driven mobility insights for specific rural regions based on determined design principles 1–3 (cf. Fig. 2)

6 Development of DSS Prototype

Next, the how-to knowledge of the specified architecture was used for developing MobiVue, a prototype of a web-based DSS applied to the German Saarland region (cf. Fig. 1). This region in South-Western of Germany was chosen due to its alignment with rural requirements [9] and the availability of data with respect to the determined factors, cf. DP1 (cf. Fig. 2). According to the defined factors (cf. DP1, Fig. 2), relevant datasets were collected as shown in Table 2.

Table 2. Data of rural region (Saarland) used in prototype with description, time horizon, number of data points (#), visualization as well as related factors (cf. Fig. 2).

Related factor(s) (F)	Description	Time horizon	Visualization	#
F9,F13	Bus stops	-	Clusters	3.836
F9,F12	Car parking lots	-	Markers	35
F5,F9,F14,F12	Car sharing stations	-	Markers	8
F5,F9,F14,F12	Park & Ride places	-	Markers	57
F9,F8,F7, F13,F15	Train stops	-	Markers	43
F9	eBike charging stations	-	Markers	77
F9,F5,F14	eCar charging Stations	-	Markers	341
F6,F8	Cities	-	Markers	17
F6,F8	Districts	-	Tiles	6
F8,F9	Companies	-	Choropleth maps	50
F8,F9	Hospitals	-	Markers	25
F8,F9	Kindergartens	-	Markers/clusters	466
F8,F9	Schools	-	Markers/clusters	346
F8,F9	Shopping centers	-	Markers	6
F9-F13, F15	Public transport app requests	09/2022-10/2023	Dashed lines	3081
F9-F15	Movement data of users	10/2023-04/2024	Heat maps	433.849
F13,F14	Speed camera locations	-	Markers	76
F12,F13,F15	Social media posts (X)	2023–2024	Markers/plots	1.111
F12,F13,F15	Newspaper articles	2022–2024	Markers/plots	2.493
F12	Weather	2010–2023	Choropleth maps	84

Data such as locations of bus and train stops, car parking lots, speed cameras, car sharing stations, park and ride facilities, charging stations for e-bikes and e-cars, locations of hospitals, Kindergartens, shopping centers and schools as well as districts and cities were obtained from GeoPortal Saarland[1]. Demographic information on citizens stem from the German Federal Statistical Office. Data on mobility patterns of citizens was gathered by trip requests of users of the public transport app in Saarland (Saarfahrplan). Furthermore, a data set of movement data of citizens in Saarland was applied, that was generated within a field study with users (n = 521) tracking all their trips with public or individual transport in Saarland with routes, duration, destination etc. by means of the MotionTag app[2] between October 2023 and April 2024 (cf. Table 2). A dataset

---
[1] https://geoportal.saarland.de/.
[2] https://motion-tag.com/.

of social media posts and newspaper articles indicating relevant content with respect to the factors *trip chaining, perceptions and comfort* was sourced from the platform X[3] as well as NewsAPI[4] [14,27]. Last, weather data were gathered from OpenWeather[5]. Then, all datasets were converted into a two-dimensional map format by means of the libraries Pandas and GeoPandas[6]. Second, geographic coordinates were assigned to each data point using the GeoPy[7] library and Nominatim API[8] if not already available. In addition, GeoPy was used to represent the Saarland region as a polygon; data points outside this polygon were filtered out. Next, all data points not located in the specific rural region, i.e., the determined polygon, were filtered out (cf. DP1, Fig. 2). Track filtering was applied to movement data of user trips in Saarland by forming intersections of paths with the polygon (cf. Table 2). Also, districts were represented as polygons by GeoPy to be able to assign data points to specific districts. Last, pre-processed data sets were mapped to be able to create a web-based interactive map (cf. DP2 and DP3, Fig. 2). According to the factors as well as characteristics of the related data, those were visualized at diverse map layers (cf. DP1 and DP3, Fig. 2) (cf. Table 2). For instance, data on weather were represented as choropleth maps; data regarding bus and train stops, social media posts and newspaper articles were clustered according to districts etc. Within generation of the interactive map, the prototypical DSS for the Saarland region is constructed by using data transformations from previous steps as data layers. By means of Folium[9], layer controls are integrated, enhancing interface clarity given the multitude of available layers (cf. DP1 and DP3, Fig. 2). This allows users to selectively view and combine layers to explore correlations between datasets and thereby factors for mode choice in rural mobility (cf. DP2, Fig. 2). Through the analyzer, users can stack one or more data layers to extract insights and identify patterns in rural mobility in Saarland (cf. DP3, Fig. 2). Figure 4 shows an example view of MobiVue in which correlations between the usage of public transport, density and infrastructure of bus stops can be examined, e.g., trips based on public transport are mainly focused on regions around cities and on routes between cities; independent of the infrastructural density of bus stops.

7 Evaluation of DSS Prototype and Design Principles

According to the applied research approach (cf. Fig. 2), we conducted a qualitative ex-post evaluation of the DSS prototype and the determined design principles that were used for its implementation [13,33]. The participating interviewees

---

[3] https://developer.twitter.com/en/products/twitter-api.
[4] https://newsapi.ai.
[5] https://openweathermap.org.
[6] https://geopandas.org/en/stable/.
[7] https://geopy.readthedocs.io/en/stable/.
[8] https://nominatim.org/.
[9] https://python-visualization.github.io/folium/latest/index.html.

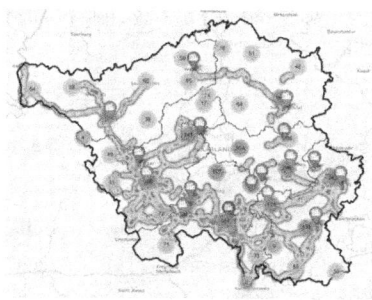

Fig. 4. DSS prototype showing correlations between usage of public transport (bus, train) (heat map) combined with city markers colored by density (green: <20k, orange: 20–100k, red: >100k) and aggregated bus stops (circles) for all Saarland districts. (Color figure online)

were experts working in mobility ministries in rural areas. The interview guideline was initially created and discussed by two senior researchers and covered 12 questions considering quality, completeness, usability, practical relevance, and decision support of the prototype [13], as well as open questions about the prototype's strengths and weaknesses. An initial test interview was conducted to determine whether the interview guideline was appropriate with respect to the design of the evaluation. All interviews were conducted in-person by two interviewers in November 2024. One interviewer introduced the prototype, posed questions, and interacted with the expert. Task of the second interviewer was to take additional notes for completing the transcripts. After a general introduction of the study objectives, age, professional experience in years, position, and field of expertise were discussed with each subject (cf. Table 3). Next, the prototype was introduced in detail by describing the general functions and specific utilization scenarios. The interviewees had the opportunity to interact with the prototype themselves. During the interview, the prototype was used and explained in more depth if necessary. Duration of interviews was 34 min on average. Ethical considerations were taken into account by obtaining consent to record the interviews from all subjects and ensuring their anonymity. The data collected was handled in accordance with data protection laws and we considered the five threats to validity within interview conduction and data analysis [17]. For the analysis with MAXQDA, thematic coding was applied, combining a priori and emergent coding[10] [10]. For coding, a pipeline was applied covering three steps: **descriptive coding, categorical coding**, and **analytical coding**. In descriptive coding, relevant sentences or phrases were summarized in a few words, e.g., *"Symbols are all very easy to understand"*, resulting in 249 descriptive codes. For categorical coding, descriptive codes capturing similar topics were combined to categories,

---

[10] A priori codes were chosen based on the interview structure, i.e., usability, practical relevance, decision support [13]. Emergent codes, such as data visualization, user interface, or analysis options, arose during categorical coding.

Table 3. Age, professional experience (PE) in years, position and field of expertise of interviewees (I) in evaluation.

#	Age	PE in years	Position	Field of expertise
I1	39	7	Deputy head of new mobility & public transport funding	Reporting for government; funding projects in sustainable mobility, on-demand transport, mobility data
I2	56	40	Deputy head of passenger transport & logistics	Project coordination in transportation planning, tariff design
I3	51	14	Public transport & new mobility advisor	Support for public transport
I4	35	9	Coordinator cycling policy	Strategies, funding guideline development, advisor cycling policy
I5	46	4	Head of new mobility, public transport & funding	Funding approval, future mobility systems and services for citizens
I6	57	21	Head of public passenger transport unit	Managing financial resources (railway, buses)
I7	31	9	Public transport advisor	Organization and support for rail transport

e.g., *"symbols are all very easy to understand"* and *"I find it clearly arranged"* was combined in the categorical code *"user interface"*. The analysis resulted in 13 categorical codes. In analytic coding, we first summarized the results from the categorical codes. Then, we examined the relationships between the categorical codes using MAXQDA's code-relations browser that visualizes quantitatively which codes overlap in the transcripts, i.e., have strong links. Those significant connections were analyzed in-depth with respect to the determined DP 1–3 (cf. Fig. 2), e.g., *"data foundation"* and *"analysis options"*.

8 Discussion of Results

The evaluation results are discussed in four parts. First, we discuss the effectiveness and applicability of the DPs. Second, we explore how the prototype supports stakeholders' decision-making in rural mobility contexts, highlighting its practical value and impact based on the evaluation. Third, we consider limitations and refinements for a second DSR cycle iteration before giving implications.

8.1 Effectiveness and Applicability of Design Principles

DP1 focuses on the integration of data on 15 socio-demographics, spatial, journey characteristics and socio-psychological factors of mobility in rural areas (cf. Fig. 2). Data provided for the Saarland region according to the given factors was characterized as interesting and useful by subjects (cf. Table 2). Especially, the integration of weather data and the provision of insights based on social media posts and newspaper articles was seen as helpful to better understand mobility behavior of individuals in rural areas. Thus, evaluation results support the effectiveness and applicability of DP1 for the design of DSS providing data-driven mobility insights for specific regions. This also holds for DP2 (cf. Fig. 2), that states that users should be able to combine data on factors (F1-F15) as they like. The combination of a multitude of data clearly arranged at district level by the prototype was appreciated by I2. Furthermore, the usage of drop-down menus and selection options for filtering data is described as a strength, helping in analyzing diverse scenarios. I4 mentioned that it is interesting to *"[...] correlate the data, to bring together different influencing variables and to be able to depict different factors in relation to each other"*. The possibility to select different types of data that can be aggregated and displayed on the map is considered as helpful by all interviewees (cf. Table 2). DP3 focused on the automatic aggregation and analysis of the heterogeneous data on factors and their user-friendly visualization by the interface (cf. Fig. 2). With respect to the user-friendly design of the interface, interviewees undermined the clear structure of the prototype's map layout; described as easy, clear, and user-friendly. The symbols used to select data to be displayed (cf. Table 2) were described as self-evident and easy to understand by most interviewees. I5 stated that users *"[...] get an initial overview of a range of data relevant to the development of mobility services without a long familiarization period."* I2 mentioned that users *"[...] have to get to know it (note: the prototype) a bit better to grasp everything straight away."*

8.2 Decision Support by Prototype

Regarding the support of decision-making processes within rural mobility contexts, results of the evaluation show that five out of seven interviewees would use the prototype in its current form within decision-making; especially for a better understanding of mobility behavior and for making decisions on future mobility services in rural areas. I6 (unit head, cf. Table 3) would use the prototype when extensive changes in traffic planning are necessary that occur on a multi-year cycle. I7 stated that especially the human movement data (cf. Table 2) would need to be more extensive and collected over a longer period of time; this would make the prototype an indispensable tool for its daily work confirming the relevance of factors F9-F15 (cf. Table 2). I1 - I5 would use the prototype on a regular basis, i.e., daily or weekly. They mentioned that in the current form, the prototype represents a well-founded basis for decision-making. I1 explained that the prototype is well suited for supporting decision-making as well as to develop and improve mobility offerings for professionals in mobility,e.g., for planning on-demand mobility services in rural areas. Furthermore, the prototype was described as useful for planning distributions of subsidies and marketing campaigns for public transport in rural areas. In total, results show that based on derived DPs 1–3 including factors that should be captured by integrated data, DSS can be designed that provide data-driven mobility insights that support decision-making of policymakers and public transport authorities in specific rural regions as defined in the research question (RQ).

8.3 Limitations

In addition, our results enable the specification of limitations and thus, refinements required for a second iteration of the DSR cycle in future work. Proposals for further development by interviewees mainly focused on integration of further data types loading on the already proposed factors (cf. DP1, Fig. 2). More comprehensive data on actual mobility behavior of individuals in rural regions was mentioned, e.g., mobile GPS data in extension to the applied movement data of users (F9-F15, cf. Table 2). Also the integration of further mobility options like scooter sharing or on-demand buses was stated by subjects in extension to already integrated data on car usage, buses and trains (F5,F7-F13, cf. Table 2). Furthermore, the need for economic and infrastructural data was mentioned, e.g., data about funding used in districts or municipalities, regarding conditions of infrastructure like streets and bridges, as well as with respect to construction sites and planned maintenance activities. Those data would support a broader analysis extending the proposed set of factors with respect to an economic and infrastructural view. In addition, interviewees asked for an integration political election results into the prototype completing it with data on additional political factors. Here, conceptual modeling methods will be applied to model further data types and to conceptualize the DSS extension with further data sources and analysis techniques. Regarding the interface (cf. DP3, Fig. 2), a more detailed filtering of data on fine-grained municipality level was requested. In this context, also the provision of meta information of the applied data by the prototype was discussed, e.g., number of data points, source, quality of data. This would further enhance the usefulness of a data-driven DSS indicating the existence of a fourth design principle that captures those aspects. Last, two interviewees mentioned that posing natural-language requests and receiving appropriate answers would improve the decision support function of the prototype.

8.4 Implications

The evaluation of the identified design principles by means of the implemented DSS prototype yields implications for both research and practice in the context of data-driven DSS for rural mobility planning. Findings underscore the practical relevance and applicability of the proposed design principles (DP1-DP3), highlighting their ability to guide the development of DSS that support decision-making in specific rural mobility contexts. The integration and flexible combination of the identified socio-demographic, spatial, journey characteristics, and socio-psychological data enables a nuanced understanding of mobility behavior, which can directly inform planning and policy interventions. The prototype's intuitive interface and visualization capabilities according to DP2 and DP3 (cf. Fig. 2) ensures its usability for various stakeholder groups, including public transport authorities and municipal planners. Consequently, DSS developed based on the proposed design principles can serve as a valuable tool in strategic decision-making processes, such as traffic planning, subsidy distribution, and service design for on-demand mobility offerings. This points to the potential for such DSS to bridge data gaps and support more targeted and region-specific mobility solutions in rural areas. From a research perspective, results contribute to the advancement of design knowledge by validating the effectiveness of the derived design principles and identifying opportunities for refinement in subsequent DSR cycles. The evaluation highlights the need for a fourth design principle focused on data transparency, provenance, and metadata provision to enhance user trust and analytical depth. Moreover, the limitations discussed point to the necessity of expanding DP1 (cf. Fig. 2) to include economic, infrastructural, and political factors, as well as fine-grained spatial resolution. Furthermore, the expressed need for natural-language interaction capabilities suggests the potential integration of conversational interfaces and large language models (LLMs) tailored to the mobility domain as an extension of DP3 (cf. Fig. 2). These insights offer concrete directions for future DSS design and iterative development cycles within Design Science Research. More broadly, this work demonstrates how regionally tailored DSS can empower local stakeholders by making complex mobility data accessible and actionable. This approach not only facilitates better-informed decisions but also promotes more inclusive, data-driven governance in rural mobility ecosystems. As such, the design principles and prototype have implications beyond the immediate case study, serving as a transferable foundation for similar contexts in other rural regions facing mobility challenges.

9 Conclusion

This work underscores the importance of addressing mobility challenges in rural regions through data-driven solutions. By exploring how DSS can be designed to generate region-specific mobility insights, we provide both theoretical and practical contributions to rural mobility planning. Through the application of a Design Science Research approach, factors influencing mobility choices were identified, leading to the development of meta-requirements and design principles for effective DSS. The implementation and evaluation of a DSS in the Saarland region based on those principles demonstrated the system's capacity to support policymakers and transport planners in making informed decisions. Findings highlight the potential of DSS designed according to the proposed requirements in enhancing accessibility, reducing car dependency, and promoting sustainable and inclusive transportation systems in rural areas.

Acknowledgement. This work was partially funded by Saarland Ministry for Economics, Innovation, Digital and Energy (MWIDE) and European Regional Development Fund (ERDF) within the research project INTE:GRATE.

References

1. Agbenyo, F., Nunbogu, A.M., Dongzagla, A.: Accessibility mapping of health facilities in rural Ghana. J. Transp. Health **6**, 73–83 (2017)
2. Alyavina, E., Nikitas, A., Njoya, E.T.: Mobility as a service (MaaS): a thematic map of challenges and opportunities. Res. Transp. Bus. Manage. **43**, 100783 (2022)
3. Andrienko, G., Andrienko, N., Chen, W., Maciejewski, R., Zhao, Y.: Visual analytics of mobility and transportation: state of the art and further research directions. IEEE Trans. Intell. Transp. Syst. **18**(8), 2232–2249 (2017)
4. Camarero, L., Oliva, J.: Thinking in rural gap: mobility and social inequalities. Palgrave Commun. **5**(1), 1–7 (2019)
5. Chen, W., Guo, F., Wang, F.Y.: A survey of traffic data visualization. IEEE Trans. Intell. Transp. Syst. **16**(6), 2970–2984 (2015). https://doi.org/10.1109/TITS.2015.2436897
6. Creswell, J.W., Poth, C.N.: Qualitative Inquiry and Research Design: Choosing Among Five Approaches. Sage publications (2016)
7. De Witte, A., Hollevoet, J., Dobruszkes, F., Hubert, M., Macharis, C.: Linking modal choice to motility: a comprehensive review. Transport. Res. Part A: Policy Pract. **49**, 329–341 (2013)
8. Eckhardt, J., Nykänen, L., Aapaoja, A., Niemi, P.: MaaS in rural areas - Case Finland. Res. Transport. Bus. Manage. **27**, 75–83 (2018)
9. Eurostat: Eurostat Urban-Rural Typology (2018). https://ec.europa.eu/eurostat/web/rural-development/methodology. Accessed 16 April 2025
10. Gibbs, G.R.: Analyzing Qualitative Data. Sage Publications (2018)
11. Gregor, S., Chandra Kruse, L., Seidel, S.: Research perspectives: the anatomy of a design principle. J. Assoc. Inf. Syst. **21**(6), 2 (2020)
12. Gross-Fengels, S., Fromhold-Eisebith, M.: Adapting transport related innovations to rural needs: smart Mobility and the example of the Heinsberg region, Germany. In: Advances in Transport Policy and Planning, vol. 2, pp. 125–162. Elsevier (2018)
13. Hevner, A.R., March, S.T., Park, J., Ram, S.: Design science in information systems research. MIS Q., 75–105 (2004)
14. Janzen, S., Saxena, P., Baer, S., Maass, W.: "listening in": social signal detection for crisis prediction. In: Bui, T.X. (ed.) 57th Hawaii International Conference on System Sciences, HICSS 2024, Hawaii, USA, 3-6 January 2024, pp. 2096–2105 (2024)
15. Kuechler, B., Vaishnavi, V.: On theory development in design science research: anatomy of a research project. Eur. J. Inf. Syst. **17**(5), 489–504 (2008)
16. Liu, Z., Zhao, P., Liu, Q., He, Z., Kang, T.: Uncovering spatial and social gaps in rural mobility via mobile phone big data. Sci. Rep. **13**(1), 6469 (2023)
17. Maxwell, J.A.: Qualitative Research Design: An Interactive Approach. Sage Publications (2013)
18. Mayring, P.: Qualitative content analysis: demarcation, varieties, developments. In: Forum: Qualitative Social Research, vol. 20. Freie Universität Berlin (2019)
19. Myers, M.D., Newman, M.: The qualitative interview in is research: examining the craft. Inf. Organ. **17**(1), 2–26 (2007)
20. Noulas, A., Scellato, S., Lambiotte, R., Pontil, M., Mascolo, C.: A tale of many cities: universal patterns in human urban mobility. PLoS ONE **7**(5), e37027 (2012)
21. Pangbourne, K.: Challenge, coordination, and collaboration for effective rural mobility solutions. In: Implications of Mobility as a Service (MaaS) in Urban and Rural Environments: Emerging Research and Opportunities, pp. 83–108. IGI Global (2020)

22. Pappalardo, L., Rinzivillo, S., Qu, Z., Pedreschi, D., Giannotti, F.: Understanding the patterns of car travel. Eur. Phys. J. Special Top. **215**(1), 61–73 (2013). https://doi.org/10.1140/epjst/e2013-01715-5
23. Parmaksız, D., Ülkü, M.A., Weigand, H.: Investigating rural logistics and transportation through the lens of quadruple bottom line sustainability. Logistics **8**(3), 81 (2024)
24. Peffers, K., Tuunanen, T., Rothenberger, M.A., Chatterjee, S.: A design science research methodology for information systems research. J. Manage. Inf. Syst. **24**(3), 45–77 (2007)
25. Poltimäe, H., Rehema, M., Raun, J., Poom, A.: In search of sustainable and inclusive mobility solutions for rural areas. Eur. Transp. Res. Rev. **14**(1), 1–17 (2022). https://doi.org/10.1186/s12544-022-00536-3
26. Porru, S., Misso, F.E., Pani, F.E., Repetto, C.: Smart mobility and public transport: opportunities and challenges in rural and urban areas. J. Traffic Transp. Eng. (English Edition) **7**(1), 88–97 (2020)
27. Saxena, P., Janzen, S., Maaß, W.: Newspaper signaling for crisis prediction. In: 2024 Annals Conference of the North American Chapter of the Association for Computataional Linguistics (NAACL-2024), Mexico. ACL (2024)
28. Schoedon, A., Trapp, M., Hollburg, H., Gerber, D., Döllner, J.: Web-based visualization of transportation networks for mobility analytics. In: Proceedings of the 12th International Symposium on Visual Information Communication and Interaction. VINCI 2019, Association for Computing Machinery, New York, NY, USA (2019)
29. Schoenau, M., Mueller, M.: What affects our urban travel behavior? A GPS-based evaluation of internal and external determinants of sustainable mobility in Stuttgart (Germany). Transport. Res. Part F: Traffic Psychol. Behav. **48**, 61–73 (2017)
30. Senaratne, H., et al.: Urban mobility analysis with mobile network data: a visual analytics approach. IEEE Trans. Intell. Transport. Syst. **19**(5), 1537–1546 (2018)
31. Stocker, A., Kaiser, C., Lechner, G., Fellmann, M.: A conceptual framework for mobility data science. IEEE Access **12**, 117126–117142 (2024)
32. Elhoseny, M., Hassanien, A.E. (eds.): Emerging Technologies for Connected Internet of Vehicles and Intelligent Transportation System Networks. SSDC, vol. 242. Springer, Cham (2020). https://doi.org/10.1007/978-3-030-22773-9
33. Venable, J., Pries-Heje, J., Baskerville, R.: FEDS: a framework for evaluation in design science research. Eur. J. Inf. Syst. **25**(1), 77–89 (2016). https://doi.org/10.1057/ejis.2014.36
34. Vitale Brovarone, E.: Accessibility and mobility in peripheral areas: a national place-based policy. Eur. Plan. Stud. **30**(8), 1444–1463 (2022)
35. Waleghwa, B., Ioannides, D.: "everyone wants to drive there": challenges to transport sustainability in rural tourism destinations. Int. J. Tourism Res. **26**(6), e2810 (2024)
36. Zeng, W., Fu, C.W., Arisona, S., Erath, A., Qu, H.: Visualizing mobility of public transportation system. IEEE Trans. Vis. Comput. Graph. **20**, 1833–1842 (2014)

Author Index

A
Abb, Luka 19
Abbad-Andaloussi, Amine 87
Aleknonytė-Resch, Milda 141
Alexeeva, Anna 290
Alter, Steven 245
Amaral, Glenda 274
Andersson, Kent 353
Andree, Kerstin 386

B
Baesens, Bart 301
Bogatinovska, Ilona 386
Borcard, Daniel 415
Bork, Dominik 335
Buchegger, Dominik Manuel 176
Bullée, Jan-Willem 274

C
Calamo, Marco 211
Cappiello, Cinzia 227
Castiglione, Pasquale 227
Chen, Qian 159

D
Daneva, Maya 274
Daubner, Lukas 257
De Laet, Tinne 301
Dhungel, Anna-Katharina 141
Dijkman, Remco 71

E
Elsaeßer, Fabian 141

F
Fill, Hans-Georg 415, 431
Forell, Martin 55
Franceschetti, Marco 176
Fritsch, Andreas 55

G
Granåker, Anders 3
Groenendal, Evelien 403
Guizzardi, Giancarlo 274

H
Hacks, Simon 290
Harašta, Jakub 257
Henoeckl, Tobias 335
Hergert, Florian 448
Hinkelmann, Knut 431

J
Jalali, Amin 3, 123
Jans, Mieke 107
Janzen, Sabine 448
Junger, Marianne 274

K
Kampik, Timotheus 19
Kautz, Tobias 368
Khaliq, Lotfy Abdel 448
Khayatbashi, Shahrzad 3, 123
Kindler, Ekkart 87
Kirikova, Marite 36
Klessascheck, Finn 386
Kunkler, Michel 193

L
Lepsien, Arvid 141
Lubane, Lauma 36
Lundberg, Jan 353

M
Maass, Wolfgang 448
Malakhova, Diana 290
Martin, Niels 107
Matulevičius, Raimundas 257
Mecella, Massimo 211
Miri, Najmeh 123

O
Oliveira, Ítalo 274

P
Pande, Charuta 431
Pathe, Thomas Ricardo 290
Pradhan, Shameer K. 107
Pufahl, Luise 386

R
Rafiei, Majid 19
Rehse, Jana-Rebecca 19
Reinhartz-Berger, Iris 318
Rinderle-Ma, Stefanie 159, 193
Roelens, Ben 403

S
Sai, Nan 71
Sales, Tiago Prince 274
Sancricca, Camilla 227
Sarmah, Dipti K. 274
Schlösser, Timo 55
Schüler, Selina 55
Seiger, Ronny 176
Sjölind, Viktor 3
Snoeck, Monique 211, 301, 318
Sorg, Thierry 87
Stein, Hannah 448
Stirna, Janis 353

T
Tiukhova, Elena 301

V
Verbruggen, Charlotte 301, 335

W
Wagner, Gerd 274
Weber, Barbara 87, 176
Winter, Karolin 71, 159
Winter, Robert 368

Z
Zdravkovic, Jelena 123

Made in the USA
Monee, IL
03 May 2026

49438657R00267